DICTIONARY OF CONTEMPORARY
SLANG

DICTIONARY OF
CONTEMPORARY
SLANG

THIRD EDITION

TONY THORNE

A & C Black • London

www.acblack.com

First published in Great Britain 1990
Paperback published 1991
Second edition published 1997
Paperback published 1999
This third edition published 2005

A & C Black Publishers Ltd
37 Soho Square, London W1D 3QZ

A CIP record for this book is available from the British Library

ISBN 0 7136 7504 7

Text production and proofreading
Heather Bateman, Emma Harris, Katy McAdam, Rebecca McKee

1 3 5 7 9 8 6 4 2

A & C Black uses paper produced with elemental chlorine-free pulp, harvested from managed sustainable forests.

Text computer typeset by A & C Black Publishers
Printed in Italy by Legoprint

INTRODUCTION: SLANG IN THE 21ST CENTURY

Slang and Society

Slang derives much of its power from the fact that it is clandestine, forbidden or generally disapproved of. So what happens once it is accepted, even in some cases embraced and promoted by 'mainstream' society? Not long ago the *Oxford English Dictionary* characterised slang as 'low and disreputable'; in the late 1970s the pioneering sociolinguist Michael Halliday used the phrase 'anti-language' in his study of the speech of criminals and marginals. For him, theirs was an interestingly 'pathological' form of language. The first description now sounds quaintly outmoded, while the second could be applied to street gangs – today's *posses*, *massives* or *sets* – and their secret codes. Both, however, involve value judgements which are essentially social and not linguistic. Attitudes to the use of language have changed profoundly over the last three decades, and the perceived boundaries between 'standard' and 'unorthodox' are becoming increasingly 'fuzzy'.

Today, tabloid newspapers in the UK such as the *Sun*, the *Star* and the *Sport* regularly use slang in headlines and articles, while the quality press use slang sparingly – usually for special effect – but the assumption remains that readers have a working knowledge of common slang terms.

There has been surprisingly little criticism of the use of slang (as opposed to the 'swear-words' and supposed grammatical errors which constantly irritate British readers and listeners). In the last five years I have only come across one instance, reported in local and national newspapers, of a south London secondary school head publicly warning pupils of the dangers of using slang in their conversation. The school in question has pupils from many ethnic and linguistic groups – which may give a clue as to why young people might opt for slang as a medium of communication and not just an embellishment. Perhaps they have come to see slang as their own common language, in which they are fluent, and which may therefore take precedence over the other varieties in their repertoires (Hindi, Gujarati, Punjabi, Creole, 'Cockney', 'textbook English' etc.). The use of slang forms part of what linguists call code-switching or style-shifting – the mixing of and moving between different languages, dialects or codes. This might be done for ease of communication, for clarification, to show solidarity or – a reason sometimes overlooked by analysts – just for fun.

In the US, on the other hand, slang and so-called 'vernacular' use is still highly controversial. This stems in part from the contest between conservatism and 'multiculturalism' or 'liberalism', which in the late 1990s focused on the stalled attempt to establish so-called 'ebonics', or black spoken English, as a linguistic variety with official status. Recently, some North American academic linguists and their students have joined with parents, teachers and adult professionals to lament the corrupting and destabilising effect of slang on young peoples' ability to manage in formal settings such as examinations or job interviews. Their fears can't simply be dismissed, but they seem to be based on a very rigid notion of language's potential. The key to effective communication is what language teachers term 'appropriacy'; knowing what kind of English to use in a particular situation, rather than clinging to rigid ideas of what is universally right and proper.

In my experience, most slang users are not inarticulate dupes but quite the opposite: they are very adept at playing with appropriacy, skilfully manipulating ironically formal, mock-technical and standard styles of speech as well as slang. If prompted they can often provide insights into their own language quite as impressive as those hazarded by professional linguists or sociologists. For this reason, for the first time in the *Dictionary of Contemporary Slang* I have sometimes included, in their own words, users' definitions of terms and comments on their usage as well as the direct quotations – 'citations' – contributed by them and featured in previous editions.

Slang versus 'Proper English'

Slang is language deliberately selected for its striking informality and is consciously used in preference to 'proper' speech (or, more rarely, writing). It usually originates in small social groups. For these groups, it is a private code that embodies their particular values and behaviour and reinforces their exclusivity. Slang expressions may escape the originating group and become more widely used, and although slang draws much of its effect from its novelty, some terms (*booze, punk, cool*) may stay in the language for many years.

This may seem a longwinded definition of a language variety that most people think they recognise, but the neater descriptions to be found in collections of quotations, such as G.K. Chesterton's 'all slang is metaphor' (much is but not all) or Ambrose Bierce's ironic 'the grunt of the human hog...'don't really succeed in nailing the phenomenon. (Definitions by academic linguists, apart from Halliday's, are entirely absent.) Slang has also been referred to as 'the poetry of everyday life' or 'of the common man'. Although it does make use of poetry's rhetorical tricks (and more devices besides), poetry is allusive while slang is anything but, depending for its power on either complete, shared understanding (by insiders) or complete bafflement (on the part of outsiders).

Ask users of slang for a definition and they might come up with: 'jargon, used playfully to prevent outsiders from intercepting the actual meaning'; 'the ever-evolving bastardisation of the written and spoken language as a result of social and cultural idolization [sic] of uneducated, unintelligable [sic] celebrities' and 'cool words, words that match the style' (all of these are from the Urban Dictionary website). One teenager I interviewed defined it simply as '*our* language'.

More specifically, slang terms have certain recognisable functions. Firstly, like any new coinage, a slang word may fill a gap in the existing lexicon. For example, there is no single verb in standard English that defines the cancelling of a romantic tryst or social arrangement, so British adolescents have adopted the words *ding* or *dingo*. To jump and hug someone from behind is rendered much more succinct in US campus speech as *glomp*.

Secondly, a slang expression may be substituted for an existing term – what linguists refer to as 'relexicalisation' – *smams* or *chebs* for breasts, *blamming* for exciting and *chuffie* for chewing gum are recent British examples. More than one motive may be in play here: renaming something makes it yours, and makes it funnier (*Ethiopia!*) or ruder (*cunted*). Using cultural allusions (*Mr Byrite*) demonstrates worldliness; rhyming slang (*Claire Rayners*) is not simply a useful mechanism, or a disguise, but may conceivably show solidarity with an older tradition.

Slang users tend to invent many more synonyms or near-synonyms than might be thought strictly necessary: for example, criminals may have a dozen different nicknames (*gat, cronz, iron, chrome*) for their guns, or for informers (*canary, grass, snout, stoolie*); drinkers can choose from hundreds of competing descriptions of a state of intoxication (*hammered, hamstered, langered, mullered*). This phenomenon is technically described as 'overlexicalisation', and it happens because the words in question have an emblematic force over and above their primary meanings. Macho would-be seducers or *studs* require a range of usually disparaging or patronising terms for their sexual conquests and more than one pet-name for their manly attributes; drug users pride themselves on being able to distinguish the nuances in different states of euphoria or intoxication; cliques and gangs enjoy inventing a host of pejorative nicknames for *dissing* those they see as outsiders. The most significant groupings of terms in the new dictionary continue to be in the same 'semantic fields' as before: the categories of drunkenness and druggedness, of terms of approval and enthusiasm, of insults and pejorative nicknames and of expressions relating to sex and partnership.

The New Dictionary

Thousands of new expressions have entered the language since the turn of the century and dozens, perhaps hundreds, more are added to the common vocabulary every week. The lexicographer has to try to identify novelties as they arise and to track the changes in the way existing words are being used. This dictionary has been regularly updated since its first publication in 1990 – but this, the first edition in the new millennium, has seen a wholesale revision of all entries and the addition of about 2,000 new terms.

One of the most painful procedures for the compiler is to decide which expressions must be deleted in order to make room for new material. Contrary to popular belief, very few slang items fall completely out of use. What happens is that certain words – *sorted* is an example – are assimilated into everyday colloquial usage, while others are abandoned by their original users as being outmoded or no longer exclusive enough, but are adopted by 'outsiders'. For example, a modish term of appreciation like *phat*, only known to a hip minority in the early 1990s, may now be heard in the primary school playground. Some words – the adjective *groovy* is one such – are recycled. Trendy in the 1960s, then sounding hopelessly outdated by the late 1970s, it was revived ironically in the later 1980s, before finally being used by some members of the new generation in more or less its original sense.

(Groovy is an interesting example in that, like lucre/*luka* and ducats/*duckets*, it seems to have been picked up by some youngsters who were unaware of its origins or 'correct' form, hearing it as *crovey*.) Seemingly archaic words may be rediscovered, as in the case of *duffer*, although there is always the chance that this is a coincidental coinage.

After much hesitation, therefore, the deletions were made on a fairly subjective basis. Genuine archaisms like *love-in-a-punt* (a comic description until the 1950s of weak beer: the joke is that it's 'fucking near water'), or *the lump*, designating a long-obsolete system of employment, were doomed, however picturesque or evocative. Terms which were always in very limited circulation, such as *puggled* (meaning tipsy or drunk) or *pipe*, in the sense of stare at, would have to go, as did others that were both dated and obvious, like the nicknames *jelly* (for the explosive gelignite) or *milko* (a milkman). Some, like *smidgin* or *channel-surfing*, are deemed to have become common colloquialisms.

The new expressions have all been collected since 2000 from a cross-section of the slang-using communities in what has come to be known as the anglosphere.

In a work of this size it isn't possible to include the entire vocabulary of every local subculture, so when a range of terms has been uncovered, we have included only those which have intrinsic interest (i.e. they are witty, inventive, particularly unusual linguistically – *Listerine* is all three), seem especially characteristic of a community (*chuddies*, *filmi*) or appear likely to cross over into wider use (*munter, hottie*). There are more British terms (although 'British' is nowadays shorthand for a multilingual mix) than North American, Australasian etc. since the bulk of the collecting was carried out in the UK. None of these criteria are in any way 'scientific', so the lexicographer is still the final judge.

One thing that has not changed since the first publication of this dictionary is the relative lack of interest shown by UK academics in this type of language, relative to their counterparts in the US, Europe and elsewhere. On the other hand, students in higher education and schoolchildren have increasingly chosen to study, analyse and research a variety of speech in which they have a special stake, while, judging by reference book sales and letters to newspapers and magazines (and to myself), the general public is hungry for any reliable information about new language and language change.

Collecting the Data

I have above all been inspired by the alternative Dr Johnson, Captain Francis Grose, who compiled the 1785 *Classical Dictionary of the Vulgar Tongue*. I have tried to emulate him, not so much in his fondness for huge meals and strong drink, but in his avoidance of print archives in favour of going out into the streets, the taverns and the barracks recording what people are actually saying.

The effect of Captain Grose's 18th-century slang dictionary was not to make respectable, but at least to treat with some respect, even to celebrate, the language of the dissolute and the dispossessed. Likewise, this dictionary applies lexicographic techniques to the speech of individuals and groups who may have little prestige in society as a whole, but who in their own environments are the impresarios of speech styles, the guardians and reinventors of subcultural mystique.

Halliday commented that of all the socialising environments (family, school, workplace) in which individuals develop their identities, the peer group is the most difficult for the researcher to penetrate. However, it is from the peer group, whether consisting of schoolkids, skateboarders or soldiers, that slang typically emerges. It is tricky for an ageing babyboomer to infiltrate these groups, to join a streetgang or even to go clubbing without attracting attention, but it's absolutely essential for the seeker of slang to get access to authentic samples of language – particularly spoken language – in their authentic settings, since much slang is never written down (calling into question the value of reference works based solely on printed examples) or only recorded in writing long after its first appearance.

When circumstances allow, listening in on conversations is an ideal approach, but as electronic eavesdropping is now forbidden except where consent has been given in advance, most of the examples collected here have been recorded and reported by users or their friends, gathered by interviews or by long-term recording of conversations in which participants gradually come to ignore the presence of the microphone. However expert the compiler, there is an obvious risk of being fed false information, so to qualify for inclusion terms must be attested by two separate sources.

Cyberslang?

The Internet has transformed the way we manipulate our systems of signs and the relationships between producers and consumers of information. Its effect on slang has two aspects. Firstly, online communication has generated its own vocabulary of technical terminology, essentially jargon (*spam*, *blogging*, *phishing*) and informal, abbreviated or humorous terms (*addy*, *noob*, *barking moonbat* etc.) which qualify as slang. The amount of new cyberslang is fairly small, but the Internet has also allowed the collecting, classifying and promoting of slang from other sources in the form of so-called dictionaries, glossaries and articles written by individual enthusiasts. Even more interesting are the online lexicons compiled wholly by contributors, who post new expressions and provide their own explanations and examples.

Many of the websites in which slang is collected and discussed are truly democratic and genuinely user-driven, but almost none of them are authoritative, in the sense that they can be trusted to have studied the words they record, to produce accurate or convincing etymologies rather than supposition, or to comment from a basis of familiarity with other sources. Two that I particularly recommend, though, are the Urban Dictionary (www.urbandictionary.com) and the Playground Dictionary (www.odps.org). It is a point of honour among lexicographers that they don't poach words from rival collections, but I have used these online glossaries to verify the authenticity and sometimes the meanings of some of the more obscure words that I have come across. One hardcopy reference work that can also be recommended is *Viz* magazine's *Profanisaurus*, a regularly updated glossary of sexual and scatological expressions and insults, donated by readers. Despite its comic intent the material is a valuable trove of contemporary folk obsessions and I have tried not to duplicate it in these pages.

It is communications technology in general and not only the Internet that is enabling slang, especially the most pervasive English-based slang, to globalise. Late one night in a hotel room in Cologne, I watched a cable TV station from Berlin broadcasting a video diary in which teenagers improvised conversations in a mix of German, English and snatches of Spanish and Turkish. The soundtrack simultaneously ran sampled sequences of rock, rap, rai etc. while subtitles provided an ironic metacommentary also blending a variety of languages. This was not an avant-garde artistic gesture as far as I could tell, but a snapshot of a genuine 'sociolect'; the creative and playful code in which this loose association of friends chooses to express itself.

Another technical development – text messaging – has triggered changes in the culture of communication, especially among young people, and brought with it, like telegrams, CB-radio or Internet chatrooms, a new form of abbreviated code. It has excited some academic linguists but it hasn't, however, contributed anything meaningful to the evolution of slang as such: no new words or radical shifts in syntax have been generated yet.

Blingage and Chavdom

Two well-known examples from early in the 'noughties' decade, already history by the time this book appears, illustrate the linguistic development and cultural resonance of slang. The first is one of the words that the south London school head singled out for disapproval. *Bling* was coined as far as anyone knows – although music lyricists and journalists often claim slang words as their own creations, the real originators often remain anonymous – either in imitation of the sound of clanking jewellery, or, less probably, to evoke its glittering appearance. The jewellery in question was part of the ostentatious display associated with black aficionados of US rap music and hip hop culture, and the word, sometimes reduplicated as *bling-bling*, came to epitomise an attitude of conspicuous and shameless consumption, aggressive flaunting of wealth and 'street' status. Young speakers in the UK adopted the expression around 2002, then the noun form began to be used adjectivally (as in 'very bling'), and by 2005, middle-aged TV presenters and middle-class parents were experimenting with the word. In slang usage, meanwhile, by analogy with other American terms, (*fundage*, *grindage*), a new noun, *blingage*, appeared in 2003.

Although black slang is the dominant influence in many youth subcultures, it is not one dialect, but rather a range of terms from a continuum incorporating US, Caribbean, urban British and South African speech. As well as words like *bling* and its derivations, which have to some extent crossed over, there are a host of other 'black' words including *skank*, *hench*, *tonk*, *mashup* and *butters* which have become common currency on the street. It's a sign of cultural importance if a trend is successfully parodied, and UK comedian Sasha Baron Cohen's fictional TV character Ali G very effectively mocked the language (not only the vocabulary but the assumed intonation) and appearance of the *wiggas* and Asians who resolutely imitated black styles from the late 1990s.

The second well-known example of media fascination with slang and cultural change is not inspired by black speech, but ultimately by the language of another oppressed minority with disproportionate subcultural capital, the Roma. In 2004 the British media became aware of a website, www.chavscum.co.uk, which was celebrating a new social category. The nickname *chav* denoted a person with the following defining attributes (according to researcher Sarah Bromley): he or she is youngish, favours sportswear, loiters in groups in town centres, may be involved in petty crime, if female wears prominent cheap jewellery (known incidentally as *Argos bling* or *bingo bling*) and has scraped-back hair (the effect has been dubbed a *Croydon facelift*), if male has a shaven head or crew cut and probably wears a baseball cap. The categorisation is complex in that it describes not only a 'look', or a so-called subculture, but in some ways resembles an old-fashioned *class* distinction. The class connotations are new, though, as, often pejorative, chav can also be used with mock-affection or even admiration by sophisticates who have extended the scope of the concept to take in reality TV celebrities and pop stars and claimed that this vulgar, feckless, assertively uncultured group are, if not the 'new ruling class' (the extreme view), then at least an unstoppable social force.

With chav, once again an ancient slang term mutates or is reinvented (*punk* is another example of this), acquires powerful if temporary social significance, and prompts excited linguistic speculation. A completely spurious folk etymology was found – the word was said by some, including some police officers, to be an acronym; 'council-housed and violent'. *Chav* is actually one version of an old Romany term meaning child and/or friend, a word previously more often recorded (and included in earlier editions of this dictionary) in the variant forms *charvie* or *charver*. The people referred to were in fact identified by slang users in the 1990s and defined by a wide range of regional nicknames, including *spide*, *steek*, *scally*, *townie*, *pikey*, *pov*, *schemie*. In the evolutionary struggle for dominance, media adoption helped *chav* to triumph, to spawn related witticisms like *chaviot* (a *chav-chariot* or cheap, over-embellished car), and become by general agreement of British journalists and lexicographers the vogue word of 2004 and 2005.

Back to the future

So to return to that question: what becomes of slang? Firstly, the general 'flattening out' of a hierarchical society and the relaxation of linguistic prejudices mean that slang may come to be seen not as something inherently substandard, but as an option among many available linguistic styles. At the same time there must always be a set of words and phrases which is beyond the reach of most speakers, that is always 'deviant', 'transgressive' and opaque. This slang must renew itself, not just in implied contrast with 'standard' language, but with earlier versions of itself. So new slang words will continue to sprout, to metamorphose, to wither and disappear or else to spread and fertilise the common ground of language. This process may now be more visible and familiar, the crossover phenomenon may happen much faster (given the complicity of the media), and the shock value of the terms themselves may be lessened (the invention and use of slang does risk becoming locked into familiarity and cliché, like the tired gestures of rock, rap, conceptual art and fashion), but it is very unlikely ever to stop.

Thanks and Acknowledgements

Thanks again to all contributors named in previous editions, especially the late Iona Opie and the late Paul Beale, and to all those who have contributed new material including Anna Merritt, Jean Saville, Danielle Dodoo, Kate Merry, Shelley Kingston, William Wentworth-Sheilds, Rebecca Gibbs, Zimarina Sarwar, Mark Smale, Benjamin Linton-Willoughby, Darren Elliott, Hattie Webster, Steve O'Donoghue, Tiffany Zwicker, Charlotte Pheazy, Sammy Wilson, Charlotte Mulley, Vicky Bhogal, Sandip Sarai, David Castell, Mathew Casey, Ross Raisin, Beatrix Agee, Anna Cook, Francis Woolf, David Mallows, Rod Murdison, Louise Marshall, Soo Rose, Anna Lisa Koppelman, Rebecca Koppelman, Christine Sarkis, Andrew Melbourne, Serena Gilbert, Nikki Follis, Victoria Milne, Louise Gage, Nicola Wardlow, Dana Stevens, Laurie Armstrong, Mark Jones, Anthony Fogg, Jan Eisby, Caroline Dunn, Chryselle Pathmanathan, David Bryan, Lisa Michelle Jenkins, Halima Jayda

Mian, Michelle Chamberlain, Rabab El Basset, Kenneth McClean Brown, Sarah Bromley, Vivian Goodman, James Womack, Simon Donald, Michael Rosen, Professor Richard Dawkins, Charlie Higson and Claire Rayner, Simon Elmes, Keith Ricketts, Colin Babb and John Goodman.

Also to colleagues at King's College London, particularly Professors Barry Ife, Linda Newson, Michael Knibb, and Ann Thompson and Dr David Ricks who have supported my research and the King's Archive of Slang and New Language. I have a very special debt of gratitude to Professor Connie C. Eble of the University of North Carolina at Chapel Hill, who generously made available the fruits of her recent research into US campus slang (complementing a tally begun in the 1970s, and her still unrivalled 1996 publication, *Slang and Sociability*).

The *Dictionary of Contemporary Slang* is an ongoing project; a survey which by virtue of its subject must be constantly updated to keep track of new coinages and changes in the status of existing terms. The idea of a reference work as something sternly authoritative and unreachably remote from its users is outmoded; thanks to electronic communications a dictionary can now interact with its readers. This was the first interactive slang dictionary and the compiler and the publishers would be very grateful for any contributions or suggestions from readers who can either mail material to: Dictionaries Department, A & C Black Publishers Ltd, 37 Soho Square, London W1D 3QZ or communicate with the author via e-mail at tony.thorne@kcl.ac.uk. (The introduction to the previous edition and related articles can be consulted at www.kcl.ac.uk/depsta/elc/slang.html.) Information about new slang terms should ideally include, as well as the meaning, details of when and where the word or phrase was used and a direct quotation if possible, together with the name of the contributor, who will be acknowledged in the next edition.

Tony Thorne
London, September 2005

HOW TO USE THIS BOOK

A typical entry in the dictionary will contain the components described below (with the typefaces explained in brackets):

The HEADWORDS are entered in alphabetical order (in primary **bold** type), together with any variant spellings or alternative forms. Next the PART OF SPEECH is given (in *italics*): these have been somewhat simplified so that an adjectival phrase appears as an adjective (*adj*), noun phrase as a noun (*n*). Unless a word is used in all parts of the English-speaking world, it is given a REGIONAL LABEL (in *italics*: *British*, *Australian*, etc.). This indicates the country of origin, or the country in which the term is most prevalent. If a particular term has more than one quite separate meaning, these meanings are NUMBERED (in **bold** type: **1**, **2**, **3** etc.). If one overall sense of a term is commonly subdivided into several slightly different meanings, these are indicated by LETTERS (in **bold** type: **a**, **b**, **c** etc.). The headword, part of speech and regional label are followed by a DEFINITION (in roman type). This in turn is followed by more information about the use and origin of the term (in roman type, unless it is a direct quote from a user, in which case it will appear in *italics*). In the explanations, foreign words are placed in *italics* and slang terms found elsewhere in the dictionary are shown in **bold** (these act as cross references throughout the dictionary). Many definitions are followed by an ILLUSTRATIVE PHRASE or sentence (in *italics*). If this example is an actual citation, its source follows in brackets.

A

aardvark *n*
1. *British* hard work, onerous tasks. A probably ephemeral pun heard among university students since the late 1980s.

> *'They're giving us too much bloody aard-vark, that's the problem.'*
> (Recorded, undergraduate, London University, 1988)

2. *American* (a male with) an uncircumcised penis. The term was used by the Dixie Chicks country rock band in interviews in 2002. It is based on the supposed resemblance to the animal's snout, and prompted by the fact that most males in the USA are routinely circumcised. **Anteater** and **corn-dog** are contemporary synonyms.

aardvarking *n American*
having sex. This term, popular among college students since the 1990s, often applies to sex in a public place, possibly evoking the animal's grubbing or rooting around in the earth or simply, as with **wombat**, heard in the same milieus, used for the sake of exoticism.

> *This semester her number-one hobby has been aardvarking every chance she gets.*

ABCD *n*
'American born confused **desi**': a designation of a young South Asian person featured in Tanuja Desai Hidier's young adult novel *Born Confused*, published in the USA in 2002

'abdabs *n pl British See* **screaming (h)abdabs**

abo *n Australian*
an Aboriginal. A standard shortening used by whites which is now considered condescending or abusive: it is often part of offensive comparisons, as in 'to smell like an abo's armpit/abo's jock-strap'.

absofuckinglutely, **absobloodylutely** *adv, exclamation*
these elaborations of the standard term are examples of 'infixing' (as opposed to prefixing or suffixing), a word-formation process unique to slang in English

> *'Are you really determined to go ahead with this?' 'Absobloodylutely!'*
> *She was absobloodylutely legless.*

Abyssinia! *exclamation British*
goodbye, a jocular farewell. The expression is an alteration of 'I'll be seeing you', sometimes further elaborated into **Ethiopia!** It is in current use among students, but may have arisen in their parents' or grandparents' generations.

AC/DC *adj*
bisexual. From the label on electrical appliances indicating that they can be used with either alternating or direct current. The slang term originated in the USA and spread to Britain around 1960.

ace[1] *n*
1. a best friend or good person. Used by males to other males, usually as a greeting or a term of endearment. In this sense the term probably spread from black American street gangs in the 1950s to working-class whites in the USA, Australia and, to a lesser extent, Britain.

> *Hey, ace!*

2. *Australian* the anus. By association with **arse** and the black mark on a playing card.

ace[2], **ace out** *vb American*
1. to outmanoeuvre, outwit or defeat

> *'I had it all figured, but those guys aced me!'*
> (*The A Team*, US TV series, 1985)

2. to succeed, win or score very highly

> *She aced / aced out the test.*

ace[3], **aces** *adj*
excellent, first class. Used extensively since the late 1950s in the USA, since the mid-1960s in Australia, and by the

1970s, especially by teenagers, in Britain. The origin of the term is obviously in the highest value playing card, the meaning now having been extended from 'best' to 'smartest', 'cleverest', etc.

an ace car

That film was really ace.

She's aces!

ace boon coon *n American*

(in the language of black males) one's best friend. An item of black street-talk combining **ace** and **coon** with 'boon' to provide the suggestion of a cherished companion and the rhyme, which was included in so-called **Ebonics**, recognised as a legitimate language variety by school officials in Oakland, California, in late 1996. A similar usage is found in the phrase 'ace boom boom'. During the 1960s and 1970s the variant form 'ace coon' was heard, often ironically referring to a self-important black male or an individual who had achieved some success, e.g. in a work-group, department, etc.

You my ace boon coon!

ace in the hole *n*

an advantage held in reserve until it is needed. From American stud-poker terminology, it refers to an ace (the most valuable card) dealt face down and not revealed.

acey-deucy *adj American*

both good and bad, of uncertain quality. The term is at least pre-World War II, but is still heard occasionally, especially amongst middle-aged or elderly speakers. It comes from a card game similar to backgammon in which aces are high and deuces (twos) are low.

acher *n See* **acre**

acid *n*

1. LSD-25, the synthetic hallucinogenic drug. From the full name, Lysergic Acid Diethylamide. This has been the standard term by which users refer to the drug since its first popularity in California in 1965, in spite of the appearance of more picturesque but ephemeral alternatives. In the late 1980s, adherents of the **acid house** cult adopted the word as a slogan (usually a cry of 'a-c-e-e-e-e-d!') and to refer to LSD or **ecstasy**.

2. *British* sarcasm, snide comments or cheeky exaggeration, especially in the expression 'come the old acid', popular in working-class usage in the 1950s and

1960s and still heard. In such phrases as 'his acid comments' the adjectival meaning is similar, but cannot be described as slang.

Don't come the old acid with me!

acid flash *n*

a sudden recurrence of a much earlier experience of the drug LSD. Some users are disturbed months or years after taking the drug by sudden disorientation which lasts from seconds to hours and which may or may not be due to its effects.

acid head, **acid freak** *n*

a user, especially a heavy or habitual user, of the drug LSD. The terms are not pejorative and were used from the late 1960s to the mid-1970s by takers of LSD or other hallucinogens about themselves and each other.

acid house *n*

a youth cult involving synthetic electronic dance music (**house**) and the taking of euphoric hallucinogens such as **ecstasy** and LSD (**acid**). This fashion, celebrated in clubs and large impromptu parties and with garish clothing and lighting effects, succeeded hip hop, **rap** and other movements in 1988. 'A-c-e-e-e-d!' (an elongated version of **acid**) was a rallying cry of celebrants, shouted and written on walls.

acid test *n*

a party or informal ritual at which a group of people take food and/or drink laced with LSD. The expression and the practice were originated by Ken Kesey and the Merry Pranksters, a group of hedonistic travellers in the USA in the early 1960s who were successors to the **beats** and precursors of the **hippies**.

'The Electric Kool-Aid Acid Test.'

(Title of a book by Tom Wolfe, 1969)

acid trip *n*

a period under the influence of the drug LSD or **acid** (which produces an altered state of awareness and, sometimes, hallucinations). The experience lasts 4–6 hours at an average dose.

ackers *n British*

money. The word, which has been in armed-forces and working-class use since the 1920s, was revived, in common with synonyms such as **pelf**, **rhino**, etc., for jocular use since the 1980s by middle-class speakers. It comes from the Egyptian word *akka*, denoting a coin worth one *piastre*.

acre, acher n
1. the buttock(s). In this sense the word is common in Australia, normally in the singular form.
2. the testicle(s). Usually in the plural, this sense of the word is typically used by British schoolboys.

'I told the estate agent I couldn't afford any land, so he kicked me in the balls and said, "There's a couple of achers for you".'
(Schoolboy joke, London, 1965)

Both senses of both words stem from the simple play on the word 'ache' which has formed part of many different puns and dirty jokes during the last forty years, involving sensitive parts of the (male) anatomy.

action gagnée n British
a literal translation into French of 'winning action', i.e. a successful sexual encounter. A humorous euphemism used by students in 2003 and 2004.

action man n British
a devotee of military exercises or strenuous physical activities, or someone who makes a show of (relentless) energy. The term is applied derisively, originally by members of the armed forces to unpopular or excessively **gung-ho** colleagues, and now by extension to anyone who is showily or mindlessly **macho**. The satirical magazine *Private Eye* referred to Prince Andrew by this name in 1986 and 1987. The origin of this piece of sarcasm is the 'Action Man' doll – a poseable commando scale model in full kit sold to children in Britain since the 1960s.

'Right little action man i'n' 'e? 'E simply wants to be prepared when the east wind blows 'ot.'
(*Minder*, British TV series, 1988)

A.D. n
a drug addict. From the first two letters of 'addict' or a reversal of the initials of 'drug addict', to avoid confusion with 'District Attorney'. The term was quite popular among addicts themselves and the police in the USA. (In Britain **D.A.** was the 1960s vogue version.)

adam n British
the drug **MDA**; methyl diamphetamine. Adam is an acronym from the initials, used by middle-class Londoners during the vogue for the drug since the mid-1980s. MDA is more commonly known to the press and non-users as **ecstasy**; to users it is also **E**, **X**, **xtc** and **Epsom salts**.

adam and eve vb British
to *believe*. Well-established rhyming slang which is still heard among working-class Londoners and their middle-class imitators, usually in the expression of astonishment 'Would you adam 'n' eve it?'.

addy n
an Internet address. The abbreviation, used in Internet communication and text messaging, is also spoken.

adhocratic adj
improvised and/or temporary, as in decisions made to suit the moment rather than as part of planned policy. The term, from Caribbean speech, has been used by white as well as black youth in the UK since 2000.

aerated adj
angrily over-excited or agitated. Perhaps originated by educated speakers who were familiar with the technical senses of aerate (to supply the blood with oxygen or to make effervescent), but usually used nowadays by less sophisticated speakers who may mispronounce it as 'aeriated'.

Now, don't get all aerated.

a few fries short of a happy meal adj
intellectually impaired, deranged, eccentric. This variation on the lines of the colloquial 'one sandwich short of a picnic' was popular among students in the UK, and also recorded in the USA in 2002. The reference is to a McDonald's fast food meal.

afro n
a hairstyle consisting of a mass of tight curls which was adopted by Afro-Caribbeans and imitated (often by perming) by white **hippies**, particularly between 1967 and 1970

afters n British
a drinking session in a pub after official closing time, **lock-in**. The term is an abbreviation of 'after hours (drinking)'.

There's going to be afters on Friday night. Are you going to stay for afters?

ag, agg n British
violence, aggression. A shortened form of **aggro**, heard in provincial adolescent slang from around 1990, and previously used by older prison inmates and members of the underworld. Like aggro, the

word may be employed with the weaker sense of trouble or irritation.

If you go to the market precinct these days it's just ag.

-age *suffix American*
a termination that became popular amongst older adolescents in the early 1990s in creating mock-serious nouns from existing slang and standard bases. **Buffage**, **grindage** and **tuneage** are examples. The tendency was popularised by its use in such films as *Bill and Ted's Bogus Journey, Wayne's World* and *California Man.*

ag-fay *n American*
a male homosexual. Usually used pejoratively and almost always by heterosexuals, this example of **pig Latin** is based on **fag**. Unlike the superficially similar **ofay**, this expression is predominantly used by white speakers.

aggers *n British*
the backside, buttocks. An item of provincial slang recorded in the *Observer* newspaper, 23 July 1994. Its derivation is uncertain.

aggie *n British*
a marble (as used in children's games). An old term, usually for a striped marble, still heard in the 1950s. From agate, the banded stone from which marbles were originally made.
See also **alley**

aggravation *n British*
serious trouble, victimisation or mutual harassment. A colloquial extension of the standard meaning of the word, used by police and the underworld. Aggravation is, like **bother** and **seeing-to**, a typical example of menacing understatement as practised in London working-class speech.

aggro[1], **agro** *n British and Australian*
aggravation. Originally the slang term was a euphemism for threatened or actual violence, offered typically by **skinheads**, although it is not clear whether they or their (typically **hippy**) victims first adopted the shortened form at the end of the 1960s. (Whichever is the case, the word is a derivation of aggravation in its colloquial sense as used by police officers and criminals since the 1950s.) Aggro, like **bother**, is a typical example of the use of menacing understatement in British working-class slang. The word was soon taken up by other users and, in informal

English, has now reverted to something like its original unspecific meaning of annoyance or trouble. In Australian usage aggro can be used as an adjective, as in 'I guess I was a bit aggro last night'.

'He's steaming drunk and well up for some agro.'
(Recorded, London student, 2001)

aggro[2] *adj American*
wonderful, excellent. This probably ephemeral term was recorded among teenagers in New York and California in the late 1980s. It is probably based on a misunderstanding or deliberate shifting in the meaning of the earlier British term.

A.H. *n American*
asshole (usually in the metaphorical rather than literal sense). A euphemistic abbreviation.
Compare **a-hole**

ah-eet *adj American*
'doing OK, feeling good' (recorded, US student, April 2002). The term, which can be used as an exclamation or greeting, is probably a humorous or mock-dialect deformation of **all right** or **awright**.

a-hole *n American*
a euphemism for **asshole**, usually in the literal rather than metaphorical sense

aiit!, ite! *exclamation American*
contracted alterations of **all right** or **awright**, fashionable since 2000

aim archie at the armitage *vb Australian*
(of a male) to urinate. A later version of the widely known **point percy at the porcelain**, popularised in Barry Humphries' *Barry McKenzie* cartoon series. ('Armitage Ware' is a brand name of toilet bowls.)

aimed *adj American*
identified, singled out and/or victimised. A slang version of 'targeted' which probably originated in the argot of black street gangs. It is now used in milder contexts by teenagers.
There's no way we'll get out of this; we've been aimed…

airball *n American*
a dim-witted, eccentric or unpleasant person. This mildly pejorative term, originating in the 1980s, is a combination of **airhead** and the more offensive **hairball**.

airbrained *adj American*
silly, frivolous, empty-headed. Slightly less derogatory than the noun **airhead**, this term has not been imported into Brit-

ain to any significant extent, perhaps because of possible confusion with 'harebrained' which is still in widespread use.

She's not just some airbrained bimbo, you know.

airhead *n*
a fool; a silly, empty-headed person. An American teenager's term heard since the mid-1970s, used for instance by **Valley Girls**; it has been adopted by British teenagers since the 1980s.

'The usual crowd of airheads, phonies, deadlegs, posers, bimbos, wallies, wannabees, hangers-on and gatecrashers...'
(Christena Appleyard, *Daily Mirror*, 11 May 1989)

air hose *n American*
shoes, typically loafers (leather moccasins), worn without socks. A **preppie** term for a preppie sartorial convention, punning on the American sense of 'hose' meaning socks, stockings, etc., and the compressed air pipe at a filling station.

airlocked *adj British*
drunk. The term occurs especially in Northern Irish use and it is possibly an inoffensive form of 'bollocked' or evoking a loss of faculties as if from oxygen deprivation.

airs *n pl American*
trainers. The word is a shortening of the trademark label *Air Jordans* which was generalised to denote any sports shoes and widely heard in 1991 and 1992. (The rare use of 'airing' in black speech to mean walking or leaving is an unconnected earlier usage, probably based on 'open air'.)

Alabama *n See* **'bama**

Alan Whickers, Alans *n pl British*
knickers, panties. The terms are non-working-class rhyming slang, heard among young people, particularly students, in the 1970s and 1980s. The reference was to Alan Whicker, a well-known punctilious and dapper television interviewer.

There was this huge pair of Alan Whickers hanging on the line.

a laugh and a joke *n British*
a *smoke*. The rhyming slang phrase generally refers to tobacco smoking. It was recorded in London in 2002.

alec, aleck *n*
a swindler's victim, dupe. This term from the early 20th century is still heard

in the USA and Australia. It is not clear whether alec derives from 'smart alec' or vice versa. The word was used for instance in the film *House of Games* (1987, David Mamet), which dramatises the world of small-time American gamblers.

aled, aled-up *adj British*
drunk. A mild and acceptable term which, although short and to-the-point, can be used in polite company or family newspapers. The expressions probably originated in the north of England where ale has been, and remains, a common all-purpose word for beer.

He's aled again.

alert *adj British*
(of a male) slightly sexually aroused. Related terms, also in use since 2000, include **lob-on** and **semi**. 'It means to be a bit turned on (i.e. having a slight erection)'. (Recorded, London student, May 2003).

alf *n Australian*
a common, foolish person. In the 1960s this term briefly vied with **ocker** as the generic term for uncouth manhood.

alkie *n*
an alcoholic, especially one who lives rough or frequents the streets. The obvious term, which usually carries overtones of contempt, has been widespread in the USA at least since the Depression; it was adopted after World War II in Australia and since the 1960s has been in limited use in Britain.

all about (it) *adj American*
enthusiastic, keen. In use among adolescents and college students since 2000.

I asked her if she wanted to hang with us and she was all about it.
I'm all about some basketball.

alley, allie *n British*
a marble (as used in children's games). Like **aggie**, the word is approximately a hundred years old and refers to a pale or white marble. Although rarely heard today, these terms probably survive where the traditional game is still played. The most likely origin of the term is a shortening of 'alabaster', from which some Victorian marbles were made.

alley apple *n American*
a lump of horse manure. A less common version of the expression **road apple**,

which is now an international English term.

alleycat vb
to prowl the streets, particularly late at night

> 'There's Arthur Smith alleycatting around, trying to pick up chicks.'
> (Kit Hollerbach, *The 39,000 Steps*, Channel 4 documentary on the Edinburgh Festival, July 1989)

alligator shoes/boots n pl
old footwear with the toes gaping open. A jocular play on (expensive and luxurious) alligator-skin shoes.

all mouth and trousers adj British
blustering and boastful, showing off without having the qualities to justify it. A commonly heard dismissive phrase, typically said by women about a loud or assertive man. There is a suggestion that this is a corruption of the more logical, but rarely heard expression, 'all mouth and no trousers', meaning full of talk but deficient in the sexual area. A less racy version is 'all talk and no action'. There is an analogy with other colourful expressions, now mostly archaic, such as 'all my eye and Betty Martin', meaning nonsense, and more abusive versions such as **all piss and wind**.

> Oh him! He's all mouth and trousers, that one.

all over the shop/show/gaff/lot/ballpark adj, adv
disorganised, in chaos or disarray. The first three versions are British, the last two American. This is a more colourful extension into slang of the colloquial phrase 'all over the place', and the first version at least dates from the 19th century. ('Shop' is a working-class catch-all for any workplace.)

all piss and wind adj
full of bluster and noise, but without real substance. This expression can have a similar meaning to **all mouth and trousers**, but can be applied for instance to a politician's speech or a theatrical performance, as well as to an individual. 'All piss and vinegar' is a rarer synonym.

all right!, awright! exclamation American
an exclamation of recognition, greeting, approval or admiration. The 'right' is emphasised, high-pitched and elongated when shouted. Used in this way the phrase was originally black American; it

was picked up by whites, especially **hippies**, in the late 1960s.

alls-bay n pl American
the testicles. An item of **pig Latin** based on **balls**.

all that n, adj American
(a person who is) exceptional, admirable. The phrase is almost invariably used dismissively or to express derision, as in 'She thinks that she's all that'. It occurs in black working-class speech and in black and white campus usage, and is probably a shortening of '(not) all that much' or 'all that great'.

all that and a bag of chips n, adj American
an elaboration of **all that** in use among college students since the late 1990s

> Wow, that movie was all that and a bag of chips.

almonds, almond rocks n pl British
socks. A London rhyming-slang term which is still in use. (Almond rock cakes were a popular working-class treat early in the 20th century.)

alms(-house) adj British
rude, disrespectful. This item of British street slang of the late 1990s is a variant form of **arms**. The reference is unclear, but the expression may have arisen in Caribbean usage.

alpha geek n American
the most technically proficient and/or knowledgeable member of a group. The term, usually but not invariably applied to males in an office or work-group, is inspired by the categorising of animal group-leaders as 'alpha males'. It was defined in *Wired* magazine in September 1995.

> 'You gotta just identify the alpha geek and fire all your questions at him.'
> (Recorded, financial trader, New York, 1996)

altered adj British
drunk, a joky euphemism from the notion of being '(in an) altered state'. An item of student slang in use in London and elsewhere since around 2000.

amagent n South African
an alternative form of **ma-gent**

amber fluid, amber nectar n
beer, Australian lager. A facetious euphemism used by Australians in the 1970s which was popularised in Britain first by Barry Humphries' *Barry McKenzie* comic strip, then by TV advertise-

ments, featuring the actor Paul Hogan, for Australian beer in the 1980s. The term was enthusiastically adopted by some middle-class British drinkers, themselves fond of mock pompous coinages.

ambulance chaser n

a lawyer, literally one who specialises in claiming on behalf of accident victims. The phrase is also applied, facetiously or critically, to any lawyer who is known for sharp practice or unethical methods. This term was originally American (dating from the beginning of the 20th century) but is now employed in other English-speaking areas.

> 'My daddy's a lawyer. Well, we often say he's an ambulance chaser.'
> (Recorded, young woman, Chicago, 1983)

amp n

1. an ampoule (of a narcotic). An obvious shortening used by drug abusers.

> I scored a couple of amps of meth[edrine].

2. an amplifier. A common shortening used by musicians and hi-fi enthusiasts since the 1960s.

> He rammed his guitar into the amp.

amped (up) adj American

excited or agitated. This term from black street slang, which can also indicate excited anticipation, may derive from an ampoule (of a narcotic) or from 'amphetamine(d)', but is equally likely to derive from the musicians' jargon 'amped-up', meaning with the amplifiers fully rigged.

> 'While they were keeping me waiting I was getting more and more amped up...'
> (Recorded, musician, New York City, 1995)

'ampsteads n pl British

teeth. Cockney rhyming slang referring to the London beauty spot Hampstead Heath. The term (which is still heard) is invariably used with the dropped aspirate.

> a lovely set of 'ampsteads
> kicked in the 'ampsteads

amscray vb

to **scram**, go away. One of the few examples of **backslang** or **pig Latin** which is actually used in speech, albeit rarely. The word is a pre-World War II Americanism

which has been heard in Australia and in Britain since the 1950s.

> We'd better amscray before he gets back.

amyl n

amyl nitrite (sometimes called amyl nitrate); a very powerful stimulant drug inhaled from a broken phial or **popper**. Amyl nitrite is prescribed for the treatment of angina pectoris, though it has been taken for fun since the 1950s, and for its supposed sexually stimulating effects, especially by **gay** men, since the late 1970s.

anal adj American

irritatingly pedantic, fastidious, conscientious, etc. This shortening of the popular psychological categorisation 'anal retentive' was a vogue term among US college students in the 1990s.

> Don't be so anal!
> That was such an anal thing to do.

anal astronaut n British

a male homosexual. A pejorative and jocular term in use among schoolboys in 2004.

anchor n British

a young person, typically a younger sibling or babysittee, who inhibits one's pleasure or freedom of movement. The term was in use among adolescents and young adults from around 2000.

anchors n pl British

brakes. Originally part of the jargon of pre-war professional drivers. The term was popular with some middle-class motorists throughout the 1950s and 1960s, usually in the phrase 'slam on the anchors', meaning to brake suddenly. It now sounds rather dated.

and relax! exclamation British

1. a warning of an approaching person
2. an exhortation to someone who is irate to calm down
Both usages have been recorded since 2000.

Andrew, the n British

the navy. A dated term which is a shortening of 'Andrew Miller' (or 'Andrew Millar'). The eponymous Andrew is said to have been a press-ganger whose name was taken as a nickname for a warship and later for the whole service.

ane n British

the backside, anus, a term used by schoolchildren since the 1990s. By extension the word can also refer to a foolish or unpleasant individual.

angel[1] *n*

cocaine. The term was recorded with this sense among clubbers in the UK in 2000.

angel[2], **angela, angelina** *n*

a passive male homosexual. These are slang terms used by homosexuals themselves and (usually pejoratively) by heterosexuals. The words may originate as terms of affection, as feminine nicknames, or possibly from an earlier slang usage denoting a (female) prostitute.

angel-drawers *n British*

a term of endearment, used especially by middle-class speakers. The phrase is typical of the jocular compounds favoured, e.g., in St Valentine's Day dedications printed in newspaper small ads but, unlike many of these, it is spoken.

angel dust *n*

the drug **P.C.P.** A powdered (usually home-made) version of an animal tranquilliser which is smoked or sniffed through a tube and which produces in the user unpredictable and extreme physical and psychological effects. Users are capable of acts of violence, hallucinations and periods of imperviousness to pain and superhuman strength. P.C.P. is easy to produce in home laboratories and became a severe social problem in US cities after 1975, principally among poorer teenagers. Fears of its spread to Britain and elsewhere were groundless. Its milieu is now largely given over to **crack**.

> 'For 15 years Washington has been struggling with abuse of PCP, also known as Angel Dust.'
> (*Independent*, 24 July 1989)

Anglo *n American*

a person of (mainly) Anglo-Saxon ethnic origin. The term came into widespread use in the 1970s, especially among Hispanics. This was the first attempt by Americans from other ethnic backgrounds to categorise white Anglo-Saxons as a subgroup. (**WASP** was first coined by Wasps themselves; **honky**, **pinkie**, etc., are terms of abuse.)

> 'They're mainly Anglos out on Long Island these days.'
> (Recorded, suburban New Yorker, 1977)

animal *adj British*

excellent, exciting. This use of the term by young people since 2000 is based on

earlier uses of the noun animal to denote an impressively excessive individual.

animal house *n American*

any dwelling, but especially a college fraternity house, whose occupants are excessively dirty and rowdy. This late 1950s campus term was revived by the film *National Lampoon's Animal House*, starring the late John Belushi in the role of a typical 'animal' in 1978.

animal night/act *n Australian*

a planned or self-conscious bout of bad behaviour or excess. The term is typically used (by and about males) with pride or admiration rather than distaste.

ankle[1] *vb*

to walk, stroll, saunter. A raffish expression heard in the USA and occasionally in Britain since the 1980s.

> Let's ankle down to the off-licence.

ankle[2] *n American*

an attractive female or females. This use of the word appears to predate its popularity among black youths and on campus since the late 1990s. The provenance is unclear and it may be a jocular reference to the archaic phrase 'a well-turned ankle' as a Victorian notion of beauty.

> She's some cute ankle.
> Check out the ankle around here.

ankle-biter *n*

a child, usually a baby or toddler. Commonly used with mock distaste by parents, sometimes with real distaste by others, ankle-biter has been heard in all social classes in Britain and Australia since the late 1970s. Synonyms are **leg-biter**, **rug rat** and **crumb-snatcher**.

annihilated *adj*

helplessly drunk, drugged or exhausted. A middle-class teenager's colloquial expression, popular in the 1970s and 1980s.

anorak *n British*

an unfashionable, studious or tedious person, usually a young male. A campus expression from the 1980s, based on the characteristic dress of these fellow-students. A sub-genre of jangling guitar pop music, supposedly beloved of such students, was dubbed 'anorak rock' in the music press in the mid-1980s.

> 'An anorak is one of those boring gits who sit at the front of every lecture with their

Pringle jumpers asking the lecturer their clever questions.'
(Graffito in the toilets at King's College, London University, July 1988)

anteater *n American*
(a male with) an uncircumcised penis. Synonyms are **aardvark**, **corn-dog**.

ante up *vb*
to pay one's contribution, put one's money in the common pot. This expression, not to be confused with 'up the ante', comes from the preliminary stage in a poker game when one or all of the players must put a stake in the pot. By extension ante up is sometimes used to mean settle accounts or (reluctantly) hand over something demanded.
OK, you guys, it's time to ante up.

(Sir) Anthony (Blunt) *n*
a very unpleasant person, **cunt**. Still in use in 2004, this rhyming slang expression uses the name of the late keeper of the Queen's pictures and traitor.

antiman *n*
a male homosexual. The term, originating in Caribbean usage and heard among young speakers of most ethnic groups in the UK, is a Creole pronunciation of 'auntie-man'. It is usually pejorative. **Panty-man** is a synonym.

an't it? *question form British*
a variation of **innit?** which, like that term, originated in black British usage and was adopted by adolescents and later by younger schoolchildren in the 1990s
We're going to the park an't it?
An't it he's the one.

antsy *adj*
1a. nervous, jumpy, agitated
'She's been getting a little antsy lately – wants me to leave my wife.'
(*The Secret of my Success*, US film, 1987)

1b. eager for sex
Both senses are derived from the older, humorous colloquial expression 'to have ants in one's pants' (meaning to be restless or agitated). Antsy is a fairly common and inoffensive term in the USA and Australia, but rare in Britain.

antwacky *adj British*
out-of-date, old-fashioned. The term, used especially in northwest England, is probably a mock ignorant alteration of antique.

ape(shit) *adj, adv*
out of control, berserk. Used especially in the expression 'go ape', the image is of a person reduced to a primal state, either by infatuation, excitement or, especially, anger. An American teenagers' term from the late 1950s, now in general currency.
He's apeshit about her.
'I go ape ev'ry time I see you smile.'
('I Go Ape', written and recorded by Neil Sedaka, 1960)
'After I'd left my last school, I pinched a wallet full of credit cards and went apeshit in about five different counties.'
(*Sunday Times* magazine, Stephen Fry, August 1989)

ape-hangers *n pl*
extra-high handlebars for motorbikes or bicycles. The style was popularised by **bikers** in the USA in the 1950s, spreading to Britain where **rockers**, **greasers** and schoolchildren had adopted the style and the term by about 1959.

apple-polisher *n*
a flatterer, someone who curries favour. The term comes from the image of the ingratiating pupil who polishes an apple carefully before presenting it to a teacher. The tradition of 'an apple for the teacher' was really practised in rural USA before World War II, but the term is common in all English-speaking areas. It is sometimes in the form of a verb, as in 'she's been apple-polishing again'. In Britain it is often shortened to **polisher**.
'I had few qualifications for Hollywood; I was immoderately slothful, had no facility for salesmanship or apple-polishing, and possessed a very low boiling point.'
(S. J. Perelman, quoted in *Groucho, Harpo, Chico & sometimes Zeppo*, Joe Adamson, 1973)

apples[1] *n pl*
1. female breasts
2. the testicles
Apples, like almost all other round fruits, have readily been used as euphemisms for these bodily parts. This type of metaphor may occur as a spontaneous coinage in any English-speaking community.

3. white people. An ethnic categorisation used by Afro-Caribbeans and South and East Asians. The reference is probably to pink skins and white flesh and is sometimes pejorative.

apples[2] *adj Australian*
fine, perfect, OK. Often used in the expression 'she's apples', meaning 'everything is all right'. This use of the word may originate in 'apples and rice' or 'apples and spice', obsolete British and Australian rhyming slang for *nice*.

apples and pears *n pl British*
stairs. One of the best-known examples of cockney rhyming slang which, although authentic, is rarely heard these days.

apricot! *exclamation British*
a generalised term of approval recorded among middle-class students in 1999. It may be a jocular version of 'peachy'.

apricots *n pl British*
the testicles
> '*Hot water has always made my apricots sag.*'
> (Pensioner Ron Tuffer, quoted in the *Eastbourne Herald*, 7 May 1994)

April fools *n pl British*
tools. Cockney rhyming slang still heard occasionally in workshops, garages and factories.

April showers *n pl British*
flowers. An item of London working-class rhyming slang which survives in market traders' jargon.

Archer *n British*
£2,000. An invention by an anonymous wit in the tradition of a **monkey**, a **pony**, etc. It refers to the sum paid by the author and Tory politician Jeffrey Archer to Miss Monica Coughlan, a prostitute, to enable her to go abroad. Her return in 1987 resulted in Mr Archer bringing a libel case against the *News of the World*, which he won. (The synonym **Jeffrey** was also heard.)
> '*The usual two Archers in a plain envelope.*'
> (*Weekending*, BBC Radio 4, 9 March 1990)

arching for it *adj British*
(of a woman) sexually aroused. 'It refers to a young woman who is sexually fired up (like a cat on heat)'. (Recorded, student, London 2004).

arctic *adj British*
1. bad. An intensified form of the vogue sense of **cold**.
2. excellent, fashionable. An intensified form of **cool** or **chilled**.

The term has been fashionable in both senses since 2000.

Argos bling *n British See* **chav**

Aristotle, arry, arris *n*
1. a *bottle*. Rhyming slang, probably dating from the 19th century, but still occasionally heard in the London area and in Australia.
2. '**arris** (usually in the sense of 'courage, nerve')

arm *n*
1. *British* power, influence, coercion. A colloquial coinage on the lines of 'hold', 'grip' or 'strong-arm'.
> *This should give us some arm.*
2. *See* **on the arm**
3. *South African* a measurement of **dagga**. Recorded as an item of Sowetan slang in the *Cape Sunday Times*, 29 January 1995.

arm candy *n*
a temporary escort, typically a fellow student or 'unattached' acquaintance, chosen to accompany to a social function. An Americanism of the late 1990s heard in the UK since 2000. **Social handbag** is a synonym.
Compare **eye candy**

armpit *n*
a very unpleasant place. The word usually forms part of the expression 'the armpit of the universe'; that is, the most unpleasant place in existence (a milder version of 'arsehole of the universe').

armpits! *exclamation British*
a less offensive alternative to **bollocks** as a cry of dismissal or derision, in use among middle-class students since 2000

arms *adj British*
offending codes of behaviour, breaking unwritten rules. This code term among teenage gangs was defined by one of its users as 'out of order'. The term was recorded in use among North London schoolboys in 1993 and 1994. It may in fact derive from the equally mysterious **alms(-house)**, which is heard in black British speech denoting rudeness or **dissing**.
> *This is/he's arms.*

'arris *n*
1. the backside, buttocks. A cockney elaboration of **arse** sometimes adopted

by middle-class speakers who want to avoid the offensive term.

a kick in the 'arris

2. courage, nerve. A London working-class term which is a more recent derivation of **arse**.

loads of 'arris

Both senses derive from a double rhyme; 'arris from **Aristotle**, meaning *bottle*, while 'bottle and glass' gives *arse*.

arse¹ *n*

1. *British* the backside, buttocks, anus. This word is not, strictly speaking, slang, but an ancient term (*aers* in Anglo-Saxon, descended from Germanic nouns related to an Indo-European ancestor meaning 'tail') which, since the 17th century, has been considered too vulgar for polite conversation. Australia follows the British spelling, while in the USA and Canada the word is spelled **ass**.

2. *British* a foolish or contemptible person. A fairly mild term of exasperated contempt, popular in upper- and middle-class speech until the 1960s, now generally replaced by stronger or more colourful alternatives. 'Silly arse!' was a favourite British rebuke.

3a. *British* courage, nerve or cheek. This has been a popular working-class usage in London and Australian slang. In Britain it has, since the 1960s, largely been supplanted by more colourful terms such as **'arris** or **bottle**, which are derived from it, or by synonyms such as **balls**.

3b. *Australian* good luck. This usage, which is more commonly expressed by the adjective **arsy**, probably derives from the previous sense, with the implication that the good fortune came as a result of daring or impudence.

4. *Australian* a synonym for **heave-ho**, **elbow** or 'the boot', usually in the expression **give (someone) the arse**

5. my arse! *British* 'Nonsense!', 'I don't believe it!' or 'It's not true!' An exclamation of angry or impatient disbelief, dating at least from the 18th century. It is probably a shortening of a longer phrase such as in the following sense.

6. kiss my arse! *British* an exclamation of defiance or contempt

7. not to know one's arse from one's elbow/a hole in the ground *British* to be incapable or incompetent, stupid

8. the sun shines out of his/her arse *British* he or she is wonderful, perfect or the favourite. The expression is used con-

temptuously or enviously of a person who, in their own opinion or that of others, can do no wrong.

arse² *adj British*
of poor quality. A vogue term (in all its senses) among younger speakers since the late 1990s, its usage popularised by cult TV comedies such as *Father Ted* and *The Fast Show*.

pure arse
That new single of hers is arse.

arse about *vb*
to fool about, behave in an irresponsible or silly way. A favourite expression of many schoolmasters, especially in the 1950s and 1960s.

Stop arsing about in there and get on with your work!

arse-about-face *adj, adv*
back to front, the wrong way round or wrongly ordered or organised

Look at the state of that shelf you just put up; it's all arse-about-face!

arse bandit *n British*
a male homosexual. The humorous but not affectionate term suggests an aggressive, predatory or desperate enemy. It is very much a term of jovial male abuse (there is no record of women saying it) in public schools, the army and the pub. Slightly less vulgar versions are 'bum bandit' and **trouser bandit**; **chocolate bandit** is another synonym.

arsed *adj British See* **can't be arsed/bolloxed/fucked/shagged**

arse-end *n*
the end, back or bottom of anything. A common vulgarism also used in the phrase 'the arse-end of nowhere', referring to a very remote and/or unpleasant place. 'Arse-end Charlie' is a more robust version of the colloquial 'tail-end Charlie', as applied to a straggler.

arsehole¹ *n British*
1. the anus. **Asshole** in American English.
2. the arsehole of the universe/earth/world an extremely unpleasant place, especially one that is dirty, smelly and hot, but now by extension anywhere awful. The phrase was probably coined by troops stationed overseas, prompted by such captions as 'the pearl of the Orient' or 'the gateway to the Pacific'.
3. an extremely unpleasant person, especially one who combines offensiveness with stupidity. The term, when used in Britain or Australia, is stronger than the

American equivalent **asshole**, and slightly different in emphasis. It shows real distaste and dislike rather than mild contempt.

**arsehole² ** *vb*
1. *British* to 'crawl', flatter or curry favour in a nauseating way. Typically used at work about a fellow employee, this is probably inspired by the now dated expressions 'arsehole-crawler' or 'arsehole-creep'.

> *There he goes, arseholing again. It makes me sick.*

2. *Australian* to throw someone out, to get rid of (an unwanted lover). The word is often used plaintively or resentfully by jilted teenagers.

> *I can't understand it. Robyn arseholed me last night.*

arseholed *adj*
1. *British* very drunk. A popular word among students, younger members of the armed forces and other heavy drinkers from the 1960s to the present. The image is of someone disgustingly or helplessly drunk, as in the expression 'pissed as an arsehole'; but the term is neutral, not usually pejorative, and is used by all social classes.

> 'Once a month he gets completely arseholed and then comes home and asks me to forgive him.'
> (Recorded, housewife, Devon, 1986)

2a. *Australian* dismissed from one's job
2b. *Australian* ejected, especially from a bar
2c. *Australian* rejected by one's partner

arseholes! *exclamation British*
nonsense. A term expressing brusque dismissal or defiance which now seems to be falling into disuse. The singer Ian Dury included it in a stream of abuse featured on a 1978 record.

arsehole to breakfast time *adj, adv British*
1. completely disorganised, 'at sixes and sevens'. A picturesque, if fundamentally meaningless expression sometimes heard in Britain, especially in the north of England.

> *It's no good, it's all arsehole to breakfast time in that office at the moment.*

2. thoroughly, constantly, or the full distance as, for instance, in the expression 'he kicked him from arsehole to breakfast time'. This may be an allusion to the complete digestive process (breakfast time

referring to the mouth), but the origins of the phrase are obscure.

arselick *vb British*
to flatter, curry favour. The verb, which may be transitive or, more often, intransitive, is a more recent back-formation from the noun form.

arse-licker *n*
a flatterer or toady, someone who is nauseatingly sycophantic. This ancient image and phrase is paralleled in many European languages (*Arschlecker* in German, *lèche-cul* in French).

arse-man *n*
a man whose favourite part of a woman's anatomy is the buttocks as opposed to a **leg-man** or **tit-man**

arse-on *n British*
a fit of bad temper, sulk. The term has been heard since 2000.

> *feeling a bit of an arse-on*
> *He's got the arse-on.*

arse over tip/tit *adv*
head over heels, upside down. The expression is typically cockney, but widespread in Britain and Australia. The American version is **ass over tincups/teacups**.

> 'She tripped and fell arse over tit down the stairs.'
> (Recorded, plumber, London, 1987)

arse up *vb British*
to make a mess of, mix up or spoil. A less common variation of **balls up** and the verb form of **cock-up**.

> *He managed to completely arse up the whole job.*

arse-up *n British*
a synonym for **cock-up** and **fuck-up**, which became popular from the mid-1990s, in common with most compounds based on **arse**

> 'It [a student union function] was quite well planned this year – unlike the last one, which was a complete arse-up.'
> (Recorded, London University student, October 1996)

arse-wipe *n*
a British version of **ass-wipe**

arsey *adj British*
truculent, aggressive, bumptious. A vogue term among young people since the late 1990s, also heard on US campuses since 2000.

arsy *adj Australian*
lucky. Usually said grudgingly or enviously about someone who has managed

to get away with something. (**Arse** in Australian slang may signify luck as well as brazenness.)

Arthur Scargill n Irish
an alcoholic drink. The name of the militant leader of the UK miners' union in the 1980s was borrowed as a rhyme for **gargle**.

artillery n
needles, hypodermic syringes and other paraphernalia used by heroin addicts. The image of an arsenal of deadly equipment is typical of addicts' own self-dramatising slang (as in **shooting gallery**, **harpoon**, etc.)

Have you got the artillery ready, man?

artist, -artist n, suffix
an expert in, or devotee of, a particular activity. The word can be added to many others, but the most popular are bull(shit)-artist, burn-artist, con-artist, **piss-artist**, **ripoff artist** and **sack artist**.
This pattern entered modern British slang via the armed forces in the 1950s and 1960s, and separately via American **hippy** terminology of the late 1960s and early 1970s. The ultimate geographical origin of the usage is obscure; it may have come into use spontaneously in several English-speaking areas, perhaps prompted by the Edwardian habit of pompously applying 'artist' or 'artiste' to performers in various fields of expertise.

arty-farty, artsy-fartsy adj
pretentious, affected, more decorative than useful. A more vulgar parallel of the innocuous 'arty-crafty', which is Edwardian in origin and was usually applied to the pseudo-rustic, as in the Arts and Crafts design movement of the late 19th century.

arvo n Australian
afternoon. An example of the Australian tendency to abbreviate even the most mundane everyday words. The tendency is shared by nursery slang in general and, in Britain, especially the slang of Liverpool. (Arvo is, however, uniquely Australian.)

'There's no excuse for being in that state in the middle of the arvo!'
(Recorded, Australian tourist, London, 1989)

asap, assap adv
immediately, as soon as possible. The spoken form of the commonly used initials a.s.a.p. (sometimes also used in speech, pronounced letter by letter or as one word).

Asian massive, the Asian invasion n British
a group, clique or gang of young (South) Asians. The phrase has been used e.g. as an ethnic or social categorisation by university students since 2000. **The innit-crowd** is a synonymous phrase. 'It's a collective term for Asian gangsters with mobile phones who hang out in the student common room'.

ass n American
1. the backside, buttocks, anus. The American spelling of the British **arse**.
2. sexual gratification. Usually used by men referring to women as anonymous sex objects.

I'm going to grab me some ass.
3. oneself, especially when thought of as an item to be manipulated

You gonna get yo' ass killed!
4. Your ass is mine! 'You are in my power!' A phrase used triumphantly, typically by representatives of authority to their victims
5. Your ass is grass. 'You are in very serious trouble'. Usually said seriously as part of a threat or ruefully by a victim.

Get it right or your ass is grass!
6. have one's ass in a sling/ass on the line to be in trouble, held responsible.
See also the entries following and **badass**; **candyass**; **kick ass**

-ass combining form
the term is used in American slang and, more recently, in Caribbean and, occasionally, British speech as an all-purpose affix denoting an individual or example, combining with a noun or adjective as in **big-ass**, 'old-ass', **lame-ass**

assap adv See **asap**

ass-bandit n American
a North American and Caribbean version of **arse bandit**

asshole n American
1. the anus. The American version of the British and Australian **arsehole**.
2. a very stupid person, someone who is pathetically or offensively foolish. This American word always implies contempt, but can also convey pity, unlike **arsehole**, which has overtones of real dislike. Since the 1960s, British and Australian speakers have adopted the American term in this sense, with its different spelling and pronunciation, for their own use. The word has become very widespread since

the late 1970s and has simultaneously become a vulgarism rather than a taboo term.

'It didn't take very long to realise that he wasn't a threat, just a total asshole.'
(Recorded, US executive, London, 1988)
3. a very unpleasant place

'On top of a bleak, snow-swept hillside in Hermon, Maine, which, if not the asshole of the universe, is at least within farting distance of it.'
(Stephen King, *Sunday Times* magazine, 15 October 1989)

asshole buddy *n American*
a very close friend or ally, a 'bosom pal'. A term that is used in both jocular and unfriendly contexts. It was coined by, and is usually about, heterosexual men.

ass-kicker *n American*
an aggressive person, a disciplinarian; someone who **kicks ass**. An armed-forces term which has been adopted by students and school pupils, among others.

ass-kisser *n American*
a sycophant, flatterer or toady. The expression is based on **kiss ass**.

ass-licker *n American*
the American version of **arse-licker**

ass-load(s) *n American*
a large amount. **Butt-load(s)** is a synonym.

an ass-load of trouble
ass-loads of money

ass-out *adj, adv American*
a synonym of **balls-out** heard in the 1990s

We've got to go ass-out to win this thing.
'It was a whole ass-out crazy attempt to just finish the job on time.'
(Recorded, art dealer, Chicago, May 1996)

ass over tincups/teacups *adv American*
head over heels. A folksy American version of the British **arse over tip/tit**.

ass-wipe *n American*
1. toilet paper. A working-class, blue-collar or armed-forces term.
2. a worthless, contemptible person. A term popular in the 1970s and 1980s.

at it *phrase British*
1. having sex. A coy euphemism typically used by schoolchildren or the middle-aged.
2. committing a crime or crimes, or engaged in a confidence trick. A mild

euphemism typically used by police officers or criminals themselves, from the common colloquialism 'at it again', referring to any repeated and troublesome activity.

'Joey Ganguli is at it all the time. He…earns his rolls of cash in the middle of the Asian gang wars…in the East End of London.'
(*Guardian*, 15 April 2004)

a touch of the tarbrush *n*
(having) a skin colour which suggests a trace of black or coloured ancestry. This euphemism, often heard in a discriminatory context, originated in the mid-19th century, when it was also used to refer to sailors (the tarbrush being used on board ship).

attitude *n American*
a bad attitude, antisocial behaviour, sullen hostility. This use of the word without 'an' or 'the' probably derives from the black American prisoners' shortening of the white authority figures' phrases 'bad/negative/antisocial attitude' or their accusation, 'You've got an attitude problem'.

Audi! *exclamation American*
goodbye. This announcement that one is leaving is probably a playful deformation of the phrase 'I'm out of here', punning on the brand of German luxury car coveted by young males. It almost certainly originated in black street slang where the variant forms 'Audi 5000!' or simply **5000!** are also heard. By the mid-1990s, the term was also in use on campuses and among high-school students.

Aunt(ie) Flo *n British*
menstruation. The expression, playing on the word flow, typically appears in the form 'Aunt Flo is round today' or 'We're expecting Auntie Flo'.

auntie-man *n See* **antiman**

Aussie *n, adj*
(an) Australian

Aussie kiss *n*
cunnilingus. By analogy with **French kiss** and the notion of 'down under', the phrase was in use among males in the UK and Ireland in 2003.

autograph *n*
a signature. Autograph is underworld argot, typically denoting a signature on a cheque or document, whether forged or genuine.

'ave it! *exclamation British*
a cry of encouragement or triumph popularised by the media during the 2004 European Football Championship

aviation blonde *n British*
a female with blonde hair that is dyed rather than natural. The male witticism refers to the combination of 'blonde hair, black **box**'.

'avin' it large, 'avin' it *phrase British*
enjoying oneself, behaving boisterously. Synonyms for **largeing it** associated especially with club culture since the later 1990s.

a walk in the park *n*
a very easy task, painless experience. The phrase probably originated in American usage.

away-day *n British*
a single dose of LSD or another hallucinogenic drug. A pun on the notion of a **trip** and the name of a cheap excursion ticket on British Rail.

away with the fairies/pixies *adj, adv*
distracted, absent-minded, in a reverie. The first version of the phrase is common in Scottish usage, the second is more often heard in Australia. Both derive ultimately from the folk belief that forces from the fairy world can abduct, enchant or derange human victims.

awesome *adj*
wonderful, excellent, very impressive. A popular teenage word, first used in the USA in the late 1970s and 1980s as part of the vocabulary of **Valley Girls**, **preppies** and hip hop music enthusiasts, among others. This use of the adjective was imported into Britain in the 1980s, especially by teenage skateboarders and **rap** music enthusiasts.

awol, A.W.O.L. *adj*
missing, not present when needed. The expression has been extended, especially by British middle-class speakers, from its original meaning in army jargon of 'absent without leave' to inexplicably absent, either with the implication of fleeing to avoid responsibilities, or wandering uncontrolled or running amok.

> *'Ollie's gone awol again; he disappeared with a bottle and no one's seen him for days.'*
> (Recorded, upper-class youth, London, 1985)

awright! *exclamation American*
an alternative spelling of **all right**. With drawn-out pronunciation, this forms an exclamatory expression of appreciation, agreement or solidarity in American English.

aws *adj American*
an abbreviated form of the fashionable slang sense of **awesome**, popular with college students, particularly females, since the 1990s

axe *n*
a guitar. The word in this sense was enthusiastically adopted by white rock musicians in the late 1960s. Black blues and jazz musicians had originally applied it to any instrument (such as a saxophone) that was held in both hands and 'wielded'. By the early 1970s the white use of the word, which had always had an element of self-consciousness, was mainly confined to rock music journalists or fans.

aya! *exclamation American*
an exclamation of amazement in vogue among teenagers in 1987 and 1988. The word may be a hearty cry or, more often, an affected shriek (possibly in imitation of Hispanic speech).

aye-aye shepherd's pie!, aye-aye Popeye! *exclamation British*
these joky expressions of agreement or compliance originated among primary and junior schoolchildren, but during the early 1990s were adopted as catchphrases by adults, particularly those working in advertising, the media and finance in London.
Compare **okey-dokey, artichokey!**; **oy-oy, saveloy!**

Ayrton (Senna) *n British*
a *tenner*, a £10 note. The rhyming slang term, borrowing the name of the late Brazilian Formula One racing driver, was still in use among London students in 2004.

> *I've only got an Ayrton left to last me the month!*

ay yo trip! *exclamation*
an exhortation or cry of solidarity used in hip hop and **rap** milieus

Aztec two-step, the Aztec two-step *n*
an attack of diarrhoea, particularly one suffered while travelling abroad. The image is of the agitation caused by impending diarrhoea or, more specifi-

cally, the frantic and undignified clenched shuffle to the nearest toilet or bush. This parody of a dance title was coined by Americans who tend to suffer while on holiday in Mexico, and is a late 1970s alternative to **Montezuma's revenge** or the British **gyppy tummy** and **Delhi belly**.

B

B *n American*
a friend, peer. The abbreviation of buddy and/or bro(ther) is used as a greeting between males, particularly in black street usage.

Hey B, how're they hangin'?
Compare **G**

B.A. *n American*
a troublesome, violent or antisocial person. An abbreviation of **badass** or 'bad attitude'. The letters were used as the initials of the surly black hero 'B.A. Baracas' played by Mr T in the US television series *The A-Team* in the 1980s.

bab *n British*
a (doner or shish) kebab. An item of student slang in use in London and elsewhere since around 2000.

We're going to pick up a bab and then back to watch the match.

babber *n British*
1a. a baby or infant
1b. a friend, companion, 'mate'
The term was in use in 2003 and 2004, especially in the Bristol area and South Wales.

babe, babes, baby *n*
1a. a sweetheart, lover. A usage imported from the USA into Britain via films, pop songs, etc. The word had begun to be used unself-consciously in Britain in the late 1970s, particularly in the form **babes** and mainly by working-class speakers. It is used by both sexes, but when used by men to women it can be considered patronising or offensive.
1b. in the form a 'babe', an attractive female. The word became a key term in male adolescent speech, first in the USA and, later, elsewhere from the late 1980s.
See also **robobabe**

babe-magnet *n*
an attractive or supposedly irresistible male. A common characterisation from

the 1990s. **Fanny-magnet** is a more vulgar British variant.

babes, the babes *n, adj*
(something) excellent, superlative. The usage, based on 'babes' as a term of endearment and by analogy with the colloquial expression 'the tops', has been recorded in Scotland and is sometimes heard elsewhere.

I tell you, it's the babes!
The do round Kirsty's last night was babes!

babia-majora *n American*
an extremely attractive woman or women. A jocular item of ersatz slang invented for the cult US TV comedy sketches and movie *Wayne's World*, by alteration of the Latin designation of the outer female genitals *labia majora*.

baby blues *n pl*
the eyes. A humorous adult phrase from the clichéd, twee or amorous description, 'baby-blue eyes'.

babydyke *n American*
a teenage lesbian or girl of 'lesbian appearance'. 'This refers to the young generation of lesbians who are currently of high-school and college age; marked by their short and/or dyed hair, multiple piercings and wallet chains. Not a derogatory term unless used in a derogatory fashion'. (Recorded, US college student, 2002).

baby giraffe *n British*
half a pint of beer. A piece of rhyming slang in vogue among pub habitués since 2000.

Babylon *n British*
1a. racist white society, Britain. The term originates in the biblical imagery of the **rastas**, but has spread, largely via the medium of reggae music, to other black youth and disaffected whites.
1b. the Babylon the police force when viewed as tokens of oppression or white racist authority. A specific usage of the

more general term for society, now widely heard among white youth.

baccy n British
tobacco. This now rather dated alteration of the standard term replaced the previous forms 'bacca' and 'bacco' early in the 20th century. (Cannabis was known jocularly in the 1960s and 1970s as **wacky baccy**.)

baccy billup n British
a cigarette. In playground parlance since 2000. **Baccy** is an old abbreviation of tobacco; billup may be an alteration of build (up) in the slang sense of construct, e.g. a hand rolled cigarette or **joint**.

bachelorette n British
a single woman. A humorous categorisation used by students since 2000.

back n American
1a. the backside, buttocks, especially if large or prominent. This term from black American usage became popularised via the **rap** lyrics to 'Baby Got Back' by Sir Mix-A-Lot (1991).
1b. a female or females seen as potential or actual sexual partners. As in the case of **ass**, the preceding sense quickly became generalised in this way.

back-assed adj American
1a. backwards, reversed
You got it all back-assed.
1b. perverse or clumsy
a back-assed way of doing things

backdoor vb
1a. to commit adultery (with)
'In Australia, you'd never get away with some of the things I've seen here because you'd get a punch in the mouth. We don't go in for backdooring someone else's woman.'
(Jamie Addicoat, fitness instructor, *Observer*, 30 April 1989)
1b. to act illicitly, covertly or deviously; to deceive or betray

backdoor man n
1a. a secret lover, especially a married woman's lover. The term is originally black American slang dating from at least the 1950s.
'I'm your backdoor man... the men don't know, but the little girls understand.'
('Back Door Man', recorded by The Doors, 1968)
1b. a man who sodomises. This usage is mainly applied to and by heterosexuals. The Australian 'backdoor merchant' means a homosexual.

backfire vb
to fart. A term which is in use in Australia and has been heard occasionally in Britain, especially among schoolchildren, since the 1950s.

back garden, back way, backdoor n
the anus. Predictable euphemisms which are invariably used in a sexual context, usually by heterosexuals.

back in the day adv, adj
'when I was younger' or 'in the past'. An item of black street-talk used especially by males, recorded in 2003. The phrase is from Caribbean usage.

back of Bourke, the n Australian
the 'back of beyond'. Bourke is a remote town in northern New South Wales.

backsiding n British
chastising, denigrating, punishing. Heard in black British usage, this term probably originated in Caribbean patois.
'She give him a real good backsiding.'
(Recorded, black female student, London, January 1997)

backslang n
backslang, in which a word or alteration of a word is reversed, enjoyed some popularity in Britain, chiefly among members of the underworld, the sub-proletariat and certain trades such as meat portering. It is also sometimes used by schoolchildren to disguise taboo conversations. Forms of backslang exist in other European languages, notably in the Parisian *verlan* which is still thriving. The only well-known 'mainstream' example of backslang is **yob** from boy.
Compare **pig Latin**

backsnurging n British
sniffing female underwear for sexual pleasure
'We've discovered how the EastEnders actor, who plays Dirty Den, is a secret backsnurger.'
(*Sunday Sport*, 9 May 2004)

back-to-back with adj, adv
showing solidarity, in full support or agreement. The usage probably originated in black speech in the Caribbean and/or North America.

back-up n, adj
(someone who is) prepared to use force on behalf of or otherwise show solidarity with (a friend). The term, deriving from the colloquial verb phrase 'back (someone) up', was first part of the vocabulary

of gangs, and since around 2000 extended to other speakers.

back way n See **back garden**

backy n British
a ride on the back of someone's bicycle. Compare **croggie**

bacon n American
a police officer or the police in general. One of several terms in underworld and student usage inspired by the 1960s epithet **pig**. It can occur in the form of '(the) bacon' for the police in general or 'a bacon', denoting an individual officer.

If you ask me he's bacon.
It's the bacon, let's book!

bad[1] adj
good. Originally from the terminology of the poorest black Americans, either as simple irony or based on the assumption that what is bad in the eyes of the white establishment is good for them, this usage spread via jazz musicians in the 1950s to teenagers in the 1970s. It is still primarily a black term, although it is occasionally used, rather self-consciously, by white teenagers in the USA and, under the influence of **rap** and hip hop, in Britain since the early 1980s. This use of bad is normally distinguished from its opposite, literal meaning by a long drawn-out pronunciation. The superlative form is 'baddest'.

'In hip hop slang "that's bad" can mean "that's good", depending on the tone of voice.'
(Evening Standard, 11 November 1987)

bad[2] n American
a fault, mistake. A key item of black street slang that was adopted by white adolescents in the 1990s, usually in the form 'my bad!', an acknowledgment of guilt or blame.

badass n, adj American
(a person who is) aggressive, antisocial or worthless. The word, first popular among black Americans, is almost always now used with an element of approval or admiration, albeit sometimes grudging. The 'ass' component simply signifies 'individual'. In the 1970s the term came into use among whites, but has not spread to Britain or Australia.

their badass biker style
He's been a badass since he was a kid.

bad-boy n British
a youth, especially a tough or admirable male. A 1990s synonym for **rude-boy** or **roughneck** first used by black gang members before being adopted by other teenagers and younger schoolchildren. Like those terms, it is typical of the tendency among transgressive subcultures to adopt for the purposes of irony and bravado the pejorative language of their critics (as in **bad**, **wicked**, etc.)

badmash n, adj
(someone who is) naughty, dissolute. A term used by Hindi speakers and by other Asians in the UK.

bad mind adj
malevolent, malicious. An Afro-Caribbean usage which has been picked up by UK **wiggas**, etc. since 2000.

badmouth vb
to insult, denigrate or disparage. An Americanism, probably originating in black speech, which was imported into British usage during the 1970s.

bad news n
a person who is unwelcome or disliked, a bore or troublemaker. A usage that was imported to Britain from the USA at the end of the 1960s.

baff vb, n South African
(to) **fart**

baffed, baft adj British
baffled, confused, incapable. This abbreviation of baffled has been a vogue word among teenagers and some young adults in the London area since the mid-1990s.

baffling adj British
difficult. The standard term became generalised as a vogue word among younger speakers from around 2000, possibly originating in Caribbean usage.

bag[1] n
1. an unattractive and/or unpleasant woman. This usage originated in the early 20th century with the idea of a shapeless, heavy or burdensome female, previously expressed as 'baggage'.
2. one's special interest or current preoccupation, sphere of activity. This usage came into vogue in Britain among the **beatniks** and later the **hippies** in the 1960s. It was derived from black American jazz terminology, where it meant a 'category' or 'style'. By the early 1980s the term had become distinctly dated.

'Papa's Got a Brand New Bag.'

(Song title, James Brown, 1965)

3. *American* a package or some measured amount of marihuana or another drug. The custom of American street dealers of **grass** was, and is, to sell small amounts in paper envelopes or cellophane bags, typically 'dime bags' or 'nickel bags'.

See also **bagger**; **double-bagger**

4. *British* the sum of £1,000 in the slang of city traders. Unlike **bar**, **pony** and other similar terms, this seems to be a fairly recent coinage. It is said to be based on the rhyme 'bag of sand': *grand*.

It'll cost you at least a bag.

bag² *vb*

1a. to arrest or catch. This subsense of the word is encountered in police usage, from the terminology of hunters.

1b. to have or take. In this sense the word is used as a synonym for 'grab' or 'cop' in such instances as 'let's bag some beers'. The usage also occurs in American adolescent argot, which includes phrases such as 'bag some z's/rays'.

2a. *American* to conceal or suppress

2b. to give up or abandon

'Maybe I should bag this tugboat business and go into politics.'

(*Legwork*, US TV series, 1986)

2c. to dismiss, fire

These usages, popular especially among teenagers, are all related by their suggestion of discarding someone or something with the trash. Similar meanings of bag were heard occasionally in Britain before 1950.

3. *Australian* to criticise. A 'bagging' is a verbal attack or strong criticism.

4. *also* **bag up** *American* to divide marihuana into small amounts and/or packages before selling it

5. *American See* **bag one's face/head**

bagaza *n South African*

a gun, especially a handgun. Recorded as an item of Sowetan slang in the *Cape Sunday Times*, 29 January 1995.

bagel *n British*

an attractive male. A term, possibly from Jewish usage, employed by young women since 2000, it was recorded in Kent in 2003, defined as denoting '**fit** men'.

Compare **baigel**

bagel-bender *n*

a Jew. A derogatory nickname, used principally in the USA, based on the

name of the baked bread rings that are a Jewish culinary delicacy.

Compare **spaghetti-eater**; **taco-bender**

bagger *n American*

an ugly, repellent person. The term is a shortening of **double-bagger** and, like that phrase, was in use among adolescent and pubescent speakers in the 1990s.

baggies *n pl*

long, wide shorts as worn by surfers since the 1960s

'We'll be wearin' our baggies, huarache sandals, too.'

('Surfin' USA', the Beach Boys, 1963)

baggy *n British*

1. (a devotee of) the Manchester music scene of the early 1990s. The so-called 'baggy scene' probably took its name from the very loose clothing affected by devotees of **rave**, **acid house** and **indie** subcultures.

For a while we were really into baggy.

2. an unfashionable, unattractive individual. In this pejorative sense the word, recorded among students and young adults since the later 1990s to refer to a supposed frump or **drabbie**, is either an elaboration of the colloquial '(old) bag', influenced by the homely images of baggy cardigans and tweeds, or possibly by **bag lady**.

bag job *n*

a theft or burglary. An underworld term heard in Britain but more widespread in the USA; not to be confused with a **paper bag job**.

bag lady *n*

a female vagrant, specifically one who through obsession or necessity collects junk and carries it in bags. The term originated in the USA in the early 1970s; by the late 1980s it was occasionally also being used, there and elsewhere, to denote any excessively scruffy female.

bag man *n*

1. someone who collects or looks after money made illegally. An underworld and police term originating in the USA between the world wars and first applied to those sent by gangsters to collect extortion payments, illicit revenues or bribes.

'Before I got promoted I used to be a bag man for Kellom – just nickel and dime stuff.'

(*The Big Easy*, US film, 1986)

2. a (male) tramp or vagrant, specifically one who collects and carries garbage in bags

bag off *vb British*

1a. to have sex

1b. to be sexually promiscuous or unfaithful

A working-class usage heard particularly in the north of England since the late 1990s.

bag of fruit *n Australian*

a *suit* (of clothes). An item of native rhyming slang.

all done up in his best bag of fruit

bag on (someone) *vb American*

to insult or deride. A term from black street slang from the 1990s, it is probably adapted from earlier slang senses of **bag** as in to dismiss, abandon, etc. but is unlikely to be related to the similar Australian use of 'bagging' to mean criticism.

bag one's face/head *vb American*

to hide one's face or oneself. Invariably used as an imperative, as in 'Go bag your face!'. This expression was popular among **Valley Girls** and other middle-class teenagers. It implies that the person in question is too hideous to contemplate and should put a bag over their head.

See also **bag someone's ass**

bagpipe *vb*

to engage in sexual stimulation using the armpit rather than the usual orifices. A term whose rarity presumably corresponds to that of the practice.

bags *n pl*

1. trousers. The word has had this meaning since the mid-19th century and survives, usually in a humorous context.

2. *American* female breasts

bag someone's ass *vb American*

to leave, go away, 'get lost'. The expression literally means to thrust into a garbage bag and throw away.

'She had no intention of having lunch with him and that was that ... Why couldn't she simply tell him to bag his ass?'

(*The Switch*, Elmore Leonard, 1978)

bag some zees *vb American*

to sleep. An alternative version of **cop some zees**.

bagsy! *exclamation*

a schoolchildren's term that indicates the speaker's choice of seat, cake, bed, etc.

Bagsy the one with the chocolate icing!

bahookie *n British*

the anus. The term, of unknown derivation, was used by the comic Scottish character Rab C. Nesbitt in the BBC 2 TV comedy of the same name in 1994.

baidie *adj British*

bad-tempered, aggressive, provocative. An obscure term which is probably a dialect version of **batey**.

baigel *n South African*

a spoilt young male. The term, which is derived from Yiddish ('bagels' are the baked bread rings often taken as emblematic of Jewish exiles' culture), has a female counterpart, which is **kugel**. Both refer to the notion of young Jewish people epitomising chic urban circles in South Africa since the 1990s.

bail *vb American*

to leave (in a hurry). A teenagers' shortening of 'bail out'. The word has been fashionable among **Valley Girls** and others since the late 1970s.

bail/bale on someone *vb American*

to oppress, burden or trouble someone. The bail or bale in question may derive from cotton picking, as in the words from *Ole Man River*; 'tote that barge, lift that bale, get a little drunk and you lands in jail', or may refer to bailing as in dumping water (on). The expression is typically used by teenagers and students.

bait *n*

an attractive potential sexual partner. This term was used in the 1950s and 1960s, either alone or in compounds such as bed-bait and the surviving **jail-bait**.

bake *n British*

a hideaway or refuge. This example of the jargon of cat burglars was recorded in *FHM* magazine in April 1996 and defined as 'a place to lay low while the constabulary run hither and thither in pursuit'. The precise origin of the term is uncertain, but it may come from the notion of the prison bakehouse as a place where inmates can withdraw or hide illicit objects.

baked adj American
stoned. The term usually refers to the effects of marihuana and implies a milder intoxication than **fried**.

baked bean, the n British
the *Queen*. An authentic item of rhyming slang.

baking brownies n American
breaking wind, farting. An expression used on campus in the USA since around 2000.

baksheesh, bakshee n
a bribe, tip or payment. From the colonial era, the word is from the Persian *bakshish*, meaning something given.

bald adj American
terrible. A vogue term among American teenagers in 1987 and 1988. The origins of this kind of appropriation from standard English are unrecorded, but often begin in gang code or street jargon.

bald-headed hermit n American
the penis. A humorous euphemism now used typically by adolescent males, although the expression seems to have originated in educated British slang of the 19th century. (Also, perhaps coincidentally, in US slang of the turn of the 20th century, 'bald-headed', as well as its literal sense, could mean both foolish and deceitful.)

Baldwin n American
an attractive male. This vogue word among Californian high-school students was featured in the 1994 US film *Clueless*, with its female counterpart **Betty** and its antonym **Barney**. The choice of the proper name may be arbitrary or may be inspired by the name of a celebrity (such as Alec Baldwin, star of romantic TV mini-series and Hollywood movies).

baldy man, the n Scottish
the penis. To 'make the baldy man cry' is to stimulate a male to orgasm. The term was posted on the b3ta website in 2004.

Bali belly n Australian
an attack of diarrhoea. The Australian traveller's equivalent of **Delhi belly, Montezuma's revenge, gyppy tummy**, etc.

ball[1] vb American
1. to have sex (with). An American term which, apart from a brief vogue in the **hippy** era, has rarely been used in Britain or Australia. Originally an item of black argot, it gained wider popularity in the

early 1960s and, as its anatomical origin suggests, is generally a male usage.

'Presley fired me because I balled his old lady.'
(The singer P. J. Proby, interviewed in 1965)

2. to behave in a boisterous, fun-loving and uninhibited way; to 'have a ball'. The term usually implies dancing, but also a degree of Bacchanalian, even orgiastic revelry far beyond that signified by the standard English (hunt or charity) ball.

'Good golly, Miss Molly, you sure like to ball!'
(Little Richard, [ambiguous] song lyrics, 1958)

3. to play basketball
4a. to behave ostentatiously
4b. to excel in a particular field
These senses of the word probably derive from black speech of the 1940s and later in which to ball meant to celebrate or enjoy oneself, itself influenced by the phrase 'have a ball'.

ball[2] n American
a stupid and/or obnoxious person. The slang for testicle has also been used as an insult by British junior-school pupils.

ball and chain n
a spouse, usually one's wife. This jocular phrase was heard in English-speaking areas throughout the 20th century and is still sometimes used ironically.

ball-breaker, ball-buster n
1a. a very aggressive, dominant or demanding woman
1b. an excessively hard taskmaster or martinet
1c. an exhausting, demanding task.
Compare **ball-tearer**
All these terms were adopted in Britain and Australia in the 1970s from American usage.

baller n American
a male who is successful and/or ostentatious. This usage, originating in black speech, probably derives from the verb **ball** and the noun **ballin'**. The word has also been used in the argot of Los Angeles gangs to mean a prominent or wealthy drug dealer. Another derivation claims that it refers to 'ball players' who have escaped the ghetto.

ballin' n
behaving ostentatiously. An Americanism of the later 1990s heard occasionally in the UK since 2000. The usage

originated in black speech of the 1940s and has been defined as '...carrying on in a flash fashion, as used by hip hop types...'.

ballistic adj

furious, uncontrollable. This use of the term, often in the phrase 'go ballistic', has become a common expression since the 1990s. It probably originated, unsurprisingly, in the slang of the armed forces, where it is still common.

'I totally choked; my father is going to go ballistic on me.'
(*Clueless*, US film, 1995)

ballisticated adj British

enraged, infuriated. A more recent formation from the earlier 'go **ballistic**', typically used by middle-class and/or middle-aged speakers.

He was totally ballisticated.

balloon n British

a boastful or loudmouthed individual, a **blowhard** or **puff-bucket**. The term is heard particularly in the Scottish Lowlands and the north of England.

Aw, take no notice of the big balloon.

balls n pl

1. the testicles. A predictable use of the word, balls was first used as a euphemism in Renaissance England, later becoming a standard, if coarse synonym. **2.** rubbish, nonsense. This use of the word, except perhaps as an exclamation, is surprisingly acceptable in middle-class speech (in such phrases as 'it's all balls'), considering its derivation.

'He was awarded a campaign medal, "but I didn't go to get mine. I wasn't interested; I thought it was all balls".'
(Falklands war veteran quoted in the *Observer* review of *The Fight for the Malvinas* by Martin Middlebrook, 9 April 1989)

3. courage, nerve. In this sense the word may now be applied to women in spite of the anatomical inconsistency.
4. a mess. This is a modern, mainly middle-class shortening of **balls-up**, usually found in the phrase to 'make a balls of it/something'.
5. *American* money, dollars. This usage was recorded in the later 1990s among adolescents. **Bollers** and **boyz** are British synonyms.

'It's gonna cost you mucho balls.'
(Recorded, teenager, North London, June 1995)

balls-ache n British

something which or someone who is very tedious or trying

balls-out adj

full-scale, full-tilt. A vulgar version of all-out, this fairly uncommon intensifying expression is normally used by males.

balls up vb

to make a mess of. In this mainly British expression, **balls** performs as a regular verb ('ballsing up' and 'ballsed up' being conjugated forms). To 'ball up' is an American alternative.

balls-up n

a mess, mistake, disaster. This expression has been in use in Britain since the turn of the 20th century.

ballsy adj

courageous, spirited. A vulgar alternative to **gutsy**. The word can be applied to either sex.

ball-tearer n Australian

1. a very demanding or exhausting task
2. something spectacular or sensationally impressive

These are versions of the international English **ball-breaker**.

baltic adj

cold, freezing. It is not clear where and when this usage originated, but it was recorded among US college students and UK adults from the late 1990s.

It's bloody baltic in here!

'bama n American

an unfashionable, unsophisticated or otherwise unfortunate person. The term, originating in hip hop culture and in more generalised usage since 2000, evokes a provincial bumpkin. In black speech Alabama was a generic term for 'the southern USA'. It means a person who cannot dress; a loser, backwards or unsophisticated person, it's rap-speak, short for Alabama.

bambaclaat, bombaclaat, bambaseed n

1a. a male homosexual
1b. a despicable (male) individual

The words are based on a dialect pronunciation of 'bum-cloth' as signifying both anal contact and something worthless.

bammy n, adj British

(a person who is) crazy, eccentric. The term, originating as a dialect version of the colloquial 'barmy', is heard particularly in the Scottish Lowlands and the north of England.

bam-stick n British

a foolish or crazy person. The phrase is derived from **bammy** (the dialect version of 'barmy'), and is used particularly in the north of England and lowland Scotland. The 'stick' component may be a combining form denoting a person, or may refer to an actual stick used to pick up barm (the froth on fermenting yeast).

banana n

1. a foolish person. This childish term of mild abuse is now obsolescent in Britain, but predictably is still heard in post-colonial English in the Indian subcontinent, Malaysia, the Caribbean, etc. The 1950s term **nana** was a shorter form.

2. the penis. The mock nursery term **tummy banana** is more common.

3. American a light-skinned black woman. A term used by black men which is both appreciative and offensive.

4. an Oriental person who affects white manners or collaborates with the white establishment. A term used by both white and Oriental-language speakers, e.g. in Hong Kong and on US campuses.

bananas adj

crazy or berserk. This now common colloquialism originated either in the notion of 'softness' (in the head) or from the archaic 'banana oil', 'soft soap' or 'balderdash'.

banana truck n American

a crazy person. An expression which evokes a whole truck-full of bananas, hence an excess of 'softness' (in the head).

bandit[1] n British

1. a homosexual. A dismissive or derisory term used by avowedly heterosexual males and deriving from longer expressions such as **trouser bandit**, **arse bandit**, **chocolate bandit**, etc.

2. -bandit an ironic or jocular combining word, added to suggest a desperate or reprehensible character or, in police jargon, literally a criminal. In his Field Manual for Police (1977) David Powis cites 'milk bandit' as an ironic term for penniless milk-bottle thieves; 'gas-meter bandit' is self-explanatory.

bandit[2] vb Caribbean

to steal or borrow without permission. The term was recorded in Trinidad and Tobago in 2003. Synonyms are **raf** and **sprang**.

bang[1] vb

1. to have sex (with), **fuck**. The association with striking (as in the origin of the word 'fuck' itself) is said to suggest the masculine role in sex, but in practice the unaffectionate term can also apply to women, especially in Australian usage where it is more common than in America. In Britain 'bang' in this sense has only been widely understood since the late 1960s. It was introduced via the phrase **gang bang** and the following expression.

'You're banging a major witness in a case you're trying?!'
(The Last Innocent Man, US film, 1987)

2. American to be an active gang member. From the parlance of Los Angeles street gangs of the late 1980s, derived from the specific sense of **gangbanger**.

He's been banging for two years now.

3. to do something stupid. An item of street slang in London since 2000.

bang[2] n

1a. a sexual act. An unaffectionate term used more often by men. In this sense the word does not seem to be older than the 20th century.

a quick bang

1b. a person rated as a sexual partner

a good bang

2. Australian a brothel. The word is now rather archaic, but is still heard among older speakers.

3a. an exciting experience, a thrill. In this sense the word goes in and out of vogue, particularly among schoolchildren in many parts of the English-speaking world.

3b. a great success, a very popular person or thing

3c. an injection of illicit drugs, especially heroin, morphine or amphetamines, or the resulting jolt of pleasure. From the lexicon of drug users and addicts, originating in the 1940s or earlier and related to the more recent verb **bang up**.

banged-up adj British

imprisoned, shut away. From the second sense of the verb to **bang up**.

'A banged-up man's no good to me. I want to enjoy life, not spend it in prison waiting-rooms.'
(Recorded, drug-dealer's girlfriend, London, 1984)

banger *n*
1. a sausage. The word has been common in this sense since the 1940s. It derives of course from the explosion of the skin during frying.
2. an old and/or decrepit vehicle

banging[1] *adj*
exciting, powerful. Like its contemporaries **kicking** and **slamming**, this term was in vogue from the early 1990s, especially among devotees of **rave** culture.

one banging gig
I tell you, it was banging.

banging[2] *n American*
a shooting. An item of black street slang of the 1990s.

bang (someone) in the boat *vb British*
to punch (someone) in the mouth or face

bangin' weights *n British*
working out as physical exercise (not necessarily referring only to weight-training). An item of black street-talk used especially by males, recorded in 2003.

bangles *n pl*
1a. female breasts
1b. the testicles. By association with the idea of adornment, as in **family jewels**, and with 'dangle'.
Both usages are most often heard among teenagers and schoolchildren all over the English-speaking world.

bang on *vb British*
to nag, harangue or talk incessantly and boringly. A popular term since the 1980s in 'respectable' usage.

She's been banging on about her bloody job all evening.

bang to Byrites *adj British*
(of a male) dressed in poor taste/cheap clothing. The phrase is a play on the expression **bang to rights** (guilty or caught in the act) and Mr Byrite, the name of a now defunct chain of men's clothing stores. 'Caught wearing cheap clothing as in footballers other than Michael Owen and David Beckham'.

He was caught bang to Byrites in that purple shellsuit.

bang to rights *adj, adv British*
caught red-handed, without hope of escape. This 19th-century expression (paralleled in American English by **dead to rights**) is usually heard in the form 'caught bang to rights' or 'we've got

him/her bang to rights' (i.e. helpless, indefensible). Until the 1970s the term was part of the restricted codes of the police and underworld; since then the phrase has been given wider currency, particularly by the realist plays of G. F. Newman.

bang up *vb*
1. to inject oneself (with heroin or another hard drug). One of many drug-users' terms with overtones of bravado. Popular in Britain in the late 1960s and early 1970s.
2. *British* to imprison, shut away. A working-class, police and prisoners' term.

'Being banged up's no joke, even in an open prison.'
(Recorded, remand prisoner, 1986)

bang-up *adj American*
excellent, exciting. The term occurred particularly in campus usage in the later 1990s, but was also recorded in British slang in the early 19th century where it was a shortening of phrases such as 'bang up to the mark'.

banjaxed *adj Irish*
defeated, overcome or overwhelmed. A humorous term from the early 20th century, often used ruefully by husbands floored or humiliated in a domestic dispute. This Irish word, probably formed by association with 'banged', 'bashed' and 'smashed', has been popularised in Britain by the Irish broadcaster, Terry Wogan, who used it as the title of a book in 1980. It can now be extended to mean stunned, flummoxed, amazed, drunk, etc.

banjo *vb British*
to force entry, break in, especially by means of the battering device to which the name has been given, based roughly on its shape. (Previously, shovels were known as banjos.) An item of police slang heard in the 1990s.

'We're going to go round and banjo the house.'
(Police officer, *Network First*, ITV documentary, February 1996)

banjo'd, banjoed *adj British*
1a. hopelessly drunk or under the influence of drugs. A jocular invention, perhaps influenced by **banjaxed** and sometimes heard among students and schoolchildren in the 1970s and the 1980s.

'...stupid how they strut, smoking Wood-bines till they're banjoed smirking at the Swedish smut'
(*Pscyle Sluts*, poem by John Cooper Clark, 1978)

1b. defeated, beaten. An armed-forces term of the late 1970s and 1980s. There may be a connection with **banjaxed** or with the archaic use of 'banjo' to mean a shovel or weapon.

bank¹ *n American*
money. A teenage vogue word of 1987 and 1988. The term was picked up by British **rap**, hip hop and **acid house** enthusiasts and was still in use in 2004.
Got any bank?

bank² *adj American*
inferior, unpleasant. A fashionable pejorative in black street slang since the 1990s, the term may be a blend of, or inspired by, terms such as **bunk** and **rank**, but the noun 'bank' was used to mean 'toilet' in black slang of the 1940s and 1950s. Yet another proposed derivation is from 'bankrupt'.

banked *adj American*
drunk. An expression used on campus in the USA since around 2000.

BAP *n American*
a 'black American princess'. A coinage based on the earlier **JAP**.
Compare **buppie**

bap-head *n British*
a foolish person. An item of playground slang in use since the later 1990s, possibly borrowed from an older generation.

baps *n pl British*
female breasts. The expression, used typically by young males in the Midlands and north of England and Scotland, borrows the name of the small, round bread bun sold in various regions of the UK. **Muffins** is an equivalent North American usage.

bar *n British*
1a. one million pounds or one million dollars in the argot of London City traders. Used in this sense the word is probably a revival of the Romany *bar* or '*baur(o)*' which used to mean one sovereign or one pound and was still heard among street traders and prison inmates in the 1960s.
1b. one pound.
See also **half a bar**

bar! *exclamation British*
an exclamation of dismissal or refusal, synonymous to its users with the collo-quial 'no way'. The term was recorded in use among North London schoolboys in 1993 and 1994.

barb *n*
a barbiturate. A shortening employed by drug abusers since the late 1950s.
'We did a load of barbs and spent the rest of the day nailed to the floor.'
(Recorded, student, Faversham, Kent, 1974)

barbie *n Australian*
a barbecue. A common term since the late 1960s, now spreading via Australian TV soap operas to Britain where it has been adopted by **yuppies** in particular.
'Australia was full of easy-going characters like Paul Hogan, who spent the day drinking Fosters and putting a shrimp on the barbie.'
(Michael Parkinson, *Daily Mirror*, 17 April 1989)

Barbie (Doll) *n*
a vacuous, passive and/or conformist young woman. Barbie is the trademark name of the well-known plastic doll originating in the USA.

bare *adj Caribbean*
1. only
There's bare wiggas here!
2. very
3. a large amount or number
He's got bare magazines.
The usage has become fashionable among young speakers of all ethnic backgrounds in the UK since 2000.

bareback riding *n*
having sex without a condom. A phrase possibly originating among prostitutes and pornographers, now widespread in colloquial speech.

barf *vb American*
to vomit. A popular student term dating from the 1950s. The word is imitative in origin and is sometimes used as an exclamation of disgust.

barf bag *n American*
1a. a disgusting or very unpleasant person. A teenagers' slightly less offensive version of **scumbag**.
'Word on the street is that you barf bags are giving the kids in the 7th grade a hard time.'
(*Vice Versa*, US film, 1988)
1b. an airsickness bag. The term is rarely used in this sense, which derives from the verb **barf** meaning 'to vomit'.

barf city *n, adj American*
(a place that is) disgusting, revolting. The expression, from **barf** ('to vomit'), is usually used as an exclamation of revulsion, typically by schoolchildren and teenagers.

barf (someone) out *vb American*
to disgust, nauseate someone. A **Valley Girl** and teenagers' term, usually heard as an exclamation, as in 'It totally barfs me out!'. It derives from **barf** meaning 'to vomit'.

bark[1] *n British*
cannabis. An item of prison slang based on the resemblance between hashish and tree-bark, and recorded in the early 1990s.

bark[2] *vb Australian*
to vomit. By extension from the earlier use of bark as a humorous synonym for 'cough'.

barking *adj British*
demented. A short form of 'barking mad', evoking utter howling craziness, this expression is typically heard in upper- and middle-class speech, often preceded by 'absolutely'.

'A friend in the Business was hugely amused when told of a forthcoming interview with Carla Lane. "She's quite barking, you know", he warned cheerfully...'
(*Sunday Times* magazine, 4 March 1990)

barking moonbat *n*
an uncontrolled, eccentric or erratic person. A term of mild disapproval or sometimes rueful affection in use among **hackers** from around 2004.

barnet *n British*
hair, a head of hair. A rhyming-slang term (from 'Barnet Fair'; both the event and the phrase in its full form were popular among Londoners in the second half of the 19th century) which is still widely used by working-class speakers and their imitators in and around London.

'I'm stayin' in tonight and washin' me barnet.'
(Recorded, social worker, Willesden, London, 1987)

barney *n British*
an argument, fight or disturbance. Perhaps surprisingly the origin of this common term is obscure. It is assumed to derive from the male forename, but the connection between Barnaby and brawl or scuffle is unclear.

I like a bit of a barney from time to time – it helps to clear the air.

Barney *n American*
an unattractive male. This pejorative term for a boy who is not categorised as a **Baldwin** was featured in the 1994 US film *Clueless*. The reason for the choice of proper name is uncertain, but may be inspired by the character Barney Rubble in the cartoon series and film *The Flintstones*, hence a primitive person. The term was still in use in 2004.

baron *n British*
a prisoner enjoying a degree of power and influence over his fellow inmates. The source of the power is usually economic, with the baron controlling trade in cigarettes (a 'tobacco baron'), drugs or other prison currency.

barrel *n American*
a gun. An item of street jargon from the 1990s employing the rhetorical device of synecdoche, i.e. naming the whole from a constituent part.

'Teachers report that teenagers talk about "packing a barrel" or "chilling someone with a pipe".'
(*Sunday Times*, 31 August 1992)

barries *n British*
fellatio. A term of unknown origin, heard since 2000 in black British usage and more recently among other young speakers.

She gave 'im barries.

Barry *n British*
a boorish, vulgar or unsophisticated male. A social categorisation said by users to be the counterpart of a **Sharon**, recorded in 2004.
Compare **Kevin**; **Wayne**

barsy, barzy *adj British*
mad, lunatic. A blend of barmy and crazy favoured by some middle-class speakers since the mid-1970s.

base[1] *n*
crack. The term is a shortening of **freebase**, a system of smoking purified cocaine which pre-dated the use of the more refined and potent crack. The word 'base' was in use among British users in 1989, together with many other nicknames.

base² *vb American*
to denigrate, criticise. A term from black street slang of the later 1990s used in the same way as **diss**.

base³ *adj American*
unpleasant, disgusting, inferior. The standard term, as in 'base behaviour', was appropriated, perhaps via black street slang, by high-school and college students in the 1980s. It is popular among female speakers.

That new diner in the mall is, like, so base!

basehead *n American*
a drug-user who **freebases** cocaine or smokes **crack**. The term dates from the early 1980s, the practice from the 1970s.

basements *n pl South African*
shoes. The term is usually applied to trainers as worn by young males and was recorded in 1994.

bash, bashy *adj British*
exciting, lively, attractive. The terms originate in Jamaican patois.

'She's goin' on like she thinks she's bashy.'

(Recorded, London student, 2002)

bashed *adj American*
drunk. One of a large number of synonyms evoking the idea of the drunkard as damaged or chastised.

basher *n British*
a shelter or shack made of cardboard, paper, plastic, etc. and lived in by a tramp or homeless person. The word is used by the 'gentlemen of the road' or **dossers** themselves.

'Their "bashers" (shacks) will be forcibly removed by police to make way for developers who want to "yuppify" the Charing Cross area.'

(*Observer*, 16 August 1987)

bashment¹ *n*
a party, dance, **rave**. The term originated in Caribbean speech and by 2003 was in general use among UK teenagers.

bashment² *adj*
lively, spirited (of a person or event)

bash the bishop *vb*
(of a male) to masturbate. The phrase, recorded in the 19th century with its synonym 'flog the bishop', was probably the precursor of many similar jocular euphemisms such as **box the jesuit**, **spank the monkey**, etc., heard in the 20th century.

basing *n See* **freebasing**

basket *n*
1. a **bastard**. A euphemism used in Britain and Australia, particularly in the 1950s and 1960s, and especially by middle-class speakers.
2. *American* the male genitals. A male homosexual term, heard in the late 1970s and early 1980s.

basket case *n*
a helpless invalid, a person who is mentally and/or physically incapacitated. Originally an Americanism, this expression (a variant of **cot-case**) has become widespread in recent years. It is now often used in journalists' jargon to refer to an irrevocably ruined enterprise.

bassed *adj British*
1. beaten up. An item of black street-talk used especially by males, recorded in 2003.
2. a variant form of **baffed**

bastard *n*
the standard term for an illegitimate person has been used as a term of abuse, disapproval, pity or even affection (particularly in British and Australian usage) since the early years of the 20th century

'Targets: banks, shops, DHSS, cop-shops, Job Centres, rich bastards.'

(*Observer*, 3 April 1988)

batey *adj British*
bad-tempered, irascible. A piece of dated, but not yet archaic public-school slang deriving from the obsolescent use of 'bate' to mean strife or argument.

bath *n British*
a girl. A term used by young street-gang members in London since around 2000.

bath bun *n British*
1. the *sun*. A less common alternative to **currant bun**.

'All this bleedin' rain. I've forgotten what the old bath bun looks like.'

(Recorded, street trader, London, 1988)

2. a *son*

Both uses are London working-class rhyming slang from the sweet fruit bun originating in the city of Bath.

bath-dodger *n British*
an unwashed or habitually dirty individual. **Soap-dodger** is a synonym.

bath(e)os *n pl South African*
shoes. The term is usually applied to trainers, and probably derives from bath-house or bathing. Recorded as an item of Sowetan slang in the *Cape Sunday Times*, 29 January 1995.

batphone *n British*
1a. a walkie-talkie
1b. a mobile telephone
The nickname, inspired by the gadget featured in the *Batman* TV series of the 1960s, was first recorded among police officers in the early 1990s. **Squawker** is a synonym.

batso *adj British*
crazy. The word, used typically by middle-class schoolchildren and adults, is an elaboration of the colloquial 'bats' or 'batty', both based on the older expression 'to have bats in one's belfry'.
'It seemed to me to be a completely batso idea.'
(Recorded, London journalist, February 1995)

batter *n British See* **on the batter**

battered, batted *adj British*
drunk. One of a host of synonyms employing the metaphor of (the drinker suffering) damage. An item of student slang in use in London and elsewhere since around 2000.

batting for the other side *adj British*
homosexual. Invariably used of males, usually pejoratively or mockingly by males, the metaphor is from cricket. The expression has become widespread since the late 1990s.

battle-cruiser *n British*
a *boozer*; the pub. This London rhyming-slang term originated, not surprisingly, in the 1940s, but is still heard, although **rub-a-dub** is probably more popular now.

battler *n Australian*
a resolute, energetic or otherwise impressive person. The term (which used to denote a prostitute operating independently of a pimp) often applies to someone who is admired for triumphing over adversity. It also occurs in the form **bottler**.

batty *n Jamaican*
the backside, buttocks. The word, usually used in a sexual context, is an item of patois based on 'bottom' which has spread into white urban slang since the 1990s.

batty-boy, battyman *n British*
a male homosexual. Nearly always used pejoratively, this is one of many terms from Jamaican patois using **batty**, a form of 'bottom', to denote sexuality.

batty-riders *n pl British*
extremely short shorts or **hot pants** worn by females. The term was associated with the ragga or dance-hall reggae movement of the early to mid-1990s whose female adherents wore provocative clothes reflecting the salacious lyrics of the music.

batty-seed *n British*
a male homosexual. This term from Jamaican patois (one of many based on **batty**, meaning the 'backside') was picked up, like the more common **batty-boy**, by London schoolchildren in the 1990s. The origin of the 'seed' element is obscure.

baunch *n American*
the female genitals. A term heard on campus since 2000, it may be an alteration of bunch.

bay *n British*
£1. The term has been in 'street' usage since 2000.
20 bays
I just need a bay for the machine.

baz, bazz *n British*
an outsider, misfit or bumpkin. One of many synonyms for **chav**, **steek**, etc. popular in 2003 and 2004.

bazeracked *adj British*
drunk. A term in use since 2000, heard especially in South West England.

bazillion *n American*
a very large number or quantity. An alternative form of **zillion**, **squillion** and **gazillion**.
'There are about a bazillion poems about trees.'
(*Clarissa Explains It All*, US TV comedy, 1994)

bazooka'd *adj British*
drunk. One of the many synonyms based on the notion of the drunkard as ruined, destroyed, etc.

bazumas, bazungas *n pl*
female breasts. Supposedly humorous coinages (also rendered in other forms such as **gazungas**, **mezoomas**, etc.) which may have originated in an elaboration of 'bosom'.

bazza n South African
a friend, fellow gang member. Recorded as an item of Sowetan slang in the *Cape Sunday Times*, 29 January 1995.

B-boy n American
a participant in hip hop street culture. This vogue term (the female counterpart is **fly-girl**) became widespread around 1982, but was first coined in the late 1970s. The initial probably stood for 'brother' as a term of address, or for 'break-dancer'.

beak n
1. the nose. Beak has been used in this obvious sense since at least the beginning of the 19th century, although other terms, such as **hooter**, **bugle**, **conk**, etc. are more popular. In Irish speech the word is also used for the mouth or face.
2. a person in authority, especially a judge or schoolmaster. This old usage is now obsolete in American English, but is retained in Britain in public-school slang and in the expression 'up before the beak' (appearing before a magistrate or someone else sitting in judgment). Attempts have been made to derive this meaning of beak from a Celtic term for judgment, but the more obvious derivation is from the intrusive beak (the nose and/or mouth) of authority. *Tatler* magazine reported in August 1989 that beak was still the standard Etonian slang for a schoolmaster.
        'Finally the beak turn his beetling brow to them and his xpression [sic] become suddenly soft, his stern eye mild.'
        (Geoffrey Willans and Ronald Searle, *Back in the Jug Agane*, 1959)
3. cocaine
4. fellatio
Senses 3 and 4 have both been in use since 2000.

beamer n American
a BMW car. A **yuppie** nickname.

beam me up, Scotty! exclamation
a request for **crack** or another stimulating drug. The catchphrase, from the 1970s TV series *Star Trek*, has been used since 2000 in **rap** lyrics.

bean-bag n British
a mild term of abuse among younger schoolchildren. Bean bags were used in throwing games and sports.

beaner, **bean**, **bean-eater** n American
a Hispanic American, a Mexican or **Chicano**. A 1970s and 1980s term, highly

offensive in the USA, which refers to poor Latin Americans' diet of *frijoles* or refried beans.

beanie n
a girl. A term used by young street-gang members in London since around 2000.

beans n pl American
dollars. A humorous synonym possibly influenced by the colloquialism 'a hill of beans', meaning something worth very little.
        'At least we're sitting on around a hundred beans from my brilliant idea.'
        (*Planes, Trains and Automobiles*, US film, 1987)

bear n American
a police officer, especially in the vocabulary of CB radio. This usage derives from the US Forest Services' fire-warning posters showing 'Smokey the Bear' in the uniform of a ranger. It was adopted by CB enthusiasts in the mid-1970s.

beard n
a male escort posing as a boyfriend, lover, husband, etc. The term (heard from the mid-1970s in showbiz and 'society' circles) may refer to a lesbian's 'official' partner, with whom she is seen in public.

beast¹ n
1. American a girl or woman. The term, typically used by male college and high-school students, may be either pejorative or appreciative.
2. the beast heroin. A drug-users' ironic nickname.
3. a sex offender, in prison slang. A more recent synonym for **nonce**.
        '20 prison officers in riot uniform were observed banging their shields in unison and chanting "Beast, beast, beast!".'
        (*Observer*, 8 April 1990)
4. also **beast man** an ugly or unattractive male. The term is used by females.

beast² vb
1. British to bully, oppress, humiliate. The word is part of the jargon of prisoners and prison officers.
2. also **beast it** to move or act quickly and/or forcefully. The term is used in this sense in the school playground and armed forces.

beast(-man) n British
a police officer or prison officer and, by extension, any figure of authority. The

word was adopted by teenage school-children in the 1990s.

beastie *n, adj American*
1a. (someone) disgusting, coarse or disreputable

1b. (something or someone) impressive, powerful or enormous. This expression, used typically by female teenagers, was a vogue term among blacks and whites in the USA in the 1980s and was adopted ironically in the name of the white **rap** group the Beastie Boys.

beasting *n British*
a 'dressing-down', humiliation or instance of physical bullying. The noun, like the verb to **beast**, is formed from the use of **beast(-man)** in British prison slang to signify an authority figure.

beat¹ *n*
a member of the 'beat generation' or aspirer to its values. The term, coined by the influential American writer Jack Kerouac and first published by John Clellon Holmes in his novel *Go*, is derived both from the notion of being beaten, downtrodden or poor, and from the notion of beatitude or holiness. The phrase 'the beat generation', coined in imitation of other literary groups such as the Lost Generation of the 1920s, originally applied to a relatively small group of writers, artists and bohemians in America immediately after World War II, whose activities and beliefs were minutely chronicled in autobiographical, mystical and experimental prose and poetry by Kerouac, Holmes, Gregory Corso, William Burroughs and Allen Ginsberg, among others. The term **beatniks** (employing the Slavonic '-nik' suffix disparagingly) was applied to these and later followers by members of **straight** society, hostile to what they saw as the licentious, irreligious and communistic aspects of the beat lifestyle. In Britain the beats were a youth subculture of the early- to mid-1960s, which co-existed with the **mods** and **rockers** and metamorphosed into the **hippies**.

> 'The most beautifully executed, the clearest and most important utterance yet made by the generation Kerouac himself named years ago as "beat", and whose principal avatar he is.'
> (Gilbert Millstein, *New York Times*, 5 September 1957)

beat² *adj American*
excellent, admirable, fashionable. A synonym for **cool**, in vogue since 2000 and used by pop singer Britney Spears among others.

beat-down *adj American*
tired, exhausted. A more recent version of the colloquial (dead-)beat.

> She was sure looking beat-down after her weekend.

beat it up! *exclamation American*
an exhortation to speak clearly. The expression has been in use since 2000.

> Come on man, beat it up! We don't have all day.

beatnik *n*
someone following a **beat** lifestyle or modes of dress. The term was coined by newspapermen to deride the self-styled members of the beat generation but was later adopted by beatniks themselves; the '-nik' suffix came from Russian and was meant to identify the beats with godless Communism (as well as being a derogatory word-ending in Yiddish terms such as **nudnik**). Aspects of the beatnik lifestyle included scruffy dress (often black), berets, modern jazz, coffee bars, a slightly more liberal attitude to sex than their contemporaries, at least a pretence at interest in modern arts and literature and a youth cult. Beatniks had passed their peak by 1960, but many of them (who incidentally referred to themselves simply as **beats**) were absorbed into the **hippy** movement in the mid-1960s.

> 'A petition signed by 2,321 residents and holidaymakers at St Ives, Cornwall was handed to the Mayor, Ald. Archie Knight during the weekend. It calls for tighter vagrancy laws to rid the town of beatniks.'
> (*Daily Telegraph*, 21 July 1969)

beat off, beat one's meat *vb*
(of a male) to masturbate. The first expression is primarily American, the second international English.

beat one's boats *vb American*
to depart, run away. A jocular term heard since the 1990s and based on 'boats' as a slang synonym for shoes or the feet.

beats, the *n*
a physical attack

> Let's give him (the) beats.

beat-up *adj American*
unfair. The term, used by younger speakers since 2000, is a transfer from

the older sense of beat(en)-up as damaged or decrepit.

beaucoup *adj See* **bokoo**[1]

beaut *adj Australian*
excellent, first-rate. A well-known Australianism which, although dated, is still in use.

beaver *n*
1a. *American* the female genitals. A term referring to the pubic hair and vagina ('a beaver').
1b. *American* a woman or women seen exclusively as sex objects
   Let's get some beaver!
These terms became known, though rarely used, outside the USA via pin-up magazines in the late 1960s.
2. a beard, especially a full or luxuriant one. A light-hearted 19th-century usage, still heard among older adults.
   He's sporting a handsome beaver.

Bedfordshire *n British*
a bed or bedtime. A nursery joke-form of the standard words, from the parents' catchphrase 'up the wooden hill to Bedfordshire', meaning '(go) up the stairs to bed'. This usage is in fact 200-year-old peasant humour.

beef[1] *n*
1. a complaint or grudge. This use of the word has occurred in American English since the early years of the 20th century, originating in the speech of criminals, pugilists and marginals, etc. Since the 1940s British speakers have also employed it and it has become a vogue term in youth slang since 2000. The relationship between this sense of the word and its literal meaning is not clear; the colloquial notion of 'brawn' may be involved.
   'I just wanna tell you, I got no beef about last night.'
   (*Miami Vice*, US TV series, 1987)
2. *British* a fight. An item of black streettalk used especially by males, recorded in 2003, based on the older colloquial sense of beef as a grudge or complaint.
   There was beef.

beef[2] *vb*
1. to complain. In the 19th-century language of street sellers, and later in the theatre, beef was associated with shouting, yelling and hence complaining. By the early 20th century the word was in use in the USA in the sense of a grudge

or complaint, but it is unclear whether the usages are related.
2. *American* to **fart**. The usage may be inspired by the rhyme or pun on 'beef-heart' (a meat product).

beef (someone) *vb*
to have sex with. A vulgarism in use all over the English-speaking world. Beef has had sexual connotations, deriving from its use as a synonym for flesh, for hundreds of years. Since the 1980s, the verb to **pork** is more common.

beef bayonet *n*
the penis. A humorous euphemism on the lines of **mutton dagger**, etc. The phrase was first popularised in Britain by Barry Humphries' *Barry McKenzie* comic strip in the satirical magazine *Private Eye* in the 1960s.

beef curtains *n pl*
the female genitals. A late 1980s vogue term among some male teenagers, particularly those affecting 'street credibility'.
   'Man, look at the beef curtains. Yeah, the blonde one, know what I mean.'
   (Recorded, youth, Baker Street station, London, 1985)

beer goggle(s) *n*
impaired judgment and/or vision due to intake of alcohol. A term popular among students and other drinkers since the mid-1990s.
   I copped off with a right munter – I was wearing the beer goggles.

beergoggle *vb*
to drink until incapacitated

beer-tokens *n pl British*
one-pound coins or money in general, in the argot of students and other adolescents since the late 1980s. 'Beer-vouchers' is an alternative form.

bees 'n' honey *n British*
money. A piece of London rhyming slang which, while never being a popular term, is still heard occasionally.

bee-stings *n pl*
small female breasts. A jocular term employed by both sexes.

beetin' *adj*
angry, annoyed. A term used by young street-gang members in London since around 2000.

beetle *vb British*
to hurry. A dated colloquialism revived by **Sloane Rangers** in the early 1980s. It is

inspired of course by the scuttling of the insects.

I had to beetle along to Jonty's before lunch.

beevo(s) *n American*
beer. A college students' term probably distantly related, via 'beverage', to the British **bevvy**. The fact that the Czech word for beer is *pivo* may be coincidental.

be geese *vb American*
to leave, hurry away, disappear. From the argot of **rappers** and hip hop enthusiasts, the phrase may be an alteration of **ghost**.

Yo, we be geese.

beggar *vb, n*
a euphemism for (to) **bugger** (except in the 'respectable' idioms 'beggar the imagination' or 'beggar description' when the meaning is to render impoverished or surpass)

beggar's velvet *n American*
another term for **dust bunny**

begiggidy *adj American*
excited, 'giddy'. An expression used on campus in the USA since around 2000.

Is she getting all begiggidy over that stud?

begonias *n pl American*
female breasts. The term is coined by analogy with other multi-syllable synonyms beginning with the letter 'b', such as **bazumas** and **bazungas**.

behind with the rent *adj*
homosexual (of a male). The phrase, which is rhyming slang for sense **2** of **bent**, has been heard in London since at least 2000.

beige *adj American*
dull, boring, insipid. A vogue term in the affected slang of West Coast adolescents, heard since the 1980s. It may have originated as a **gay** disparagement of **straight** taste in decor, clothing, etc.

bell *vb, n British*
(to make) a telephone call (to someone). A working-class usage which has become almost universal since the 1970s in the form 'give someone a bell' or, more racily, 'bell someone'. It is also in Australian use.

I got a bell from old Milward yesterday.
(Recorded, businessman, London, 1988)

bell-end[1] *n British*
the (tip of the) penis. A vulgarism popularised by *Viz* comic. **Helmet** is a synonym.

'He's scared to get his bell-end out!'
(*Away The Lads*, BBC 2 TV documentary, February 1993)

bell-end[2], **bell-ender** *n British*
a stupid and/or obnoxious person. The terms refer to the tip of the penis.

bellyflop *n*
1a. a shallow dive, landing stomach-first on water

1b. an ignominious or total failure

belter *n*
something wonderful, excellent or exciting. An expression of enthusiasm, heard predominantly in the north of England, which can be applied equally to a girlfriend, a car, party, etc. This noun derives from the colloquial senses of the verb 'to belt', denoting thrashing, speeding, etc.

Just look at her. She's a right belter isn't she?

belting, beltin' *adj British*
excellent, exciting. A synonym for the more common **blindin'** popular among **chavs** in 2005.

ben, benner *n British*
a £10 note or the sum of ten pounds

bender *n*
1. a bout of heavy drinking, a riotous spree. The term may have originated in North America in the mid-19th century when 'hell-bender' meant any event or spectacle which was outrageous, aggressive or exciting. An alternative derivation is from **bend the elbow**. In its narrower sense of an unrestrained spree, the word was introduced in Britain at the end of the 19th century.

'When his marriage collapsed, Dick went on a four-day bender.'
(Recorded, business executive, London, 1986)

2. *British* a homosexual. A term of contempt, originally for a passive male homosexual who supposedly **bends over**. The term is now probably heard less frequently than in the late 1960s and early 1970s.

'It's not every day that a man wakes up to find he's a screaming bender!'
(*Blackadder II*, BBC TV comedy, 1988)

3. *British* a makeshift shelter. The word derives from the 'bender tents' used by gypsies or other travellers and made by stretching cloth or tarpaulin over bent-over saplings. It was brought into common currency by the women peace protesters camped outside the US base at Greenham Common in the mid-1980s.

bendered adj British
drunk. A back-formation from the older noun **bender**, used by students since 2000.

bend one vb
to have sex. A vulgarism used typically by and about males since around 2000.

I was bending one and she just lost interest.

bend over, bend down vb
1a. to invite or submit to **buggery**. A euphemism popular among all social classes in Britain in the 1960s and early 1970s.

'He'd bend over on Blackfriars Bridge for ten bob.'

(Recorded, public schoolboy, London, 1970)

1b. to yield or submit to abuse or attack, by extension from the first sense. A term popular among businessmen in the 1980s. This may be a shortening of the phrase 'bend over backwards' and is a more brusque version of 'take it lying down'.

'I'm certainly not going to bend over for them.'

(Recorded, company director responding to takeover attempt, London, 1988)

bend the elbow vb
to drink alcohol. A hearty euphemism used by habitués of bars all over the English-speaking world since the 19th century.

Benjamin n American
1a. a one hundred dollar note, from the image of Benjamin Franklin thereon
1b. Benjamins money in general

Man he's really rakin' in the Benjamins.
'When I'm rollin' in the Benjamins I will throw you and your dog a bone.'
(*School of Rock*, US film, 2003)

bennie n
a tablet of Benzedrine, a trademark for a variety of amphetamine used and abused from the 1940s to the 1960s

Benny, Bennie n British
a foolish, clumsy person, misfit. The name of a slow-witted male character (played by Paul Henry) in the long-running TV soap opera *Crossroads* was adopted as a nickname for unfortunate males and lasted into the late 1990s. The word became notorious when it was applied by British servicemen to inhabitants of the Falkland Islands in 1983. *See also* **throw a Bennie**

Benny Hill n British
a *till* or cash box. An item of market-traders' rhyming slang based on the name of the late comedian and recorded in the mid-1990s. A synonym from the same environment is **Buffalo Bill**.

Just hold on while I unlock the Benny Hill.

bent adj
1a. criminal, crooked, dishonest. This usage has been widespread in Britain at least since the beginning of the 20th century. It is still used by the police to refer to anyone who is not **straight**, and by criminals and others to refer to corrupt police officers (often by the cliché phrase 'a bent copper' – 'bent coppers' were damaged coins that could not be used in public lavatories in the 1950s and 1960s). A more colourful embroidery sometimes heard in Britain is 'bent as a butcher's hook'.

'Remember, this happened in the 1960s when many detectives were bent.'
(Former detective quoted in *Inside the Brotherhood*, Martin Short, 1989)

1b. stolen, forged
a bent motor

2. sexually deviant, homosexual. A common term in Britain, mainly in working-class usage, since the 1940s. A London variant popular in the 1960s was 'as bent as a nine bob note' (a non-existent, obviously forged denomination).

3. American drunk or under the influence of drugs. This usage is rather archaic, but the longer 'bent out of shape' is still heard among college students and **preppies**.

4. American angry, furious. This seems to be an armed-forces term in origin. It is also more usual in the form 'bent out of shape'.

be out! exclamation British
an all-purpose cry of encouragement or enthusiasm in use among dancefloor-culture devotees in London since the mid-1990s

beresk adj
berserk, out of control. A humorous corruption perhaps inspired by a genuinely mistaken pronunciation, or possibly by the influence of 'bereft'. An alternative is 'besrek'. Both forms have been heard, mainly among middle-class speakers in

Britain and Australia – students and rugby players are typical users – since the early 1970s.

berifta *n, adj*

(something) disappointing, depressing. The word may be a deformation of, or influenced by 'bereft'. It seems to have operated as an antonym of the equally mysterious **bifta** in the speech of middle-class adults since 2000.

berk *n*

a fool. This word, which has been widespread since the early 1960s in Britain and Australia (where it was introduced via British TV comedies), is used as a form of mild derision by many speakers who would be shocked by its original meaning in rhyming slang. The origin is 'Berkeley hunt' or 'Berkshire hunt', meaning **cunt** which, in the late 19th and early 20th centuries, was a cockney synonym for a fool.

> 'How tempting it must have been to add: "...despite what you may gathered from that posturing berk, Chirac".'
> (Quentin Letts writing in the *Daily Mail*, 24 June 2005)

berko, berco *adj Australian*

enraged, uncontrollable. The term may originate as a contracted form of 'berserk'. It is also heard in Ireland where it can also denote drunk.

> *He went completely berko!*

berlimey! *exclamation British*

an expression of surprise or wonder, sometimes feigned. An item of student slang in use in London and elsewhere since around 2000. It is an exaggerated pronunciation of the old 'blimey'. It was still in use in 2005.

bernie *n British*

the sum of £1 million. In UK financial slang the term commemorates the attempt by motor racing impresario Bernie Ecclestone to donate this sum to the Labour Party in 1997.

bertie *n British*

1. a male homosexual. The connection between the name and the subject is unclear.

> *He looks a bit of a bertie to me.*

2. a fool, dupe. In this sense the word (probably based on the names Albert and **Herbert** as supposedly epitomising foolish individuals) is typically used in London working-class speech.

> 'We're going to get a right pounding and they'll [the IRA] make berties of us.'
> (Londoner calling an *LBC* radio phone-in programme, 25 October 1993)

3. *See* **do a Bertie**

berties *n pl British See* **take berties**

besrek *n See* **beresk**

bessie *n British*

best friend. A term which probably originated in North West England but which, since 2000, has become widespread, especially in the speech of younger females. **Bra** is a contemporary synonym.

best! *exclamation British*

an ambivalent exclamation that may indicate approval or the sarcastic reverse; in these senses it has been defined by one of its users as 'that's good, ain't it?' 'Not!'. The term recorded in use among North London schoolboys in 1993 and 1994.

bestie *n British*

an unpleasant or despicable individual. A term of playground abuse from 'bestiality'.

Betty *n*

a girl, particularly a non-participant in sports such as skateboarding. A mildly derisory usage among some teenagers, possibly inspired by the character played by Michelle Dotrice in the TV comedy series *Some Mothers do 'ave 'em*. In the late 1980s Betty became a vogue word in the USA, often used to mean an attractive or popular girl. (In East Anglian dialect Betty – perhaps coincidentally – is a prefix signifying female, as in 'Betty-cat'.)

Betty Bracelets *n British*

a police officer or the police in general. A jocular and ironic nickname bestowed by members of the **gay** community from the later 1950s. (Bracelets is archaic slang for manacles or handcuffs.)

> 'I was sitting there minding my own business when up comes Betty Bracelets looking all obstreperous ...'
> (Recorded, male transvestite, London, 1992)

beverage *n*

alcohol. This (uncountable) usage is popular with young males.

> *Let's get some beverage.*

bevvied *adj British*

drunk. From the increasingly popular use of the noun and verb shortenings of 'beverage'.

bevvy, bevvie *vb, n British*
(to take) an alcoholic drink. A predominantly working-class abbreviation of 'beverage' in use since the 19th century, usually referring to beer. The term gained a new popularity among students, etc. from the end of the 1980s.

They've been bevvying since lunchtime.
'We had a few bevvies on the way here.'
(Recorded, workman, York, 1986)

beyond the black stump *adj Australian*
See **black stump**

Bezz, Bezzie *n British*
a cloddish, unsophisticated person. This term from the 1980s street slang of Manchester probably derives from an eponymous individual who bore this nickname, such as Mark Berry of the band the Happy Mondays. The music impresario Tony Wilson, when reminiscing, commented of the band New Order, 'They were all Bezzies'.

B.F., b.f. *n British*
'bloody fool'. A pre-World War II, mainly middle-class, euphemism, now sounding rather dated. The initials have sometimes been used with more vehemence, probably on the assumption that the 'f' in question stood for **fucker**.

B.F. Egypt *n American*
a disguised version of **Bumfuck Egypt**

B-girl *n American*
1. a prostitute or woman of dubious morals who frequents bars
2. the female counterpart of a **B-boy**. **Fly-girl** is a more common synonym.

bi- *n, adj*
(a person who is) bisexual

bible *n See* **Tijuana bible**

bible-basher *n*
an over-enthusiastic evangelist Christian

bicycle *n See* **town bike/pump**

bif, biff *n British*
1. a cigarette. A vogue term among adolescents from the later 1990s, the derivation is given at **bifta**.

Chas's just caned my biffs.

2. an Internet user deemed to be embarrassing or unfortunate, in the patois of **cyberpunks** and **net-heads**. This categorisation is defined in *Surfing on the Internet*, by J. C. Hertz (1994), as 'the archetypal ultimate loser-cum-cyber-punk-wannabee stuck in the fantasy world of low-end equipment, limited software and all-caps mode'.
3. the vagina

biff *vb British*
to have sex (with). A rarer alternative form of **boff**, heard particularly among male adolescents since the early 1990s. The word can be used both transitively and intransitively.

biffa, biffer *n British*
1. an ugly or unattractive female. Biffa is sometimes used as a children's nickname, usually denoting a burly, boisterous individual, so probably from the colloquial verb 'biff' meaning to hit. It is also the name of a UK waste disposal company. 'Biffa Bacon' is the name of a male cartoon character in *Viz* comic.
2. the vagina. A vulgarism heard in the North of England.
3. a **spliff**

biffage *n British*
an attractive female or females in general. The usage derives from **biffa 2**. **Damage** is a synonym.

biffie *n Canadian*
a toilet. The origin of the word, heard in the 1960s and currently popular among male adolescents, is obscure. It might possibly be a corruption of the French *buffet* in the sense of a bench or stool.

bifta[1] *n*
1a. a cigarette
1b. a marihuana cigarette
1c. marihuana, cannabis

In the sense of cigarette the word originated in playground slang in the 1970s. It is a deformation of the medical term *spina bifida*.

bifta[2] *n, adj*
(something) wonderful, impressive. In this sense the word is of uncertain origin. It often occurs in the phrase 'the full bifta'.
Compare **berifta**

biftad *n American*
a male **preppie**. This comic but probably ephemeral coinage was recorded in use among American teenagers in 1987. It is a combination of two supposedly archetypal preppie nicknames, as in the exchange:
'Say, Biff…'
'Yes, Tad?'

big A, the n Australian
a shortened form of the phrase 'the big arse', meaning the **heave-ho** or the **elbow**.
See also **arse**[1] 4

Big Apple, the n American
the nickname for New York City. It seems to have originated among jazz musicians, perhaps from the notion of 'a bite of the apple' meaning a chance of success.

big-ass adj American
very large

big cack, the n Australian
a wild celebration, an enjoyable experience. **Cack** in this case is probably a short form of 'cackle' with a nod to its other ruder sense. The term was popularised by Australian revellers in London in 1994. It denotes, according to the Sunday Express, 'the holy grail of funlovers, the ultimate party experience'.

big E, the n
the **elbow**.
See also **arse**[1] 4

big enchilada n American
an important or self-important person, the boss. A humorous phrase from the 1970s. An enchilada is a Mexican filled pancake. The term is a later imitation of the pre-World War II colloquialisms 'big cheese/potato'.

big fuck-off adj
enormous, excessive, impressive

big girl's blouse n British
a weak, ineffectual or pathetic male. A phrase usually heard in the north of England. It first came to prominence in the late 1960s.
    'Naff ballet roles – the big girl's blouse in "Les Sylphides".'
    (The Complete Naff Guide, Bryson et al., 1983)

big hair n American
a spectacular teased or bouffant female hairstyle. This Americanism, dating from the 1950s, began to be used in other English-speaking areas in the 1990s, usually sarcastically.

big house, the n American
a prison, especially a federal prison. This underworld euphemism was publicised by its use as the title of an Oscar-winning film of 1930 starring Wallace Beery.

big jimmies n Scottish
a large backside, prominent buttocks. Jimmies refers to the actor/musician Jimmy Durante, whose name was borrowed as a rhyme for pantie(s) in Glaswegian slang. The phrase big jimmies was used by Scottish singer Sharleen Spiteri in 1999.
    Look at the big jimmies on those two.

big jobs n pl British
excrement, defecation. A mainly middle-class nursery term, in use since the 1940s.

big licks n pl
(a display of) enthusiasm or energy, e.g. on the dancefloor. A term from late 1990s club culture.
    She was givin' it big licks.

big man on campus n American See **B.M.O.C.**

big-note vb Australian
to boast or to praise. The term probably referred originally to large denomination bank notes.
    'I big-noted myself.'
    (Mel Gibson, Australian actor, 1987)

big-noter n Australian
a braggart, boastful person. From the verb form.

bigs, biggins n British
something of no importance, often as a dismissive exclamation, probably from the phrase '(no) big deal'. Others claim a reference to the ubiquitous minor celebrity and party-goer, Christopher Biggins.

big spit, the n
an act of vomiting

Big Swinging Dick n
a forceful, powerful individual. The term evokes a large virile male and is in use particularly among financial traders, first in Wall Street, and subsequently in the City of London. Impressive female colleagues were known in London as Honorary Big Swinging Dicks. The term was sometimes disguised as **B.S.D.**

big time adj
very much, a lot
    'Have you got a lot of work?' 'Yeah…big time!'
    You're in trouble big time.

big (someone) up vb British
to boost someone's confidence, praise someone. This fairly widespread slang

phrase of the late 1990s probably originated in black British usage.

'She were biggin' 'im up, goin' gwaarn, gwaarn! at 'im...'
(Recorded, black teenage girl, London, March 1997)

bike *n See* **town bike/pump**

biked *adj British*
deceived or defrauded. This item of taxi-drivers' jargon often refers specifically to the driver's dilemma when the passenger disappears into a building without paying. It was recorded in the *Evening Standard*, 22 April 1996.

biker *n*
a motorcycle rider, a member of a motorcycle gang. This American usage was unknown in Britain until the late 1960s when biker style and hardware began to be imitated.

bikie *n Australian*
the Australian version of **biker**

bill¹ *n British*
1. a £100 note or an amount of one hundred pounds. An item of black street-talk used especially by males, recorded in 2003.
I gave him two bills to take care of it.
2. the penis. The word was used in this sense by adolescent males in 2000.

bill² *vb*
1. *American* to depart, leave. One of many fashionable synonyms in use in black street slang, later adopted by white adolescents in the late 1990s. It is probably an alteration of the earlier **bail**. A variety of euphemisms (like its contemporaries **bail**, **book**, **jam** and **jet**) for 'run away' are essential to the argot of gang members and their playground imitators.
Someone's coming, we better bill!
2. *British* to have sex (with). The word was used in this sense by adolescent males in 2000.

Bill, the Bill, the Old Bill *n British*
the police. A working-class London term which slowly entered common currency during the 1970s, partly owing to television police dramas. The term's origins are obscure. It seems to have passed from 'Bill' or 'Old Bill', a mock affectionate name for individual police officers, via 'the Old Bill', a personification of the police force as a whole, to 'the Bill'. It can also be used in expressions such as '(look out) (s)he's Bill!', mean-

ing he or she is a police officer. Coincidentally or not, in 1917 the Metropolitan Police used Bruce Bairnsfather's famous cartoon figure *Old Bill* (he of 'If you know of a better 'ole, go to it') on a recruiting campaign. It may also be significant that when the Flying Squad was first motorised, all their licence plates had BYL registrations.

'A banner was draped from cell windows [at Wandsworth prison where police had taken over from striking warders] reading: support the screws – Old Bill out.'
(*Guardian*, 3 January 1989)

Bill and Ben *n British*
yen (Japanese currency). An item of rhyming slang from the lexicon of London City traders in the 1990s. The names are those of the two 'Flowerpot Men', heroes of a 1950s children's TV puppet show.

billiards *n pl See* **pocket billiards/pool**

billies *n pl American*
money, dollar bills. A popular term among **Valley Girls** and other teenagers since the early 1980s.

billit *n British*
a marihuana cigarette, **spliff**. A term used by young street-gang members in London since around 2000.

bills *n pl British*
male underpants. The term, in use in the Liverpool area in 2003, is said to refer especially to boxer shorts. It has given rise to the expression **chill one's bills**; relax, calm down.

bill up, build it up *vb British*
to construct a **spliff**
You built up yet?

Billy *n British*
speed. The term is a shortening of 'Billy Whizz', the name of a character from the children's comic *Beano*; whizz is an earlier nickname for the drug.

Billy (Bunter) *n British*
an ordinary member of the public, a customer. This item of rhyming slang meaning **punter** – borrowing the name of the fat schoolboy hero of children's stories – was widely used in the service industries in the 1990s.

'Billies is our name for the clients...no disrespect.'
(Club 18–30 representative, *Sunday Times* magazine, 24 September 1995)

Billy-and-Dave *n*
a friendless individual, misfit, outsider.
The phrase is formed from the witticism
'Billy no-mates, Dave all gone!'. An item
of student slang in use in London and
elsewhere since around 2000.

Billy no-mates *n*
a friendless individual, misfit, outsider. A
very widespread usage since the late
1990s. **Norman no-mates** is synonymous.

bim *n*
a shortened form of **bimbo** and **bimboy**

> *'He wanted some bim to be skating down
> the slopes in a bikini.'*
> (*Blind Date*, TV dating show, March
> 1997)

bimbette *n*
a silly, empty-headed young girl. A jocular diminutive of **bimbo**, popular in the
mid-1980s, first in the USA and then, via
magazine articles, in Britain, where it has
been enthusiastically taken up and over-
used in the tabloid press.

bimbetude *n*
combined physical attractiveness and
intellectual vacuity. This humorous combining of **bimbo** and 'pulchritude' was
briefly recorded in the early 1990s.

bimbo *n*
1. a silly, empty-headed or frivolous
woman. This is the sense of the word in
vogue since the late 1980s, imported to
Britain and Australia from the USA. The
origin is almost certainly a variant of
bambino, Italian for baby. In the early
1900s a bimbo, in American colloquial
use, was a man, especially a big, unintelligent and aggressive man or a clumsy
dupe. By the 1950s the word was used
as a nickname for boys in England, perhaps inspired by a popular song of the
time. By the 1920s bimbo was being
applied to women, especially by popular
crime-fiction writers, and it is this use
that was revived in the 1980s with the
return to fashion of glamorous but not
over-cerebral celebrities. In the late
1980s the word was again applied occasionally to males, although with less brutish and more frivolous overtones than
earlier usage.

> *'Daryl Hannah plays an interior designer
> and Gekko's part-time mistress who
> turns her attention to Bud Fox's apart-
> ment and bed. She's meant to be a rich
> man's bimbo.'*
> (Oliver Stone, US film director, *Sunday
> Times* magazine, February 1988)

2. *British* the bottom, backside. A nursery and schoolchildren's word of the
1950s, now rarely heard.

bimboid *adj*
vacuous, having the attributes of a **bimbo**

bimboy *n*
a male **bimbo**. This humorous item of
journalese is a synonym for the (possibly
more common) **himbo**.

bin[1] *n*
1. a pocket, usually in trousers. This
example of the jargon of cat burglars was
recorded in *FHM* magazine in April
1996.
2. the bin *British* a mental hospital or asylum. A shortening of **loony bin**.

> *'If she goes on like this she's going to end
> up in the bin.'*
> (Recorded, housewife, London, 1988)

bin[2] *vb British*
to throw away, reject. A sharper or more
imperious version of 'chuck it' or 'dump
it' is 'bin it', heard since the late
1980s, especially in offices and in a
broader business context.

bin-diving *n British*
rummaging in rubbish in search of food
or valuables

bingle *n Australian*
a car crash

bingo *n British*
an arrest, a successful search. A customs officers' term employing the tri-
umphal cry from the popular game of
chance.

> *We got a bingo finally after three weeks.*

bingo bling *n British*
cheap, ostentatious jewellery as worn,
e.g., by **chavs**. A synonym of **Argos bling**
recorded in 2005.

bingo wings *n pl British*
flabby upper arms. The mocking pejorative term is typically applied to females.
It was popularised by the TV comedy *Bo
Selecta* in 2003 and 2004. The bingo
reference may be to elderly women wav-
ing their arms at bingo sessions.

binner *n British*
a vulgar person. A middle-class term of
social denigration 'used about people in
tracksuits on council estates' since
2000.

bins n pl British
1a. glasses, spectacles. A cockney short-ening of binoculars, sometimes spelled **binns**. The term has been in use at least since the 1930s and is still heard.
1b. the eyes. An extension of the previous usage.
2a. headphones. Part of the jargon of recording engineers and rock musicians in the late 1960s; the term was eagerly picked up by hi-fi enthusiasts and **musos** in the 1970s, although **cans** is more prev-alent in this context.
2b. hi-fi or concert speakers. By exten-sion from the above sense.

bint n British
a girl, a (young) woman. *Bint* is Arabic for daughter or girl; the word was adopted by soldiers serving in Egypt and became widespread in Britain from the 1920s to the 1960s. In English the word nearly always had, and still has, deprecatory overtones.
'I've got to keep him and that Russian bint one step ahead of the police.'
(*Room at the Bottom*, TV comedy, 1987)

binter, binta n British
a girl. A variant form of **bint** heard since 2000.

binting n British
pursuing or seducing females. A term used by (generally unsophisticated) young males, from the noun form **bint**.

bio-head n American
an unstylish person, a **nerd**. The expres-sion was recorded in the late 1990s among college students and Internet users.

biotch n American
1a. an unpleasant female
1b. a female
An alteration of **bitch** in use among stu-dents since 2000.

bird n British
1. a girl. A very common term in the late 1950s and 1960s, it is now somewhat dated and considered offensive or pat-ronising by most women. The word was first a 19th-century term of endearment, ultimately from Middle English, in which bird could be applied to young living things in general, not merely the feath-ered variety.
2. a prison sentence. From the rhyming slang birdlime: *time*.
He's doing bird in Wandsworth.

birdbath n British
a silly person. A humorous variant form of the colloquial 'birdbrain' typically used since the 1970s by parents and children.

bird droppings n pl British
an adolescent euphemism for **chickens-hit** in the sense of something derisory or pitiful

birding n British
pursuing or trying to 'pick up' women. A northern English working-class term of the 1960s and 1970s, from the more widespread use of **bird**.

birf n British
a coy or jocular shortening of 'birthday', used typically by teenage magazine journalists since the 1980s

birl n See **burl**

biscuit n American
1. an attractive person. The term, heard in the late 1990s, can be used by, and of, either sex.
Wow, a total biscuit!
Compare **earth biscuit**
2. the head
The result was Chrissie bumped her bis-cuit.

biscuits n pl American
the buttocks
Man, scope those biscuits.

bish-bash-bosh adv, adj British
quickly, efficiently, in quick succes-sion. A vogue catchphrase in use among fashionable young professionals in Lon-don in the mid-1980s and still heard.
It was bish-bash-bosh/a bish-bash-bosh job.
Compare **bosh**

bit adj American
disappointed, resentful. A folksy version of 'bitter' or 'bitten' used by country peo-ple and poor blacks (in pre-war slang it usually meant 'cheated'); adopted as part of **preppie** language in the 1970s.
She sure was bit when she found out she hadn't been chosen.

bitch n
1a. a pejorative term for a woman which, although not strictly speaking slang, is normally highly offensive. As a term of denigration bitch, like its alternatives 'sow', 'vixen', etc., has been widespread since the Middle English period. In black American speech 'bitch' can be used with proprietorial or condescending over-

tones rather than with personalised malice.

> *'Ultimately, it [N-W-A's album]'s just another extension of the black under-class machismo which casts all women as "bitches".'*
> (*Independent*, 8 September 1989)

1b. a spiteful or vindictive male homosexual

1c. an infuriating or gruelling task

1d. something impressive, admirable. This is another example of a negative term being employed in a contradictory sense (compare **bad**, **wicked**, etc.) It usually occurs in the appreciative phrase 'it's a bitch!' in American speech.

bitch-bag *n*
an unpleasant female. The term, heard since 2000 and used both pejoratively and sometimes affectionately, is an elaboration of **bitch**.

bitchin' *adj American*
excellent, first class. From the colloquial phrase 'it's a bitch!', expressing great enthusiasm.

bitch (someone) out *vb American*
to criticise, nag, denigrate

> *Do you expect me to just go home and have the wife and kids bitch me out?*

bite *vb American*
to be repellent, inferior, worthless. Since around 2000 'it bites' has been synonymous with 'it **sucks**'.

bite me! *exclamation American*
a cry of contempt or defiance

biting *n*
selling a graffiti artist's pen name to another young person. Usually seen in this form rather than the verb 'to bite'. It is a specialisation of the colloquial sense of bite meaning 'coercion'.

bit of fish *n British*
sexual contact with a female. The fish reference is to the supposed smell associated with female sexuality. This vulgarism is a successor to the obsolescent 'handful of sprats'.

bit of fluff, bit of stuff *n British*
a woman, seen as attractive but frivolous, or not to be taken seriously. A condescending male term from the early 1900s, still fairly widespread in the 1960s and not yet quite obsolete.

bit of rough *n British*
a lover of either sex who exhibits or feigns primitive, aggressive or socially inferior characteristics. A phrase often used joc-

ularly in the 1980s, originally a variation of the prostitutes' and homosexual term **rough trade**.

> *She's always preferred a bit of rough.*

bits *n pl British*
1. primary sexual characteristics. In origin possibly a shortening of 'naughty bits', the word has become popular with all age groups since around 2000.

> *Show us yer bits!*
> *He was doing acrobatics and his bits fell out.*

2. *See* **in bits**

bitser, bitza *n*
a mongrel (usually a dog). A witticism based on the idea that the animal's pedigree is composed of 'bits of this and bits of that'. The expression, which probably originated in Australia, can also be applied to anything put together from disparate components.

bivvy[1] *vb British*
to bivouac, make camp. A shortening used by scouts and the armed forces in the 1970s and 1980s.

bivvy[2] *n British*
1a. a bivouac, camping place

1b. a tent, especially a small tent. Both terms are, predictably, part of the vocabulary of soldiers, scouts, campers and ramblers, etc.

2. an alternative form of **bevvy**

biz, the biz *n*
1a. show business. A term used by the self-consciously theatrical, originating as 'show biz' in the style of journalese popularised by *Variety* magazine.

1b. any sphere of activity, such as the music biz, the public relations biz, etc., by extension from the first sense. It is often used ironically to add a sheen of cheap glamour to difficult or thoroughly mundane jobs. In the company of cognoscenti, any such group may be referred to as **the biz**.

1c. a term of approbation, as in 'this is the biz' or 'he's the biz'

bizatch, biznatch *n American*
1a. an unpleasant female

1b. a female

Altered pronunciations of **bitch** heard for example on campus since 2000.

blab *vb*
to inform (on someone), to tell tales or reveal information. The term often has the sense of a garrulous or inadvertent revelation of a secret or confidence.

Like blabber, the word has meant '(to engage in) voluble or indiscreet talk' since the 16th century.

blabber *n Australian*
a TV remote control. This item of domestic slang of the 1980s refers to the mute capability. No universal slang term for the remote control has yet emerged, though **zapper** is a recorded alternative.

black bag job *n American*
a break-in or other covert operation carried out by a government agency. A piece of jargon from the time of the Watergate scandal.

black bombers *n pl British*
capsules of Durophet (a form of amphetamine popular among drug abusers in the 1960s), named for their colour and their powerful effects

black-hole-Bill *adj British*
depressing, miserable. An expression heard, especially among males, since around 2000.

> *The weather's black-hole-Bill today.*
> *I'm feeling black-hole-Bill.*

black maria *n*
a prison van or police car or van. The nickname originated in the USA in the mid-19th century (Maria is probably an arbitrary borrowing of a female name as a familiarising device).

black rat *n British*
a traffic patrol officer. An item of police slang recorded by the *Evening Standard* magazine in February 1993. The black refers to the uniform and the rat to other officers' and motorists' dislike of the traffic police.

black stump *n Australian*
a very remote region. The mythical starting point for 'the back of beyond'.
See also **Woop-woop**

blad *n British*
an Afro-Caribbean pronunciation, or imitation thereof, of **blood**, in the sense of 2

bladdered *adj British*
drunk. An increasingly common term among middle-aged speakers as well as students, etc., since the early 1990s. It was used in the TV soap opera *Brookside*.

> *'"What I like to do on a Monday night is go out and get bladdered", says Mick.'*
> (*Daily Telegraph* magazine, 15 June 1996)

> *'... the conversation begins to steer bladderedly through a number of topics ...'*

(*Q* magazine, March 1997)

blade *n*
a knife, particularly when used for protective or offensive purposes

blag *n, vb British*
1a. (to carry out) a robbery. This is the sense of the term familiar to most people since its use in TV shows of the 1970s giving a realistic perspective on criminal milieus.

1b. to scrounge, cadge, deceive or bamboozle, or the booty from such an activity
The word 'blag' has been in widespread use in both sub-senses in underworld and police circles since the early 1950s. It is presumed that it derives from the French *blague*, meaning a joke or blunder, but the details of this etymology are unclear. There have been suggestions that it is more simply an elaboration of to **bag**.

blah *n, adj*
(something) dull, tedious, listless, inert. A pejorative term deriving from an exclamation of boredom or resignation. The word spread from the USA to Britain before World War II.

blair, blare (out) *vb British*
to criticise, denigrate, belittle. A word of obscure origin (it precedes the media attention paid to the Labour leader Tony Blair), it may have originated in black speech and may simply be an appropriation of the standard meaning of blare, i.e. to shout, trumpet. The term was recorded in use among North London schoolboys in 1993 and 1994.

blamming *adj British*
exciting. Like its earlier synonyms **banging** and **slamming** the usage (among students, urban gang members, etc. since around 2000) derives from the equation of percussion or explosion with physical and/or emotional stimulus ('blam' being imitative of gunfire in cartoons).

blang *n American*
a later variant form of **bling**, recorded in 2004

blank (someone) *vb British*
to snub or refuse to speak to someone or acknowledge them. A mainly working-class expression becoming increasingly popular in London since the later 1980s. The past participle form 'blanked' in particular is a vogue term among schoolchildren.

> *'Donna went to see her and she totally blanked her.'*

(*EastEnders*, British TV soap opera, March 1988)

blast *n*

1a. a party or celebration

1b. any enjoyable or exhilarating experience

2. an inhalation of cannabis or another euphoric drug

3. *British* a gun. A term used by young street-gang members in London since around 2000.

blat *n Australian*

a short trip on a bicycle. The word, which was featured in the long-running soap opera *Neighbours* in 1996, has been adopted by British schoolchildren.

blatant *adj*

1. obvious. Can be used to express surprise, as in: 'What the blatant pantsgan do you think you're doing?'.

2. outright

3. excessive, outrageous. A vogue term (invariably used to indicate approval) among adolescents since the mid-1990s.

> '*Crispin was being blatant again as usual when we went to TuTu's.*'
> (Recorded, London University student, December 1996)

4. Blatant! an exclamation of agreement

blates *adj, adv British*

a short form of **blatant** or **blatantly** in their slang senses

blathered *adj British*

drunk. The term has been used by students since 2000. Synonyms include **bladdered**, **blatted** and **lathered**.

blatherskite, blatherskate, bletherskite *n*

1a. a boastful or bombastic person, a 'windbag'

1b. a villainous or disreputable person

This picturesque word is the American and Australian version of the Scottish dialect word 'bletherskate'. Although it is a fairly innocuous term of mild abuse, it derives from 'blether' meaning a bladder or to blather, and 'skate', a dialect variant of **shit**. The image evoked is of someone who is 'full of shit'. During the War of Independence, Americans became familiar with the word from the Scottish song, *Maggie Lauder*.

blatted *adj British*

intoxicated by drugs or alcohol. A popular word among adolescents since the 1990s. Like many synonyms, the word evokes the notion of someone struck (down) or punished (which has been

rendered by 'blat' and 'blatter' in dialect for centuries).

blaw *n British*

cannabis, marihuana. An altered pronunciation of **blow**, heard since 2000.

blazed, blazed up *adj*

1a. intoxicated by drink or drugs

1b. in a heightened state of excitement, anger, etc.

bleak *adj South African*

depressed, disappointed

bleeder *n British*

an individual, particularly an unfortunate or despicable person. This working-class term often conveys strong dislike or contempt. It dates from the 19th century, but has lost popularity since the 1960s.

bleeding *adj British*

an intensifying term, currently out of fashion except in the expression '(the) bleedin' obvious', but widespread in the 1960s when it was significantly stronger than **bloody**. This usage probably dates from the 19th century in working-class speech.

Blighty *n British*

Britain. An anglicisation of the Hindustani *bilayati*, meaning foreign. The word was originally used with some affection by the pre-World War I colonial army, but is now used only to suggest mock jingoism.

> '*I was blown through the door and put my hand to my head. It was covered in blood, but we had no thoughts of Blighty. We didn't want to go back, we'd only just come.*'
> (World War I veteran David Watson, *Independent*, 12 November 1988)

blim[1] *n British*

a very small portion of a drug, usually hashish. A coinage recorded among drug users and dealers in London from the late 1980s.

blim[2] *vb British*

to drop burning embers of cannabis

> '*You're not skinning up in here, you blimmed the carpet last time.*'
> (Recorded, Southampton, 2000)

blimp *n*

a fat person. A favourite American college-student term of derision, also heard among British schoolchildren and others since the 1980s. From the name of the World War I barrage balloon.

*'When I was playing tennis I was just a fat
blimp waddling round the court.'*
(Annabel Croft, *Today*, 7 February 1989)

blimp out *vb American*
to become sated and/or collapse from
overeating. An elaboration of **blimp** in the
sense of a fat person. In black street
slang of the 1990s it was often shortened
to 'blimp'.

blind *adj South African*
unpleasant, painful. Recorded as an
item of Sowetan slang in the *Cape Sunday Times*, 29 January 1995.

blinder *n British*
an impressive or exciting action, thing
or person. The word, which is often used
for a sporting feat, commonly in the
phrase to 'play a blinder', implies something 'visually stunning'.

Blind Freddie *n Australian*
the personification of a slow-witted,
ignorant individual. The term is usually
employed in phrases such as 'even
Blind Freddie knows that'.

blinding *adj, exclamation British*
excellent, outstanding, astonishing. This
old term of approbation from the language of middle-aged Londoners was
adopted as a vogue term by adolescents
in the 1990s, sometimes in the form of an
exclamation. (The colloquial **blinder**,
meaning a dazzling feat, has been popular since the 1970s.)
It was a totally blinding bop.
*'Recently I bought a copy of the Big
Issue. The man took the money and then,
instead of the usual "Cheers!" or even
"Thank you!", he said, "Blinding!"'*
(*Daily Telegraph* magazine, September
1996)

bling, bling-bling *n*
1a. jewellery
1b. ostentation, conspicuous display.
See also **chav**
These terms, from US hip hop and street
usage, became emblematic of an assertive
vulgarity and conspicuous consumption in
popular culture and the media from
around 2000.

blingage *n American*
a more recent version of **bling**

blinglish *n British*
an imitation by white or Asian speakers of
black speech patterns, especially of hip
hop slang and a Caribbean accent. The
term was reported in the *Observer* news-

paper in February 2004.: it refers to **bling**
as an emblematic term of youth affiliation.

blissed-out *adj*
ecstatic, euphoric or in a trance, specifically as a result of a religious experience. The term is from the jargon of
transcendent 'fringe' or alternative religious cults of the late 1960s.

blitzed *adj*
very drunk or **stoned**. The usage ultimately derives from the German *Blitz*
(lightning) and *Krieg* (war).
*'Jesus, she was completely blitzed, abso-
lutely out of her head.'*
(Recorded, photographer, London,
1989)

bloater, bloat *n British*
a fat or overweight person. A bloater is
an edible fish, but the slang term is
probably derived from 'bloated'.

blob *n British*
1. a corpse, road-accident victim. An
unsympathetic term used by ambulance
men, the police and tramps.
2. an ulcer, excrescence
3. a bodily protuberance, a breast or a
testicle
4. a condom.
See also **on the blob**
The second and third senses of the word
are recent mock-childish coinages in use
particularly among schoolchildren and
students.
In archaic British slang, blob has been
used in a variety of sexually related contexts, e.g. 'on blob', meaning sexually
aroused, and 'blobbing', meaning suffering from a venereal infection.

blobocracy *n British*
members of middle management or
office workers, especially those considered unimaginative and undynamic.
This dismissive epithet was heard in the
office slang of the 1990s, typically
used by senior executives of their subordinates.
*'If you want to get anything done, the
simplest thing is just avoid the blobocracy and push it upstairs as fast and hard
as you can.'*
(Recorded, advertising sales executive,
London, 1995)

blob-strop *n British*
a bout of bad temper on the part of a
female. The term, from **on the blob** and

strop, refers to pre-menstrual tension and is used by speakers of both sexes.

She threw a terrible blob-strop.

Sorry, it's just a blob-strop.

blob wagon *n British*

an ambulance. From the language of tramps and **dossers**.

'Being rescued by the "blob wagon" for hospital treatment.'

(*Observer*, August 1987)

block *n British*

1. the head. Since the early 1950s this old term has only been used as part of phrases such as 'knock someone's block off' or 'do one's block'.

2. the block solitary confinement. A prisoners' term which is a shortening of 'punishment block'. **Down the block** denotes being sent (sent) in(to) solitary confinement.

block (in) *vb British*

to have sex (with). A working-class male vulgarism heard from the late 19th century until the 1960s. It may now be obsolete.

blocked *adj British*

under the influence of drugs, especially **pep pills** or amphetamines. This word was popular in the early 1960s among **mods**, who used it to refer to the state of intoxication caused by 'pep pills' or amphetamines, such as **purple hearts**, **blues**, **black bombers**, etc. The origin is probably in the idea that one's **block**, or head, is completely taken over and partly incapacitated by the drug. This is reinforced by the fact that a side-effect of amphetamines is to make the user tongue-tied, so that communication is literally blocked.

'"Does that mean you're blocked out of your mind on stage?"

"It means we're blocked out of our minds all the time".'

(Pete Townshend of The Who, interviewed on the television programme *A Whole Scene Going*, 1966)

bloke *n*

a man. The most widespread slang term in Britain and Australia from the 1950s, when it superseded 'chap' and 'fellow', to the 1970s, when 'guy' began to rival it in popularity amongst younger speakers. The exact origin of the word is mysterious. It seems to have entered working-class slang from vagrants' jargon; either from Shelta, the Irish travellers' secret language, or from Romany.

Romany has a word, *loke*, which is derived from the Hindustani for a man; in Dutch *blok* means a fool. Whatever its ultimate origin, bloke entered British usage early in the 19th century and is still thriving in colloquial speech.

'I went into the boozer the other day and there was this bloke I hadn't seen for 25 years.'

(William Donaldson, *Independent*, 26 August 1989)

blonde *adj*

slow-witted, vapid, scatterbrained. The pejorative use followed the rash of jokes which circulated internationally from around 1999, based on the supposed vacuity of blonde females and reinforced by Hollywood comedies such as *Legally Blonde*. 'Blondespeak', recorded in 2004, denotes simplified language as supposedly used by or to blondes.

Don't be so blonde!

That was real blonde.

blood *n American*

a term of endearment or address used by black men to fellow males, it is a shortening of 'blood brother', or a version of 'young blood' as applied to tribal warriors. By 2005 it was a common greeting among youths in East London, usually pronounced 'blad'.

blood-house *n Australian*

a squalid, disreputable establishment, usually a bar, pub, café or hotel. The term probably arose in the 19th century. An East London theatre specialising in gory melodramas was nicknamed 'The Blood-hole' in the late 1800s.

bloody *adj British*

an intensifying adjective which is now considered fairly mild, but which was held to be taboo in many circles until the later 1960s. The standard folk etymology is from the oath 'by our lady', but the word is more probably a simple extension of the literal meaning.

blooper *n American*

a mistake, blunder. A coinage influenced by 'bloomer'.

'TV Censored Bloopers.'

(US TV programme featuring humorous out-takes from films and TV series, 1988)

blooter *n British*

a failure, mess, an instance of excessive behaviour. The origin of the word is unclear, but it is presumably related to 'bloomer' and **blooper**.

blootered *adj British*
drunk. The term is heard particularly in the Scottish Lowlands and the north of England, and is perhaps influenced by the noun **blooter** or by **blotto**.

blot *n Australian*
the anus. One of many Australian vulgarisms for this.

blotto *adj*
drunk. The word appeared around 1905. It implies that the person in question has soaked up alcohol in the manner of blotting paper.

blow¹ *vb American*
1. to leave, go suddenly. A shortening of 'blow away'.

I better blow town before the cops come looking for me.

2. to perform fellatio (upon someone). In this sense the term may either derive from **blow job** or may be the source of that expression.

'Who blew and were blown by those human seraphim, the sailors, caresses of Atlantic and Caribbean love.'

(*Howl*, poem by Allen Ginsberg, 1956)

3a. to smoke. In this sense the verb is typically used by devotees of cannabis.

Let's get together and blow a couple of numbers.

3b. to sniff, **snort**. A cocaine (and occasionally amphetamine) users' term for inhalation.

4. to be repellent. A rarer synonym of to **suck**, heard among school and college students.

'Nice party, Dorothy'

'It blows.'

(Valentine, US film, 2001)

5. to play a musical instrument (not necessarily a wind instrument) in **hip** talk

blow² *n*
1a. cannabis for smoking (hashish or marihuana). A drug users' term.

1b. tobacco. A usage encountered especially in the speech of prison inmates.

Both instances are based on the use of the verb to **blow** to mean smoke.

2. cocaine. The use of blow to mean cocaine spread from the USA to Britain in the later 1970s.

From the slang use of the verb to **blow** to mean both inhale and consume.

blow (someone) away *vb*
to kill someone, especially by shooting them. A widespread euphemism originally in American underworld and military usage.

blower, the *n British*
a telephone. A slang term which was common by the 1940s and is still heard. It may originate in 'blow' as an archaic term meaning 'to talk', or from the habit of blowing into an old telephone mouthpiece before speaking.

Get Nelson on the blower, will you.

blowfurt, blowfoot, blue foot *n British*
a white person who affects black mannerisms, clothing, etc. A highly pejorative term of uncertain derivation used by black teenagers in the early 1990s; it may originate in Caribbean patois. Mild disapproval is indicated by the more widespread **wigga**.

blowhard *n*
a pompous and/or aggressive person, a blusterer. The term seems to have arisen in American speech but is now heard in all English-speaking regions. **Puff-bucket** is a near synonym.

blowin' *adj*
angry or annoyed. An item of black street-talk used especially by males, recorded in 2003.

blow-in *n Australian*
a newcomer and/or interloper. The noun, usually referring to an unwelcome visitor, is based on the colloquial verb 'to blow in' meaning to arrive unexpectedly.

I've got enough to do without having to deal with bloody blow-ins.

blow job *n*
an act of fellatio. This term, now widespread in English-speaking countries, spread from the USA in the 1960s. A puzzling misnomer to many, to **blow** in this context is probably a euphemism for ejaculate, a usage occasionally recorded in the 1950s. This may itself be influenced by the 'there (s)he blows' of whaling cliché. An alternative and equally plausible derivation of blow job is from the black jazz musicians' **hip** talk expression **blow**, meaning to play (an instrument). This term probably caught on in Britain and Australia simply because there was no well-known alternative in existence.

blown away *adj*

1. killed. A cold-blooded euphemism on the same lines as **dusted**.

2. (pleasurably) surprised, 'transported', **gobsmacked**

blown out *adj*

1. *American* tired, exhausted or hung over. A high-school and **preppie** term probably adapted from the following sense.

2. *American* intoxicated or euphoric after taking drugs, **high**. This use is still heard, but less commonly than during the **hippy** era.

3. *American* ruined, failed. Used typically of an event or an opportunity.

4. full of food, gorged. From the verb to **blow out**.

5. rejected, cast aside, expelled. From the verb to **blow out**.

Her past is littered with the corpses of blown out lovers.

blown-up *adj American*

1a. excessive, impressive. An expression used on campus in the USA since around 2000.

That party sure was blown-up; there must've been two hundred people there.

1b. strong, powerful

Man that spliff was blown-up.

blow off *vb*

1. *British* to **fart**. A children's term of the 1950s which was revived in the 1980s.

'We were right in the middle of the restaurant and Kitty blew off in front of them all.'
(Recorded, father, London, 1986)

2. *American* to reject, get rid of someone or something. A less common variant of **blow out**.

3. *American* to absent oneself, avoid, waste time. The verb, popular in campus usage, can be employed transitively or intransitively.

We decided to blow off the class and hit the beach.

Don't go to the office today; blow off instead.

blow one's cookies/doughnuts/ groceries/lunch/grits *vb American*

to vomit. Colourful euphemisms from the lexicon of high-school and college students.

blow one's mind *vb*

to be transported beyond a normal state of mental equilibrium, experience sudden euphoria or disorientation. A key term from the lexicon of drug users of

the 1960s, this phrase was rapidly generalised to cover less momentous instances of surprise, awe, admiration, etc. Now dated, the expression is still in many people's passive vocabulary, allowing it to be used, e.g., in advertising copy as late as 1989.

'Happiness is hard to find – we just want peace to blow our minds.'
(Lyrics to *Revolution* by Tomorrow, 1967)

'She blew my nose and then she blew my mind.'
(*Honky Tonk Woman*, Rolling Stones, 1971)

'The way she came on to me – it completely blew my mind.'
(Recorded, student, London, 1976)

blow out *vb*

1a. to reject someone (especially a lover) or something. From the image of violently expelling something.

1b. to cancel, especially unexpectedly. In this sense the phrase applies typically to a pop group cancelling a tour or concert.

2. to over-eat as a matter of sensual indulgence. From the image of the stomach being blown out like a balloon.

blow-out *n*

an occasion of over-indulgence, particularly excessive eating and drinking

'Have a blow-out at Les Trois Marches.'
(*Mail on Sunday*, *'You'* magazine, March 1988)

blow someone's mind *vb*

1a. to give someone a hallucinogenic drug

1b. to astound, transport, bamboozle or overwhelm someone, or in some other way to radically and rapidly alter their mood or consciousness. An extension of the first sense.

'We're not out to blow people's minds however. We're out to get through to them.'
(Pete Townshend, *Oz* magazine, June 1969)

Both senses of the phrase were part of the **hippy** lexicon of the 1960s and are now dated. (The Beatles were castigated for their ambiguous use of 'I want to blow your mind' in the lyrics of *A Day in the Life* in 1967.)

blow the gaff *vb*

to give away information, reveal a secret, inform on someone. This picturesque phrase was derived from the archaic term 'gaff' meaning a trickster's strategy or paraphernalia. Although it dates from the early 19th century and often evokes the world of **spivs** or gangsters, the expression is still used. Confusingly, blow the gaff could conceivably also now mean 'leave (**blow**) the premises (**gaff**)'.

blub *vb British*

to cry, weep. A middle-class children's and public-school term, typically used derisively. It is a shortening of the collo-quial 'blubber'.

> *'But the boiled egg made his gorge rise, and it was as much as he could do to stop himself blubbing over the toast and marmalade.'*

(*Scandal*, A. N. Wilson, 1983)

bludge *vb Australian*

to cadge, scrounge, shirk or loaf. Origi-nally the word meant to bully and was a shortening of bludgeon. It later meant to live off immoral earnings. The word, which has given rise to the more com-mon **bludger**, was introduced to Britain via Australian TV soap operas in the late 1980s.

bludger *n Australian*

a cadger or scrounger, a disreputable or despicable person. (A **dole-bludger** is the Australian equivalent of the British 'dole scrounger'.)

blue *n*

1. *Australian* a violent row or fight

> *'They got into a blue – Kelly pushed Char-lene into a gooseberry bush.'*

(*Neighbours*, Australian TV soap opera, 1987)

2. *British* an amphetamine tablet. A term from the 1960s when these tablets were light blue in colour and also known as 'French blues' and 'double-blues'. (Strictly speaking blues were tablets of drinamyl, a mixed amphetamine and barbiturate preparation, prescribed for slimmers.)

3. a police officer. A rare usage, but occa-sionally heard in all English-speaking countries; it is usually in the plural form.

4. *Australian* a red-headed man. A nick-name mentioned in Rolf Harris's well-known song 'Tie me kangaroo down, sport!'.

blue balls *n*

a condition of acute (male) sexual frus-tration, jocularly supposed to bring on a case of orchiditis, the testicles swelling to bursting point. This American expres-sion of the 1950s, popular then among college students, has since spread to other English-speaking communities.

bluebottle *n British*

a police officer. A term popular in the 1950s and still heard. It has been used in Britain since the 16th century, well before policemen wore uniforms, and indeed existed in any organised form, which suggests that the original refer-ence was to an annoying pestilential presence.

> *'Before you could turn round the place filled up with bluebottles.'*

(Recorded, pub habitué, London, 1987)

blue foot *n British*

a prostitute. An ephemeral word of uncertain origin.

> (Recorded by Deputy Assistant Commis-sioner David Powis in his *Field Manual for Police*, 1977)

bluie, bluey *n*

1. *British* a five-pound note or an amount of £5, from the turquoise colour of the banknote. A term used by young street-gang members in London since around 2000.

2. *Australian* a red-headed man. A com-mon facetious nickname also rendered as **blue**.

blunt *n*

a marihuana cigarette, **joint**. This term, fashionable in the USA and the UK since the early 1990s, originally referred to a cigar hollowed out and filled with a com-bination of cannabis and cocaine.

> *We prefer to spark up a blunt and kick back.*

blunts *n British*

cigarette papers. The term was recorded in 2001.

B.M.O.C. *n American*

'big man on campus'; a **preppie** and stu-dent term for an influential fellow stu-dent.

Compare **B.N.I.C.**

B.M.W. *n American*

a successful black male. The initials, punning on the brand name of a favourite German car, stand for 'Black Man Work-ing'. An item of black street-talk included in so-called **Ebonics**, recognised as a legitimate language variety by school offi-cials in Oakland, California, in late 1996.

Compare **B.N.I.C.**

B.N.I.C. *n American*

a successful or dominant black male. The initials stand for 'Boss Nigger In

Charge'. An item of black street-talk that was included in so-called **Ebonics**, recognised as a legitimate language variety by school officials in Oakland, California, in late 1996.

Compare **B.M.O.C.**; **B.M.W.**

boak *vb British*
to vomit. The term, probably echoic in origin, is heard particularly in the Scottish Lowlands, the north of England and Northern Ireland. It occurs in the work of the Scottish novelist James Kelman and the Northern Irish poet Tom Paulin.

It makes me want to boak.

We could hear him boaking in the next room.

boat *n American*
a desirable, attractive individual. This item of adolescent slang is a clipping of the colloquial **dreamboat**.

boat (race) *n British*
the *face*. A piece of London rhyming slang which is still heard in both the shortened and full form. (The Oxford and Cambridge boat race provided an annual excursion for many East Enders.)

'Nice legs, shame about the boat race.'
(Sexist catchphrase from the 1970s)

bob[1] *n*
1. *Canadian* a fat or well-built woman. The term, which can be used pejoratively or with mild affection (usually condescending), is an abbreviation of 'big ol bitch'.
2. *British* the male genitals as visible through tight clothing. The term was inspired by the pop musician and impresario Bob Geldof. The female counterpart is **Paula**.

bob[2] *vb American*
to have sex (with). This fairly inoffensive term, heard among American adolescents, began to be used by younger speakers in Scotland and the north of England in the late 1990s. Like many similar terms (**boff**, **biff**, etc.) it probably derives from the use of the same word (in this case in British dialect) to denote a jab or punch.

'You hear lads saying they just want to bob her. Not me, mate.'
(*Guardian*, 15 July 1996)

bobbins *n British*
rubbish, worthless items. This usage arose in the north of England, referring originally to the waste bobbins in the wool mills, and is still heard in its generalised sense.

bobble ((hat) and scarf) *vb, n British*
(to) *laugh*. A rhyming slang phrase heard since around 2000. **Bubble-bath** is a synonym.

You're 'avin a bobble mate.

bobby *n British*
a policeman. A widely known nickname, usually applied to constables or uniformed officers. Rarely heard except in jest since the 1960s, the word derived from the Christian name of Sir Robert Peel, who founded the Metropolitan Police in 1828.

bobbydazzler *n British*
something or someone impressive or dazzling. The word dates from the late 19th century.

bobby soxer *n American*
a teenage girl. The phrase referred to the short white socks worn as part of a standard ensemble in the 1930s and 1940s. The term itself survived until the 1960s.

BOBFOC *n British*
a female with an attractive body but an ugly face. A very widespread male pejorative. The expression, popular since 2000, has been defined as '...a woman with a great rack and pegs, but a face like a builder'. The letters stand for 'body off *Baywatch*, face off *Crimewatch*'. It is pronounced as a word rather than letter by letter.

Bob Hope *n British*
cannabis, **dope**. Rhyming slang from the name of the British-born American comedian. The term is usually said in full, as in 'We've run out of Bob Hope, let's call the man'. The 'H' is often dropped, in self-conscious imitation of the appropriate accent (compare the self-conscious glottal stop in, e.g., **bottle**). This is an example of rhyming slang used, and probably coined, by young middle-class soft-drug users in imitation of traditional working-class cockney rhyming slang.

bobo *n*
a 'bourgeois bohemian' (person who simultaneously favours materialistic behaviour and 'alternative' tastes). The word began to be used in New York in 2001, although it originates in French as *bohème bourgeois*.

bob oneself *vb British*
to **shit** oneself. A vulgarism recorded in 2001.

bocat *vb*
to perform oral sex. A term used by young street-gang members in London since around 2000.

bock *n British*
bad luck. This obscure term, cited as an example of the jargon of cat burglars, was recorded in *FHM* magazine in April 1996.

bod *n*
1. the body. The short form is usually heard in American speech, as in 'check out his great bod'. In British middle-class speech it refers to an individual, as in 'odd-bod'.
2. *British* a tedious, intrusive, pretentious or otherwise irritating person. A vogue term among the fashionable young in the later 1980s. The word may be a shortening of the synonymous 'wimp-bod'.

> 'We are going to create a club without bods…No bods. Bods being the sort of chaps who've got onto the scene and just stuck like glue.'
> (*Evening Standard*, 12 June 1989)

bodacious, boldacious *adj*
fearsome, enormous, impressive, **feisty**. The word is now often used in black speech and by teenagers and has spread from American usage (where it originated) to the language of British teenagers. It appears to be a blend of bold and audacious, but Chapman's *New Dictionary of American Slang* derives it from 'body-atiously', meaning bodily.

bodge *n, vb Australian, British*
(to do) a slapdash job, especially in constructing something. The term may be a back-formation from 'bodger', a rural craftsman who works out-of-doors in primitive conditions roughly shaping and turning, e.g., chair-legs and spindles, or may be from the related standard verb to 'botch'.

bodge-up *n British*
1. a makeshift repair, a ramshackle construction. The result of someone bodging a job.
2. a mess or disaster. A variant of **balls-up** or 'botch-up' influenced by the above sense.

bodgie *n Australian*
a male member of a youth cult, similar to the British **teddy boys** of the 1950s. (The

female counterpart was a **widgie**.) In the 1930s bodgie was apparently used in American **jive talk** to denote a male jitter-bug (dance) fanatic; some authorities dispute this and derive bodgie from the British and Australian verb to **bodge**.

bodgy *adj British*
inferior, malfunctioning or out of order. A late-1980s adolescent term based on **bodge-up**.

> 'Hey mate, your machine's bodgy!'
> (Recorded, video arcade habitué, 1989)

B.O.F., b.o.f. *n British*
a 'boring old **fart**'. An expression of derision institutionalised by rock-music journalists in the mid- and late 1970s, usually applied by devotees of **punk** music to musicians of the **hippy** era who were entering middle age.

> 'Taking all my B.O.F. records and paper-backs down to [the] jumble sale…'
> (*Sincerely yours, Biff*, Chris Garratt and Mick Kidd, 1986)

boff[1] *vb*
1. to hit, punch. A nursery variant of **biff**, occasionally used semi-facetiously by adults.
2. to have sex (with), **fuck**

> '"He's a logical choice".
> "So the fact he's boffing her has nothing to do with it?"'
> (*Vice Versa*, US film, 1986)

The term boff came to temporary prominence in Britain in 1974 when newspapers reported it as current among the upper-class set of which Lord Lucan (fugitive and alleged murderer) was a member. This gentle-sounding word, with its suggestions of 'puff', 'buff' and 'buffer', next appeared as a convenient euphemism employed in US TV series, such as *Soap*, of the late 1970s and 1980s, where verisimilitude would demand a more brusque alternative. It is unclear whether the word is American or British in origin or a simultaneous coinage. It may derive from its nursery sense of 'to hit'.

boff[2] *n*
1. *British* the backside, buttocks

> 'A kick up the boff.'
> (*Only Fools and Horses*, British TV comedy series, 1989)

2a. *American* a successful joke
2b. *American* a hearty laugh

Both senses of the word are part of the jargon of the entertainment industry and are probably imitative of an explosive chortle, or else like 'biff' denote a 'hit'.

3. *British* a **swot**. The word is probably a shortening of the colloquial 'boffin'.

> *'Some took so much pride in never being seen with a book, they had virtual slaves carry their books to and from school…the worst thing you could be was a "boff" or an "anorak".'*
> (*Independent*, 17 November 1996)

4. *British* a sweet. In this sense the word has been used by schoolchildren since 2000.

> *Crash me some boffs.*

boff³ *adj American*
a variant of the vogue term **buff**

> *'You sure look boff to me.'*
> (*California Man*, US film, 1992)

boffo *adj American*
excellent, first-rate. A piece of jargon from the entertainment world (derived by most experts from 'box-office') which has entered popular journalese.

boffola *adj, n American*
an uproarious joke or laugh. The word is a form of **boff** with the Spanish **-ola** suffix denoting large-scale or extra.

bog *n British*
a mess, disaster. The word occurs in the phrase 'make a bog of (something)', popular in the 1980s.

bog(s) *n British*
a toilet. A widespread vulgar term, probably coined by students or servicemen in the 19th century in the form of 'boghouse' to describe foul communal lavatories. The term is used in Australia, too.

> *'"I ran into Shane", said Spider Stacey, "at a Ramones gig at the Roundhouse. He was standing on top of the bog, for some reason".'*
> (*Evening Standard*, 17 March 1988)

bog (up) *vb British*
1a. to make a mess of, spoil. Usually heard in the form 'bog it' or 'bog it up'. A term especially popular in public schools and the armed forces.

1b. to make the end of a cigarette or **joint** wet and mushy while smoking it

bog-all *n British*
a synonym for **fuck-all**, **bugger-all**, 'naff-all', etc.

bogan *n Australian*
a member of a social group first identified by journalists in the 1970s, consisting of uneducated working-class young adults,

roughly the equivalents of US **trailer trash** and the more recent UK **chavs**

> *'Identifying a Bogan is not difficult. Males sport a distinctive hair growth called a "mullet"…Female Bogans are entrusted with the raising of multiple offspring.'*
> (www.effect.net.au, September 2004)

bogart *vb*
to monopolise or fail to pass on a **joint** or cigarette during communal smoking. This popular **hippy** term of the late 1960s was prompted by the actor Humphrey Bogart's habit in films of keeping a cigarette in his mouth for long periods. The verb originated in the USA and quickly spread to other English-speaking areas.

> *'Don't Bogart that Joint.'*
> (Song title, The Holy Modal Rounders, featured on the soundtrack to the film *Easy Rider*, 1969)

bogey *n*
1. *British* a police officer. Probably from the notion of the 'bogey man'.

2. an enemy aircraft or other enemy presence; a service term from the notion of the 'bogey man'

3. *British* a piece of mucus from the nose

bogging, boggin' *adj British*
stinking, filthy, disgusting. The term is heard particularly in the Scottish Lowlands and the north of England, and is probably based on **bog** in the sense of toilet.

> *'My jeans are just boggin'.'*
> (Singer Sharleen Spiteri, 2000)

boggo *adj, n British*
standard, ordinary (merchandise). This variation of the colloquial 'bog-standard' has been recorded among adult speakers since the 1990s.

> *'It makes me laugh all this fuss in the papers about Porsches and Mercs being what we're after – we're coming for your boggo stuff.'*
> (Car thief, quoted in the *AA Magazine*, 1995)

bog in *vb Australian*
to begin (a meal), to eat with relish. A vulgar alternative form of the colloquial 'tuck in'.

bog off *vb British*
to leave, go away. Nearly always used as an aggressive exclamation or instruction. A vulgar term that existed in armed-service use before becoming a vogue successor to **naff off** around 1980. In spite of the

brusque nature, the phrase is not taboo and is used by women.

'If he's going to treat her like that he can just bog off.'
(Recorded, secretary, York, 1981)

bog-roll *n British*
1a. a toilet roll
1b. paperwork or a computer printout

bog-trotter *n British*
an Irish person. A pejorative term heard since the 17th century. The alternative form 'bog-hopper' is sometimes used in the USA.

bogue *adj American*
1. suffering from drug withdrawal. An obsolescent term of unknown origin from the jargon of narcotics addicts.
2a. worthless, counterfeit. From underworld usage.
2b. unpleasant, insincere. An adolescent term.
2c. inferior, ersatz. A vogue term among adolescents, it is a shortening, like the two preceding senses, of **bogus**, itself a key item of fashionable youth slang.

bog-up *n British*
a mess, a badly improvised job. A more vulgar form of 'botch-up' and **bodge-up**.

bogus *adj American*
unpleasant, unacceptable. The standard meaning of bogus (the word is said to have been the name of a counterfeiting machine) was adapted in adolescent usage to become an all-purpose vogue term of disapproval.

'Bill and Ted's Bogus Journey'
(Title of US film, 1991)

bog-wagon *n Australian*
a private van, particularly one which has been customised and/or decorated inside. Like **shaggin' wagon**, it sometimes denotes a vehicle equipped for seduction.

boho *adj*
bohemian, often in the sense of scruffy and/or irresponsible. This Americanism was fashionable from the late 1980s among London journalists.

bohunk *n American*
an East European immigrant. This old term deriving from Bohemian/Hungarian is offensive and occasionally still heard. It is synonymous with 'oaf'.

boiler *n British*
a woman. A contemptuous, derogatory term, implying a lack of both attractiveness and intelligence, commonly used by young working-class males. The phrase 'dodgy boiler' suggests the extra possibility of sexually transmitted diseases. The word in this sense originated pre-World War II when it referred to an older woman with the dimensions and explosive attributes of the contraption. An alternative derivation is from 'boiler' as used to denote a tough or scrawny chicken.

boink *vb American*
to have sex (with), **fuck**. A 1980s variation of **bonk**, sufficiently inoffensive to be used in TV series such as *Moonlighting*.

bokoo[1] *adj American*
very. This facetious adoption of the French *beaucoup* ('much' or 'many') probably originated in black bebop or white Cajun usage, but by the 1990s was fashionable among hip hop aficionados and white adolescents. (Some authorities claim alternatively that it was adopted by US servicemen from the French-speaking Vietnamese. The same French word appeared in British slang after World War I in the form 'boko', now obsolete.)

The program was, like, bokoo boring.

bokoo[2] *n American*
a large quantity or a number of items. The noun form is probably less common than the adjectival.

She said how much did you want and I said, bokoo.

bold *adj British*
flamboyant, daringly fashionable. A vogue word of the mid-1960s, originating as a **camp** code word for a fashionable or overt **gay**. The word was adopted by **mods** as a term of approbation in 1965 and was used as the name of a chain of men's boutiques.

bolid *n British*
hashish. The word is an alteration of the earlier **solid**, in use among students in the south of England in 2002.

bollers *n British*
money. The term is probably a humorous alteration of dollars, perhaps influenced by **boyz**. It may mean simply money or a large quantity of money, as in 'He's got bollers'. The term was recorded in use among North London schoolboys in 1993 and 1994.

bollixed, bollixed-up *adj*
ruined, messed up. A derivation of **bollocks** which, in American English, is used

as a less offensive version of 'ball(s)ed-up'.

bollock[1] *n British*
a ball (in the sense of a dance). A **Sloane Ranger** witticism said quite unselfconsciously by girls as well as boys, Hunt bollocks and Charity bollocks being regular features in the annual social calendar.

bollock[2] *vb British*
to chastise, severely scold or dress down. The word has been used in this way since the early years of the 20th century.

bollocking *n British*
a severe telling-off, chastisement or dressing-down
    'He was all set for giving me a bollocking for parking where I shouldn't.'
    (*Guardian*, 12 December 1987)

bollock-naked *adj British*
completely nude. A more vehement version is 'stark bollock-naked'. In spite of its etymology, the expression may on occasion refer to women.

bollocks
1. *n pl* the testicles. A version of this word has existed since Anglo-Saxon times; in Old English it was *bealluc*, a diminutive or familiar elaboration of *bula*, meaning ball. For much of its existence the word, usually spelled 'ballocks', was standard (if coarse) English.
2. *n pl British* rubbish, nonsense. Often used as an exclamation or in expressing derision or dismissal such as 'a load of (old) bollocks', this sense of the term has existed since the early 20th century.
    'Never Mind the Bollocks, Here's the Sex Pistols.'
    (Title of LP, 1977)
See also **bollock**[1]
3. *n, adj* **the bollocks** *British* (something) excellent. A shortened form of **the dog's bollocks**, used by younger speakers since around 2000.

bollocksed *adj British*
drunk. An item of student slang in use in London and elsewhere since around 2000.

bollocky *adj Australian*
a variant form of **bollock-naked**

bollox, bollocks *adj British*
bad. An adjectival form of the earlier noun, used by younger speakers since 2000.

bolt *vb American*
to leave, go away. A **Valley Girl** and teenagers' expression usually denoting a leisurely departure.

bolted-up *adj British*
a synonym for **fitted up** or **framed**, in criminal jargon of the late 1980s
    'I've got about 30 previous – about half of those, I was bolted-up.'
    (Recorded, bag snatcher, London, 1988)

bom *adj British*
exciting, impressive. The term, used by young black speakers in London since 2000, may be a form of **bomb** or **boom**.

bomb *vb*
to put one's **tag** (personal signature) on a building. From the jargon of graffiti artists.
    'Welcome to a freshly-bombed station.'
    (Graffito, East Putney underground station, London, 1988)

bomb, the *n, adj*
(something) superlative. A vogue term in the USA in **hip** talk, teenage and campus slang since the later 1990s, now also heard in other English-speaking areas. It is often rendered as 'da bomb' in imitation of Afro-Caribbean speech or hip talk.

bombaclaat *n See* **bambaclaat**

bombed *adj*
drunk or **stoned** on illicit drugs. 'Bombed out of one's mind/skull' is a common elaboration.
    'Harvey decided his only real option was to get bombed out of his skull; some things never went out of style, thank God…'
    (*The Serial*, Cyra McFadden, 1976)

bomber *n*
1a. a pill or capsule of an illicit drug, especially amphetamines.
See also **black bombers**
1b. a **joint**, especially a large or powerful one
2. a graffiti artist. From the verb to **bomb**.
3. *South African* a train. Recorded as an item of Sowetan slang in the *Cape Sunday Times*, 29 January 1995.

bona *adj, exclamation British*
excellent, fine, the real thing. An all-purpose term of approbation increasingly heard among working-class Londoners in the 1980s, probably derived from 'bona fide' or from the Spanish and Italian words for good (*buena* and *buona*). In the 1960s bona was part of the **camp** lexicon (popularised in Kenneth Horne's

radio comedy shows), originating in theatrical performers' and prostitutes' argot of the 19th century, in which it often meant 'beautiful'.

a bona geezer

bonce *n British*

the head. Bonce was a mid-19th-century dialect and schoolboy term for a big marble. The word was soon adapted to mean the head, and in that sense remained popular in young people's usage until the 1960s. It now sounds old-fashioned or affectedly upper class, but may be due for revival, in common with other obsolescent but 'jolly' words.

bone[1] *vb*

to have sex. A vulgarism, originating in American speech, in use in many English-speaking areas. Common from the mid-1980s, it was recorded among black Londoners in 1999. This usage may be a back-formation from **boner**.

> '*I hate them.*
>
> *Yeah but would you bone them?'*
>
> (*Buffy the Vampire Slayer*, US film, 1992)

bone[2], **bones** *n*

the drug **crack**. In this sense the usage appeared around 2000.

bonehead *n British*

1a. a complete fool

1b. a **skinhead** of unusually low intelligence and/or extremely right-wing views. The expression was used by skinheads themselves to characterise their more brutal fellows, who may also differentiate themselves by having almost completely shaven heads.

boner *n*

1. a clumsy error, serious mistake. The origin of the term is not clear; it may be inspired by 'bone-headed' or by a 'bone-jarring' blow.

2. an erection. 'Bone', 'hambone' and 'jigging bone' are all archaic slang terms for the penis.

> '*Do you really want to get all dressed up so some Drakkar Noir-wearing Dexter with a boner feels you up?'*
>
> (*10 Things I Hate About You*, US film, 1999)

bones *n pl*

1. dice

2. *American* money

3. the drug **crack**

boneyard *n*

a cemetery

bong[1], **bhong** *n*

a water-pipe for smoking cannabis, strictly one with a carburation hole so that the smoker can add air at will to the smoke. The typical bong is smaller than a hubble-bubble but larger than a pipe. A part of late 1960s drug paraphernalia. From the late 1980s the word referred also to a **crack** pipe.

bong[2], **bong on** *vb*

1a. *Australian* to smoke cannabis in a water-pipe (a **bong**)

1b. *American* to smoke **crack**

bonged *adj*

stoned after smoking cannabis or **crack**

bongo'd *adj British*

thoroughly intoxicated by an illicit drug or, less commonly, alcohol. A variant form of synonymous terms such as **bombed** and **banjo'd**.

bonk *vb British*

to have sex (with). A vogue word of the late 1980s; first heard in the late 1970s and quickly picked up by the media as a useful, vigorous, but printable euphemism for **fuck**. (The word was first broadcast in a British TV comedy series; at a later date, the tennis champion Boris Becker was dubbed 'Bonking Boris' by the gutter press.) It is a childish synonym for 'hit'; the sexual sense may derive from the sound of energetic bouncing. Alternatively, an extended correspondence in *Private Eye* magazine suggested that this had long been a schoolboy term meaning to masturbate or ejaculate. It may also be significant that the immediately precedent vogue word for copulate among teenagers was **knob**, which in **backslang** would give bonk.

> '*They do call it bonking after all, which, as everyone knows, is THE word used by promiscuous people who DON'T REALLY LIKE SEX.'*
>
> (Julie Burchill, *Elle* magazine, December 1987)

bonkers *adj*

1a. crazy. A common colloquialism in Britain since the mid-1960s (it seems to have existed in restricted use since the 1920s), bonkers has more recently been adopted by American teenagers. The inspiration behind it is uncertain, but it may refer to a bang ('bonk') on the head.

1b. fun. Influenced by the associated notions of wild, excessive and unrestrained, this adapted sense of the term has been popular among adolescents since 2000.

We had a bonkers day out.

bonzer *adj Australian*
excellent, great. A word sometimes adopted for humorous use by British speakers. It may derive from bonanza or from Latinate words for 'good'.

boo *n American*
1a. a term of endearment, especially towards a partner of either sex
1b. a 'significant other', e.g. a partner, girl/boyfriend
An expression used on campus in the USA since around 2000.
2. marihuana. A former black slang word, adopted by **hippies** in the late 1970s. It is possibly a pre-World War II adoption of *jabooby*, an African term for fear, or else derives from the adjectival sense.

boob¹, boo-boo *vb*
to blunder, commit a gaffe or error. The verb to boob, based on the earlier nouns 'booby' and 'boob' in the sense of a fool, has been in use since before World War II, the reduplicated form boo-boo since the 1960s.

boob² *n British*
jail. An item of prison slang from the 1990s, probably a shortened version of **booby hatch** in the sense of an institution in which one becomes crazy.

boobs *n pl*
female breasts. The only slang word for the breasts which is currently acceptable in 'polite circles'. (It is also used in the singular form, 'boob'.) It is a less brusque variant of the more vulgar **bubs** or **bubbies** which probably derive from the noises made by suckling babies. Boobs has been a fashionable term since the mid-1960s; bubbie since the 17th century.

> *'Gimme the good old days – when a pair of boobs was a couple of dumb guys.'*
> (*Smokey and the Bandit III*, US film, 1983)

booby hatch *n*
a psychiatric hospital. A jocular term, originally from North America. The association with **boob** and 'booby' is obvious; hatch or hutch is an archaic term for many different enclosures and containers.

boo-coo(s) *n, adj American*
variant forms of **bokoo**

boof, boof-head *n Australian*
a stupid person. The terms are heard throughout the English-speaking world, but probably originated in Australian usage before World War II.

boog *n British*
a foolish, unfortunate or unpleasant person, a misfit. In use among adolescents since 2000. It is probably an arbitrary coinage, possibly influenced by **booger** and/or **bugger**.

booger *n American*
a piece of mucus from the nose. This is the American version of **bogey**.

book *vb American*
to depart, leave. A fashionable term of the 1990s in black street usage and also heard among white adolescents. A variety of euphemisms (like its contemporaries **bail**, **bill**, **jam** and **jet**) for 'run away' are essential to the argot of gang members and their playground imitators. The origin of this usage is not certain; it may derive from an earlier phrase 'book it', meaning that someone has to return home quickly in order to record a transaction.

boom¹ *n*
1. *American* a stereo cassette player, particularly one fitted in a car. A teenagers' term recorded in California in 1987.
2. a party. A teenagers' term in use in Britain and the USA since the early 1980s.

boom² *adj*
1a. excellent, exciting
1b. sexually attractive
The usage, popular since 2000, probably originated in Afro-Caribbean speech. In 2005, pupils at a South London secondary school excused their apparent booing of Prime Minister Tony Blair by claiming that they were in fact chanting 'boom!'

boomer *n*
1. *Australian* a particularly large kangaroo. 'Boom' is an archaic term meaning to rush or move forcefully.
2. *Australian* something excellent, admirable, exciting
3. *American* a member of the so-called baby-boom generation born between 1945 and 1960. The term came into prominence in the 1990s as the adult lifestyle of this age-group came under renewed scrutiny.

boom-ting *n British*

something excellent or impressive. An item of black British slang adopted by adolescents during the 1990s, combining the slang sense of **boom** and the Afro-Caribbean pronunciation of 'thing'.

boondocks, the boondocks *n American*

an out-of-the-way place, a rural community, the back of beyond, **the sticks**. In Tagalog, a language spoken in the Philippines, *bundok* means a mountain (area). The word was picked up by US service personnel in World War II.

> *He comes from somewhere out in the boondocks.*

boong *n Australian*

a coloured person. An offensive racist epithet based on an Aboriginal word, but used as a catch-all term regardless of nationality.

Compare **choong**

boonies, the *n pl*

shorter forms of **boondocks**

boost *vb*

1. *American* to steal. Originally from black slang, perhaps influenced by **lift**, **hoist** and **heist**, the term is now in general use among young people. It usually refers to petty theft, often shoplifting.

> *'Some gals go in for boosting, or paper-pushing or lifting leathers. Others work the chloral hydrate.'*
> (*Wild Town*, Jim Thompson, 1957)

2. *South African* to assist or help. Recorded as an item of Sowetan slang in the *Cape Sunday Times*, 29 January 1995.

boosted *adj*

pleased, proud. This slang usage, recorded among London students in 2001, may derive from phrases such as 'boost one's self-esteem'.

boot *vb*

1. *American* to vomit. This **preppie** expression is either echoic or is a blend of **barf** and 'hoot'.

2. to leave, depart. Like **bail**, **book**, **break** a key term in the argot of street gangs.

booted *adj*

1. *American* expelled, 'booted out' (of school or college). A **preppie** term of the 1970s.

2. *British* ugly. One of a set of terms, including **busted** and **kicked**, in vogue since 2000 and employing a damage metaphor.

bootie call *n*

a request or demand for romance or sex. An expression from the lexicon of **rap** and hip hop, adopted by UK teenagers from around 1999.

bootleg *adj American*

inferior, of poor quality, malfunctioning. A generalisation of the term as previously used for recordings, branded clothing, etc.

booty, bootie *n*

1a. the backside, buttocks

> *Check that booty.*

1b. sex

> *Get some booty.*

Since the late 1990s this US variant form of the Caribbean **batty** has become an emblematic item in the lexicon of **rap**, hip hop, R 'n' B, etc.

booze *vb, n*

(to drink) alcohol. 'On the booze' may mean habituated to alcohol or on a drinking binge. The word originated in Middle English as *bousen*, from the Middle Dutch and Flemish *busen*, a word based on the root *bus-*, meaning 'swelling'.

booze-up *n*

a drinking bout or drinks party

bop¹ *vb*

1a. to dance

> *'Bop till you drop.'*
> (Record title, Ry Cooder, 1974)

1b. to move in a fast but relaxed way. This usage became popular in Britain in the late 1960s and is still heard.

> *Why don't we bop down to the supermarket and grab some beers.*

2. to hit or punch

> *Say that again and I'll bop you a good one.*

bop² *n*

1. a fast, **cool** style of modern jazz introduced in the 1940s; also known as bebop. Bop was accompanied by rapid nonsense lyrics and dancing.

2. a dance. A word from 1950s America, revived in the 1970s and still popular in Britain, among teenagers and students in particular.

> *Are you going to the art school bop?*

bopper *n*

1. *American* a **cool** musician, dancer or devotee of **bop**

2. a **teenybopper**. This shortened form of the word was especially popular in Britain in the 1970s to describe a vivacious, party-loving (usually small or childlike) young girl; a **raver**.

boracic, brassic(k) adj British
penniless, broke. The word is a shortening of the rhyming slang 'boracic lint': **skint**. A genuine example of London working-class argot, this term was adopted into raffish speech in general from the early 1970s. (Boracic is an older name for boric acid used as a weak antiseptic impregnating bandages, etc.)

borer n British
a knife, especially when carried or used as a weapon. An item of black street-talk used especially by males, recorded in 2003.

born-again combining form British
an intensifying phrase used to prefix another pejorative term, the usage (which may have arisen in armed-services' speech) is based on the notion of a 'born-again Christian' being a particularly extreme or intense example of the variety

　　*'In my humble opinion he behaved like a
　　born-again bastard.'*
　　(Recorded, executive, Guildford, England, 1995)

See also **ocean-going**

BORP n British
an unattractive person of the opposite sex. The initials stand for 'big old rough piece', and are typically used by males of a female. An item of student slang in use in London and elsewhere since around 2000.

bo selecta!, bo! exclamation
an expression of enthusiasm, approval, etc. The phrase, from the garage music scene, literally meaning 'excellent DJ', was popularised by the comic persona Ali G played by Sasha Baron Cohen and then by its use as the title of an anarchic UK TV comedy starring Avid Merrion.

bosfotick adj British
drunk. An item of student slang in use in London and elsewhere since around 2000.

bosh vb British
an all-purpose verb which, in club and DJ culture, can replace, e.g., play, consume, go, finish, etc. The term was posted on the b3ta website in 2004.

boss[1] adj
excellent, first-rate, superlative. Currently a fashionable word among teenagers all over the English-speaking community, boss originated in American black street jargon of the early 1960s. It was picked up by other speakers, but it remained an Americanism. (The music industry attempted to promote the 'Boss town sound' in order to establish Boston as the US equivalent of Liverpool in 1964; Duane Eddy had a 1960s hit with *Boss Guitar*.) In the 1970s and 1980s the usage spread through the language of disco, **funk** and **rap** to the young of Britain and Australia.

boss[2] n
a term of address for a stranger or friend, like **blood**, **bredren**, **cuz**, **bro'**, etc. An item of black street-talk used especially by males, recorded in 2003 in the UK.

bostin' adj British
excellent. The word may be a form of 'bursting', or derive from **bust** which, since the 19th century, has had the slang sense of a wild spree or party. Bostin' is common in northwest England and the East Midlands.

bot vb, n
1a. *Australian* (to behave as) an irritant or cadger. A shortening of 'bot-fly' (a native parasite) or 'botulism'.
1b. *British* a shortened form of 'bottom', **arse**

bother n British
trouble, violence, aggression. A typical example of menacing understatement as it occurs in London working-class speech (**spanking**, **seeing-to** and 'have a word with (someone)' are other examples). The use of bother by police officers and thugs as a euphemism for violence reached public notice in the late 1960s when it became a **skinhead** rallying cry, usually rendered as **bovver**.

bottibasher n See **botty-basher**

bottle[1] n British
courage, bravery, 'nerve', especially in the phrases to 'have a lot of bottle', to **lose one's bottle** and 'his/her bottle's gone'. It derives from 'bottle and glass', rhyming slang for **arse**. Most users of **bottle** are ignorant of its derivation (compare the earlier **berk**). The word is long-established in the repertoire of South and East London rhyming slang, but surfaced in widespread usage only in the mid-1970s

(probably via television renderings of police or criminal speech) to enjoy a vogue culminating in the adoption of the slogan 'Milk has gotta lotta bottle' for a nationwide advertising campaign in 1985. The word is pronounced with a medial glottal stop by cockneys and their imitators.

> 'If you've got an old PC trained twenty years ago and he's got no bottle, then you have to have somebody chase and get it [a stolen car].'
> (*Inside the British Police*, Simon Holdaway, 1983)

bottle² *vb British*
1. to hit with a bottle. A widespread brawler's tactic which seems to have become less widespread since the 1960s.
2. to collect money on behalf of a busker or other street entertainer

bottle and glass *n British*
arse. The rhyming slang phrase, still heard in 2004, probably dates back to the 1960s, if not earlier. It is also the origin of the better-known **bottle**, meaning courage.

bottle it *vb British*
a later synonym for the more widespread expression **bottle out**, recorded among London football hooligans in the late 1980s

> 'Blair had decided to cancel his reshuffle. After last year's fiasco...he effectively "bottled it", knowing that the wheels were already coming off.'
> (*Sunday Times*, 25 July 2004)

bottle out *vb British*
to lose one's nerve. From **bottle** in the sense of courage.

bottler *n Australian*
a powerful, forceful or impressive person. It is probably an alteration of **battler**.

> 'You're an absolute bottler, you are – the most powerful woman I've ever...!'
> (*Let The Blood Run Free*, Australian TV comedy, 1993)

bottom burp *n British*
a **fart**. An example of 'schoolboy humour' not confined solely to schoolchildren.

bottom-feeder *n*
an individual engaged in 'doubtful', sordid or disreputable activities. The image evoked is of a scavenging fish (swimming in murky waters) and the phrase is used

in the slang of the workplace, sometimes as a synonym for **bottom-fisher**.
Compare **pond scum**

bottom-fisher *n*
a trader in cheap and/or disreputable shares or commodities in the jargon of financial traders of the 1990s

> 'The bottom-fisher pulled an archer from his bag.'
> (*Evening Standard*, 9 December 1994)

botty-basher, botty-bandit *n British*
a male homosexual. A term of abuse among hip hop aficionados and schoolchildren.

boughetto *adj American*
materialistic, fashion-obsessed. A blend of **bourgie** and **ghetto**. An expression used on campus in the USA since around 2000.

> 'As boughetto as Shannon is, she's still my friend.'
> (Recorded, US student, 2002)

boulder-holder *n*
a brassière. A supposedly humorous phrase used invariably by males since the 1960s.

bounce
1. *vb* to leave
> I'm bored. Let's bounce.

2. *vb* to behave aggressively. The word has been used in this sense by London teenagers since the 1990s, but bounce denoting swagger dates from the late 17th century.
> Look at that plum bouncing.

3. *n* **the bounce**
3a. the sack (from one's job) or a rejection (by a sweetheart). A later version of 'the boot'.
3b. one's fate, an inevitable result. Usually in expressions of resignation, such as 'that's the bounce'.

bounced (out) *adj*
fired from one's job, ejected, expelled or rejected. The image is one of forcible and speedy ejection resulting in one bouncing off one's backside on the floor or pavement.

bouncer *n*
a dud cheque, in debt collectors', underworld and police jargon all over the English-speaking world

bouncy-bouncy *n*
an act of sexual intercourse. A coy or joky euphemism invented by adults in imitation of children's language. It is

usually used in the expression 'play bouncy-bouncy'.

bounty bar n British
a black person who apes white manner-isms or collaborates with white society, an 'Uncle Tom'. Bounty bar, derived from the trademark name of a type of confec-tionery, like the synonym **coconut**, implies that such people are dark (like the chocolate) outside and white inside. The term is typically used by black or Asian teenagers.

bourgie, boojie adj
supposedly middle-class in taste and/or behaviour, materialistic, snobbish. The pejorative words, from bourgeois, origi-nated in US speech.

Bourneville boulevard n
the anus. The vulgarism (Bourneville is a trademark for Cadbury's chocolate) is heard in such phrases as 'cruising the Bourneville boulevard', referring to 'active' and 'predatory' male homosexual behaviour, and was reported by the former *Sun* journalist and *LBC* radio pre-senter, Richard Littlejohn. **Marmite motorway** is a contemporary British syno-nym; **Hershey highway** is the American equivalent.

bovver n British
trouble, **aggro**. A spelling, in imitation of a London accent, of **bother** in its menacing euphemistic sense of physical violence or extreme aggravation. 'You want bovver?' was the standard challenge issued by **skinheads**.

bovver-boots n pl
heavy boots as worn as part of the **skin-head** uniform in the late 1960s. Skin-heads first wore army surplus boots, later adopting 'Doc Martens' (DMs).

bovver-boy n
1a. a youth, particularly a **skinhead**, who enjoys fighting and conflict and is always attempting to provoke trouble. A coinage, based on the noun **bovver**, from the late 1960s.
1b. someone who is brought in to do a difficult job, a trouble-shooter. By humor-ous analogy with the above.

bowl[1] vb
1a. to leave in a hurry
1b. to swagger, adopt an aggressive gait
   Look at him bowling along.

bowl[2] n
an exaggerated walk. The walker falls to one side and swings his arms. An emblematic term from youth slang in the UK and USA since the late 1990s.
   Mmm, have you seen that bowl!

bowler n British
a **chav**. The term may refer to a suppos-edly characteristic **bowl** or swagger. The term was posted on the b3ta website in 2004.

bowser n British
an ugly or unattractive woman. A male term of contempt coined on the basis of **dog** and the later **bow-wow**.

bow-wow n
1a. an unattractive woman
1b. anything inferior, unappealing or worthless
Both senses of the nursery word are more recent synonyms for **dog** in its (originally American) slang sense. In City slang '**bow-wow** stocks' are poorly performing shares.

bow-wows n pl American
dogs in the sense of the feet

box n
1a. the anus. An old term popularised by male homosexuals in the 1970s.
1b. the male genitals. A term occasionally used by British schoolboys (influenced by 'cricket box', a protective shield for the genitals) and by male homosexuals.
1c. the vagina. An uncommon, but per-sistent usage since the 1950s in all parts of the English-speaking world. The origin may be an unaffectionate reference to a 'container' or may derive from 'box of tricks'.
2a. a coffin
2b. a safe. Used by criminals, among others, throughout the 20th century.
3. a guitar. This usage was adopted by British rock musicians in the late 1960s from America, where it was originally used by black jazz and rock musicians in the 1950s.
4. *American* a portable cassette/radio player. A version of the longer 'ghetto/beat/rasta box', heard in the later 1970s.
5. the box television. No longer really slang, but a common colloquialism, especially in Britain.

boxed-up adj
1. *British* comfortable, content. This vogue term of the early 1990s probably derives from the notion of a homeless person comfortably accommodated in a squat or a **basher**, etc., but was general-ised to refer to any state of contentment.

Made-up is a near synonym from northern English speech.

A new girlfriend and a flat and a car; I'm well boxed-up.

2. *American* intoxicated by drugs or alcohol. This usage may be related to the earlier 'boxed out', meaning uninhibited or wild (by contrast with the colloquial 'boxed-in').

boxhead *n Australian*
a stupid person. The term was one of many insults employed by the former Australian prime minister, Paul Keating, in outbursts in Parliament during the 1990s.

box the jesuit *vb American*
(of a male) to masturbate. The phrase was coined by analogy with the earlier **bash the bishop** and was adopted as the name of a 1990s rock band.

boy *n*
heroin. Although this coded use of the standard word became common in the 1990s, it originated in US street slang of the 1920s. Its ultimate derivation is obscure, but may possibly evoke the image of a boy as an ever-present servant or a term of address for a slave.

He was trying to score some boy.

boyf *n*
1a. a boyfriend
1b. a boy
The abbreviation may have occurred in teenage usage, but in the UK was notable as an example of journalese attempting to replicate adolescent speech. The more generalised later sense mirrors this.

boy racer *n British*
an irresponsible young car owner. A term of contempt applied to youths who characteristically decorate or customise cars and drive dangerously.

boystown *n*
the male homosexual **scene**, the **gay** milieu or part of town. A code term from the 1970s gay lexicon derived from the cult 1938 film *Boys' Town*, dealing sentimentally with juvenile delinquents.

boyz *n British*
£1. The term always appears in the seemingly plural form, so that one boyz = £1, ten boyz = £10. It was recorded in use among North London schoolboys in 1993 and 1994. **Bollers** and **luka** are contemporary synonyms.

bozack *n American*
the backside, buttocks. A term from hip hop vocabulary recorded in 2002.

bozo *n*
a buffoon, a clumsy or foolish person. A mild term of contempt which can sometimes sound almost affectionate. It has been widely applied to the former US president Ronald Reagan. Originally from the USA and Canada, and dating from at least the 1920s, the word is now in limited use in Britain and Australia. Before the 1960s it meant a man or simple fellow, since then it has been adopted as a name for circus clowns. Attempts have been made to derive the word from Spanish origins such as *vosotros* (the familiar plural form of 'you') or a Mexican slang term for facial hair. In Italian *bozo* means a lump or bump.

'Capable of putting up with every bozo and meathead who comes his way.'
(Jonathan Keates reviewing Malcolm Bradbury's *Unsent Letters*, *Observer*, 5 June 1988)

bozo-filter *n*
an alternative name for a **killfile** in the 1990s patois of **cyberpunks** and **netheads**

bra *n British*
best friend. The word has been popular among younger speakers since the late 1990s. **Bessie** is a synonym.

brace *vb American*
to accost, **shake down**. A rather old-fashioned underworld term.

brackers *adj British*
broke, penniless. A word heard in the 1980s which is an invention based on **boracic** or a deformation of 'broke'.

Brad (Pitt) *vb, n*
(to) **shit**. '(An attack of) the Brad Pitts' denotes a case of diarrhoea. An item of student slang borrowing the name of the Hollywood movie star, in use in London and elsewhere since around 2000.

Brahms (and Liszt) *adj British*
drunk. Rhyming slang for **pissed**. A fairly popular cockney term since the 1930s which was given wider currency by its use in television comedies of the early 1970s.

brainless, braindead *adj British*
drunk. The term is heard particularly in the Scottish Lowlands and the north of England.

brallin' n British
fighting. An item of black street-talk used especially by males, recorded in 2003. It is an Afro-Caribbean pronunciation of 'brawling'.

bran n British
1a. cannabis
1b. heroin for smoking
The term is an alteration of **brown**.

brandy n British
the backside, buttocks. Used in this sense the term has been heard among the London **gay** community since the 1960s and may have originated from the rhyming slang expression 'brandy and rum': **bum**.

brasco n Australian
a toilet

brass[1] n British
1. money. Brass has been an obvious metaphor or euphemism as long as the metal has been used in coins. The word is currently more widespread in northern England.
2. a prostitute. Originally in the form 'brass nail', this working-class usage is rhyming slang for **tail**, in its sexual sense.
3. a shorter form of **brass neck**

brass[2] adj British
1. broke, penniless. Pronounced to rhyme with 'gas', never the southern English 'class', this is a short form of **boracic** or **brassick** heard among teenagers in the 1990s.
2. a shorter form of **brass-monkeys**

brass eye n British
the anus. This obscure vulgarism, used by schoolboys, was adopted as the name of a controversial satirical TV comedy in 1997.

brassick adj British
broke, penniless. An alternative spelling of **boracic**.

brass-monkeys adj British
extremely cold. A shortening of 'brass-monkey time' or 'brass-monkey weather', this phrase refers to the widely known vulgar saying 'cold enough to freeze the balls off a brass monkey!'. A rather far-fetched explanation of the catchphrase is that a 'brass monkey' was a rack of cannonballs on board a warship.

brass neck n British
an intensive form of **neck** in the sense of 'cheek' or 'nerve'

breachen n Jamaican
friend(s), brother(s). A term from reggae music culture synonymous with **bredren**, **hidren**, **idren**.

bread n
money. In the 1960s this usage supplanted the earlier **dough** in **hip** parlance; by the late 1970s the word was dated and in the 1980s had largely been replaced by a variety of colourful alternatives (in Britain, words like **dosh**, **rhino**, etc.)

'This year two chicks and I got enough bread together and flew to Eilat (Israel) to see what was happening out there.'
(Reader's letter in *Oz* magazine, February 1970)

breadbasket n
the abdomen. A pugilists' euphemism, first recorded in 1753.

breadhead n
someone who is motivated by money, a mercenary person. A term of disapproval from the **hippy** era, applied to those professing loyalty to the counterculture but who openly or covertly sold out to commercialism or profit.

'Bob Geldof, then an impoverished photographer's assistant, sold him photos of Jagger and Pete Townshend which are still reproduced. Goldsmith, always an unrepentant "breadhead", parted with ten quid.'
(*Sunday Times* magazine, June 1989)

break vb American
to leave, depart. A synonym for **boot**, **jam**, **jet**, **bail**, heard since 2000. It may be influenced by the phrase 'make a break for it' or possibly 'break for the border'.

breakers adj British
excellent, exciting. A vogue term among clubbers, hip hop aficionados, etc., since the later 1990s.

breakfast n
1. *British* ketamine. The drug is also nicknamed 'Special K' after a breakfast cereal, hence this play on words.

'...you got any breakfast? ...Man, you look like you already had yours...'
(Recorded, art student, UK, 2002)

2. *See* **dingo's breakfast**; **dog's breakfast**; **Mexican breakfast**

break it down vb British
to enjoy oneself, act boisterously. A vogue term among teenagers and devotees of dancefloor and **acid house** culture from the end of the 1980s. The term, perhaps American in origin, was also

recorded in use among North London schoolboys in 1993 and 1994, sometimes as an exclamation.

break north vb American
to depart, leave. A vogue term in black street slang of the 1990s, the origin of the term is obscure but may evoke the escape of a slave from the southern states. A variety of euphemisms (like its contemporaries **bail**, **book**, **jam** and **jet**) for 'run away' are essential to the argot of gang members and their playground imitators.

breathing out of one's arse/hoop/ring adj
tired, exhausted. The phrase, evoking a desperate need for extra oxygen, is in army and Officer Training Corps usage.

bred vb British
to behave in a sycophantic manner, curry favour, 'suck up'. A term in use among schoolchildren and students from around 2002.
Stop bredding Mr Green.

bredder n British
a sycophant
top bredder

bredgie n British
a friend. The word is an alteration of **bredren**. A term from Caribbean speech, also heard in the UK since 2000, especially among younger speakers.

bredren n British
a good friend, welcome stranger. A term from Caribbean speech, also heard in the UK since 2000, especially among younger speakers. **Hidren** and **idren** are alternative forms.

breed vb American
to make (a woman) pregnant. An item of black speech probably originating in the Caribbean. It occurs in the cult novel *Yardie* (1993) by Victor Headley.

breeder n
a heterosexual. A pejorative term in use among **gay** speakers, quoted by the San Francisco writer Armistead Maupin.

breeze vb
to move quickly, rush, run. A term used by young street-gang members in London since around 2000.

breeze! exclamation American
an exhortation to relax, calm down. An expression used on campus in the USA since around 2000.
No need to get so aerated – just breeze.

breezy adj, exclamation American
excellent. The term was fashionable among adolescents in the early 1990s, often used as an all-purpose exclamation of approval.

Brendon, Brendan n British
a misfit, outsider, unattractive person. A synonym for **Billy no-mates** recorded in 2002. The original reference is unclear.

brer n
a friend. The term of address originated in southern US and black speech as a dialect pronunciation of brother. It is now widely used in the UK by **chavs**.

brew n
1. beer or a drink of beer. A word used by northern British drinkers (usually without the indefinite article) and by American college students (usually in the form 'a brew').
2. British tea. A term popular in institutions, especially in the 1950s.

brewer's droop, brewer's n, phrase
impotence, usually temporary, caused by drinking alcohol. The term is common in Britain, where it is now sometimes shortened to brewer's, and in Australia. (Brewers featured in many comic or ribald expressions from the 16th to the 19th centuries.)

brewin' adj British
annoyed, infuriated. A term from black speech adopted by white and Asian speakers since 2000.

brewski n American
a beer. An elaboration of **brew** popular with students.

Brian n British
a boring, vacuous person. Supposedly a typical name for an earnest and tedious working-class or lower-middle-class male. The term was given humorous currency in the late 1970s and 1980s by joky references to the TV sports commentator Brian Johnson and a well-known sketch in the TV series *Monty Python's Flying Circus* concerning footballers. However, it was already heard among schoolboys in London in the late 1960s.
'Educating Brian.'
(Title of an article on 'academic' footballers, *You* magazine, March 1988)

brick n British
a mobile phone

brick it *vb British*

to be extremely nervous, overcome with fear. A recent usage derived from the vulgarism **shitting bricks**.

 'Although I was bricking it, when the light came on on top of the camera, it was like this fifth gear…'

 (*Evening Standard*, 2 September 1988)

brickwit *n British*

a fool. A less offensive version of **fuckwit** recorded since 2000.

brief *n British*

1. a lawyer. Derived from the 'briefs', or documents containing a résumé of each case, with which the lawyer is prepared or 'briefed'. A working-class term used since before World War II by both police officers and criminals.

2. a passport. A word from the lexicon of drug smugglers, among others.

 'They picked him up with a suitcase full of cash and three false briefs.'

 (Recorded, convicted cocaine smuggler, London, 1987)

brights *n American*

intelligence, awareness. The term is a near synonym for **smarts** and is often used in the admonition 'turn up your brights!'.

brill *adj British*

wonderful, exciting. A teenagers' shortening of brilliant, used as an all-purpose term of approval since the late 1970s.

 'They are a wicked group and steam up the charts with brill singles in the US'

 (Heavily ironic reader's letter, *NME*, 8 July 1989)

 'I am having a completely utterly brill time…'

 (Postcard from a 9-year-old, London, 1989)

brillo-pads *adj British*

excellent. An elaborated form of **brill**, used by London schoolchildren from the late 1980s, borrowing the trademark name of kitchen scouring pads.

bring down *vb*

to depress or disappoint. A black American and **beatnik** term, like the other phrasal verbs 'come down' and **put down**, adopted in Britain in the early 1960s by jazz enthusiasts among others. The phrase became one of the standard items in the **hippy** vocabulary. The past form 'brought down' was also used in Britain to mean suddenly depressed, especially after an initial drug **high**.

 'Don't Bring Me Down.'

 (Title of song by the Pretty Things, 1964)

bringdown *n*

1a. a disappointment, a depressing experience. A black American and **beatnik** term popular among **hippies** in Britain. The word implies high expectations unfulfilled, or depression following elation.

 'What a Bringdown'

 (Title of song recorded by Cream, 1969)

1b. a depressing or morose person

 Don't invite John – he's a real bringdown since Sally dumped him.

bring it on! *exclamation British*

a cry of defiance, encouragement or invitation, in vogue in 2004

bristols *n pl British*

female breasts. A common vulgarism, from the rhyming slang 'Bristol City': **tittie**. (Bristol City is the name of the city's chief football team.)

Britney (Spears) *n pl British*

beers (rhyming slang). From the name of the American singing star.

 Are you coming out for a few Britneys?

bro' *n American*

a shortening of 'brother'. An affectionate term of address used typically by black Americans to each other.

broad *n American*

a woman. A disparaging term in that it is exclusively used by men and implies a lack of respect for the woman in question. The origin of the word is not documented but is probably from 'broad-**ass**' or something similar, denoting an accommodating woman. (Immorality is not an integral part of the meaning in modern usage.)

 'We've got Dustin Hoffman fighting Meryl Streep for a four-year-old in "Kramer vs Kramer"…Thirty years ago, the Duke would have slapped the broad around and shipped the kid off to military school.'

 (*Real Men Don't Eat Quiche*, Bruce Feirstein, 1982)

broccoli *n*

1. money

2. marihuana

Both usages, inspired by the colour of the vegetable, are popular in the argot of hip hop aficionados and on campus.

brok *adj British*
broken, damaged, in disarray. This alteration of 'broke(n)' probably originated in black dialect. It was a vogue term among teenage gangs (**bruck**[ers] is an alternative form). The term was recorded in use among North London schoolboys in 1993 and 1994.

Bronx cheer *n American*
a **farting** noise made with the lips and tongue; a **raspberry**. The Bronx is a mainly working-class borough of New York City.

broom-broom *n British*
a car. A nursery word sometimes used facetiously by adults.
He's got himself a new broom-broom.

brothel creepers *n pl British*
shoes with thick crepe soles, fashionable among **teddy boys** and others in the 1950s ('brothel stompers' is an American version). Brothel creepers has sometimes also denoted suede shoes or 'desert boots'.
'Red tiger-stripe brothel-creepers are all the rage.'
(*Tatler*, March 1987)

brother *n*
1. a friend, often shortened to **bro'** in **rap** and hip hop parlance
2. *British* a lesbian. Although a fairly predictable coinage, it may in fact be an ironic male response to the feminist use of 'sister' to indicate solidarity.
'They're all brothers in the canteen.'
(Recorded, London student, September 1995)

brown[1] *n*
1. *American* the anus. In this sense the word is probably an abbreviation of **brown eye**.
in/up the brown
2. *British* a ten pound note or an amount of £10, from the colour of the banknote
3. *British* a cigarette, almost invariably used in the plural form, presumably from the colour of the tobacco
I'm going to pick some browns.
4. *British* heroin

brown[2] *vb American*
to sodomise, perform anal intercourse
The idea of browning really geeks me out!

brown bread *adj British*
dead. A rhyming-slang expression which probably originated in the 1960s and which is still in working-class use in London.

brown envelope *n British*
a full confession. The term, used by criminals and police officers in the 1990s, derives from the phrase 'to give (someone) a/the brown envelope' and typically describes the action of a 'supergrass' who confesses in return for a light sentence. The envelope in question probably evokes a mysterious package (e.g. containing a note or payment).

brown eye *n*
the anus. An Australianism also heard in Britain, not to be confused with 'big brown eyes', a colloquialism denoting female breasts or nipples.

brown hatter *n*
a male homosexual. A derogatory term from the 1950s, still occasionally heard. The term refers both to the idea of contact between the head of the penis and excrement and to the archaic upper-class notion that the wearing of brown hats on certain formal occasions marked out a man as socially unacceptable.

brownie *n British*
a Scotch, drink of whisky. A word used by middle-class and usually middle-aged drinkers.

brownie-hound *n*
a male homosexual. One of several 1980s epithets combining humour and hostility and evoking an image of a predatory sodomite ('chasing' or 'stealing' excreta). **Turd burglar** and **chocolate bandit** are synonyms.

brownie points *n pl*
credit for good deeds, an imaginary award for virtuous actions. An American colloquialism which has caught on in Britain since the late 1970s.

brown-nose *vb, n*
to flatter, behave sycophantically (towards), or a flatterer or sycophant. A vulgarism common in all English-speaking countries at least since World War II. 'Brown-noser' is an alternative version of the noun form. From the image of kissing another person's backside. (*Private Eye*, the satirical magazine, has instituted a regular column in which the 'order of the Brown Nose' is awarded for nauseating sycophancy.)
brown-nosing the boss
'Now he is on his knees, brown-nosing with the rest of them.'
(*Private Eye*, 1 April 1988)

brown trousers n, adj British
(a situation that is) very frightening. A light-hearted reference to the terrified person losing control of their bowel movements. Now mainly middle class in usage, the term probably dates from World War II, but has not previously been recorded in writing.

a brown trouser job
Getting up in front of all those people was brown trousers.

bruck adj British
broken, destroyed. A dialect form of 'broken' in the speech of the southern USA and of the Caribbean, this term passed from black British usage into general adolescent usage in the 1990s. 'Bruckers' is an elaborated form of the same word.

bruck out vb
to dance, especially frenetically. The phrase, heard since around 2000, originates in Jamaican usage and is a dialect pronunciation of 'break out', in the sense of erupt, burst free.

bruck up vb British
to beat (someone) up. Originally from black speech, the phrase was adopted by younger speakers of other backgrounds from around 2000.

Brummie, Brummy n, adj British
1a. (someone) from Birmingham. From the city's nickname **Brummagem**.
1b. the speech of Birmingham

brutal adj
excellent. A typical appropriation of a negative (compare **bad**, **wicked**, **chronic**) as a faddish adolescent form of all-purpose approval. Brutal has been recorded at different times in the UK, USA and Australia.

B.S.D. n See **Big Swinging Dick**

bubba n American
a young man, especially an uncomplicated extrovert. The jocular term, evoking beer- and sport-loving, possibly well-to-do **redneck** youths, was applied in the mid-1990s to US president Bill Clinton and there was a brief attempt to promote the idea of a new social category under the same name (a magazine called *Bubba* was published) along the lines of the **laddish** tendency in the UK. The word originated as a 'baby-talk' pronunciation of 'brother' used as a nickname or term of endearment applied to young adult males in the southern states of the USA.

bubble[1] n British
a *Greek*. Rhyming slang from 'bubble and squeak', an inexpensive dish of fried leftover mashed potatoes and greens. The term probably dates from the 19th century, but is still in use in London. In spite of its friendly sound, bubble is not a jocular term and can be used abusively.

'They also call him [George Michael] the bubble with the stubble.'
(*News of the World*, 29 May 1988)

bubble[2] vb British
to weep. The term is now heard particularly in the Scottish Lowlands and the north of England. It occurred in public-school slang as long ago as the 1920s.

For God's sake, stop your bubbling, you big softie!

bubble-bath vb, n British
laugh. **Bobble hat (and scarf)** is a contemporary synonym, **tin bath** an archaic version.

You're havin' a bubble-bath, aren't you?

bubble-head n
a version of **airhead**

bubbly n
Champagne, or any other sparkling wine
a bottle of bubbly

bubkes n American See **bupkes**

buck n
1. *American* a dollar. A buckhorn knife handle was used apparently as a counter in 19th-century card games and 'buckskins' were earlier traded and used as a unit of exchange in North America.
2. a young male gang member. A term adopted by British black youth and football hooligans from the street gangs of the USA, who themselves appropriated a word applied to young Red Indian braves.

bucket[1] n
1. a pejorative or humorous term for a car or boat
2. *British* the mouth. In this sense the word is typically heard in working-class speech in such phrases as 'shut your bucket!' or 'stick this in your bucket!', recorded in the mid-1990s.
3. *American* an unfortunate person. An item of possibly ersatz slang from the lexicon of the cult 1992 film, *Wayne's World*. **Pail** is a synonym.
4. *British* the vagina. A vulgarism used by males and females since around 2000.

bucket[2] *vb*

1a. to move quickly. Usually, but not always, in the phrase 'bucketing along'. This usage dates from the 19th century.
1b. to pour (with rain). Usually heard in the expression 'it's bucketing down'.
2. *Australian* to criticise or denigrate. This use of the word probably arose from the image of tipping a bucket, e.g. of excrement, over a victim, although the noun 'bucketing' was recorded in England in 1914 in the sense of a harsh or oppressive task.

bucket shop *n*

an establishment selling cheap and/or low quality items in large quantities. The phrase has become a standard British colloquialism for a cut-price travel agency. The expression originated in the USA in the 1880s when it referred to share-selling operations, by analogy with cheap saloons.

buckfucker *n British*

an unpleasant and/or obnoxious person. In playground usage since 2000.

Buckley's hope/chance *n Australian*

no chance at all or very little chance. The eponymous Buckley was an escaped convict who surrendered to the authorities after 32 years on the run, dying one year later in 1956.

bucko *n*

a term of address or affection between males. The word was popular in club culture from around 2000.

buckshee *adj*

free, without charge. Like baksheesh, meaning a bribe or tip, this word derives from the Persian *bakshish*, denoting something given or a gift, and dates from the colonial era.

buck-wild *adj American*

uncontrolled, uncontrollable, running amok. The term uses the intensifying combining form 'buck-' which probably originated in the speech of the southern USA.

bucky *n British*

a gun. An item of black street-talk used especially by males, recorded in 2003. The same word is a term of endearment or address among males in the southern USA.

bud *n American*

cannabis, marihuana. The use of the word is probably inspired by the appear-ance of the flowering heads and round seeds of marihuana plants.

bud (accent) *n*

used by young British Asians to describe a very strong Indian accent. It comes from the racist term 'bud bud' denoting any Indian or Pakistani accent.

buddha *n*

marihuana. In the 1970s 'Thai sticks', then one of the strongest strains of mar-ihuana, were also known as 'Buddha sticks'.

buddy *n*

1a. *American* a male friend, from 'butty', a British dialect or gypsy diminutive of brother. 'Butty', or 'but', is heard in parts of Wales to mean a close friend (of either sex).
1b. a volunteer companion to an AIDS patient

budgered *adj British*

drunk. Probably a comical mispronunci-ation of **buggered**, it is an item of student slang in use in London and elsewhere since around 2000.

buff[1] *n*

1. an enthusiast, expert or aficionado. An American term which, in forms such as film-buff, opera-buff, etc., has become established in other English-speaking countries. The word is said (by American lexicographer Robert L. Chapman among others) to be inspired by the buff-col-oured raincoats worn by 19th-century New York firemen, later applied to watch-ers of fires, hence devotees of any activ-ity.

> *'Having your life dragged through the popular press for scrutiny by a nation of voyeurs and trivia-buffs...'*
> (*London Australasian Weekly*, 4 Septem-ber 1989)

2. the buff the nude. From the colour of (white) skin.

buff[2] *adj American*

1a. excellent, attractive. A vogue term of appreciation or approval in use among adolescents since the early 1990s, first associated with the **slacker** and **grunge** subcultures as well as the language of college students. **Boff** is a variant form.

> *'She's buff!'*
> (*Sneakers*, US film, 1993)

1b. physically fit

In both senses, the word had been adopted by UK adolescents by 2000. The superlative form is **buffest**

buffage n American
an attractive person or persons. A vogue term of 1993 using the **-age** suffix, as in **grindage**, **tuneage**, etc., with the vogue term **buff**, especially in the appreciative description or exclamation 'major buffage!', popular particularly among females.

Buffalo Bill n British
a *till* or cash box. An item of market traders' rhyming slang recorded in the mid-1990s. A synonym from the same environment is **Benny Hill**.

> *Just hand it over and I'll bung it in the old Buffalo Bill.*

buffaloed adj American
1a. bullied, cowed, overwhelmed or bamboozled
1b. knocked flat or knocked out
Both senses of the word evoke the crushing force of a stampede.

buffet vb American
to have sex. The term was recorded on campuses in the 1990s.

bufty n British, esp. Scottish
a male homosexual. It is possibly an altered pronunciation of **poof(tah)**.

bug¹ n
1a. an insect
1b. a covert listening device
1c. a virus or infection
1d. a fault or flaw in a machine or system
1e. an enthusiast, devotee. A racier synonym of **buff**.
The word 'bug' originates in the Middle English *bugge*, meaning a hobgoblin or scarecrow.

bug² vb American
to irritate or annoy. The image is of a crawling, buzzing or biting insect. The use of this term spread to Britain in the **beatnik** era but has never fully established itself.

> 'Stephenson said Mark Allen had "kept bugging them to burn down his neighbour's flat".'
> (*Independent*, 1 November 1989)

bug³ n, adj American
(something) excellent, superlative. In the expression 'it's the bug!'.

bugged adj
1. angry, irritated. From the verb to **bug**.
2. suffering from abscesses. A prisoners' and drug addicts' term.

bugger¹ n
1. a sodomite. The Bogomil ('lovers of God') heretics sent emissaries from their base in Bulgaria in the 11th and 12th centuries to contact heretics in Western Europe. These travellers were known as *Bulgarus* (late Latin), and *bougre* (Middle French), a name which was imported into Middle English along with a loathing of the heretics and their practices. One offence which heretics of all persuasions were accused of was unnatural vice, hence the transformation of Bulgarians into buggers. The word is now a very mild pejorative often meaning little more than 'fellow'.
2. an awkward or difficult task or person
> *This is a bugger to get open.*

bugger² vb
1. to sodomise
2. to ruin, wreck, incapacitate, thwart. This figurative application of the term is several hundred years old.

bugger-all n British
nothing, none. A synonym of **sod-all** and **fuck-all**. It occasionally denotes almost or virtually nothing.

buggeration n, exclamation British
ruin, confusion. The word is often used as an exclamation of impatience by middle-class and upper-class speakers.

buggered adj
incapacitated, ruined, useless. This usage is encountered in British and Australian speech.

buggerise vb Australian
to damage, mishandle, etc. The term is also used in the phrase 'to buggerise around', meaning to waste time.

bugger off vb, exclamation
to leave, go away. A common verb and expletive in British and Australian speech.

buggery n
1. anal intercourse. The word is still, in Britain, the official designation of the act in legal terminology.
2. British oblivion, destruction, ruin. The word usually appears in phrases such as 'all to buggery'.

bugging adj American
irritated, agitated, discomfited. This vogue term, fashionable among adolescents at the end of the 1990s, may have originated in prison or underworld usage, itself derived from the verb to **bug** or the adjective 'bugs' in the sense of crazy.

*'Those guys were all looking at me like I
was a freak and I didn't belong there and
I was like totally bugging…'*
(Recorded, female student, California,
1995)

Buggins' turn *n British*
an automatic privilege that comes in turn
to members of a group, regardless of
merit, seniority, etc. A piece of bureau-
crats' slang. Buggins is an imaginary
name, perhaps inspired by **muggins**. The
term probably dates from the 1940s and
is still heard in local government and
civil-service circles.

*'The committee's leader is still selected
on the principle of Buggins' turn.'*
(Recorded, member of Brent Council,
London, 1987)

bug house, bug hutch *n American*
a mental hospital

bugle *n*
the nose. An old London working-class
usage, paralleled in Canada, Australia
and elsewhere.

*'If you go on doing all that cocaine, you'll
perforate your bugle!'*
(Recorded, artist, Vauxhall, London,
1976)

bugle-duster *n*
a handkerchief

bug out *vb American*
1. to leave hurriedly. The **bug** component
in this adolescent expression is essentially meaningless.
2. to go crazy, become enraged. A **hipsters'** expression revived by clubbers and
hip hop aficionados since 2000.

bugs bunny *n British*
money. A rhyming-slang term heard in
raffish and underworld use since the
1960s.

buick *vb, n*
(to) vomit. An imitative term employing
the name of an American make of auto-
mobile and recalling such words as **puke**
and **hoick**.

builds *n British*
the components needed to construct a
joint. The term may apply to cigarette
papers alone or to the tobacco, cardboard, etc. required.

'I've got the puffy, I just need the builds.'
(Recorded, university student, London,
1995)

built *adj*
physically well-developed; statuesque
or strong. An American term of the

1970s, now heard in Australia and Britain. It is used to express appreciation of
sexual attractiveness by men of women
and vice versa.

Man, is she built.

built like a brick shithouse *adj*
heavily, strongly or solidly built. The
term is used usually of people; when
referring to men it is generally appreciative, when used of women it is more
often disparaging. This is a very popular
expression in Australia, but it is used
throughout the English-speaking world.
In polite company 'outhouse' can be
substituted for 'shithouse'.

bull[1] *n*
1. a uniformed policeman. A 200-year-
old term still heard in North America and
Australia, but never in Britain.
2. a shorter and more acceptable version
of **bullshit**. In armed-service usage it particularly refers to excessive regimentation
of unnecessary formalities; in civilian
speech it often denotes empty talk.

bull[2] *adj*
bad. In this sense the word, probably a
shortening of **bullshit**, has been used in
several English-speaking areas since
2000.

some bull weed
That band is bull.

bull and cow *n British*
a noisy argument, a fight or brawl. Still
thriving London rhyming slang for **row**.

*There was a right bull and cow in the pub
last night.*

bull artist *n*
a more polite form of 'bullshit-artist'

bulldyke *n*
a masculine, dominant or aggressive lesbian. An offensive term which was commonly heard until the late 1960s (by
which time **gay** women's styles had
largely moved away from imitation of
male roles). Bulldyke was almost invariably used by men and was invariably pejorative; it was sometimes extended to
apply to any lesbian.
See also **dyke**

bulling *n Irish*
behaving aggressively, obstreperously

bullong *n British*
a large penis. An item of black street-talk
used especially by males, recorded in
2003. **Wullong** denotes an even larger
member.

I gave her the bullong/ma bullong.

bull session n

a period of earnest or bombastic but shallow conversation; talking **bull**. The expression usually refers to energetic group discussions between friends (usually males).

bullsh n

an abbreviated, euphemistic version of **bullshit**, which seems to have originated in Australian usage

bullshit[1] n

nonsense or falsehood, especially when blatant or offensive; empty, insincere or bombastic speech or behaviour; tedious attention to detail. The term has become particularly widespread since the late 1960s, before which it was more often heard in American speech than British (where it was, however, a well-known part of armed-service language).

'I'm not allowed to talk about it …[Roald] Dahl grumbled from his Buckinghamshire home. It has something to do with security or some such bullshit.'

(*Evening Standard*, 8 September 1989)

bullshit[2] vb

to try to impress, persuade, bamboozle or deceive with empty, boastful or portentous talk. Whereas the noun form is sometimes shortened to the less offensive **bull**, the verb form, especially in American speech, is shortened to **shit(ting)**, as in 'come on, you're shittin' me'.

Don't try to bullshit me, I know the score.

bullshitter n

a bombastic, verbose or insincere person; a habitual source of **bullshit**

'"Mi-Lords! Laydees! and Gentlemen!!!" A VOICE FROM THE DARK SHOUTS, "Go home you Welsh bull-shitter!"'

(Spike Milligan, *Adolf Hitler, My Part in his Downfall*, 1971)

bum[1] n

1. *British* the bottom, backside, buttocks. From the Middle English period to the end of the 18th century it was possible to use this word in English without offending respectable persons. By the 19th century it was considered rude, perhaps unsurprisingly, in that its suggested origin was in 'bom' or 'boom', an imitation of the sound of flatulence.

2. a tramp, down-and-out, wastrel. This sense of the word is probably unrelated to the previous one. It is a 19th-century shortening of 'bummer', meaning an idler or loafer, from the German *Bummler*, meaning a 'layabout' (derived from *bummeln*, meaning 'to dangle, hang about').

'It kind of upsets me that they talk about him as if he's a hopeless bum.'

(Recorded, Canadian teenage girl, London, April 1996)

See also **on the bum**

3a. sodomy or the opportunity thereof. A vulgarism used mainly by heterosexuals, referring to homosexual activity.

3b. an act of sexual intercourse. A heterosexual synonym for **tail**.

bum[2] adj

1a. worthless, inferior, bad

a bum cheque/trip

1b. incapacitated, out of order

a bum ankle

These usages are inspired by the American noun sense of tramp, meaning an idler.

bum[3] vb

to cadge or scrounge. From the noun form **bum** meaning a down-and-out or beggar. This use of the word is predominantly British.

Can I bum a cigarette from you, man?

bumbass, bum-ass n British

an unpleasant and/or obnoxious person. In playground usage since 2000, the second 'b' is sometimes sounded, sometimes silent.

bumblefuck n American

a less widespread synonym for **Bumfuck Egypt**

bumboy n British

1. a homosexual or a youth (not necessarily homosexual) who consents to buggery. A term of contempt, originating several hundred years ago and widespread since the 1950s, especially among schoolchildren.

2. a sycophant, an **arse-licker**. The term is rather archaic, having been supplanted by stronger alternatives.

bum chum n

a male homosexual partner. A schoolchildren's term, usually used jokingly to jeer at close friends.

'Those two are supposed to be definite bum chums.'

(Recorded, female care-worker, London 1993)

bumf, bumpf, bumph n British

information on paper; forms, instructions, brochures, etc., especially those considered unnecessary, annoying or in excessive quantity. This term is now an acceptable middle-class colloquialism although its origin is more vulgar. It derives from 'bum fodder', a pre-World War II public-school and armed-forces term for toilet paper. This was applied scornfully in wartime to excessive bureaucratic paperwork. In Australia the usage is sometimes extended to mean unnecessary or verbose speech. The phrase 'bum fodder' in full is now obsolete, but was used from the 17th century to refer to waste paper.

> 'A glimpse of the unpestered life you lead at Cap Ferrat, deluged with fan mail, besieged by the press, inundated with bumpf of one sort or another.'
> (Ian Fleming in a letter to Somerset Maugham, quoted in John Pearson's biography, 1966)

bumfluff n British
light facial hair on a pubescent boy. Usually a term of mild derision, especially referring to a youth's first attempts to grow a moustache or beard.

Bumfuck Egypt, bumfuck n American
a very remote and/or backward place. The phrase apparently originated among British military personnel serving overseas as an imaginary address or location evoking squalor, ignominy and obscurity.

> They're sending you away to Cow College? Man, that's Bumfuck Egypt.
> I had to park in bumfuck because all the good spots were taken.

bummed out adj American
disappointed, dejected, having suffered a **bummer**

bummer n
1. a bad experience, a disappointment. An American expression (said to have originated in the jargon of the racetrack where it meant a loss which reduced one to the status of a **bum**) which spread to Britain and Australia in the **hippy** era of the late 1960s. It is still heard, although by the late 1980s it was dated. The meaning of the term was reinforced by the expression 'a bum trip', referring to an unpleasant experience with LSD.

> 'So okay, it looks like a bummer. But maybe...maybe you can still get something out of it.'
> (The Switch, Elmore Leonard, 1978)

2. British a male homosexual, in playground usage

bump vb
1a. to remove someone surreptitiously from a waiting list, in order to substitute a more favoured client. A piece of jargon from the world of air travel which entered the public consciousness in the late 1980s due to the prevalence of the practice.

> We were bumped at the last moment.
> They offered to bump someone to get us on.

1b. British to cheat, swindle. This sense of the word, popular among London schoolchildren since the mid-1990s, may derive from the earlier jargon sense.

> Yeah! He's trying to bump you.
> We got bumped.

2. American to kill. An item of street slang, abbreviating the now dated colloquialism **bump off**.

3. a shortening of **bump 'n' grind** used by adolescents and **rappers** in the mid-1990s

bumper n Australian
a cigarette end

bumpers n pl
1. female breasts
2. tennis shoes or baseball boots, especially those (in the style of the 1960s) with extra-thick rubber round the toecaps, resembling the bumpers of American automobiles

bumph n British
an alternative spelling of **bumf**

bumpin' adj
exciting. A vogue term, especially in dancefloor culture, from black speech heard since the late 1990s. Synonyms are **banging**, **rinsin'**.

bump 'n' grind vb, n
(to make) pelvic motions in simulation of sexual thrusting, usually as part of dancing or of 'heavy petting'. The term is North American in origin.

bump off vb
to kill. A 'tough-talking' euphemism now largely replaced by more sinister locutions such as **blow away**, **waste**, etc.

bump one's gums vb American
to talk, speak or converse. An item of black street-talk which was included in so-called **Ebonics**, recognised as a legitimate language variety by school officials in Oakland, California, in late 1996. A variant of the earlier **flap/snap one's gums**.

bumps *n pl*
female breasts. A mock-childish term.

bump tummies *vb*
to have sex (with). A humorous euphemism invented by adults in imitation of nursery language. Usually said by middle-class speakers.

bum's rush, the *n*
an unceremonious ejection. This is North American saloon terminology of the early 20th century, referring to barmen or doormen grabbing undesirable customers (such as **bums**) by the collar and the seat of the pants and bodily hustling them out into the street. The phrase is almost always used in the expressions 'give someone the bum's rush' or 'get the bum's rush'.
'Personally I think Ange should have given Den the bum's rush.'
(*Biff* cartoon, 1986)

bum tags *n pl British*
another term for **dingleberries**

bumwad *n*
toilet paper. A vulgarism heard in Britain and Australia.

bunce *n British*
money or profit. A word dating from the 19th century and almost obsolete by the 1960s, except among street traders and the London underworld. In the late 1980s the word was revived by middle-class users such as alternative comedians in search of colourful synonyms in a climate of financial excesses. Bunce may originally have been a corruption of 'bonus'.

buncey, buncy *adj British*
profitable, lucrative. The adjectival use postdates the noun **bunce**.

bunch of fives *n British*
a fist. A 19th-century pun on a hand of cards (or, later, a handful of banknotes), typically used in describing threatening or violent behaviour.

bunch-punch *n American*
a **gang bang** or **train**

bunco *n American*
a swindle, fraud. A version of 'bunk' or 'bunkum' which has not been exported.

bundle *n*
1. a large quantity of money or of something else desirable, such as narcotics
I lost a bundle.
2. *British* a fight, brawl or rough-and-tumble. Used especially by schoolchildren from the 1950s onwards, typically as a cry or chant to attract onlookers to a playground or street fight, it is the British equivalent of the American **rumble**. Bundle is also used as a verb.
3. the male genitals, normally as seen through tight clothing. A term used by homosexuals and heterosexuals since the mid-1960s.
4. *American* an attractive woman. A condescending term which is probably a shortening of 'bundle of joy'.
See also **drop a bundle**

bundle of sticks *n American*
a male homosexual, a humorous definition of **faggot**. An expression used on campus in the USA since around 2000.

bung *n British*
a bribe. A term used by police officers and criminals, almost always to refer to a bribe being given to a policeman. This normally implies something more substantial than a **drink**. The earlier verb form to **bung (someone)**, meaning to bribe or pay protection money to, is now rare but not yet obsolete.
He wants a bung of a monkey to square it.

bung (someone) *vb British*
to bribe, pay protection money to. An item of underworld and police jargon.
We're going to have to bung him if we want to stay out of trouble.

bunghole[1] *n*
the anus. A vulgarism found in the works of the celebrator of low life, Charles Bukowski, among others.

bunghole[2] *vb*
to sodomise, **bugger**

bung it on *vb Australian*
to behave in a presumptuous or pretentious manner. The term denotes 'putting on airs', from which phrase it may derive.

bungled *adj*
ugly. One of a set of terms including **cruttess**, **off-key** and **cake-up** which have been in vogue among street-gang members, hip hop aficionados and students in the UK since 2000.

bung on a blue *vb Australian*
to lose one's temper, indulge in a display of irritation

bungy, bungie, bunjie *n British*
a rubber eraser. A schoolchildren's term since at least World War II, it was in use among office workers as early as the

1930s. The sound of the word is intended to convey the shape and consistency (influenced by words such as bung and spongey). The 'g' is usually soft.

'If i thro a bit of bungy at peason he will bide his time and thro an ink bomb back [sic].'
(*Back in the Jug Agane*, Geoffrey Willans and Ronald Searle, 1959)

bun in the oven *n British*
'to have a bun in the oven' has meant to be pregnant in working-class British usage since the 19th century. The comparison of the stomach or abdomen with an oven is older still.

bunjie *n British*
an alternative form of **bungy**

bunk[1] *adj American*
unfashionable, **uncool**. A teenage vogue word from 1987 which is a deliberate shifting of the standard sense of bunk and bunkum (as signifying nonsense). It was still in use in 2005.

a real bunk thing to do
That's bunk, man.
See also **bank**[2]

bunk[2] *vb American*
to cheat. A verb formed from the colloquial nouns bunk and bunkum and the slang term **bunco**.

bunk in *vb British*
to gatecrash, enter illicitly or surreptitiously. Bunk in occurs in many contexts as a version of bung, meaning to throw forcibly; here the image evoked is of being lifted or hoisted, e.g. through a window.

'I told him I'd never been to drama school, so he said: "RADA the Royal Academy of Dramatic Arts is just down the road. Let's go and bunk in".'
(Philip Roth, *Observer*, Section 5, 9 April 1989)

bunk off *vb British*
to play truant or absent oneself. A term now heard mainly among schoolchildren, bunk off is a variant of 'do a bunk' which has been a common expression since the 19th century. There is no connection with bunk bed, but rather with the sense of bunk (like 'bung') meaning 'to hoist or toss'.

bunk-up *n British*
1. an act of sexual intercourse, especially when furtive and/or brusque. A term influenced more by the notion of being 'up someone' than the erotic possibilities of bunk beds.

a bunk-up behind the bike sheds
2. a lift, help in climbing something
Give me a bunk-up over this wall and I'll scrump us some apples.

Both uses were common schoolchildren's currency in the 1950s and 1960s. The sense of bunk evoked is hoist or throw; it is a variant form of 'bung'.

bunnin' *n*
smoking (cannabis or, less commonly, tobacco). A term from Caribbean speech, also heard in the UK since 2000, especially among younger speakers.

bunny *n*
1. *British* incessant talking, chatter. This is a later version of **rabbit** (a shortening of the rhyming slang 'rabbit and pork': *talk*). As rabbit entered non-cockney colloquial speech, so working-class Londoners adopted this more raffish alternative. It is sometimes used in the verb form.

2a. *Australian* a dupe or victim. Partridge dates this usage to the 1920s, although the word was briefly used in a similar sense by British **teddy boys** in the 1950s and by the US novelist Sinclair Lewis.

2b. a girl or young woman. A patronising male term with similar implications to the previous sense.

bunny-boiler *n*
a vengeful, dangerous female. The reference is to the 1987 film *Fatal Attraction* in which a jilted woman kills (by boiling) the pet rabbit belonging to her ex-lover's family. The term has become very widespread.

'Coronation Street bunny-boiler Maya Sharma tries to wreck love rival Sunita Pareklis' wedding plans...'
(*Daily Mirror*, 16 July 2004)

buns *n pl*
1. *American* the buttocks. A popular term since the early 1970s which is not particularly vulgar and which is gaining currency outside North America. The origin may be an obsolete northern British dialect term for 'tail', a variation on **bum**, or may simply refer to the parallels in form and texture with edible buns.

2. *Australian* sanitary towels or tampons. A shortening of 'jam buns' used almost exclusively by men. ('To have the buns on' is to be menstruating.)

bupkes, bupkiss *n American*
1a. an insignificant amount or trivial matter
1b. nothing or none
The words are a borrowing from Yiddish, which adopted them from the Russian for 'beans', a term widely used colloquially (in expressions such as 'not worth a hill/row of beans') to suggest items of little value.

buppie *n*
a member of the black middle class, a black **yuppie**. An American categorisation of the late 1980s also heard in Britain and still in use over a decade later.

> *'Establishing a black middle class won't help anybody except a few buppies – all yuppies, black and white, are scum.'*
> (Reader's letter, *NME*, 8 July 1989)

burb *n British*
a stylish or good-looking male. The derivation of the word, recorded in 2000, is obscure, although it may refer to the Burberry brand.

burbs, the *n pl American*
the suburbs. A vogue word of the later 1980s.

burg *n American*
a town, place. From the Germanic component added to many American place-names.

> *Let's split this burg for good.*

burl *n Australian*
a try. Usually in the phrase 'give it a burl', meaning to make an attempt at, to try (a task or activity). Probably a blend of the colloquial expressions 'have a bash' and 'give it a whirl'. Give it a burl is one of many Australian expressions given currency in Britain by the cartoon strip *The Adventures of Barry McKenzie*, written by Barry Humphries, which ran in the satirical magazine *Private Eye* between 1965 and 1974. Some of the more colourful of these expressions were in fact coined, or embellished, by Humphries himself, but this phrase was well established in Australia by the early 1960s.

burly[1] *n, adj American*
(something) difficult, hard to achieve, problematical. A teenage vogue term from 1987, in use among the successors of **Valley Girls** and **preppies**, among others. It may originate in black street slang, where standard terms are often appropriated for use as gang code words, or from surfers' slang.

burly[2] *adj*
excellent. A reversal along the lines of **bad**, **wicked**, **brutal**, etc., heard in youth slang since the late 1990s.

burn[1] *n*
1a. tobacco
> *Got any burn?*
1b. a cigarette
1c. a smoke
> *a quick burn*
The first sense is in use in prisons in the UK; the others are also heard in other English-speaking areas.
2. *American* a **hit** of crack
> *I just need a burn.*

burn[2] *vb*
to record on CD-Rom or DVD. An item of **hacker** slang that, by 2004, was appearing in advertisements for IT hardware, etc.

burn (someone) *vb*
1. to cheat financially. An Americanism that was part of the **hippy** vocabulary (typically referring to selling phoney drugs) and hence spread to the UK. It is now archaic in Britain.
2. *American* to kill someone. A 'tough guy' euphemism.

burner *n*
a firearm. An item of American teen gang language probably postdating the verb form to **burn (someone)**, reported in the *Sunday Times*, 8 March 1992.

burn off *vb British*
to overtake, outstrip and thus humiliate another driver. A term from the language of **ton-up boys** and **boy racers**.

burnt[1] *n British*
glass. The term is a shortened form of the London rhyming slang 'burnt grass', meaning *glass*, or 'burnt cinder', meaning *winder* (window). It is used in the jargon of criminals and glaziers, decorators, etc. to refer to glass panels in windows and doors. The word was cited as an example of the jargon of cat burglars recorded in *FHM* magazine in April 1996.

burnt[2] *adj American*
terrible, hopeless. A teenage vogue term of the late 1980s which is an extension of the earlier slang senses of cheated or 'burnt out'.

BURP *n*
a 'big ugly rough piece'. An unattractive person of the opposite sex. An item of student slang in use in London and

elsewhere since around 2000. It is said as a word rather than letter by letter.

bush¹ *adj*

provincial or primitive. A term that can mean either rural or second-rate, or both. Much used in Australia in expressions such as 'bush scrubber' and 'bush lawyer' and, to a lesser extent, in the USA where it is often in the form **bush-league**, meaning small-town or small-time.

bush² *n*

1. the pubic hair area. The term is used more often by men of a woman's pubic hair than vice versa.

> '*Naff things the French do on a beach:
> …display enormous pubic bushes.*'
> (*Complete Naff Guide*, 1983)

2. marihuana, **grass**. A common term among smokers in the Caribbean and Britain. Bush refers especially to cannabis leaves and seeds sold unsorted and uncleaned.

> '*Prisoners cut off the cannabis leaves
> and dry them before smoking the drug in
> a form known as "bush".*'
> (*Observer*, 12 June 1988)

bushie *n Australian*

a provincial, rural or barbaric person; a yokel

> '*He thought the stereotype of the sporty,
> outdoorsy Australian began with the
> romantic 19th century image created by
> artists like Banjo Paterson, who had tried
> to convince us that we were "bushies".*'
> (*Southern Cross* magazine, July 1987)

bush-league *adj American*

provincial, amateurish, unsophisticated, inferior. The term derives from the categorisation of minor-league baseball teams, and is sometimes shortened to **bush**.

> '*"I can't handle the shit anymore".
> "You're bush-league, that's why".*'
> (*Pay Dirt*, US film, 1992)

business

1. *n* a hypodermic syringe. A drug user's euphemism.

2. *n* an act of defecation. To 'do one's business' was a nursery expression epitomising Victorian notions of duty and hygiene.

3. *n* **the business** *British* a thrashing, a thorough dressing down or beating up

> *We gave him the business. He won't try
> that again.*

4. *adj* **the business** *British* the very best, the acme of excellence

You should try some of this gear – it's the business.

busk it *vb British*

to improvise. From the standard English 'busker', referring to a wandering street musician. Busk it at first was a musician's, later a theatrical performer's, term, referring to improvisation ('I don't know it, but if you hum a few bars I'll busk it'), but is now widely used in other forms of endeavour, such as business. The word 'busk' seems to have originated in an 18th-century borrowing from a Latin language: the Spanish *buscar*, meaning to search or the archaic French *busquer*, meaning to cruise, etc.

> *If they don't accept our agenda we'll just
> have to busk it.*

buss, buss out, bust out *vb*

to express oneself, especially forcefully and/or publicly. The term, which can also be used transitively to mean show off, is fashionable in hip hop and **rap** culture.

> '*Sometimes I act individually and buss
> out with my own lines [improvisations].*'
> (Recorded, contributor to www.wass-up.com, November 2003)

> '*Buss that jacket.*'
> (Recorded, London student, 2003)

buss juice, bust juice *vb British*

to ejaculate. An item of black street-talk used especially by males, recorded since 2000.

bust¹ *n*

1. an arrest, especially for possession of illicit drugs. An item of **hippy** jargon which originated in the early 1960s and which by the late 1980s had become a common enough colloquialism to be used in the written and broadcast media. In American street-gang and underworld usage the word already had the sense of 'catch in the act' by the late 1950s.

> '*The busts started to happen. People
> started to go to prison. People started to
> die. But by then you were too far in.*'
> (Female ex-drug addict, *Independent*, 17 July 1989)

2. *American* a spectacular achievement or successful coup. A teenage term of approbation of the late 1980s, coming from the jargon of basketball, where it means a good shot.

3. a wild party or celebration

4a. *Australian* a break-in, burglary

4b. a break-out, an escape from prison

bust² *vb*
1. to arrest, especially for possession of illicit drugs. In the USA the word was being used in this sense by the 1950s.

> 'And then I went and got busted, my old mother was disgusted. I'm never ever going to be trusted, by anybody anymore.'
> (Lyrics to 'Busted' by the Bonzo Dog Band, 1970)

> 'What I say [is] if guys get busted in North Africa and end up in their shitty prisons they got to be dumb in the first place.'
> (Letter to *Oz* magazine, June 1969)

2. *American* to demote. The word is used in this sense in armed-forces jargon, as in 'busted down to sergeant'.

busta *n*
a key term from the **rap** and hip hop lexicon, defined in 2000 as 'a man who thinks he is the best but is in fact the opposite'

> What a busta, I can't believe he thought he could hit on me!

busted *adj*
1. caught out
2. ugly

> Man that chick is just plain busted.

bust on (someone) *vb American*
1a. to punish, attack, kill someone. An item of youth slang of the late 1980s. Christian Brando, son of the actor Marlon Brando, was reported by his sister Cheyenne to have said he was going to bust on her boyfriend, Dag Drollet, whom he was later convicted of shooting and killing.
1b. to criticise, harass

> Quit bustin' on me, will you?
> Her parents are always busting on her.

bust one's buns *vb American*
to exhaust oneself by working, to make great efforts. **Buns** in this expression means the buttocks, and the phrase is roughly equivalent to the British 'work one's arse off'.

bus up *vb*
to attack, beat up. A term used by young street-gang members in London since around 2000. It is probably an Afro-Caribbean pronunciation of 'bust up' or imitation thereof.

butch *adj*
1a. tough, strong and assertive. The term is now often used humorously or to express mild derision; it probably comes from 'Butch' as a male nickname first heard at the end of the 19th century in

the USA, which in turn probably derives from butcher.
1b. assertively masculine in behaviour and/or appearance. The term, typically applied disapprovingly or derisively, is used about heterosexual women, lesbians and **gay** men. During the 1950s the word had a narrower sense of a 'masculine' (active) rather than a 'feminine' (passive) partner in a homosexual relationship, or of a lesbian who behaved and dressed like a man; in this sense butch was also used as a noun.

butcher's *n British*
a *look*. Nearly always in the phrases 'have a butcher's' or 'take a butcher's (at this)'. From the rhyming slang expression 'butcher's hook', which is at least eighty years old and is still heard in the unabbreviated form.

butch up *vb*
to become more assertive, tougher or more masculine. The expression, heard since the early 1980s in Britain, is often used as an exhortation, normally to a man who is behaving in a weak or cowardly way. (The antonym is **wimp out**.)

butt *n*
the backside, buttocks. In the USA, butt is the most common colloquial term for this part of the body. Although slightly vulgar and generally the monopoly of male speakers, butt, unlike **ass**, is permissible in 'polite society' or broadcasts. It is rarely heard in Britain or Australia. Butt is historically related to 'buttocks' and in British, Australian and American English is still used to denote the thick end of something, such as in the butt of a cue or a rifle, or simply the end, such as in a cigarette butt.

butta *adj British*
1a. (of, e.g., a task) easy, painless
1b. (of a person) suave, seductive, 'smooth'
A term used by young street-gang members in London since around 2000.

butter *adj American*
1a. attractive, beautiful, stylish
1b. lucky, fortunate
An expression used on campus in the USA since around 2000.

butterball, butterbutt *n American*
a fat person, a **lard-ass**

butternutsquatch, butternut squash *n*
a penis or dildo. The term was in use among adolescents in London in 2002,

but is probably American in origin. The butternut squash is a long bulbous vegetable.

butters¹, butter *adj British*

ugly. A term from black Caribbean usage that was adopted by UK adolescents from the mid-1990s. It is probably related to 'buttocks'.

> *'It's not surprising she got upset; they were calling out at her, "Hey, butters!"'*
> (Recorded, London schoolgirl, 1994)

butters², but-a-boy *n British*

a newly qualified taxi driver. This item of taxi drivers' jargon may derive from the catchphrase 'a driver now – but for how long?'. Recorded in the *Evening Standard*, 22 April 1996.

buttfuck¹, butt-fuck *n American*

1a. a male homosexual. A heterosexual term of abuse.

1b. a despicable or contemptible person

Both senses of the term play on the idea of someone who will submit to anal intercourse.

buttfuck², butt-fuck *vb American*

to sodomise, **bugger**. An expression typically used by heterosexual males who are repelled or fascinated by the practice.

> *'"Go butt-fuck yourself, Fruitfly". Milo smiled tightly.*
> *"If I were you, I'd worry about my own anal sphincter, Ernie".'*
> (*Over the Edge*, Jonathan Kellerman, 1987)

buttie, butty *n British*

a sandwich. From Liverpool working-class slang (a shortening of 'buttered bread'). The term spread throughout Britain in the 1960s, largely through the influence of the 'Mersey boom'.

> *a chip buttie*

See also **buddy**

buttinsky, buttinski *n American*

someone who interferes, someone who 'butts in'. A humorous imitation of a Yiddish or a Slavic surname. The jocular **-ski** suffix is popular among high-school and college students, for instance.

> *'This is probably not any of my business, in fact I'm sure that it's not my business, and you're probably going to get very mad at me for being a buttinski, but I really couldn't live with myself if I didn't say something.'*
> (*Moonlighting*, US TV series, 1989)

butt-load(s) *n American See* **ass-load(s)**

buttmunch *n*

a foolish, irritating individual. An Americanism also heard in the UK since 2000.

button *n*

1a. the clitoris. An obvious reference which has been recorded in English since 1879. It gave rise to the now archaic 'buttonhole' for the vagina.

1b. the chin. Most often heard in the phrase 'right on the button', used of a punch that finds its target.

2. a section of the peyote cactus resembling a button, ingested for its hallucinogenic effect

button it *vb*

to shut up, keep quiet, **zip one's lip**. A shortening of **button one's lip** which is heard as a peremptory imperative.

button one's lip *vb*

to shut up, keep quiet

butt out *vb American*

to stop interfering, keep out, leave somewhere. Usually in the form of an instruction to remove oneself, butt out is a fairly mild, if brusque expression. The **butt** component is interesting in that it is probably inspired by 'butt in', in which case it derives from 'butt' meaning to strike or push with the head. (It is commonly assumed to derive from **butt**, meaning the backside.)

buttplug *n American*

a slightly milder version of **buttfuck**. A term of abuse among schoolchildren.

> *'Sit on this, buttplug!'*
> (*My Science Project*, US film, 1985)

butt-ugly *adj American*

a stronger version of the colloquial 'plug-ugly'

butt-wad *n*

a foolish and/or contemptible person. The insult, originating in the USA, employs the widespread combining form **-wad**.

buy a woof ticket *vb American*

to pretend to make a threat. An item of black street-talk that was included in so-called **Ebonics**, recognised as a legitimate language variety by school officials in Oakland, California, in late 1996. The verb to 'woof', now somewhat dated, has been used in black slang to mean aggress or threaten.

buy it *vb*
to die or meet disaster. A euphemism often ascribed to airforce pilots in war comics and films. It may derive from the expression to buy or pay dearly (i.e. with one's life) or may be a shortening of the American **buy the farm**.

I'm sorry, Madge, but Archie's bought it.

buy the farm *vb American*
to die. An expression which is said to have originated with barnstorming or fighter pilots. The farm in question is either a 'worm farm' (i.e. a grave) or an ironic reference to a symbol of retirement (if a pilot survived he would often literally buy a farm).

buzz¹ *n*
1. a rumour. A usage now so widespread as to be a colloquialism rather than slang.
2. a pleasurable sensation, stimulation. In the jargon of drug users, especially the **beats** and later the **hippies**, the word referred to a surge of lightheadedness, a **rush** or **high**. It sometimes also refers to the use of alcohol.

buzz² *vb*
1. *British* to become intoxicated from sniffing solvents. The term is heard particularly in the Scottish Lowlands and the north of England. (**Huff** is an American synonym.)
2. to experience a sense of exhilaration, a **rush** or **high**

buzz-crusher *n American*
a killjoy or 'wet blanket'. A teenage vogue term of 1988.

buzzed, buzzing *adj*
excited, exhilarated, stimulated

buzzin' *adj*
1a. cool, **hip**
1b. excellent
2. high on drugs or alcohol
3. joking
You're buzzin'.
The word, in all these senses, has been fashionable since 2000.

B.V.D.s *n pl American*
male underwear. From a trademark name.
I was standing there in my B.V.D.s.

C

cabbage *n British*
1. money. This is a lighthearted 1950s expression rarely heard today. The term was used for instance by 'Flash Harry' (played by George Cole) in the film *The Pure Hell of St Trinians* in 1960. **Lettuce** was a more popular alternative, with the same derivation from the 'green and leafy' nature of banknotes.
2. a brain-damaged, inert or incapable person

cabbaged *adj British*
drunk. An item of student slang in use in London and elsewhere since around 2000. It probably derives from the colloquial use of 'cabbage' or 'vegetable' to denote someone who is mentally incapacitated or comatose.

cable *n American*
a golden chain worn as decoration, especially by males. The use of the word and the practice arose in the hip hop black street subculture of the early 1980s in which heavy gold chains (also known as **ropes**) and (often improvised) medallions were an essential part of the paraphernalia.
Compare **bling**

ca-ca *n British*
excrement, **shit**. A word generally used by parents and children in the home. For the derivation see **cack**.

cack¹ *vb, n*
(to) **shit**, (to perform) an act of defecation. A word which, in Britain, is fairly rare (it is heard more often in the north of England than in London and the southeast), but remains common in Australia. Cack is a variation of **ca-ca**; both are usually nursery words and come from a common and very ancient Indo-European base. There are equivalents in Latin (*cacare*) and many modern European languages – *caca* in French, *kaka* in German, *kakani*

in Czech. *Cakken* was the Middle English verb.
> *'He cacks on your "originals", you pee-pee on his boots.'*
> (*Psycle Sluts*, John Cooper Clarke, 1979)

cack² *adj*
awful, inferior, despicable

cack-handed *adj British*
clumsy, inept. The term originally meant left-handed, probably deriving from the idea of handling **cack** (excrement). Although the connection seems obvious, this expression is probably too old to be influenced by reports of the Muslim practice of eating with the right hand, wiping away excrement with the left. This pejorative adjective seems to be country dialect in origin; it is now fairly widespread and not particularly offensive.
> *a cack-handed attempt at patching up the dispute*

cacks *n pl Irish*
trousers. An Irish version of **kecks**.

cad *n British*
an unprincipled, contemptible fellow. A word applied in the 19th century by privileged school pupils and students to their 'common' counterparts. It came to mean an often plausible but dishonourable male. Unknown to most of its users, the word is a short form of 'caddie', a Scottish and northern English dialect word meaning a junior or unskilled helper, itself from the French *cadet*.

caffle *vb British*
to become entangled, snagged. In playground usage since 2000, especially in Wales.

cagoule *n British*
an unfashionable, tedious individual. The usage (a cagoule is an unflattering hooded cape) is a more recent version of **anorak**.

caj *adj See* **cas**

cake¹ *n American*
money. The term has occurred particularly in adolescent and campus usage since the 1980s, but was first recorded in adult black street slang of the 1960s.

'My ride [car] has to make a point – and the point is that I have cake...'
(Damon Dash, hip hop record producer, quoted in the *Sunday Times*, 6 June 2004)

cake² *n, adj British*
(something) easily achieved, often as an exclamation by school-age children. A shortening of the colloquial phrase 'a piece of cake'.

cake³ *vb American*
1a. to lavish attention and/or gifts upon
1b. to spend time with
An expression used on campus in the USA since around 2000.

cake-boy *n American*
a **gay** male. An item of black street slang adopted by high school and college students in the 1990s, probably from the earlier term 'cake(-eater)' meaning a 'ladies' man' or fop.

cakehole *n British*
the mouth. A slang term which was extremely widespread (and considered by many to be vulgar) in the 1950s and 1960s. It survives in the argot of schoolchildren.

cake-up, caked up *adj*
ugly, unattractive. One of a number of terms (including **off-key** and **bungled**) fashionable among gang members, hip hop aficionados, etc. since 2000.

call for Hughie/Charlie/Ruth, etc. *vb*
to vomit. These are variations of **cry Hughie**, etc.

call-girl *n*
a prostitute who makes assignations by telephone. The term became popular after streetwalking was outlawed in Britain.

Calvin Klein *n British*
a *fine*. The rhyming phrase borrows the name of the fashion designer.

Only doing 5mph over the limit and I got a bloody Calvin Klein.

camel-jockey *n American*
an Arab, Middle-Eastern person. A pejorative term widely employed during the Iraq conflict of 2004. **Dune-coon** was a synonym.

camel toes *n pl American*
the female genitals, as visible through tight clothing. The phrase, which appeared in the late 1990s, is the counterpart of the male **basket**, **packet** or **bob**.

camp¹ *adj*
homosexual, effeminate or affectedly theatrical in manner, gesture, speech, etc. A word which emerged from theatrical slang into general use in the 1960s. The sense of the term has moved from the specific (a (male) homosexual) to the general (affected, exaggerated, parodic). The word was adopted by the theatrical world some time after World War I from London slang, but the ultimate derivation of the adjective is obscure. It may come from the French *camper*, meaning to portray or pose, or from the dialect term *kemp*, meaning uncouth. In the late 1970s the **gay** phrase 'as camp as a row of tents', referring to a person who is outrageously or blatantly camp, crossed over into general usage. The word 'camp' was adopted in Australia and the USA before World War II.

'To be camp is to be mannered, affected, theatrical. To be camp is to be effeminate.'
(*About Town* magazine, June 1962)

camp², camp about, camp it up *vb*
to behave in a **camp** way, using exaggerated, 'effeminate' gestures, speech mannerisms, etc. The phrase 'camp it up' is particularly used to indicate a scene-stealing or outrageous piece of theatrics (literal or figurative) without necessarily any sexual overtones.

camping *adj British*
exciting, stimulating, dynamic. The term, heard since the late 1990s, is a facetious pun on the (vogue) term 'intense' (from 'in tents').

'Wow, that movie last night was mega camping.'
(Recorded, London student, March 1996)

can¹ *n*
1. *also* **the can** a toilet. Now a less-than-respectable term, but originally an accurate description of the buckets, tin containers, etc., used in, e.g., outdoor lavatories. The word was more common in the USA than Britain (except in armed-forces usage) until the 1970s.
2. *also* **the can** a jail, prison. In this sense, dating from the late 19th century, the

word is more common in Australia and the USA than it is in Britain.

3. *American* the backside, buttocks. An inoffensive euphemism.

She fell on her can.

can² *vb American*

1. to dismiss from a job, fire. The term probably derives from the American sense of **can** meaning the buttocks or **ass**, and the notions of 'kicking one's ass out' or 'thrown out on one's ass'.

'I got some more news, I got canned last week.'

(Recorded, female executive, Chicago, 1983)

2. to stop, suppress or conceal something. This sense is normally expressed in the phrase 'can it!'.

Canadian *n American*

a black person. A racist term in use on campuses.

canary *n*

an informer. An underworld term originating in the USA, based on the notion of **singing** (like a bird).

'Mob canary slain in Rolls – Had testified in bootleg gas probes.'

(*New York Daily News*, 3 May 1989)

cancer stick *n*

a cigarette. A middle-class irony, used by smokers and non-smokers alike since the late 1960s.

candy *n American*

1a. an illegal drug, particularly cocaine or heroin. This use of the word originated before World War I as a specialisation of the figurative use of candy as anything enjoyable. (The word was used in black street slang with sexual connotations.)

1b. a dose of liquid LSD on a sugar cube. This vogue term was heard in Britain about 1967 when LSD was still taken in this form.

See also **nose candy**

candyass *n American*

a weak or effete person, usually male

candyman *n American*

a **pusher** or **dealer** of illicit drugs, especially heroin or cocaine. Originating in black street usage, in which candy could also signify sexual gratification, this expression became part of the addicts' lexicon in the USA by the 1950s. (The original 'candyman' was an innocent peddler of sweets in the early 1900s.) The word features in numerous blues and folk songs.

cane *vb British*

1. to beat up, assault. A working-class brawlers' and prisoners' term. It is probably a back-formation from the more widespread colloquialism a 'caning', meaning a trouncing or defeat.

2. to devour or consume. A vogue term from the language of adolescents since the later 1990s, it is an extension of the colloquial sense of 'cane' as meaning to punish or subject to heavy use. Among students it typically applies to excessive or spectacular use of cocaine, cigarettes, etc.

Rachel was telling Phil off for caning the blow.

3. to cadge, borrow. A vogue term among British adolescents since the later 1990s, this is an extension of the preceding sense of the word.

Can I cane some chuddie off you?

caned *adj British*

intoxicated by drugs or drink. A popular term among adolescents since the 1990s, like many synonyms evoking the notion of punishment.

caning it *adj British*

1a. behaving extremely or excessively energetically

1b. achieving success, doing well

The term has been popular among younger speakers since 2000.

canned *adj*

drunk. The word seems to have originated in the USA, but had spread to other English-speaking countries before the 1950s.

cannon *n See* **loose cannon**

canny *adj British*

sharp-witted, 'street smart', attractive. This term from standard English is applied, particularly in Newcastle and the north of England, as a general term of approval, especially in the phrase 'a canny lad/lass'. Canny is an irregular adjectival form of the verb to 'can', thus meaning able, probably influenced by the dialect term 'ken', meaning to know (how).

cans *n pl*

1. *American* female breasts. Although the names of receptacles are often appropriated as euphemisms for the breasts, this usage may in fact be an alteration of **cones**.

2. headphones

cantaloupes *n pl American*
female breasts. (The cantaloupe is a type of melon.)

can't be arsed/bolloxed/fucked/ shagged *exclamation, phrase British*
slang equivalents of the informally dismissive phrase 'can't be bothered'

> *'I'm an incompetent fuckwit who can't be arsed to find decent solutions to problems.'*
> (Message posted on b3ta website, February 2004)

Canuck *n*
a Canadian. The only widespread slang term for Canadians, whether French or English-speaking, it is rarely used by the British. The word has usually been used in a derogatory sense. (The -uck ending is probably an imitation of an Amerindian form, as in Chinook, the name of a North American Indian tribal group and jargon.)
Compare **Canadian**

canvas *n See* **on canvas**

cap[1] *n*
a capsule of an illicit drug. The word appeared in the 1960s and was sometimes applied to a dose of LSD, even when this did not come, strictly speaking, in capsule form.
> *She scored a few caps of acid.*

cap[2] *vb American*
1. to insult, humiliate, **put (someone) down**. A teenage vogue term of the late 1980s. It presumably originates in the idea of capping someone's best stories or achievements, i.e. going one better.
2. to kill someone. An item of underworld and street-gang parlance. **Tag** and **clip** are contemporary synonyms.

capeesh?, capeeshee? *question form American*
do you understand? The words are anglicisations of the Italian *capisci*?
> *'You dig? Capeesh? Understand? Dig? Didn't they teach you that in Kiev?'*
> (*Red Heat*, US film, 1988)

cappella *n British*
a hat. Part of the **parlyaree** lexicon used, e.g., by London **gays**, in the 1960s; it is from the Italian *cappello*.
> *She's swishing about in her bona cappella.*

Captain Cook *n British and Australian*
a *look*. An old piece of rhyming slang, still in use in 2004. It is typically used in expressions such as 'take/have a Captain Cook (at this)'.

captain's log *n British*
a toilet. The term is rhyming slang for **bog**.

cark, cark it *vb Australian*
to die. The origin of the word is obscure; it may be a deformation of **croak** or of **cack**. Like other items of current Australian slang, the word has been introduced to Britain via TV soap operas.
> *'They break down in the middle of nowhere and before you know it they've carked it.'*
> (Recorded, Australian visitor, London, 1988)

carked *adj*
1. (of a situation) ruined or destroyed
2. (of a person) exhausted, **pooped**
This word may simply be an invention, or may be derived from **croak**, **cocked (up)** or, more plausibly, **cack** (excrement, **shit**, by analogy with **poop**). It is heard in Britain and Australia, but not in the USA.

carn *n British*
cash, money. A distorted pronunciation of coin, probably taken from, or in imitation of, black speech. The word was heard in teenage circles from at least 1990.
> *You got nuff carn, guy?*

carnaged *adj British*
1a. drunk
1b. hung-over
An item of student slang in use in London and elsewhere since around 2000.

carpet *n British*
1. a period of three months' imprisonment. This term, dating from the early years of the 20th century, is based on the supposition that it would take three months for an inmate to weave a carpet.
2. the sum of £3. In use among gamblers, market traders, etc. This sense of the word may be inspired by the preceding one.

carpet-muncher *n*
someone who performs cunnilingus. The term is usually used by males referring to **gay** women. **Rug-muncher** is a synonym.

carpet rat *n*
a less common version of **rug rat**

carpy *n British*
incarceration. This item of prisoners' jargon refers to the period of the day in which prisoners are locked in their cells. It has been derived from the Latin injunc-

tion *carpe diem* ('seize the day') but may alternatively be a form of **carpet**.

> *'I just need a scratcher for a burn, before carpy.'*
> (*Evening Standard*, September 1995)

carrot-top *n*
a red-haired person. The expression is used all over the English-speaking world; in Britain the earlier 'carrot-nob', like **copper-nob**, is now almost obsolete.

carrying *adj*
1. in possession of illicit drugs or firearms. An international English usage.
2. *British* solvent, 'flush', having plenty of cash on one's person. A London working-class term.

car surfing *n*
riding on the roof of a moving car. A dangerous teenage fad of the late 1980s, influenced by the US film *Teenwolf*.
See also **train surfing**

carsy, carzie *n British*
alternative spellings of **khazi**

cart *adj British*
high on drugs or alcohol. **Buzzin'**, **blazed (up)**, **mashed(-up)** are synonyms. The term may be an alteration of **cat 5**. It has been in vogue since around 2000.

carve *vb British*
to attack with a knife, to slash or cut (someone). From the vernacular of thugs, street gangs and professional criminals.
They threatened to carve him.
She got carved.

carve-up *n British*
1. a swindle or conspiracy that ruins one's chances. A rueful London working-class term probably inspired by a greedy carving up of a chicken or joint of meat and the use of **carve** to mean slash (someone) with a knife. The word was especially popular in the 1950s.
'Wot A Carve-Up!'
(Title of British comedy film, 1962)
2. a sharing-out of loot or booty. A term used by criminals and police officers, especially in London.

carvie-diesel *n British*
tea. The term is heard among inmates referring to the tea brewed in a prison canteen. It was recorded in the 'London Lingo' section of the *Evening Standard* in 1995. 'Diesel' is a mocking reference to the consistency of the brew, 'carvie' is archaic slang for a fellow inmate (itself

from the earlier 'carving-**china**': 'friend who shares').

cas, caj, caz *adj*
1. *American* relaxed, nonchalant
2. *American* good, acceptable
Both senses of the word, which is a shortening of casual and pronounced 'cazz' or, more frequently, 'cazh' or 'caj', are teenage terms of approbation from the late 1980s.
3a. *British* a shortening of 'casual' in the sense of a relationship which is not yet serious. The term was part of the teenage dating lexicon of the later 1990s.
Is this a cas thing you've got?
Are you two just caj?
3b. *British* a shortening of 'casual' in the sense of informal as applied to clothing or appearance. The word is usually used mockingly between adolescents.
A caj jacket/outfit.
She's trying to look très caz tonight.

case¹ *n See* **get on someone's case**

case² *vb*
to reconnoitre (premises) in preparation for subsequent robbery. The well-known phrase 'case the joint' has existed in underworld slang since before World War II. It originated in American usage, first being used with a generalised meaning of to assess.

cashed *adj*
empty, depleted. The term originates in American usage where it can typically refer to, e.g., money or marihuana.

cashish *n American*
money. A play on cash and hashish and/or **baksheesh**, heard on campus in 2003.

cassava *n American*
1a. the female genitals. A euphemism used by men and heard in the 1980s. It may come from the Caribbean, where the cassava root is eaten as a staple.
1b. a woman, especially an available one. By extension from the more specific first meaning.

casual¹ *n British*
a member of a working-class subgroup of the early 1980s who were to some extent successors to **skinheads** and 'suedeheads'. The characteristic of a casual was that he or she wore fairly expensive designer sports clothes in imitation of Italian or US **preppie** looks. The musical accompaniment to this style was generally home-produced soul or disco music.

Casuals were a more materialistic and conformist manifestation from the skinhead and **mod** milieus. Optional elements of the lifestyle included football hooliganism and shoplifting for clothes or profit. Casuals were personified by the 1988 comic character Eddie Loadsamoney, created by Harry Enfield.

casual² adj South African
excellent. The standard adjective has been borrowed for use as a fashionable all-purpose term of approbation among younger speakers since the 1990s.

cat n
1. a person. In the parlance of **beatniks**, **hipsters**, etc. Deriving from black musicians' argot, cat was an approving form for a fellow (almost always male – females were **chicks**). The word is still in use, unself-consciously among American blacks and jazz aficionados, and self-consciously in **hip** circles in Britain and Australia.

'All the cats and chicks/gonna get their kicks/at the hop.'
(Lyrics to At the Hop, recorded by Danny and the Juniors, 1959)
2. a spiteful woman. This sense is now so widespread as to be a colloquialism rather than true slang. It is probably derived from 'catty' rather than vice versa, although cat meant a prostitute until the end of the 19th century.
3. American the female genitals. A rarer alternative to **pussy**.
4. Australian a passive male homosexual. This sense of the word probably, although not certainly, originated as an abbreviation of catamite.
5a. British a person under the influence of drugs, particularly when rendered agitated or erratic. In this sense the term is said to be a contracted form of **paracat**.
5b. British someone craving a drug or drugs. A synonym of **cretin**.
A term used by young street-gang members in London since around 2000.

catalogue man n British
a conformist, dull or unstylish male. The phrase, defining, according to the user, 'an Alan Partridge-type male wearing classic trousers and a puffa jacket', was in use among students in 2001. The suggestion is that the person in question orders his clothes from a catalogue rather than exercising originality or individualism in choice/purchasing.

catbird seat, the n American
a very advantageous or privileged position. The catbird is a black and grey songbird which characteristically sings from a high perch.

catch a cold vb
to suffer a financial loss or setback. This expression, from business jargon, implies a temporary rather than terminal affliction.

catch some z's vb American
a version of **cop some zees**

cathouse n
a brothel. A widely known expression, although it is mainly used in the USA, cathouse is based upon cat in its now archaic sense of a prostitute (current in British English from the 16th to the early 20th century).

cavalier n British
(a male with) an uncircumcised penis. This term is from the argot of schoolchildren.
Compare **roundhead**

caveman mode n
obsolete, outdated. A dismissive term from the jargon of computer users in the mid-1990s.

caz adj See **cas**

cementhead n American
a stupid person. A coinage on the lines of **rubblehead**, **rock-head**, etc. (The notion of 'rocks in one's head' in place of brains is a well-known American concept.)

centurion n British
someone in possession of £100. An item of student slang in use in London and elsewhere since around 2000.

century n
£100 or $100. The word has been common in the argot of criminals, among others, for the last hundred years.
I put a century on it and it lost.

cereb n American
a **swot** in the language of the more sophisticated **preppies**. The word is from cerebral and may be pronounced 'seereb' or 'sareb'.

cessy adj British
foul, repugnant, disgusting. A fairly rare, and usually middle-class usage, derived from cesspool or cesspit.
Honestly, the whole thing was cessy!

cha-cha n British
a friend, peer. The term is used by British Asians.

chad n
rubbish, debris, worthless information. The term derives from computing jargon in which it denotes the waste paper discarded from a printer.

chai n British
a girl, female. An item of **parlyaree** first recorded in the 19th century and still used by older members of the **gay** community in London in the 1980s. An alternative spelling is **chy**. The term derives from Romany.

chai-klom, chy-clom n British
a female wig or hairstyle. An item of **parlyaree** recorded since the 1960s. The second part of the compound is of uncertain origin. The first is the parlyaree (originally Romany) term for a girl.

chair, the n American
the electric chair. Used for the execution of criminals in many parts of the world.

Chalfonts n pl British
'haemorrhoids'. Rhyming slang for piles, from the small town of Chalfont St Giles in Buckinghamshire. **Farmers** and **nauticals** are synonyms.

 'Stan was around yesterday, complaining about his Chalfonts.'
 (Recorded, pensioner, Bristol, 1989)

chandies n South African
a difficult situation, trouble. Recorded as an item of Sowetan slang in the *Cape Sunday Times*, 29 January 1995.

chang, charlie chang n
cocaine. A term used by young streetgang members in London since around 2000. The coinage may be an invention or a deformation or mis-hearing of the name – Charlie Chan – of a fictional 1940s detective.

chap vb American
to irritate or provoke. A term heard in adolescent usage since the 1980s, deriving from the sense of the standard term signifying 'to chafe'.

 Quit chappin' me!

chap-esse n British
a woman. The word became popular in ironic and facetious middle-class speech and in the slang of the armed services in the early 1990s.

 Now here's something special for all you chaps and chap-esses out there…

char, cha n British
tea. The words for tea in almost all Eastern languages, from Slavonic through Indian to Chinese, are variants of 'ch'a' or 'chai'.

 a nice cup of char

chara' n British
a motor coach. From the word charabanc (in French *char à bancs*, meaning a carriage with benches), widespread from at least the 1920s into the 1950s as a rather pretentious alternative to coach, and used by tour operators and their customers. The word in full was pronounced 'sharrabong' or 'sharrabang', and the shortening likewise. Elderly speakers still occasionally use the term.

charfing n South African
joking, teasing. Recorded as an item of Sowetan slang in the *Cape Sunday Times*, 29 January 1995.

charge n British
hashish or marihuana. The word was popular in the 1950s and 1960s, especially among **beatniks**, students, etc., who generally did not use hard drugs. This term, no longer heard, refers (rather inappropriately perhaps in the case of cannabis) to the 'charge' or sudden electrifying sensation felt by the drug user, possibly reinforced by *charas* (the Hindi word for cannabis, used by some English speakers in the 1960s). In American usage it was originally applied to the effect of a heroin injection.

 Got any charge, man?

Charles n British
cocaine.
See also **charlie**[1] 2

charlie[1] n
1. *British* a foolish person. This innocuous word, often encountered in the expression 'a right/proper charlie', is in fact derived from the more vulgar cockney rhyming slang Charlie Hunt: **cunt**. In pre-World War II cockney usage cunt merely meant a fool, rather than the modern sense of a thoroughly unpleasant person.

2. cocaine. A euphemism from the international alphabet designation for the letter 'C', or simply a nickname. (The full form of the proper name, Charles, is occasionally used, usually facetiously, in Britain in this sense of the word.)

 'She came steaming into the room when I had a massive great pile of charlie drying out on the floor.'

(*News of the World*, 29 October 1989)

3. *American* the Viet Cong personified. During the Vietnam War the military alphabet designation 'Victor Charlie' was shortened thus.

4. *South African* a friend. Recorded as an item of Sowetan slang in the *Cape Sunday Times*, 29 January 1995.

5. *British* the penis

charlie² *adj British*

cheap and nasty, flashy or in bad taste. A public-school and **Sloane Ranger** term of disapproval, heard in the early 1980s.

> *He's really awfully charlie.*
> *The flat's a bit charlie, if you ask me.*

Charlie (Chester) *n British*

a *child molester*, paedophile. The rhyming slang phrase, used by schoolchildren, borrows the name of a UK comedian of the 1950s.

charlies *n pl*

female breasts. A word used (almost exclusively by men) since the 19th century. There have been many attempts to explain this term by deriving it from rhyming slang (Charlie Wheeler: **Sheila**), from Romany or from the habits of Charles II. It is more probably simply a personification which implies affectionate familiarity.

charver, charva *vb, n British*

(to have) sexual intercourse. A word that was almost unknown by the 1980s, but which was used in criminal, theatrical and other circles in the 1950s and early 1960s. It is Romany in origin (from *charvo* meaning to interfere with), and refers to the 'taking' of a woman by a man, so, by extension, it has been used to portray a woman as a sex object.

chase the dragon *vb*

1a. to take heroin by smoking it. The specific meaning of this expression (the arrival of which coincided with an influx of cheap heroin into the UK in the late 1970s) is to inhale fumes from a piece of the vaporising drug through a tube, often literally chasing the smoke across the sheet of foil on which the drug is 'cooked'.

> *'Carmella never injected heroin, her serious involvement came with "chasing the dragon", inhaling a burning trail from a piece of tin foil.'*
> (*Independent*, 17 July 1989)

1b. to flirt with death by using heroin. This more generalised meaning of the sinisterly colourful phrase was adopted by middle- and upper-class drug users when heroin spread to these circles in the early 1980s.

(le) chat *n British*

seductive talk or flattery. From 'chatting up', often pronounced jocularly as the French word for 'cat'. An item of student slang in use in London and elsewhere since around 2000.

chat *vb*

1a. to speak, talk

> *'...u chat out ur ass.'*
> (Recorded, contributor to www.wassup.com, November 2003)

1b. to say

> *'Jus because we use slang doesn't make us dumbasses...so stop chattin fluff!'*
> (Recorded, contributor to www.wassup.com, November 2003)

1c. to contribute to an online chat room

chateau'd *adj British*

drunk. A colourful upper-class and **yuppie** expression of the late 1980s playing on 'shattered' and implying that it is an expensive claret (Bordeaux) or other château-bottled wine which has caused the inebriety.

chav, charv, charva *n British*

a vulgar person, representative of the working class or underclass. A vogue term and concept from 2004, defined by the *Sunday Telegraph* as '...the non-respectable working classes: the dole-scroungers, petty criminals, football hooligans and teenage pram-pushers'. The word originates as Romany for 'friend'. The chav's appearance typically incorporates (for both sexes) white trainers, a tracksuit, heavy jewellery (known as **Argos bling** after the catalogue chain store), baseball caps and often the scraped-back hairstyle dubbed a 'Croydon facelift' (Croydon being a London suburb considered emblematic of brash unsophistication).

> *'The cultural phenomenon that is "chav" was kicked off by www.chavscum.co.uk, a site billing itself as a humorous guide to Britain's burgeoning peasant underclass.'*
> (*Guardian*, 10 March 2004)

chavvie *n British*

a friend, 'mate'. The word probably comes from Romany.

Compare **chav**

cheaters n pl American
sunglasses or glasses. A word now popular with schoolchildren but which probably originated with cardsharps, who supposedly used 'magic spectacles', or with fraudsters who wore dark glasses as a disguise.

chebs n pl British
female breasts. One of a set of synonyms popular among younger males since 2000. **Wabs**, **waps**, **baps** and **smams** are others.

check vb British
to visit, especially one's girl/boyfriend. In this sense the term, popular since 2000, has been defined as 'seeing someone, not officially going out'.
Seb's checkin' Rachel, so I hear.

check! exclamation American
yes. A jargon expression of affirmation (based on the mark of verification on a checklist, for instance) carried over into popular speech.
'Hey you, stay cool!
Check!'
(*Panic on the 5.22*, US film, 1974)

check out vb
to die. The notion of leaving a hotel or motel has been carried over into an eternal context. An old euphemism in American English which is now international.

cheddar¹ adj
cheesy. A pejorative vogue term in use in the USA and UK since around 2000.

cheddar², **cheddars** n American
money. An expression used on campus in the USA since around 2000.
I need to grab some cheddar before we hit the bars.
'Don't take all my cheddars.'
(Recorded, US student, 2003)

cheeba n See **chiba**

cheekies n pl British
alcoholic drinks, especially pints of beer. The term, popular particularly in the southwest of England, was recorded in 2001. In 2004 the b3ta website reported its use in Australia.

cheese¹ n Australian
one's partner or one's wife.
See also **cheese and kisses**

cheese²
1. n **a cheese, the cheese** an important person. This is a shortened version of the colloquial 'big cheese'.
2. n something or someone unpleasant or unsavoury, particularly distasteful bodily secretions. From the smell and texture of ripe cheese.
3. n, exclamation British another spelling and/or pronunciation of **chiz!**
4. n a Dutch person. A humorous or derogatory term heard in one form or another ('cheese-head' or 'John Cheese' are alternatives) since the 19th century.

cheese and kisses n Australian
one's wife. This rhyming slang for *the missus* is probably the origin of the synonymous **cheese** and **old cheese**, referring to a mother.

cheeseball n
an unsavoury or contemptible person. An all-purpose term of abuse borrowing the name of the cocktail biscuit and the notion of **cheesy**.

cheese it vb American
to beware, hide or run away. This old phrase, normally used in the form of an exclamation such as 'cheese it – the cops!', has become a comic cliché in the USA. It may once have been used by members of the underworld (in Britain) or it may be a pre-1900 invention by writers or journalists. In any case it is actually heard in use today, usually somewhat facetiously by adults and straightforwardly by children.

cheesy adj
1a. unpleasant, unsavoury, squalid, disreputable, underhanded. The original notion of smelly cheese has encompassed a number of nuances of distaste. The word became extremely fashionable in 1990s youth slang.
a cheesy place
a cheesy thing to do
'It was a degrading, lying, cheating piece of cheesiness.'
(John Lydon [characterising Alec Cox's film *Sid and Nancy*], BBC television, 1989)
1b. outdated and/or in poor taste in a pleasant or amusing way

cheesy quaver n British
1. a *raver*, in the sense of a devotee of post-1980s dance culture
2. a *favour*
The rhyming slang borrows the name of a

savoury snack.

chernie n British
a stupid person. In playground usage since the 1980s, the term dates from the nuclear accident at the Chernobyl power station in Ukraine and the associated notions of contamination, genetic defects, etc.

cherries n pl American
flashing lights on a police car. 'Hit the cherries!' is the command to turn them on.

cherry¹ n
1a. a young girl, a virgin. This is an extension of the last sense, although modern users of the word may derive it simply from the notion of something sweet or delicious.
1b. South African an attractive young female. Recorded as an item of Sowetan slang in the Cape Sunday Times, 29 January 1995.
1c. maidenhead, virginity. The word is usually part of the phrase 'to lose one's cherry', said normally of girls but occasionally of boys. The expression is old (dating at least from the late 19th century) but has not been superseded. It derives from the supposed similarity of the fruit to the hymen.
2. British the tip of a lit cigarette

cherry² adj
new, fresh and attractive. A term used by teenagers and young adults since the 1970s in the USA and subsequently elsewhere. It evokes both the shininess of the fruit and the figurative sense of virginity.

cherry³, **cherry up** vb British
to blush. In playground usage since 2000.

Chevy Chase n British
the face. The rhyming-slang phrase uses the name of the US comic actor, who borrowed the name of a suburb of Washington DC (itself named after the site of a battle in Northumberland, UK).

chew (someone) out, **chew (someone's) ass**, **chew** vb American
to chastise, tell off, give someone a severe 'dressing-down'. A colloquial expression heard typically in educational institutions and the armed services.

chi-ack, **chi-ike**, **chiake** vb
to tease or taunt. A rather dated term derived from 'to cheek'. It has been

more common in Australia where the noun form, meaning impudence or insolence, is also heard.

chiba n
cannabis, marihuana. A fashionable term heard among hip hop and **rap** aficionados since the early 1990s. It was first recorded in the 1970s and may derive from Hispanic slang.

Chicano n
a Mexican American. Méjicano or Méxicano in Spanish has been anglicised to this word which, by the 1980s, had few pejorative overtones. It has to a large extent been superseded by **Latino** or 'Hispanic'.

chi-chi adj
excessively cute, pretentious or twee. The word is a direct borrowing from French.

chi-chi man n Caribbean
a homosexual male

    'The worst thing is when you see children
    of three or four singing songs about killing
    the chi-chi man.'
    (Guardian, 26 June 2004)

chick n
1a. a girl, girlfriend. The word has been used as a term of affection for hundreds of years, but was readopted by British slang from America in the **teddy boy** era. It was used unself-consciously by **hippies** until the mid-1970s, since when it has been disapproved of by the majority of women. The term is now dated.

    'This year two chicks and I got enough
    bread together and flew to Eilat (Israel) to
    see what was happening out there.'
    (Reader's letter, Oz magazine, February
    1970)

1b. American also **chickie**, **chicken** a passive homosexual partner or sodomised victim of a **rooster**. An American prison term of the 1970s and 1980s.

chicken¹ n
1. a coward. In this sense the word has been in use for several centuries, although the children's taunt or exclamation was an Americanism of the early 1950s.
2a. a young male who is, or is likely to be, preyed on by an older homosexual, in **gay**, police and prison usage.
Compare **chickenhawk**
2b. an under-age girl as a sex object or partner in the jargon of pornography. ('Chicken' was a common term of

endearment, especially to a younger or vulnerable lover, in the 19th and early 20th centuries.)

2c. a girl

3. a game in which young people dare one another to attempt something dangerous (e.g. to stand in the path of an oncoming train or car); the chicken, or first to withdraw, is the loser. When motor vehicle races are involved **chicken run** is the usual phrase.

chicken² *adj*

afraid, cowardly

chickenhawk *n*

1a. a male homosexual who 'preys on' younger men. This American term from the **gay** lexicon was given wider currency by press articles in the late 1980s when Scott Thurston, the entertainer Liberace's lover, referred to him as a chickenhawk in revelations after his death.

1b. a heterosexual seducer or exploiter of under-age girls

'Lolita at twelve, thirteen, fourteen, fifteen – and chickenhawk Charlie [Chaplin] never far away, mistily watching the bud unfold.'

(*Hollywood Babylon*, Kenneth Anger, 1975)

chicken-head *n American*

a foolish female

chicken oriental *adj British*

crazy, deranged, **mental**. The rhyming-slang phrase (using the name of a popular Chinese takeaway dish) is often used in the cry 'mental, mental, chicken oriental!'. From the end of the 1990s it was popularised by celebrities such as Next of Kin, Denise Van Outen, Pete Tong and 'lots of clubby types'.

chicken run *n American*

a teenage game in which drivers aim their cars at each other to see which one will swerve first; **chicken** is used here in the colloquial sense of coward(ly)

chickenshit¹ *n*

anything worthless, petty or contemptible. In American usage the word originally had the specific meaning of oppressive minor regulations and other effects of bureaucracy, particularly in the armed forces in World War II. The noun sense is now rarer than the adjectival use of the word, except when describing paltry amounts of money.

chickenshit² *adj*

1a. cowardly, afraid. An Americanism which was adopted in Britain, mainly by schoolchildren and teenagers, in the late 1980s.

1b. petty, contemptible. This sense derives from the American and Canadian armed-forces' expression to describe small-minded regulations, orders, etc.

chief¹, chief-bod *n*

a foolish or obnoxious individual, a misfit. A vogue term from the language of adolescent gangs, also recorded in the late 1980s among aficionados of dance culture. The term was in use among North London schoolboys in 1993 and 1994. ('Chief' occurs in North American usage, the 'bod' form is exclusively British.)

chief² *adj British*

stupid or pretentious. The adjectival use has been fashionable among younger speakers across the UK since the late 1990s.

chill¹ *vb*

1. to kill someone. A 'tough-guy' euphemism originating in US street slang.

'Teachers report that teenagers talk about "packing a barrel" or "chilling someone with a pipe".'

(*Sunday Times*, 31 August 1992)

2. to relax, become calm. This shortening of the earlier **chill out** (itself adopted from American usage) became popular among British adolescents during the 1990s.

chill² *adj*

1. relaxed, relaxing, unstressed. Derived from the verb form, this adolescent vogue term has been in use since the 1990s.

feeling chill
a chill party

2. *American* excellent. An expression used on campus in the USA since around 2000.

Hey, your new car is chill.

chillax *vb American*

to 'take it easy'. A blend of **chill** and relax used by teenagers in 2004.

chilled *adj*

excellent, admirable. A teenage vogue word of the later 1980s. The term is a synonym for **cool**, influenced by the verb form to **chill out** (relax, unwind). British fans of **rap** and **acid house** music and skateboarding introduced the word to schoolchildren's slang.

chilled article, the n Australian
a cold beer. A mock-pompous euphemism used by drinkers.

chillin', chilling adj American
1. relaxing. Chillin(g) is a teenagers' shortening recorded in the late 1980s.
2. excellent. An expression used on campus in the USA since around 2000.

chill one's bills vb British See **bills**

chill out vb American
to relax, take it easy. A popular phrase since the 1980s, first among teenagers but later among adults too, it comes from black street talk and is a later variation of **cool out**.

chillum n
a type of container (usually ceramic, but sometimes made of wood or stone) which is packed with marihuana or hashish (often mixed with tobacco) for smoking. This item from the lexicon of **hippies** and other cannabis users is not a pipe but a hollow cone held cupped in both hands, with a 'chillum stone' lodged in it to prevent the contents being sucked into the lungs of an enthusiastic user. Chillum is not, strictly speaking, a slang word, but Hindi in origin. It is, however, the only name for the object in question.
Compare **bong**

chilly adj British
excellent, fashionable. A British teenagers' term of all-purpose approval based upon **chill (out)** and **chilling out**, recorded in 1991.

chimney-wok n British
a satellite dish affixed to the exterior of a house. The joky nickname was heard from the early 1990s, sometimes abbreviated to **wok**.

chin vb British
to hit someone (by implication on the face or head, although not necessarily on the chin). An old working-class term still heard in or around bar brawls, playground fights, etc.
'He called me a poof, so I chinned the bastard.'
(Recorded, pub habitué, London, 1988)

china n British
a friend, *mate*. Rhyming slang from 'china plate'. An example of London rhyming slang which has survived from the 19th century and is still in working-class use today, albeit often ironically or self-consciously. It is usually part of the phrase 'me old china'.

Chinese adj See **get Chinese**

ching n British
a five-pound note or an amount of £5. An item of black street-talk used especially by males, recorded in 2003.

chink n
1. a Chinese person. The word (possibly inspired by Chinese words for their own country and people, actually pronounced 'Joong-') has been used in American and Australian speech since the turn of the 20th century; in Britain it is slightly more recent.
2. money, change. From the sound of coins.

chinkie, chinky n British
1a. a Chinese restaurant or takeaway food service
1b. a Chinese meal
I don't feel like cooking. Let's grab a chinky on the way home.
1c. a Chinese person. A more patronising or dismissive version of **chink**.

chinless wonder n British
an effete or gormless youth, particularly a vacuous upper-class male. The pejorative expression is applied to those literally weak-chinned, but more often to young men, usually in a privileged position, who are irresolute, offensively presumptuous or absurd. **Debs' delight** and **pedigree chum** have similar overtones.

chip vb British
to leave, run away. Like its synonym **duss**, a vogue term among teenage gang members since the 1990s.
'Let's chip, it's the beast.'
(Recorded London schoolboy, 1994)

chippie, chippy n
1. *British* a fish and chip shop. A nickname which appeared to spread from Liverpool in the early 1960s.
2. *British* a carpenter
3. *American and Australian* a prostitute or promiscuous woman. The etymology of this sense of the word is unclear.

chipping n American
1a. the occasional use of illicit drugs (as opposed to regular use by addicts)
1b. secret and sporadic use of illicit drugs while under surveillance, for instance in prison or while undergoing a drug rehabilitation programme

chippy adj
aggressive and hypersensitive, irritatingly resentful. The word is based on either the 19th-century 'chip in', mean-

ing to interfere, or the later notion of having 'a chip on one's shoulder'.

> 'He's chippy. I find that small people are often chippy.'
> (Recorded, **Sloane Ranger**, London, 1984)

> 'Mr Kinnock appears to be sinking under a barrage of criticism to the effect that he is an ill-educated Welsh windbag carried high by chippy class hatred.'
> (*Evening Standard*, 25 July 1988)

chips n pl British
money. Rather than referring to the tokens used for gambling, this is probably derived from the earlier and synonymous use of **potatoes**. Like that term it occurred several times in the telephone conversations between Sarah Ferguson, Duchess of York, and her psychic advisor, Madame Vasso, published in Vasso's memoirs and in the UK press in 1996.

chirps vb British
to flirt, 'chat up', attempt to seduce. The term, usually describing male behaviour, has been popular among students and others since the 1990s. Its derivation is unclear but some users claim that it is inspired by the 'charming' chirping of birds.

> He's been chirpsing her all night but I bet he's not going to score.

chiv n, vb
(to) knife (someone). A word originating in Romany (gypsy) speech, used particularly in criminal argot of the 1950s. The word, also written and pronounced **shiv**, often referred to a home-made knife or razor blade used for instance by prisoners or street gangs.

choad[1], **chode** n Canadian
1a. the penis
1b. a stupid and/or obnoxious person. The origin of this term is unclear, but (particularly in the second, figurative sense) it has become popular among college students and Internet users since the late 1990s, also in combinations such as 'dick-chode' and 'chode-lick/wad'.

choad[2], **chode** adj Canadian
unpleasant, worthless, inferior. The adjectival form derives from the noun. It was defined on the Internet by *Play Time* in March 1997 as 'so bad it's good'.

chocaholic n
a person with an inordinate fondness for chocolate in all its forms. A jocular term punning on alcoholic. Colloquial and slang terms relating to food and indulgence (**foodie**, **couch potato**, etc.) were a feature of the 1980s.

chocolate bandit n British
a male homosexual. Like **brownie-hound**, **turd burglar**, etc., this unaffectionately jocular term portrays the sodomist as a covert thief of excrement.

chocolate cha-cha n American
anal intercourse. One of many vulgarisms in use among heterosexuals and based on the faecal aspects of (not necessarily homosexual) sodomy.

> If you ask me, they've been doing the chocolate cha-cha.

chocolate-dipper n
a male homosexual. One of many supposedly humorous but pejorative phrases, invariably used by heterosexual males and based on the faecal aspects of sodomy. (**Brownie-hound** and **chutney-ferret** are others.)

chocolate drop n
a black or coloured person. A usually unaffectionate term used mainly by schoolchildren.

chocolate frog n Australian
1. a foreigner, immigrant, not necessarily someone non-white. A piece of purely Australian rhyming slang for **wog**.
2. an informer, **stool pigeon**. In this sense the word is probably rhyming slang for *dog*, as in 'dirty dog', 'low dog', etc.

chocolate soldier n
a weak, ineffectual or cowardly person. The phrase was at the centre of a court case in February 2002 when the black model Naomi Campbell alleged unsuccessfully that the *Daily Mirror* had used it in a racist slur against her. In fact the expression probably dates back to the late 19th century and originally referred to a purely decorative or excessively fragile soldier. 'Chocolate fireguard' and 'chocolate teapot' were used in the 1950s to describe useless items.

chocolate starfish n British
the anus

chode n, adj Canadian See **choad**[2]

choirboy n American
1a. an innocent, naïve or young male
1b. a new recruit to the police force, a **rookie**

1c. someone feigning innocence or naïvety. In this ironic sense the word was used by the ex-police officer Joseph Wambaugh as the title of his 1973 novel, *The Choirboys* (filmed in 1977).

choke a darkie *vb Australian*
to defecate. A vulgarism heard since the 1960s.

choked, choked-off *adj British*
overcome with indignation, fury, rancour or another strong emotion. Choked is a very widespread working-class usage, especially in London speech. Choked-off is a less common and more recent variant.

> *I tell you I was choked, really bloody choked, when she told me they'd given the contract to someone else.*

choke (someone) off *vb*
1a. *British* to discourage, repudiate or reject someone. This term is used in a fairly specific sense in the context of prisons, where it usually means to frustrate someone who is attempting an official complaint or application.
1b. to aggress, castigate

> *'She [his wife] choked me off yet again.'*
> (Recorded, London taxi driver, June 2005)

choke the/one's chicken *vb*
(of a man) to masturbate. A teenagers' and students' variant of **jerkin' the gherkin**, **flogging the lizard**, etc.

choking *adj British*
desperate for relief, typically in the form of alcohol or sex. The widespread term, popular, e.g., among university students since the late 1990s, is a shortening of the colloquial phrase 'choking for (the specified item)'. The phrase 'choking for it' invariably refers to sex. **Gagging** is a contemporary synonym.

choky, chokey *n British*
prison or a cell. A word which was still in use in the late 1980s, although sounding rather dated. The term comes from the Hindi *chauki*, meaning a shed or police compound, and was imported from India in the mid-19th century by members of the armed forces.

chomp¹ *vb*
to fellate. This usage is a specialisation of the colloquial sense of to eat.

chomp² *n British*
food. From the colloquial verb which imitates the sound of eating.

chompers *n pl*
the teeth. A jocular term inspired by the verb to **chomp** and the earlier **choppers**.

chones *n pl American*
the testicles. A corruption of the Spanish **cojones**.

chong *adj British*
a variant form of **chung**

chonged *adj*
1a. stoned
1b. tired
The term, still in use in 2005, may derive from *Cheech and Chong*, the names of two marihuana-loving comedians of the 1960s.

choo-choo *n*
a train. Like **chuffer** or **chuff-chuff** this is a nursery phrase often used facetiously by adults.

chook *n Australian*
a chicken. This is an alternative pronunciation of an old dialect term, imitating the clucking of hens, which gives **chuck** in British English.

> *'I hope your chooks turn to emus and kick down your dunnee.'*
> (Rural Australian curse)

choom *n Australian*
an English person. Now usually pejorative, the term seems to have appeared during World War I and was probably an imitation of the northern English pronunciation of 'chum'.

choong, chung *n Australian*
a Chinese person. A derogatory racist term which may be an imitation of Oriental speech or a deformation of **chink** or **jungle bunny**.

chop¹ *n*
a cut-down, customised motorcycle. A shortening of **chopper 2a**.

> *'Sarah belongs to the distinctly laid back, Harley-Davidson inclined "lifestyle" bikers. Soon she will be appearing on a customised 550 cut-down "chop".'*
> (*Independent*, 6 April 1988)

chop² *vb*
1a. to attempt to seduce
> *That guy was chopping me all evening.*
1b. to succeed in seducing, **pull**
> *Man, I chopped her at last.*
1c. to have sex
> *I just want to chop.*

In all these senses the term has been used, mainly by males, since around 2000.

chopper n
1. a helicopter. This was probably originally a children's version of the longer word, reinforced by the sound and scything action of the rotor blades. It was adopted by adults in World War II.
2a. a customised motorcycle, usually one having high **ape-hangers** and lengthened front forks, as ridden by Hell's Angels. It is derived from 'chopped hog' or chopped (meaning cut down, altered). Nowadays it is often shortened to **chop**.
2b. a young person's tricycle or bicycle designed and manufactured to look like a customised motorcycle, that is with a large back wheel and long front forks. From the 1970s when such bikes became popular.
3. British the penis. A working-class vulgarism dating from at least the 1940s and still heard.
4. American a machine gun. Although this use of the word is familiar to many people through films and crime fiction, it has been obsolete in spontaneous speech since before World War II.

choppers n pl
the teeth. A lighthearted term used all over the English-speaking world, often referring to false teeth.
    a new set of choppers

chops¹ n
the mouth or jaws. The word has been heard since the 18th century, before which it was usually in the form 'chaps', referring to the jaws of animals.

chops² vb British
to talk too much or to cheek. In playground usage.

chop shop n American
a customising workshop for cars or motorcycles. To **chop** in this case means to cut down or alter.

chopsy adj British
garrulous, inclined to talk out of turn, argumentative, **mouthy**. From the use of **chops** to designate the mouth or jaws.
    'Spurs have turned into a really chopsy team since Venables took over.'
    (Recorded, Welsh football supporter, London, 1989)

chore vb British
to steal. In this sense the word may be Urdu in origin.

chow n
1. food. The word is about a century old and derives either from the Far Eastern

pidgin English term 'chowchow', meaning a mixture, or from *jiao(ze)* (pronounced 'jowzer'), which is Mandarin Chinese for a dumpling.
2. a Chinese person. The term is usually used derogatively.
3. British a vulgar person. This is a social designation possibly based on the greeting/farewell ciao! It was defined as a 'person who wears lots of gold and speaks with an almost cockney/Essex accent'.

chow down vb American
to eat, sit down to a meal, 'tuck in'. From **chow** meaning food.
    'While we're here let's chow down, hey?'
    (*Real Men*, US film, 1987)

Christian Slater adj British
later. The rhyming slang borrows the name of the Hollywood actor.

Christmas! exclamation
an inoffensive euphemism for Christ, mainly used by British and Australian speakers

Christmas-crackered adj British
exhausted, worn out. Rhyming slang for **knackered**; a less common version than **cream-crackered**.

chrome n American
a gun. A term from the argot of street gangs.

chrome-dome n
a bald person. A humorous derogatory term referring to the polished sheen of a hairless head. In their 1977 book, *The Boy Looked at Johnny*, Julie Burchill and Tony Parsons consistently referred to the balding musician Brian Eno as a chrome-dome.

chronic, cronic, kronik adj American
excellent, powerful. One of many appropriations of negative words as vogue terms of approbation in adolescent speech, such as **bad**, **wicked**, **brutal**, etc. Chronic appeared in the late 1990s.
    Wow, this sure is some chronic blow.
    'Try some of this cake – it's cronic.'
    (Recorded, London student, 2003)

chubbette n
a 'well-built' or shapely young woman. A vogue term of the early 1980s among some American and British speakers.

chubby n American
an erection. An item of teenage slang often heard in the phrase 'crack/pop a chubby'. It may derive from the earlier synonym **crack a fat**.

'Hi boys, don't pop a chubby on our account.'
(*Meet the Applegates*, US film, 1991)

chubby-chaser n
someone who is sexually interested in or attracted to large or obese people. 'Chubby Checker' has also been recorded in London speech for a male who enjoys looking at 'well-built' women. The phrase was an American-ism of the early 1960s and was adopted as the nick-name of the American soul singer who popularised the 'twist'.

chuck¹ n
a term of endearment literally meaning chicken in northern English speech. It was originally a rural dialect term imitating the sound of clucking (**chook** in modern Australian English).

chuck² vb
1. to vomit. A moderately respectable euphemism probably abbreviated from the more common **chuck up**.
2. to throw out; specifically in police and underworld jargon to reject (an appeal), dismiss (a case) or acquit (a defendant)
3. *British* to stop, desist. In this sense the word has been used particularly in working-class slang of the north of England.

   'Chuck hassling me, will ya!'
   (*Your Cheating Heart*, British TV drama, 1990)

4. to eat excessively. In this case the verb is synonymous with 'chuck out' or **pig out**.
5. to **fuck**. The variant form is used euphemistically as an exclamation or intensifier.

   'They say it is, is it chuck!'
   (Gary Crowley, *The Beat*, British TV music programme, 25 October 1993)

6. *South African* to leave, hurry away
   Let's chuck.

chuck a cheesy vb Australian
to grin. The colloquial cliché 'a cheesy grin' has given rise to this more recent expression, in use since the mid-1980s among adolescents.

chuck a hissie vb British
to become enraged, lose control. Heard since 2000, the phrase derives from the earlier **hissie(-fit)**.

chuck a mental vb
to become enraged, agitated, disoriented. The term was featured in the Australian soap opera *Neighbours* in

1991, and is also in use among British and Scottish schoolchildren.

chuckle-dust n American
any illicit drug in powder form. The phrase seems to originate from the early 1990s when it was used to refer to **angel dust** or cocaine and was subsequently also recorded among North London schoolboys in 1993 and 1994.

chucklehead n American
a foolish, silly or eccentric person

chuck up vb
to vomit. **Upchuck** is a later variant form.

chuddie n
chewing gum. In the form 'chuttie' the term was first recorded in American speech as long ago as the 1920s; it was very probably originally a nursery form of the verb to chew. In the late 1990s it became a vogue term among UK adolescents. **Chuffie** is a synonym.

chuddies n pl British
underwear. The term seems to have originated in South Asian speech and has been popularised by TV comedy series such as *Goodness Gracious Me* and *The Kumars at No. 42*. By 2004 it was also in use in school playgrounds among other ethnic groups.

   Eat/kiss my chuddies!

chuff n British
1. the anus, backside. A word which has been heard since the 1940s and which is innocuous enough to use where other synonyms are taboo. The etymology of the word is obscure, but it may be from the dialect meaning plump (which is related to **chuffed** meaning pleased).

   'As tight as a badger's chuff.'
   (*Room at the Bottom*, British TV series, 1988)

2. a **fart**. A schoolchildren's and students' vulgarism recently popularised by *Viz* comic.
See also **chuffing**

chuff-chuff n British
a synonym of **chuffer**

chuffed adj British
delighted, pleased. The word's meaning stretches from flattered to excited. It probably originates in northern English dialect (meaning puffed-up and proud) and is still most frequently heard in the North and Midlands. Embellished forms are 'dead chuffed', 'chuffed pink' and 'chuffed to arseholes'. The TV soap opera *Coronation Street*, which is set in

the north of England, has 'chuffed to little mint-balls'.

chuffer n British
a train. A quasi-nursery word used facetiously by adults.

  'I'm catching the chuffer down to Bath.'
  (Recorded, journalist, 1987)

chuffie n British
chewing gum. An alternative form of
chuddie, heard in school playgrounds
since 2000.

chuffing adj British
a polite or disguised form of **fucking** as an
intensifying adjective. It is heard most
often in the north of England.

chuff-nuts n pl British
another term for **dingleberries**

chug vb
1. British to drink (alcohol). A coinage,
derived from the drinkers' toast or chant
'chug-a-lug', fashionable among young
people in London from the late 1980s.

  *'Sloane Rebs all support Chelsea F.C.,
  and can be seen every other Saturday
  lunchtime "chugging brew" and getting
  hammered at any number of pubs in the
  Fulham Road, before charging down to
  Stamford Bridge for a "frightfully good
  game of footy".'*
  (I-D magazine, November 1987)

2. American to throw away, reject. The
term was recorded in 2001.

chummer n British
a male homosexual. The term, recorded
among schoolboys in 2000, is possibly
influenced by **bum chum** and **bummer**.

chummy n British
a term of address used typically by
police officers to or about suspects.
This condescending word is representative of the menacing use of terms of
endearment, understatement, etc.
favoured by London police and underworld.

  *I think chummy here has got something
  he wants to tell us.*

chump[1] n British See **off one's block/
chump/crust/head/nut/onion**

chump[2] vb American
1a. to cheat or dupe
  The guy was chumpin' me.
1b. to steal, appropriate
  *First they chumped my car, then they
  came back for the fuckin' furniture!*
In both senses the term was popular in
black street slang from the 1990s. It is
formed from the colloquial noun sense

denoting a 'sucker'.

chunder vb Australian
to vomit. This term, in use among Australian **surfies** and others in the 1960s,
was imported into Britain later in the decade by the strip cartoon *The Adventures
of Barry McKenzie*. The writer, Barry
Humphries, derives it from the warning
cry 'Watch under!', perhaps used by sailors. An alternative derivation is from
'Chunder Loo' as rhyming slang for *spew*,
from the name of a character used in
advertisements for boot polish fifty years
earlier. Already established in Britain,
especially among young sportsmen and
drinkers, there are signs that this and
other Australianisms are making headway in the USA following the success of
the Australian comedy film *Crocodile
Dundee* in 1987.

chung adj British
physically attractive. A vogue term
among schoolchildren in 2005.

chunk vb American
1. to throw away, reject
2. also **chunk it** to vomit. The term, used
by adolescents, is probably derived from
the earlier **blow chunks**.
  Cissie chunked all over the couch.

chunker n American
an obese or heavily built person

chunky adj British
an all-purpose term of approbation briefly
in vogue among London **mods** in 1966
and 1967

chunter, chunner vb British
to nag or complain, especially incessantly and in an undertone. Chunter is a
common form throughout Britain, while
chunner is a northern and Midlands variant. The word is imitative of the sound.
  What are you chuntering on about?

church key n
a bottle opener. A (mainly middle-aged)
drinkers' witticism.

chutney-ferret n British
a male homosexual. One of a set of synonymous phrases (**fudge-nudger**, **turd
burglar**, etc.) based on the faecal aspects
of sodomy.

chutney-locker n British
the anus. A euphemism appearing in
London speech around 1990.

chutzpah n
daring effrontery, impressive cheek.
The word, pronounced 'hootspar', is via
Yiddish from the Hebrew *huspah* (bra-

zenness, audacity); it has been in use among non-Jewish Americans since at least the mid-1960s, but only appeared in the mid-1970s in Britain.

> 'I have valued my fleeting acquaintance with Larry Adler over the years because it has always given me an easy way of explaining the meaning of the Jewish word chutzpah to those who have not met this valuable term. As far as I can define it briefly, it's an elegant opportunism, so fast as to deceive the eye, and so successful as to be totally disarming. Or what cockneys call bloody cheek.'
> (Miles Kington, Independent, 27 January 1989)

cider-punk n British
a **crustie**. The phrase was used (unlike crustie itself) by members of the early 1990s subculture which included militant beggars, homeless vagrants and their weekend emulators. Cider was a preferred (cheap) stimulant and **punk** the music of choice.

cig, ciggie n
a cigarette

-city combining form American
a situation or a state of affairs, as in **barf city** (something revolting) or **edge city** (anxiety)

clack n, vb British
(to) chatter, talk incessantly. A mainly working-class word, popular in the north of England. 'Clack on' is an alternative verb form.

clackers n pl Scottish
balls (in both the literal and figurative slang senses). The word, recorded in the early 1990s, was the name of a fashionable children's toy of the 1970s consisting of two plastic balls on a string wound round the fingers and knocked together. **Conkers** is a synonym of similar provenance.

clag n British
bad weather. A rural dialect term for clay or mud, clag was first adopted in airforce slang to refer to thick cloud or fog. More recently, TV weather forecasters have employed the term lightheartedly.

Claire Rayners n pl British
trainers. The rhyming-slang phrase, first recorded in the late 1990s, borrows the name of the broadcaster and agony aunt.

clam n American
a dollar. Invariably used in the plural, this is a racier alternative to **buck**, etc.

clambrain n American
a foolish or stupid person. The image evoked is of someone with the brain power of a mollusc.

clamped adj
(to be) caught out

clam up vb
to keep quiet, refuse to speak. Originally an Americanism (clams are a popular oyster-like seafood), the term is now widespread.

clang vb British
to commit a gaffe, make a mistake. A back-formation from the colloquial phrase '(drop) a clanger', which shares the meaning of the shortened form.

clanking adj British
stinking. An item of student slang in use in London and elsewhere since around 2000. Synonyms are **bogging**, **minging**.

clanking for it adj British
sexually aroused, desperate for sex. In playground and campus usage since 2000, the phrase is an alternative to the contemporary **arching for it** and the earlier '**gagging** for it'.

clap, the clap n
venereal disease, gonorrhoea. The only widespread slang term for the condition, this word was derived from French (clapoir, meaning a swelling, or clapier, meaning a brothel) in the late 16th century. It became a taboo, and therefore slang term only in the 19th century. The specific reference to gonorrhoea had widened to include other venereal diseases by the 1950s.

> 'For while he nibbles at her Am'rous Trap
> She gets the Mony but he gets the Clap.'
> (Poor Pensive Punck, poem by John Dryden, 1691)

> '"Ain't got the clap have you?"
> "God no! It's just a sense of cosmic boredom".'
> (Robert Crumb, cartoon in Head Comix, 1968)

clapped[1], **clapped out** adj
worn out, exhausted. The second of these essentially British terms has been adopted in the USA since the 1950s. They are normally applied to machines, particularly cars, although they derive originally from the idea of a person debilitated by the **clap** (venereal disease). As

the origin has been forgotten, the terms are now colloquial rather than vulgar.

clapped², clapped up *adj*
infected with venereal disease, suffering from gonorrhoea. These rather old-fashioned forms have largely been replaced by 'got the clap'.

claret *n British*
blood. Originally an upper-class theatrical and boxing euphemism, this word is now heard mainly in London police and underworld circles.

'If you prick me do I not spill claret?'
(The character 'Arthur Daley' in *Minder*, British TV series, 1983)

clart, clarts *n British*
trouble, a mess. This dialect term from the north of England and Scotland – probably a variant of 'clot' or 'clod' (of mud, slime, excrement) – is heard occasionally in other parts of Britain, usually in expressions such as 'too much faff and clart' or '(dropped) in the clarts'. 'Clarty', the dialect adjective meaning dirty, sticky and messy, is also still heard.

class *adj British*
excellent. Deriving from the colloquial 'classy' and top-class, class act, etc., this use of the word has been a vogue term among younger speakers since the mid-1990s – a successor to **wicked** and **safe** and a contemporary synonym of **sound** or **the bollocks**.

clat *n British*
a dirty and/or obnoxious person. The term, which is related to the dialect **clart**, is heard particularly in the Scottish Lowlands and the north of England.

'The little clat gets right up my nose.'
(Recorded, middle-aged woman, York, 1995)

clat-tale *n British*
a tell-tale. A northern English children's variant of the standard terms 'tattle-tale' or 'tell-tale'.

clattering *n British*
a kicking. The term is from the jargon of football fans and refers not to kicks in the course of play, but a personal attack by one or more players during a match and, by extension, also by brawlers, hooligans, etc., off the field.

clemmed, clemped *adj British*
starving, hungry. An old term which is a survival of northern dialect (from the Middle English *clemmen*, meaning 'to pinch'). Clemmed is still heard occasionally among older speakers (and, incidentally, in the TV soap opera *Coronation Street*); clemped has enjoyed a revival among younger speakers since 2000, sometimes in the form 'clemped dief' – 'to death'.

click¹ *n American*
a clique, a small group of friends or confederates. A favourite word with high-school and college students.

click² *vb British*
1. to catch someone (doing something they shouldn't)
I clicked him sconned on peeve. [I caught him drunk]
2. to make contact with a potential romantic or sexual partner, **score**, **pull**.
See also **get a click**

clink *n*
1a. jail, prison. The most common (in Britain) and least racy synonym; it was the name of a prison on Clink Street in Southwark, London, from at least 1509 until the 18th century. The term may also be inspired by the sounds of metal keys, doors and manacles.
You'll end up in the clink.
1b. *British* detention, in schoolchildren's jargon
I'm in Saturday morning clink again.
2. *British* money, change. Like **chink** it is imitative of the sound of coins.
I'm a bit short of clink.

clinker *n American*
a failure. A word used particularly with reference to a film or play. In this sense it has been adopted by some British writers; in the USA it may occasionally denote other types of failure or incompetence. The slang use is based on the word's standard meaning of coal residue or cinder.

'Most of Hollywood, and especially John's brother Jim, refused to have anything to do with this clinker, adapted from the book by crusading Bob "I've been played by Robert Redford" Woodward.'
(*Tatler*, October 1989)

clinkers *n pl British*
another term for **dingleberries**

clip *vb*
1. to take (someone's) money dishonestly by sharp practice, deceit or fraud. The word is a euphemism from the jargon of

tricksters, with the image of 'trimming' someone of their 'excess' wealth.

2. *British* to hit someone a glancing blow with an open hand, to smack

I clipped him round the ear.

3. *American* to kill, execute. An item of black street slang from the early 1990s. One of many short 'tough-guy' euphemisms such as **tag**, **cap**, **off**, etc.

clip artist *n American*
a fraudster, cardsharp or confidence trickster. A dated term derived from the verb **clip 1**.

clip joint *n*
originally a club or bar which employs hostesses who encourage clients to buy them (inevitably hugely overpriced) drinks in the expectation, rarely fulfilled, that their generosity would be reciprocated with sexual favours. The phrase may now be applied to any overpriced, low-quality establishment. **Clip**, like 'trim', is an old euphemism for 'relieve someone of their money'.

clipping *n British*
a particular kind of cheating in which a prostitute takes a client's money but does not provide sex in return. A specific sense of the more general slang meaning of **clip**.

clobber *n British*
clothes, accessories or equipment. The word is now so widespread as to be colloquial rather than slang. It dates from the 19th century but its origin is obscure; it may be an invention, a dialect form of 'clothes', or from the Yiddish *klbr*.

clock *vb British*
1. to notice or see, to look at. A working-class usage widespread, especially in southeast England, since World War II. The middle-class fashion since the late 1980s for imitating working-class speech brought the word into some prominence and greater respectability. It probably derives from the obsolete use of 'clock' to mean a person's face.

'Villains call it clocking in Leeds, eyeballing in Manchester and screwing in London's East End…It came as a shock: juries can be intimidated by a stare.'
(*Sunday Times*, 5 June 1988)

2. to hit. A usage that was, and is, popular in Australia and which has been adopted in Britain (where it may have originated) and the USA. This term, used almost exclusively by men, probably also derives from the archaic term 'clock' meaning a person's face; hence the verb meaning to punch (in the face).

He finally lost his temper and clocked him one.

3. to tamper with the mileometer of a car in order to show a low mileage. A piece of dealers' jargon which has passed into common currency due to the wide extent of the practice.

clocking *n American*
selling **crack**. A street-slang term of the late 1980s.

'Some of them wear tiny gold charms that look like miniature watch faces – a dealer's trademark, which is probably where the term clocking came from.'
(*Sunday Times*, 10 September 1989)

clock it *vb*
to defeat one's opponent, win a contest. The term may have derived from the jargon employed in the Nintendo Game Boy computer games, or from the colloquial Americanism 'to clean someone's clock', meaning 'to defeat or confound'.

clodhopper *n*
1a. a clumsy or boorish person. The term originally (two hundred-odd years ago) referred to a ploughman or rustic (treading clods of earth in the fields).
1b. *British* a policeman. Rhyming slang from **copper**, rather than a simple pejorative.

clog¹ *vb British*
to kick

clog², cloggy *n British*
a Dutch person. This humorous or derogatory word may date from the 1940s when clogs were still widely worn. **Cheese** is a synonym.

clogger *n British*
someone who kicks people. The term is usually used dismissively of soccer players whose game is based more on violence than competence.

That team are nothing but a bunch of cloggers.

cloggy *n See* **clog²**

clogs *n pl See* **pop one's clogs**

clone *n*
1a. a **gay** man of stereotyped appearance. In the gay male community of the 1970s a 'uniform' of working clothes, leather caps, moustaches, etc., developed. Indistinguishable conformists to this standard code were referred to by

others and themselves as clones. In this sense the word is not necessarily pejorative.

1b. any fashion-follower or imitator who is indistinguishable from others, or is blindly conformist to a dress code. A derogatory term since the late 1970s, often added to a prefix to form such epithets as '*Madonna-clone*', '*Michael Jackson-clone*', etc.

clone-zone *n*
the male homosexual milieu or **gay** area of a town where **clones** congregate. A term from the late 1970s.

closet case, closet queen *n*
a homosexual who conceals his or her homosexuality; the second version of the phrase refers only to men. Originally part of underground **gay** terminology, this phrase became well known in the early 1970s when many previously secretive homosexuals decided to **come out**. The term was first widely used in the USA although its precise time and place of origin is obscure. The connection between closet and secrecy is obvious; compare the phrase with the well-known 'skeleton in the cupboard'.

clouts *n pl British*
underpants, especially female. The term is currently in use among, e.g., middle-class adolescents, but dates back to at least the late 18th century when it denoted a handkerchief, later a sanitary napkin.

Club Fed *n American*
prison, especially a federal, rather than state institution. A 1980s pun on Club Med(iterranée), which continues the time-honoured metaphor of a prison sentence as a vacation.

clucky *adj Australian*
broody, pregnant. From the image of a mother hen clucking over her clutch of eggs, the word has now been extended to mean pregnant, wanting to be pregnant, or merely eagerly anticipating something.

clue-ie *adj Australian*
bright, alert, well informed. The term is derived from the colloquial 'clued up' and has been used in Australian TV programmes such as *Police Rescue*, also broadcast in the UK.

When it comes down to it, she's not too clue-ie, is she?

clueless *adj American*
unfashionable, unpopular, unattractive. The standard colloquialism was adopted as a vogue term among Californian high-school students from the early 1990s, often in order to categorise a person excluded from the in-group. The word provided the title of the 1994 US film which featured the pampered successors to the earlier **Vals**.

cluffy *n British*
a foolish, unfortunate or unpleasant person, a misfit. In use among schoolchildren and adolescents since 2000.

clumping *n British*
a beating or maiming. The term, used typically by criminals to indicate physical punishment or a revenge attack, was recorded in the ITV documentary, *The Cook Report*, 6 June 1995.

clunk *n American*
1. a stupid, dull-witted person
2. an old, dilapidated car or truck

clutch *n British*
a cheek-to-cheek or arm-in-arm dance. A 'society' word, used by **Sloane Rangers** among others, which is a specialised use of the colloquial meaning of 'embrace'.

clutched *adj American*
tense, agitated. The term refers to the physical symptoms of anxiety in the form of tension in the abdomen and chest.

There's no need to get so clutched, it's only a math test.

Clyde *n See* **Clydesdale**

Clydesdale *n American*
an attractive male. A humorous term of the late 1980s based on the supposed suggestion of heroic **WASP** maledom inherent in the Christian names 'Clyde' and 'Dale'. The word, which probably originated on the streets ('Clyde' was used by **hipsters** in the 1950s to categorise an archetypal **square**), was used by **Valley Girls** and **preppies** among others from the early 1980s. (The literal meaning of Clydesdale is a form of large, handsome, pedigree horse; strong, hardworking and enormously expensive.)

c-note *n*
£100 or $100 (not necessarily always in the form of a hundred-denomination bill). From the Latin numeral C, meaning one hundred, this amount is also known as a **century**.

coasting *adj American*
under the influence of illicit drugs, moving around in a drug-induced daze or stupor. By extension, being in a euphoric state after listening to jazz, rock music, etc.

coating *n British*
abuse, insults. This use of the word has been recorded since the 1990s among middle-aged speakers and either refers to the grabbing by the lapels, or is based on the notion of **pasting** and the colloquial slang sense of 'paint' (to beat up). The archaic verb to 'coat' was also recorded in Britain and Australia in the sense of to reprimand.

cob *vb, n American*
(to give someone) a pinch or poke in the buttocks. In this sense the word, originally a dialect term for a lump or a protrusion, can be dated back to the English slang of the later 18th century.
See also **get/have a cob on**

cobber *n Australian*
a friend, 'mate'. An unsophisticated term of address among men, which is now virtually obsolete. There are two possible derivations proposed for this well-known Australianism: the archaic English dialect verb to 'cob', meaning to take a liking to (someone) or the Yiddish word *chaber* (from Hebrew, meaning comrade).

cobblers *n British*
nonsense, rubbish, **balls**. A popular example of rhyming slang (from 'cobbler's awls') which is often used in ignorance of its vulgar derivation. Formerly used literally by cockneys to mean the testicles, the word is old, but was given widespread currency in the 1960s by such TV comedies as *Steptoe and Son*.

> *'He is dismissive about awards: "A load of cobblers".'*
>
> (*Observer*, Section 5, 9 April 1989)

cob-on *n British*
a fit of ill-temper. A term heard predominantly in the north of England.

cock *n British*
1. a term of address (for men). It probably derives from 'cock-sparrow', or from the image of a brave fighting-cock. Typically, the word is used in an affectionate, bantering way in expressions such as the dated cockney 'wotcher cock!' or '(my) old cock'. Cock has been used in this

general sense for at least three hundred years.
2. nonsense, rubbish. This sense of the word has been in use since the 1940s and may be a shortening of 'poppycock' (from the Dutch *pappekak*, meaning 'soft shit' or absolute rubbish), 'cock and bull' or a euphemistic variant of **cack**.
3. the penis. In this sense the word is used all over the English-speaking world. In Britain the usage dates from the 17th century. Its origin is in the image of the male member either as a strutting fighter or as resembling a chicken's neck or water-valve. (In the USA the word rooster is usually prudishly substituted when referring to the male bird.)

cockblock *n*
1. an obstacle to seduction by a male, typically an obstructive or intrusive female friend of the intended seductee. The term was posted on the Internet in 2003.
Compare **grenade**
2. the protruding dividing barrier between male stand-up urinals

cock diesel *n American*
a powerful, attractive male. The term, usually employed appreciatively, but sometimes ironically, was heard in black street slang and on white campuses in the 1990s. The 'diesel' element (as in **diesel-dyke**) suggests the unrefined power of a diesel-engined vehicle.

cocksucker *n*
a despicable, contemptible person. This expression is almost always used in this sense rather than its literal meaning of someone who performs fellatio; it is generally an Americanism, applied to males as a term of abuse. The implication is of a person who is willing to stoop (metaphorically) to disgusting or debasing acts.

cock-tease, cock-teaser *n*
a slightly more polite version of **prick-tease(r)**

cock (something) up *vb British*
to make a mess of, to mismanage disastrously. As in the noun **cock-up**, the precise origin of the expression is uncertain. It is common in Britain and Australia, but not in the USA.

cock-up *n British*
a mistake, blunder or shambles. Many different sources have been posited for this expression; 'cock' may refer to some

obscure piece of professional jargon (it occurs in the vocabularies of printers, hunters, brewers and others), to the penis, or it may be an alteration of **cack**. Alternatively, 'cock' may simply have been chosen as a more acceptable complement in a phrase synonymous with **balls-up** and **fuck-up**.

> *'Mercifully these cock-ups don't happen too often.'*
> (Jeremy Paxman, Breakfast TV, November 1988)

coco[1] *n British*
a black or coloured person. A pejorative or patronising term used especially by middle- and upper-class speakers since the 1960s.

> *'And there were two cocos changing a wheel in the outside lane.'*
> (Recorded, public schoolboy, London, 1971)

coco[2], **cocoa** *vb British*
almost always used in the phrase 'I should coco(a)!', expressing disbelief or indignation. This is London rhyming slang for *say so* (as in 'I should say so!').

cocoa-shunter *n British*
a male homosexual. One of many vulgarisms (**fudge-nudger**, etc.) playing on the notion of sodomy and faeces, this expression was used in the TV comedy spoof *Brass Eye* in March 1997.

coconut *n*
1. *British* a non-white person who collaborates with the white establishment, an 'Uncle Tom'. This expression, used by young Asians and blacks since the 1980s, refers to the idea that such people are, like the coconut, black on the outside but white on the inside. **Bounty bar** is an alternative.
2. one's head. An obvious, but probably obsolescent usage.
3. *American* a dollar

cocooning *n American*
staying at home with one's partner and children (as opposed to going out or socialising in the evening). A **yuppie** term from the late 1980s.

cod *adj British*
excellent. The word has been used in this sense by schoolchildren since the mid-1990s.

code brown *n*
an instance of faecal incontinence or diarrhoea in medical slang, given wider currency by its use in the US TV series

ER. Sometimes extended to refer to a moment of panic.

cods *n pl British*
the testicles. The singular form 'cod' is an archaic word for the scrotum; it is an Anglo-Saxon word meaning 'bag' (seen in the obsolete terms pease-cod and codpiece). Since the era of Middle English the plural has had this meaning in British and, later, Australian usage, although not in the USA.

> *He got kicked in the cods for his efforts.*

codswallop, cods *n British*
nonsense, worthless rubbish. A dismissive term, typically applied to something purporting to be true. There is more than one theory as to the origin of the word; the most fanciful is that it referred to the 'wallop' (gassy drink) produced by Mr. 'Codd' (inventor of a patent ginger-beer bottle). Alternatively, it may refer to the testicles (**cods**) as in **balls**.

> *'Equal opportunities? That's a load of old codswallop!'*
> (Recorded, office worker, London, 1986)

coffee-spitter *n*
a shocking action, event or piece of information. This item of office slang, reported in the London *Evening Standard* in March 2004, refers to something so outrageous or upsetting that it causes spluttering and/or expulsion of a drink.

coffin-dodger *n British*
an elderly person. A sometimes humorous pejorative.

> *'My four sons and their friends, all in their mid-twenties, refer to the likes of me, a mere 60 year old, as "nearly-deads" and "coffin-dodgers".'*
> (Reader's letter to the *Independent*, 4 September 1992)

coffin nail *n*
a cigarette. The jocular term pre-dates the public concern over the effects of smoking on health in the last three decades.

cog[1] *n British*
1a. a gear, in the jargon of motorcyclists and other drivers
> *Drop down a cog and rev up.*
1b. power, acceleration
> *Give it some cog.*

cog[2] *vb British*
to move, go, act energetically. The word also occurs in the verbs **give it some cog** and 'get cogging'. The term, used in this

way, particularly in working-class speech, is derived from subsense **b** of the noun form.

coinage n
money. A vogue term among younger speakers since 2000.

cojones n pl
1a. courage, 'guts'. A word (pronounced 'co-honays') introduced to many English speakers by Ernest Hemingway, it is the Spanish slang word for **balls** in both the literal and metaphorical senses.
1b. the testicles. The word sometimes has its literal sense in American English, especially when spoken by Hispanics.
  She kicked him in the cojones.

coke n
cocaine
  'If somebody come and sell coke on our street we kill 'em or beat 'em up bad.'
  (13-year-old US dealer, *Independent*, 24 July 1989)

cokehead, cokie n American
a (habitual) user of cocaine.
See also **head**

cold adj
1. untraceable. The opposite of **hot** in its criminal sense, often applied to weapons or cars.
  It's OK, these guns are cold.
2. *British* bad. A vogue term in black speech and club-culture usage since the late 1990s. An intensified form is **arctic**.
3. good

cold turkey n
a sudden withdrawal from hard drugs, typically heroin, with the attendant hot and cold flushes, goose-pimples, discomfort, etc. The expression is originally American, from the 1940s or earlier, and in the late 1980s was increasingly used, often ironically, to describe a sudden withdrawal from any habitual activity. The phrase refers either to 'goose flesh' or to the general pallor and consistency of cold turkey meat.
  to go cold turkey/go through cold turkey
  They gave him cold turkey treatment.

collar n, vb
(to) arrest (someone). The noun form is a later coinage from the verb, meaning to 'catch', and the idiomatic expression 'to feel someone's collar', meaning to arrest them. Collar is another police jargon term which has passed into general use.

'Forget it Friday, this is our collar.'
(*Dragnet*, US film, 1987)

colon crusader n British
a male homosexual. In playground usage since 2000, often used as a non-specific insult.

come[1] vb
to experience an orgasm. A Victorian euphemism for a physiological fact that has no other name (apart from the also euphemistic 'climax') in standard English; this use of the word in fact dates back at least as far as Shakespeare and occurs subsequently in the (now archaic) form 'come off'.

come[2]**, cum** n
semen. A later derivation from the verb to **come**.

come across vb
to consent to sex, especially after initial reluctance. A phrase widespread in the English-speaking world since the 1960s, originating from the more general sense of come across, meaning to accede, give or agree.

come a gutser vb Australian
1a. to have an accident
1b. to commit a blunder, fail
The phrase functions similarly to the colloquial 'come a cropper', the 'gutser' originally denoting a heavy fall onto one's stomach.

comedown n
a period of physical and mental depression and exhaustion following a bout of elation from drugs, specifically the after-effects of amphetamine use
  That stuff's terrible – the comedown lasts longer than the high.

come on vb
to start to menstruate. A euphemism used by women and men.

come out vb
to reveal oneself as a homosexual, declare one's homosexuality. The expression is a shortening of 'come out of the closet', dating from the period in the early 1970s when liberalisation encouraged more openness among **gay** men and women in their relations with each other and the **straight** world. Subsequently the term has sometimes been extended to mean 'to declare one's real position' in non-sexual contexts.

come the raw prawn vb Australian
to try to take advantage of or deceive someone. This colourful expression

probably originated in the 1940s and is still heard. The precise connection between the uncooked crustacean and deceitfulness is not clear, but the suggestion is of cadging by feigning innocence or naïvety.

come untied vb See **untied**

commodore n British
the sum of £15. The item of financial slang is inspired by the Commodores' hit single 'Three Times a Lady' (a **Lady (Godiva)** being £5 in rhyming slang).

completely cute adj American
suitably attractive, handsome and/or sexy. An expression used by upper- and middle-class young women to indicate approval of a potential male partner. A code term in the **preppie** lexicon.

compo n Australian
(unemployment) compensation. A typical Australian shortening.
Compare **arvo**

con[1] vb, n
(to perpetrate) a swindle or fraud, obtain money by false pretences. This venerable colloquialism (regarded as slang in the 1950s) is simply a shortening of 'confidence-trick'.

'A crazy au pair girl planned to con superstar Eric Clapton out of a fortune by claiming another couple's baby was THEIR love child.'
(News of the World, 1988)

con[2] n American
a convict or ex-convict, felon or prisoner

conch n American
a **swot**. A **preppie** shortening of 'conscientious'.

conchie n
an alternative spelling of **conshie**

cone-head n American
1a. an intellectual or **swot**
1b. a stupid, socially inept person. The term is a more recent version of **pointyhead**. Its latter sense, as used in adolescent speech, was adopted as the title of a comedy film starring Dan Ackroyd in 1993.

cones n pl
female breasts

conk n
1a. the nose. The generally quoted origin for this comical word is the conch shell (often collected as a curio since the 17th century), or a learned play on the Latin concha, meaning shell in general, or a trumpet.

'This face, embossed as it is with a vast fleshy conk.'
(Observer magazine, 15 May 1988)
1b. the head. A less common use of the word.
2. American a 'process' hairstyle (one where the hair is straightened by the application of chemicals and/or heat) as worn by **hip** young blacks from the 1930s until the 1960s when it was superseded by the racially affirmative **afro** styles

conkers n pl Scottish
balls (in both the literal and figurative slang senses). Like its contemporary synonym **clackers**, the expression borrows the name of a children's game.

connection, connexion n
a drug supplier, a **dealer** or **pusher**. Originally from the language of American drug users of the late 1950s and 1960s, the term has become part of the international jargon of illicit drug users. It particularly refers to a source of heroin. ('Connection' was used ambiguously as the title and in the lyrics of a 1967 song by the Rolling Stones.)

conniption n
a fit of irritation, agitation. The geographical origin and derivation of the word is obscure (it is fairly common in Australian and North American speech) but it is most often heard among middle-aged speakers.
to have/get into a conniption

content adj
attractive, pretty. The term has typically been used by younger males for describing females since 2000. It is probably a transferral of the idea of pleased from subject to (pleasing) object.

contrasexual n
a person, usually female, who prefers domestic comforts to sexual display or activity. The semi-technical term from psychology and anthropology (originally denoting someone who displays traits of the opposite sex) was borrowed in 2004 for this jocular social categorisation on the lines of **metrosexual** and **retrosexual**.

coo[1] n
gossip, news. The term, usually in the form 'What's the coo?', has been used in London since 2000. Its origins are obscure, but it may be the same word as **ku**, or derive from the adjectival sense. It has also been suggested that it is

inspired by the cooing of congregating birds.

coo² *adj American*
a deliberately lazy pronunciation of **cool** in the sense of relaxed, congenial, etc.

coochie *n American*
1a. the female sex organs
1b. a female or females as sex objects
This item of black slang is probably a shortening of **hoo(t)chie-coochie**, which has denoted sexual activity since the 19th century.

cookie-pusher *n American*
an unmanly man, an effete or sycophantic male (the word never seems to be used of women). The image is of someone who spends his time passing cookies at tea parties, either because he enjoys such 'effeminate' activities, or in order to curry favour or further his career.

> *some little State Department cookie-pusher trying to persuade them all to play ball*

cooking *adj American*
going well, moving fast, succeeding. Originally from pre-World War II street language, this usage spread, especially via jazz musicians, to young whites. It is still often used to refer to musicians who are performing well and generating excitement. A stronger form is 'cooking with gas'.

cool¹ *adj*
1a. unflappable, imperturbable
1b. excellent, admirable, acceptable
One of the key items in the vocabulary of jazz musicians, **hipsters**, **beatniks** and **hippies**, cool, with its original suggestion of calm disinterested serenity, is a word which has not dated. It is as much in vogue with teenagers in the early 21st century as it was among the 1930s jazz musicians who probably coined it (to denote gentler, progressive jazz, as opposed to 'hot' jazz).

cool² *n*
sang-froid, imperturbability. A back-formation from the adjective.

cool³ *vb*
to calm down. A more fashionable abbreviated form of the colloquial 'cool down', heard since 2000.

> *Just cool!*

cool it, cool out *vb*
to relax, unwind, defuse a situation. A **hipsters**' term which has become a common colloquialism.

coon *n*
a black person. Originally (and still) a term of racist abuse common in the southern states of the USA, from 'raccoon' (a black-faced rural pest). The word has been adopted in Britain and Australia to refer to a person of any supposedly inferior race. In Britain it is a widespread racist epithet in use by the police and other working-class whites; **egg and spoon** is the rhyming-slang version.

> *'There were a couple of coons shouting at each other and it's difficult in these circumstances, I suppose.'*
> (Police officer, quoted in *Inside the British Police* by Simon Holdaway, 1983)

coot *n*
a foolish person, idiot

cootie *n American*
a head or body louse. The word was originally armed-forces slang, from the Polynesian *kuty*, meaning 'parasite'.

> *'Here you are.*
> *No, not if it has cooties on it.*
> *I don't have cooties!'*
> (*Roseanne*, US TV comedy series, 1989)

cooze *n American*
1a. a woman. A fairly vulgar term, used almost exclusively by men and having overtones of 'sex object', 'victim' or 'slut'.
1b. the female sex organs. The origin of the word is obscure.

cop¹ *n*
a police officer. A shortening of **copper**. In Britain, until the 1960s **cop** was felt to be an Americanism and only in the late 1980s did it find its way into print, albeit in the gutter press.

> *'Don't cry/Gotta go bye bye/SUDDENLY:*
> *DIE DIE/COP KILL A CREEP! pow pow pow.'*
> ('Concentration Moon' written by Frank Zappa, recorded by the Mothers of Invention, 1967)

cop² *vb*
to buy illicit drugs, to **score**. A specialisation of the general use of 'cop' to mean obtain.

> *'You wanna take a walk,*
> *You wanna go cop,*
> *You wanna go get*
> *Some chinese rock?'*

('Chinese Rock' by Dee Dee Ramone and Richard Hell, recorded by the Heartbreakers, 1977)

copacetic, kopasetic adj American
excellent, satisfactory, hunky dory. Used usually of a situation or state of affairs, copacetic is as likely to be said by a college professor as a New York **cop**. The college professor might think he is using a newish slang term; the cop may suspect that a word ending in -ic derives from Greek or Latin. Both would be wrong. This bizarre word has rarely been written down, but was recorded as early as 1919. Attempts have been made to derive it from Latin, Yiddish or even Amerindian roots, but its true origin is unknown. It has not crossed the Atlantic in its comparatively long history.

'What's your sign, love?'
'Stop.'
'Well that's copacetic.'
(*Beach Party*, US film, 1981)
'You stick with me and everything will be copacetic.'
(*The Secret of My Success*, US film, 1987)

cop a feel vb American
to grope (someone) sexually; succeed in heavy petting. A (mainly male) teenagers' term from the 1950s, when this might be the goal, rather than a way-stage in the process of seduction.

I didn't even get to cop a feel.
'Then when they start gettin' passionate, start coppin a few feels.'
(High-school student, *IT* magazine, June 1972)

cop a plea vb American
to plead guilty to a lesser offence than the one which is charged to speed up the judicial process (for the prosecutors) and avoid a heavier sentence (for the defendant). A strategy which forms the basis of plea bargaining, a peculiarity of the US legal system.

The guy copped a goddam plea and only went down for three.

cop off vb British
to find a sexual partner, to **pull** someone. A term from the north of England that had become widespread elsewhere by the 1990s.

'Cop off...that beautiful moment when you finally get some snog action...'
(*Just Seventeen* magazine, August 1996)

cop-out vb, n
(to be guilty of) an evasion, avoidance of responsibility. This expression (almost always heard in the noun form) was American slang until the late 1970s, at which time it suddenly gained widespread currency, even among 'respectable' speakers in Britain. The phrase arose in the 1960s meaning specifically to 'duck out' of one's obligations to one's peers.

copper n
a police officer. The word originated in Britain in the 1840s, from 'to cop' as a humorous or racier alternative to 'to catch'.

coppish? question form American
an alternative spelling of **capeesh**

copshop n British
a police station. Currently mainly a children's expression.

cop some zees vb American
to sleep. The phrase, which also occurs in the form **stack some zees/zeds**, uses the repeated letter 'z' as a cartoon representation of snoring.

corgis n pl British
(a) 'couple of really ghastly individuals'. Another in the series of joky acronyms (on the lines of **yuppie**, **dinkie**, etc.) coined by professionals and the media to epitomise special subgroups of the population in the late 1980s.

cork up vb British
to keep quiet. A phrase briefly in vogue among adolescents in the mid-1960s, usually in the form of a brusque imperative.

corn n
money. A variant form of the Caribbean form **carn** which was said to have been the favourite word of the black British boxer Frank Bruno in 1982.

corn (on the cob) n British
the penis. Rhyming slang for **knob**.

corn-dog n American
1. a **swot**. One of many synonyms used in the USA (**throat**, **grind**) and UK (**Wendy**, **spod**), principally by male school students, to ostracise misfits. The reference is to a bland-tasting variety of hot-dog.
2. (a male with) an uncircumcised penis. The expression trades on the supposed resemblance to a type of hot-dog. **Aardvark** and **anteater** are contemporary synonyms.

cornflake n American

an eccentric, crazy or silly person. An elaboration of the widespread term **flake** (which has the same meaning). The pun is on the name of the breakfast cereal; 'corn' is otherwise meaningless.

corn-hole n American

1a. the anus

1b. a pinch or poke in the anal region. In this sense the phrase has been recorded since the early years of the 20th century.

Cornish pasties n pl British

a style of men's shoe considered deeply unfashionable or indicative of a certain social subgroup in the 1970s and 1980s (specified by Judy Rumbold, fashion editor of the *Guardian*, as 'maths teachers countrywide'). The pastie was so-called because of the supposed resemblance of the moulded-soled, heavily stitched shoe to the meat and vegetable savoury.

corpse vb British

1. (in acting) to be rendered unable to speak or act by the onset of uncontrollable hysterical laughter, in rehearsal or before an audience. The word has been used in the theatre since the 19th century.

2. to cause another actor to break down with laughter or giggling during rehearsal or performance

These meanings are also true of performers in operas and musicals.

cory, corey n British

the penis. A vulgarism used particularly by marginals and the poorer elements of the working class. The word, which is from the Romany word for thorn, *kori*, was more widely used in the 1950s and 1960s than today.

costered up adj British

solvent, wealthy. A phrase from the East End of London, probably based on the old word 'costermonger' for a fruit-seller.

costume n See **in costume**

cosy n British

an act of sex. A **Sloane Ranger** euphemism, used by girls and perhaps revealing of sexual attitudes in that milieu.

cot-case n

an invalid or someone who has been mentally and/or physically incapacitated. A usually heartless and often derogatory expression, used in Britain and Australia

typically by health-care personnel or relatives. The similar term 'stretcher-case' has become an acceptable colloquialism, whereas **basket case** remains slang.

cotch vb

to relax

> *'I've got some pot, want to cotch round mine tonight?'*
> (Recorded, student, Devon, 2002)

cotchin' n

relaxing. A vogue term since 2000 among young speakers of all ethnic groups.

cottage n British

a public lavatory, in the language of the homosexuals who made contact there. The word and the practice were more common in the 1950s and 1960s before the liberalisation of anti-homosexual laws, but are still in evidence. The term is also used in Australia.

cottaging n British

visiting, or hanging around in, public lavatories to make sexual contacts. A male homosexual's term from the 1950s which was still in use in the late 1980s.

cotton-top n American

an old person, especially one with white hair. **Frost-top** and **moss-back** are synonyms.

cotton wool n British See **on the cotton wool**

couch potato n American

a lazy, greedy person. This expression from the late 1980s describes a person whose only activity is to lie in front of a television and eat and drink. ('Couch' is an American synonym for sofa.)

> *'"Couch-potato", according to Lindsey Bareham "is American for a television addict": the potato, once again, is defamed as a symbol of dull lethargy.'*
> (Patrick Skene Catling, *Daily Telegraph*, Christmas Book Review, 1989)

cough vb British

to confess to a crime, to reluctantly give up information. A police and underworld term influenced by the notion of coughing up something stuck in the throat.

> *'Look, many times I have known prisoners who have coughed to seven or eight jobs when they have been given a quick thump.'*
> (Police officer quoted in *Inside the British Police*, Simon Holdaway, 1983)

council *adj British*
inferior, of poor quality, shabby. The
term, recorded since 2000, is inspired
by council estates as a habitat of poor
people.

   *Those big gold hoop earrings make her
look so council.*

Compare **village**

cow *n British*
1a. an unpleasant or obnoxious woman
1b. a placid, drab or humiliated woman
The word is often used with real malice or,
alternatively, can be said with fellow feeling by a sympathetic woman, especially in
the phrase 'poor cow'. Cow is not a universal term of abuse (in French for instance it
can be a term of affection). It is said that
the synonym **moo** was used in the 1960s
because cow was still considered beyond
the pale for family TV.
2. an unpleasant or extremely irritating
task, experience or sensation, etc. In this
sense the word is often used in the
phrase 'a cow of a job', etc.

Compare **mare**

cowboy[1] *n*
1a. a reckless or irresponsible person,
especially someone young, inexperienced and/or wild. The term is typically
used by older workers referring to
younger ones, or by police about a delinquent loner. The term originated in the
1950s, drawing comparisons with western film heroes or with pre-war gangsters'
use of 'cowboy job' or the verb 'to **cowboy**'
to refer to a particularly messy or violent
crime.
1b. *British* a bad workman. The above
sense of cowboy has been extended and
popularised in colloquial language to
refer to anyone who does a shoddy job in
order to make a quick profit.

   a cowboy plumber/plasterer

cowboy[2] *vb British*
to behave or perform recklessly. The
word is now used in two main senses; to
drive dangerously or to perform a professional task in a slapdash and/or haz-
ardous way.

cowboy job/operation *n*
1. an unauthorised scheme, as in, for
instance, the field of espionage
2. *British* a badly finished or skimped
example of workmanship
3. *See* **cowboy**[1] **1a**

cowboy outfit *n British*
a firm or organisation which specialises
in shoddy workmanship or dubious

business practices. The punch-line of a
familiar joke among disgruntled businessmen is that a doting millionaire,
when asked by his infant son for a cowboy outfit, buys him the company in
question.

coyote *n American*
a person who preys on those illegally
immigrating to the USA from Mexico. The
word (literally, prairie wolf) is used in
Spanish to describe unscrupulous
agents, mainly Mexican, who offer to help
wetbacks cross the border, but instead
rob, defraud, denounce or even kill them.
A term from the late 1970s and 1980s.

coz *n See* **cuz**

cozzer *n*
a police officer. An item of London
working-class slang. The word might
have originated in the archaic market
porters' term 'cozza(r)', from the
Hebrew *chazar* meaning pork or pig.
London's first black policeman, Norwell
Roberts, was known as 'Nozzer the cozzer'.

   *'I didn't want to see the shit-eating grins
on the cozzers' faces.'*
   (Jimmy Robinson, released prisoner,
speaking on the BBC TV programme
Panorama, 24 February 1997)

crabs *n pl*
pubic lice, a case of *pediculosis pubis*.
The louse is popularly known as the
crab louse from its resemblance when
viewed under magnification.

   a dose/case of crabs

crack *n*
1. a purified, addictive form of cocaine.
When pellets of crack are smoked they
fizz and crackle, which is probably the
origin of the name, reinforced by the
precedent of **smack**. The drug became
popular in the USA in 1985, but was first
described in *The Gourmet Cookbook, a
Complete Guide to Cocaine*, published in
California in 1972.

   *'Crack – cocaine mixed with baking soda
and cooked in microwave ovens – has
been described as the "fast food of
drugs".'*
   (*Independent*, 24 July 1989)

2. the vagina. An obvious vulgarism,
occasionally heard in all English-speaking areas.
3. *Irish and British* a good time. From the
adjective cracking and the Irish notion
(sense **4**).

'It's a right crack.'
(Snooker hall manager, ITV telethon, May 1988)

4. the crack *Irish and British* what's going on, the latest news or the current ambience. This word is used all over Ireland and in the late 1980s spread to Britain. The all-purpose term, usually in phrases such as 'what's the crack?' or 'that's the crack!', seems to combine two very old, popular unorthodox senses of the word: to talk, gossip or boast, as in **crack on**, and the adjective crack meaning first-rate, excellent.

'This is the only place to live. I tried Australia but I came back because I missed the crack.'
(Belfast resident, *The Crack: a Belfast Year*, Sally Belfrage, 1987)

'Big Alex is a minder and a fixer. In his words, he knows all the crack.'
(*Guardian*, 12 December 1987)

crack a brown *vb Australian*
to **fart**. A fairly rare post-World War II male vulgarism.

crack a chubby *vb See* **chubby**

crack a fat *vb Australian*
to have an erection. A vulgarism known in Britain through Barry Humphries' *Adventures of Barry McKenzie*. There are a number of mostly obsolete expressions in Australian English using the word 'crack' to mean achieve or produce.

crack a stiffie *vb British*
to have an erection. An expression used in **Sloane Ranger** and **yuppie** circles.

cracker[1] *n American*
1. a white person. In black street argot the term, from the colour of savoury biscuits, is almost invariably pejorative and often refers to an unsophisticated or bigoted white person.
2. a computer programmer who breaches systems for fun or profit, in the patois of **cyberpunks** and **net-heads**. *Compare* **hacker**

cracker[2] *adj British*
excellent. A vogue adjectival version of the colloquial noun usage (denoting something or someone outstanding, admirable) which dates back to the late 19th century.

crackerbox *n American*
1a. a psychiatric hospital
1b. a crazy person

'I'm stuck in some private crackerbox.'
(*Man Trouble*, US film, 1993)
The terms are a pun on the colloquial adjectival sense of 'crackers'.

crack house *n*
a place where the drug **crack** is prepared, sold or consumed

'In the depressed inner-city areas of Los Angeles or New York, crack is frequently consumed in "crack houses" or "rock houses" – derelict buildings, often occupied by squatters, where addicts can buy and consume the drug.'
(*Sunday Times*, 10 September 1989)

crack it *vb British*
to succeed in a seduction. Used by and about men, this is a specific use of the general colloquial sense of to succeed, especially to suddenly succeed after long effort, as in 'cracking' a safe or a code.

crackle *n British*
money, banknotes. A word used by street traders, bookies, **spivs**, etc., particularly in the 1950s and 1960s. An alternative to **crinkle**, similarly inspired by the sound of crisp new notes.

crackling *n British*
an attractive female, or women in general seen as sex objects. This male expression was particularly popular in the 1950s and early 1960s, usually in the phrase 'a bit of crackling'. It derives from the idea of pork crackling being a 'tasty morsel', perhaps reinforced by the vulgar sense of **crack**.

crack on *vb British*
1. to talk incessantly, browbeat or boast. The phrase, which is now generally used by middle-class speakers, is a successor to a colloquial use of **crack** to mean gossip, brag or tell tales which is at least 300 years old and survives in Scottish and American speech.

'He was cracking on about his job and his responsibilities.'
(Recorded, city financier, London, 1987)

2a. to establish contact with a potential romantic partner, seduce

'You can't crack on to that many people here.'
(*Away the Lads*, BBC 2 TV documentary, February 1993)

2b. 'crack on someone': to flirt with, have and/or express an infatuation with someone. An item of slang in use in girls' public schools in the early 1990s.

crack wise *vb*
to make witty or cheeky remarks. A back-formation from the noun and verb 'wisecrack'.

crafty butcher *n British*
a male homosexual. The pejorative expression is inspired by the notion that 'he takes his meat in through the back door'. The term was posted on the b3ta website in 2004.

crank *n*
1. the penis. A rare usage, mainly heard in the USA among sailors, truckers, 'hard-hats' and others in the 1960s and 1970s.
2. speed (methedrine or amphetamine), heroin. A drug users' term from the late 1960s which could also be used to refer to any drug which 'cranks up' or re-stimulates a person's system.
3. *American* an irritable, bad-tempered person. The slang noun is derived from the colloquial adjective 'cranky' (itself from the Scottish dialect word for bent or distorted).

cranking, cranked *adj*
exciting, stimulating, powerful. The words come from the image of cranking up an engine and, by extension, the colloquial 'cranking up the volume'.

crank up *vb*
to inject (a dangerous drug). A **junkies'** term from the early 1970s derived from the image of inserting a handle into an engine to jerk it back into life.
crank up some smack
They're going to crank up.

crap¹ *n*
1a. excrement, **shit**
1b. dirt, rubbish
1c. worthless nonsense, **bullshit**
In modern usage crap is generally seen as a more moderate synonym for **shit**; in fact the word comes from Middle English *crappe*, which meant scrapings, scale, residue or chaff; this in turn came from words existing in Old French, German and Dutch, distantly related to 'crop' and 'crabbed'. (The fact that the flush toilet was invented by a Thomas Crapper appears to be pure coincidence.)
2. oppressive, petty or unpleasant behaviour; by extension from **crap 1a** and **1b**. This idea is usually expressed in such phrases as 'he doesn't take any crap from anyone' or 'she's not going to put up with this crap any more'.

crap² *vb*
to defecate, **shit**. The verb form, which began to be used in the late 18th century, is derived from the earlier noun **crap**, which originally meant rubbish, rather than excrement.

crap-ass *adj*
very bad. An intensified form of **crap**, using the American **ass** as a combining form. The term was in use among British speakers in 2003.

crap on *vb British*
to nag, harangue or talk incessantly. A near synonym for the verb to **bang on**, with the added suggestion that the content of the monologue or harangue in question is worthless or frivolous.
'The only moments of light relief we get are when you come in and we crap on about anything we like.'
(Recorded, London University student, July 1988)

crapper, the crapper *n*
a toilet. This vulgarism appears to derive from **crap** and not from the name of Thomas Crapper, a Victorian manufacturer of lavatories who is claimed to be the inventor of the flush toilet.

crappy, crappo *adj*
worthless, contemptible, of very low quality. From **crap**. Crappo is a more recent variant.

crash¹ *vb*
1. to go to sleep, lie down and lose consciousness. This word was very popular in the **hippy** era, perhaps because the suggestion of sudden collapse coincided with drug-induced sleep or simply curling up on a floor exhausted. Crash sounded rather dated by the late 1990s; it originated in armed-services slang in World War II, probably among airmen, and was adopted by bohemian travellers and **beatniks** during the 1950s.
2. to gatecrash. A word made especially popular by the teenage custom (from the 1960s onward) of arriving uninvited at parties.
3. *British* to cadge, borrow or lend. In use among working-class speakers and members of the armed services in the 1950s, this term became popular among adolescents in the 1990s. It is heard particularly in the Scottish Lowlands and the north of England.
Can you crash me a tenner?
I just wanted to crash a couple of biffs.

crash² *adj*
excellent, attractive, exciting. In this sense, fashionable since 2000, the word may be a shortening of **crash-hot** or an unrelated coinage.

crash and burn *vb*
to fail spectacularly. A military metaphor which became an item of journalese in the early 1990s.

crasher *n British*
a (crashing) bore. An upper- and, more recently, middle-class term. It has existed in limited circulation since the 1950s and has been fashionable among **Sloane Rangers**, **yuppies**, etc.

crash-hot *adj Australian*
excellent, first-rate. This fairly popular expression is probably a euphemism for **shit-hot**.

crashpad *n*
a place to sleep (temporarily). This term, combining **crash**, meaning to sleep, and **pad**, meaning a home or shelter, was popularised by the **hippies**; it usually referred to a communal building where sleeping space was available to travellers.

crater-face *n*
a person suffering from facial acne or spots. 'Pizza-face' is a synonym, similarly used by or of adolescents.

cream¹ *n South African*
an attractive young female. Recorded as an item of Sowetan slang in the *Cape Sunday Times*, 29 January 1995.

cream², **cream one's jeans** *vb*
to have an orgasm or to become sexually excited (while dressed). The vulgarism can be used of either sex (and now, by extension, can even sometimes mean to become over-excited or over-enthusiastic without the sexual connotation). Cream has been a euphemism for semen or sexual lubricant for at least a century. Cream one's jeans dates from the late 1960s.

cream-crackered *adj British*
knackered; exhausted, worn out. A humorous rhyming-slang version of the more common word. It was probably coined in the 1970s, inspired by the savoury dry biscuits called 'cream crackers'.

crease *n British*
the anus, buttocks, the female genital area. The vulgarism, in use especially in the northwest of England, is often heard in phrases such as 'a kick up the crease'.

creasing, creasing up *adj British*
overcome by laughter. The terms have become fashionable, especially in black speech, since 2000.
> '*You tell me it's OK for whites to imitate black culture? I'm creasin'.*'
> (Recorded, black female, London, March 2004)

creature-features *n*
a mild term of abuse among schoolchildren. It may originate in 'creature-feature', a show-business jargon term for a horror film of the 1950s.

creatures, the creatures *n pl British*
prison warders. A prisoners' term conveying more bitterness than the more usual **screws**.

cred *adj, n British*
(having) 'street credibility'. A 1980s adolescent vogue term inspired by the earlier cliché.

creep *vb*
1. *American* to attempt to seduce, make unwelcome sexual advances (towards)
2. to cheat on a man
An expression used on campus in the USA since around 2000.

creeping Jesus *n*
an unpleasantly insincere, untrustworthy or complaining person; a creep, sneak or **whinger**. This strange expression of distaste is mainly heard among middle-class speakers in Britain and Australia; it dates, according to the *Oxford English Dictionary*, at least to 1818.

creep (someone) out *vb*
to disgust, disquiet someone. Formed from the colloquial 'creepy', the phrase is popular among younger teenagers.
> '*I don't care: he creeps me out, plus he smells gross...*'
> (*The X-Files*, US TV series, 1996)

creepshow *adj*
frightening, grotesque or merely unpleasant. An American teenagers' word, from the title of a horror film released in 1982. The adjective is an elaboration of 'creepy' and the earlier term 'creepsville', and has been heard among British teenagers since the late 1980s.
> *a creepshow party*
> *her creepshow boyfriend*

cremated adj British
ruined, destroyed, defeated, trounced. A coinage of the 1980s combining the notions of 'killed' and **burned**. The term was briefly in vogue among **yuppies**.
'If the market moves in a big way we'll get cremated.'
(*Serious Money*, Caryl Churchill, 1987)

creps n pl British
trainers, sports shoes. Heard in London since 2000, the word may derive from 'creep' or, conceivably, from 'crêpe(-soles)'.

cretin n British
someone who is craving a drug or drugs. A term used by young street-gang members in London since around 2000.

crew[1] n
1a. *British* a gang. A word used since the 1960s by street gangs, especially **skinheads** and football hooligans, to refer to themselves. It was a synonym for a band (of ruffians) 300 years earlier.
1b. *American* a group of young people. Unlike the British sense which implies violence, this 1980s usage usually referred to hip hop artists, break dancers or **scratch** musicians.

crew[2] vb American
to belong to a gang or social group. An item of black street slang of the 1990s, the verb is formed from the earlier noun usage.

crib n
1a. *American* a home, flat or accommodation. A common term in black street slang sometimes adopted, usually facetiously, by white adolescents.
I'm going crib.
1b. a room in a student hostel
1c. *American* a person from the same home-town
He's my crib.
This extended sense of the term has been heard since the end of the 1990s.

crim[1] n
a criminal. A term heard increasingly from the late 1980s; it is probably originally an Australian usage.

crim[2], **crimble, crimbo** n British
Christmas. These are adults' nursery words (probably originally from Liverpool) which were popularised, particularly by radio disc jockeys, in the 1970s.
'Stevie's determined to have a well wacky Crimble do – even by his standards.'

(*Just Seventeen* magazine, December 1987)

cringe (someone) vb British
to embarrass, discomfit or excruciate. A mainly middle-class usage of the late 1980s.
'Would it cringe you too much if I used my [cell-]phone here?'
(Recorded, yuppie to companion in opera-house bar, London, June 1988)

crinkle n British
banknotes, money. This term was used by bookies, **spivs**, etc. in the 1950s and is now probably obsolete. **Crackle** was a synonym.
I need some crinkle in a hurry.

crinkly n British
1. an elderly person or adult. A young person's dismissive (or sometimes grudgingly affectionate) term. It forms part of the group of post-1970 vogue terms which includes **dusty, crumbly** and **wrinklie**.
2. a banknote, especially formerly a £1 banknote. The term was used by **Sloane Rangers** in the late 1970s.

crippled adj
drunk. An item of student slang in use in London and elsewhere since around 2000.

cris, criss, crissed, crisp adj
1. excellent, attractive
That dress is so cris.
2. suffering from a hangover or exhaustion
I woke up feeling really criss.
In both senses the words have been in vogue since around 2000.

crispy adj American
1a. suffering from a hangover. A teenage and adolescent vogue word of 1988. Its provenance is uncertain; it may evoke the notion of 'brittle' or 'fragile'.
1b. unpleasant, inferior. The generalised term, in use among American adolescents in the 1990s, seems to postdate the more specific sense above.
2. smart, neat

criss-kross n
a foolish and/or obnoxious person. A term used by young street-gang members in London since around 2000.

critter n Canadian
an unattractive, unsophisticated male. The usage, recorded in 2004, employs the North American dialect pronunciation of 'creature'.

croak *vb*
1. to die. An unsentimental term presumably derived from the choking death rattle or rasping dying words. The usage dates from the 19th century.

He croaked before he could tell us anything useful.

2. to kill. An American gangster and prison term.

The guy threatened to croak his business partner.

croaker *n British*
a doctor who prescribes for addicts. A drug addicts' and prisoners' term in use since the 1960s, although the notion of the death-dealing doctor thus expressed goes back to the 19th century.

croc(k) *n British*
a stupid and/or irritating person. The word occurred in the speech of London schoolchildren in the early 1990s. Its exact etymology is uncertain, although in early 19th-century dialect the word denoted a worthless or worn-out animal and it was later used in public-school slang to refer to a weak or unsporting fellow pupil.

crock, crock of shit *n American*
nonsense, something worthless and unpleasant. 'It's a crock!' is an expression (inoffensive enough to be used on TV) which was employed in the 1970s and 1980s to dismiss, deride or reject something such as false information. In North America the word crock, for container, is not archaic as it is in Britain and Australia.

crocked *adj*
1. *American* drunk. A word used, e.g., by college students, in the 1980s. It probably comes from the old use of 'crocks' as containers for pickling or preserving in alcohol or, particularly in Canada, as containers for whiskey. Alternatively, the derivation may be the same as that of the following sense.
2. *American* angry. This use of the word is connected with an archaic or dialect use of 'crock' and 'crook' to mean an old, infirm, cantankerous and complaining person.
3. *British* broken or injured, used particularly of sportsmen incapacitated through injury. From the standard English sense of crock as a potsherd, or from a dialect term for a decrepit animal.

croggie *n British*
a ride on the crossbar or handlebars of another rider's bicycle. An item of schoolchildren's slang recorded in 2003.

Come on, give us a croggie home will you?

cron(z) *n American*
a gun. The term, which usually refers to a handgun, originated in black street argot in the 1990s. Its derivation is obscure.

cronk *n, adj American*
(something) excellent, powerful. In use since 2000, the word may be an alteration of **chronic**, as applied, e.g., to high-grade marihuana. It might alternatively be related to **crunk**, but that seems to be a more recent coinage.

crook *adj Australian*
unwell, unhealthy, wrong, dubious. A common term in Australia, crook is either an alteration of the archaic slang term 'cronk' (from the German and Yiddish *krank*) meaning ill, or of crooked, meaning bent out of shape. By 1988, due to the influence of Australian soap operas, the word could be used in a British newspaper or magazine, although it has not as yet penetrated British speech.

crovey *adj British*
excellent. A term of unknown origin in use among teenagers since the late 1990s. It could conceivably be a deformation of **groovy**.

Croydon facelift *n British*
a tightly scraped-back hairstyle such as a ponytail or bun.
See also **chav**

crubbing *n*
a less common synonym for **grinding**

crucial *adj British*
a Jamaican code word from the radical self-dramatising slang of **rude boys** and reggae devotees, crucial became a vogue term of appreciation in London around 1979, first among black youth and later their white imitators. Lenny Henry, the black comedian, brought the word to a wider audience by including it in the scripts of his television series, in the mouth of the character 'Delbert Wilkins'.

crud *n*
1a. anything filthy, disgusting or worthless, including excrement, any encrusted or coagulated substance and (in Ameri-

can English) the effects of skin infection. Crud is from the Middle English *crudde*, a dialect word related to the standard English 'curd'.

1b. a worthless, despicable person (usually male). A word used widely in the 1960s, in place of taboo synonyms such as **turd**.

cruddy *adj*
unpleasant, inferior, worthless. A word in vogue in the mid-1960s. It is now heard mainly among schoolchildren.

cruel *vb Australian*
to spoil, frustrate, defeat. This use of the word often occurs in the phrase 'to cruel it' meaning to ruin or jeopardise an enterprise.

cruise *vb*
1a. (used intransitively) to move around in search of a sexual partner. The word was first used by prostitutes seeking clients then, in the 1960s, by **gays**, and subsequently in the 1970s by heterosexuals, especially those frequenting singles bars.
1b. (used transitively) to actively try to attract a particular potential sexual partner. The overtones of cruising a person are a discreet display of oneself with some unmistakable hints or 'come-ons'.

crumb (it) *vb American*
to ruin, mess up. From 'crumble' in its standard sense, reinforced by the notion of acting like a 'crumb' (the obsolescent noun form denoting a worthless person) and by **crummy**.

> *'You crumbed the play.'*
> (*House of Games*, US film, David Mamet, 1987)

crumble *n British*
a generic term for old or senile people. Used since the 1980s in the expression 'a bit of crumble' for instance, or by nursing staff to refer contemptuously to their elderly patients.

crumbly, crumblie *n British*
1a. an old person. In spite of the suggestion of crumbling or falling apart, the term is only mildly contemptuous and may even be used affectionately. Coincidentally, the 1960s French slang term for old or 'past it' was *croulant*, meaning crumbling.

> *'Senior citizens, inevitably, watch 37 hours a week. "Audiences are getting crumbly", says Street-Porter in media-speak.'*

(*Independent*, 23 March 1988)

1b. a parent or adult. Used by children and teenagers since the mid-1970s. A fairly inoffensive middle- and upper-class word favoured by **Sloane Rangers** among others.
See also **wrinkly**; **crinkly**; **dusty**

crumb-snatcher *n*
a baby or small child. Like **ankle-biter**, **rug rat**, etc., the phrase can be used affectionately and/or ruefully.

crummy, crumby *adj*
dilapidated, dirty, worthless. By the mid-19th century this word was in use in Britain as a literal and figurative synonym for 'lousy', apparently due to the resemblance of body lice to crumbs. The word (usually spelled with double 'm') has remained in widespread use in Britain and the USA.

crump *n, adj British*
(something) unpleasant, of poor quality, disappointing. A vogue term among teenagers in 2005, it may be a variant of **crumby** or ironically of **cronk**.

crumpet *n British*
a woman, or women viewed collectively as sex objects. 'Crumpet' or 'a bit of crumpet' date from the last decade of the 19th century and conform to a much older pattern of likening women to cakes (e.g. **tart**), delicacies (e.g. **crackling**), etc. The terms 'crumpet' or 'a bit of crumpet' are now likely to offend most women although both are still widespread, mainly in working-class usage. Women are now beginning to use the terms to refer to males.

> *'I don't think we should condemn a doctor simply because he made a wrong diagnosis of what is, or is not, crumpet.'*
> (*Carry on Again, Doctor*, British comedy film, 1969)

crunchie *n American*
a lesbian, particularly a lesbian with austere habits and 'utopian' views. 'Crunchies' were one faction of lesbians at Yale University in the late 1980s, the other being so-called **lipsticks**.

crunk *adj American*
1a. enjoyable, fun, spirited

> *'...we the type of people make the club get crunk...'*
> (From *Rosa Parks*, single by US band Outkast, 1998)

1b. popular

1c. a variant spelling of **cronk**

2. intoxicated by drink or drugs

The term, in all its senses, has been in vogue since the late 1990s. It may originate as a blend of crazy and drunk.

crush *vb*

1. *American* to eat

Man, she crushed that whole pizza in, like, 30 seconds.

2. *American* to have sex (with)

3. *British* to disturb, annoy

Quit crushing me, bro'.

All usages date from around 2000.

crusher *n British*

a boring, tedious person; a 'crushing' bore. An alternative to **crasher**, typically used by middle- and upper-class speakers since the 1980s.

crust *n British*

(one's) head. This London working-class usage is almost always heard in the forms **off one's crust** or **do one's crust**.

crustie *n British*

a homeless person and/or beggar, especially a member of a militant subculture of importunate vagrants of the early 1990s, centred on the English West Country, who practised deliberate self-degradation and embraced personal filthiness (hence the name, from the encrustations on bodies and clothing). Other names for members of the same subculture were **fraggles**, **hedgers**, **scrotes**, **smellies**, **soap-dodgers** and **cider-punks**.

'The Crusties of Bath are, with their counterparts at the other end of the social spectrum, the smooth lawyers and medics, considerably more redolent of the city Jane Austen knew than anything else the tourist is likely to see.'

(Reader's letter to the *Independent*, November 1991)

crut *n*

dirt, distasteful material or unpleasantness in general. A version of **crud** (normally felt to be less offensive than that word).

crutching, crotching (it) *n British*

smuggling illicit substances (tobacco, drugs, etc.) in bodily crevices. An item of prison slang recorded in the 1990s.

cruttess *n, adj*

(someone who is) ugly, repellent. One of a number of synonyms (including the adjectives **off-key** and **bungled**) in use

among gang members, hip hop aficionados, etc. in the UK since 2000.

cry Ruth/Hughie/Ralph *vb*

to vomit. All these humorous equivalents attempt to imitate the sound of hearty or sudden retching. They have been popular, particularly with students, all over the English-speaking world since the 1960s.

crystal *n*

an amphetamine, or cocaine. An item of drug users' jargon.

cube *n*

an extremely **square** person. A derogatory **hipsters'** and **beatnik** term last heard in the early 1960s.

cubehead *n American*

a user of the hallucinogenic drug LSD (lysergic acid diethylamide). A term used in the mid-1960s, when LSD was frequently taken orally on sugar cubes.

cubicle monkey *n American*

a desk-bound office worker or IT specialist. A derisive term used both by the victims of workplace tedium and happily peripatetic colleagues.

cum *n, vb See* **come**[1]

cumulonimbus *n British*

cunnilingus. A usage recorded by *Viz* comic's *Profanisaurus* in 2001.

cunt *n*

1a. the vagina. This taboo word has ancient origins; related words exist in other European languages (French *con*, Spanish *coño*, etc.) and it seems that, in the unwritten prehistoric Indo-European parent languages, *cu* or *koo* was a word base expressing 'feminine' or 'fecund' and associated notions.

1b. a woman or women in general. An extension of the above sense which is probably most commonly heard in the USA.

2. a very unpleasant person. As well as being the most 'obscene' of the common set of sexually related taboo words, 'cunt' is also used to indicate extreme distaste or dislike. This usage, which is more noticeable in British and Australian English than American, is presumably inspired by deep-seated fear and loathing of women's sexuality, although in practice the word is usually applied to men.

From Anglo-Saxon times until the 14th century the word was in standard use, but was then replaced by euphemisms in all but rural dialect speech. Most dictionaries refused to acknowledge the word until the 1960s and it is probably the only word that is still banned from most British newspapers and television.

cunted *adj British*

1a. exhausted

1b. intoxicated by alcohol or drugs

'I went to a bop last night and got totally cunted.'

(Recorded, female university student, London, 2000)

A term which, although forceful, has no sexual or taboo connotations. Used by speakers of both sexes. **Twatted** is a contemporary synonym.

cupcake *n American*

1. a cute or attractive woman. A deliberately humorous or (consciously or unconsciously) patronising male term of endearment. 'Cupcakes' are small, usually iced, buns.

2. an eccentric person

curling *n British*

drinking alcohol, especially beer. The expression is a synonym for **bend**(ing) **the elbow**, heard in the Midlands and north of England.

currant bun *n British*

1a. the sun

1b. a son

Both rhyming-slang uses have been in evidence in London working-class use since at least the 1940s.

2. a *nun*. A rare item of rhyming slang heard occasionally from at least the 1950s.

curry-queen *n*

a **gay** male who is attracted to South Asian partners.

Compare **rice-queen**

curse, the curse *n*

menstruation, a monthly period. This is the standard term used by schoolgirls and women; its probable origin is in Genesis, in which Eve is 'cursed' by God who promises to 'multiply thy sorrow and thy conception: in sorrow thou shalt bring forth children'. The 'curse of Eve' thus became a euphemism for the most troublesome aspect of femininity.

I've got the curse, I'm afraid.

cushdy, cushti, kushti *adj British*

fine, wonderful. An all-purpose term of approbation or agreement. This working-class term (recently brought to a wider audience by the television comedy *Only Fools and Horses*) is related to 'cushy', the colloquial term for easy or comfortable. Both words derive ultimately from an archaic Persian word *khosh*, meaning 'pleasant', either via the Hindustani *khush*, or the Romany *kushto*, or both.

cuss (someone) off *vb*

to criticise, denigrate someone. The phrase is in black usage in Britain and the USA and may have originated in Caribbean speech.

custard *n British*

a very unpleasant person. The playground term of abuse, in use since 2000, is a blend of **cunt** and **bastard**.

cut[1] *vb*

to dilute or adulterate (illicit drugs), usually with the intention of increasing weight and hence profit

The coke was cut with lactose.

cut[2] *adj*

circumcised

'Everyone knows what cut and uncut means.'

(Male prostitute, Channel 4 documentary *Hookers, Hustlers, Pimps and their Johns*, October 1994)

cut (someone) a little slack *vb American*

to relax regulations, to make allowances for or give room to move. The image is of tailoring something for relatively unrestricted ease of movement.

Come on, cut me a little slack will you?

cut a rug *vb*

to dance. A lighthearted expression which was fashionable in the jitterbug era and in the post-war language of rock and **jive**. It still survives in jocular use.

cute *adj See* **completely cute**

cut it *vb*

to succeed, manage. A shortened form of 'cut the mustard' or 'cut some ice'.

'Her experience among women rappers trying to cut it in the macho world of hip hop led Charlotte to look again at the girl groups from the Seventies she'd always loved.'

(*Ms London* magazine, 4 September 1989)

cuz *n American*

a term of address (derived from 'cousin') for a stranger or friend. An expression used on campus in the USA since around 2000.

cuzzer n British
a curry meal. The standard word has been modified with the suffix indicating familiarity and/or affection.

c-word, the n British
cunt

cyberpunk n
an enthusiast for information technology, a **net-head**. The term arose in the 1980s to describe young fans of the science-fiction writer William Gibson, who combined a fascination for computing and youth culture with a supposedly **punk** attitude. In the later 1990s the word usually referred to a nonconformist user of the Internet.

'Just launched, Cyberseed describes itself as Britain's first Cyberpunk event, which will, it is hoped, one Friday every month, present a vision where man, music and machine contrive to be one.' (*Sunday Times*, 12 December 1993)

D

D, d *n*
1. dope, illicit drugs. The predictable abbreviation was typically used by British cannabis smokers in the early and mid-1970s.

Hey, man, got any d?

2. *Australian* a detective. This abbreviation dates from the 19th century and is now almost archaic. It has metamorphosed into **demon**.

D.A. *n British*
1. a hairstyle in which the hair is scraped back and greased into a curl on the nape of the neck. It is an abbreviation of **duck's arse**. The style was popular among **teddy boys** in the 1950s and, to a lesser extent, with the **rockers** of the early 1960s.
2. drug addict. An abbreviation used, generally facetiously, by drug users themselves in the mid- and late 1960s.

da bomb *n, adj See* **bomb**

dabs *n pl British*
1. fingerprints. The term has been used by police officers, criminals and crime writers since the 1930s at least. It derives from the fingerprinting process in which the suspect presses his or her fingers on an ink pad.

We managed to lift some dabs from the wine glasses.

2. money, pounds. The term is usually, but not invariably, heard in the plural form, especially in the north of England.

Daddies, the *n pl British*
a group of respected or prestigious males, the 'in-crowd'. From army and Officer Training Corps usage.

daddio, daddy-o *n*
a man, usually one who is old. A variant of 'Dad' and 'Daddy', used as a term of address. It originated in the **jive talk** of black jazz musicians in the 1940s, and was adopted by the **beatniks** of the 1950s. The word implied a degree of respect or affection, usually for someone older or in authority. In later use, e.g. by

British **teddy boys** and **beatniks**, it was often a teasing or mocking form of address.

daddy *n British*
1. a dominant inmate among prisoners
2. an older and/or dominant male homosexual in a relationship, group or institution

daffy *adj*
silly, eccentric. The rather dated colloquialism was revived by adolescents from the later 1990s. Its ultimate origin is the Middle English *daffe*, meaning a 'fool'.

dag *n Australian*
1. (a piece of dried) sheep dung. This sense of the word dates from the 16th century, but has become archaic in Britain. It usually refers to the dried flakes adhering to tail wool.
2. a stupid or unpleasant person, by extension from the first sense. By the late 1980s 'dag' had become a fairly mild all-purpose insult or description, freely used for instance in television soap operas such as *Neighbours*.

dagga *n South African*
cannabis, marihuana. This is the most common term for these drugs in South Africa and it derives from local African languages. It is occasionally heard elsewhere among drug users.

daggy *adj Australian*
stupid, unpleasant. From the noun **dag**. A brusque but fairly mild expression of distaste (deemed suitable for inclusion in the scripts of TV soap operas, for instance).

dago *n*
1a. a person of Hispanic origin (Spanish or Latin American). This derogatory meaning is probably the original sense of the word in that it derives from the Hispanic proper name 'Diego' (James). The word usually has this sense when used by British speakers.

1b. an Italian. This has become the most common American sense of the word. 'Dago' is sometimes used as an indiscriminate insult to persons, usually male, of Mediterranean origin.

dainties *n pl*
(women's) panties, knickers. A jokily coy euphemism heard in both America and Australia from the mid-1970s.

dairybelle *n South African*
an attractive woman, especially one with large breasts. The term is an adoption of the brand name of milk and cheese products.

daisy *n*
a male homosexual or an effeminate man. The word in this sense is not common, but occurs occasionally in British, American and Australian usage.

daisy chain *n*
a group of people taking part in 'serial' sexual activity; cunnilingus, fellatio, penetration, etc. in series

daks *n pl*
trousers. From the trademark name of a brand of casual trousers sold since the 1930s in Britain and Australia. The word's popularity was boosted by its use in the *Barry McKenzie* cartoon series in *Private Eye* magazine, usually in the phrase **drop one's daks**.

damage *n British*
an attractive female or females in general. A male usage recorded in 2004. **Biffage** is a synonym.
  major damage
  Check out the damage.

dame *n*
a woman. An Americanism usually identified with the criminal, musical, etc. milieus of the 1920s, 1930s and 1940s. The usage obviously derives from the original British 13th-century title of 'Dame' (itself from the Latin *domina*, via Old French), which quickly became a synonym for a woman in dialect and rural speech. Like **doll**, **broad** and, to some extent, **chick**, the term now sounds dated.

damn skippy! *exclamation American*
a strong expression of agreement. It is a more recent version of colloquial phrases such as 'darn tootin' (right)' or 'damn straight'.
  'Did you nail that cute co-ed?' 'Damn skippy!'

damp *adj*
1. *British* a middle-class synonym for **wet** in the sense of ineffectual or feeble
  I always found Jenny's husband a bit damp.
2. (of a woman) sexually aroused
  'On the Jonathan Ross show one night I saw a female comic asked how she viewed the prospect of the next guest, a renowned male hunk. "I'm damp", she replied, and went on to repeat the assertion a few times. "Damp. Yes, I'm really damp". There was no joke as such, no turn or twist or wit, just a blank description.'
  (Sebastian Faulks, *Independent* magazine, 28 October 1989)

d and d *adj*
drunk and disorderly. The phrase in full is police or judicial jargon; the abbreviation is a euphemism used by police officers in the USA and, in Britain, facetiously by drinkers.
  Terry was completely d and d again last night.

dang *n American*
1. the penis. A rare variant of **dong**.
2. a euphemism for 'damn'

dangleberries *n pl*
a variation of **dingleberries**

dangler *n*
1. the penis. A nursery euphemism also used facetiously among adults.
2. *Australian* a **flasher**, a male sexual exhibitionist
3. *British* a trailer, when attached to a truck or tractor
4. *American* a trapeze artist

danglers *n pl*
the testicles. An old and predictable euphemism heard, e.g., in British public schools and the armed forces.

dank[1] *adj American*
excellent. This sense of the word may be influenced by its use as a nickname for potent marihuana.

dank[2] *n American*
(high-grade) marihuana. So called because of its dark colour and moist, sticky consistency.

Danny (La Rue) *n British*
a **clue**, invariably as part of a phrase in utterances such as 'Don't ask me, I haven't got a Danny La Rue'. The rhyming slang uses the name of the female-impersonating UK variety star. **Scooby(-doo)** is a synonym.

da nuts *n, adj*
the best or the greatest, excellent. The phrase, poular since around 2000, is a euphemism for **the dog's bollocks**.

That man is da nuts.

dap *adj American*
elegant, smart, fashionable. The term, heard in black and campus speech, is a shortening of 'dapper'.

dap-dap *n, adj American*
(an individual considered) attractive, well dressed, fashionable. An elaboration of **dap** favoured by younger teenagers in California and featured in the 1996 US film *Clueless*.

dapper *n British*
a stylish, successful or dominant male. The noun form of the standard adjective has existed in London street slang since 2000, probably originating in black usage.

dappy *n, adj British*
(a person who is) silly, clumsy, eccentric. This blend of dippy and daffy was in use among schoolchildren and teenage speakers in the early 1990s.

daps *n pl British*
tennis shoes, plimsolls. The word may echo the sound of light footfalls or derive from an archaic dialect verb meaning to 'dart' or 'pad'. 'Daps' was a particularly popular term among teenagers and schoolchildren in Wales and the Southwest in the 1960s.

darb¹ *vb British*
to have sex. In this sense the word was recorded among London schoolgirls in 1993. Its origins are unknown and it seems not to be related to the identical American noun.

darb² *n, adj American*
(someone or something) excellent or admirable. The word seems to have originated in the 1920s and is said to derive from Ruby 'Darby', the name of a popular showgirl.

dare *adj British*
good, fantastic. A vogue term in use among teenage gang members. The term, sometimes in the form of an exclamation of approval, was recorded in use among North London schoolboys in 1993 and 1994.

dark *adj*
1. *British* behaving harshly, unfairly or unpleasantly (to another person). Used in this way the term is part of the slang code heard among London teenagers since the 1990s. It probably originated in the black Caribbean community, although the same word was employed to mean stupid or obtuse in 17th-century English slang.

'I didn't like it that he was actin' dark.'

(Recorded, North London schoolboy, 1993)

2. stylish, impressive. This sense of the word derives from its use to describe 'moody, deep' drum 'n' bass music in the later 1990s.

Darren *n British*
an uncouth, unfashionable and/or unfortunate male. A synonym, in use since around 2000, for the earlier **Kevin** and **Wayne** and the contemporary **Trev**, playing, like the female **Sharon**, on the supposedly negative social connotations of some common first names.

dash¹ *n*
money, a bribe or tip. The term is from West Africa, where it derives from *dashee*, a local African dialect term. It may be the origin of the more common **dosh**.

dash² *vb British*
to throw away. A usage recorded among young Londoners in 2004.

date *n*
1. *Australian* the anus. Presumably by association with the colour of the fruit, or just possibly from the archaic British rhyming slang 'date and plum' meaning **bum**.

2. *British* a stupid, silly or weak person. This rare usage (probably by association with the texture of an over-ripe date) is now nearly obsolete, but was heard until the 1960s, especially in the phrases 'you soft date' and 'you soppy date'. Such phrases now survive only in nursery language.

3. a prostitute's assignation with a client. An item of police slang recorded by the London *Evening Standard* magazine, February 1993.

date roll *n Australian*
a *toilet roll*. Derived from **date 1**.

David *n British*
semen. This 1996 term from the language of adolescents puns on the surname of the sports hero and Arsenal and England goalkeeper, David Seaman.

David (Gower) *n British*
a *shower*. An instance of educated rhyming slang which borrows the name of the cricketer, heard among university students from the 1990s.

David (Mellor) *n British*
(a drink of) *Stella* Artois lager, playing on the name of the notorious Tory politician turned journalist. **Nelson (Mandela)**, **Paul (Weller)** and **Uri (Geller)** are synonyms, all popular with students since the late 1990s.

Davy Crockett *n British*
pocket. A piece of rhyming slang inspired by the cult film about the American pioneer for which there was a craze in 1956. **Sky rocket** and **Lucy Locket** are synonyms.

dawg, dog *n American*
a friend. This term of affection, originating in southern speech, became one of the most widespread slang vogue words in US usage from around 2000.

daylighting *n*
working (usually illicitly) at a second job during daylight hours. An obvious derivation from the colloquial 'moonlighting'.

deacon *n British*
a stupid person, **Benny**, **spack**. Allegedly from 'Joey Deacon', an elderly cerebral palsy victim featured on TV in the early 1980s. The term is used by schoolchildren.

deadass *n, adj American*
(a person who is) very boring, feeble or very stupid
  He's a real deadass.
  What a deadass town.

dead bang *adv, adj American*
caught in flagrante or red-handed. An American police version of **dead to rights** or the British **bang to rights**.
  'I got you dead bang for breaking into Eddie's apartment.'
  (*The Rockford Files*, US TV crime series, 1979)

deadbeat *n*
1a. a poor or homeless person
1b. a penniless scrounger, a freeloader
1c. a worthless or stupid person
All these senses derive from a 19th-century Americanism in which 'dead' means 'completely' and 'beat' is not 'exhausted' but a 'loafer' or **hobo**.

dead-crack *adj British*
penniless, broke

deadhead[1] *n*
1. a very stupid, lifeless or boring person. An obvious derivation of its component parts, this phrase is reinforced by its 19th-century American meaning of non-paying passengers or non-participants (from a 'dead head' of cattle).
  'This is a stoners' western for crystal-dangling deadheads.'
  (*Evening Standard* film review, 22 July 2004)
2. *Australian* an idle person, a good-for-nothing
3. a fan or devotee of the San Francisco rock group The Grateful Dead, who were popular in the late 1960s and early 1970s, and enjoyed a revival in the 1980s

deadhead[2] *vb American*
(of a vehicle) to run or drive empty or without passengers. This meaning, a relic of 19th-century cattle drives, is now rarely heard.
See also **deadhead**[1] 1

deadleg[1] *n British*
1. a feeble, lazy or disappointing person. This word has been used from the 1950s and may derive from an earlier armed-forces term 'deadlegs', meaning a cripple or someone who refuses to rise from bed.
  'The usual crowd of airheads, phonies, deadlegs, posers, bimbos, wallies, wannabees, hangers-on and gate-crashers.'
  (Christena Appleyard, *Daily Mirror*, 11 May 1989)
2. a numb feeling in the leg following a kneeing in the thigh by an attacker

deadleg[2] *vb British*
the action of kneeing someone in the thigh. A popular school playground tactic.

deadly *adj Irish*
excellent, **cool**. The term was recorded with this sense in 2003.

dead meat *n*
a person who is dead, about to die or inevitably doomed. Dead meat is an old and heartless euphemism for a corpse. Now the phrase usually forms part of a threat.
  Do that, baby, and you're dead meat!

deadneck *n American*
a variant of **deadhead**, **deadbeat**, etc.

dead presidents *n pl American*
money, banknotes

deadshit n, adj Australian

(a person who is) contemptible or very unpleasant

That was a deadshit party.

dead soldier n

an empty bottle (of alcohol). The phrase was first used by members of the British armed forces about 200 years ago, likening the aftermath of a drinking bout to a battlefield littered with corpses.

I'll clear up the dead soldiers while you fumigate the place.

dead to rights adv, adj American

an American version of the British **bang to rights**. 'Dead to rights' is probably the original form of the phrase, dating from the 19th century and now rarely, if ever, heard in Britain.

'Dead' is used here in its common colloquial meaning of 'completely'.

deal[1] n British

a portion or amount of a drug, especially hashish. Before decimalisation in 1971, very small amounts of cannabis were bought or referred to as a 'five-bob deal' or 'ten-bob deal'.

deal[2] vb

to sell (drugs). The verb is used intransitively, as in 'does he still deal?', and transitively, as in 'she deals dope at the weekend'.

dealer n

a supplier of illicit drugs. The term, imported into other English-speaking areas from the USA in the early 1960s, is a neutral one, implying someone who sells on demand without coercion. It replaced the earlier, pejorative word **pusher** among users themselves.

dealing adj British

involved in a relationship, 'seeing someone'. A fashionable term from the older adolescent's lexicon of dating, heard from the later 1990s. The word had been used in the same sense by public schoolgirls in the 1960s.

deal with (someone) vb British

to beat up. A term used by young street-gang members in London since around 2000.

deb n

1. a debutante; a young girl being introduced into the social season. Although principally identified with an upper-class London milieu, the adoption of *débutante*, French for 'beginner', may have occurred in the USA in the first decade of the 20th century.

2. *American* a female member of a street gang. A term used in the 1960s, usually in the plural, probably originating in 'debutante', perhaps reinforced by the prevalence of the Christian name Deborah or Debbie. 'Deb' resurfaced in the gang argot of Los Angeles in the 1980s.

de-bag vb British

to remove (someone's) trousers. The phrase originated among 19th-century university students but quickly spread to schoolboys for whom the ritual humiliation of fellow pupils by de-bagging was a popular diversion up to the late 1960s at least. **Bags** was a 19th-century slang term for trousers which survived until fairly recently.

debs' delight n British

an upper-class young man, especially one who might be considered an eligible partner or escort by parents (of debutantes), in spite of low intelligence. The phrase was used pejoratively and/or enviously and was popular in the 1960s. A more recent version is **pedigree chum**.

deck[1] vb

to knock (someone) to the ground. A variant of 'to floor'.

deck[2] n

1. a portion or package of illicit drugs, especially heroin. The term, from American addicts' jargon of the 1960s, spread to Britain and Australia where the meaning was sometimes amended to refer to an injection, or the amount (of heroin) necessary for an injection.

2. a skateboard or surfboard in the jargon of aficionados

deck up vb

to prepare for injection or to inject a drug, usually heroin. A phrase from the jargon of drug users and prisoners in the UK The verb derives from the noun **deck**, meaning a quantity of a narcotic.

decorators n pl British See **have the decorators in**

deep-sea diver n

a £5 note, *fiver*. A piece of London rhyming slang heard occasionally since about the mid-1970s.

deep-six vb American

to bury, dispose of. The verb form, which has been common in American speech since the 1950s, derives from the earlier noun form 'the deep six', an underworld euphemism for the grave. The ultimate origin is nautical; burials at sea have to be made in water that is more than six fathoms deep.

'I've got to exchange all this money!' 'You can deep-six it, sir.'
(*M.A.S.H.*, US TV series, 1977)

def *adj*
excellent, wonderful, 'the real thing'. A late 1980s vogue term of approbation deriving from the language of hip hop. The word is a shortening of 'definitive' or 'definite'. The use of the word as the title of a BBC2 'youth slot' programme (*DEF II*) in 1988 marked its apogee. **Det** is a more recent synonym.

'This month's music selections are frightfully def, totally treach and all those other hip hop clichés.'
(*I-D* magazine, November 1987)

de facto *n Australian*
a live-in lover, one's unmarried partner. This phrase is one Australian solution (since the 1970s) to the problem of finding an acceptable term to describe what the British judicial system calls a 'common-law spouse'.

'My de facto's out buying groceries.'
(Recorded, young woman, Melbourne, 1978)

de-frosted *adj American*
heated, agitated. An adolescents' term, inspired by the opposite notion of **cool** or **chilled out**.

Come on, don't get all de-frosted.

dekko *n British*
a look, glance. A word that probably originated in the jargon of tramps, taken from the Romany word for 'look', *dik*, in the late 19th century. British soldiers overseas also encountered the Hindustani version *dekko*. The word is now less popular than in the 1950s but is still heard in the phrase 'take/have a dekko (at)'. The word is not unknown, but is rare in American slang, where it has been recorded as 'decko'.
See also **dick² 2**

Delhi belly *n*
an attack of diarrhoea. Since the era of British colonialism this has been the South Asian equivalent of **gyppy tummy**, **Montezuma's revenge**, etc.

delicious *adj British*
(of a person) attractive, often deliberately mispronounced as 'delshous'. The

term is used typically by teenage girls and students of both sexes.

dementoid, demental *n, adj American*
(a person who is) crazy, demented. A high-school term of the 1980s that expressed contempt, grudging admiration or both. The word is also used adjectivally, as in 'that was a totally dementoid movie'.

demon *n Australian*
a detective. This probably originated in the simple abbreviation D, which then passed via 'd-man' to demon. The word is fairly rare; when it does occur it is often in the plural form.

Dennis (Law) *n British*
hashish or marihuana. The term is rhyming slang for **draw**. The name of the footballer was evoked by adolescents at the end of the 1980s.

Has anyone seen Dennis? [Have you got any smoke?]

dental floss (pants) *n British*
variant forms of the American **floss**

derk, durk *n British*
a stupid person. Used by younger teenagers, the words are formed from or influenced by **dork**, **nerd** and **durr-brain**.

dero *n Australian*
a homeless person or tramp, a derelict. The term has been in use for about twenty years. It is also heard as a fairly mild insult among children and adolescents.

derro *n British*
1. an unfortunate, inferior or unpleasant person. A derivation from 'derelict', used either of vagrants or of someone pitied or disliked.

'And touching someone when you're dancing, Caris intimates, is the act of a derro, a flo-to-tin' yup, a deadbeat, a homebug and a commuter.'
(*Observer*, Section 5, 7 May 1989)

2. a **derry**

derry, deri *n British*
a derelict building or similar location, used as a temporary shelter by tramps, etc.

'It's not a derry, guy, there are people living there.'
(Recorded, vagrant, Waterloo, London, 1988)

desi *n, adj South Asian*
(someone who is) local, indigenous. The term is used in the UK, sometimes pejoratively, by younger or supposedly

sophisticated speakers to refer to traditionalists or recent immigrants.
Compare **freshi**

Desmond *n British*
a lower second university degree, a 2.2 (two-two). This is a student's witticism playing on the name of the black South African community leader Bishop Desmond Tutu. The word was in vogue in 1986 and gave rise to a number of other joky euphemisms, such as **Douglas**, **Pattie**, **Taiwan**, **Richard**, etc.

> 'We all expected Penny to get a James but she ended up with a Desmond.'
> (*Evening Standard*, June 1988)

destroyed *adj*
intoxicated by alcohol or illicit drugs. A widespread colloquialism which has been particularly popular among middle-class speakers since the late 1960s. The word continues the dramatic tendency evidenced by such usages as **smashed**, **bombed**, **wrecked**, etc.

det, dett *adj*
excellent, physically attractive. A vogue term, pronounced with a glottal stop at the end and never a 't' sound, since 2000, it may be a variant form of the earlier **def**.

detox *n, vb*
(to undertake) a course of withdrawal from 'hard' drugs or alcohol; a detoxification, to detoxify. A term from health workers' jargon which is now standard among drug users and patients.

deuce *n*
1a. two dollars or two pounds
> *Just let me have a deuce till tomorrow.*

1b. a two-year prison sentence
> *He pulled a deuce in Club Fed.*

devo *adj American*
apparently 'robotic' or depersonalised. The name of the avant-garde late-1970s band (who presented themselves as near-automatons and semi-retards due to 'devolution') is now used to describe a 'somnambulistic', expressionless person or behaviour. **Stepford** is used in a similar context.
> *acting devo*
> *I don't know what her problem is but she is so devo.*

dex, dexie, dexo *n*
a pill or capsule of Dexedrine, a trademark for an amphetamine (**pep pill**) frequently prescribed and abused in the 1950s and 1960s. Yellow pills of Dexe-

drine were popular among English **mods** of the mid-1960s. Dexy's Midnight Runners, a phrase adopted as the name of a late 1970s white soul group, was an elaborate nickname for the drug.

Dexter *n American*
a conventional and/or boorish male. The pejorative term has been in vogue among adolescents since the late 1990s.

Dezzy *n British*
an alternative form of **Desmond**

dialog(ue) *vb*
to engage in conversation, particularly with the intent to trick, seduce, etc.

diamond *adj British*
first-rate, superb, admirable. A London working-class and underworld term, often heard in the appreciative phrase 'a diamond geezer'.

dib[1] *n*
a contribution, portion, amount of money. This word was in use in Britain in the late 19th century, but is now heard mainly in the USA, typically in children's street or playground games. The plural form was common in England until the late 1950s and survives especially in the expression 'to have dibs on something', meaning to reserve or have first rights to something.

dib[2] *vb, n British*
a partly smoked cigarette saved for relighting later, or the act of extinguishing it. This term, which may originate in a dialect verb meaning to 'pinch' or to 'stub', is used for instance by workmen, labourers and the armed forces.

dick[1] *n*
1. the penis. This use of the word has been widespread in the English-speaking world since the end of the 19th century. It is probably an affectionate personification in origin in the same way as **willie**, etc. This sense of the word is sometimes extended to mean sex in general, as in 'Suzy loves dick'.

> 'Not all women in pop are, or ever have been, brainless bimbos lured into lurex by cynical rock business shitheads with one eye on their cheque books and the other on their dicks.'
> (*Ms London* magazine, 4 September 1989)

2. a fool (invariably male). Dick has this secondary sense in common with most slang terms for the male member, such as **prick**, **tool**, etc.

3. nothing at all. A vulgar emphatic more commonly heard in America and in vogue since the mid-1970s. Its sense is roughly equivalent to the British **bugger-all**.

> *'What do those gimps do all day?' 'They do dick.'*

4. a detective. Almost invariably in the phrase **private dick**. This Americanism, popularised in crime fiction, originated in underworld jargon as a corruption of the word 'detective' itself.

See also **dickless Tracy**

dick² *vb*

1. to have sex (with), penetrate. A predictable but rare term, generated from the noun sense of **dick**.

2. *British* to look at. A variation of the Romany *dik*, meaning to look, from which **dekko** may be derived. This rare term is occasionally heard among tramps, street traders, etc.

See also **dekko**

3. to mess up, mess around (with). A variant of **dick around** or **dick up**.

> *She completely dicked the project.*

dick around *vb*

to mess around (with), behave in a disorganised or aimless way. The expression employs **dick** (the penis) in the same way as **cock**, **prat about**, etc.

dickbrained *adj*

stupid, extremely foolish. A term popular among young people since the 1980s. The adjective is American in origin and the sense of **dick** employed, deriving from 'penis', may be reinforced by the German sense of 'thick'.

dickhead *n*

a fool, an idiot. An old, folksy Americanism which became a vogue term among British youth from around 1980. It may be applied to males or females. Abusive compound words ending in '-head' have proliferated since the end of the 1970s.

> *'The outcome of being a dickhead is that I don't possess any Aretha Franklin singles and make do with compilations.'*
> (John Peel quoted in *New Musical Express*, 7 February 1987)

dickless Tracy *n Australian*

a policewoman. A humorous coinage playing on **dick** (the penis) and 'Dick Tracy', the American comic-strip detective hero created by Chester Gould.

dick up *vb*

to make a mess of. A variant of **cock up** occasionally heard in Britain and Australia.

dick-wad, dick-weed *n*

a despicable, obnoxious or contemptible person. Teenage insults using the combining form **-wad** and its euphemistic version **-weed**.

dicky *adj British*

shaky, insecure, faulty. A colloquialism whose origin is obscure but which dates back at least 150 years. Its original meaning of 'ill' survives in the modern phrase 'a dicky heart'.

> *'Oh, my dicky ticker!'*
> (Catchphrase from *'Allo 'Allo!*, British TV comedy series of the 1980s)

dicky bird *n British*

a *word*. A piece of London rhyming slang which has become a widespread colloquialism, especially in the phrase 'not a dicky bird'. Unlike most modern examples of rhyming slang, it is invariably used in full, presumably to avoid confusion with 'dickie' and **dick**.

did *n British*

a form of **didicoi**

diddle *vb*

1. *British* to cheat. A common colloquialism recorded since the early 1800s.

> *'Comedian Ken Dodd insisted on cash for shows to diddle the taxman, his former agent told a jury yesterday.'*
> (*Daily Mirror*, 5 July 1989)

In Old English *dydrian* meant to deceive or delude; Jeremy Diddler was a fictional swindler (in the 1803 farce *Raising the Wind* by James Kenney).

2a. to have sex with. This sense probably derives from a nursery sense of diddle meaning fiddle with or agitate (*see* **diddle 2b**).

2b. to sexually stimulate (a woman) with the fingers. (In Middle English *dideren* meant to quiver.)

diddlo, didlo *adj British*

crazy, silly or unhinged, 'daft'. An inoffensive Londoners' word popularised by the ITV series *Minder* from the late 1970s.

> *'Right bunch of diddlos, this lot!'*
> (*Minder*, British TV series, 1986)

diddly (squat) *n American*

nothing at all, or something very insignificant, petty or small. Diddly is a nursery term akin to tiddly. The word has been used by adults, alone or in conjunction with other nursery terms (**squat**, **shit**, 'whoop', 'doo', etc.) to express dismissive contempt. A variant form is **doodly squat**.

diddly-dum *adj British*
perfect, fine. A term used typically by students in the 1970s and 1980s, usually in phrases such as 'everything's (just) diddly-dum'. The phrase resembled other mock-nursery inventions such as **dinky-di** and **fair dinkum**.

diddy¹ *n*
1. *British* a fool. A lighthearted term of abuse, heard particularly in Scotland and the north of England.
2. *British* a **didicoi**
3. *Irish* the penis

diddy² *adj British*
small, cute and appealing. A variant of **diddly** popularised by the Liverpool comedian, Ken Dodd.

didicoi, diddicoy, diddyguy, did *n British*
a gypsy or a half-gypsy. The word derives from the Romany *didakeis*, meaning the offspring of a marriage between a full-blooded gypsy and an outsider. The word, which can be spelt in many ways, is often used in country districts to denote any type of gypsy or traveller.

> 'There was this didicoi used to go down our snooker club – couldn't sign his own name but he always had a roll of money on him.'
> (Recorded, carpet fitter, London, 1989)

diesel *adj See* **smutty**

diesel (dyke) *n*
a lesbian who behaves aggressively and/or has a rough masculine appearance or heavy build. The word, which is pejorative and generally used by men, carries overtones of engineers, engines, trucks and other **butch** associations and perhaps also refers to the overalls, dungarees, etc. worn by some lesbians. The term originated in the USA but was heard in Britain in the 1980s as a pejorative term and also as a simple descriptive phrase used by lesbians themselves.

dig *vb*
to understand, appreciate or enjoy. A word from the slang of American swing and jazz musicians which was adopted by the beat generation and thence by teenagers all over the English-speaking world. It is now almost always used iron-ically or facetiously (except in the question form, 'you dig?'). The ultimate origin is perhaps a metaphorical or religious sense of dig (into), meaning 'to apply oneself to (a task)'.

> 'The Seventies were not a decade in which a young artist could kid himself his creative idealism could best be fulfilled grovelling in a muddy field digging Hendrix through a bad acid haze.'
> (*Platinum Logic*, Tony Parsons, 1981)

digerati *n pl*
members of a suppose elite made up of the 'digitally literate'. A cyber slang and journalistic term, based on the notion of the 'literati', heard since 2000.
Compare **liggeratti**

digger *n Australian*
an Australian. The word was used by gold prospectors in the latter half of the 19th century to address or describe one another. It was adopted by British, Canadian and American servicemen in the First World War. **Aussie** has largely replaced digger since the 1960s.

digits *n pl*
a phone number
> *Gimme your digits.*

digs *n pl British*
excitement, thrills. A more recent synonym for **kicks**, used by adolescents during the later 1990s.

dike *n*
a variant spelling of **dyke**

dilbert *n British*
a foolish person. A teenage term of mild abuse from the late 1980s, it is probably a blend of **dill** and the (supposedly comical) Christian names 'Gilbert' or 'Herbert'.

> 'No I'm not – and definitely not with a dilbert like you.'
> (Recorded, schoolgirl, London, 1989)

dildo *n*
1. an artificial penis. The word is approximately 200 years old and probably originates in *diletto*, Italian for (a) delight or darling. Alternatively the term may simply be an invention.
2. a fool, an offensively stupid person. This sense of the word, popular among teenagers since the mid-1970s, may be an embellishment of **dill** as much as a derivative of **dildo 1**.

> 'Oh, come on, he's such a dildo!'
> (Recorded, schoolboy, London, 1988)

dilemma n British
a fight. An item of black street-talk used especially by males, recorded in 2003. It often occurs in the form **mad dilemma**.

dill n
a fool, idiot, silly person. A word which has been recorded in Australia and the USA since at least the early 1950s, and in Britain since the mid-1970s when it was popular among schoolchildren. The word may be a shortening of 'dill pickle' (gherkins may also be the source of **wally**, used to describe a fool), or of 'dilly'.

dillberries, dilberries n pl
a variant of **dingleberries**

dimbo, dimmo n
an unintelligent or dull-witted person. These embellishments of 'dim' (also influenced by 'dumb', **dumbo** and **bimbo**) have been favourite words with British schoolchildren since the late 1970s.

> 'He [Bruce Springsteen] is just dead popular with a lot of dimmos because of the unchallenging nature of what he does.'
> (Alexei Sayle, Great Bus Journeys of the World, 1988)

dim bulb n American
a dimwit or dullard. The phrase evokes a low-wattage light bulb.

dime (someone) vb American
to inform on someone, betray to the police. A back-formation from **dime dropper**, used especially by prison inmates.

dime dropper n American
an informer. An underworld phrase derived from the 'dime' (ten cents) dropped into a payphone when calling the police.

dimlow, dinlow n British
a dim-witted, foolish person. A term of playground abuse of uncertain derivation.

dimmock n British
a dull-witted person. The use of the term, which is based on **dim(mo)** and terms such as **lummock** and **pillock**, predates the television fame of the busty female gardener Charlie Dimmock.

dimp n, vb British
a cigarette end which can be retrieved, typically from the street, and relit. The word, now part of the language of tramps, is also heard as a verb meaning to extinguish (for later smoking). The term seems to be an invention, possibly influenced by 'crimp' and 'damp'.

dimstick n British
a stupid person. The word, used by younger teenagers in the 1990s, is a blend of **dimbo** and **dip-** or **bam-stick**.

din-dins n
dinner or another meal, food. A nursery word which, like many others ('choo-choo', **gee-gee**, **wee-wee**, etc.), is used facetiously by teenagers and adults. The conversion of dinner into din-dins is by a familiar process known as reduplication.

ding[1] adj British
execrable, inferior, unpleasant. The word was recorded in provincial English usage in 2004.

ding[2] n
1. Australian an Italian person or person of Italian descent. The word, of obscure origin and usually pejorative, was also used in the 1940s and 1950s to refer to Greeks.
2. British a stupid person. In playground usage since the 1980s.

ding[3] vb
1. to hit
2. to single out for a reprimand, rejection or for an onerous duty. This use of the word occurs in institutional life in both Britain and America, but its origin is obscure.
> They dinged me.
> He was dinged.
3. to cancel a date (with someone). A variant form of **dingo** heard in 2005.

dingaling, ding-a-ling n
1. an eccentric, crazy or foolish person. A word which originated in the USA and was enthusiastically adopted by schoolchildren in Britain in the late 1960s.
2. the penis. This obscure nursery word was popularised by Chuck Berry's hit song of 1972, 'My Ding-a-Ling'.

dingbat n
1. an eccentric, crazy or foolish person. Originally this was an Australian word, probably derived from 'dingbats' as an adjective (an embellishment of the colloquial 'bats'). The word is now popular in Britain and the USA.
> 'In fact, editing and voice-over combine to ensure that the man never looks a real dingbat.'
> (Independent, 23 December 1988)
2. Australian a Chinese person
3a. any unnamed or unnameable thing. This mainly American sense is influ-

enced by the Dutch and German *ding*, meaning 'thing'.

3b. a typographical symbol, a printers' device. A specialised use of sense **1**.

dingleberry *n*

1. a piece of dung or excrement clinging to hair or wool around the anus. This originally rural notion (applied to sheep and, by extension, to humans) has curiously given rise to a very large number of colourful terms throughout the English-speaking world. Others are **dangleberries**, **dillberries**, **clinkers**, **winnets** and **wittens**, **bum tags**, **chuff-nuts**, etc.

2. a crazy or eccentric person, a fool. Most commonly heard among American high-school and college students; it is inspired by the previous sense (although users may be unaware of the fact).

dingo¹ *n British*

a stupid person. This schoolchildren's word of the 1990s is an alteration of **dimbo**.

dingo² *vb British*

to cancel (a date). The term was recorded among teenagers and university students in 2004.

dingo's breakfast *n Australian*

a **piss** and a look around. A humorous coinage on the lines of **Mexican breakfast** or 'pelican's breakfast'.

dingus *n*

a thing, an obscure or unnamed object. Originally a South African and American version of 'thingy' or 'thingummy', it derives from the Dutch and German *ding*, meaning 'thing'.

dink *n*

1. a silly person, fool or eccentric. The word has been used especially by children and young people in both Britain and America, although possibly coined separately in each.

2. a South-East Asian person. The racist term, probably an arbitrary alteration of **chink**, has been applied in Australia to people of Chinese origin and in the USA to Japanese and Vietnamese.

3. *also* **dinky** *American* one of a childless **yuppie** couple; an acronym for 'double (or dual) income, no kids', coined in New York in 1986. Dink is an example of the American use of acronyms to describe social subgroups. This tendency, which produced **WASP**, **JAP** and, later, yuppies in the 1970s, became a vogue among New Yorkers in the mid-1980s. In spite of

enthusiastic use by some journalists and imitation by their London counterparts, this term, like **guppy**, has achieved only limited currency.

'Take Dink, for instance, which I always thought meant idiot. The other day I heard a girl refer to a yuppie couple as "dinks".'

(*Evening Standard*, 22 January 1987)

4a. *American* the penis. A fairly rare teenage term.

4b. *American* nothing at all. In this sense the equivalent of **dick**.

dinkum *adj Australian See* **fair dinkum**

dinky *n*

1. *British* a car, particularly a large, impressive car. Said self-deprecatingly or admiringly by nouveau-riche working-class speakers and **Sloane Rangers**. Dinky Toys were a brand of miniature model cars popular among children in the 1950s and early 1960s.

2. a **dink 3**

'I have had my year of being a dinky (double income, no kids) and I lost all my friends of any worth to it.'

(Richard Jobson, *Sunday Times*, 9 July 1989)

dinky-di *adj*

1a. *Australian* the real thing (pronounced 'dinkee-die'). Perhaps an embellishment of **fair dinkum**.

1b. *British* perfect, fine (pronounced 'dinkee-dee'; the spelling is arbitrary). A pseudo-nursery term like **diddly-dum**, probably invented by students.

Don't worry, everything's dinky-di.

dip *n*

1. a fool. This word, first heard in the 1970s, is either a back-formation from **dippy** or a short form of **dipstick** or **dipshit**.

'All those people out there, they're just complete dips.'

(Recorded, American teenager, London, 1988)

2. a pickpocket. A Victorian term, still in police and underworld use.

3. *British* an act of sex. The vulgarism usually refers to male sexual activity and was used, e.g., by the stand-up comedian Frank Skinner in stage monologues in 1992. It is derived from the phrase **dip one's/the wick**.

dip (out) *vb American*

to depart, leave. A vogue term from black street slang of the 1990s. The variant form 'do the dip' has also been recorded. A variety of euphemisms (like its contemporaries **bail**, **book**, **jam** and **jet**) for 'run away' are essential to the argot of gang members and their playground imitators.

dip one's/the wick vb
(of a man) to have sex. A vulgar euphemism which is about a century old. 'Wick' is either a shortening of the rhyming slang **Hampton Wick**: **prick**, or a straightforward metaphor from candle wick. Originally British, the term is now used, albeit less commonly, in the USA and Australia.

dip out vb Australian
to fail

dipping n
picking pockets. The term has been in use since the middle of the 19th century.

dippy adj
eccentric, silly or slightly deranged; daft. A British term now in use throughout the English-speaking world. It seems to be an invented word rather than a derivation.

dipshit n
a fool. This vulgarism is sometimes said to be a euphemism for a male homosexual or the male member (compare **dungpuncher**, etc.), but may simply be an elaboration of **dip**.

dipso n
an alcoholic or drunkard. A shortening of the term 'dipsomaniac' (from the Greek *dipsa*, meaning thirst).

dipstick n
a fool. The word is probably a euphemism for **dipshit**, but with less unpleasant overtones. It has been popularised by television series and films in both Britain and the USA since the early 1980s and is a favourite with teenagers.

dipsy n, adj American
1. (an) alcoholic or drunk. In this sense the word is based on 'dipsomaniac', as are **dipso** and 'tipsy'.
2. (a person who is) foolish

dirtbag, **dirtball** n American
a despicable person. These terms of abuse, being strong but not obscene, are frequently heard in films and TV programmes, such as the police series *Hill Street Blues*.

'All right dirtbags, I've had enough.'
(Psychopath in *Beer*, US film, 1985)

dirter n British
an all-purpose term of abuse popular among UK schoolchildren in 2003

dirty adj
1a. possessing or containing illicit drugs, a jargon term used by the police, customs officers and drug users
    His suitcase came through dirty.
1b. British unsafe, illicit, **hot**. This general sense is employed typically by criminals and the police.
2. Australian annoyed, resentful. In this sense the word is often used in the phrase 'to be dirty on (someone)'.
3. excellent. A vogue word in club culture since 2000 by analogy with **bad**, **brutal**, etc. **Filthy** is a synonym. 'It refers to dance music considered so exciting it's positively rude, as used by DJ Brandon Block'.

dirty old man n See **D.O.M.**

disco-biscuits n pl British
tablets of **ecstasy**. The nickname was in use from 1990 and provided the title for an anthology of drug-related writing published in London in 1997.

discombobulated adj
confused, discomfited or distracted. An invented pseudo-Latinate word, normally heard in the adjectival form. It dates from the 19th century when such portmanteau words were popular.
    I've been feeling discombobulated since we got back.

discuss Uganda vb British
to have sex. A euphemism coined in the 1970s by the British satirical magazine *Private Eye*. It has become one of the magazine's long-running jokes and is said to stem from a party at which a female journalist was alleged to have explained an upstairs sexual encounter by saying 'We were discussing Uganda'. (Idi Amin's regime was in the news at the time.) The term 'Ugandan Affairs' is also derived from this source.

dish[1] n
1a. a very attractive woman. This appreciative term (though offensive to most modern women) is one of many that liken a woman to a tasty snack or meal. Unlike **tart** or **crumpet**, e.g., dish was introduced, or perhaps reintroduced (the metaphor was not unknown in earlier times) into Britain from the USA in the 1930s.
1b. a very attractive man. Since the mid-1960s the word has also been used of

men by women and this usage may now be more common than the original.

> *'And those photographs of Mustapha – he was so unattractive, and because you'd had him they said "what a dish".'*
> (Kenneth Halliwell, quoted in Joe Orton's diary, 2 May 1967)

2. *American* gossip. From the phrase **dish the dirt**.

> *'Oh my, this is prime dish. I can't wait to tell the girls.'*
> (*Cheers*, US TV comedy series, 1989)

dish² *vb*

to defeat, destroy or ruin. The original sense of this British term of the 18th century was to swindle, deceive or make a fool of. The image behind the expression was probably that of 'serving up' something (or someone) that has been well and truly 'processed', exploited, etc.

dish the dirt *vb American*

to spread scandalous or malicious gossip. 'Dish' here is, of course, dish up in the sense of 'serve' to an eager audience.

dishy *adj*

very attractive, handsome or beautiful. The adjectival form of **dish** is currently more often used by women than men and is so common in Britain as to be a colloquialism rather than true slang.

diss *vb*

to scorn, snub, belittle. This vogue word of the late 1980s entered adolescent speech via the hip hop and **rap** subcultures originating in the USA. A typical 'clipping', like **def**, **treach**, etc., it is based on the verbs to dismiss, disapprove or disrespect [sic] (perhaps influenced by **dish**).

distress *vb*

to annoy (someone). A vogue use of the standard term, heard since 2000 and probably originating in black speech.

ditch *vb British*

to play truant, **bunk off**. The term has been used (intransitively) by schoolchildren since at least 2000. It may be a transferral of the older colloquial sense of 'ditch' meaning to abandon or dispose of. **Mitch** is a contemporary synonym.

ditsy, ditzy *adj*

silly, eccentric, twee or frivolous. An invented term, popular especially in the USA since the mid-1970s. The word,

which is obviously influenced by 'dizzy', is generally applied to females.

ditz *n*

a silly, eccentric and/or frivolous person; someone who is **ditzy**. An Americanism picked up by some British speakers in the mid-1980s.

div *n British*

a person who is odd, stupid, weak or deviant in some way. This shortening of **divvy** has become popular among young people of all classes since the 1980s. Before that it was part of the lexicon of criminals, tramps, street-traders and workmen.

> *'Him, he's a bit of a div, isn't he?'*
> (Recorded, student, London University, 1986)

dive *n See* **take a dive/tumble/fall**

divebombing *n British*

1. attacking something with spray paints in order to cover it with graffiti. Since the late 1970s the term has been used by young graffiti artists or vandals. **2.** picking up cigarette ends from the street (to relight and smoke). A term used by vagrants in the 1980s.

diving *n American*

picking pockets. An underworld term which is the equivalent of the British **dipping**.

divot *n American*

a toupée or hairpiece. The standard word, denoting a clod of earth and grass dug out by a golfing stroke, has become part of the adolescent lexicon of mockery (like its UK counterparts **syrup (of figs)**, **Irish**, etc.) 'Divot' itself is an old Scottish word of unknown origin.

divvy *adj British*

odd, stupid, deviant, weak or pathetic. This term, of uncertain origin, has existed in the vocabulary of society's 'marginals' since at least the late 1950s (it is unlikely to derive from deviant or be related to 'daft' or **daffy**, or even by a tortuous etymology from 'divine' in the sense of possessed). It has recently been revived as a vogue term by schoolchildren, although the short noun form **div** is more common. (Divvy itself has occasionally been recorded as a noun.)

> *'Who's your friend with the glasses? 'E looks a bit divvy.'*
> (Recorded, street-gang member, London, 1967)

diz n American
a foolish, eccentric or disoriented individual. The term, in use among US teenagers in the 1990s, was probably a variant form of **ditz** or may be based upon 'dizzy'.

dizzle n American
1. an unnamed or unnameable thing
   Help me get rid of this dizzle.
2. the penis
   She got a squint at his dizzle.
3. a friend
   Yo, how's it hangin' my dizzle?
These usages, all recorded in 2003 and 2004, may involve words like deal, **dong** and **dawg** with the substitute syllables -**izzle**.

d.k. vb American
to snub someone or renege on something or to feign ignorance of someone or something. The letters (pronounced 'dee-kay') are an acronym of 'don't know'.
   'He d.k.'d me.'
   (*Wall Street*, US film, 1988)

do¹ vb
1. to have sex with. More a shorthand vulgarism than an evasive euphemism, the term was widely used in the USA from the late 1960s and since the 1990s has been popular among adolescents in Britain.
   'Debbie does Dallas'
   (Title of 1970s US porno film)
   'Is she really doing that dreamboat in the sixth form?'
   (*Just Seventeen* magazine, August 1996)
2. to kill. A term used by criminals and street-gang members and their fictional counterparts.
   He didn't say a goddam word, he just went and did her.

do² n American
a hairstyle. This shortened form of hairdo originated in black slang. It is now also heard among younger British speakers.

do³, **doo** n
excrement. A nursery word used all over the English-speaking world, although in Britain the plural form **dos** is probably more common. The word in this sense is probably pre-World War II and derives from the Victorian notion of doing or performing one's bodily functions dutifully.

do (drugs) vb
to take drugs. The term can apply to single instances or to habitual use. Originally an Americanism, it was adopted by British speakers in the **hippy** era.
   *'Well the one [**trip**] that stopped me from doing acid forever was when I dropped seven tabs.'*
   (Zodiac Mindwarp, *I-D* magazine, November 1987)

D.O.A. adj
unconscious, inert. A facetious use of the American police and hospital jargon 'dead on arrival' to mean 'dead to the world', particularly after taking drugs or alcohol.

do a Bertie vb British
to turn Queen's Evidence, to inform on one's accomplices. A fairly rare piece of criminal jargon of uncertain origin. It is possibly from the Edwardian era, when turning King's Evidence would have been joining 'Bertie's' side, and seems to have existed before the days of Bertie Smalls, a 1970s criminal supergrass (a high-level informer).

do-able adj American
sexually attractive. This term, used to categorise a potential partner, was popular among female Californian highschool students in the 1990s and was featured in the 1994 US film *Clueless*.
   'There's no getting round the style question. If you want to be "do-able"…you cannot afford to dress "random".'
   (*Sunday Times 'Style'* magazine, 22 October 1995)

do a duck vb British
to escape, conceal oneself. A term that may originate from the colloquialism 'ducking and diving', or simply 'ducking out of sight'. It was used by London criminals, including Johnny Bradbury, a member of the Richardson gang of 1960s notoriety.

do a job on (someone) vb
to deceive, thoroughly overwhelm, devastate someone. Originally an Americanism, this unspecific phrase is now in fairly widespread use in Britain and Australia.

do a number on (someone) vb
to cheat, frustrate, defeat, demoralise someone. Like the previous phrase, this expression, the precise meaning of which depends on its context, originated in the USA and is now used elsewhere.
   'A talk that made it clear that Ari intended "to do a number on Bolker, he wanted to

hurt the fellow, not do him in, but certainly to harm him in some way".'
(Nigel Dempster, writing in the *Sunday Times*, 24 September 1989)

do a runner *vb British*
to escape, run away or disappear. A phrase from semi-criminal and subsequent working-class usage which has become a generally popular term since the early 1980s. It originally referred specifically to the practice of leaving a restaurant, bar, etc. without paying.

'I decided to "do a runner", i.e. to leg it out of the restaurant without paying the bill.'
(*Great Bus Journeys of the World*, Alexei Sayle, 1988)

dob, dob in, dob on *vb Australian*
to inform (on someone), tell tales. A schoolchildren's term since the late 1970s which was previously, and still is, part of underworld terminology. 'Dob' was a British dialect word meaning something between drop and lob (it survives in the noun form in colloquial expressions such as 'a dob of butter'). 'Dob in' has been introduced to British audiences via Australian soap operas of the 1980s.

'I tell you what you do, dob her in to the governor.'
(*Prisoner, Cell Block H*, Australian TV series, 1982)

dock asthma *n British*
gasps of (usually feigned) surprise and disbelief by prisoners in the dock. A part of police and prison jargon since at least the 1950s.

docker *n British*
a partly smoked cigarette, put out for later relighting. This word, which is more common in the north of England than elsewhere, originates in 'dock', meaning to cut short, or the related archaic use of dock, meaning the 'solid part of an animal's tail'.

Doctor Feelgood *n American*
a doctor or other person who freely prescribes pleasurable drugs. The name has been used in several blues and soul songs since World War II, but probably pre-dates them as a black underworld term, where it had a more generalised meaning of someone who could provide euphoria or comfort. It was later applied as a nickname, e.g. to Dr Max Jacobson,

physician to President Kennedy, famous for his disbursement of amphetamines to New York high society.

doctors and nurses *n*
sexual activity or sex play. To 'play (at) doctors and nurses' is a humorous euphemism, sometimes used by adults, deriving from the children's game which often involves sexual experimentation.

dodgy *adj British*
1a. doubtful, suspect. A common term in British English and nowadays hardly slang. It arose in the later 19th century and derives from the sense of dodge as an artful or risky ruse. In the 1960s 'dodgy!' was the counterpart of 'swinging!' in the catchphrases of TV compère Norman Vaughan.
1b. stolen, illegal. A narrower sense of **dodgy 1a**, common since the 1960s in such euphemisms as 'dodgy gear/merchandise'.

doer *n American*
a perpetrator of a crime, suspected criminal. The term, a synonym of **perp**, is probably a shortening of 'wrongdoer' in police jargon.

dog[1] *n*
1a. an ugly, unpleasant or unattractive woman or girl. This sense of the word was in common use in the USA from the 1950s. It was adopted by British speakers in the mid-1970s.
1b. *American* something unpleasant or worthless. Expressions in which 'dog' signifies distaste or contempt are almost all American in origin, presumably reflecting the cliché that the British are a nation of dog lovers. Nevertheless there are occasional instances of this sense in British English.
This car's a dog!
1c. a company or share that performs badly on the stock exchange, a worthless piece of stock (these are also known as **bow-wow** stocks)
2. *British* a wig, toupée. The word usually implies a ragged, ill-fitting or generally unconvincing hairpiece. It has been in use among teenagers at least since the early 1970s.
3. a rogue, (likeable) reprobate. A 19th-century usage, now a colloquialism usually surviving in the form '(you) old dog!'.
4. *British* a **dog-end**
5. *See* **dogs**

dog[2] *vb American*
to abandon, reject, get rid of. The word in this sense has been used by teenagers and college students since the late 1980s.

'Dog the dorm rules now!'
(*A Different World*, American TV series, 1987)

dog (and bone) *n British*
a *telephone*. An example of rhyming slang which is still used today. It is usually used of the appliance rather than the action.

Get on the dog to him and find out when he's coming.

dog (it) *vb British*
to play truant. The term is heard particularly in the Scottish Lowlands and the north of England.

dog-and-boned *adj British*
stoned. A cannabis smoker's term from the 1960s and early 1970s, now heard in the form **doggo**.

dog (someone) around *vb American*
1a. to pester someone. An expression inspired by the same images as to 'dog someone's heels'.
1b. to behave badly, cruelly, irresponsibly or unfaithfully, especially to one's partner. This Americanism seems to have its origin in black street-talk of the late 1950s, perhaps inspired by the notion of an errant or 'dirty dog'.

dog-ass *adj American*
worthless, inferior, bad. A vulgarism in use for instance among military personnel and college students since the 1950s.

dog-botherer *n British*
a humorous and meaningless term of abuse, inspired by **God-botherer**, but without the connotations of religious zeal, bestiality or indeed specific wrongdoing

dog-box *n British*
a mess, a confused situation. An item of middle-class family slang heard in the 1990s.

dog-end *n British*
a cigarette end. The word usually describes a stubbed-out butt, rather than a partly smoked cigarette put aside for later relighting (a **dimp** or **docker**). It has been in use since at least World War II.

dog-esse *n American*
an obnoxious and/or unattractive woman. A supposedly humorous synonym for **bitch**.

dogflop *n American*
1a. excreta, usually but not necessarily from a dog
1b. something worthless
The term is used facetiously or euphemistically.

(all) dogged-up *adj*
dressed smartly or extravagantly. The term is probably inspired by 'decked out' or 'dolled up', or by the expression **dog's dinner**.

I don't want to have to get all dogged-up just to go out to dinner.

dogger *n British*
a truant. The term is heard particularly in the Scottish Lowlands and the north of England, and derives from the earlier verb to **dog (it)**.

doggett *vb British*
to scrounge. An arcane piece of London rhyming slang. Thomas Doggett, an actor, on the occasion of George I's accession in 1715, endowed a prize for an annual race for Thames watermen between London Bridge and Chelsea. The prize for the race, which is still rowed, is a coat and badge, hence 'Doggett's Coat and Badge': *cadge*. The word is also used as a noun to mean a scrounger.

'He's meeting me at the Hong Kong. He's only trying to doggett a Chinese [meal].'
(Recorded, pensioner, Bristol, 1989)

doggie-do/dos *n*
1a. dog excrement
1b. something worthless and/or repellent
Both meanings are used, generally facetiously, among adults, though the term originated as a nursery word.

doggie-fashion, doggy-fashion *adv*
(sexual intercourse) involving penetration from the rear

They like to do it doggy-fashion.

dogging *n British*
a (hetero)sexual practice whereby strangers meet at prearranged or well-known rendezvous such as car parks to have sex *in situ*. The term was popularised in 2003 when the footballer Stan Collymore admitted engaging in dogging. It derives from the notion that participants – or voyeurs who spy on them – pretend to be 'walking the dog'.

doggo *adj*

1. *American* worthless, inferior, bad. A variation of **dog-ass**.

2. *British* intoxicated by marihuana. This unusual term derives from a now obsolete piece of rhyming slang **dog-and-boned**: **stoned**, perhaps reinforced by the immobility and furtiveness implied in the colloquial phrase to 'lie doggo'.

dog it *vb American*

to perform badly, fail to do one's best. A campus and high-school expression from the 1970s.

> *If you dog it again this time, you're off the team.*

dog out *vb American*

to get **(all) dogged-up**

dogs

1. *n pl*

1a. the feet. Of obscure origin, this usage has persisted in British and American usage at least since World War II. It usually implies tired, sore feet.

> *'Ooh, that feels better – my dogs are barking today!'*
> (*Planes, Trains and Automobiles*, US film, 1987)

1b. slippers, shoes or boots

1c. *American* trainers. An item of black street-talk that was included in so-called **Ebonics**, recognised as a legitimate language variety by school officials in Oakland, California, in late 1996.

2. *n pl* **the dogs** *British* greyhounds or greyhound racing

3. *adj* **the dogs** (something) excellent. A shortening of **the dog's bollocks**.

dog's bollocks, the *n British*

a superlative thing, situation, etc. This widespread vulgarism was given wider currency by its use in *Viz* comic from the early 1990s, and its first broadcast use in the TV comedy series *Hale and Pace* in 1997.

dog's breakfast *n*

a mess, a confused mixture. From the image of a mishmash of unappetising scraps. The expression (compare the roughly contemporaneous **dog's dinner**) is commonly applied to a misconception or botched plan or display. The phrase dates from the 1930s.

> *'My God, he made a real dog's breakfast of that presentation.'*
> (Recorded, publisher, London, 1986)

dog's breath, dogsbreath *n*

a repellent, contemptible or unpleasant person. A term of abuse popular in the 1980s, probably because it is colourful without being obscene; another factor in its spread is its usage in TV shows, particularly by the cult character Mick Belker in the US TV police series *Hill Street Blues*. It originated in American teen usage in the late 1970s.

See also **dog**[1] **1b**

dog's dangly bits, the *n, adj British*

the best, exceptional. It is a version of **the dog's bollocks**.

dog's dinner *n*

1a. an extravagant display, especially a vulgar, misguided or unsuccessful attempt at smartness. The expression, which dates from the late 1920s, usually forms part of a phrase such as 'all done up like a dog's dinner'.

1b. a mess. In this negative sense **dog's breakfast** is currently more fashionable.

do-hickey *n American*

1a. an unspecified thing, thingummy

1b. a spot, pimple or skin blemish. **Hickey** alone is a common teenage term for a spot or lovebite; the prefix is an embellishment.

1c. the penis. A children's term that is probably a specific application of **do-hickey a**.

doink *vb*

1. to hit

2. to have sex. The term is a variant form of **bonk** and **boink**.

do it *vb*

to have sex. An evasive or coy euphemism used by children, those too embarrassed to be more explicit or, often, facetiously by adults.

do-it fluid *n American*

alcoholic liquor. An item of black street-talk which was included in so-called **Ebonics**, recognised as a legitimate language variety by school officials in Oakland, California, in late 1996.

dole-bludger *n Australian*

a person who claims unemployment pay which they are not entitled to, a 'dole scrounger'. This common term is sometimes extended to encompass any idle or shiftless person.

> *'Newspapers are always whingeing about the dole bludgers.'*
> (*Girls' Night Out*, Kathy Lette, 1989)

doley, dolie n Australian
someone who is on the dole (drawing unemployment pay)

doll n
a woman. A fairly dated Americanism adopted into British working-class usage in the 1950s and again in the 1970s, since which time it may also be used by women of men. The word has condescending or proprietorial overtones when used by teenagers.

doll city n American
1a. a beautiful person (of either sex but implying idealised cuteness, femininity or passivity)
Wow, check the new boy out – doll city!
1b. a pleasant situation or attractive idea. The expression is often an exclamation of approval.
Paris in the fall – doll city!
Both instances of the phrase typically occur in adolescent speech.

dollface n American
an attractive or cute person. A term of affection used especially by women to men.

dolls n pl American
pills of amphetamine or barbiturate drugs. A term adopted by middle-class users of (often prescribed) drugs. The word was popularised (and probably invented) by the author Jacqueline Susann in her sensationalist novel *The Valley of the Dolls* in 1965. The inspiration for the term is presumably the fact that the pills and capsules are colourful and comforting.

dollsome adj American
attractive. The term typically refers to a male and was popularised by its use in the US TV series *Buffy the Vampire Slayer* from 1997.

dolly adj British
excellent, attractive, cute. A vogue word of the mid-1960s, enshrined in the title of Adam Diment's fashionable novel *The Dolly Dolly Spy*. The word passed from **camp** theatrical and homosexual use to general currency for a year or so. It survives in middle-class speech as an ironic or scathing synonym for 'twee'.

dolly bird n British
an attractive girl. This expression, which would now appear hopelessly dated and offensive to many women, briefly epitomised the ideal gamine of the mid- to late 1960s. The word was used only fleetingly by the fashionable young themselves before becoming a journalistic cliché.

dolly-mixtures n pl British
pictures. Often used by criminals and police officers to describe mugshots, crime-scene photographs, etc., the rhyming slang expression refers to sweets popular among children since the 1950s. As an example of the jargon of cat burglars, the phrase was cited in *FHM* magazine in April 1996.

D.O.M. n
a 'dirty old man'. A middle-class and **Sloane Ranger** version of the colloquial expression, D.O.M. is applied, usually by females, to anyone male and lecherous regardless of age.

do me something! exclamation British
a phrase used by teenage gangs as a provocation or invitation to fight. A synonym is **what to go?** Both phrases are often followed by 'then?!' The term was recorded in use among North London schoolboys in 1993 and 1994.

don¹ adj
excellent, fashionable, admirable. A vogue term of approbation which originated in American usage in the early 1990s and by 1995 had been adopted for fashionable speech by British and Australian adolescents. It may derive from 'the Don' in the sense of a powerful or exceptional individual.

don², the Don n British
1a. a pre-eminent, successful or admirable person
1b. an excellent thing, the best
Both senses derive from the use of the word to refer to a criminal boss, originally from the title of a Spanish gentleman.

don³ vb British
to steal, defraud. In this sense the term was used by London schoolchildren in the early 1990s. Its derivation is uncertain. One user defined it as 'a rip-off' and claimed it as a deformation of **con**.

Donald Duck, Donald n
a **fuck**. A piece of rhyming slang, based on the cartoon character, that is heard in Australian and British English. It was popularised by the UK TV black comedy *The Estate Agents* in 2002.

done up adj British
an alternative form of **fitted up** or **stitched up**

dong¹, donger *n*

1. the penis. This word is common in current Australian English but is also heard in Britain and North America. Its origin is unclear but it resembles synonyms such as **whang**, **schlong**, etc. Unlike most similar terms its use has not been extended to mean a 'fool'. This hearty, brusque word is usually used by males.

2. a blow, strike. From the verb form.

dong² *vb American*

to have sex (with). The term can be used transitively or intransitively, like many of its synonyms it is also based on the notion of striking. An expression used on campus in the USA since around 2000.

donging *n British*

living outside society in makeshift shelters, teepees, trees, etc. The term was a back-formation from the 'Dongas Tribe' of environmental protesters who came to prominence in the summer of 1994.

donk¹ *n*

1. *Australian* a car engine. This is probably a shortening of 'donkey', which the late Eric Partridge recorded as being in use in British navy jargon for a ship's engine. The term 'donkey engine' is often used for small, portable or auxiliary engines such as an outboard motor or miniature shunting locomotive.

2. *Australian* a foolish person

3a. *American* excrement, **shit**

3b. *American* a prominent or well-shaped backside

donk² *vb American*

to have sex (with). An expression used on campus in the USA since around 2000.

donnybrook *n*

a brawl, free-for-all. Donnybrook Fair, held near Dublin, was often the scene of uproarious behaviour.

doob *n*

1. *British* an amphetamine pill. The singular form of the more common **doobs**.

2. the penis. This rare usage is either an invention or a shortening of **doobry**.

doobie, dooby *n*

1. *American* a marihuana cigarette, a **joint**

2. *British* a stupid or foolish person. The term is heard particularly in the Scottish Lowlands and the north of England.

doobry *n British*

1. an unspecified thing, thingummy, or a person whose name is forgotten or unknown. This invented word has existed at least since the 1950s.

2. an amphetamine tablet or other pill. This is probably a narrowing of the preceding sense and was popular among the **mods** of the 1960s, although the plural **doobs** was the more common alternative. 'Doobry', in this drug-related sense, has also been derived from 'double-blues', a particular type of **pep pill**.

doobs *n pl British*

tablets or capsules of amphetamine (later known generically as **speed**). This was the 1960s **mods**' own favourite term for the pills known to the popular press as **purple hearts** or **pep pills**.

doodad *n*

an unspecified thing, thingummy. The word is American, dating from before World War II. 'Doodads' are bits and pieces, odds and ends.

doodah *n*

an unspecified thing, gadget, thingummy. The British and Australian form of the American **doodad**.

doodle *n*

1. the penis. A nursery word.

2a. excrement

2b. nonsense, rubbish

doodly squat *n American*

1a. excrement

1b. nonsense, nothing at all. The expression is a common variant form of **diddly (squat)**.

'Shoot – I wouldn't tell you doodly squat after the way you've behaved.'
(*Night Game*, US film, 1988)

doody, doo-doo, do-do *n American*

excrement. A nursery word used facetiously by adults, this is one of many similar words, perhaps inspired by the older usage **do** or **dos**.

doofer, doofa *n*

1. *also* **doofa** *or* **doover** an unspecified thing, thingummy

Hand me that doofer.

2. a partly smoked cigarette; a pun on '(it will) do for later'. A wartime term that remained in use in the 1960s and may still survive.

doofus *n*

an alternative spelling of **dufus**

doofy *adj American*

foolish, clumsy. The term is probably derived from the earlier term **doofus**.

> 'He looked pretty doofy to me.'
> (New York paparazzo talking of actor Michael J. Fox in *True Stories*, Channel 4 TV, April 1993)

dook *n*

1. a hand, fist. A variation of the better-known **duke(s)**. In rustic and working-class Australian speech this form survives from archaic British usage.

2. *See* **dukes**; **duke it**; **duke on it**

doolally *adj British*

deranged, crazy. A very popular term derived from the location of a colonial army sanatorium and rest camp at Deolali, Bombay, where soldiers exhibiting signs of fatigue, heat exhaustion, etc. were sent. An early form which is still heard occasionally was 'do(o)lally-tap', the 'tap' meaning 'fever' in Hindi.

dooley, doolie *n British*

a stupid or contemptible person. This term of abuse, probably originating in Scottish usage, was featured in the ITV drama *Your Cheating Heart*, written by Johnny Byrne in 1990. The term is now heard particularly in the Scottish Lowlands and the north of England.

do one *vb British*

to depart, run away. In the slang of street gangs, homeless persons, etc. since 2000. The expression probably originated in northern usage, sometimes used as an imperative, as in 'OK, you've had your fun so go on – now do one!'.

do one's fruit *vb British*

to become enraged, lose control. A variant of the colloquial version 'do one's nut', punning on the fruit-and-nut chocolate bar, this item of middle-class, middle-aged jocularity was recorded in the early 1990s.

> 'When they finally said the train was cancelled, I just did my fruit...'
> (Recorded, male commuter, London 1991)

do one's nut/block/crust/pieces/taters *vb*

to lose control, to become furious. Originally working-class alternatives for to 'lose one's head' or to 'blow one's top', all in use in Britain and Australia; the more colourful second, third, fourth and fifth variants are currently in vogue among young people.

> 'Funny you should say that, because these days I find I do my nut very easily.'
> (*Alfie*, British film, 1966)

> 'Men are always saying they can count the number of times they've cried on the fingers of one hand. Well, I reckon women can count the number of times they've really done their blocks.'
> (*Girls' Night Out*, Kathy Lette, 1989)

doover *n*

an alternative form of **doofer 1**

dooze[1] *n American*

1. something which is very easy to accomplish, an attractive proposition

2. an alternative form of **doozer**

dooze[2] *vb American*

to bamboozle, flatter

doozer, doozie, doozy *n*

something or someone very impressive, remarkable or exceptional; a 'humdinger'. This is probably an invented word (though some authorities derive it from a spectacular pre-World War II car, the 'Duesenburg'). The term is certainly American in origin.

dope[1] *n*

1. an illicit drug, narcotics. The word was first applied to stupefying drugs such as opium and heroin at the turn of the 20th century, and remained limited to this context until the 1960s. In the late 1960s **hippy** drug users began to apply the then almost archaic form ironically to their preferred soft drug, cannabis (marihuana and hashish), and this remains the most common use today.

> 'He said: "You know how you leave dope lying around? Well, she ate some and she went berserk. She hasn't liked it much since".'
> (*News of the World*, 29 October 1989)

2. information, news. In this sense the word has been used at least since World War I, especially in America. The word is derived from the idea of something dense or viscous, embodied in the Dutch word *doop*, meaning dip (in the sense of a sauce in which other food may be dipped).

3. a foolish or stupid person

dope[2] *adj*

excellent, fashionable, admirable. A vogue term of approbation which originated in American usage in the early 1990s and by 1995 had been adopted for fashionable speech by British and Australian adolescents.

'He's dope – I'd go out with him.'
(*California Man*, US film, 1992)

'Bangin' sounds and dope d.j.s.'
(Disco poster at King's College, London
University, September 1995)

doped-up *adj*
under the influence of a (stupefying or
tranquillising) drug

dope-on-a-rope *adj*
an elaborated form of **dope** in the sense
of 'excellent'. The term was defined as
follows by a user in 2001: '...as used by
various **rap**, R 'n' B and pop types. If
something is really cool, it can be
described as dope-on-a-rope'.

dope out *vb*
to work out, discover information. A
phrase derived from the noun **dope 2**, it
is more common in American English
where it originated before World War II.

doper *n*
a user of illicit drugs. The word, from
dope, has been in vogue since the early
1970s. It is used about, rather than by
drug users, and is applied indiscriminately to users of hard and soft drugs.

He's a doper from way back.

dopper *n British*
1. the penis
2. a fool or contemptible person. The earlier sense seems to have fallen into disuse but, like many synonyms (**prick**,
plonker, etc.), has been adopted to
denote a stupid person. The word 'dopper' itself occurred in Norfolk dialect,
meaning a thick blanket or sweater, but
this is unlikely to be the origin of the
derogatory usage which is probably
related to the archaic 'dobber', referring
to the male member.

do-re-mi *n American*
money. A pun on **dough**.

Doris *n British*
1. a frumpy or unattractive older woman
in the slang of City traders from the
1990s. Such women, especially if
thought to be unglamorous or too serious, are typically dismissed by males as
'a bit of a Doris'. **Nora** is a synonym.
2. a girlfriend or wife

dork *n*
1. the penis. A term popularised first
among American adults then among
teenagers in the 1970s, it is probably
inspired by **dick** and, perhaps, **pork**.
2. a fool, an offensive buffoon. This is a
predictable second (and now more wide-

spread) sense of the word, on the same
pattern as **dick**, **prick**, etc. It is not used
affectionately (as **plonker**, for instance,
is), but is only mildly offensive. Since the
late 1970s this term has been in vogue in
Britain and Australia as well as in its
country of origin.

*'I love your husband, but he's a real
dork.'*

'Yes, but he's my dork.'
(*Someone to Watch Over Me*, US film,
1987)

dorky *adj*
dull, offensively gauche, silly. From **dork
2**.

dos *n pl*
a version of **do** (in the sense of excrement)

It is pronounced 'dooze'.

dose *n*
a venereal infection. Until the 1960s
the word most often referred to a bout of
gonorrhoea.

*'Don't Give A Dose to the One You Love
Most.'*
(Song written and recorded by Shel Sil-
verstein, 1972)

dosed (up) *adj*
1. infected with a venereal disease
2. drugged illicitly (as in the case of, e.g.,
a greyhound or racehorse) or unwittingly
(in the case of a person). The expression
in this sense is a synonym for 'spiked',
and in the 1970s often referred to LSD.

dosh *n British*
money. This is a working-class term from
the early 1950s which was falling out of
use in the 1960s, but which, like many
similar words (**bunce**, **loot**, **lolly**, etc.),
was revived in the money-conscious late
1980s. It is a favourite with alternative
comedians and 'professional cockneys'.
The original would seem logically to be
the old African colonial term **dash**, denoting a tip or bribe, but other authorities
claim that it is influenced by **doss**, in the
sense of the price of a bed (for the night).

doss[1] *vb*
1a. to sleep

*I need a place to doss for a couple of
nights.*

1b. to move from place to place, sleeping
in borrowed or low-class accommodation

*'Old Shawie's been dossing for the last
three weeks.'*
(Recorded, London student, 1988)

1c. to relax, **chill**. A fashionable usage since 2000.

A 19th-century term which may derive from the Latin *dorsum*, for 'back'. The verb forms, as opposed to the noun forms of the word, are mainly encountered in British English.

doss² *n*

1a. a place to sleep, especially a temporary, free and/or makeshift bed. This word, from 19th-century tramps' jargon, was probably originally a corruption of the Latin *dorsum*, for 'back'. Tramps are unlikely to have coined the term; it may have come from the jargon surrounding pugilism (meaning 'flat on one's back') which was a sport subscribed to by aristocrats and students, among others.

1b. a period of sleep, a nap

2. a very easy task, a pushover. In this sense the word, although based on the notion of lying down, may be influenced by 'toss', as in easily tossing off a piece of work.

You mustn't see this purely as a doss.

doss around *vb British*
to do nothing in particular, lead an aimless existence. From **doss 2**.

dossbag *n British*
1. a sleeping bag
2. a scruffy, lazy or slovenly person

doss down *vb British*
to lie down to sleep (usually on the floor), to bed down
Just doss down anywhere you like.

dosser *n British*
1a. a homeless person, vagrant, or down-and-out who sleeps wherever space is available
'We are not tramps, winos or even dossers, we are gentlemen of the road – and we refuse to be moved.'
(Homeless man, *Observer*, 16 August 1987)
1b. a slovenly, irresponsible person. A favourite term of affectionate abuse between young (usually male) people since the 1980s. (From the noun **doss** or the verb **doss around**.)

doss house *n*
a dormitory for vagrants or a cheap, shabby hotel
I don't know how you manage to live in this doss house you call a flat.
'I felt like pissing off and spending the night in some Arab dosshouse.'
(Joe Orton's diary, 14 May 1967)

dot *vb*
to hit. Usually used in the phrase to 'dot (someone) one', meaning to land a heavy and precise (on the 'dot') blow, or to blacken someone's eye.

do the wild thing *vb American*
1a. to run amok
1b. to have sex
An item of black slang which may have given rise to the widely reported **wilding**.

do time *vb*
to serve a prison sentence

double-bagger *n American*
a hideous or repellent person. A phrase from the vocabulary of **Valley Girls** and other American teenagers from the mid-1970s, probably originating in earlier surfers' slang. The image evoked is of a person who must wear a bag over their head ← and provide one for the onlooker too, or alternatively wear *two* bags. The expression, in this humorous usage, was first borrowed from the language of baseball, where it describes a hit which allows the hitter to advance two bases or 'bags'.

double-munter *n British*
a particularly ugly or unattractive female. An intensified form of the vogue term **munter**, popular among students and others since 2000.

double result *n British*
in the jargon of football hooligans this denotes a victory against both an opposing team's supporters and the police

douchebag *n American*
a contemptible or very unpleasant person. The expression is usually a strong term of abuse, indicating real distaste, although like comparable words it is sometimes used lightheartedly, typically by high-school and college students. Rubber bags were a part of douching paraphernalia when that form of contraception was widespread, especially among prostitutes. The word is applied to males and females.
'OK, we're going in there and anyone who doesn't act elegant is a douchebag.'
(*Satisfaction*, US film, 1988)

dough *n*
money. This was the most popular American slang term for money from the 19th century until the mid-1960s when it was supplanted by **bread**.

doughboy *n*
1. *American* an army private. The word was most popular at the time of World

War I but is still occasionally used. The original doughboy was a sort of suet dumpling served in the armies and navies of the 19th century in Britain and the USA.

2. *British* a blow, a heavy punch. In working-class and cockney jargon this rare sense of the word is occasionally recorded. Its derivation may be from the (heavy) dumpling referred to above.

> *He landed him a real doughboy round the chops.*

Douglas *n British*
a 3rd, a third-class university honours degree. A student witticism of the late 1980s playing on the name, Douglas Hurd, of a long-serving member of Mrs Thatcher's Conservative cabinet (a **Richard** is a synonym).
Compare **Desmond**; **Pattie**; **made-in**

do up *vb*
1. to inject or inhale (a drug). An embellishment of **do** in the sense of 'take (drugs)' common among illicit drug users since the early 1970s.
2. *See* **done up**

do (someone) up *vb British*
to discomfit, defeat, confound
> *'Those long-haul flights really do you up.'*
> (Recorded, female traveller, London, 2003)

dout, dowt *n British*
a cigarette end or stub. A word like **dub**, used by vagrants and working-class speakers. The *Oxford English Dictionary* first recorded the word in use in Glasgow in 1975. It may be a dialectal form of 'dowse(d)' or a contraction of 'stubbed-out'.

down *adj American*
1. authentic, trustworthy, sound. The usage may derive from the appreciative sense of **down-and-dirty** or the phrase **down with** (someone).
> *'You're a down girl.'*
> (*Clueless*, US film, 1995)

2. in agreement, interested
> *I'm down with that.*

down-and-dirty *adj American*
1a. deceitful, corrupt, savage. An exclamation used in poker (when cards are dealt or slapped on the table) extended to describe base or brutal behaviour.
1b. basic, primitive, authentic, 'rough and ready'. In this sense the phrase is usually appreciative rather than pejora-

tive; in rock music jargon it denotes healthily authentic or **funky**.

downer *n*
1. a tranquillising or sedative drug (especially a barbiturate) in the language of illicit drug users (as opposed to **uppers** or stimulant drugs)
> *She's on downers.*

2. a depressing or boring experience. From the slang of American **hipsters** of the 1950s, widespread in the English-speaking world since the 1960s, but now sounding rather dated in British English; although the phrase 'on a downer' (going through a depressed or unlucky phase) is currently widespread.

downhome *adj American*
rustic, ethnic or (agreeably) simple and neighbourly. The word was first used by urbanised northern blacks to refer to their southern roots.

downstairs *adj, adv*
(in) the genital area or the buttocks. A coy euphemism which was probably inspired by the earlier **upstairs**, relating to the brain or head.

down the block *adj, adv British*
in solitary confinement, being punished. A prisoners' term.

down the road *adj, adv British*
dismissed, rejected. An item of working-class slang.
> *'I want him down the road as soon as possible.'*
> (Recorded, labouring gang leader, London, 1992)

down the tubes/flush/chute *adv*
ruined, abandoned, beyond hope. These are racier versions of 'down the drain', 'down the pan' or 'down the toilet', heard in the USA since the late 1970s and in Britain since the early 1980s.
> *'Bright enough to realise he is going down the tubes, he is still drawn to a prodigal self-destruction.'*
> (*Sunday Times*, 26 July 1987)

down with *adj*
close to, supportive of. An item of black street argot popular among **rappers** and hip hop aficionados.
> *My crew, they're all down with me.*

dozy *adj British*
slow-witted, foolish. The word is now a colloquialism; in the 1950s it was part of 'vulgar' speech. Originally it meant sleepy or lazy and was (and still is) a favourite term of abuse employed by

sergeant majors and officers in the armed forces, teachers and other authority figures.

drabbie n British
a 'frump', 'bluestocking' or puritanical person, usually female. A middle-class term of mild derision or disapproval, based on 'drab' and applied, often by journalists, in the 1980s to literary, academic or other professional women who deliberately eschewed a glamorous appearance.

drack[1] n Australian
rubbish. An Australian variant form of the more common **dreck**.

drack[2] adj Australian
scruffy, shabby, dowdy. The adjective is formed from the earlier noun, itself a variant of **dreck**.

drag n
1. women's clothing, as worn by men, especially homosexuals, transvestites or female impersonators. Originally theatrical slang of the early 20th century in Britain, signifying a long dress (dragging along the ground), the phrase 'in drag' crossed into popular terminology in the early 1960s. In the case of women wearing masculine clothing, 'man-drag' or 'male-drag' is usually specified.

> 'Marlene in man-drag.'
> (Caption to photograph of Marlene Dietrich in Kenneth Anger's *Hollywood Babylon*, 1975)

2. a thing, event or person considered to be boring or depressing. An Americanism, probably originating in the late 19th century and remaining in marginal use until the 1960s, it was adopted into teenage currency in Britain and Australia in the late 1950s and was widespread by the mid-1960s.

> 'What a drag it is getting old.'
> (*Mother's Little Helper*, Rolling Stones, 1965)

3a. *British* an inhalation of cigarette smoke, a puff

> Give me a drag on that.

3b. *British* a marihuana cigarette, a **joint**. A prisoners' term.

4. a street, especially a long or important street, usually in the form **main drag**. This Americanism gave rise to 'drag racing' to describe unofficial races from a standing start over a short, straight stretch of public road. Drag racing is now also an

organised sport run over custom-built private 'dragstrips'.

drag-arsing n British
lingering, delaying or prevaricating. An item of student slang in use in London and elsewhere since around 2000.

drag ass vb American
1. a variant of **haul ass**
2. to move unwillingly, lazily or slowly

drag-ass adj American
boring, tedious, onerous. The word is applied to people as well as to tasks.

dragged-up adj
1a. dressed in **drag**
1b. dressed, clothed (especially in flamboyant or unusually expensive clothing). By extension from the first sense to the heterosexual world (although the term does not seem to be applied to women). Dragged-up is a racier version of 'dolled-up'.

> Here he comes, all dragged-up in his best things.

draggy adj
tedious, slow or depressing. Deriving from the second sense of **drag**, the word is now rather dated. In the 1960s and 1970s it was more popular in Britain than in the USA.

> It was a totally draggy scene.

dragon n British
a formidable (and therefore unattractive and/or unavailable) female. The earlier colloquialism was adopted as a code term by male financial traders in the City of London and was recorded (with other categorisations such as **oof**, **mum**, etc.) by psychologist Belinda Brookes in the *Independent on Sunday*, 9 July 1995.

drag queen n
a male homosexual who wears women's clothing. The phrase now has overtones of flamboyant, exhibitionist 'femininity' rather than mere cross-dressing.

> 'Kenneth Williams then gave a long portrait of a dismal drag queen writing a witty letter requesting employment.'
> (Joe Orton's Diary, 13 April 1967)

> 'The most important week in my life and I'm going to be spending it with a drag queen?!'
> (*He's My Girl*, US film, 1987)

drainpipes, drainpipe jeans, drainies, drains n pl British
very tight trousers fashionable in the 1950s among **teddy boys** and, later, **rockers**. Although the terms have been fash-

ionable subsequently (during the glitter craze and **punk** era, for instance), they are now more rare.

drain the lizard/dragon/snake *vb*

to urinate. Colourful euphemisms popular with (invariably male) college students, hearty drinkers, etc. These expressions entered the slang lexicon of teenagers and college students in the late 1960s and early 1970s, although they are probably older, adult coinages on the pattern of **siphon the python**. It is not clear where in the English-speaking world the pattern originated, but it is thought by many to be typically Australian.

> 'He can't come to the phone right now, he's in the can draining his lizard.'
> (*Friday 13th Part VI*, US film, 1986)

draipsing *n British*

extorting money or items of value from a weaker person. The synonym of **taxing** was employed in the 1970s among comprehensive-school pupils in London and referred to using a threat rather than actual violence to bully younger pupils into giving up items of value. Its derivation is uncertain.

drama queen *n*

a self-dramatising or hysterical person. The expression was originally (in the 1960s) applied by male homosexuals to their fellows. In the 1970s the phrase was adopted by heterosexuals and applied to women and, sometimes, to **straight** as well as **gay** men.

drape(s) *n*

1a. clothes, a suit or outfit. The word was in use in the USA (where 'drapes' are curtains) in the 1950s among black musicians, **hipsters** and **beatniks**. It was then adopted by **spivs** and prisoners in Britain, where it is still heard.

1b. *British* a drape jacket, the top half of a 'zoot suit' and part of the uniform of the **teddy boy** in the 1950s. (The drape had wide shoulders and was almost as long as a frock-coat, but loose and unwaisted.)

draw

draw[1] *n British*

1a. tobacco. In this sense the word, derived from the action of inhaling, dates from the 1950s. It occurs in prison jargon in particular.

1b. cannabis (hashish or marihuana). Since the mid-1970s this word has been in vogue for smokable cannabis.

> 'By the time he returned home hours late, Robert was intoxicated with cider and high on 'draw' (cannabis cigarette).'
> (*Sunday Times*, 28 January 1996)

draw[2] *n British*

a 'two-one' honours degree in the late 1980s parlance of university students. (The joke is that a draw means 'two won'.) Alternative names for the same award are **made-in** or **Taiwan**.

Compare **Desmond**; **Douglas**; **Pattie**; **Richard**

draw[3] *vb British*

to attract (an admirer). A term used by young street-gang members in London since around 2000.

> 'Round here we draw more black guys than white ones.'
> (Recorded, teenage female gang member, East London, 2001)

dread[1] *adj*

1. *Jamaican* an all-purpose word implying authentic, impressive, etc., in connection with the black reggae and **ganja** culture and Rastafarian religion of Jamaica. The word first conveyed the power and awe felt and inspired by the (dreadlock-wearing) devotees of Rastafarianism.

> *He's dread.*
> *It's real dread.*

2a. *British* good

> *Well dread sounds.*

2b. *British* bad

> *Some dread shit.*

Shorn of its Rasta associations the word had, by 2000, become popular among UK adolescents. Like its synonym **rough**, its meaning changed according to intonation.

dread[2], **dred** *adj British*

awful. Employed by middle-class speakers since around 2000, this usage of the term is more likely to be an abbreviation of 'dreadful' than the Rastafarian key-word.

> *I'm feeling dread, man.*

dreamboat *n*

a very attractive person of the opposite sex. The word, redolent of Hollywood in the 1940s, is still used, especially in the USA and usually, but not always, facetiously as a description or term of endearment.

dreck *n*

rubbish, a worthless thing, **shit**. From the Yiddish *drek* and German *dreck*, which have the same meaning.

'Here's some news to gladden the hearts of all devotees of dreck – the world première of "Prisoner Cell Block H".'
(*Time Out* magazine, July 1989)

dreg *n British*
a despicable or worthless person. A middle-class term of abuse or disapproval which has been rare since the late 1960s. It is a modern back-formation from the standard plural 'dregs', which itself derives from an Old Norse term for oil or wine residues.

dreich *adj Scottish*
dreary. A dialect term which was occasionally heard as a colourful new colloquialism in self-conscious use amongst middle-class inhabitants of England in the late 1990s.
The weather is rather, as they say, dreich.

dribbler *n British*
an unpleasant, obnoxious and/or unfortunate person. In playground usage since 2000.

drift *vb*
to leave, go away, escape. The word is sometimes in the imperative form, meaning 'get lost'; otherwise it is a **cool** or 'tough-guy' synonym for to 'go'.

drill *vb*
1. *British* to sleep. A middle-class and public-school term deriving from the phrase 'blanket drill', a facetious army expression for sleeping.
2. to shoot (usually to kill). A now dated Americanism adopted by crime and western movies and fiction.
3. to have sex with. A rare usage on the same pattern as **screw**.

drink *n British*
a small bribe, tip or other financial inducement. Originally, in London working-class usage, it meant literally the price of an (alcoholic) drink. Now it usually refers to a more substantial sum and is sometimes extended to a share in an attractive venture, or a 'piece of the action'. As an item of British police and underworld slang, it was given wider currency by TV series such as *Minder*.
Brian will need a drink, too.

drinkable *adj British*
attractive and/or available. The term was popular among City traders, **Sloanes** and **yuppies** from the later 1980s and could be applied equally to a potential sex partner, usually by males, or to an investment opportunity.

drinking vouchers *n pl British*
coins or banknotes. An alternative version of 'beer-vouchers' or **beer-tokens**.
'Our Rebels are more likely to be huddled inside an SW William Hill putting plenty of "drinking vouchers" (cash money) on Chelsea thrashing Man United. They can often be spied at pubs like the White Hart.'
(*I-D* magazine, November 1987)

drink-link *n British*
a cash dispenser. A term in use among college students since 2000.

drip¹ *n*
1. an insipid, unassertive or boring person. This common colloquialism is probably British in origin, but is also used, especially by school and college students, in the USA and Australia. It is one of many terms (**wet**, **damp**, **dripping**) equating weakness with water.
2. the drip *British* hire purchase, paying by instalments. The phrase is usually part of the longer expression **on the drip**.

drip² *vb British*
to complain. The term was recorded on the Royal Marines website in 2004, where it was defined as 'moan incessantly, usually a sign that the blokes are happy'.

dripping *adj British*
weak, irresolute, pathetic. An upper- and middle-class term of mild contempt from the late 1970s. It is inspired by the popular colloquialism **wet.**
Her husband's absolutely dripping.

drive the porcelain bus/great white bus/ big bus *vb American*
to vomit. A popular expression among college and high-school students. The image is of a helpless drunk or hangover victim kneeling before the toilet pedestal, clutching the rim of the bowl in both hands like an oversized steering wheel, as the room spins. (**Kiss the porcelain god** is an alternative form.)

droid *n American*
a stupid, slow or completely unimaginative person, in the language of teenagers and students. It is a shortening of 'android', of which both the full and abbreviated forms have been used extensively in science-fiction books and films since the mid-1970s.
'Man, he's a total droid.'
(*Zombie High*, US film, 1987)

drongo n

a foolish, unfortunate or unpleasant person. An Australian word which was adopted by British speakers in the early 1970s, probably introduced to it by an influx of young Australian travellers. It is a term of scathing contempt which may have been inspired by a spectacularly unsuccessful racehorse of the same name in the 1920s, although 'drongo' is also the name of an Australian bird. The word seemed to be declining in popularity by the late 1980s.

droob n Australian

a dullard. This word is probably a blend of **drip** and **boob(y)**.

drooly adj

very attractive, appealing or appetising. A less usual synonym of **dishy** or 'yummy', often used by adolescent females.

drop[1] vb

1. to take (an illicit drug) orally. The word was most often encountered in the phrase 'drop acid', meaning to take LSD by mouth. Originally an American term, 'drop' replaced the neutral 'take' in Britain around 1966.

'Well, the one that stopped me from doing acid forever was when I dropped seven tabs. I completely lost my mind and went to Muppetland – the whole trip lasted for about six months.'

(Zodiac Mindwarp, *I-D* magazine, November 1987)

2. to knock (a person) down

He threatened to drop him.

3. to give birth to. A shortening of **drop a pup**.

Has she dropped it yet?

She's going to drop in August.

4. *American* (of a record, film) to appear, be released. From the earlier sense of to 'give birth to'. An expression used on campus in the USA since around 2000.

That Outkast track dropped last week.

drop[2] n British

news, requisite information. The word usually occurs in the question 'What's the drop?', recorded among UK adolescents in the early 1990s.

drop a bollock vb British

to commit a blunder; a vulgar alternative to the colloquial 'drop a brick' or 'drop a clanger'

drop a bundle vb

to lose a large amount of money (by gambling or speculative investment, for instance).

See also **drop one's bundle**

drop a pup vb Australian

to give birth to. A vulgar and/or humorous euphemism used mainly by men.

dropdead adj

stunning, extreme, sensational. A vogue word since the mid- to late 1980s among those concerned with fashion. The usage is American in origin.

a dropdead blonde

dropdead gorgeous

drop-kick n Australian

a 'low', worthless or miserable person. This relatively mild epithet, used, e.g., in television soap operas of the 1980s, is probably a descendant of the vulgar rhyming slang (based on soccer), 'drop-kick and punt': **cunt**.

This makes me seem like a real drop-kick or something.

drop off the twig vb

to die. A lighthearted expression in vogue in Britain since the late 1980s. Bird imagery features in several colourful, predominantly working-class phrases in British colloquial use, such as 'sick as a parrot' or **rattle someone's cage**.

drop one out vb British

to exclude someone (such as a suspect) from one's list, surveillance or enquiry. A piece of police jargon presumably based on the notion of people being **in the frame** or out of it.

drop one's bundle vb Australian

to panic. The bundle in question may originate in a **hobo's** pack, or may be a reference to fright's tendency to empty the bowels.

drop one's daks vb Australian

to take off one's trousers. An Australianism (Daks is a trademark for a brand of casual slacks especially popular in the early 1960s in Britain and Australia). A catchphrase from *The Adventures of Barry McKenzie*, the cartoon strip published in *Private Eye* magazine in the late 1960s was 'drop your daks and say the magic word'.

drop out vb

to withdraw from conventional society, opt out. The motto of the **hippy** movement, coined by Dr Timothy Leary in 1967, was '**turn on**, **tune in**, and **drop out**' (take drugs and/or become enlightened; make contact with like-minded people or the life force; and leave society behind). The phrase survives in the specific sense of abandon one's education.

'Since I dropped out in September last year I have come to the conclusion that the city drop-out scene is a pathetic one.'
(Letter to *Oz* magazine, June 1968)

drop-out *n*
someone who has opted out of society. In this sense the word and the concept date from the late 1960s when **hippies** renounced capitalism, the education system, etc. to form an 'alternative society'. The term was quickly picked up by the press and others who disapproved and it became a pejorative description. In the USA in the 1950s and early 1960s drop-out was used to refer specifically to those who had left full-time education before graduating from high school.

dropped on *adj*
punished, reprimanded. The expression in full is 'dropped on from a great height'; the 'dropping' in question may refer to the weight of authority, or may be a euphemism for **shitting**. Predominantly a middle-class term, it is generally used in the context of a hierarchy.

drop trou *vb American*
to take down one's trousers, usually as part of an undergraduate ritual or **hazing**, as an expression of high spirits sometimes, but not necessarily, involving **mooning**; or in preparation for sex. A **preppie** term.

drossy *adj British*
unpleasant, inferior, disappointing. Formed from the noun, this term has been in use among students since around 2000.

druggy, druggie *n*
a user of illicit drugs. The term has been used by disapproving commentators such as concerned parents, teachers, etc. since the mid-1960s, when **beatniks** were the culprits.

drum *n*
1. *British* a house, home or building. The word, which is used especially in police and underworld circles, may come from the Romany word *drom*, meaning 'highway', but is possibly a back-formation from **drummer**, referring to someone who knocks ('drums') on people's doors, either to buy or sell goods or to find some-

where unoccupied to rob. In the past the word has also meant 'prison cell' and 'brothel', especially in Canada and Australia respectively.

'Go and turn over his drum while we keep him locked up here.'
(Recorded, Detective Sergeant, Canterbury, 1971)

2. *Australian* a tip, piece of information or news, probably from the notion of 'jungle drums'

I got a drum that she was in town.

drummer *n*
1a. a door-to-door salesperson, peddler or buyer of junk
1b. a housebreaker or burglar

This now obsolescent term derives either from knocking ('drumming') on doors or from **drum** as a vagrants' and criminals' synonym for house.

drumming *n British*
1a. selling door-to-door
1b. housebreaking or burglary

Both senses of the word derive from **drum** as a slang term for house or home, or from **drum** in the sense of knock.

drumsticks *n pl South African*
legs. The word is used typically by young males commenting mockingly on young females. It was first recorded in this sense in English slang of the 18th century and later in black American argot of the 1940s.

dry *n British*
rubbish, **shit**. The origin of this vogue term among adolescent gangs is uncertain. The term was recorded in use among North London schoolboys in 1993 and 1994 as an all-purpose adjective signifying anything unpleasant, disappointing, etc. It was in vogue in 2005.

dry-hump, dry-fuck, dry root *n, vb*
(to perform) a sexual activity (often while standing up) in which the partners simulate intercourse while they (or at least their genitals) are fully clothed. The term usually describes the behaviour of consenting heterosexuals rather than 'perversions' such as frottage (where the activity is performed on an unwilling victim, as for instance in a crowded lift or train), tribadism (between lesbian partners) or frictation (between male homosexual partners). Dry root is an expression peculiar to Australian speakers.

*'You can't dry hump good in the car.
Unless you're a midget.'*
(High-school student, *IT* magazine, June
1972)

*'...for £20 a head the "cuddle party" is
bringing together lost souls...there are
strict rules: no alcohol, no nudity and
emphatically no "dry humping".'*
(*Sunday Times*, 25 July 2004)

D.T.s, the *n*
delirium tremens; trembling as a result
of alcohol abuse

dub[1] *n*
1. a kind of heavy reggae music in which
instrumental tracks already recorded are
electronically altered and overlaid
('dubbed' one on another) with vocals
and sound effects to create a new piece
of music. The form was popular in
Jamaica and Britain in the late 1970s
and early 1980s.
2. *American* a cigarette
3. a fool, an incompetent. An almost
archaic word which survives among older
speakers in the USA and Australia.

dub[2] *adj American*
fashionable, aware. In this sense the
word was a vogue term of the lexicon of
the grunge movement originating in Seattle in 1993 and functioned as a synonym
of **hip** and **dope**, etc.

dubbed (up) *adj British*
locked up, incarcerated. A 1950s underworld usage probably deriving from an
archaic use of dub to mean 'key' or 'lock'.
Tucked up is a more recent alternative.

dubber *n American*
a cigarette. The word's etymology is
unclear.

dubbo *n Australian*
a fool. An embellishment of the archaic
dub meaning an awkward or incompetent
person, especially a rustic simpleton.

ducats *n pl American See* **duckets**

duchess *n British*
a woman, usually one's wife. The image
is of a dignified, respectable female
who is no longer young. This cockney
usage is still in evidence although
roughly a century old. The word is either
a straightforward simile or a shortening
of a rhyming-slang phrase, 'Duchess of
Fife': *wife*.

duck[1], **duck egg** *n*
a score of nil or zero in sport, especially
cricket. The term is at least a century
old and derives from the resemblance

between the written or printed 0 and the
egg.

duck[2] *n American*
an unattractive female. The term, which
may be connected to the notion of a waddling gait, is in use among college students. In the late 1950s and early 1960s
the same word was used by **beatniks** as a
neutral synonym for **chick**.
Compare **mucky duck**

duckburg *n American*
a rural, provincial town. A mildly contemptuous term.

duckets *n pl American*
money, dollars. An appropriation of the
archaic 'ducats' (Venetian gold coins
used all over Renaissance Europe)
heard in black street argot and campus
slang, and high-school slang from the
1990s.
*'He earns minor duckets in a thankless
job.'*
(*Clueless*, US film, 1995)

ducks, ducs, duc-duc *n pl American*
variant forms of **duckets**

duck's arse *n British See* **D.A.** 1

duck's breakfast *n*
a drink of water. A humorous expression
on the pattern of **Mexican breakfast**, 'pelican's breakfast', etc. The geographical
origin of the phrase is obscure.

duck shoot *n American*
an exceptionally easy task. From the
image of shooting sitting ducks.

duck-squeezer *n American*
an enthusiast for environmental issues. A
pejorative categorisation heard particularly on campuses, the term is part of a
set including **eagle freak**, **tree-hugger**,
earth biscuit, **granola**, etc.

ducky *adj*
cute, delightful. A word which today is
almost invariably used ironically or
facetiously. It derives from 'duck' as a
term of endearment.

dude *n*
a man. The 19th-century American
sense of dude as a 'fop', an overdressed
city dweller, etc. (familiar from westerns
and 'dude ranches') gave rise to a 20th-
century black usage meaning first pimp
or 'fancy man', then simply a (male) person. The term came into vogue in the
1970s and spread to Britain, where in
1973 it was briefly adopted by the **gay**
and teenage milieus (appearing for
instance in the title of the David Bowie

song 'All the Young Dudes'). In the late 1980s the word had again surfaced in teenage parlance, inspired by its continuing presence in black American street speech. Dude was originally a German rustic term for a fool.

> 'There were more commercials…but no more crime…nothing about two dudes in Halloween masks breaking into a Bloomfield Village home.'
> (*The Switch*, Elmore Leonard, 1978)

duds *n pl*
clothes. A word (the plural is usually used) which is approximately three hundred years old, deriving from the Middle English *dudde*, meaning a coarse cloth cloak. The plural of the word later came to mean rags or clothes and now sometimes has the extended sense of an outfit and/or set of accessories.

duff¹ *n*
1. the backside, buttocks. Duff is a 19th-century word for boiled dumpling or pudding (surviving in the British 'plum duff'), from which this usage was probably derived.

> 'Come on you turkeys, get off your duffs and give me some info.'
> (*Buck Rogers in the 25th Century*, US film, 1979)

2. *See* **up the duff**

duff² *adj*
useless, inferior. The word derives from a piece of 18th-century thieves' jargon meaning worthless or counterfeit, related to **duffer** which originally denoted a seller of supposedly stolen goods.

duff³ *vb Australian*
to steal. A verb formed from the generalised negative sense of duff. The usage is now fairly rare.

DUFF *n*
an unattractive female. The letters stand for 'designated ugly fat friend'. Pronounced as a word, not letter by letter, this pejorative epithet has been used by younger males since around 2000.

duffer *n British*
an ugly or unattractive female. An item of student slang in use in London and elsewhere since around 2000.

duffies *n pl Australian*
underpants, usually male

duff up/over *vb British*
to beat up. Mild-sounding terms for what may be anything from a children's scuffle

to a murderous attack. The modern sense, in vogue since the 1950s, seems to derive from an earlier sense meaning to 'ruin' which is related to the adjective **duff**.

> 'Michael threatened to duff him up if he ever did anything like that again.'
> (Recorded, teenage girl, London, 1986)

dufus, doofus *n American*
1a. an eccentric person
1b. a foolish or gauche person
1c. a gadget, intriguing object, thingummy
All three senses are typically used on college campuses. The origin of the term is obscure. It is probably an invented word with a mock Latin suffix, although there is a possible connection with *doofart*, a Scandinavian word for 'fool'.

duke it, duke it out, duke it up *vb*
to fight, brawl or box. Later formulations from the noun **dukes**, meaning fists.

duke on it *vb*
to shake hands. A slang version of 'shake on it', from **dukes**, meaning fists.

dukes *n pl American*
fists. This has been part of the jargon of streetfighters and pugilists since the turn of the 20th century. It originates either in the rhyming slang Duke of York: *fork*, i.e. a hand or finger, or from a Romany word meaning palm or hand. The word is most commonly heard in the challenge 'put up your dukes' or the phrase **duke it out** (to engage in a fist-fight).

duke someone *vb*
to slash someone across the legs with a sharp instrument as, e.g., a gang punishment. Recorded among Asian youths in Oldham, UK, 2003.

dukey rope *n*
a gold chain as worn by males. It is an emblematic accessory among **rap** and hip hop aficionados.

dumbass *n, adj American*
(a person who is) stupid. A relatively modern extension of dumb.
See also **dumbo**

dumb cluck *n*
a stupid or gormless person. In origin a rustic Americanism, probably inspired by the supposed stupidity of chickens.
See also **dumbo**

dumbell *n American*
a stupid person.
See also **dumbo**

dumb-head n

a stupid person. An elaboration of the American sense of dumb which is a direct translation of the German *Dummkopf*: fool.

dumbo n, adj

(a person who is) stupid. The American use of dumb for stupid, reinforced by the German *dumm*, is as old as the British sense of mute. Since the 1960s the American sense has been adopted in colloquial British English. This variant word may have been reinforced by the Walt Disney film *Dumbo* (which was itself inspired by 'Jumbo', the name of an elephant at London Zoo).

dumdum, dum-dum n

a stupid person. An embellishment (by the linguistic process known as 'reduplication', which is common in nursery words) of dumb.

See also **dumbo**

dummy n American

a fool, simpleton or dupe. From 'dumb' in the American sense.

> *'The dummy got too chummy in a Bing Crosby number.'*
> (*Salome Maloney*, John Cooper Clarke, 1978)

See also **dumbo**

dummy up vb

to keep silent; refuse to speak. A more robust alternative to **clam up**, used for instance by underworld characters in fact and fiction.

dump n

1. a dirty, messy or dilapidated place. The word in this sense is now so common as to be a colloquialism rather than slang (which it would have been considered to be, say, in the 1950s).
2. an act of defecation, usually in a phrase such as 'take or have a dump'

> *'What are you doing back there, taking a dump?'*
> (*Friday 13th Part VI*, US film, 1986)

dumper n American

a violent male devotee of aggressive sexual practices. The term is used by police and pornographers to describe males indulging in rough sexual treatment of women.

dump on (someone) vb

to criticise or chastise, heap blame or responsibility on, denigrate. This expression is now often used as an innocuous

colloquialism, although it derives from the decidedly vulgar sense of **dump 2** above.

dun vb British

to criticise, denigrate, berate (someone). The usage was recorded among middle-class adolescent males in 2000.

dune-coon n American

an Arab, Middle-Eastern person. A derogatory term recorded in armed-forces' use during the Iraq conflict of 2004.

dung-puncher n

a male homosexual. A highly pejorative term paralleling **fudgepacker**, **browniehound** and **turd burglar** in the reference to the faecal aspects of sodomy.

dunkie n British

a girl. The word is probably an abbreviation of 'dunkin' donut', a trademark name of an American chain of doughnut and coffee shops, although there may be a connection with the sexual sense of **dunking**. The overtones of the expression, used by teenagers in the 1970s, were not respectful.

dunking n British

sex. A euphemism which was in middle-class and 'society' use in the early and mid-1970s. It now seems to have fallen out of use but might be revived (on the pattern of similarly predictable terms which are periodically rediscovered). The origin is of course in the practice of dunking biscuits (in Britain) or doughnuts (in America) in tea or coffee.

dunky n British

a condom. The term is a back-formation from 'dunk' as a sexual euphemism.

dunnee, dunny n Australian

a toilet, especially an 'outhouse' or outside lavatory. The word was reintroduced to some British speakers via the Australianisms in the cartoon strip *The Adventures of Barry McKenzie* in *Private Eye* magazine in the late 1960s. In fact this term has existed for approximately 200 years in British English as 'dunnakin' (spelt in various ways, including 'dunnigan' in Ireland) and had become obsolete. The ultimate origin of these words is obscure but seems to be related to archaic dialect words for excrement such as *danna*, or its colour ('dun').

dunning n British
an admonition, telling-off, humiliation.
The term has been recorded since
2000, but may relate to a much older
use of the word to mean 'harass or
importune'.

'Three duhs in quick succession indicate
a relatively light dunning, but said more
slowly and forcefully the dunning
becomes more severe.'

(Recorded, London student, 2000)

durk n British See **derk**

durr-brain, durb n British
a foolish, slow-witted person. This popular term of abuse among schoolchildren probably imitates the hesitation
noise supposedly made, e.g., before
responding of a simpleton or dullard,
but might possibly be a version of the
American 'dough-brain'.

duss, dust vb
to depart, leave. In this sense the word
dust was recorded among black Americans as long ago as the 1930s, the
expression deriving from the image of a
cloud of dust being thrown up. As
'duss', the term was fashionable among
gang members and schoolchildren in
the UK from the mid-1990s.

It's the beast-man, let's duss!

dust¹ n
angel dust, P.C.P. Among young people
the shortened form was considered
cooler than the full phrase in the late
1980s

'Johnny does dust.'

(Graffito, Hammersmith, London, 1987)

dust² vb American
to kill. A 'tough-guy' euphemism implying the casual elimination of nuisances,
typically in a gangland or military context. The origin is probably in a now-
obsolete use of dust, meaning to 'hit',
which survives in the expression 'dust-
up'.

dustbin lids n pl British
children, *kids*. A piece of fairly modern
rhyming slang which has spread beyond
its working-class London context. The
singular form exists, but is rare. 'Saucepan lids' is an alternative form.

dust bunny n American
a ball of fluff lurking in an undusted part
of a household. (Also known as **dust kitty**
and many other terms.)

'She won't make the bed, she won't
sweep up the dust bunnies or nothin'.'

(*The Rockford Files*, US TV series, 1980)

dust kitty n American
1a. a ball of fluff, found for instance
under a bed or in another undusted part
of a household. This domestic phenomenon has given rise to a number of colourful expressions in American English (**dust
bunny, beggar's velvet**, 'house moss' and
ghost turds are others), but none in British English.
1b. the navel. So-called due to its being a
repository for fluff, etc.

dusty, dustie n British
1. an old person. A term of mild contempt
or even affection to their elders among
Sloane Rangers and other young people
of the late 1970s, becoming more widespread since. A less common alternative
to **wrinkly**. In *The Official Sloane Ranger
Handbook* (1982) Ann Barr and Peter
York attempted to define the ages of
adults as follows: **wrinkly** (40 to 50 years
old); **crumbly** (50 to 70 years old); and
dusty (70 and above).
2. a dustman. Not as common an abbreviation as **postie** for postman, for
instance.

Dutch¹ n British
1. one's wife. This hundred-year-old
piece of cockney usage is still heard
(invariably in the form 'my old Dutch'),
although now often used facetiously or
self-consciously. It may be a shortening
of **duchess** (originally 'Duchess of Fife',
rhyming slang for *wife*), or she may be so-
called after 'an old Dutch clock' (a
homely piece of furniture with a broad
open dial).
2. a friend, *mate*. A second cockney
sense of the word comes from the rhyme
'Dutch plate'.

Dutch², Dutch fuck vb American
to have sex by putting the penis
between the female breasts. Dutch here
is used as in other expressions, like
'Dutch auction', 'go Dutch', etc., to
mean unorthodox. In British armed-
service slang Dutch fuck referred to
lighting one cigarette from another.

dweeb n
a foolish, gormless or unpopular person.
An American campus and high-school
word of the late 1980s, adopted by British youth since 1988.

'I didn't even tell her my name – I am a
dweeb!'

(*18 Again!*, US film, 1988)

dwem *n*

a 'dead white European male'. A key term in the 'politically correct' lexicon of the mid-1990s; a dismissive categorisation of members of the supposed literary canon, such as Shakespeare.

dyke, dike *n*

a lesbian. The only common slang term to describe a female homosexual; it was first used derogatorily by heterosexuals, but it is now used by **gay** women themselves, though often wryly. When said by a heterosexual the word usually still carries overtones of the 'aggressive masculine' stereotype of a lesbian. No one has satisfactorily explained the term's ultimate origin; it might be from an old pejorative euphemism for a woman's genitals. Another, rather far-fetched, theory is that it is inspired by the story of the little Dutch boy with his finger in the dyke. Whatever its origin the word seems to have been imported into British English from America between the world wars.

dykie, dyky *n, adj*

1a. like a **dyke**, a lesbian

1b. (of a woman) 'masculine' in behaviour and/or appearance

dykon *n British*

a lesbian. A variant form of **dyke** in use among schoolchildren since the 1990s. It may have originated as a blending of 'dyke' and 'icon', thus referring to the object of **gay** females' admiration rather than the females themselves.

dynosupreme *adj American*

excellent, perfect, outstanding. Often an exclamation, this is a teenage vogue elaboration of supreme using a mock-prefix based on 'dynamo' or 'dynamic', or a contraction of 'dynamite'.

E

E *n*

1. (a dose of) the drug **ecstasy**. An abbreviation in vogue in the UK since the late 1980s.

   She's on E.

2. *See* **big E, the**

eagle freak *n American*

an enthusiast for environmental issues. A pejorative categorisation heard particularly on campuses, the term is part of a set including **duck-squeezer**, **tree-hugger**, **earth biscuit**, **granola**, etc.

earache *n British*

incessant chatter, complaining or nagging. The expression usually occurs in working-class speech.

   Will you stop giving me all this earache about being late and let me eat my tea in peace.

ear-basher/-banger/-bender *n*

someone who talks incessantly, a person who harangues, nags or bores. Earbasher is heard in Britain and Australia; ear-banger and ear-bender are predominantly American.

earlies *n pl British*

underpants, knickers. A fairly obscure but surviving instance of 19th-century London rhyming slang. The rhyme is 'early doors': *drawers*. 'Early doors' is from theatrical jargon.

earner *n British*

a scheme or situation which brings financial advantage, especially when unexpected or illicit. Originally from the language of police and thieves, the term, especially in the vogue phrase 'a nice little earner', entered general circulation in the profit-oriented society of the late 1980s.

   'The job's hard work, long hours and pretty boring – but at £70 a week it's a nice little earner if you're 15 and living at home.'

   (Teenage truant, *Observer*, February 1988)

earnings *n pl British*

the proceeds of crime or dishonesty. An item from the language of adolescent gangs. The term was recorded in use among North London schoolboys in 1993 and 1994.

ear'ole[1] *n British*

a dull, gormless or exasperating person. A word used typically by working-class schoolchildren in the 1970s to refer to tedious fellow pupils or adults.

ear'ole[2] *vb British*

1. to 'buttonhole' (someone); in other words, to detain (someone) in conversation

2. to scrounge; from **on the earhole/ear'ole**, which earlier in the 20th century meant to try to swindle

3. to nag, shout at, talk incessantly

4. to listen to, eavesdrop

All these senses of the word are in mainly working-class use and are most commonly heard in London.

earth biscuit *n American*

an enthusiast for environmental issues. A pejorative categorisation heard particularly on campuses, the term is part of a set including **duck-squeezer**, **tree-hugger**, **eagle freak**, **granola**, etc.

earwig *vb British*

1. to eavesdrop or listen out for news, danger, etc. A working-class word used by the underworld and, more innocuously, by or about neighbourhood gossips, etc.

   'You cunning git! You was earwiggin' my conversation.'

   (*Only Fools and Horses*, British TV comedy series, 1989)

2. to understand, realise. A less common sense of the word in this rhyming-slang expression (from **twig**).

ear-wigging *n British*

a synonym for 'ear-bashing', punning on the earwig insect and the 19th-century colloquial use of 'wig' to mean scold

'That didn't stop [David] Puttnam giving [Christopher] Patten a severe ear-wigging from the green pulpit last week.'
(*Sunday Times*, 26 November 1989)

ease down! *exclamation*
calm down, relax

easy *adj British*
good, acceptable, pleasant. An all-purpose term of appreciation, used especially in provincial England since 2000, this adjectival usage is inspired by the earlier usage as an exclamation.

an easy night out
She's easy, man.

easy! *exclamation*
1. *British* a generalised cry of derision, triumph, joy, etc. The word is usually lengthened to 'eezee!' It originated on football terraces in the 1960s, and is often heard in repetitious crowd chants at sporting events.
2. an all-purpose greeting or farewell which probably originated in gang usage whence it was adopted by adolescents in the 1990s.
Compare **easy-seen!**

easy meat *n*
1a. a person who is easy to seduce or take advantage of
1b. something easy to achieve or acquire. The phrase has been in currency since the 1920s.

easy-peasy *adj British*
very easy indeed, posing no problem. A popular phrase with younger schoolchildren since the early 1980s, although common in Scotland and northern England for decades.

easy rider *n British*
(a drink of) *cider*. Rhyming slang employed by students since the later 1990s, using the name of the 1969 movie.

easy-seen! *exclamation British*
an elaboration of **seen**, used as an all-purpose exclamation of greeting, thanks, approbation, etc. The term was recorded in use among North London schoolboys in 1993 and 1994.

eat, eat out, eat someone out *vb*
to perform cunnilingus. These Americanisms of the 1960s are heard in Australia and, to a lesser extent, in Britain.

eat dirt *vb See* **eat shit**

eat it! *vb, exclamation American*
a euphemism for **eat shit!**

eat my shorts! *exclamation American*
an exclamation of defiance or contempt, popular among male high-school and college students from the 1980s. The shorts in question are of course (unsavoury) male underwear.

eat shit *vb*
1a. to submit to humiliation, to abase oneself. Until recently the phrase had more currency in the USA and Australia than in Britain.
1b. **eat shit!** an American exclamation of defiance or contempt

Ebonics *n American*
a variety of English mainly consisting of street slang and in use among young blacks in the late 1990s. The word is constructed from 'ebony' and 'phonics'. The school board in Oakland, California, was the first to recognise Ebonics, also known as 'black-speak' or **jive talk**, as a legitimate language variety.

ecaf *n British*
the face. An item of **backslang** which became part of the **parlyaree** in use among London **gays** from the 1950s.
Slap some make-up on your old ecaf.

eco-freak, eco-nut *n*
a person concerned with ecology and the environment. These dismissive or patronising terms, used by critics or mockers, surfaced in the 1970s.

ecstasy *n*
the drug MDMA (3,4 methylene dioxy methamphetamine). A preparation which was synthesised and patented in 1914 and rediscovered for recreational use in 1975 in the USA. The drug, related to **speed**, remained a minority taste until the early 1980s; it was used by Californian therapists among others and was legal until 1985. It is also known as **E**, **Epsom salts**, **X** and **adam**.

'Every generation finds the drug it needs...the cold, selfish children of 1985 think ecstasy will make them loved and loving.'
(*Republican Party Reptile*, P. J. O'Rourke, 1987)

edge city *n*
a sensation or situation in which one experiences tension, dread or anticipation. A dramatising of 'edgy' heard among drug users and progressive music fans.

edged *adj American*
nervous, anxious, irritated. This adaptation of the colloquial 'edgy' and the slang **edge city** was heard in black speech and campus slang from the early 1990s.

Edwardian *n British*
a **teddy boy**. A variant form of the name used seriously on occasions by journalists and facetiously by teddy boys themselves.

eek, eke *n British*
1a. the face. A word heard in London theatrical and **camp** slang from the late 1950s. The etymology is obscure. One suggestion, unfortunately rather far-fetched, is that it is from the scream of fright occasioned by glimpsing the said visage leering through the limelight.
1b. face-paint, make-up. Also a theatrical term, presumably derived from the first sense. **Slap** is a more common alternative.

eff *vb*
a euphemism for **fuck** heard in America and Australia but more popular in Britain. It is most often encountered in the phrase 'eff off' and 'effing and blinding' (cursing, using bad language).

> '*Mr … put his arms around my waist and tried to kiss my neck. I told him to eff off.*'
> (Victim of sexual harassment, *Daily Mirror*, 31 March 1989)

effect *n See* **in effect**

effort *n British*
1a. something or someone considered worthless, disappointing
1b. an exclamation of derision or schadenfreude
Both senses of the word form part of playground slang: the first probably originating in adult speech, where it was an all-purpose term for any unnamed object or person.

egg *n See* **lay an egg**

egg and spoon *n British*
a black person. Rhyming slang for **coon**; this picturesque working-class expression, its origin in children's egg-and-spoon races, usually implies contempt and dislike.

eggplant *n American*
an Afro-Caribbean person. The analogy is with the shiny, dark skin colour of the vegetable.

eggs-up *adj British*
intrusive, nosy. The term was recorded in West London in 1998. **Extra** and **inna** were contemporary synonyms.

eggy *adj British*
1. moody and/or agitated
> *He got really eggy when I said his new single was crap.*

2. excellent, in playground parlance
In both senses the word has been fashionable among schoolchildren since the late 1990s.

ego-trip *n*
an exhibition of self-aggrandisement, self-indulgence or other selfishness. The term dates from the late 1960s and derives from the notion that under the influence of LSD (on a **trip**) enlightened persons will lose their ego, while the unenlightened may experience a concentration of selfish impulses. **Trip** later took on the generalised idea of behaviour or idée fixe, and ego, simply egomaniacal or egotistic.

Egyptian PT *n British*
sleeping. A joking and contemptuous expression dating from before World War II. It derives from the feats of legendary laziness imputed to Arabs in general by the British forces overseas. The phrase survives, mainly in public-school and army slang.

elbow *vb British*
to dismiss (someone), to dispose of or reject (something). A more modern version of 'give it/them the elbow'. It is often in the passive form 'get elbowed'.

> '*OK, elbow the buskers, we haven't got time.*'
> (TV studio crew, *One Day in the Life of Television*, 1 November 1989)

elbow bender *n British*
a habitual imbiber of alcoholic liquor; a drunk. From the phrase to **bend the elbow** (in lifting a drink to the lips).

> '*Sam Brown admits she became a big-time boozer when she was a schoolgirl and is still a solid elbow-bender.*'
> (Photo caption, *People*, 23 April 1989)

electric soup *n*
alcoholic drink, a strong alcoholic punch. The phrase is predominantly heard in middle-class circles. It belongs to a set of synonymous phrases including **lunatic soup** and **giggle water**.

elephant n British
an unattractive female (not necessarily heavily built). In playground usage since 2000.
Compare **nellie**

elephants, elephant's trunk adj British
drunk. A piece of 100-year-old London rhyming slang which is still heard, although usually used facetiously.

> I seen him down our local again – completely elephants.

elf n British
an unpleasant and/or obnoxious person. In playground usage since 2000.

el ----o n
a Spanish pattern applied jocularly to English words mainly by American speakers. The meaning is 'the supreme ----', 'the quintessential ----' or just 'the ----'. It appears in 'el creepo', 'el sleazo', 'el cheapo', etc. This tendency (in imitation of Hispanic 'low life' speech) has been in evidence since the early 1970s.
See also the entries following

el primo n American
the very best, top quality. From Spanish in which it means the first (quality). The expression is used by **Anglos**, blacks, etc. in imitation of Hispanic speech.

el ropo n American
a cigar or **joint**, especially a large and noxious one, from the idea of low-grade tobacco resembling **rope**

elven adj British
a less common version of **elvish**

elvish, elfish adj British
bad, unpleasant, of poor quality. The term, of uncertain derivation, has been in playground usage since the late 1990s. It is probably unrelated to the Elvish language invented by J. R. R. Tolkien.

embalmed adj
drunk. A now fairly rare, predominantly middle-class euphemism, it is an old usage, probably coined in the 19th century and inspired by 'balm' (as a euphemism for comforting liquor), 'balmy' and the early 20th-century Americanism 'embalming fluid', meaning whisky.

embrocation n British
alcoholic drink. A humorous borrowing of the word for rub-on liniment, said mainly by the middle aged.

> I think a spot of embrocation might be in order.

Emma Freuds n pl British
haemorrhoids. An item of rhyming slang popularised by the comic Viz in its feature 'Nobby's Piles'. The name is that of a female TV presenter.

emmet n British
a tourist, an unwelcome stranger. A dialect word (meaning 'ant') used in Cornwall since the 1950s to refer disparagingly to swarms of holidaymakers. **Grockle** is another regional term with a similar meaning.

enchilada n American See **big enchilada**

ends n pl American
money. The term, probably originating in black street argot in the 1950s, was later adopted by college students. It may have begun as 'N's', referring to (bank)notes, or possibly derived from the cliché 'to make ends meet'. It is also said to be a shortening of 'dividends' or from 'ends and means'.

endsville n, adj American
the ultimate; the best or the worst. From the language of **hipsters** and **beatniks** in the late 1950s, already sounding dated by the 1960s.

eppy n British
an instance of uncontrolled behaviour, fury, tantrum. The shortening of 'epileptic fit' has been part of playground parlance since at least the 1980s.

> He threw an absolute eppy when he found out.

Epsom salts n British
the drug **ecstasy**. A vogue term on the **acid-house** scene in 1989. The expression was borrowed from the name of the old-fashioned purgative medicine (hydrated magnesium sulphate).

ept adj British
skilled, competent. A jocular back-formation from 'inept', heard in middle-class speech since the 1990s.

> 'I've got to say she's not very ept, is she?' (Recorded, office manager, London, 1996)

Compare **ert**

equipment n
1a. the male sex organs. An unromantic euphemism used by males and females alike.

1b. a woman's breasts. A rarer vulgarism, usually indicating unromantic appraisal.

'erb *n See* **herb**

'erbert *n British*
a foolish person, a cheeky, unwashed child. For many years, in London working-class slang, Herbert or 'Erbert was used to refer to any otherwise unnamed man or boy. Gradually, probably by being used in phrases such as 'silly 'erbert', it came to have the more pejorative sense. There probably never was an eponymous Herbert; it was merely a common working-class name from the Edwardian era.

erdie *n British*
a tedious, orthodox, **straight** individual. The origin of the term is mysterious: Eric Partridge's dictionary derives it somewhat unconvincingly from the German *Erde*, meaning 'Earth', as in earth-bound.

> 'Most managers were erdies; agents ditto.'
> (Rolling Stones' manager Andrew Oldham in 1965, quoted in Christopher Sandford's *Mick Jagger: Primitive Cool*, 1993)

eric *n British*
1. an erection. A schoolboy term.
2. a foolish, gauche or unpopular male. This sense of the word also occurs in school argot and may be a corruption of **erk** or **oik**.

erk *n British*
a vulgar, inferior or tedious person. A piece of armed-service and public-school slang which some authorities derive from aircraft. It may in origin be a version of **oik**.

erp, earp *vb American*
to vomit. The word is echoic and has been recorded among teenagers of both sexes.

> *Someone's erped in the parking lot.*

-ers *n, suffix British*
a termination added to all or part of a standard word. In public-school, armed-forces' or middle-class speech it confers familiarity or affection. The core-word is sometimes preceded by **harry-**, as in **harry-starkers** for stark naked. This speech-pattern, found risible by many since the 1960s, arose at Oxford and in public schools in the late 19th century.
See also **preggers**; **honkers**; **starkers**

ert *adj British*
alert, lively, aware. A humorous backformation from the standard term inert, heard in middle-class adult speech since the 1990s.

> *You've got to try to be a bit more ert!*
Compare **ept**

Ethiopia! *exclamation British*
a jocular farewell, coined by analogy with **Abyssinia!**

Eurotrash *n*
the European 'jet-set' and their hangers-on. A version of 'international **white trash**', heard in 'society' and journalistic circles.

> 'I enjoyed it, famous bits of Eurotrash enjoy it, but Miss Mouse might not feel altogether comfortable.'
> (Rupert Christiansen, *Harpers and Queen*, November 1989)

eve *n British*
the drug MDEA, a stimulant related to **ecstasy** which is known as **adam** (from MDMA)

evil *adj American*
impressive, admirable. This use of the word originated in the jargon of black musicians; a rarer variant of **bad** or **wicked**. It is now used by teenagers of all ethnic origins, in Britain and Australia as well as the USA.

evil(s) *n See* **give someone evil(s)**

eviling *n*
adopting a menacing attitude, glaring, frowning. The word, used intransitively and transitively, is part of the post-2000 lexicon of teenagers and younger schoolchildren in the UK **Giving someone evil(s)** is an alternative form.

ex *n See* **X**

excrement *exclamation, adj British*
excellent. A jocular usage among students since 2000.

exercise the ferret *vb Australian*
to have sex. An unromantic male expression equating the penis with the aggressive, hyperactive animal and its well-known proclivity for wriggling into crevices and tunnels.

exes *n pl British*
expenses. A variant form of **eckies**.

extra *adj British*
intrusive, nosy. In this sense the word was recorded in West London in 1998. Contemporary synonyms were **eggs-up** and **inna**.

extract the Michael vb British
to **take the mickey**; to mock. A humorously pedantic version of the well-known colloquialism.

extract the urine vb British
to **take the piss**; to mock. A mock-pedantic version of the common, more vulgar expression.

eyeball[1] vb
to look at, stare at or inspect. The expression probably originated in the USA in black usage in the late 1940s. By the 1970s it was heard in Britain and Australia, especially among teenagers and the police. In the form 'eyeballing' the term can have the specific meaning of staring threateningly or provocatively.

> 'Villains call it clocking in Leeds, eyeballing in Manchester and screwing in London's East End…It came as a shock: juries can be intimidated by a stare.'
> (Sunday Times, 5 June 1988)

eyeball[2] n British
1a. a surveillance operation, in the jargon of the CID and the Flying Squad in particular

> We've been on eyeball for a week now.

1b. 'visual contact', a sighting. Another police term, employed, e.g., during a stakeout or surveillance operation.

> Do you have an eyeball on suspect one?

eye candy n American
1a. something decorative, visually attractive, often with the implication that it is not to be taken seriously

> 'The panoramic shots of the scenery is [sic] basically just eye candy for the audience.'
> (Recorded, film maker, London, 2004)

1b. an attractive person (typically of the opposite sex). The term can be either appreciative or mocking in the case of someone who is considered merely decorative and lacking other qualities.
Compare **arm candy**

eyetie n, adj
(an) Italian. A rather unimaginative and dated soubriquet, but fairly inoffensive, as opposed to **spaghetti-eater** or **wop**. The term arose at about the time of World War I.

F

F.A., Fanny Adams, sweet F.A./Fanny Adams
n British
1a. nothing at all. Fanny Adams is a widespread euphemism for **fuck-all**.

1b. a pitifully small amount. In 19th-century naval slang, Fanny Adams was tinned or cooked meat, a sardonic reference to a girl of the same name who was murdered and dismembered in 1867. The name was later matched with the initials of **fuck-all** and used euphemistically in its place.

> 'He says Eve behaved like a complete bitch over the kids' custody...and he'll get sweet F.A. out of the sale of the house.'
> (Party gossip in cartoon by Posy Simmonds, *Guardian*, 1979)

fab *adj*
brilliant, wonderful. This abbreviation of fabulous was adopted as an all-purpose term of approbation by teenagers in the 1960s from **camp** adult parlance and a local usage in Liverpool. The word has become popular again since the late 1980s, often ironically, but is also used in its original sense.

> 'No need to phone me, a text would be fab.'
> (Recorded, female executive, London, May 20005.)

fabe, fabe-o *adj British*
variant forms of **fab**, occurring in London **parlyaree** in the 1960s and recorded in the TV documentary *Out* in July 1992

face *n British*
1. an outstanding person, someone who is more sophisticated, better dressed, etc. than the rest. A vogue word among **mods** in 1963 and 1964, probably originating from the idea of a well-known or recognisable face in the crowd, or possibly from a 'face card', an expression occasionally heard in the USA, indicating an extraordinary, important or famous person.

2. a synonym for 'cheek' or **front 1**. This use of the word was popular in raffish speech from the late 1980s.

> '"A really good beggar makes maybe £50", Brian says. "I haven't got the face to do it".'
> (Homeless youth, *Independent*, 22 December 1989)

3. *See* **give (someone) face**
4. *See* **jump in (someone's) face**

faceache *n*
1a. an ugly person. A term of mild derision or abuse, now mainly confined to children's badinage.

1b. an indicated but unnamed person, a 'whatsisname'

> Old faceache's back again.

face-case *n American*
a teenage synonym for **faceache**, heard from the late 1980s

faced *adj American*
1. drunk. A **preppie** term which is a milder shortening of **shitfaced**.

> 'Get a six-pack of tall-boys, get faced and hit on the girls.'
> (*3rd Rock from the Sun*, US TV comedy, 1996)

2. humiliated, snubbed. This teenage term of the late 1950s describes the result of having been **put down**: it derives from 'losing face'.

face man *n American*
a male, especially an attractive male, considered to have a bland, insipid personality

fade *vb*
1. *American* to leave (a place), go away. A piece of **hipster** and **beatnik** language

from the 1950s which has been revived by teenagers since the 1980s.

Come on guys, let's fade.

2. *American* to meet or cover a bet. From the language of the dice game craps.

Ten bucks says he doesn't make it. Who'll fade me?

3. to kill, eliminate. A term from the argot of street gangs and other criminals.

'I feel like I can't be faded...just the hardest nigger around!'

(*Gang War*, Channel 4 TV documentary, August 1995)

faded *adj American*
inferior, unpleasant, tedious. An expression used on campus in the USA since around 2000.

fadge *n*
the vagina. A vulgarism in use among adolescents in the 1990s and listed in *Viz* comic in 1994. **Vadge** is an alternative reading.

faff, faff about *vb British*
to behave in a confused, disorganised or indecisive way. The expression usually indicates exasperation at another's incompetence.

'Stop faffing about and play the bloody thing forwards!'

(Recorded, football spectator, North London, 1988)

fag *n*
1. *British* a cigarette. In Middle English *fagge* meant, as a verb, to droop or, as a noun, a flap or remnant. These notions gave rise to 'fag-end' and subsequently, in the 19th century, to fag as a stubbed-out or limp, low-quality cigarette. In the 20th century the word was generalised to refer to any cigarette.

'"Come on darling give us a fag", says a brass to an elderly tom. "Have pity on a destitute prostitute!"'

(*Sunday Times* colour supplement feature on the East End of London, 2 June 1968)

2. *American* a male homosexual. This is generally taken to be a shortened version of **faggot**, but may pre-date it. (There is no discernible connection with the British public-school term meaning a junior boy performing servant duties.)

'I'm led into a room where a short fag doctor and a big bull-dyke nurse are waiting for me.'

(Bill Levy's journal in *Oz* magazine, February 1970)

faggot *n*
1. *British* an unattractive or disreputable woman. This now outdated term, some three hundred years old, is still heard in the phrase 'old faggot'.

2. *American* a homosexual man. It is not certain whether this term is an embellished version of **fag**, derives from the old British sense of the word (above), or is a native American invention. The second alternative appears the most likely.

'You know I'm a faggot?
Well, congratulations.'

(*Kiss of the Spider Woman*, film by Hector Babenco, 1985)

faggy *adj American*
camp, effeminate. The adjective is formed from the earlier noun.

'Just a faggy little leather boy with a smaller piece of stick.'

('Memo from Turner', song recorded by Mick Jagger, 1969)

fag-hag *n*
a woman who prefers the company of homosexual men. The expression became popular in the late 1960s with increased awareness of the **gay** community among **straights**. The phrase quickly spread from the USA to Britain and Australia. Although originally and usually used pejoratively, it can now be used neutrally, or by a woman of herself.

'She [Edith Olivier] became the supreme fag-hag of the 1920s and 1930s, the older woman who acts as mother-confessor and salonnière to a group of young homosexual men.'

(Bevis Hillier writing in the *Sunday Times*, 26 November 1989)

fagmonkey *n British*
an unpleasant and/or obnoxious person. In playground usage since 2000.

fag-stag *n American*
a heterosexual male who enjoys the company of **gay** males. The coinage is by analogy with the earlier **fag-hag**.

fains!, fainites!, faynits! *exclamation British*
a cry demanding a truce or exemption from something (such as being caught or penalised in a playground game). The various forms of the word are a survival of the archaic 'fains' or 'fains I' which means forbid and is related to the standard English fend.

'The air echoed with cries of pax, unpax, fains, roter, shutup.'

(*Back in the Jug Agane*, Geoffrey Willans and Ronald Searle, 1959)

fair dinkum *adj Australian*
just, honest, equable, worthy of approval. This well-known Australianism originated in a Victorian British dialect version of 'fair play' or 'fair share'. (The exact origin of the 'dinkum' component is not clear.)

fair go/goes *phrase Australian*
an interjection demanding fair or reasonable behaviour
   Come on, fair goes, give us a break.

fair suck of the pineapple/sauce stick
phrase Australian
elaborations of the colloquial 'fair crack of the whip'

fairy *n*
a male homosexual. The word in this sense probably originated in the American West around the turn of the 20th century. It was commonly heard in Britain by the 1920s.

fairy money *n British*
vouchers or coupons. The derisive phrase appeared in the mid-1990s, often referring to the redeemable but almost worthless tokens given out with petrol sales in garages.

fall *n See* **take a dive/tumble/fall**

fall guy *n American*
a dupe, victim or scapegoat. A pre-war Americanism deriving from the phrase 'to take a fall' (to be caught, arrested or imprisoned).
   'I'm the fall guy: I'm the one who'll take the fall if it all blows up.'
   (Recorded, security guard, Detroit, December 2004)

falsies *n pl British*
a padded brassiere or other padding worn to make a woman's breasts appear larger

family jewels *n pl*
the male genitals, more specifically the testicles. A jocular expression which may be Victorian in origin. Now sometimes shortened to 'jewels'.

fan *n*
1. an aircraft propeller
2. *American* the backside, buttocks. A shortening of **fanny 2**.
   She fell on her fan.

fang-farrier *n Australian*
a dentist. A humorous coinage: a farrier is a blacksmith.

fang it *vb Australian*
to drive fast, accelerate

fanny *n*
1. *British* the female genitals. This old and relatively inoffensive euphemism is possibly derived from the well-known erotic novel, *The Memoirs of Fanny Hill*, by John Cleland, published in 1749, or is perhaps simply an affectionate personification of the sex organs, using the short form of Frances. The word is used by women as well as men.
2. *American* the backside, buttocks. The American sense of the word probably derives from the earlier British sense. Fanny is sometimes confusingly used with this meaning by middle-class speakers in Britain too.

fanny about *vb British*
to **faff about**, dither. The **fanny** element may be present merely for its sound, its proximity to fuss or **faff**, or as a suggestion of femininity, rather than as a direct reference to the buttocks or genitals.

Fanny Adams *n British See* **F.A.**

fanny-fit *n British*
a bout of consternation or agitation. This term, based on fussing as described in the phrase **fanny about**, became popular amongst all age groups in the 1990s. **Hissie-fit** is a similar usage from the same period.

fanny-magnet *n British*
an attractive young male. This racier version of the widespread phrase **babe-magnet** was posted on the Internet by Bodge World in 1997.

fanny merchant *n British*
someone who behaves in an indecisive, weak or supposedly effeminate way
   'Stop pratting about, Hoddle, and get stuck in. You're nothing but a fanny merchant.'
   (Recorded, football supporter, North London, 1985)

fanny rat *n British*
a womaniser or seducer. A term used with either contempt or admiration by other men.
   'A policeman accused of drowning his wife in a holiday villa's Jacuzzi bath was branded "King Fanny Rat" by his colleagues because of his womanizing.'
   (*Daily Mirror*, 15 April 1989)

fanny-toots *n British*
an unnamed or unnameable person, so-and-so. The term, recorded in Edin-

burgh in 2001, is a synonym for collo-quialisms such as 'thingummybob' and 'oojamaflip'.

fantabuloso *adj British*
exceptionally good and/or spectacular. An item of **parlyaree** recorded in the TV documentary *Out* in July 1992.

farley, farly *n American*
a man or boy, a **gay** male, a ridiculous or unattractive person. A **Valley Girl** term used in the early 1970s.

> *'I can't get behind London. There are all these crazy farleys everywhere.'*
> (Recorded, Californian teenage girl, 1970)

Farmer Giles *n See* **farmers**

farmers *n pl British*
haemorrhoids. Rhyming slang from Farmer Giles: *piles*. The eponymous farmer is a common personification of bucolic heartiness. The longer version, Farmer Giles, was heard, particularly among schoolchildren, until at least the late 1970s.

> *'Send your farmers packing with "Prepa-ration Ouch".'*
> (*There's a Lot of it About*, British TV com-edy series starring Spike Milligan, 1989)

far-out, farout *adj*
1a. extreme, eccentric, unconventional
1b. wonderful, remarkable. By extension from the first sense, usually as an excla-mation in the approval of anything extraordinary.

> *'Marlene's entire range of expression was pretty much limited to "far out", "super" and "gross".'*
> (*The Serial*, Cyra McFadden, 1976)

Both senses of the phrase, originally an Americanism, were beloved by **hippies** from the late 1960s, but far-out was sounding dated by about 1974.

fart¹ *n*
1. an expulsion of intestinal gas from the anus. Not really a slang term, but often included as such because of its vulgar overtones. (For the etymology see the verb form.)
2. a term of abuse, sometimes dismiss-ive, now sometimes almost affectionate, heard especially in the expressions 'old fart' and 'boring old fart' (**B.O.F.**) Fart in this sense suggests someone inconse-quential, ineffectual or otherwise worthy of mild contempt.

fart² *vb*
to 'break wind', expel intestinal gas through the anus. The word is a descendant of an old Germanic verb *fer-zan* which in turn comes from an Indo-European root *perd-* or *pard-* (giving modern French *péter* among others). In English fart has never been genuine slang, but is sometimes considered to be so because it is taboo in polite com-pany. This was not the case until the 18th century.

fart around/about *vb*
to mess around, waste one's time or play the fool

> Come on you guys, stop farting around and get down to business.

fart-arse, fartarse about/around *vb British*
to waste time, behave ineffectually or indecisively. A common, mildly vulgar term in British and Australian English. It is an elaboration of **fart around**.

> I wish they'd stop fart-arsing around and make their minds up.

fartleberries *n pl*
another term for **dingleberries**

fashionista *n*
a fashion expert or arbiter of taste. The term employs the Spanish '-ista' suffix by analogy with 'Sandinista' (Nicara-guan freedom fighter of the 1970s).

fast-ass, fast-arse *n, adj British*
(a person who is) clever, socially adept. A term of approbation from the slang of London schoolchildren in the 1990s, often pronounced (like the similar smart-ass/arse) in the American way.

> Sarah just thinks she's such a fast-ass, but she isn't.

fat *adj*
excellent, fashionable, **hip**. A vogue term of approval in youth subcultures of the 1980s. **Fattier** and **fattiest** are derived terms. The word is sometimes spelt **phat**.

fat city *n American*
1. a state of contentment and/or material repletion, a very satisfactory situation

> Wait till you see the set-up there – he's in fat city.

2. obesity or an obese person. A high-school and college term of the 1970s and 1980s.

> Get a load of fat city, here!

fat farm *n*
a health farm or slimming centre

fatso n
a fat person. This unfriendly term from the USA largely superseded the more typically British 'fatty' in the 1960s.

fave, fave rave n
a favourite thing or person. The expression was first used in the 1960s. Nowadays it is almost always used humorously or ironically, typically surviving in the journalese of teenage magazines.

fax (someone) vb British
to **fuck**. A euphemism first heard in upper-class, media, and show-business circles.

But darling I'm quite sure she's faxing him.

faynits! exclamation British
an alternative form of **fains**

Feargal Sharkey adj British
chilly, cold. The rhyming slang (for the colloquial *parky*) uses the name of the Irish **punk** singer.

-features suffix
'-face'. In British and Australian English it is often added to other, usually offensive, words as an insult or mock insult as in **bum**-features, **creature-features**, **cunt**-features, etc.

feature with (someone) vb Australian
to have sex with, succeed in seducing someone. A favourite expression of *Barry McKenzie*. Popularised by the cartoon strip in *Private Eye* magazine in the 1960s, it was briefly current as a result among students and others. It is probably inspired by the journalese 'featuring' as in 'starring', or as in being the main protagonist of a scandal.

If I don't feature with this tart tonight the Pope's a flamin' Jew.'
(*Barry McKenzie*)

feck! exclamation Irish
an alteration of **fuck** which pre-dates its popularisation by the TV comedy *Father Ted*

Fed n See **Club Fed**

Feds, the n pl American
law enforcers, FBI agents. The word, used especially by lawbreakers in the USA, was briefly and inappropriately picked up in Britain as a euphemism for police in the early 1970s.

feeb n American
a feeble-minded person, a **twerp**. A teenagers' term. This is one of a series of expressions for social misfits or peer-group outcasts coined by American school and college pupils. Earlier words such as **wimp** and **nerd** have entered world English, others like **dweeb**, which immediately pre-dated feeb, are rarely heard outside North America.

feek adj Irish
attractive, 'enchanting'. The word may be a variant form of fake used to mean magic(al).

feel n
a sexual contact, a **grope** or caress. In American teen jargon the word is often heard in the phrase **cop a feel**.

feel froggy vb American
to want to fight. An item of black street-talk which was included in so-called **Ebonics**, recognised as a legitimate language variety by school officials in Oakland, California, in late 1996. It comes from the catchphrase used as a challenge to fight: 'If you feel froggy, leap!'.

feel someone's collar vb
to arrest or take someone into custody. An item of police jargon, now more often expressed by the noun **collar**.

feenin' n
a variant form of **fiendin'**, recorded in the USA in 2004

feisty adj
spirited, tough and assertive, quarrelsome. The word looks like Yiddish, but is in fact from a southern American English dialect word for a small, fierce dog (a 'feist' or 'fice'), the name of which is distantly derived from 'fist', a variant of **fart**.

It was this feisty creature [Pamella Bordes] who ended a relationship with Andrew Neil by redecorating the walls of his Kensington flat with obscene graffiti.'
(*Private Eye*, February 1989)

felching n
the insertion of a live animal into the anus as a form of sexual stimulation. The practice was reported from California in 1993 and the word briefly became a vogue source of humour among UK adolescents.

The term may also be applied to other practices involving digital or anal contact with the anus.

femme, fem n, adj
1a. a lesbian accustomed to playing a passive, female role in relationships; the opposite role to **butch**
1b. an effeminate or passive male homosexual

Both terms are from the French for woman or wife (*femme*), and have been in fairly widespread use since the turn of the 20th century. Femme (or fem) was a slang term meaning woman in the 17th, 18th and early 19th centuries.

fence *vb, n*

(to act as) a receiver of or dealer in stolen goods. The word was generally considered slang until the 1960s; there being no equivalent shorter than the definition above. Fence is now a universally understood term. It is at least 350 years old, apparently originating as a shortening of 'defence', although the precise relationship to that word is unclear.

fender-bender *n American*

1a. someone who poses as a road-accident victim or stages an accident in order to claim compensation. A law enforcers' and lawbreakers' term.

1b. a minor traffic accident or 'shunt' in which a car or its wing or bumper is slightly dented

ferret *n See* **exercise the ferret**

fess up *vb American*

to confess, own up

> 'We want the truth!' 'What time is it?' 'Time for you to fess up!'
> (*Out of the Dark*, US film, 1988)

fidget *n British*

a secret, 'wrinkle', edge or angle. A mainly working-class term used, among others, by fraudsters and petty criminals.

> He's got a few fidgets worked out.

fiendin' *n*

craving. The vogue term from club culture was defined by the *Observer* in 2002 as '...hungry, thirsty but not for a sandwich or cup of tea'. It probably originated among drug users in the USA.

fierce *adj*

excellent, stylish. A term used by young street-gang members in London since around 2000.

fifi[1] *n American*

sex, sexual gratification. A humorous euphemism heard among middle-aged speakers, often in the phrase 'getting some fifi'. It was featured in the US film *Extreme Prejudice*, 1987.

fifi[2] *adj*

'prissy', conceited. This usage is probably inspired by the earlier use of the

word as a nickname for a female or a lapdog.

fifth wheel *n*

a superfluous or intrusive extra person, an unnecessary thing. The phrase is American in origin.

filleted *adj British*

a late 1980s version of **gutted**. A fashionable way of conveying intense (or exaggerated) disappointment, bitterness, etc.

> When she said she was going and taking the kids, I tell you, I was filleted.

fill someone in *vb British*

to beat someone up. A phrase dating from before World War II.

filmi *adj South Asian*

glamorous. A word evoking the glamour, ostentation and drama of Bollywood movies, now used by South Asians in the UK.

filth, the filth *n British*

the police, especially those in plain clothes. A thoroughly derogatory term coined in the 1950s and enthusiastically adopted by radicals, student demonstrators and criminals alike in the 1960s.

> 'I didn't realise he [an ex-boyfriend] was filth.'
> (Recorded, nurse, London, 1985)
> 'They don't call us the filth for nothing.'
> (Comedian Julian Clary, in police uniform, on *Friday Night Live*, April 1988)

filthy *adj British*

1. extremely wealthy. A shortening of 'filthy rich'.

> I tell you, she's absolutely filthy.

2. excellent. Like **dirty**, a vogue word in club culture since 2000. In Seattle it is always pronounced 'filty'.

fin *n American*

a five-dollar bill. From the Yiddish *finif*, meaning five.

See also **finski**

finagling *n*

devious machination, manoeuvre or manipulation. The word, which is sometimes used as a regular verb ('to finagle'), is well established in the USA. It is said to derive from the archaic British dialect word *fainaigue* (meaning to cheat).

financial *adj Australian*

well-off, in funds, solvent

> He's fairly financial just at the moment.

finesse (someone) vb American

to outmanoeuvre, cleverly manipulate or cheat someone. From the technique in contract bridge. Originally a cardsharps' term, now in general use.

finger¹ vb

to inform on someone. From the action of pointing out a culprit.

> They fingered him for the Jamaica Avenue job.

finger², finger fuck vb

to sexually stimulate (vaginally or anally) with the finger(s)

fink n American

an informer or any untrustworthy, reprehensible person. In the late 19th century the word was used for spies, informers, policemen and strikebreakers. It is the German word for finch and was presumably imported by German or Yiddish-speaking immigrants, although the exact meaning is obscure. (It appears not to be related to 'singing like a canary'.) Less plausibly, the name of the Pinkerton detective agency has also been suggested as a source.

See also **ratfink**

finski n American

a **fin** (five-dollar bill). An embellished form of the word used typically by high-school or college students. The **-ski** ending (in imitation of Slavic languages or Yiddish) is thought to add raciness to short everyday words.

> 'See what a finski can do for a man's attitude?'
> (Ferris Bueller's Day Off, US film, 1986)

fired-up adj

1a. angry, furious

1b. sexually aroused

1c. stimulated by illicit drugs

1d. enthused, aroused, excited

All these senses of the word are American slang in origin, based on the 'firing-up' or 'revving' of an engine. The term is now a common colloquialism.

fireman's hose n British

the nose. A piece of authentic rhyming slang, still heard occasionally in London.

> 'He had to stick his fireman's hose into it, didn't he?'
> (Recorded, hairdresser, Richmond, 1988)

firkin' adj

fucking. This word is generally thought of and used as a joky euphemism, inspired by the similarity of the taboo word with the archaic name for a cask of ale. In fact 'firk' existed as a verb in its own right in early modern English. It meant to strike, and also to copulate, and may even have been in origin a distortion of 'fuck'. The word is typically used as an intensifier, as in 'firkin' cold'.

firm, the firm n

1a. British a criminal gang or organisation. Also used by and of teams of football hooligans, such as the Inter-City Firm, a much-publicised gang of older West Ham supporters.

1b. an insider's, or would-be insider's, euphemism for an official but clandestine organisation, such as a secret-service department or undercover police group

first base n American

kissing, necking. The first stage in the process of seduction, as described by teenagers and students (usually from the male point of view). The image is taken from baseball, where to get to first base is the first step towards scoring a run; stretching the analogy, a **home run** or **homer** is full sexual intercourse.

fish n

a woman. The term is typically used pejoratively by **gay** males, referring to the supposedly characteristic smell of the female genitalia.

fishing expedition n

an attempt to gather information while purporting to be doing something else. An expression used in general conversation and, recently, specifically in business jargon where, e.g., a company will advertise for personnel in order to interrogate interviewees about rivals' plans.

fishing fleet n British

a group of females arriving en masse in search of partners or husbands. The expression is applied today mainly to visitors to the outpost of upper-class society in Hong Kong; it formerly referred to the same social phenomenon occurring in India, etc. in the colonial era.

fishwank adj British

inferior, disappointing, poor. A meaningless compound used especially by males since 2000.

fit¹ adj British

excellent, fashionable. A vogue term among adolescents in the early 1990s. Synonyms are **mint** and **top**.

fit² *n*

1. a set of clothes

I say rid [get rid of] the fit right now!

2. *British* the materials needed to prepare and inject heroin; the ligature, burner and hypodermic. An item of prisoners' and addicts' slang of the 1990s.

In both senses the word is a shortening of 'outfit'.

fit-chased *adj American*

drunk. A disguised form of **shitfaced** used by college students since the late 1990s.

fitted *adj American*
elegant, well dressed

fittie *n British*

an attractive person, usually referring to a female. A synonym of **hottie**, in use since 2000, based on the slang sense of **fit**.

fit up *vb British*

to **frame**; to manufacture evidence to procure a (false) conviction for a criminal offence. A piece of police and underworld jargon, which by 1990 had become widely known through its use by journalists, scriptwriters, etc.

fit-up, fit *n*

a **frame-up**, a situation in which an innocent person is accused or incriminated on the basis of false evidence, perjury, etc. The noun derives from the verb form.

'It was an obvious bloody fit-up, but they let it go through anyway.'

(Recorded, pub customer, London, 1987)

Five-O *n American*

the police force or an individual police officer. The usage originated in the TV series *Hawaii Five-O*, broadcast in the early 1970s.

five by five *n American*
a short, fat person

five-finger discount *n American*

something stolen, especially a shoplifter's booty. This is the thieves' own term, popular, especially in New York, in the 1970s and 1980s.

five-pinter *n British*

an ugly or unattractive female. The pejorative term was defined by the Student World website in 2001 as 'an ugly girl you'd only chat up after five pints'. **Ten-**

pinter is an alternative form of the expression.

five thousand!, 5000! *exclamation American*

goodbye. A variant form of **Audi!**

fix *n*

an injection of a narcotic. Originally an Americanism, by the 1960s it was in use throughout the English-speaking world. The word is now also used metaphorically or ironically to describe any habitual action, such as taking a fix of nicotine, or any pleasure which the speaker would not willingly forgo, as in a weekly fix of a television programme.

fizzy pop *n British*

alcoholic drink. A jocular euphemism as used by parents and adolescents.

Too much fizzy pop, mate!

flack *n See* **flak**

flag *vb American*

to fail. In high-school and college usage, the term refers to an F grade attached to an assignment.

I knew they'd flag me.

Erin got flagged again.

flagged *adj American*

nabbed, reprimanded, identified and/or warned. It is the custom in American-football matches for the umpires to throw a flag (a sort of yellow duster) when they spot an infringement, to mark the spot where it took place. This is known as there being 'a flag on the play'. Flagged sometimes has the very specific senses of having been refused further drinks in a bar or being arrested.

flak *n*

criticism, antagonism, aggression, trouble. The terms *Flugabwehrkanone* and *Fliegerabwehrkanone*, given to German World War II anti-aircraft guns, provided this acronym which was adopted as an English colloquialism. It is now sometimes spelt flack.

We've had to take a lot of flak over this.

They've been getting a lot of flak from head office recently.

flake *n*

1. *American* an eccentric or crazy person. A later formation from **flaky**. The origin is obscure.

'Marx stands out as refreshingly creative and literate among a batch of flakes.'

(Robert Conquest, *Independent*, 27 January 1989)

2. *Australian* shark meat

flake and chips

3. *American* cocaine. High-quality Peruvian cocaine, e.g., is often sold in the form of small flakes.

4. *Australian* an unscrupulous, untrustworthy person

5. *Scottish* an unreliable or dangerous individual.

See also **flaking**

flaked, flaked out *adj*
exhausted, collapsed

flake out *vb*
1. *American* to leave (a place). An American teenagers' idiom in use since the late 1970s.
2. *American* to act eccentrically. From **flake** and **flaky**.
3. to collapse from weariness, fall asleep. In this sense the word is now a common colloquialism. Its derivation is uncertain.

flakers *adj British*
exhausted. A term from armed-forces' usage, from the colloquial 'flake out' (collapse from fatigue).

They were all flakers after the manoeuvres.

flaking *n American*
doctoring, manufacturing or planting evidence to secure an arrest and/or conviction. Police jargon of uncertain derivation.

flaky[1], flakey *adj American*
eccentric, crazy, unstable and irresponsible. This Americanism was given wider currency when President Ronald Reagan referred to Colonel Gaddafi as 'flaky' in January 1986; the word had to be translated in the press for British and Australian readers. The original connotations of the word are obscure. Suggested derivations are from **flake** as a word for cocaine, or from 'flaking' or 'crumbling' stucco, stone, timber, etc. This second derivation, with overtones of disintegration and splitting or dividing, is more plausible.

flaky[2], flakey *n British See* **throw a flaky**

flame *vb*
to attack verbally and/or humiliate by sending an Internet or e-mail message. An item of **net-head** slang dating from the later 1980s.

She got flamed.

flamer *n*
1a. *American* a flagrant or obvious solecism or blunder
1b. *American* a person who commits a gaffe or error

Both these sub-senses of the word are campus terms, used especially in **preppie** jargon.

2. a flagrant male homosexual, in American and Australian slang of the 1970s and 1980s. Since the beginning of the 19th century the word had been employed in British English to refer to something conspicuous.

flaming[1] *n*
1. *American* (of homosexual males) behaving in a provocative or flamboyant manner

2a. using computer links and networks to carry on obscene or sexually titillating conversations. A term of the late 1980s. This noun form preceded the later use of **flame** as a verb.

2b. posting verbal attacks upon an Internet user, in the 1990s patois of **cyberpunks** and **net-heads**

flaming[2] *adj*
an intensifying adjective; an alternative to **bloody** or a euphemism for **fucking**. The word is mainly heard in Britain, where it is rather dated, and in Australia, where it is fairly common. Especially in the north of England it forms part of several colourful but inoffensive oaths such as 'flaming heck', 'flaming 'eck' and 'flaming Nora'.

flange *n British*
the vagina. The phrase 'piece of flange' is armed-forces' slang for (an attractive) woman. In its primary sense flange was publicised by its use in 2003 TV revelations of drunken revelling by young UK tourists in Ibiza.

Show us your flange!

flanked *adj American*
drunk. An expression used on campus in the USA since around 2000.

flannel *vb, n*
(to subject someone to) talk intended to flatter, deceive, bamboozle, cajole, etc. This term is now a well-known colloquialism for waffle or nonsense. It was originally (in the 19th century) a scathing term for the pretentious ornamentation on commercial letterheads, etc.

He gave me a load of old flannel.

flapdoodle n
fuss, agitation, consternation. An invented nonsense word dating from the 19th century.

flap one's gums vb American
to talk, speak or converse. An item of black street-talk that was included in so-called **Ebonics**, recognised as a legitimate language variety by school officials in Oakland, California, in late 1996. 'Flap one's lips' is a less common variant, **snap/bump one's gums** are synonyms.

flaps n pl
1. ears, especially large or protruding ears
2. the female labia

flash¹ n
1. a glimpse of, or deliberate exposure of, the genitals, breasts, underwear, etc.
2a. the sensation felt immediately after the injection of a narcotic; the sudden, initial effect of a drug
2b. also **acid flash** a sudden recurrence of a previous experience of the drug LSD (lysergic acid diethylamide)
3. British a street trader's display of goods
4. an ugly or unattractive female, **minger**. The derivation 'because she mings mercilessly' is from the Flash Gordon cartoons and film in which the villain is 'Ming the Merciless'.

flash² adj
ostentatious, showing off. Since the 1960s, especially in Britain and Australia, this form has tended to replace the earlier 'flashy'.

> 'Why do you bring horses if not to sell? It's flash.'

(Recorded, gypsy boy, Appleby horse fair, 1988)

flasher n
a sexual exhibitionist, a man who deliberately exposes his genitals in public. The word was slang or police jargon until the 1960s when the prevalence of the activity and a lessening of verbal prudishness brought it into common currency.

Flash Harry n British
a show-off, a flamboyant or boastful person. The identity of the eponymous Harry is unknown.

flash the ash vb British
to offer a cigarette. Usually the expression is in the form of a request or demand.

flat adj British
penniless. A shortened form of the colloquial 'flat broke', heard in raffish speech of the late 1980s.

flatlining adj
drunk. The term is medical jargon for the state of a patient whose vital signs have disappeared, leaving only a flat trace on monitoring screens.

flave adj American
fashionable, stylish, **cool**. A vogue term among **rappers** and hip hop aficionados in the early 1990s, the word is an abbreviated form of the earlier word 'flavor', denoting personal style.

flavour of the month n
the current favourite or fashionable person or thing. An expression which usually expresses a scathing or critical attitude to fads or ephemeral popularity. (It derives from the use of the phrase in advertising ice cream in the USA in the 1950s and 1960s.)

fleabag n
1a. a cheap, dirty hotel
1b. a scruffy, dirty person or animal
1c. an old sleeping bag or bed

fleapit n
a cheap, dirty cinema. Originally the term usually referred to the front-stalls section and the 'pit' in front of the screen. Before World War II, in the case of rural cinemas especially, the term was often a literal description.

flex n British
energy, enthusiasm. A term from the jargon of dancefloor and **acid house** aficionados in the 1990s.

> Give it flex!

flexin' n
showing off, acting ostentatiously. A vogue term in club culture since the later 1990s, by 2001 also in use among UK schoolchildren.

flick n
a film. This word was first common slang, then trade jargon in the film business and now, via such American magazines as Variety, is emerging again as a general term for a film. (For the derivation see **flicks**.)
See also **skinflick**

flicking adj British
an intensifying adjective, a euphemism for **fucking**. It is used, e.g., by schoolgirls and adult women.

*'I can lay any amount of hands on them –
no flicking danger.'*
(*An Evening with Victoria Wood*, British
TV programme, 1988)

flicks, the flicks *n pl*
the cinema, films. An early slang term in
all English-speaking countries, derived
from 'flicker' or from the homemade
moving pictures made by flicking cards.
This form of the word is now obsolete in
the USA and has rarely been heard in
Britain or Australia since the early 1960s.
The singular form **flick** is still current.

*We're going down the flicks tomorrow
night.*

flid *n British*
a stupid person. The word was reported
as being in use among schoolchildren
by the sociolinguist Peter Trudgill in his
1990 work *Bad Language*, but seems to
have arisen in the 1970s. It may be an
arbitrary coinage, an obscure dialect
term or, alternatively, a conflation of
'flip one's lid' or, some suggest, of 'tha-
lidomide (victim)'.

flim-flam *vb, n*
(to attempt) trickery or deceit, specifically a confidence trick involving a tall
story. The word, which is in use in Britain, but more widespread in the USA,
probably comes, via Scottish dialect,
from an old Scandinavian word *flim*
meaning mockery. The added second
syllable is an example of a common linguistic change in comical words (such
as knick-knack, etc.) known as 'reduplication'.

*'I can smell flim-flam, right down to the
paperclips you make me buy.'*
(*Columbo*, US TV series, 1976)

fling *vb, n British*
1. (to give someone) a bribe, illicit payment. A piece of criminal and police jargon which is a more recent coinage
inspired by **bung**.

We'll have to fling him to square it.
I'd need a fling in that case.

2. an affair, usually extramarital

flip, flip out *vb*
to lose control, either through delight,
anger, etc., under the influence of an
illicit drug, or during the course of a nervous breakdown. Both words spread from
American English to world English in the
1960s and derive from the earlier 'flip
one's wig' or 'flip one's lid', in use in the
late 1940s and 1950s among **hipsters**,

jazz enthusiasts and **beatniks**. To flip out
was used to describe temporary insanity
caused by LSD in the early days of the
hippy era. The term is now old-fashioned
(although surviving in French, particularly in the form *flippé*).

*'He was worried about his mother,
though. The old lady was flipping out.'*
(*Requiem for a Dream*, Hubert Selby Jr.,
1979)

flipping *adj British*
a euphemism for **fucking** used as a mild
intensifier, especially in such phrases as
'flipping hell' or 'flipping heck'

*'"Stop standing there dreaming, lass",
shouts Dad, "and get the top orf this flipping bottle of 'arp".'*
(*Town* magazine, May 1964)

FLK *n*
'funny looking kid' in medical shorthand, a jocular version of 'possible dys-
morphology' as written, e.g., on a
paediatric patient's notes

floating *adj*
euphoric, especially from the effects of
illicit drugs. A now dated term common
in the late 1950s and early 1960s.

flob *vb British*
to spit. An echoic term heard among
schoolchildren since the 1950s.

flog *vb*
to sell. A common colloquialism in Britain which would still be considered
slang by some speakers. The word originally referred to selling off military
stores illicitly and is said to derive from
a 19th-century army expression to 'flog
the clock', meaning to put the clock forward to shorten the working day, later
extended to other devious behaviour.

**flog the   lizard/log/dong/meat/mutton/
bishop** *vb*
to masturbate. Colourful expressions
used of, and usually by, men. The verb
to flog was employed in the formation of
a large number of slang terms in the
18th and 19th centuries.

flook *n American*
an unattractive and/or unpopular person. An expression used on campus in
the USA since around 2000.

floored *adj British*
drunk. An item of student slang in use
in London and elsewhere since around
2000.

floozy, floosie *n*
a disreputable, immoral, 'loose-living' or frivolous female. A late-19th-century word which is still in use (now usually said lightheartedly). The word originated in the USA, but by the end of World War II was in widespread use elsewhere. It is probably a deformation of 'flossy', an archaic word for a prostitute (itself deriving from 'flossy', meaning 'showy', or from the female nickname).

flop¹ *n*
1. a place to sleep, a temporary bed or shelter. Especially in the USA the term has been used by vagrants since the early 20th century.
2. excreta. Probably originating in the USA, where **dogflop** is heard, this euphemism is paralleled by the British **plop(s)**.

flop² *vb*
1. to collapse exhausted, go to bed
2. to consent to sex. In this sense the word has been used, albeit rarely, in the USA at least since Raymond Chandler's private eye Philip Marlowe said of a woman that she would 'flop at the drop of a hat'.

flophouse *n*
a cheap hotel or dormitory for vagrants. Originally an Americanism, the word is now part of international English.

floss¹ *n American*
abbreviated female underwear; a G-string or thong. The colloquial shortening of 'dental floss' was used by females from the late 1980s to refer to thongs (in the sense in underwear).

floss² *vb American*
(of a female) to behave ostentatiously and/or offensively, usually in public. The term was popularised by its use by singer Jennifer Lopez. By 2002 it was also heard in the UK.

flossie, flossy *adj, n*
(behaving like) an ostentatious, pretentious or otherwise obnoxious female. Said to derive originally from **floss** in the sense of thong underwear, the term is used by females in the UK and USA of those they disapprove of.

flub *vb*
to fail, blunder. The word, of uncertain origin, was recorded among computer specialists and **rave** devotees in the 1990s.

fluff¹ *n*
1. nonsense, rubbish
'…so stop chattin' fluff!'
(Recorded, contributor to www.wass-up.com, November 2003)
2. *See* **bit of fluff**

fluff² *vb*
1a. to stimulate sexually. The term, from the jargon of pornographers, refers to assisting the male performer to an erection before filming.
1b. to arouse, excite
'Here, fluffing the crowd for Thirteen Senses, Liverpool's Afterkicks steal the night.'
(*NME*, 28 March 2005)
2. *British* a euphemism for **fuck**, used in the form **fluffing** as an intensifying adjective or in the expression 'fluff off!' (an exclamation delivered at journalists by Prince Philip in October 1987)

fluff³ *adj American*
easy, unchallenging. An expression used on campus in the USA since around 2000.

fluffing *adj British*
a mild euphemism for **flaming** or **fucking**, when used as intensifiers

fluffy *n British*
marihuana. The term was recorded in 2002.

fly¹ *adj American*
streetwise, fashionable. A vogue term in black street slang of the mid-1980s, later used by whites.
'You fly, you cool: too much macho man fu' one woman.'
(*LA Takedown*, US film, 1989)

fly² *n American*
1a. a **cool** male
1b. an unfortunate male who thinks he is **cool**

fly a kite *vb*
to issue a worthless cheque. Originally an underworld term from the jargon of fraudsters, the expression is now a common colloquialism with the meaning of presenting any dubious scheme or idea for approval. It retains its original meaning in criminal and police parlance.

fly-girl *n American*
the female counterpart of a **B-boy**

FMBs *n pl British*
calf-length boots for females. The abbreviation is for 'fuck-me boots' and was recorded in 2000.
See also **fuck-me shoes**

fod *n British*
the forehead. A schoolchildren's conflation.

fodder *n British*
food. A lighthearted or hearty usage, heard typically among middle- and upper-class speakers.

folderol *n*
fuss, complications, 'argy-bargy'. 'Folde-rol' and 'falderal' are nonsense words used in popular songs in former times.

folding stuff, the folding stuff *n*
money, banknotes. A common lighthearted euphemism.

> *'The Cali cartel has a gentler reputation, first offering large amounts of the folding stuff and abhorring murder unless it is absolutely necessary.'*
> (*Independent*, 12 September 1989)

fomp *vb American*
to engage in sexual horseplay, heavy petting. The word was popular among college students in the later 1990s but its derivation is unclear.

foodist *n Caribbean*
a glutton

foo-foo *n See* **fufu**

foofy *adj*
'prissy', conceited

fool around *vb American*
to commit a sexual indiscretion, typically adultery. A common euphemistic use of the expression, heard particularly among middle-class and middle-aged speakers since the 1960s. The term in this specific sense has not caught on outside the USA.

foolio *n*
a foolish person. A lighthearted insult in use since 2000, employing a mock-Italian termination (as in Coolio, the nickname of a well-known US **rapper**).

footsie *n See* **play footsie**

footy *n*
football. An abbreviated form popular in Australasia and in Britain where it is now more common than the older **footer** (which persists in public-school usage).

foozling *adj*
1a. clumsy, bungled

1b. trivial, footling. From the verb foozle meaning to play or move clumsily or bungle; itself from the German *fuseln*, meaning to work carelessly.

form *n British*
a criminal record. A police and underworld term derived from the language of the racetrack where it refers to a record or reputation based on past performance.

> *Has he got any form?*

fornicating *adj British*
a jocular euphemism for **fucking** (as an intensifying adjective)

> *I'm fed up hearing about his fornicating job!*

foul *adj American*
immoral, unacceptable. The standard term was appropriated by black street slang as a general indication of disapproval.

four-by-two, forby *n British*
a *Jew*. London rhyming slang in current usage. A descriptive, rather than an intrinsically offensive term. A four-bytwo is a standard size of timber plank used for rafters, etc. (In the USA it is known as a two-by-four.)

four-on-the-floor *adj, adv*
flat out, extremely, excessively. This term, used typically by the young in the 1980s, comes from the hot rodders' term for a 'stick shift' or four-speed gear system.

> *When I realised I wanted it, I tell you, I went at it four-on-the-floor.*

fox *n*
a person who is sexually attractive. The word was used in black American slang of the 1940s by men of women (who were also known as 'minks'). Fox was adopted by white speakers in the 1960s and can now also be said of men by women.

> *'She's a fox and she knows it too.'*
> (Lyrics to 'Deborah', written by Dave Edmunds and Nick Lowe, 1978)

foxy *adj*
attractive in a 'feral', sexually exciting way. Usually, but not invariably, used of women by men. The word was originally a black Americanism derived from the noun form **fox**; it is now widely known and used.

> *'Lookit all these foxy chicks! Everywhere I turn.'*

(Robert Crumb, cartoon in *Head Comix*, 1970)

fraff *n*

spoken nonsense. An item of London youth slang recorded for the film *Backslang* in 2003.

You're talking fraff.

fragged *adj American*

ruined or badly damaged. The term derives from the Vietnam-era practice of 'fragging' or killing one's own officers, itself based on 'fragmentation grenade'.

The fraternity house was totally fragged.

fraggle *n British*

a new-age traveller or **crustie**. The term, from the lexicon of the homeless, neo-**hippies**, etc., denotes an unkempt and/or seemingly deranged youth. It is inspired by the TV puppet series *Fraggle Rock*.

framed *adj*

falsely accused, incriminated or convicted of a crime. The term was first used in the USA in the early years of the 20th century.

frame-up, frame *n*

a situation in which someone is **framed**. Originally an Americanism from the early years of the century.

francis, frances *n American*

the buttocks. The derivation of this term, heard in the armed forces and on college campuses, is obscure but it may be a euphemism for **fanny**.

franger *n Australian*

a condom

Frank *n British*

a TV remote control. The reference is to the late musician Frank Zappa and **zapper**.

Pass the Frank, will you.

frass *adj*

1. untidy

2. smelly, repellent

His crib is well frass.

An item of London youth slang recorded for the film *Backslang* in 2003.

frat *vb, n*

1. *British* a schoolchildren's alteration of **fart**

2. (to indulge in) fraternisation

freak¹ *vb*

to lose control of oneself, become hysterical. A shortening of **freak out**, this term came, in **hippy** usage of the late 1960s

and early 1970s, to have a negative connotation of alarm or over-reaction.

I told her I was leaving home and she completely freaked.

freak² *n*

1. a **hippy**, a long-haired (if male), non-conformist member of the 'alternative society' of the late 1960s and early 1970s. Freak was originally a term of abuse directed by **straights** at homosexuals and later at those guilty of outlandish behaviour and/or bizarre appearance. The term was quickly adopted by the objects of abuse and used as a badge of pride in themselves. (Hippies almost never referred to themselves as hippies after 1966; freak remained the acceptable epithet until the movement faded in the early to mid-1970s.) The word has now reverted to its original derogatory sense and is applied for instance to sexual deviants.

'I feel like lettin' my freak flag [i.e. long hair] fly.'

(Song lyric, Crosby, Stills, Nash and Young, 1970)

2. (as a suffix **-freak**) an enthusiast, devotee. From the mid-1970s the word was used in this sense, as in health-freak, **eco-freak**, etc. It was originally a **hippy** usage, as in acid-freak. The term now sounds dated and has partially been replaced by the less radical **buff**.

3. *American* a sexually active or promiscuous person. This item of black street slang may be used pejoratively or appreciatively.

See also **freaky-man**

freaking *adj*

an intensifying adjective, a euphemism for **fucking**

'You're a narc, you're a freaking narc!'

(*Magnum*, US TV series, 1981)

freak out *vb*

to lose one's self-control, to behave in an outrageous, frantic way. The phrase first described the alarming effect of hallucinogenic drugs such as LSD on some users, but was soon extended to any wild behaviour (whether viewed positively or negatively) such as ecstatic dancing. The expression originated in the USA among the first **hippies** and quickly spread to other English-speaking areas; it was sounding dated by the mid-1970s.

freak-out, freakout *n*

a bout or scene of wild abandon, self-expression or loss of control. Originally, in

hippy terminology, it was the result of ingesting hallucinogenic drugs, but later came to refer to any simulation of their effects.

'These guys that come up and say: "Wouldn't it be a mind-blower if we got 6,000 million kids in red uniforms and had a big freak-out in the middle of Ealing Common".'
(Pete Townshend of The Who, interviewed in *Oz* magazine, June 1969)

freak someone out *vb*
to alarm, traumatise or 'transport' someone. A transitive form of **freak out**.

'Coming up next on channel 4: a task that freaks out one of the girls on Big Brother.'
(UK TV announcement, 20 June 2005)

freaky *adj*
1a. unorthodox, non-conformist, pertaining to **freaks**
Their awful freaky dancing.

1b. amazing, outstanding, **far-out**. A term of approval used by **freaks**.
this freaky chick

2. *American* upset, unsettled. A 1990s synonym for **freaked out** or **freaking out**, used by neo-**Valley Girls**, e.g., 'When I saw him I was, like, freaky'.

freaky-deaky *adj*
a later elaboration of **freaky** in both senses. This form of the word was generally used pejoratively, condescendingly or sarcastically.

freaky-man *n Caribbean*
a male homosexual. A pejorative term, like the contemporary **chi-chi man**.

freckle *n Australian*
the anus. One of many Australian vulgarities (**ace**, **date**, etc.) to denote this anatomical feature.

freebasing *n*
taking cocaine by mixing the crystals with various volatile solvents, including ether, to form a **base** which is then smoked in a pipe. This activity is also known as 'basing'.

'…the technique known as freebasing, a method of separating the base cocaine from the hydrochloride salt…the result is pure crystals of cocaine…'
(*Guardian*, 5 September 1989)

french *vb*
1. to perform oral sex. A jargon term from the world of prostitution and pornography. The word may refer to cunnilingus or fellatio and derives from the British

notion that all forms of 'deviant' sexual behaviour are widespread among, if not invented by, the French. This may originate in the widespread accusation or supposition of the spreading of venereal disease by foreign neighbours.

2. to engage in **French kissing**, in the language of teenagers. In this sense the word is most commonly heard in the USA.
See also **Frenching unit**

frenchie, frenchy *n*
a condom. From the now obsolescent 'French letter', one of many examples of ascribing anything with sexual connotations to the French. (In French the equivalent is *une capote anglaise*, meaning an English bonnet or overcoat.)

Frenching unit *n American*
the mouth or tongue. A humorous euphemism, popular among college students for instance, and derived from the verb, to **french**, in the sense of tongue kissing or oral sex.

French kiss *n*
an open-mouthed kiss with tongue contact. A phrase which appeared in British and American speech shortly after World War I, before which there was, perhaps significantly, no equivalent term. Later alternatives were 'soul kiss' and **tongue sushi**.

French safe *n Canadian*
a condom. The phrase has been heard since the 1970s.

fresh *adj American*
excellent. A vogue term among teenagers in 1987 and 1988. Teenage argot is in constant need of new terms of approbation but this fairly obvious example (derived probably from its over-use in advertising hyperbole rather than its standard American colloquial sense of cheeky) was still in use after 2000.

'I've got to have that [red carpet] in my crib in LA. That's fresh to death!'
(Damon Dash, hip hop record producer, quoted in the *Sunday Times*, 6 June 2004)

freshi *n British*
a newcomer, unassimilated immigrant, unsophisticated person. An abbreviation of the dismissive phrase 'fresh off the boat', used by British Asians.
Compare **desi**

friar tuck n British
an act of sexual intercourse. A rhyming-slang form of **fuck**.

fridge n British
a male. An item of rhyming slang ('fridge freezer', meaning **geezer**) heard since the 1970s.

fried adj
suffering from the effects of drug intoxication. The term probably derives from the notion of 'frying one's brains', and denotes a state of dangerous disorientation, physical collapse, etc. **Baked** and **toasted** are used in the USA in similar senses.

frig vb
1. to masturbate (oneself or another person). The ultimate origin of the word is the Latin *fricare*, meaning to rub (from which friction is derived), via the Middle English *friggen*.

> 'Friggin' in the rigging 'cause there's fuck-all else to do.'
> (Chorus from the rugby song 'The Good Ship Venus')

2. to have sex (with). Since the 19th century the word has been used as a slightly less offensive alternative to **fuck**, although this was not its original sense.

The verb is nowadays rarely used in either sense except in the noun or adjectival form **frigging**.

frigging adj
an intensifier used with adjectives and nouns for emphasis in the same way as **bloody** or **fucking**. It is considered substantially more offensive than the former and slightly less offensive than the latter.

> 'I was talking to my Canadian niece this very weekend; she (a devout Mormon, 22-ish, not given to profanity) used the word frigging and said, "I'm sorry. I keep forgetting it's a bad word over here" or words to that effect.'
> (Recorded, editor, London, 1989)

frighteners, the n pl See **put the frighteners on (someone)**

frill n American
a girl or woman. A condescending male term which may be related to the archaic 'frail' rather than to a more obvious origin.

frog, froggie n, adj
1. (a person who is) French. The only slang term for this particular nationality dates from the end of the 18th century

when the French were known as 'frog-eaters'.
2. *Australian* a condom.
See also **frenchie**

frog (and toad) n British
a *road*. A piece of London rhyming slang which is occasionally still heard.

> 'I'm off down the frog for a pint of pig's.'
> (Recorded, financial journalist, York, 1980)

froggy adj American
aggressive, willing to fight. This item of black street-talk of the 1990s was probably derived from the phrase **feel froggy** rather than vice versa.

front, the front n British
courage, cheek, effrontery, **chutzpah**. This use of the word, as opposed to the colloquial senses of bearing or façade, occurs in phrases such as 'loads of front' or 'he's got more front than Harrods' (a reference to the large, impressive frontage of the London store).
See also **front out/off/it**

front (someone) vb Australian
to confront. This abbreviated form from the speech of adolescents was featured in Australian soap operas from 1990.

> 'Why don't you just front her about it.'
> (*Neighbours*, Australian TV soap opera, December 1991)

front bottom, front bum n
the female genitals. A term used by young children of both sexes and, often jocularly, by some adults in Britain and Australia.

front out/off/it vb
1a. to face up to someone or something, either with courage or bluff
> She decided to front him out.

1b. to behave aggressively or over-assertively. An activity of young working-class males, often containing an implicit invitation to violence.

> 'He was fronting out down our boozer, so me and a couple of mates gave him a good kicking.'
> (Recorded, youth, London, 1988)

The phrase in both its senses was popular in the 1980s in Britain, and became a vogue term in US black slang of the 1990s.

front-wheel skid, front-wheeler, fronter n British
a Jew. A racist London rhyming-slang term of the 1970s and 1980s. The rhyme is on **yid**.

frost¹ *vb*
1a. to snub or ignore
1b. to anger or irritate
Both senses have been in use (based on social coolness, 'chilling' or 'freezing') since the 19th century. The word is currently fashionable in teenage use in the USA.

frost² *n*
1. a failure, a woeful example of inadequacy. This fairly rare usage of the word occurs in educated speech, particularly in reference to a disappointing performance (e.g. in the theatre; it may originate in a literary or Shakespearean 'killing frost').
2. a snub or silent rebuff. This sense of the word derives from the verb form, currently in vogue among adolescents, particularly in the USA.

frost-top *n American*
an elderly person. This item of adult and family slang often refers to a relative. Synonyms are **cotton-top** and **moss-back**.

frowdy *n, adj British*
(someone) dull, unattractive. The term, probably a blend of 'frump(ish)' and 'dowdy', was in use among teenage girls in 2001.

frowsy *adj*
unpleasant, nasty. The word, used by UK adolescents since around 2000, may be an alteration or mis-hearing of the archaic 'frowsty' which, since the 19th century, has meant smelly, stuffy, oppressive.

fruit *n American*
1. a male homosexual. From the idea of exotic, 'ripe', etc. A common term of abuse in the USA since the early 20th century.
2. an eccentric person. A shortening of **fruitcake**.

fruitcake *n*
1. an eccentric or crazy person. This is a term from the late 1960s, originating in the 1950s catchphrase, 'as nutty as a fruitcake'.
2. *American* a male homosexual. An elaboration of **fruit**.

fruit-fly *n American*
1a. a male homosexual. An elaboration of **fruit** and synonym of **fruitcake**.
1b. a woman who frequents or escorts male homosexuals, a **fag-hag**

fruity *adj*
1. *British* sexually suggestive or provocative. In the former sense the word has become a common colloquialism, as in fruity jokes/stories, etc. In the latter sense it remains a more restricted slang term in use especially among British cockneys and their imitators.
2. *American* strange or eccentric. The word is often used adverbially as in 'acting fruity'. It presumably derives from the noun **fruitcake**.

fry *vb American*
1a. to execute someone by electrocution in the electric chair
1b. to punish or chastise someone. A college students' and armed-forces recruits' term, used in such expressions as 'he got fried' or 'they fried her ass'.

fubar *n*
a spectacular instance of incompetence, a hopeless mess. The term originated as an acronym standing for 'fucked up' or 'fouled up beyond all recognition'. It probably originated in armed-forces usage like the similar **snafu** and is now heard particularly in US campus and office speech.

fuck¹ *vb*
1. to have sex with. The most commonly used 'four-letter' word, used intransitively ('let's fuck') and transitively ('he fucked her/him'); now also used of women ('she fucked him/her'). Surprisingly, the age and origins of this word are obscure. It may not be Anglo-Saxon as is often supposed (it was not recorded in writing until the 16th century) and does not occur in Chaucer and Shakespeare, but may have been borrowed from Norse (*fukkar* in Norwegian, *fockar* in Swedish). Wherever and whenever the word entered English, it is undoubtedly related to a pattern of words in Indo-European languages which give, among many others, the Latin *pungere* (meaning to prick), the German *ficken* (meaning to fuck or strike) and the French *foutre* (meaning to fuck). The common semantic feature of these words is that they all contain the meanings strike, push or prick.
Fuck has always been a taboo word in all English-speaking countries and is still omitted from broadcasts and generally asterisked if written in the press. In the late 20th century the verb often had the more specialised sense of 'habitually copulate' or 'be sexually willing' as in 'does she

fuck?'.

2. to make a mess of, destroy. A 1980s shortening of **fuck up** with slightly more emphatic or drastic connotations.

They fucked the experiment totally.

3. to damn or disregard

'Fuck art, let's dance!'

(T-shirt slogan of the 1970s)

fuck² *n*

1a. an act of sexual intercourse. The noun postdates the verb by at least three hundred years.

1b. a person when evaluated as a sexual partner

a good fuck/an easy fuck

1c. a person, especially when viewed as a fool, victim, villain, etc.

The poor dumb fuck didn't have a chance.

fuck-a-duck! *exclamation*

a virtually meaningless expression of surprise or disbelief

fuck-all *n British*

nothing or almost nothing. An emphatic vulgarism.

'He walked away with two hundred thousand and I got fuck-all.'

(Recorded, businessman, London, 1987)

fuck around/about *vb*

to play the fool, behave irresponsibly or irresolutely

OK, let's stop fucking around and get down to work.

fucked *adj*

1a. (of things) ruined, destroyed, rendered useless

This typewriter is completely fucked.

1b. (of people) completely exhausted, beaten or at a loss

I'm feeling fucked.

fucked-up *adj*

1a. (of things or situations) in a mess, destroyed, spoilt or ruined. Originally the expression meant seduced and abandoned.

1b. (of people) psychologically disturbed, traumatized

'Sadowitz will soon revert to being the fucked-up nonentity he must have been before people like you started dressing him up in the Emperor's New Clothes.'

(Letter to *Time Out*, December 1987)

1c. (of people) temporarily deranged by drugs or drink (not necessarily a negative term)

I got really fucked-up on that dope.

fucker *n*

a person. the word does not invariably imply dislike or contempt, although it may.

The poor fucker never stood a chance.

See also **motherfucker**

fuckhead *n*

a stupid or unpleasant person. A term of abuse popular since the 1980s and usually applied to males.

fucking *adj*

an intensifier used with other adjectives for emphasis. Like **bloody** it is also one of the very few examples of an 'infix' (a word component inserted before the stressed syllable in the middle of a polysyllabic word) in English.

Jesus, it's fucking cold in here.

Abso-fucking-lutely!

fuck-me shoes *n pl*

provocative female footwear. This obscure term received extensive publicity at the end of 1995 when the former feminist writer Germaine Greer accused the *Guardian* columnist Suzanne Moore of betraying feminist principles by wearing 'fuck-me shoes' among other items. The phrase probably originated in American usage but may be a confusion with 'fuck-you shoes', implying a disregard for convention or propriety, or 'fuck-off shoes', where fuck-off means both outsize and aggressive.

fucknuckle *n*

a term of abuse, used of males. The second component is included merely for the purpose of reduplication of sound and signifies nothing.

fuck off *vb*

to leave, go away. A vulgarism that is used in regular verb forms and as an interjection.

Why don't you just fuck off!

fuckoff *n American*

a useless, hopeless or idle person

fuck-off money *n*

funds with which to escape, retire, etc.

fuck (someone) over *vb*

to humiliate, discomfit, distress or destroy someone or something

'Once the income tax guys get their hands on you they can really fuck you over.'

(Recorded, self-employed male, London, 1988)

fuckpig n
a very unpleasant, worthless or contemptible person. This is the British version of the American **pigfucker**. It has been part of the London working-class slang repertoire since the 19th century.

fuck truck n
another term for **passion wagon**

fuck up vb
1. to make a mess of things, commit a serious error or blunder
  Don't tell me, you've fucked up yet again.
2. See **snafu**
3. also **fuck (someone) up** to create an emotional disturbance (in someone), traumatise
  'They fuck you up, your mum and dad.'
  (Philip Larkin, *This be the Verse*)

fuck-up n
1a. a disaster, blunder, error or failure
1b. a bungler or blunderer
1c. someone who is emotionally or psychologically disturbed

fuckwit n
an idiot, a halfwit. An Australianism which has caught on in British use since the late 1970s. It usually expresses exasperated contempt.
  The guy's a complete fuckwit.

fuckwitted adj Australian
hopelessly stupid, dim-witted

fudge-nudger n British
a male homosexual. The term was one of many synonyms based on the notion of excrement (others include **turd burglar**, **chutney-ferret** and **jobbie-jabber**), denoting 'active' or 'predatory' homosexuality, heard since the 1990s.

fudgepacker n British
a homosexual. A derisive late 1980s term employing fudge as an image for excrement and equating homosexuality with buggery, on the same pattern as **browniehound**, **chocolate bandit**, etc.

fudge-tunnel n British
the anus. The vulgar euphemism was adopted as the name of a British **grunge** band in the early 1990s.

fufu n
the vagina. The term has been recorded in the USA and UK since 2000. It may originate as, or imitate, baby talk.

fuggin' adj
a euphemism for **fucking**

fugly adj American
ugly, repellent. Although the word, which is popular in campus speech, is blended from 'fucking ugly', it is generally milder than its components imply.
  God, that's some fugly dog she's got.

full (as a boot/bull/bull's bum) adj Australian
drunk. Full or 'full as a tick' were euphemisms for drunk in Britain in the 19th century, but are now obsolete. Earlier Australianisms on the same pattern were 'full as an egg' and 'full as a goat'.

full as a state school adj Australian
drunk. A more recent variation of expressions based on the notion of full (of drink), heard during the late 1980s, but perhaps older.

full monty, the n British
all that is desired and/or required. The previously obscure phrase suddenly became extremely popular in 1990 and 1991 and many derivations were proposed, ranging from a nickname given to inhabitants of the Potteries region of England to a comment on the quality of the wartime briefings given by the British General Montgomery in North Africa. In fact, the most likely explanation of the phrase is that it is a piece of gamblers' jargon meaning the entire kitty or necessary 'pot' to be bet, from the Spanish *monte* (mountain). In the US 'monte' was adopted as the name of a risky card game, while in Australian horseracing circles 'monty' used to mean an accurate tip or certain bet.
  'We had starters, main course, wine, you name it – the full monty…'.'
  (Recorded, financial consultant, London, May 1993)

full-on adj, adv British
exciting, powerful, with maximum effort. A vogue term among students, particularly in the Midlands during the later 1990s. The expression is used in the same way as the colloquial 'all-out'.

funbag n
1a. a woman, particularly an attractive woman or a potential sexual partner
1b. American a prostitute, in 1980s police jargon

funbags n pl Australian
female breasts. A vulgar term from the 1960s inspired by children's 'lucky dip'

sweet packets on the same lines as **mystery bags**.

fundage n

money. One of many formations using **-age** for mock pomposity. This example was not confined to North America and was recorded among British students in the 1990s.

fundamental adj American

excellent. A fashionable usage, often in the form of an exclamation, among adolescents from the early 1990s.

funk n

1a. heavily rhythmic, 'earthy' music, particularly soul or disco music. A term applied to varieties of urban black music since the 1950s.

1b. an authentic feeling, earthiness, a quality of unsophisticated, raw vitality. The noun form is a back-formation from the adjective **funky**.

2. British cowardice, fearfulness, a fit of panic. A word which is quite unrelated to the musical sense. Funk here comes from the Flemish fonck, meaning worry or agitation. (A blue funk is a state of extreme fear.) It has been in use since the 18th century.

3. British **skunk** marihuana. The term has been in use since around 2000.

funky adj

1a. earthy, raw in the style of **funk** music (characteristically having heavy rhythm and bass and simple repeated melodies). This term, applied to urban soul-music which contained elements of African, jazz, blues and rock music, has been heard since the 1950s. It is sometimes elaborated to 'funky-butt'.

1b. vital, raw, energetic in an unsophisticated way. A term of approval applied to people, objects, ideas, etc. by extension from the musical sense.

2. smelly, fetid. This is the original sense of the word, dating from the early 17th-century British noun funk, meaning a stink or 'fug' of tobacco smoke. This in turn probably derives from the Latin verb fumigare (to smoke or fumigate), via French. Senses **1a** and **b** originate in this meaning.

funny farm n

a psychiatric hospital or home for mental patients

'They're coming to take me away, ha ha, to the funny farm, where life is beautiful all the time.'

('They're coming to take me away, ha-haaa!', song by Napoleon XIV, 1966)

funny money n

1a. counterfeit money

1b. worthless denominations

1c. foreign currency

1d. excess or unearned wealth. The words in this sense express disbelief or resigned acceptance in the face of 'unthinkably' large amounts of money.

furburger, fur-doughnut, furry hoop, fur pie n

the vagina. Expressions which have been part of the male repertoire of vulgarisms since the 1960s. In the USA, furburger and fur pie are sometimes used to refer to a female or females in general.

furiously adv American

extremely. A hyperbolic vogue term in use among the **Vals** of the 1990s and featured in the 1994 US film Clueless.

furphy n Australian

a lie, malicious rumour, tall story. The term is said to originate in Irish usage, but has also been derived from a person of the same name, the contractor who supplied garbage disposal wagons for the army camps in Australia during World War I. An alternative eponymous source is the writer Joseph Furphy.

furry monkey n British

the vagina. A jocular euphemism as used by presenter Daisy Donovan on the late night review The 11 O'clock Show on UK TV in 2001.

furry muff! exclamation British

'fair enough'. An item of student slang in use in London and elsewhere since around 2000.

fusion n British

a state of unhappiness, irritation or agitation. This term became popular among teenagers in the 1990s, who had probably picked it up from an older generation among whom this shortening of the word 'confusion' had become almost obsolete. The usage was recorded among North London schoolboys in 1993 and 1994.

She's in a fusion again.

futz[1] n American

1. the vagina

2. a disreputable and/or unpleasant male These noun forms are related to the verb form.

futz[2] *vb American*

to mess or fool around. The word is a deformation of a Yiddish verb *arum-fartzen*, meaning literally and metaphorically to **fart around**.

fuzz, the fuzz *n*

the police. A 1960s buzzword nowadays only likely to be used by a hopelessly out-of-date adult attempting to communicate ingratiatingly with young people (who will either not understand at all, or regard the dated term with contempt). It derives either from the likening of a worthless person to mould, fluff or dust, or it is a black reference to white men's 'wispy' head and body hair.

'You're more likely to be damaged permanently in a tangle with the American fuzz though, if you see what I mean.'
(Terry Reid, interviewed in *Oz* magazine, February 1969)

fuzz-butt *n American*

a novice. The term is used especially to refer to inexperienced members of the armed forces and it refers to the notion of an adolescent with downy hair on the buttocks.

f-word, the *n British*

a coy reference to the taboo word **fuck**

'He was very coarse, always scratching himself and saying the f-word.'
(Recorded, middle-aged female bus passenger, London, 1989)

G

G¹ *n American*

a friend, peer. This all-purpose greeting used among black speakers (usually, but not necessarily, male) is probably an abbreviation of **guy**, although **gangsta** has been suggested as an alternative.

G² *n*

1. a gram (of some illicit substance). The abbreviation is typically used in referring to cocaine, which is sold in grams.

2. a thousand, a **grand**

It cost me two g's.

3. *American* a friend, peer. The abbreviation (probably of 'guy') is used as a greeting between males, particularly in black street usage.

gadger *n British*

a male friend, unnamed male. A term of address or affection between males, heard predominantly in the north of England.

He's a good gadger.

gadgie, gadgy *n, adj British*

(an) old, infirm or senile (person). A schoolchildren's word mainly heard in the north of England. The source is in dialect of the 19th century or earlier but the precise original meaning is lost.

gaff *n British*

a home or house. In 19th-century slang a gaff was a fair, fairground or any place of cheap entertainment. These notions were expanded in the argot of actors, tramps, market stallholders, criminals, etc. and the word came to be used to describe any place or location, hence the current meaning which was racy underworld jargon from the 1920s to the 1950s when **spivs**, **teddy boys**, etc. gave it wider currency. (It is still mainly used by working-class speakers.)

Nice gaff you've got here.

'If I was you I'd go round his gaff and pour brake fluid all over his paintwork – see how that goes down.'

(The Firm, British TV play, February 1989)

See also **blow the gaff**

gaffer *n*

1a. a boss. A rustic term of address or descriptive word for an old man or master current in Britain since the 16th century, gaffer is a contraction of 'grandfather'. It is still widely used, particularly by working-class speakers.

If I were you I'd go and fetch the gaffer; he's the only one who knows what's going on.

1b. an old man. This is probably the most common sense of the word in the USA, where it is also used to refer to a father (but rarely specifically a grandfather), and to a foreman as in the first sense.

1c. *British* a police officer. The term was recorded among London criminals in 1993.

gaffle *vb American*

1. to confound, defeat, cheat. A term heard in black street slang in the 1990s, perhaps derived from the use of 'gaff' in black slang to mean a swindler or crooked betting scheme.

2. to steal, take without permission. An expression used on campus in the USA since around 2000.

Hey, who gaffled my smokes?

gag *vb*

to vomit. A teenager's specialised use of the colloquial term for choking or retching. Its use is not entirely restricted to the speech of teenagers.

gaga *adj*

senile, crazy, besotted. The word has come into world English from French, via upper-class or educated British English of the 1920s. In French it was probably originally a nursery word, influenced by *grand-père* (grandfather) and *gâteux* (feeble-minded, infirm).

'She's gone completely gaga over this appalling creep.'

(Recorded, wine bar habituée, London, 1986)

gage, gauge n

marihuana or hashish. Gauge is a now obsolete slang term for an alcoholic drink and later also for a pipe or a pipeful of tobacco, coming presumably from the idea of a 'measure' (of something intoxicating). The survival of these senses in American and Jamaican English led to the use of the same word for cannabis.

'You want to blow that gage this way? We'd love it.'

(Chrissie Hynde of the Pretenders rock group, shouting from the stage at Glastonbury music festival, 25 June 1994)

gagging adj British

desperate (for relief, typically in the form of sex or alcohol). Like its synonym **choking**, gagging (literally, retching) became a popular vulgarism in all social circles during the 1990s. The phrase 'gagging for it' refers specifically and invariably to sex.

gag me with a spoon! exclamation American

a favourite **Valley Girl** expression of exaggerated or thrilled disgust or astonishment

Wow, gag me with a spoon! How gross can you get?

galah n Australian

a fool, a silly, empty-headed person. The galah is a species of Australian cockatoo which characteristically congregates with others and 'chatters'. A rural catchphrase in currency before World War II was 'as mad as a (gum)tree full of galahs'. The word is pronounced with the stress on the second syllable.

'Let's forget the whole thing, I feel like a right galah.'

(*The Flying Doctors*, Australian TV series, 1987)

gallis n

a group of females, girls. In black British speech since 2000 the term is the female counterpart of **mans**. It may derive from the Scottish **gallus**.

gallus adj Scottish

cheeky, assertive, **feisty**. A Scottish dialect term applied particularly to women, it was used specifically to refer to TV presenter Muriel Gray in 1995. It is said to derive from the observation that someone was 'fit for the gallows'.

gam vb British

to perform oral sex. A shortening of *gamahucher*, a 19th-century French term for this practice which was adopted into the specialist jargon of prostitutes, pornographers and their customers. The word is now a rather old-fashioned working-class and schoolchildren's vulgarism.

game adj British

working as a prostitute, available for sex. The word in this sense is a back-formation from the earlier 'on the game'. It is used by **punters** and those involved professionally in prostitution.

She's game.

game on! exclamation British

a cry of enthusiasm or encouragement. Since the late 1990s the phrase has been used in association with competition and merrymaking, or as a euphemistic reference to sex. It was the title of a TV comedy series.

game over! exclamation

an assertion that an attempt has failed or that an activity has been definitively terminated. The expression, first featuring on pinball machines, has been a catchphrase since the mid-1990s.

gamer n American

an irritating, foolish and/or inept person. An expression used on campus in the USA since around 2000. The word first described a devotee of video games, thus someone despised by would-be sophisticates.

gams n pl

legs, especially a woman's legs when considered shapely. A jocular word which now sounds old-fashioned, unsurprisingly in that it originates in the medieval heraldic term for leg, *gamb*, which in turn comes from Old Northern French dialect *gambe* (modern French is *jambe*, Italian is *gamba*). Gams is sometimes thought to come from 'gammon', a word which features in several cockney slang expressions; it does not, but it is distantly related etymologically. It is still heard occasionally throughout the English-speaking world.

'Oo Nudge, check out those gams.'

(*Beach House*, US film, 1981)

gander n

a look. The word, which is usually part of phrases such as 'take/have a gander at this', comes from the bird's characteristic craning of the neck.

Gandhi *adj See* **Mahatma (Gandhi)**

ganef, gonef, gonof *n American*
a thief, petty criminal. A word from the Hebrew *gannath*; thief, via Yiddish. In the 19th century variant forms of this word were heard in Britain and South Africa, but are now archaic.

'I'm curious, what do you remember about the man who robbed you...I want to know what the ganef looked like.'
(*Hill Street Blues*, US TV series, 1986)

ganga, ganger *adv American*
extremely. A campus synonym for **hella** and **grippa** recorded in North Carolina in 2002.

gang bang¹ *vb, n*
(to take part in) sex involving several males sequentially with one woman; group sex. The word received publicity in the 1960s, largely as a result of articles describing the rituals of Hells Angels and others.

gang bang² *vb American*
to take part in the activities of a street gang. A term from the 1980s which is a play on the well-known sexual term, and bang in the sense of gunshot. The word has been brought to public attention by TV documentaries describing the activities of such gangs in the era of **crack**. (The phrase is now sometimes shortened to **bang**.)

gangbanger *n American*
a loyal and committed member of a street gang. This 1980s term is used by and about the members of street gangs in Los Angeles. The bang in question is a gunshot; shooting a victim is often part of the initiation process.

gangbusters *n pl, adj American*
(something) superlative, excellent, impressive. A schoolchildren's word which is a shortening of the jocular adult phrase 'like gangbusters', meaning very strongly, energetically or dynamically. The terms originate in the violently heroic actions of the anti-mob law enforcers (nicknamed gangbusters) of yellow journalism and crime fiction.

Hey you know, that set they played was gangbusters!

gangie *n Australian*
a **gang bang** or **group-grope**

gangsta *n, adj American*
(someone) belonging to black street-gang culture. The term, which denoted an admirable gang member, became generalised as an all-purpose categorisation in street-gang, hip hop and **rap** culture.

ganja *n*
marihuana. This is one of the many names for cannabis which has been heard in various milieus over the last fifty years or so. At present the term is popular in the Caribbean and among blacks and young white smokers in Britain. It comes originally from the Sanskrit *gañja*, via Hindi.

gank *vb American*
to steal or borrow without permission. An expression used on campus in the USA since around 2000. It may be a blend of 'grab' and 'yank'.

I can't believe she ganked your boyfriend.
Stop ganking my clothes.

gannet *n British*
a person who eats greedily, someone who bolts their food. Gannet is a 1970s and 1980s term derived, possibly via comics' adaptation of navy argot, from the voracious habits of the fish-gorging seabird.

'If you've got any sense you'll keep the best stuff away from those gannets.'
(Recorded, teacher, York, 1981)

garbo *n Australian*
a garbage man, dustman. The word's first use seems to have coincided with the height of the fame of the Swedish movie actress, Greta Garbo.

garbonzas *n pl American*
female breasts. One of many invented terms used lightheartedly by males (**gazungas** is another version). This may conceivably be influenced by the Spanish *garbanzos*: chickpeas.

gargle *n Irish and British*
(an) alcoholic drink. A joke on the lines of **lotion** and **tincture** which is at least 100 years old and is still commonly heard in Dublin, for instance.

'Fancy a gargle, John?'
(Posy Simmonds cartoon, *Guardian*, 1981)

'I'll have some gargle, if you don't mind, sir.'

(Recorded, Irish pub habitué, London, 1987)

See also **Arthur Scargill**

garms *n pl*
clothes. The clipped form of 'garments' was an important part of the hip hop and **rap** subculture's lexicon from the 1980s, later crossing the Atlantic and eventually heard among UK adolescents. Older synonyms were **rags**, **threads** and **vines**.

'Grab your flash garms!'
(*Touch* magazine, September 1993)

Gary Glitter *n British*
the anus. The vulgarism uses the name of the disgraced 1970s rock star as rhyming slang for **shitter**. (Previously the name of the cowboy star of the 1950s, Tex Ritter, had been employed.)

'What male priests can do – give choir-boys one up the Gary Glitter.'
(Comedienne Jo Brand, Christmas 1994)

gas *n*
1. something which is exhilarating, stimulating or highly enjoyable. In the phrases 'it's a gas' and 'what a gas!', this word became one of the clichés of the **hippy** vocabulary. It probably originated in American black street slang of the late 1950s, inspired by the exhilarating effects of nitrous oxide (laughing gas), although the same word, with the same meaning and origin, already existed in Irish speech.

'But it's all right now, in fact it's a gas…I'm jumping Jack Flash, it's a gas, gas, gas.'
('Jumping Jack Flash', Rolling Stones, 1968)

2. an idle conversation, a period of empty chatter

gas guzzler *n*
an uneconomical car. A term originally applied to American non-compact cars of the 1970s.

gash[1] *adj British*
1. spare, available. This now almost obsolete use of the word was common in the armed services in the 1950s and probably has the same origins as the following senses.
2. attractive, impressive. The origin of this sub-sense of gash is obscure, but may be inspired by the attractiveness of 'spare' or available women. It was heard

among working-class Londoners until the late 1960s.
3. useless, worn out, broken. In this sense gash is still heard, especially in London, among workmen, technicians, musicians, etc. and in the armed forces.

'There's nothing in there but a pile of gash tapes.'
(Recorded, video technician, London, 1988)

The various meanings of the term probably all derive from a 19th-century adoption of the French word *gâcher* (to waste or spoil) or *gâchis* (mess) for rubbish on board ship. The meaning was ironically extended to cover extra portions, then anything spare. The original French is preserved in the third sense above.

gash[2] *n*
1a. a woman or girl. A male term of sexual origin but not necessarily used with sexual connotations. The term existed in the argot of the streets in the 1950s, both in the USA and in working-class Britain (where it usually occurred in the phrase 'a bit of gash'). It was revived in the 1980s by aficionados of **rap** music and hip hop as a fashionable synonym for girlfriend. The origin of the word lies in **b**, which is unknown to many users.
1b. a woman's genitals, or women as sex objects. The fearful or dismissive male image of a woman's external sex organs as a wound is an ancient one. Gash in this sense was a widespread vulgar euphemism in the 19th century.

gasper *n*
1. a cigarette. An ironic witticism from the days before the anti-smoking lobby, when shortness of breath was still a possible subject for levity. (It is probably unconnected with the more recent British cliché 'gasping for a fag'.) The word was at its most popular in the 1950s in the language of **spivs**, **cads**, etc., but is not yet obsolete.
2. *British* a devotee of self-asphyxiation as a sexual stimulus. The term, from the lexicon of prostitution, received publicity at the time of the death in 1994 of the Tory MP Stephen Milligan while indulging in this practice (known in slang as **scarfing**).

gassed *adj*
drunk. A popular word among middle-class, middle-aged drinkers in the USA from the mid-1960s, gassed was also a synonym for tipsy in Britain after World

War I (probably from 'laughing-' rather than 'mustard-gas').

gasser n

1. something which is highly amusing or impressive. This sense of the word is inspired by the properties of laughing-gas and is used to denote, e.g., a good joke. This is an Americanism which is also heard in Britain and may have been coined there independently. It was first used before World War II, and is now heard particularly among teenagers.

2. American a depressing experience, person or situation. The word is rare in this sense, in which the image evoked is presumably of a poisonous, asphyxiating or anaesthetic gas.

gat n

a pistol, revolver. A piece of obsolete underworld slang from the early 1900s derived from 'Gatling' gun (an early revolving-barrel machine-gun). The word is occasionally resurrected by writers invoking the atmosphere of the gangster era, and was the trademark name of a cheap British air pistol of the 1950s.

gata n South African

a police officer. Recorded as an item of Sowetan slang in the Cape Sunday Times, 29 January 1995.

gate fever n British

terror at the prospect of release from prison. An item from inmates' jargon describing a familiar condition.

gatted, gattered adj

drunk, possibly from the notion of 'gunned down' from **gat**, a gun. An item of student slang in use in London and elsewhere since around 2000.

gay adj

1. homosexual. In late-medieval English gay often had the sense of showy or affected as well as happy and light-hearted. In British slang of the 18th and 19th centuries it was a euphemism for sexually available or living an immoral life, and was invariably applied to women, usually prostitutes. In the early 20th century it was adopted as a code word by the British and American homosexual community, an innocent-sounding term which they could use of themselves and each other. The word had the secondary purpose of reinforcing homosexuals' positive perception of their sexual identity as opposed to the derisive or disapproving terminology of the heterosexual world. Gay was widely used in the theatrical milieu by the mid-1960s and, when homosexuals began to assert themselves openly in the later 1960s, it supplanted all alternatives to become the standard non-discriminatory designation.

2. bad, in poor taste, socially inept or unsophisticated. This non-homophobic use of the term has been in vogue among teenagers in the USA and UK since 2000.

That show was, like, so gay.
Don't be gay!

gaydar n

the (supposed) ability to detect homosexuality in others. The blend of **gay** and 'radar' suggests an instinctive appreciation of invisible qualities.

gaylord n British

an effete or homosexual male. A schoolchildren's term of the late 1980s. The word, which is an embellishment of **gay**, may derive from Jamaican argot.

gazillion n American

a very large number or quantity. An alternative form for **zillion**, **squillion** and **bazillion**.

gazing n British

relaxing. A fashionable term among adolescents from the later 1990s, the word may be related to 'shoe-gazing', a phrase earlier used to describe the posturing of **indie** musicians who would slouch almost motionless while performing staring down at the stage.

gazump vb British

to cheat (in a house purchase) by raising the price at the last moment, after agreement has been reached but before contracts have been formalised. An old expression from the language of swindlers, revived to denote a practice which became widespread during and after the dramatic rise in property prices in 1972. The word formerly existed in several forms (gazumph, gazoomph, gazumf, etc.) and is from Yiddish.

gazumped adj British

drunk. An item of student slang in use in London and elsewhere since around 2000.

gazunda, gazunder, gazunta, gozunder n

a chamber pot. A perennial humorous euphemism heard in Britain and Australia, based on the fact that the unnameable article in question 'goes under' the bed. By extension these words are sometimes used to refer to other un-named gadgets, containers, implements or contraptions.

gazungas *n pl*
female breasts. A male term.

gear[1] *adj British*
excellent, absolutely right, first rate. An ephemeral vogue word that spread with the popularity of the Beatles and the 'Mersey sound' from Liverpool in 1963 to be picked up by the media (a fact which incidentally marked its demise as a fashionable term). It is related to 'the gear', meaning the 'real thing' or top quality merchandise.

gear[2] *n*
1. clothes, accessories. Now a widely used colloquialism, gear was slang, in the sense of being a vogue word in restricted usage, in the early 1960s, when its use paralleled the new interest in fashion among **mods**.
2. illicit drug(s). Since the early 1960s gear has been used by drug abusers, prisoners, etc. to denote, in particular, cannabis or heroin. In this sense the word is a typical part of the drug user's quasi-military or workmanlike vocabulary (**works**, **equipment** and **artillery** are other examples).
Got any gear, man?
3a. top quality merchandise, the 'real thing'
3b. stolen goods. A specific usage of the standard colloquial sense of the word.
Stash the gear in the garage.

gee *n American*
a version of **G**

geeb *n American*
an unfortunate, inept and/or unattractive individual. It is probably a blend of **geek** and **dweeb**.

gee-gee *n British*
a horse. A nursery term adopted by adults to refer ruefully or facetiously to racehorses. In British films of the 1950s the word was characteristic of **spivs** and **cads**.
I lost thirty quid on the gee-gees.

geek[1] *n*
1. *American* a freak, an insane or disgusting person. This old word originated with fairground folk to describe someone willing to abase themselves or perform disgusting acts, such as biting the heads off live chickens, or a grotesque person

exhibited for money. The word is now firmly established in teenage and schoolchildren's slang, helped by the preponderance of geeks in the horror films of the late 1970s and 1980s. It may be derived from German, Dutch or Yiddish words for 'to peep', or from Dutch and English dialect words for a fool.
'I'm gonna marry the geek tycoon.'
(*Cheers*, US TV series, 1988)
2. a menstrual period. This use of the word, indicating distaste and/or fascination and used by both sexes, originated in the USA. 'On the geek' (having one's period), 'geek pains' (period pains).

geek[2], **geek out** *vb American*
1a. to behave eccentrically, like a **geek**
1b. to search desperately for drug remnants, particularly **crack**. This sense is a specialisation of the first, used by drug users since the late 1980s to describe the actions of a crack addict *in extremis*.
'You just want more and more. That's when you go geeking – looking for specks on the floor, just to get some more.'
(Drug-user, *Guardian*, 5 September 1989)

geek collector *n*
a panty liner or tampon

geek rock *n American*
another name for **crack**. **Rock** is a generic term for narcotics in (lumpy) powder or granule form; **geek** is a crazy person.

geet *n British*
a contemptible and/or tedious person
'Those geets at the ACF [Army Cadet Force] deserved what happened. If they want to join the army, why don't they go and do it.'
(Delinquent youth quoted in the *Daily Telegraph* magazine, 15th June 1996)

geeze bag *n American*
an old **fart**, old **geezer**. A term of mild abuse or derision, mainly in adolescent use in the 1990s.

geezer[1] *n*
a man. A common word in Britain, where slang users often assume that it derives from a bathroom geyser (water heater), by analogy with **boiler**. In fact it probably originates in 'guiser' or 'gizer', a word for a masquerader or mummer who wears a (dis)guise. In the 19th century geezer could be applied to women. The word is also used in the USA, where it is regarded as rather colourful.

geezer² *adj American*
excellent, in hip hop and **rap** parlance

geezerbird *n British*
a girl with a masculine appearance and/or supposedly male attitudes or behaviour. The term has been common among all age groups since the later 1990s.

'Some people call me a geezerbird and I suppose I like it, I'm proud of it.'
(Recorded, female DJ, London, 1999)

geezing *n American*
injecting heroin, **shooting up**. An item of addicts' and underworld slang, also used by the police, which appeared in the 1960s.

gelt *n*
money. The word is taken directly from Yiddish or German and has been used in all English-speaking areas since at least the 17th century, at first probably in allusion to Jewish moneylenders.

gendarmes *n pl British*
the police. A middle-class appropriation of the French word in an attempt at raciness.

Had a spot of bother with the gendarmes as I was driving down.

Generation X *n American*
a journalese coinage describing the supposedly listless, apathetic post-**yuppie** generation of young people who were entering adulthood in the early 1990s. The phrase was borrowed, in 1992, by the Canadian author Douglas Coupland, from earlier use as the title of a 1960s sociological analysis of youth rebellion and in the 1970s as the name of a would-be **punk** band.

gentleman of the road *n British*
a tramp, vagrant. A euphemism first applied to highwaymen and later by tramps to themselves.

Geoff (Hurst) *n British*
a *first* (class degree). The rhyming slang uses the name of the England football star of the later 1960s.

geordie *n British*
a native or inhabitant of Newcastle or Tyneside in the northeast of England. The word is a Scottish dialect version of George and probably first arose as a nickname for one of the Hanoverian kings, used by, and later applied to, soldiers billeted upon Newcastle. The

name refers also to the distinctive speech patterns of the area.

george¹ *adj American*
excellent, first-rate, fine. A word from teenage slang of the late 1950s which is periodically revived by modern schoolchildren and college students. It probably derives from gorgeous or is an expansion of the letter 'g' (for good).

george² *vb American*
to have sex, the term is used particularly by adolescents and refers to heterosexual activity by either sex

George Melly *n British*
belly, paunch. This item of rhyming slang employs the name of the corpulent old-Etonian jazz singer and writer.

George Raft *n British*
a *draught* (of air). A fairly widespread piece of jocular rhyming slang inspired by the American actor of the same name (famous for his tough-guy and underworld roles on and off screen).

Blimey, there's a bit of a George Raft in here, ain't there?

germ *n British*
an irritating, unpleasant or contemptible person. A schoolchildren's term of criticism or abuse, typically applied to fellow pupils or younger children.

gerry, geri *n British*
an old person. A short form of 'geriatric', typically said without affection by teenagers or schoolchildren.

gertcha! *exclamation British*
a cockney cry, roughly equivalent to 'get away!', 'give over!', or 'get out of it!' and expressing disbelief or gentle mockery. The dated expression was revived for use in the musical accompaniment (by Chas and Dave) to a television advertisement for Courage Best Bitter screened in 1983.

'"Gercher", wheezes Dad convulsively over the debris of the saloon bar.'
(*Town* magazine, May 1964)

get *n British*
a bastard, literally or figuratively; an unpleasant or stupid person. This word is more widespread in the Midlands and north of England, generally in working-class usage. In the south of England **git** is more common. Get was originally a derivation of 'beget' and meant a (begotten) child.

get a click *vb British*
to succeed in picking up a partner. The term is heard particularly in the Scottish Lowlands and the north of England.
I hear Jillie managed to get a click last night.

get a job *vb, exclamation American*
(to) fulfil oneself. A joke variation on admonitions such as **get a life** or **get real**, which enjoyed a vogue in the 1990s.

get a life *vb, exclamation*
(to) fulfil oneself. An admonition, originally American, that became a vogue term from the early 1990s. **Get a job** is a jocular alternative.

get a rift/rush/hustle on *vb British*
to hurry up, make haste. These are more colourful working-class London variants of the colloquial 'get a move on'.

get a room *vb American*
to behave more discreetly, remove oneself from sight. The phrase is applied, usually but not always lightheartedly, when a couple are publicly and/or embarrassingly engaged in love-play.
Come on you two, get a room!
Sheena and Damian are always at it in the corner of the bar. They should get a room.

get a twitch on *vb British*
to become agitated and/or furious. An item of London working-class slang heard among, e.g., football supporters from the 1990s.

get beats *vb*
to be beaten up (by someone). A term used by young street-gang members in London since around 2000.

get behind *vb*
to approve of, support, empathise with. A phrasal verb (originating in the USA) of the sort popular with the 'alternative lifestyle' proponents of the early 1970s.
I can't really get behind the idea of God as some bearded dude sitting on a cloud.
Compare **get off (on)**; **get down**

get boots *vb American*
to have sex. A vogue term in black street slang in the 1990s. **Knock boots** is an alternative, and probably original, version of the phrase.

get busy *vb*
1. to have sex
2. to eat, gorge oneself

get Chinese *vb American*
to get very **stoned**, become euphoric and/or semi-conscious by smoking mari-

huana. This **preppie** expression is based on the premise that their stupefaction will rival that of Chinese opium addicts or that their glazed serenity will result in an Oriental demeanour.

get cogging *vb British See* **cog²**

get corrugated ankles *vb British*
to get drunk. An item of student slang in use in London and elsewhere since around 2000.

get down *vb American*
to let oneself go, begin something in earnest. This phrase was originally a piece of black slang, inspired by 'get down to business' (probably first used as a euphemism for beginning sexual activity, then transferred to musical activity). The expression is still heard in a musical context, referring for instance to musicians improvising successfully or to disco dancers 'letting go'.

get dribbly *vb British*
to become intoxicated by drink or drugs. The phrase usually, but not necessarily, implies being visibly uncontrolled. It was in use among middle-class students in 2001.

get/have a cob on *vb British*
to become angry, display irritation. The term has been used in the Channel 4 TV soap opera *Brookside*. Eric Partridge dated the phrase to the 1930s: the 'cob' in question is probably originally a dialect term for a lump or a protrusion, and can be dated back to English slang of the later 18th century.

get (someone) in *vb*
to engage in lesbian sex
'They're all getting each other in, didn't you know that?'
(Recorded, London student, September 1995)

get in! *exclamation British*
the phrase was defined by a user in 2001 as: 'fantastic! Result! That was tremendous! Said after something quite brilliant has happened or if you hear good news'. **Hop on!** is a synonymous expression.
'"I've managed to get front-row tickets for Steps". "Get in!"'
(Recorded, London teenager, 2001)

get in (someone's) eye/face *vb American*
to behave intrusively and annoyingly (towards)

get into bed (with) *vb*
to merge or agree to liaise closely with. A piece of jargon from the business

world which has become widely known since the late 1970s.

get it on *vb*

1a. to succeed in having sex, to achieve (mutual) sexual gratification. An American euphemism dating from the 1960s.

'I'm gonna ask you something right up front. Are you getting it on with that dude with the dog parlor or not?'

(*The Serial*, Cyra McFadden, 1976)

1b. to succeed in something pleasurable or desirable. A generalisation of the first sense which was used, sometimes as an exhortation, in the **hippy** era. Both senses became known, and to some extent used, in Britain after 1970, but had largely fallen out of use by the end of the decade.

get it together *vb*

to organise oneself, one's life and/or environment. A vogue term and cliché from around 1969. The 'it' refers to one's 'act', one's life, one's head, or to things in general.

get it up *vb*

to achieve an erection. A common vulgarism.

get laid *vb*

to have sex. A derivation from **lay**, which spread from the USA to Britain around 1968.

'Young guys in their twenties, of course they're going to try and get laid, and even if they don't succeed it's hardly big news.'

(Lenny Henry, *Time Out* magazine, 26 July 1989)

get licks *vb British*

to be beaten up (by someone). A term used by young street-gang members in London since around 2000.

get messy *vb British*

to become intoxicated by drink or drugs. An item of student slang in use in London and elsewhere since around 2000.

get next to (someone) *vb*

to strike up a relationship (with someone). The phrase has been used by frequenters of discos since the late 1980s.

get off (on) *vb*

1a. to achieve satisfaction, exhilaration or inspiration (from). This American expression of the early 1970s is an extension of an earlier purely sexual sense of the phrase in which get off means to achieve orgasm. This concept was modified by the drug users' image of leaving terra

firma, of flying or floating in a state of euphoria. Since the late 1970s the term has been generalised (in Britain and Australia) to include finding pleasure from more innocuous sources, such as music.

Did you manage to get off on those mushrooms?

I really get off on that guitar solo.

1b. to **get someone off** retains the sexual sense of bringing someone to a climax: this use of the phrase is fairly rare

get off one's case *vb British*

to become intoxicated by drugs, to **get high**. An item of prison slang.

get one's act/head/shit together *vb*

to organise oneself, arrange one's affairs, start to perform efficiently or effectively. A euphemism from the era of alternative therapy which likens one's behaviour to a performance (it may in fact have originated in theatrical or musical circles); unlike many such phrases it is still in widespread use.

get one's arse in(to) gear *vb*

to prepare oneself, get organised and get going. A phrase which appeared in Britain and America (with **ass**) seemingly simultaneously around 1974. It is usually employed as an exhortation to someone who is disorganised or wasting time.

get one's beans *vb British*

to have sex. An item of student slang in use in London and elsewhere since around 2000.

get one's end away *vb British*

to have sex, succeed in seduction. A masculine vulgarism in widespread use since the 1960s, this is a variation on 'get one's end in', a euphemism dating from the early years of the 20th century.

get one's head together *vb*

to collect one's thoughts, achieve a state of equanimity. A cliché of the 'alternative society' of the early 1970s (members of rock groups, suffering from the excesses of social and professional life, typically spoke of going to the countryside to get their heads together). This phrase is still heard, albeit more rarely, usually in the sense of pull oneself together or **get one's act together**.

You know you really should try and get your head together if you intend to carry on in this business.

get one's jollies *vb*

to derive enjoyment, obtain sensual satisfaction. The gratification referred to in this phrase is often less innocuous than the lighthearted nature of the words might imply.

It's not my idea of a good time, but if that's how you get your jollies, I won't stand in your way.

get one's knickers in a twist *vb British*
to become agitated, flustered or over-excited. This picturesque vulgarism originated in the late 1950s with a purely sexual sense. Now widely used, it is generally heard in the negative form, exhorting someone to calm down.
See also **get one's panties in a bunch**

get one's knob polished *vb American*
to receive fellatio

get one's leg over/across *vb British*
(of a male) to have sex, to succeed in seduction

You [Colin Moynihan, then minister for sport] can be honest with us. Did you get your leg over or not?
(*Private Eye* magazine, April 1989)

get one's oats *vb British*
to achieve sexual satisfaction. The phrase originates in the idea of 'sowing one's wild oats', especially in the sense of sexual adventuring outside marriage. Since the 1960s the phrase has been applied to both men and women, and to sex in general rather than adultery in particular. It is heard in all social classes in Britain and Australia.

If he plays his cards right, he should end up getting his oats tonight.
(Recorded, teenage drinker, London, 1986)

get one's panties in a bunch *vb*
the Australian equivalent of **get one's knickers in a twist**

get one's rocks off *vb*
to obtain sexual satisfaction, achieve orgasm, ejaculate. An American vulgarism which became part of the **hippy** linguistic repertoire; some British users of the expression are unaware that **rocks** is a direct euphemism for testicles. (In American usage **nuts** or other terms could be substituted for rocks.) In the later 1970s the phrase was extended to mean to indulge oneself or enjoy oneself generally rather than in a specifically sexual sense. It now sounds dated.

But I only get my rocks off while I'm dreaming.
(Lyric from 'Rocks Off', The Rolling Stones, 1972)

get on one's wick/tits *vb British*
to irritate, annoy or vex. The 'wick' in question, unknown to many speakers, is a now rather archaic shortening of **Hampton Wick**, rhyming slang for **prick** (which is nowadays more usually shortened to **hampton**). In spite of the implied gender difference, both versions of the expression are used indiscriminately by both men and women.

It really gets on my tits when someone calls me a career woman.
(Recorded, female journalist, London, 1986)

get on someone's case *vb American*
to harass, badger or interfere. A phrase used with indignation or resentment, typically by an 'underdog' to or of an authority figure. The notion on which the expression is based is that of a judge or law-enforcer examining one's case. 'Get off my case' is a widespread negative form.

get on the bag *vb American*
to act in a more mature or 'manly' way. A phrase used exclusively by males, particularly on campus. The bag reference is unclear.

get over *vb American*
to become a success in white society. An item of black street slang.

get real *vb, exclamation*
to face up to reality, to behave rationally. A vogue term originating in the USA and widespread elsewhere since the 1980s. Near synonyms are **get a life** and **get a job**.

get some poot *vb British*
to have sex. An item of student slang in use in London and elsewhere since around 2000.

get tapped up *vb British*
to succeed in meeting/seducing a partner. The phrase is used in working-class speech, particularly in the northeast of England.

Couldn't even get tapped up last night.
(*Away The Lads*, BBC 2 TV documentary, February 1993)

get the ass *vb American*
to become angry, irritated or furious. An item of black street-talk included in so-called **Ebonics**, recognised as a legitimate language variety by school officials in Oakland, California, in late 1996.

get the horn *vb*
to achieve an erection. A vulgarism employing the horn as a penis metaphor, heard more commonly in the adjective **horny**. 'Get the horn' is now mainly heard in uneducated adult speech and the language of schoolchildren. To be 'on the (h)orn' is an alternative form.

get the hump *vb British*
to become bad-tempered, morose or offended. This common expression is at least 100 years old. The origin of this sense of hump is not clear, although it may refer straightforwardly to a hunchback's deformity, to a back bent with care, a head dropped in gloom, or a traveller's burden. In modern cockney usage the phrase is often abbreviated to the adjective **humpty**.

get the needle, get the dead needle *vb British*
to become irritated, bitter or vindictive. This expression is one of a number referring to needle in the sense of provoke or annoy. This particular form of words has survived as a working-class Londoners' phrase since the late 19th century.

get the salmon on prawn *vb British*
to have an erection. A piece of rhyming slang based on the phrase **on the horn**. The phrase was chosen as the title of an exhibition of paintings by the young artist Sarah Lucas in London in 1995.

get up one's nose *vb British*
to irritate, annoy. A colourful vulgarism used by both sexes since its popularisation in TV comedies of the late 1960s, notably *Steptoe and Son* and *Till Death us do Part*.
> It really gets up my nose the way he harps on about his work.

get wood *vb British*
to have an erection. A phrase popularised by *Viz* comic from the 1990s.

ghetto *adj American*
cheap, of poor quality, in poor taste, old, broken down. The term is not racist, but is primarily in use among white adolescents.

ghora, gora *n*
a white person. A Hindi word used by South Asians of several ethnic backgrounds in the UK.

ghora-fied *adj*
seen as typical or representative of white culture. A term, often pejorative

or at least critical, used by British Asians.

ghost[1] *vb American*
to depart, leave. This item of black street slang, adopted also by white adolescents in the 1990s, is probably related to the phrase **git ghost**.

ghost[2] *adj American*
absent, missing, unseen. A key term from the lexicon of street gangs and aficionados of **rap** and hip hop since the 1990s. Used in this way the word has evoked disappearance and invisibility in black speech for two decades or more.
> *They came for us but we was ghost.*
> *Get ghost!*

ghost turds *n pl American*
another expression for **dust bunnies**

gib *vb British*
to talk gibberish. An item of student slang in use in London and elsewhere since around 2000.

G.I.B. *adj American*
sexually accomplished and/or sexually active. The euphemistic abbreviation of 'good in bed' is spoken as its constituent letters, not as an acronym.

gibbing *n British*
gatecrashing. This term was in use among bouncers and security men during the 1990s. Its origin is obscure.

gig[1] *n*
1a. a musical engagement or performance. One of many terms, originating among pre-World War II jazz musicians in the USA, which were adopted by the rock-music milieu in the 1960s. The exact origin of the word is obscure, but may be related to 'jig' in the sense of a dance.
> 'These lads are professional musicians and gigs are their bread and butter.'
> (*News of the World*, 29 May 1988)

1b. an appointment, session, stint or activity. Particularly in the 1970s, the musicians' term was extended to refer to any one-off engagement or event (thus sometimes performing as a synonym of **trip** or **scene**).
> I've got the feeling this party isn't really my gig.

gig[2] *vb*
to perform at a **gig** or (more often) a series of gigs. An item of musicians' jargon.
> 'These guys [The Grateful Dead] will be gigging beyond the grave.'

(*Independent*, 26 February 1988)

gigantic *adj British*
excellent. A vogue term among British adolescents in the 1990s as an adjective or exclamation.

giggle-stick *n*
a **joint**, cannabis cigarette. A jocular expression, typically used by middle-class students or otherwise respectable adults since the early 1970s. It is not part of the lexicon of hardened drug users.

giggle water *n*
alcoholic drink, particularly champagne or exotic spirits. An ingenue's jocular expression for the potential cause of unaccustomed hilarity.

gilbert *n British See* **green gilbert**

gimme five! *exclamation*
an invitation to slap palms as a ritualised greeting or sign of solidarity

gimmer, gim *n British*
a foolish, clumsy or unfortunate person. The words originated as Scottish and northern English dialect terms for a helpless young ewe or old sheep. They are still used primarily as contemptuous descriptions of females.

gimp *n*
1a. a crippled or lame person, especially an old one. The term is thought to derive from a blend of grandfather and limp. The adjective 'gimpy' is applied, often derisively, to anything or anyone clumsy or crippled.
1b. an awkward, ineffectual or clumsy person. By extension from the first sense above. The word is popular among schoolchildren.
2. a sexually promiscuous male

gimpiny *n British*
a version of **gimp 1b** in use among students in 2005

ginger *n, adj British*
(a person who is) homosexual. Rhyming slang from 'ginger beer': **queer**. A piece of pre-World War II London working-class argot which is very much alive in spite of the decline in ginger-beer drinking.

gink *n*
1. an awkward, ugly, foolish or clumsy person. The word is at least 100 years old in Britain and America, but its origin is obscure; it may be an invention, or derive from either Scottish dialect or Turkish or Arabic via Romany. Before the 1950s the word also meant simply a person, without the pejorative overtones.
Who's the shortsighted gink in the corner?
2. *British* a bad smell, stink. The word, which is probably lowland Scottish in origin, also occurs in the form of the verb 'to gink'.

Giorgio Armani *n British*
a sandwich. A rhyming slang phrase heard since the late 1990s. The rhyme is with **sarnie** and the name of the Italian fashion designer.

gippo *n See* **gyppo**

gippy tummy *n See* **gyppy tummy**

girl-cott *vb*
to boycott. A feminist alternative, coined in the 1980s and used both facetiously and seriously.

girlfriend *n American*
a female companion, member of one's circle or gang. This use of the word arose among black adolescents in the late 1970s and by the 1990s had become a common term of address among younger females across the USA. The word is sometimes abbreviated to 'girlf'.

girlie *n British*
a weak or effeminate person, a sissy. A schoolboy expression of derision adopted facetiously by some adult males.

girl's blouse *n British See* **big girl's blouse**

gism *n*
an alternative spelling of **jissom**

gismo, gizmo *n*
a gadget, unnamed object. An American armed-forces' term adopted in Britain since the 1960s.

git *n British*
an unpleasant or worthless person. Many saloon-bar lexicologists have claimed that this word is an Arabic term of abuse, meaning 'pregnant camel', which was imported by servicemen who had been stationed in Egypt. The Arabic word does exist, but was probably noticed by British soldiers because the word git, a southern pronunciation of **get** (bastard or fool), was already part of their stock of vulgarisms.
'A frightfully clever chap called Stephen Fry, sending up all those smug gits who present kids' TV. (Hmmm... comes across as a bit of a smug git himself.)'
(*News of the World*, 15 May 1988)

git ghost vb American
to behave discreetly, 'keep a low profile'.
An item of black street-talk that was
included in so-called **Ebonics**, recognised
as a legitimate language variety by school
officials in Oakland, California, in late
1996.

git-go n American
the outset, beginning. The term is usually heard in the phrase 'from the git-
go'.

git wid it vb American
to become alert, streetwise, adapt to the
current situation. An imitation of the earlier colloquial phrase 'get with it', spoken
with an Afro-Caribbean accent. An item
of black street-talk that was included in
so-called **Ebonics**, recognised as a legitimate language variety by school officials
in Oakland, California, in late 1996.

give (someone) a portion vb British
to have sex. The vulgarism describes
the sex act from the male point of view
and has been popularised in the broadcast media, e.g., by the TV comedy
series Hale and Pace in 1996.

give a toss/fuck/flying fuck vb British
to concern oneself, care. Almost invariably used negatively, these phrases,
recorded since the early 1970s, but
perhaps slightly older, are successors to
the old dismissive or insouciant expressions '(don't) give a damn/fig'.
See also **Kate Moss**

give (someone) face vb American
to affront, provoke, deride. An item of
black street slang heard in the 1990s.

    'Are you giving me face?
    What the hell does that mean?'
    (Made in America, US film, 1993)

give head vb American
(to be willing) to perform fellatio. A male
term from the 1950s and 1960s, used
typically by college students or servicemen during the **hippy** period of sexual
experimentation. The phrase, and indeed
the practice, seemed to assume a real
and symbolic importance in male sexuality in the USA, far greater than in Britain
and Australia. The term has occasionally
been applied to cunnilingus. (Since the
1980s the words **skull** or 'some skull'
have occasionally been substituted for
head.)

    'But she never lost her head, even when
    she was giving head.'

('Walk on the Wild Side', written and recorded by Lou Reed, 1972)

give it a burl vb See **burl**

give it beans vb British
to perform energetically, as in dancing
or sex. The term was recorded on the
Student World website in 2001.

give it large vb British
an alternative form of **large it**

give it one, give her one vb British
to have sex (with a woman). A male vulgarism which has been commonly heard
from the 1980s, both in boastful or
assertive male conversation and in parodies thereof. A common elaboration is
'Give her one for the boys'.

give it some cog vb British
to accelerate, increase power and speed.
A motorcyclist's term since the 1980s.
Cog is jargon for gear.

give it some wellie vb See **wellie**[1] 1a

give it the berries vb British
to act energetically, increase power
and/or speed. The phrase was used by
presenters on the tv car programme Top
Gear in 2005.

give it toes vb British
to run away, escape. Recorded from the
mid-1980s and heard particularly in the
Merseyside area, this is a synonym for
the London criminal slang **have it away
on one's toes**.

give it up vb
to accede to a request for sex
    That slapper gives it up easily.

give it up! exclamation
1a. a demand by a mugger to give up
one's money, possessions, etc.
1b. an exclamation of joy or solidarity
In the second sense the phrase became a
fashionable cry uttered by aficionados of
dancefloor culture since the mid-1990s.

give someone evil(s) vb British
to look menacingly or angrily at. An item
of playground slang. **Eviling** is an alternative form.

**give (someone) the arse/boot/heave-ho/
elbow** vb Australian
to get rid of, jilt or dismiss someone; variations of **give someone the wellie**

give (someone/something) the wellie vb
British
1a. to dismiss (someone) from work
1b. to reject (a partner)
1c. to discard (an object).
Compare **wellie**

In all senses the expression is a variant form of the colloquial **give someone the boot**.

give (someone) togg outs *vb British*
to attack, beat up. An item of teenage playground slang of the 1990s, recorded among schoolboys in North London. The origin of the phrase is obscure: tog(g)s might logically mean 'blows/punches' but the word has not been recorded in that sense previously; it may have arisen in black British street slang.

glar, glah *n British*
paint. A term used by house painters and artists in London which has not apparently been previously recorded in writing. The origin is obscure, although some connection with glare, gloss or glue seems possible.

> 'Go on, slop on some more of the old glar.'
> (Recorded, mural artist, Vauxhall, London, 1974)

glare *vb British*
to intimidate. A term used by young street-gang members in London since around 2000.

> He was glaring her.

Glasgow kiss *n British*
a head-butt. The term, sometimes also expressed as 'Glasgow handshake', dates from the 1960s. **Gorbals kiss** is a synonym.

glass *n*
diamonds or other gems in underworld argot

glasshouse *n British*
an army prison. The military detention centre at Aldershot barracks had a glass roof in the early years of the 20th century and was notorious for the severity of its regime. Known as the 'Glass House' to inmates, it gave its name to other similar establishments.

Glen *n British*
an easy task. The phrase is based on the rhyme Glen Hoddle (the UK soccer star and manager) and the colloquial term 'doddle'. An item of student slang in use in London and elsewhere since around 2000.

glitch *n*
a snag, an unforeseen fault or malfunction. This piece of aerospace technicians' jargon from the late 1960s has entered the common vocabulary in the era of high technology, referring particularly to computer problems. It is either a blend of **gremlin** and hitch, or from a Yiddish version of the German *glitschen*, meaning to slip.

glitz *n*
glamour, (pseudo)sophisticated showiness. The word is a blend of glamour, ritzy and glitter and is probably a back-formation from **glitzy**. The term is usually used with a degree of implied criticism; it evokes superficiality and 'brittleness'. The word seems to have been an invention of journalists and writers in about 1984. In 1985 it was used as the title of a crime thriller by the American author Elmore Leonard.

> 'Here [Liberia] there is little glitz to the evangelical churches.'
> (*Sunday Correspondent*, 17 September 1989)

glitzy *adj*
glamorous, showy. A vogue word from 1985 to 1987, used particularly by journalists, evoking materialistic but superficial glamour. It is generally more negative than positive in its connotations.
See also **glitz**

glomp *vb American*
to jump and hug someone from behind. An expression used on campus in the USA since around 2000.

glop *vb British*
to drink alcohol, particularly to swill beer. A student term of the 1980s.

> 'Glop, don't stop.'
> (Slogan in urinal, University of Essex, 1987)

glory-hole *n American*
a hole in a partition between two toilet cubicles, enabling voyeurism or communication by (usually male) **gays**

glug *vb, n*
(to take) a drink or drinks of alcohol. A word which imitates the gurgle of pouring or swallowing.

gnarly *adj American*
1. excellent
2. awful, inadequate
Both senses of the word have been beloved by **Valley Girls** and their teenage imitators in the USA since the mid-1970s. The word is thought to have originated in surfing jargon in the 1960s, referring to the texture of waves. By 1989 *Tatler* magazine reported the word as being in use among

schoolboys at Eton. It is sometimes spelt **narly**.

go *vb*
to be sexually active and/or enthusiastic. The word is used in this sense, particularly in Britain, of women by men; its vulgarity was highlighted in the 'Nudge nudge, wink, wink' sketch by Eric Idle in the British TV series, *Monty Python's Flying Circus* (1970), in which he badgers a fellow drinker with importunate questions such as:

Your wife...does she go? I bet she does.
See also **goer**

go ape *vb See* **ape(shit)**

goat heaven *n*
a state of unfettered freedom, enjoyment, indulgence. The phrase, in use since 2000 and of uncertain geographical origin (it is popular in the Caribbean), evokes both bliss and excess.

go at it *vb British*
to have sex. A vulgar euphemism popular with adolescents in the mid-1990s. The colloquial phrase denotes any vigorous performance, but its meaning has become specified in slang usage.

'*They can't wait to go at it, both of them!*'
(Recorded, London University student, October 1996)

gob[1] *n British*
the mouth. The word was originally Irish and Scottish Gaelic for beak or mouth, becoming a British dialect term in about the 16th century. It is still more widespread (and considered less vulgar) in Ireland, in Liverpool, where the influence of Irish speech is strong, and in the north of England, where the influence of post-Gaelic dialect lingers. In southern England it is mainly a schoolchildren's word.

gob[2] *vb*
to spit. The ritualistic spitting at groups performing on stage indulged in by **punks** from 1976 onwards was known as 'gobbing'.

gobble, gobble off *vb, n*
(to perform) oral sex, particularly fellatio. A vulgarism which is most widespread in Britain.

gobby *adj British*
excessively loquacious, boastful. Based on **gob**, the term is a slang version of the colloquial 'gabby'.

go belly-up *vb*
1a. to die

'*Just another fat junkie who went belly-up.*'
(*Tatler*, October 1989)

1b. to fail or collapse. Said typically of a business or other venture.

'*He lost all his equity when the firm went belly-up in the recession of '81.*'
(*Wall Street*, US film, 1987)

These senses are based on the image of a dying fish or a supine dead animal.

1c. to give in, yield, submit. This refers to the animal behaviour whereby the soft underparts are exposed to an adversary as a sign of submission.

gob-grabbing *n British*
passing illicit objects or substances covertly from mouth to mouth. An item of prisoners' slang.

'*If you went to hug a fellow-prisoner, wouldn't he suspect you of attempting a "gob-grabbing"...?*'
(Will Self writing in the *Evening Standard* magazine, September 1993)

gob job *n British*
an act of oral sex, usually referring to fellatio. A vulgarism from the late 1960s.

go blow! *exclamation*
used for telling someone to go away

'*So take a piece of u own medicine and GO BLOW (oops did dat offend u?).*'
(Recorded, contributor to www.wass-up.com, November 2003)

go Borneo *vb American*
1a. to get drunk
1b. to behave outrageously, go too far

Both senses are **preppie** terms indicating a regression to a supposed primitive jungle mentality, influenced by the numerous 'wild men of Borneo' featured in travelling freak shows and the wrestling ring over the years. (The original tales of wild men living in the unexplored jungles of Borneo probably arose from the first reports of the orang-utan.)

gobshite *n British*
a contemptible person. A Liverpudlian and northern term of abuse which, since the 1960s, has spread to other areas of Britain including London. It usually indicates great distaste or contempt (**gob** refers to the mouth and **shite** to excrement; both are regional vulgarisms).

gobslutch *n British*
a slovenly, messy person; someone with dirty personal habits, especially eating habits. A term from the north of England,

heard in the long-running TV soap opera *Coronation Street*. (**Gob** refers to the mouth, 'slutch' is a variant form of slush.)

gobsmacked, gob-struck *adj British*
astonished, struck dumb, left open-mouthed in amazement. From **gob**. These are originally Liverpudlian terms and are now widespread, used even by **Sloane Rangers** and **yuppies**, thanks initially to usage on TV comedies set in Liverpool. The expressions enjoyed a vogue in popular speech and journalistic use from 1988. The phrases originally referred to a victim gaping after literally being punched in the mouth.

> *'He had expected to pay one tenth of the price and was said to be "gobsmacked" at the final cost.'*
> (*Independent*, 21 September 1989)

gobsmacking *adj British*
astonishing. A more recent derivation of **gobsmacked**.

> *'... but when Casaubon observes, "Life isn't simple, the way it is in detective stories", the gobsmacking banality can only be the author's.'*
> (Hugo Barnacle reviewing Umberto Eco, *Independent*, 14 October 1989)

go bush *vb Australian*
to go native, become countrified. *See also* **bush[1]**; **bushie**

go commando *vb British*
to dispense with underwear when otherwise clothed. The expression probably did originate in military usage but by 2005 was in use among fashion designers, journalists etc.

God-botherer *n British*
an excessively pious person or a clergyman. A mainly middle-class expression applied particularly to institutional holy men such as prison and army chaplains, or to members of evangelical movements. The phrase has inspired the more frivolous non-specific insult, **dog-botherer**.

God forbids *n pl*
children, *kids*. The rhyming-slang phrase is synonymous with **saucepan lids** and **dustbin lids**, and was still in use in 2004.

> *Try not to wake up the God forbids.*

go down *vb American*
to take place, happen. A phrase from black street slang which became widespread in the later 1960s.

go down (on) *vb*
to perform oral sex. The term is used by, and applied to, both sexes; until the late 1960s it was a predominantly American expression. Elaborations used by high-school and college students included 'go down like water/like a submarine' (usually indicating shock at a person's readiness to indulge in this behaviour).

God squad, the *n British*
the forces of organized religion, especially in evangelical form. The phrase has been applied scornfully to the Salvation Army, doorstep zealots and university Christian Unions alike, from the late 1950s to the present.

goer *n*
a sexually active and enthusiastic person; in the past, almost always said of women by men. The word can express admiration and approval or astonishment, though rarely moral disdain.

gofer *n*
a minion or assistant who runs errands or delivers messages, etc. The word, originally an Americanism from the film industry (where it is now a job title), is a pun on 'go for (something)' and gopher, the North American burrowing rodent.

gogglebox *n*
a television set. This term has been in use since the late 1950s. At first used pejoratively by those disapproving of TV, then ironically by viewing enthusiasts, the word is now semantically neutral.

goggles *n pl*
spectacles, or someone wearing them. A schoolchildren's word.

goggy *n British*
a misfit, a pupil rejected by schoolfellows. This invented term was reported by *Tatler* in September 1989 to be in current use at Eton College. (Synonyms are **gunk**, **spod**, **Wendy** and **zoid**.)

go home *vb*
to shut up, cease, desist

going for gold *vb British*
expending maximum energy, displaying maximum effort. This 1990s usage borrows the cliché phrase from the language of sports and competitions.

> *'Everyone's up by the speakers, going for gold.'*
> (New Age tribal dancer, *Exodus: The Diary*, Channel 4 TV documentary, 12 November 1995)

going in *n British*

'chatting up' a stranger of the opposite sex. The term is part of the language of dating in use among adolescents in the later 1990s and was included in *Just Seventeen* magazine's 'lingo of lurve' guide to teenage jargon in August 1996.

going through *n British*

engaging in an argument or dispute, usually with a romantic partner or close friend. The term is part of the language of adolescents in use in the later 1990s and was included in *Just Seventeen* magazine's 'lingo of lurve' guide in August 1996.

goit *n British*

a foolish and/or grotesque person. The term, possibly based on 'goitre', was used in and possibly coined for the cult BBC TV comedy series, *Red Dwarf*.

G.O.K. *adj*

undiagnosable or undiagnosed, it is an abbreviation of 'God only knows'. Jocular medical shorthand, e.g. as written on a patient's notes.

goldbrick *vb American*

1. to shirk, idle or loaf. In this sense the word is often used in an armed-service context.

2. to swindle. The reference is to painted 'gold' bricks sold by fraudsters.

golden *adj American*

exceptional, superlative. The standard adjective used figuratively (as in a 'golden opportunity') was adopted as a vogue term by Californian high-school students in the 1990s, particularly to categorise a valued or admired friend. The term was featured in the 1994 US film *Clueless*.

golden showers *n*

urine or urination. A joky euphemism derived from the jargon of prostitution, in which urination is part of the sexual repertoire. An alternative term is **water sports**.

gome, gomer *n American*

a tediously studious fellow pupil or student, a **swot**. A **preppie** and teenage term based on the name ('Gomer' Pyle) of a fictional comic television character who personifies cloddishness. Perhaps coincidentally, *gomeril* or *gomerel* are archaic British dialect words for a simpleton.

gomey *n Irish*

a stupid person. The word is related to the Scottish **gommie** and the American **gomer**, all deriving from older dialect words for a simpleton which in turn come from the Old English *guma*, meaning man, which is a cognate of the Latin *humanus* and the word from which (bride)groom derives.

gommie *n British*

a foolish, stupid or gormless person. The term is heard particularly in the Scottish Lowlands and the north of England. It is related to the Irish **gomey** and the American **gomer**.

gone *adj*

1a. in a euphoric state; ecstatic from the effects of drugs or music. The term is from the slang of jazz musicians of the 1950s, adopted by **beatniks** and **hipsters**. It now seems comically dated.

> *I tried talking him out of it, but he was totally gone on booze and reefer.*

1b. inspiring ecstasy or euphoria; said especially of music and usually preceded by 'real'

> *some real gone jazz*
> *a real gone chick*

gonef *n American*

an alternative spelling of **ganef**

gong *n*

1. *British* a medal. The use of the word derives predictably from its resemblance to the metal gong which was ceremoniously sounded in colonial days, itself named from an echoic Malayan word.

> *'Tony Hart, Tory leader of Kent County Council, may not be in line for the usual gong dished out to holders of his office.'*
> (*Private Eye*, April 1989)

2. *South African* a Chinese person. Recorded as an item of Sowetan slang in the *Cape Sunday Times*, 29 January 1995.

gongol *n British*

an idiot, an unfortunate simpleton or buffoon. The word is a blend of **goon** and 'mongol' and was briefly a vogue term among London schoolchildren from 1979.

gonk *n British*

a dull-witted, buffoonish or grotesque person. Gonk was services' slang in the 1950s for sleep (probably from 'conk out'), but the word was used as a trademark name for troll-like dolls in the late 1960s. It is from this source that the word as a term of abuse or contempt arose, just as **muppet** did in the late 1970s. Gonk was applied by schoolchildren to unfortunate fellow-pupils and by hospital staff and police to the mentally retarded.

gonof n American
an alternative spelling of **ganef**

gonzagas n pl American
female breasts. Gonzaga is a Spanish proper name, but is used in this sense by analogy with earlier humorous synonyms **garbonzas** and **gazungas**.

gonzo adj
unrestrained, hedonistic, extremist as a style, particularly a journalistic style popularised by the late Hunter S. Thompson in his articles for Rolling Stone magazine in the early 1970s. Gonzo is said to be an earlier **hipster** term made up of **gone** and the '-o' ending (with a median s or z to aid pronunciation), but is more likely to be a straightforward borrowing of the Italian gonzo, meaning foolish.

> 'He was responsible for pioneering the style of modern journalism known as "Gonzo": the freewheeling and often self-indulgent method which has been copied by countless writers.'
> (I-D magazine, November 1987)

goobatron n
a foolish person, a **nerd**. An adolescent elaboration of **goober** heard in the late 1980s.

goober n American
1a. a spot or pimple
1b. a foolish person, especially one small in stature
1c. a gob of spit
All senses of the word are derived from a southern American term for a peanut which is an Americanisation of the Kongo word nguba.

good afternoons n pl South African
prominent buttocks. The term is used appreciatively and jocularly, invariably by males, of a female's posterior. It was recorded as an item of Sowetan slang in the Cape Sunday Times, 29 January 1995.

good oil, the n Australian
the truth, an utterly accurate and/or admirable statement

good plan, Batman! exclamation British
a cry of agreement or approval. An armed-forces and public-school version, possibly earlier, is 'Good plan, that man!'.

goods, the n
1. the real thing, first rate merchandise
2. incriminating information, evidence

goody-goody, goody-two-shoes n
an offensively virtuous or diligent person. The second phrase is more often heard in the USA; it derives from the heroine of a children's story and implies a dislikable prissiness.

> 'Superman's naïve, a goody-two-shoes. Batman busts heads.'
> (Joe Lihach of Village Comics, Observer, July 1989)

gooey n American
a girlfriend. A fashionable, but probably ephemeral term among teenagers in late 1987 and 1988. It was probably influenced by 'gooey-eyes' (romantic looks).

> How's your gooey?

gooey nectar n American
an attractive girl, a particularly good-looking girlfriend. A teenagers' vogue word from late 1987 combining **gooey** (a girlfriend) with 'nectar' (a pretty girl).

goof[1] n
a gormless, awkward or foolish person. Originally a rural British dialect word, goof became widely used between the two world wars all over the English-speaking world, particularly in the USA.

goof[2] vb American
1. to blunder, make a mistake, fail. The verb postdates the noun form of the word.
2. to stare or look vacuous. A teenage term from **goofy**.
3. to indulge in wordplay, improvise poetry. A word and an activity popular with the more literary **beats** in the 1950s.

goofball n American
1. a slow-witted and/or clumsy person. A mildly derogatory term derived from **goof** and **goofy**.
2. an illicit drug, typically a tranquilliser or barbiturate which renders the user slow or inert

go off vb
1. American to express enthusiasm and/or excitement, give vent to strong feelings. An expression used on campus in the USA since around 2000.
2a. to be lively, exciting. Usually referring to a party or dance, the phrase can also denote, e.g., exciting surfing conditions.

> It was going off down the boathouse bar last night.

2b. *British* to erupt into violence

'Then Jimmy spilled Bob's beer and it all went off.'

(Recorded, Southampton, 2000)

go off on (someone) *vb American*

to criticise, denigrate, **diss**. An item of black slang of the 1990s, also adopted by younger white speakers.

goof off *vb American*

to avoid responsibility, refuse to take things seriously. An Americanism since the 1940s, the word was briefly adopted by British **beatniks** in the early 1960s but did not establish itself.

goof up *vb American*

to make a mistake, blunder. An elaboration of **goof**.

goo-gobs *n American*

a large quantity of money, used in the phrase 'to make goo-gobs'. An item of black street slang that was reported by US linguists to be obsolete by the end of the 1960s, but which was revived in 1990s usage.

googy-egg, googie, goog *n Australian*

an egg. A piece of 'baby talk' transferred from the nursery to facetious adult usage.

gook *n*

1. *American* a North Vietnamese or any Oriental person. A derogatory term widely used by American soldiers in the Vietnam War, but originating much earlier, probably in the Filipino uprising of 1899 in which US troops referred to Filipinos as 'gugus', from a native word meaning tutelary spirit. Coincidentally, *kuk* is a Korean word-ending meaning person, and gook was also heard in the Korean conflict.

'...dinks, gooks, slopes – all sorts of slang to dehumanize them.'

(Veteran of My Lai massacre, Channel 4 TV, 22 June 1988)

2. an alternative spelling of **guck**

goolies, ghoulies *n pl British*

the testicles. In northern Indian languages *gooli* means pellet or pill. The word was picked up by British colonial troops at the turn of the 20th century as a euphemism for testicle. This sense was reinforced by a more circuitous route; the gypsies' language, Romany, also adopted the Indian word *gooli*, from which the English and Australian schoolchildren's word 'gully', for a marble, derived. **Marbles** itself was a common euphemism for the testicles.

'The temperature further increased each time we dipped a deep fried fish ball into the special Oh' Boy sauce. "It's enough to take your goolies off", gasped my sister-in-law.'

(Craig Brown, *Sunday Times* magazine, 8 October 1989)

goomba, gumba *n American*

a friend or associate. The word has been widely used, mainly by males, in many social contexts. It is often assumed to have an Afro-Caribbean origin, but one authority, Robert L. Chapman, derives it from a dialect pronunciation of the Italian *compare* (a 'comrade' or 'relation').

goon *n*

1a. a foolish, clumsy or clownish person. This sense of the word was popularised in Britain by the zany radio series *The Goon Show* in the 1950s, and was earlier used in the *Popeye* cartoons for 'Alice the Goon', a huge dull-witted character. This in turn was probably influenced by a pre-existing word in British dialect meaning vacuous or simple (and distantly related to 'yawn'). Since 2000 the expression 'you goon!' has been used by British adolescents to indicate strong dislike or disdain.

1b. a thug. The word was already being used in this sense in the USA in the late 1930s, typically of hired strike-breakers. It was later applied particularly to strong-arm men of low intelligence used by gangsters to intimidate or punish.

'Tell Simpson to get his goons to lay off – then we'll talk.'

(*Rockford Files*, US TV series, 1978)

go (out) on the cotton wool *vb See* **on the cotton wool**

goony *n American*

a foolish person. A variant form of **goon**, mainly heard among children and teenagers.

gooper *n American*

a gob of spit. This is probably a variant form of **goober**.

goopy *adj*

foolish, clumsy or unfortunate. An uncommon adjective influenced by **goop** and **goofy**.

'To keep goopy stills from love scenes out of circulation, his contracts stipulate that the studio can't release his photograph without his approval.'

(*Elle* magazine, May 1989)

gooseberry n British See **play gooseberry**

goosegog n British
a gooseberry, in the literal sense. A nursery term also used by adults and teenagers.

go pear-shaped vb British See **pear-shaped**

go postal vb See **postal**

gopping adj British
1. dirty, disgusting
2. drunk
A term popular (in both senses) among younger speakers since 2000. Its derivation is obscure.

gora n See **ghora**

go raggo vb See **raggo**

Gorbals kiss n British
a head-butt. The phrase, a synonym of **Glasgow kiss**, refers to the formerly notoriously violent working-class district in that city.

gorge adj
very attractive. A shortened form of 'gorgeous' used especially by middle-class speakers in both the UK and the USA since 2000.

gorilla-finger n Australian
a **joint**, especially a large one. The phrase was recorded in the early 1990s.

'When we've packed up, we'll roll up the first gorilla-finger of the evening.'
(Recorded, Australian sound engineer, London, September 1993)

gorked out, gawked out adj American
incapable, intoxicated, disoriented. The word was featured in the 1990 US film, *Donor*.

goss n British
gossip (in the sense of rumour, scandal and chatter, not of a person). A vogue term which appeared around 1988 and established itself in the language of teenagers and writers in teenage magazines. Although the shortened form resembles the abbreviated journalese of *Variety* magazine in the USA, it appears to be a native British coinage.

'A triff new weekly mag with all the goss on your fave TV stars.'
(BBC TV advertisement for *Fast Forward* magazine, 1989)

go the full distance vb
to be arrested, tried, convicted and sent to prison. A euphemism heard among the criminal fraternity and the police in

the 1970s and 1980s. The metaphor is taken from boxing jargon.

go through the slips vb British
to renege on (a deal). An item of underworld slang from the 1990s. The term refers either to a cricket ball passing near the wicket or to an escape near the 'slips' (wings) of a theatre.

go tits-up vb American
1a. to die
1b. to be ruined, bankrupted, defeated, etc.
In both senses the expression is a vulgar version of the more common **go belly-up**.

go troppo vb Australian See **troppo**

go twos vb
to share, 'go halves/half-and-half'
'Lets go twos on the shopping.'
(Recorded, London student, 2003)

gouge vb American
to intimidate, damage, do down. A business term of the 1980s.

gouged adj British
intoxicated by drugs, the term especially denotes someone **stoned** on **ecstasy**

gouger n Irish
a **yob**, lout or thug. The word is Dublin slang, heard since the 1980s.

gouing n British
lying. A term of uncertain origin in use among West London students in 2000.

gourd n American
the head. The word is almost always heard in the phrase 'out of one's gourd'.

governor n British See **guvnor**

go walkabout vb
to daydream, lose concentration. The term derives from the Australian Aboriginal practice of leaving the community to go into the bush on a mystical quest (when they are said to 'go walkabout'). It was applied by journalists to the tendency of the tennis player, Evonne Goolagong, to allow her concentration to slip during matches and now is applied to any sort of aberrant mental behaviour.

gozunder n See **gazunda**

grab vb
to kiss. In this sense the word has been used by British adolescents since the late 1990s.

graft[1] n
1a. work, particularly hard, unrelenting or persistent work

1b. a job, one's occupation

2. *American* dishonesty, bribery, or peddling influence in public or political life

Both the British and American senses of the word ultimately derive from a British dialect word descended from the Anglo-Saxon verb *grafan*, related to grave and meaning to dig.

graft² *vb British*

1a. to work, in particular to work hard and constantly

1b. to engage in clever, devious or dishonest money-making schemes, especially those involving selling in street markets, fairs, etc.

1c. to pursue criminal activities

All the senses of graft originate in a dialect word meaning to dig, from the Anglo-Saxon verb *grafan*.

grand¹ *n*

a thousand pounds or a thousand dollars. The word originated in the jargon of American sportsmen, gamblers and, later, criminals. It was adopted in the same milieus in Britain by 1950.

> *'Zackerman rings and – this'll make you smile – he goes, he goes, I'll give you a hundred grand plus the car and that, and fifty in your hand.'*
> (*Serious Money*, play by Caryl Churchill, 1987)

grand² *vb South African*

to appreciate. In this sense the word was recorded as an item of Sowetan slang in the *Cape Sunday Times*, 29 January 1995.

> *Well, I don't grand your joke.*

grandstand *vb American*

to put on a bravura display, show off to an audience. The expression comes from the world of sport and was originally an Americanism. It is often used as an adjective as in 'a grandstand play'.

granola *n American*

a keen environmentalist or a person dressing like one. This campus categorisation (often pejorative) appropriates the name of a health-food cereal. It is a synonym for **earth biscuit**, **duck-squeezer**, etc.

grass *n*

1. herbal cannabis, marihuana. British smokers traditionally preferred hashish, but began to import more marihuana in the mid-1960s. Grass was the predominant American term and had largely supplanted **bush**, **pot**, **herb**, etc. in British speech by 1970.

> *'They're saying cannabis drives you crazy, but I can't see that applying to just grass.'*
> (Teenage smoker, London, June 2005)

2. *British* an informer. Originally the expression was 'grasshopper' as rhyming slang for *copper*; the meaning was then transferred to the 'copper's nark' or informer and by the 1940s grass had become established in the underworld lexicon. By the 1970s the word was also widespread among schoolchildren and others. 'Supergrass' was a journalese elaboration denoting a highly significant informer.

grass (someone up) *vb British*

to inform on or betray (someone) to the police or authorities. The usage was originally to 'grass on someone' or to 'grass to the authorities'. From the 1980s the London underworld expression to 'grass someone up' has been used, not least among schoolchildren, who had adopted it from TV police dramas and documentaries. For the etymology see the noun **grass**.

graunch *vb South African*

to engage in 'heavy petting', fondling or sex play

graze *vb*

to eat while standing up and/or occupied in some other activity. A piece of **yuppie** jargon from the late 1980s.

grease¹ *n American*

money. An underworld term of the early 20th century, adopted by **beatniks** among others and, more recently, by teenagers. From the notion of greasing the wheels of commerce, or money as a social lubricant.

> *If we had some grease we could hit town this weekend.*

grease² *vb American*

to kill. The word appears to have had the specific meaning of shoot (probably inspired by 'grease-gun') until the 1970s when it acquired its additional and more general sense.

> *One move and we grease your friend.*

greaseball *n American*

1a. a person of Hispanic or Mediterranean origin or appearance. An offensive term which has been in use since before World War II.

1b. a person, such as a cook or mechanic, who works in literally greasy conditions

grease-monkey n
a mechanic. Partridge dates the term to around 1910. It was still in use in 2004.

greaser n
1. *British* a **rocker**, motorcycle enthusiast, a scruffy unfashionable person. A scathing term adopted by **mods** and students to refer to rockers in 1964. The word has gradually fallen out of use since that time.
2. *American* a person of Hispanic or Mediterranean origin or appearance. The term refers to a supposedly greasy complexion; it implies great contempt and causes offence.

> 'Crazy greasers – they've always got bees in their panty hose about something.'
> (P. J. O'Rourke writing on Panama in *Holidays in Hell*, 1988)

3. a petty criminal, juvenile delinquent, etc., specifically one who wears hair oil, a leather jacket, etc.
4. a toady, sycophant or hypocrite, from the notion of greasiness equated with unctuous, devious behaviour

greasy spoon n
a transport cafe, diner or other cheap restaurant. A mildly derogatory but generally affectionate term for the kind of eating place where most, if not all, of the hot dishes are fried in animal fat. The expression seems to have originated in Canada or the USA in the 1930s.

> 'There's nothing for breakfast except toast. Let's go down the greasy spoon – I fancy a good grease-up.'
> (Recorded, teacher, London, 1987)

grebo, greebo n *British*
a scruffy young rock-music enthusiast, typically long-haired, unkempt and leather-jacketed. The word was coined in 1985 in the Midlands to describe a youth subgroup of gauche but earnest heavy-rock devotees. Grebo does not so much denote a separate cult (its proponents displayed characteristics of **rockers**, **hippies**, goths and **punks**), but is a new term for a pre-existing phenomenon (as in the case of **anorak**).

> 'Greboes drink stout and snakebite, smoke Players No.6 (packets of ten), wear y-fronts and dirty torn jeans, drive big bikes, and go out with girls who don't shave their armpits.'
> (*I-D* magazine, November 1987)

greek vb, n *American*
(to engage in) anal sex. The term, from the euphemism 'greek love', is invariably used for referring to homosexual behaviour between males.

green[1], **green stuff** n
money. Banknotes of all denominations are green in the USA. In Britain, pound notes were green until replaced by coins in the 1980s.
See also **long green**

green[2] n
1. a £5 note or the sum of five pounds. The UK banknote is dark turquoise in colour.
2. weed, from the usual colour of herbal cannabis. A fashionable synonym for the earlier **grass**, heard especially since 2000.

> That was a tasty price for that green.

green (out) vb *British*
to vomit, especially after smoking cannabis. In use among students since 2000.
Compare **white-out**

greenback[1] n *American*
a banknote. US paper money is predominantly green in colour.

greenback[2] vb *American*
to subsidise, underwrite, finance. A recent derivation of the well-established noun form, greenback is employed as a novel synonym for bankroll.

green gilbert n *British*
a thick piece of mucus from the nose. A schoolchildren's term which has been in use since the 1950s and is now considered respectable enough to be said on television. The choice of Gilbert is due to the supposed inherent comicality of the name and to its echoes of gobbet, glutinous, etc.

greenie n
1. *British* an old term for a one-pound note. From the predominant colour.
2. *American* a (Heineken) beer. A **preppie** term, often extended to refer to other brands, from the colour of the bottle and label of the popular import.

green welly, green-welly brigade adj, n *British*
(in the style of or characteristic of) upper-middle-class young people who indulge in country pursuits such as rid-

ing and hunting and who typically wear Barbour jackets and green wellington boots. The term 'green-welly brigade' is used pejoratively to refer to wealthy townspeople who visit the country at weekends (usually staying in second homes), and comments on their habit of 'dressing-down' in a pseudo-country style.

greezy adj
excellent. The vogue term is used by UK adolescents and may be a blend of great and easy. 'It means I'm doing well, everything is good'. (Recorded, student, London, 2003).

gregory n British
a *cheque*. A piece of rhyming slang from the late 1980s, playing on the name of the film star Gregory Peck. The same rhyme has also been recorded with the alternative meaning of 'neck', but this, given the rarity of conversations concerning that part of the body, seems unlikely to supplant the financial sense.

'I'm just popping out to sausage [and mash: cash] a gregory.'
(Recorded, property speculator, Bath, 1988)

greldge, grelge n American
an unpleasant substance, dirt. An item of middle-class slang used by adults as well as adolescents. It was recorded from the early 1990s and appears to be formed from such terms as grease, filth and **grunge**.

grem, gremmie n Australian
1a. a novice or incompetent surfer
1b. a novice or incompetent skateboarder
A teenage term imported into Britain in the late 1970s. The variant forms are probably based on **gremlin**.

gremlin n
an unexplained flaw, malfunction or error. A word used particularly by British soldiers in World War I and American airmen in World War II, evoking a malicious spirit. (The word is a form of the Irish *gruaimin*, meaning a bad-tempered little fellow.)

grenade n
an unattractive female, especially one who has to be placated in order for a more attractive female to be approached. The use of the term derives from the notion of a heroic act of sacrifice whereby an individual falls upon a live grenade, thereby saving his comrades.

OK, it's your turn for the grenade.

grey, the grey n
1a. British a conventional, conformist person. A vogue term in British counterculture circles from about 1966 to 1968. The word had the same dismissive or pitying overtones as **straight**, which had supplanted it by the end of the 1960s.
1b. British **the grey** the collective mass of conformists, dullards and authority figures, as opposed to the (literally as well as metaphorically) colourful **hippies**
2. American the 'white' man. A derisive term used by blacks.

greybar n
a period of inactivity. An item of **net-head** jargon referring to sitting before a grey screen waiting for a display.

greybeard n
1. an 'old-timer'. The word probably originates (as 'graybeard') in the USA where it is a jargon term for a long-serving senior officer in various fields, such as civil aviation, from the literary term for an old man.
2. See **longbeard**

grid n British
the mouth. The term, which is heard in northern speech, is almost invariably heard in the phrase 'shut your grid!'.

G-ride n American
a stolen car. An item of black street-talk that was included in so-called **Ebonics**, recognised as a legitimate language variety by school officials in Oakland, California, in late 1996.

griefy adj British
depressing, troublesome. A fairly rare middle-class teenage and student term from the early 1970s.

'I mean we've all tried to fly from upstairs windows…we know those griefy scenes, man!'
('American ethno-botanist' in cartoon by Posy Simmonds, *Guardian*, 1980)

grievous adj British
1a. annoying
1b. unattractive or unappealing
The standard term was adopted as a vogue term of disapproval by adolescents in the later 1990s.

grifter n American
an untrustworthy, suspect or dishonest person, typically a gambler or minor fraudster. Grifter is a word from the

early 20th century which is a blend of 'graft' and 'drifter'. It was used by Raymond Chandler in his detective fiction and was still occasionally heard in the late 1980s.

grill[1] *vb*
1. to interrogate. Police and armed-forces slang of the 1950s which has become a widely used colloquialism.
2. *American* to intrude upon someone's personal space, from the noun form. A fashionable usage among adolescents since around 2002.

grill[2] *n American*
1a. the teeth, mouth. The reference is to the radiator grille of a car, often in the form '(all) up in someone's grill' (engaged in confrontation or harassment).
1b. one's personal space, **face**. The word has been in vogue in hip hop and **rap** milieus since around 2000.

grim *adj British*
extremely unpleasant, disgusting. The standard term was adopted as a vogue term of disapproval by adolescents from the later 1990s.

grimy *adj American*
thuggish in demeanour, from the language of hip hop. The term can be used appreciatively or, probably less often, pejoratively. An expression used on campus in the USA since around 2000.

grind *n*
1. an act of sexual intercourse. A widespread vulgarism since the 1960s, the word has been used with a sexual connotation since the 16th century.
2. *American* a **swot**, a tediously diligent student, in high-school and college terminology
3. the quotidian reality, an oppressive routine, as in the 'daily grind'

grindage *n American*
food. One of many items of adolescent slang using the **-age** suffix, fashionable in the 1990s.

grinding *n*
rubbing one's body against a partner for sexual stimulus. The term applies particularly to dancing and usually refers to males. **Crubbing** is a synonym.

grip[1] *vb*
to steal. A term used by young street-gang members in London since around 2000.

grip[2] *n American*
1. a large crowd
  a grip of people
2. money. In this sense the word was recorded in student usage in 2003.

grippa, gripa *adv American*
extremely. A vogue synonym of **hella** and **ganga** recorded on campus in 2002.
  Hey that ride is grippa tight!

grizzer *n South African*
a mother, matriarch or elderly lady. Recorded as an item of Sowetan slang in the *Cape Sunday Times*, 29 January 1995.

gro, groe *n American*
a black person. The racist epithet is a clipped form of 'negro'. In the UK **groid** has been used in the same way.

grobber *n British*
an obnoxious, repulsive individual. The term was first recorded in the 1960s and may be related to the verb 'to grub'.

groceries *n pl See* **blow one's cookies/ doughnuts/groceries/lunch/grits**

grockle *n British*
an unwelcome outsider, tourist or visitor. A Devon dialect term applied contemptuously to summer visitors by local residents since the 1960s. The word has been adopted by the many non-native **hippies** and travellers living in the West Country to refer to anyone who is not approved of. (The term has also been heard in other parts of Britain.) Grockle is claimed to derive from the name of the famous clown 'Grock'. In Cornwall the equivalent is **emmet**.
  'That unmistakable grockle smell – stale fat and farts.'
  (Recorded, resident of Torquay, 1976)
  'We never go in that pub – full of grockles.'
  (Recorded, resident of Parracombe, North Devon, 1986)

grody *adj American*
an American version of **grotty**, used typically by **Valley Girls**. A word dating from the mid-1970s which now seems established in the teen lexicon. It is often intensified in the phrase 'grody to the max'.

grog
1. *vb*, *n* (to indulge in) alcoholic drink. The noun form, from the rum and hot water served in the British navy since the 18th century, can now refer to any strong drink, or even beer. It is generally heard among middle-aged speakers. The verb

'to grog/grog up' (in Australian English to 'grog on') is rarer and restricted mainly to a younger age group. It implies heavy and constant imbibing. 'Old Grog' (from the grogram, or silk and wool cloak he wore) was the nickname of Admiral Vernon who aroused his sailors by ordering the dilution of their rum ration in 1740.

> *'Not realizing one's dependence on the grog is where the wheels touch the road, eh?'*
> ('Edmund Heep' in a cartoon by Posy Simmonds, *Guardian*, 1979)

2. *vb British* to spit. The term is heard particularly in the Scottish Lowlands and the north of England.

groid *n*
a black person. This racist term of abuse, a shortening of the adjective 'negroid', was particularly prevalent in police usage in London in the late 1980s. It also exists in American speech.

> *'Travelling around – being an International Knee-grow (or a "groid" as the Met would have it) – thanks chaps!'*
> (Lenny Henry, *Time Out* magazine, 26 July 1989)

grolly *n, adj British*
(someone (usually a male) who is) dull, unattractive, 'frumpish'. An item of student slang in use in London and elsewhere since around 2000.

grommet, grom *n Australian*
a young and/or inexperienced person. The term is used by surfers to denote novices, especially those under 16.

gronk *n British*
an unattractive female. In armed-forces' usage since the 1990s.

groove¹ *n*
1. an enjoyable experience or situation. An Americanism derived from the verb to **groove** (on) and the adjective **groovy**. The word was **hip** jargon of jazz musicians since the 1930s, later becoming part of the **hippy** lexicon and as such was also heard outside the USA until the mid-1970s. It now sounds very dated.
2. *See* **in the groove**

groove² *vb*
to experience a sensation of well-being, fellow-feeling, to feel in tune with one's surroundings. This well-known and characteristic **hippy** term originates in the slang of jazz musicians and others for whom being in the groove meant being at one with the melody, with one's fellow players, etc. (like a needle in the groove of a record). The word subsequently became a pivotal one for hippies, for whom it expressed a notion of enjoyable one-ness with one's environment that hitherto lacked a name. The expression was hackneyed by the time James Taylor was ridiculed by British rock journalists for his declaration at a mid-1970s concert at the Royal Albert Hall that he 'grooved to the vibes'. To 'groove on something' was another typical form.

> *'Groovin' down a crowded avenue/ doin' anythin'/ we like to do.'*
> ('Groovin', recorded by the Young Rascals, 1967)

groover *n*
1. a fashionable, dynamic, **hip** person. A 1960s formation from **groovy** and the verb to **groove**.
2. a tedious person, a **swot**. A probably ephemeral usage of the late 1980s, based on the newly pejorative teenage sense of **groovy**.

> *'Charmless college swots are no longer known as "nerds" but are on the receiving end of a whole variety of new insults including "dweeb", "geek", "goober", "wonk", "corn-dog", "goob-a-tron" and "groover".'*
> (*Independent* magazine, 24 December 1988)

groovy *adj*
1. satisfactory, satisfying, fine. A term of approval, sometimes in the form of a mild exclamation, from the **hippy** era. The adjective is derived from the verb to **groove**; originally an American term, it was adopted by British rock musicians, **beatniks** and, later, hippies from about 1965. Sounding risibly dated in the 1970s and 1980, groovy was revived first for ironic, then appreciative use from around 2000.

> *'You see we have a lot of other groovy things going for us, and not just concerning music.'*
> (Mick Jagger, *Record Mirror*, 26 August 1967)

2. *American* tedious, dull. A vogue word among adolescents from 1988. It is probably inspired by the ironic use of the dated term of approbation.

> *'Another 1960s catchword, "groovy", has mysteriously turned into its opposite, now signifying stodgy or old-fashioned.'*

(*Independent* magazine, 24 December 1988)

gross *adj*

disgusting, distasteful. An Americanism of the mid-1960s, particularly popular among teenage girls. It is a fashionable usage of the standard term (from Latin *grossus*, meaning thick, via French and Middle English) in its sense of excessive, vulgar or obscene.

'Like Joan's, Marlene's entire range of expression was pretty much limited to "far out", "super" and "gross".'
(*The Serial*, Cyra McFadden, 1976)

gross (someone) out *vb American*

to disgust or repel (someone). The expression is normally used by a speaker to refer to their own distaste. It is a teenagers' term, popular since the late 1960s.

'Would you move your socks. Like out into the patio or something? I mean they're really grossing me out.'
(*The Serial*, Cyra McFadden, 1976)

gross-out *n American*

a disgusting act or situation. A favourite term of teenagers since the mid-1960s, usually said with excited or exaggerated distaste.

'After totting up the score-sheet of exposed breasts ("garbonzas"), mutilations, rolling heads, gross-outs, auto-collisions, he awards a number of stars and puts his seal of approval on a film.'
(*Observer*, 9 April 1989)

Grosvenor Squares *n pl British*

rhyming slang for *flares*, i.e. bell-bottom trousers. This phrase was an ephemeral youth term of the late 1970s used contemptuously of the (by then) unfashionable style and the remnants of the **hippy** movement who still favoured it. London's Grosvenor Square, the site of the US embassy, was the scene of peace demonstrations by students and hippies during the Vietnam war. A later, more lasting, alternative piece of rhyming slang for the same item was **Lionel Blairs**, followed by **Tony Blairs**.

'Belinda has discovered an important pair of "jeans" dating from the late 1960s. These are most certainly rare items, known by collectors as "Grosvenor Squares".'
(Caption to cartoon by Posy Simmonds, *Guardian*, 1981)

grot *n British*

1a. dirt, squalor, unpleasantness. Although this word was a back-formation from the adjective 'grotty', it no longer reflects that word's origin in 'grotesque'.

I can't go on living among all this grot.

1b. a dirty, slovenly or disreputable person

He really is an awful grot.

grotty *adj British*

unpleasant, revolting or distasteful. The word became extremely popular in the early 1960s and quickly passed into the middle-class lexicon where it is still found. Grotty, a typically Liverpudlian shortening of 'grotesque', became popular among young people, via the influence of the 'Mersey boom' in the early 1960s. It was adopted by some Americans in imitation of British usage, although an American form, **grody**, arose in the 1970s.

grounded *adj American*

confined to one's home, deprived of one's car keys. A popular parental means of chastising American teenagers. The image is of course that of a plane and/or pilot prevented from flying.

'I can't go out tonight, I'm grounded too, you know.'
(*The Stepford Children*, US TV film, 1987)

group-grope *n*

a group 'heavy-petting' session. A teenagers' term from the early 1960s. The phrase was later applied to full-scale **gang bangs** or orgies and, scathingly, to group therapy sessions.

groupie *n*

a girl who associates with or follows a musical group or star. The term originally assumed, and still implies, the sexual availability of the girl. The word and the phenomenon were publicised in the late 1960s, particularly in the semi-autobiographical book *Groupie* by the British writer Jenny Fabian in 1968 and the US film *Groupie Girl*, 1969.

grouse *n, adj Australian*

(something) excellent, superlative. This use of the word probably derives from the notion of the bird as a delicacy; also used figuratively to denote an attractive woman since the pre-war period.

grub *n*

1. food. The word has existed with this meaning since at least the 17th century, inspired by the action of grubbing around.

> *"At the weigh-in, Reynolds, in the red corner, weighed eight stone, two pounds.' 'Give the poor sod some grub!'*
> (*Adolf Hitler, My Part in his Downfall*, Spike Milligan, 1971)

2a. *Australian* a dirty, slovenly person. This sense of the word was in British use until the early 20th century, but is now obsolete there.

2b. *British* a younger child, especially a grubby or defiant one. From the terminology of prep and public schools.

Both these senses of grub derive from the lowly insect larva.

grues *adj British See* **gruse**

gruff *vb, n British*
(to) **fart**

grundies *n pl British and Australian*
underpants, perhaps related to the earlier **undie-grundie**

grunge *n*
1a. *American* anything dirty, distasteful, squalid or sordid. This adolescent coinage is now heard in Britain.

> *'For Martin Amis is the Wodehouse of grunge…'*
> (David Sexton, *Sunday Correspondent*, 17 September 1989)

1b. *American* a boring or irritating person or task

2. a genre of rock music and subsequently a youth subculture and fashion movement, originating in Seattle in 1992. The earlier senses of the word were applied to the heavy, fuzzy sound of the musical style and to the deliberately scruffy image cultivated by its adherents.

> *'Sure, even before Kurt Cobain took his own life last year, whispers of grunge's death had been patently acknowledged.'*
> (*Guardian*, 25 March 1995)

grunt *n American*
1. a soldier, an army private. A derogatory term sometimes used ironically by the soldiers themselves, deriving from the supposedly low intelligence and predilection for grumbling of the humble enlisted man or conscript.

> *'The grunts were conscious that they were involved in a drug-and-rock 'n' roll extension. Most of the combatants, black and white, came from the working class.'*

> (Michael Herr, *Observer*, 15 January 1989)

2. power. The term is used particularly by car enthusiasts to refer to engine power.

> *'The engine size has gone up from 3.4 to 3.6 so there's plenty of grunt.'*
> (*Top Gear*, BBC 2 TV motoring series, 13 February 1997)

gruntled *adj*
satisfied, gratified. A jocular back-formation from the standard 'disgruntled' (in which 'gruntle' in fact means grumble and is related to grunt). This rare word is typically used by educated speakers, saloon-bar philosophers and amateur or professional comedians.

> *I was feeling extremely gruntled following my success.*

grunt-work *n American*
menial or demeaning job(s)

> *'You know, I used to do the grunt-work around here. Now I own the place.'*
> (*Double Cross*, US film, 1994)

gruse *adj British*
unpleasant, repellent. The term is an abbreviation of 'gruesome'.

> *'I watched my mate get her tongue pierced and it was well gruse.'*
> (Recorded, London student, 2002)

G-thing, G-thang *n American*
1. a subject or activity characteristic of a **gangsta**

> *'Nothin' but a G-thang.'*
> (Title of a **rap** recording by Dr Dre, 1992)

2. a subject or activity characteristic of males, from the phrase 'it's a guy's thing'

> *You wouldn't understand: it's a G-thing.*

gub *vb British*
1a. to hit (someone), especially in the mouth or face

> *The geezer kept at him and finally Mickey gubbed him.*

1b. to defeat

> *Our team got well and truly gubbed.*

Both senses of the verb derive from a dialect form of **gob** meaning mouth. The terms are heard particularly in the Scottish Lowlands and the north of England.

gubbing *n British*
a beating. The term, from the verb to **gub**, is almost always used literally, but can also be used figuratively to mean a verbal attack.

Gucci *adj*

flashy, materialistic. The name of the Italian design company, usually employed with (mildly) critical intent, was adopted for use in street and, later, campus slang in the USA in the 1980s. Gucci shoes and handbags were part of the accessories favoured by devotees of the hip hop and **rap** subcultures. In the slang of the British Officer Training Corps the phrase **Gucci kit** is used to mock those who bring expensive luggage and accessories to training camps.

guck *n*

a sticky substance, muck. A mainly American nursery word blending 'goo' and 'muck'. Also spelt **gook**.

guff *vb, n British*

(to) **fart**. An old childish vulgarism which has been revived since the late 1980s as part of a vogue for pseudo-nursery slang among students and others.

> 'The force of the gigantic guff you used has wrecked the entire drainage system.'
> (*Johnny Fartpants, Viz* comic, April/May 1988)

guffie *n British*

a **fart**. A variation of **guff**.

guinea *n American*

an Italian. An offensive term, the origin of which is obscure, but which might derive from a proper name such as Gianni or Giovanni, or else by a tortuous process from the name of the African country (whence slaves were exported).

gumby *n*

an aggressively gormless, clumsy and/or dull person. From the name of a character personifying these qualities in the TV comedy series *Monty Python's Flying Circus* in the 1970s (in turn partially inspired by Peter Cook's earlier invention 'E. L. Wisty'). The personification and name were taken up by British and American teenagers in particular.

gump *n American*

1. a foolish, clumsy person, a simpleton. This widespread term pre-dated the 1994 film *Forrest Gump*. It originated in Yorkshire English dialect, in which it denoted a 'dolt' and was probably related to the colloquial 'gumption'.

2. a male prostitute, particularly a transvestite male prostitute, from the slang of Chicago police, recorded in the non-fiction work *Pure Cop*, 1991. By 2000 it was also in use in the UK.

gumshoe *n*

a detective, private eye or plain-clothes police officer. The term was first used in the USA early in the 20th century and referred to the silent rubber-soled shoes that detectives supposedly wore, as opposed to uniformed police officers' heavy boots.

gunge *n British*

a sticky substance, muck. A slang term of the 1960s which has become a middle-class colloquialism.

gung-ho *adj*

excessively eager, enthusiastic and/or assertive, especially in the context of patriotism, jingoism and military aggression. This phrase was thought to be a Chinese rallying cry. (The words 'gung ho' were part of the Chinese title of an Industrial Cooperative and were assumed wrongly to mean 'work together'.) It was adopted by the Marine Corps and later for general American military use in World War II. It became known outside the USA to a limited extent during the Korean war and more particularly during the Vietnam war, now being so well known as to constitute a colloquialism rather than a slang term.

gunk *n*

1. muck, goo, sticky stuff. An American version of the British **gunge**, now heard in Britain, too. By extension it can also mean debris or rubbish.

2. *British* a school misfit. A schoolboy term reported to be in use in Eton College by *Tatler* magazine in September 1989.

gunsel *n American*

1a. a callow youth

1b. a gunman

The latter meaning is now more widely encountered, but the former, with overtones of punkishness, comes from the Yiddish slang for young man (*gantsel* or *ganzl*: 'gosling') and was the sense in which it was used in crime novels and *film noir* in the 1930s. The second meaning is based on a misreading of the first.

guns of Navarone *n pl South African*

female breasts. The jocular expression from the 1990s borrows the title of a 1961 film featuring giant cliff-top cannons.

guppy n
an environmental **yuppie**. A journalese coinage blending 'green' and 'yuppie', inspired by the popular tropical fish.

gurgle n British
(an) alcoholic drink. A fairly predictable euphemism, used typically by pub habitués and other hearty drinkers. It is probably influenced by **gargle**.

> 'Fancy popping down to the Swan for a bit of a gurgle?'
> (Recorded, middle-aged drinker, Pangbourne, 1986)

gurgler n Australian
a toilet. The term is sometimes used figuratively in the phrase 'down the gurgler', meaning ruined, lost or failed.

gurk vb, n
1a. British (to) belch, burp
1b. Australian (to) **fart**
Imitative words used, mainly by children, since the 1950s.

gurner n
a tablet of **ecstasy**. The term was in use among UK students and others from the late 1990s.

gurning adj British
intoxicated by drugs or drink. The term was popular among adolescents and students from the later 1990s and refers particularly to someone feeling the ill effects of drugs. It is inspired by the verb to 'gurn' (from Middle English girn, a form of 'grin'), which means to pull grotesque faces.

> 'Look at Gemma, she is properly gurning man...'
> (Recorded, art student, UK, 2002)

gussied-up adj
smartly dressed, neatly turned out. The term is common in American speech and is heard elsewhere. It may have originated in Australian usage and is possibly based on the names Augustus, Gus or Gussie as supposedly denoting an effeminate or fussy male.

> 'Well, you're all gussied-up.'
> (Curaçao, US film, 1993)

gut-rot n
a cheap, low-quality alcoholic drink. This phrase is probably more widespread in Britain and Australia than the alternative **rot-gut**. Unlike rot-gut, it is occasionally also used to refer to food.

gutsache n
a miserable, complaining person, a **misery-guts**. The expression is particularly

popular in Australia, but is also heard in Britain. The image evoked is of someone perpetually suffering from dyspepsia or provoking indigestion in others.

gutser, gutzer n Australian See **come a gutser**

gutted adj British
1a. devastated, deeply disappointed, saddened or shocked. A vogue word among working-class and lower-middle-class speakers since the late 1980s, perhaps encouraged by the over-use of the word by sportsmen and sports commentators. The concept has also been expressed subsequently by the alternatives **kippered** and **filleted**.

> '24 hours before work on the commercial was due to start the answer came from Central. It was no. After all those years – just no. I was gutted.'
> (Paul 'Benny' Henry, News of the World, 8 January 1989)

1b. used as an exclamation. By the end of 1990 the term had become a schoolchildren's catchphrase, used as a shout of victory or defiance, meaning 'I have humiliated you' or 'you have been shamed'. The form 'gutted out' is also heard.

gutters n British
an unattractive female. A synonym for **butters** and **dog**, in the jargon of clubland recorded from the early 1990s.

> 'An out and out gutters.'
> (Touch magazine, September 1993)

gutty, gutsy adj British
bold, brave or 'bolshie'. A late 1980s coinage, popular in unsophisticated speech, which is a back-formation from the well-established colloquial sense of guts denoting courage.

guv n British
a respectful term of address to a male, in working-class usage. Said invariably by, as well as to, men, guv is a shortening of the almost equally widespread **guvnor**, meaning boss.

guvnor, governor n British
a boss, chief or leader. A descriptive term or term of address used by, to and about males in working-class speech. This widespread colloquial form of governor arose in the early 19th century and shows no sign of dying out. Governor, then spelt correctly, was recorded as a slang term for one's employer as early as 1802; Charles Dickens later

referred to it as a slang synonym for 'old man' or 'boss' when referring to one's father. In the 1980s it acquired a further nuance in the form 'the guvnor' as an acknowledged expert or leading exponent (for instance among rock musicians and fans).

'I'll be alright 'cos I believe in the life here-after. I mean, Jesus was the governor wasn't he?'
(East Ender, *Sunday Times*, 2 June 1968)

gweeb, gweebo *n American*
a stupid, dull person. A late 1980s variation on **dweeb**, coined by teenagers. It is probably unrelated to the British **grebo**.

gwot *n American*
a contemptible person. This high-school term of great distaste, heard since the late 1980s, is an invention, obviously influenced by other evocations of unpleasantness such as grotesque, **weed**, **twat**, etc.

'Oh God, not him, he's such a gwot.'
(*Some Kind of Wonderful*, US film, 1987)

gyppo, gippo *n*
1. a gypsy
2. an Egyptian. A neutral rather than pejorative term in origin, gyppo was, and is, sometimes extended in uneducated speech to encompass other Arabs or Muslims.
3. *British* a vulgar, poor and/or unsophisticated person. One of a number of pejorative terms (such as **chav**, **pikey**, **skeg**) in vogue since 2003.

gyppy tummy *n British*
an attack of diarrhoea. A phrase from the colonial era. The equivalent of **Delhi belly**, **Montezuma's revenge**, etc.

H

H *n*

heroin. This was the most popular term among British drug users in the 1950s and 1960s before being supplanted by **smack**, **scag**, **brown** etc.

He's been on H for years.

habit *n*

an addiction, a 'drug habit'. A drug-user and law enforcers' term, sometimes extended to refer to more innocuous addictions.

a $100 a day habit

hack *n*

1. a journalist, professional writer. The word, inspired by the image of a worn-out workhorse, has traditionally denoted a disreputable, unprincipled, mercenary reporter or writer. Since the late 1960s, if not earlier, journalists have appropriated it to refer to themselves proudly rather than self-deprecatingly. Hack is still used in publishing as a simple descriptive term for a journeyman writer prepared to tackle any subject, as distinct from a specialist.

2. *British* an excessively ambitious student. In the slang of Oxford and Cambridge universities this is the undergraduate equivalent of the many schoolchildren's synonyms for **swot**.

3. a cough, particularly a dry, rasping cough. The word imitates the sound in question.

hacked-off, hacked *adj*

annoyed, irritated, resentful. From the late 1980s, this phrase has enjoyed something of a vogue as a replacement for the better-known 'brassed-off', 'cheesed-off' and as a euphemism for **pissed-off**. It has been recorded in both the USA and Britain since the early 1950s.

hacker *n*

1. someone who **hacks into** a computer system. The hacking in question is the evocation of a person chopping their way through dense undergrowth to their destination. Hacker in this sense appeared as part of data-processing jargon in the early 1980s. Spectacular instances of the penetration of computerised systems brought the word to public awareness.

2. a taxi driver. A 'hackney cab' (the archaic version of taxi cab) takes its name from 'hackney', meaning a horse used for transportation. The short version of the phrase survives in this sense.

3. a clumsy worker. Here hack evokes chopping clumsily, rather than handling or cutting finely.

hackette *n British*

a female journalist. A jocular term coined by journalists (on the basis of **hack**) and popularised in the 1980s by *Private Eye* magazine (who referred to society gossip columnist Lady Olga Maitland as 'the fragrant hackette') among others.

hack into *vb See* **hacker**

hack it *vb*

to succeed, to manage (in spite of adversity). A slang usage which remained relatively obscure until the early 1980s, since when it has become a common colloquialism. The original sense of hack is uncertain here; it may mean to drive, to strive or to chop (one's way through).

The poor guy's finished, he just can't hack it anymore.

hag *n*

a disreputable, promiscuous and/or irritating female

hagsay *n, vb British*

(a) **shag** in **pig Latin**, in secondary school usage

ha-ha *n British*

marihuana or hashish (cannabis), or another 'euphoric' drug. A light-hearted reference by middle-class soft-drug users to the hilarity induced by smoking, ingesting or sniffing the chosen substance.

hairball n American
an unpleasant and/or despicable person, by analogy with something vomited by a cat. The phrase owes its usage from the 1980s partly to the fact that, while offensive, it is not obscene and can therefore be used in television dramas and by children in the presence of adults.

hairy¹, hairie n British
a bearded, long-haired person and, by extension, a **beatnik**, 'bohemian' or intellectual. A disparaging term typically used by middle-class speakers in the mid-1960s.

> Honestly, she spends her time with all these weirdos and hairies.

hairy², herry, herrie n Scottish
a female. The term is almost invariably pejorative and often refers to an unattractive or troublesome young woman. It is said to derive from the fact that the poorer female inhabitants of Glasgow in the 1930s and 1940s could not afford hats (then de rigueur for respectable women), thereby exposing their hair to onlookers.

> Mick was off wi' a wee herrie, so I'm told.

hairy-arsed, hairy-assed adj British
wild, primitive, uncouth or rugged. A term in armed-forces and middle-class use which is often, but by no means always, appreciative in tone.

> 'I am not some hairy-arsed Viking from the North bent on a bit of rape and pillage.'
> (John Ashworth, Director of the LSE, quoted in the Independent, 5 January 1995)

half a bar n British
before decimalisation in 1971 half a bar was ten shillings; since then it has meant fifty pence. The phrase is London working class or cockney. 'Bar' is an archaic term, still occasionally heard in London, coming from a Romany word (bar or baur(o)) meaning a sovereign and, later, one pound.

half-arsed, half-assed adj
ill-considered, incomplete, ineffectual. An expression which appeared in British and American usage around the turn of the 20th century. The term may originate in the notion of something which has less than a whole solid base or, according to a more fanciful theory, derive from a jocular deformation of 'haphazard'. In modern British speech it is sometimes used as a more vulgar version of half-hearted (its more probable inspiration).

> 'I'd rather write nothing than something half-arsed. There are far too many half-arsed books in the world.'
> (Novelist Dan Rhodes, interviewed in the Guardian, 9 April 2003)

hamburger n British
the vagina. A vulgarism in use among adolescents in the 1990s and listed in Viz comic in 1994. **Furburger** is a (probably earlier) synonym.

hammer n
1. a male who behaves excessively, a heavy drinker. In this sense the word has been used by US college students and some British adolescents since 2000.
2. a gun. A term used by young street-gang members in London since around 2000.
3. See **put the hammer on (someone)**

hammered adj British
drunk. A fashionable word among mainly middle class young people since the 1980s.

> 'Sloane Rebs all support Chelsea FC, and can be seen every other Saturday lunchtime "chugging brew" and getting hammered at any number of pubs in the Fulham Road, before charging down to Stamford Bridge for a "frightfully good game of footy".'
> (I-D magazine, November 1987)

> 'First things first: I'm a bit hammered and a bit dyslexic.'
> (Posted on online student blog, October 2004)

Hampsteads n pl British
a short form of the cockney rhyming slang 'Hampstead Heath': teeth

hampton, Hampton Wick n British
the penis. Hampton Wick is a southwestern suburb of London, providing a rhyme for **prick**. In modern usage the short form of the phrase is usually preferred. Since the mid-1970s the term has been considered well established and inoffensive enough to be used in television comedies.

> 'Then there were these telephone calls from…groupies. Somehow they'd learned a hell of a lot of cockney slang. They'd phone up and say "Hi Jeff Beck, how's your 'Ampton Wick?" Ridiculous!'
> (Jimmy Page, Oz magazine, April 1969)

Compare **ted**

ham shank n British
an act of male masturbation, rhyming slang for **wank**. An item of student slang in use in London and elsewhere since around 2000.

hamstered adj British
intoxicated by drugs or drink. An item of student slang in use in London and elsewhere since around 2000.

handbag[1] n British
a male escort, a 'walker'. Handbag refers to a 'decorative appendage' to a fashionable lady, often a homosexual male. The term was popular in high society and journalistic circles in the mid-1980s.

handbag[2] vb British
to frustrate, obstruct or attack. A jocular version of **sandbag** seen in the 1980s, often in journalistic references to Margaret Thatcher. The term evoked shrewish intransigence.

handbag situation, handbags at ten paces n British
a scene of provocation, a confrontation and/or feigned violence. These sarcastic phrases are typically used by football supporters to describe a scene in which players make a show of menacing or jostling each other. The reference is to a supposed brawl between middle-aged women.

'A handbag situation – when players square up and scuffle (supermarket style) but the ball is too far away for them to kick each other…'
(*Evening Standard*, 26 May 1994)

hand-job n
an act of manual sexual stimulation, usually masturbation of a male by a female. A common vulgarism in use since the mid-1960s.

handle n
a name, nickname, alias or title. The first sense of the word was that of title (an appendage to one's name) in the early 19th century.

hand shandy n British
an act of (male) masturbation. The term became widespread in the 1990s.

handsome adj British
excellent, impressive. An all-purpose term of approval used by cockneys and other Londoners, sometimes standing alone as an exclamation. The 'h' is usually dropped.

handy adj British
1. a catch-all London working-class term, invariably pronounced without the 'h' and signifying adept, devious, virile, brutal, etc., usually in a context of immorality or illegality
2. a term from teenage sexual slang, invariably applied to boys and defined by *Just Seventeen* magazine in August 1996 as 'a bit too tactile under a girl's T-shirt for her liking'

hang vb American
1. to consort with, frequent. This black street usage is a shortening of the colloquialism 'hang out' and was adopted by white adolescents from the 1990s.
He's been hangin' with the homeboys.
Those betties hang down at the mall.
2. to relax. This usage is probably a shortening of the phrase **hang loose**. Originating in black street slang, it was adopted by white adolescents from the 1990s.
I'm inclined to tell them all to go to hell and just hang for a while.

hang a louie vb American
to take a left turn. A teenage expression from the early 1970s.

hang a ralph vb American
to take a right turn. A teenage expression from the early 1970s.

hang a yooie/u-ie vb British
to make a U-turn when driving a car. A mock-racy expression from the 1980s.

hang five vb
to ride a surfboard (at near-optimum speed or full stretch) with the toes of one foot hooked over the front. From the jargon of American surfers since the early 1960s.
See also **hang ten**

hanging adj British
1. ugly, usually applied to females. In this sense the word was recorded in South Wales in 2000.
2. tired, exhausted. From army and Officer Training Corps usage.
Compare **hooped**
This may be a shortening of the synonymous expression *hanging out of my hoop*, where 'hoop' signifies 'anus'.
3. drunk

hang loose vb American
to stay relaxed, keep **cool**, **chill out**. A vogue term from the late 1950s and early 1960s when it characterised the nonchalant state of detachment aspired to by **beatniks**, jazz musicians, etc. The phrase

(still heard occasionally) is often an exhortation to a friend on parting. It probably originates in the use of 'loose' to describe a free, unstructured style or mood (although some have interpreted it as referring to the male genitals in an unencumbered position).

hang one on *vb*
an alternative form of **tie one on**

hang one on someone *vb*
to hit, punch someone. An expression, used particularly by brawlers, which may also be expressed with the verbs 'land', 'stick' or 'put'.

hang out *vb See* **let it all hang out**

hang ten *vb American*
to ride a surfboard (at near-optimum speed or full stretch) with the toes of both feet hooked over the front. From the jargon of American surfers since the early 1960s. The phrase is sometimes used figuratively to mean something like 'go full-tilt on a risky course'.

hang-up *n*
a neurosis, obsession. From the image of being hung on a hook. This **beatnik** term was seized upon by the **hippies** to describe the concerns of the **straight** world. Unlike many contemporary terms, hang-up has not dated significantly and is still in use today.

He's got a hang-up about young chicks in uniform.

hank *adj British*
extremely hungry. Recorded in London in 1994, the word is a shortening of the rhyming slang phrase 'Hank B. Marvin', meaning *starvin(g)*, borrowing the name of the lead guitarist of the *Shadows* pop group.

'Can you hurry up, we're all bloody hank in here.'
(Recorded, builder, southeast London, July 1994)

hankie-head *n*
an Arab. The term, which probably post-dates the more widespread synonyms **rag-head** and **towel-head**, was popularised by the comic writer P. J. O'Rourke in the 1980s.

happening *adj American*
exciting, stimulating and/or up-to-date. A fashionable term from the vocabulary of teenagers since the mid-1970s. It is influenced by the earlier black catch-phrase greeting 'what's happening?' and the **hippy** cliché, 'it's all happening'.

a really happening band

happy dust *n*
a narcotic in powder form. The term has been applied to cocaine, **PCP** and amphetamines among others.

happy slapping *n British*
a transgressive fad of 2005 whereby a random victim is attacked and the attack photographed or videoed on a mobile phone. The coinage is probably influenced by the phrase 'slap-happy'.

'Let's happy slap that bloke there.'
'Ha! Aye!'
(*Viz* magazine, June/July 2005)

haps *adj British*
an abbreviation of happy

'We're really haps to be in the Smash Hits Pop-o-Saurus.'
(Pop group Fierce, speaking in 2000)

hard-arse, hardass *n*
a tough, unyielding and/or severe person, a martinet. This noun form post-dates the adjectival form hard-arsed.

hardass *n American See* **hard-arse**

hardball *n See* **play hardball**

hardcore[1] *adj*
1. thoroughly criminal, deviant or sexually debauched. This is a specific sense of the colloquial meaning of hardcore (committed or uncompromising, as applied, e.g., to political beliefs or pornography). In the 1970s in the USA the word took on a narrower connotation in the jargon of the street and underworld, coming to mean irredeemably criminal. It was often used in this sense to indicate admiration or awe.

the hardcore life
That guy's real hardcore.

2. excessive, outrageous, relentless. This vogue term in adolescent speech in the later 1990s was often used to indicate appreciation or admiration. It is based on the earlier uses of the word to characterise pornography and rock music and, according to its users (one of whom defined the usage as referring to 'somebody who stays up all night, is violent, or drinks everyone under the table or takes loads of drugs'), its antonym is **lightweight**.

a hardcore guy/scene
acting/playing hardcore.

hardcore[2] *n*

a style of fast, loud, aggressive music, a development of **punk**. The term originated in America in the early 1980s, perhaps influenced by the adjectival use of **hardcore** to mean (uncompromisingly) rebellious, anarchic or criminal, spreading to Britain around 1985. The genre has since spawned subcults such as 'deathcore' and 'speedcore'.

hard-off *n American*

an unstimulating, disappointing person, experience or sensation. The term, coined by analogy with **hard-on**, is used by members of both sexes.

hard-on *n*

1a. an erection. To 'have a hard-on' has been the most common way of expressing male sexual tumescence since the early 20th century. It derives from a slightly earlier adjectival form (to be 'hard-on') which follows a pattern of Victorian euphemism which includes 'fetch off' (to have sex or an orgasm), etc.

> *'Don't go home with your hard-on/It will only drive you insane.'*
> (Lyrics from 'Don't go home with your hard-on', Leonard Cohen and Phil Spector, 1977)

1b. a sudden strong desire or affection. This specialised sense is a piece of **macho** business jargon from the late 1970s. It suggests an aggressive and uncompromising wish to acquire or cement relations with, e.g., a business partner.

> *I think Ingrams is nursing a hard-on for United Mills.*

hard word, the *n*

1a. a rejection or condemnation

> *'It was the one thing that would bring Christina [Onassis] and her father together again. It was only a matter of time before Christina gave me the hard word.'*
> (Joseph Bolker quoted in *Heiress*, by Nigel Dempster, 1989)

1b. a difficult request or ultimatum, particularly a demand for money or sex

The phrase is normally part of longer expressions such as 'put the hard word on' or 'give someone the hard word'. The origin of the expression is obscure, but it is most prevalent in Australian use.

harf, hark *vb American*

to vomit. Echoic terms in use among students in 2003. **Hork** is a variant form.

haricot (bean) *n Australian*

a male homosexual. Rhyming slang on **queen**.

Harold Ramp, Harold *n British*

a rhyming slang term for *tramp* or homeless person, popular since 200. The proper name seems to be an invention for the purposes of the rhyme.

harolds *n pl Australian*

trousers or underpants. The etymology of this jocular usage is unclear: it is thought to originate in rhyming slang based on a real or imaginary proper name such as 'Harold Taggs/Wraggs': **bags**.

harp, harpoon *n*

a harmonica. Long known as a 'mouth harp' among black American blues musicians, the harmonica became known worldwide as a harp during the rhythm and blues boom of the early 1960s. Harpoon is a later and fairly rare elaboration.

> *'Seriously he [Stevie Wonder]'s a knockout harp player, but this singing-only effort is a swinger.'*
> (*Rave* magazine, March 1966)

harpic *adj British*

crazy, deranged. A pun which was popular for instance among schoolchildren in the 1960s. The person so described was 'clean round the bend', from the slogan of the Harpic toilet cleaning preparation which claimed in a TV advertisement to 'clean round the hidden bend'. The word was used on *Whacko!*, a parody of public-school life starring the late Jimmy Edwards.

harpoon *n*

1. a hypodermic syringe. Another example of the self-dramatising language of drug abusers.

Compare **artillery**; **shooting gallery**

2. a version of **harp** in the sense of harmonica

harry *n British*

heroin. An addicts' term from the 1960s, personifying the drug in the same way as **charlie** for cocaine.

harry- *prefix British*

a prefix used in public-school, university and armed-services' slang, almost always by males, to add jocular familiarity to a standard term. It is often used in conjunction with the **-er(s)** word ending. The **-er(s)** form is probably earlier; 'harry-'

seems to have originated in armed-forces speech pre-World War II.

Fiona's harry-preggers again.

harry-starkers *adj British*
naked. An upper-class or armed-services jocularity.

harsh *adj*
1. *American* unpleasant, inferior. An all-purpose negative, briefly a vogue term among Californian adolescents in the mid-1990s.
2. good, impressive. In this reversed or ironic sense, recorded among British **mods** of the 1960s and US high-school and college students of the 1990s, the word is one of a large set of near-synonyms including **savage**, **brutal**, **tough**, etc., which have been adopted into adolescent codes.

hash *n*
hashish (cannabis resin). Hashish from North Africa, the Middle East and the Himalayas is the most widely used form of cannabis in Britain, especially among white smokers, while **grass** (herbal cannabis) is more common in the USA. This shortened form of the word was probably the most widespread term in use among British cannabis smokers in the early 1960s. It was then largely supplanted by more colourful terms such as **charge**, **shit**, **dope**, etc.

'Hash smoking is now a widespread social habit, almost in the same class as whiskey and soda.'
(Letter to *Oz* magazine, June 1969)

hassle *vb, n*
(to subject someone to) bother, harassment, intrusive complications. This term had existed in American English since the 19th century; in the 1960s it formed part of the **hip** and counterculture jargon which became established throughout the anglophone community. In origin it is either a blend of 'harass' or 'haggle' and 'tussle' or 'wrestle', an anglicisation of the synonymous French verb *harceler* or, more convincingly, a version of **hustle**. In Britain hassle replaced hustle as a vogue term among **beatniks** and **mods** in about 1967.

hat *n American*
a condom. **Jim(my)-hat** is an alternative form.

hatch *vb British*
to drink, drain one's glass. A matter-of-fact beer-drinkers' term, derived from the exclamation 'down the hatch!'.

'I think we'd better hatch these [beers] and get going.'
(Recorded, wedding guest, Bristol, 1988)

hatchback *n South African*
a female with prominent buttocks. An appreciative term used by young males in the 1990s and inspired by the designation of cars.

hate on (someone) *vb American*
to be jealous of (someone). An expression used on campus in the USA since around 2000.

hater *n American*
a jealous or envious person. An expression used on campus in the USA since around 2000.

hatstand *adj British*
crazy, eccentric, deranged. The nonsense term was invented by the comic *Viz* for the character Roger Irrelevant and was adopted into student slang in the late 1990s.

He's completely hatstand and always has been.

haul ass *vb*
to get moving, go into action. An Americanism, usually in the form of a command or exhortation, which has been heard in British and Australian speech since the 1980s.

haul off *vb American*
to get ready to strike someone or to launch an attack. The term may be used literally (of leaning back before aiming a blow) or figuratively.

have a cow *vb American*
to throw a tantrum, become extremely agitated. An expression used on campus in the USA since around 2000. The analogy is probably with the colloquial 'having kittens'.

have a lend (of someone) *vb Australian*
to deceive, bamboozle, lie about. The phrase is related to older locutions such as 'get a lend of/have a loan of' which refer to a dishonest individual taking advantage of another by borrowing from them.

'You better be sure he's having a lend of you.'
(Recorded, Melbourne bus driver to adolescent passenger, 1995)

have a mare vb British
to become angry, infuriated. The mare in question may be a shortening of nightmare, or the phrase is possibly a version of the American **have a cow**, evoking the pain of giving birth to something enormous. The expression was in use among London teenagers in 2000.

have a scene (with someone) vb
to have a sexual relationship, have an affair (with someone). This phrase, now sounding rather dated but as yet lacking a more fashionable alternative, was the standard term throughout the late 1960s and early 1970s for an unmarried relationship. The expression, particularly popular with middle-class British **hippies**, avoided the juvenile, frivolous or banal implications of 'going out with' and the middle-aged overtones of the word 'affair'.

have it away, have it off vb
to have sex. These phrases, which have been commonly used in Britain and Australia since the 1940s, seem to derive from an earlier sense of the same terms meaning to succeed in stealing or succeed in accomplishing (something illicit). There is also significant similarity with 19th-century sexual euphemisms such as 'fetch off'. Both expressions are used by all social classes.

    'He later told me he'd had it off with a photographer the previous night and so wasn't much concerned with having it away himself.'
    (Joe Orton's Diary, 14 May 1967)

have it (away) on one's toes vb British
to escape, run away. A phrase from the repertoire of criminals, prisoners and the police since the early 1950s. It was still current among these and working-class Londoners in the late 1980s.

have (someone) over vb British
1a. to trick, dupe, deceive. A working-class euphemism related to the colloquialism 'get one over on (someone)'.

    'Similar themes run through stories about social workers who are reckoned to be easily "had over" by "villains" and even by juvenile offenders.'
    (*Inside the British Police*, Simon Holdaway, 1983)

    'I was a young geezer and I was trying to have the police over.'

(Vincent Hickey, released prisoner speaking on *Panorama*, 24 February 1997)
1b. to seduce. A specialised sense of the preceding usage, invariably referring to a male 'taking advantage of' a female.

have the bomb vb Australian
to be exhausted. The phrase may be related to the use of **bombed**, meaning incapacitated by drink or drugs.

have the decorators in, have the painters in vb
to menstruate. A women's euphemism; both phrases are heard in Britain and Australia, the second version in the USA.

have the hots (for someone) vb
to nurse a sexual desire for someone, to lust after. The phrase is a variation of other, now obsolescent phrases (to 'be hot for', to 'have the hot ass', etc.) in which hot equates with sexually excited. First heard in the USA in the 1960s, the term quickly spread to other English-speaking countries.

having it large, having it n See **'avin' it large**

Hawaii n British
a £50 note or the sum of fifty pounds. A raffish expression inspired by *Hawaii-Five O*, the title of an American TV crime series of the 1970s.
    I got him to do it, but it cost me a Hawaii.

hawk one's fork, hawk the fork vb Australian
to sell one's body, engage in prostitution. A colourful vulgarism playing on the medieval sense of fork as the join of the legs. In archaic British slang 'hawk one's mutton' and 'hawk one's meat' were terms with the same meaning.

hay n
1a. a homosexual person
1b. a heterosexual with **gay** mannerisms or appearance.
Compare **metrosexual**

hazing n American
teasing or humiliation, especially as part of a student initiation rite. An American version of the British 'ragging', but often with less light-hearted overtones. The word originated in naval use where it meant to oppress or harass. It probably has no etymological connection with other senses of haze, deriving instead from the archaic French *haser*, meaning to irritate.

head *n*
1. an aficionado of the drug-using counterculture, a drug-user. A word used by **hippies** to refer to themselves. The term originally simply meant a person or individual in the slang of black jazz musicians and, later, white **hipsters**.

'Those were the days of heads and freaks. And if getting high was where it was at, then Vietnam was the ultimate trip.'
(Michael Herr, *Observer*, 15 January 1989)

2. a toilet. This is the singular form of **the heads**, the earlier designation for shipboard latrines.
3. oral sex, particularly fellatio. The word in this sense is usually encountered in the phrase **give head**.

headbanger *n*
1a. a devotee of heavy metal rock music who expresses excitement by frenzied shaking and even literal banging of the head in time to the music. The practice and term originated in the early 1970s.
1b. a person who behaves in a relentlessly frenzied or dangerous way. This usage, deriving from the first sense of the term, usually expresses a certain shocked admiration. It has been current among British schoolchildren and students since the late 1970s, and is rapidly becoming 'respectable' by its use in the press and elsewhere by adults, typically with reference to political extremists.

'I'd like to meet her father; he sounds like a right headbanger.'
(Contestant on *Blind Date*, TV show, September 1989)

1c. a madman, psychotic, **headcase**

headbanging *adj*
1a. shaking or banging one's head in response to rock music
1b. behaving in a wild, unrestrained, relentless or excessive manner. The second, generalised sense is an extension of the first and was coined to describe the behaviour of (mainly male) rock-music fans in the early 1970s.

headcase *n*
an unhinged or deranged person. The word, originally an Americanism of the early 1970s, is typically used by teenagers to indicate awe or dismissive contempt; it rarely refers to the genuinely insane.

header *n Irish*
an unhinged, deranged or unstable person. A version of the earlier **headcase**, recorded in 2004.

head honcho *n*
1. the top person in a hierarchy, the most important boss
2. *See* **honcho**
I can't be bothered dealing with assistants. Who's the head honcho around here?

headlamps, headlights *n pl*
female breasts. These are jocular male terms from the earlier 20th century when large, raised car headlamps were the norm. The first version is British, the second American and Australian. **Bumpers** and **hooters** are other slang terms for the breasts using automotive analogies.

heads, the heads *n pl*
a toilet, latrine. This plural form is now rather dated, except in armed-services' usage. It originated in naval terminology where it referred to the for'ard location of the privies on a ship. **(The) head** is more common.

headset *n*
someone's attitude, way of thinking. This version of the colloquial 'mindset', punning on headset as, e.g., a virtual reality helmet, is heard in British campus slang. It may have originated in the jargon of psychotherapy.
'If you want to understand them, you've got to try to relate to a completely different headset.'
(Recorded, postgraduate student, Warwick University, November 1995)

headshrinker, headshrink *n*
a psychiatrist, psychoanalyst. A jocular term of the 1950s originating in the USA and reflecting the mild contempt, tinged with fear, felt towards the practitioners of these professions. Since the late 1960s both terms have normally been shortened to **shrink.**

heat, the heat *n American*
the police. A black street form of the early 1960s (using the image of heat as pressure, oppression, something stifling) which was adopted by **hippies**. 'The heat's on the street!' was a warning among black communities and white activists alike.
'Her man got took away by the heat/we're lost and incomplete.'
('Endgame', song by Doll by Doll, 1979)

heater n American

a handgun. A pre-World War II term which was appropriated by writers of crime fiction.

heatseeker n American

a dynamic person. The usage derives from the phrase 'heat-seeking missile' as used in news reports, etc., from the 1970s, and was heard in the 1990s in a professional context and among students.

heave vb

to retch or vomit. A literal, rather than metaphorical usage.

heave-ho, the old heave-ho, heave-o n

a rejection or dismissal. A worldwide English expression, typically referring to being jilted by a lover or being fired from one's job. It originates in the shouts of exhortation made by men engaging in physical exertion. It was a sailors' call in the 17th century.

'It was evens…four men had broken her heart and she had given another four the old heave-ho.'

(*A Touch of Spice*, British TV comedy, 1989)

heaves, the heaves n

an attack of retching or vomiting. A literal description of these spasms, although the expression is, by its context, considered slang.

heaving adj

1. *British* stinking. The term, in use in working-class speech in the north of England and Scotland, possibly evokes the notion of something so rotten as to be infested with maggots and literally pulsating, or else evokes the heaving (i.e. retching) of the person sensing the odour. Slightly less overwhelming experiences are evoked by **minging** and **howling**.

I couldn't stay in the flat more than five minutes – it was fuckin' heavin' in there…

2. *British, Irish* very crowded with people
It was heaving in there last night.

heavy¹ n

a thug, **minder**, someone employed for their intimidating physical presence rather than their intellectual qualities. Originally an Americanism, the term has spread to world English via crime fiction and films. In current British colloquial speech it is sometimes used in the phrase 'come the heavy', meaning to act in a threatening manner.

heavy² vb

to intimidate, threaten or pressurise (someone). The verb forms (expressed as 'to heavy someone', 'to heavy someone into (doing) something' or to 'come the heavy') postdate the adjective and noun forms.

heavy³ adj

1. violent, oppressive, intimidating, powerful

2a. (of a situation) emotionally charged

2b. (of a person) difficult to cope with, having a powerful personality

These senses of the word, which were slang terms of the 1960s, have become common colloquialisms.

hebe, heeb, heebie n

a Jew. Based on the word Hebrew, these words originated in the USA. They have been heard in Britain and Australia since the early 1970s, sometimes jocularly lengthened to 'heebie-jeebies'. Hebe is less offensive than **yid**, **kike**, etc., but discriminatory nonetheless.

hectic adj British

excellent, exciting. A vogue term of approbation among adolescents and schoolchildren since 2000.

hedger n British

a rural vagrant. The term, from the lexicon of the homeless, travellers, etc., denotes a **crustie** who prefers to live rough in the countryside. It was first recorded in the early 1990s, although phrases containing 'hedge' – like 'ditch' for a scene of sordid or dishonest behaviour – were common from the 16th century.

heel n American

someone who behaves in an unworthy or base way. This use of the word appeared at the turn of the 20th century.

heesh n American

an altered pronunciation and spelling of **hash** (hashish). The term was used on the street in the 1960s and 1970s, since when it has been adopted by schoolchildren and **preppies** in imitation of more louche speakers.

heifer n

1a. a young woman. A usage which is mainly restricted to the slang of the USA and Australia. In Britain the word was common in the 19th century, but has been archaic since before World War I.

1b. an unattractive, clumsy or unsophisticated young woman

I feel like such a heifer.

height *adj American*
excellent, first-rate. A term of approbation from the hip hop youth culture of the 1980s, coined by black teenagers (as a shortening of 'height of fashion') in the USA and spread with the music and dance trend to Britain where it enjoyed a brief vogue.

'Don't reach for a tape measure the next time someone refers to your bullet-proof safari jacket as "height". They just mean it's cool.'
(Charles Maclean on New York terminology, *Evening Standard*, 22 January 1987)

heimie *n*
an alternative spelling of **hymie**

heinie *n American*
the backside, buttocks. A coy diminutive of hind(quarters) or behind, although spelt as if it were Yiddish. The term is innocuous enough to be used by mothers and children.

'He hit me daddy – and then he kicked me in the heinie.'
(*Date with an Angel*, US film, 1987)

heist *vb, n*
(to commit) a robbery or hold-up. The word, redolent of American gangsterdom, dates from the first two decades of the 20th century. It is probably a variant form of **hoist** which, like 'lift', is a 200-year-old euphemism for steal, influenced by German and Yiddish speakers who would know the verb as *heisst*. Heist in its current usage usually suggests a carefully staged major robbery or criminal operation.

helicopter *n American*
a temporary visitor. In middle-class adult slang of the 1990s the word would be applied to a neighbour who drops in just to eat and then disappears or, as in the phrase 'helicopter-parents', by school staff referring to parents who stay only long enough for a brief consultation or complaint.

helicopters, the *n British*
a bout of dizziness.
See also **whirling pits, the**

helioproctosis *n British*
arrogance, overweening self-assurance. In medical slang the supposed condition in which 'the sun shines out of someone's **arse**'. Also known as **proctoheliosis**, from the Greek *helios* – Sun and *procto* – rectal.

hella, hellov *prefix American*
very. A variant form of 'helluva' and 'hellish', influenced by the fashionable prefix **mega**. The first popular use of the device was in the combination 'hellacool', heard among American teenagers in 1987 and 1988. By 2000 the variant form hellov was also in use.

hellacious *adj American*
1a. appalling, awful, horrifying. A hyperbolic term mainly used and presumably coined by educated speakers, this is an invented elaboration of 'hellish'.

'Well, we made it but we had a truly hellacious flight.'
(US visitor to the UK, June 2005)

1b. impressive, excellent. The term, like **bad, wicked,** etc. has since the early 1980s been used by the young to indicate approval.

Hey, they're a hellacious band.

hench *adj British*
muscular, well-built. A term from Caribbean speech, also heard in the UK since 2000, especially among younger speakers. It may derive from henchman (itself from the Old English *hengestman*, a groom, where *hengest* meant 'stallion').

heng *vb British*
to stink. The term was posted on the b3ta website in 2004.

Hennessey *n*
1a. alcohol
1b. marihuana

For US **rappers** and hip hop aficionados the French cognac brand Hennessey became a generic term for (expensive) alcohol. Among black British adolescents in London in 2001, probably in ignorance of its origin, the word could be used of both alcohol and cannabis.

hep *adj*
aware, in touch with the latest (cultural) trends. An Americanism from the jargon of jazz musicians in the early part of the 20th century, hep was adopted by the white intellectuals of the **beat** generation in the mid-1950s and slightly later by teenagers. The word metamorphosed into **hip** (although the two terms co-existed in the early 1960s), which itself prompted the coinage of **hippy**. The precise dates and derivation of hep are somewhat obscure, although it almost

certainly originates in a shout of exhortation or encouragement: either the noise used by riders, ploughmen, etc. to horses, or (perhaps more likely, given the importance of marching bands in the early history of jazz) that used by parade leaders, drill sergeants, etc. to keep time. To 'get hep' or 'be hep' signifies to be working in harmony or in step.

hepcat *n*

an aficionado of **jive**, jazz and other aspects of progressive popular culture of the 1940s and 1950s. Originally a black term combining **hep** (fashionably aware) and **cat** (a man), it was adopted by white bohemians, intellectuals and proto-**beatniks** and used until replaced by such terms as **hipster** in the 1960s. British jazz fans also picked up the expression and used it self-consciously or humorously until the mid-1960s.

herb *n*

1. marihuana, herbal cannabis. This is probably the most common name for the drug in Caribbean use (usually pronounced **'erb**). The word has been given especial prominence since the early 1970s by reference to it (in popular songs and elsewhere) by Jamaican Rastafarians, for whom it is sacramental. White British cannabis smokers adopted the term as an alternative to the more commonplace **grass**, **bush**, etc. in the mid-1970s.

2. *British* a street urchin. A rare shortening of **Herbert**, typically pronounced **'erb**.

3. *American* a dupe. This term, heard in the 1990s in street argot, is probably taken from the proper name supposedly denoting a quintessential 'sucker'. **(H)erbert** is the British equivalent.

herbal, herbals *n*

marihuana. The term is a predictable borrowing of one component of the official designation 'herbal cannabis' for the leaves and flowers of the plant sold and consumed loose, as opposed to compacted into hashish. It had partly supplanted the form **(h)erb** by the later 1990s.

> *'Didn't any of them enjoy a lug on the herbals?'*
> (*Q* magazine, March 1997)

Herbert *n British See* **'erbert**

her indoors *n British*

one's wife, female partner or boss. A London working-class circumlocution which was popularised by its use in the TV series *Minder* (broadcast between 1979 and 1988). The expression has established itself as a facetious or ironic reference to an unseen (and by implication oppressive) female presence.

> *'All right I'll stop off for a quick drink, but for God's sake don't tell her indoors.'*
> (Recorded, teacher, London, 1988)

Hershey highway *n American*

the anus. The expression, usually heard in connection with homosexual behaviour, uses the brand name of chocolate bars like its British equivalent, **Bourneville boulevard**.

het *n, adj British*

(a person who is) heterosexual

> *They wouldn't understand, they're all hets.*
> *It's a strictly het affair.*

hey diddle diddle *n*

an act of urination, a **piddle**. A piece of rhyming slang in use in London and Australia. (**Jimmy Riddle** is a more common alternative.) The words are from the first line of a well-known nursery rhyme.

hickey *n American*

1a. a love bite

> *'I like your date, Sam. Be careful she doesn't lose a baby tooth when she's giving you a hickey.'*
> (*Cheers*, US TV comedy series, 1986)

1b. a spot or other skin blemish

Hicksville *n American*

a backward provincial place. A racier version of 'hick town', based on 'hick' meaning rustic or unsophisticated. (Hick was originally a diminutive of Richard, influenced by 'hickory'.)

H.I.D. *n British*

an abbreviated form of **her indoors** used by City financial traders during the 1990s

hide the sausage/salami/weenie *vb*

to have sexual intercourse. Usually preceded by 'play', these phrases are adult imitations of baby talk, used facetiously since the late 1960s. The first version is British and Australian, the second and third American.

hidren *n Caribbean*

a good friend. The term is an alteration of, or synonym for, **bredren**. **Idren** is an alternative form.

high *adj*

intoxicated by alcohol or drugs, euphoric. The expression 'high as a kite' preceded the shorter usage which became widespread in the late 1960s.

high on life
I feel like getting high.

high five (someone) *vb American*
to slap raised palms and fingers together as a ritual greeting. The custom and the expression appeared in the black community in the 1970s and was subsequently adopted by sportspeople and adolescents in general.

high-hat *vb American*
to behave condescendingly or 'high-handedly' (towards someone). A fairly rare but long-established expression. The silent-film star Clara Bow claimed that more sedate members of the Hollywood community high-hatted her.

high muckamuck *n American See* **muckamuck**

hike *vb, n*
(to make) a departure or journey

Take a hike.
It's time to hike.

hill-billy *adj British*
chilly. An item of rhyming slang that probably originated in Glasgow rather than London.

It's a bit hill-billy in here.

hilljack *n American*
a redneck, hillbilly, person from the 'deep south' of the USA. The term was in use on campuses in 2002.

himbo *n*
a male **bimbo**. An item of journalese that was adopted into general speech in the 1990s. **Bimboy** is a synonym.

hinky, hincky *adj American*
1. inspiring doubt or suspicion; of uncertain loyalty, origin, etc. This term of unknown derivation is roughly equivalent to the British **dodgy**.
2. cute and/or neat

hip *adj*
1a. in touch with current trends, up-to-date, culturally aware. This word co-existed with, and then supplanted, **hep** in the 1960s in the argot of musicians, **beatniks** and other bohemians. It implied identification with an ideal of **cool** behaviour characterised by a nonchalant, enlightened detachment and a rejection of 'bourgeois' values.

'Now, the truly hip stay at home with the baby and open a bottle of wine with a couple of friends; if they do go out, they dress down in T-shirts, jeans and sneakers.'
(Sunday Times, 9 July 1989)

1b. aware, 'in the know'. Hip, now divested of its counterculture overtones, is used in popular speech to denote an unspoken understanding of a certain state of affairs.

There's no need to give me all this bullshit, man. I'm hip to what's going down.

hippie *n American*
a term of address or endearment, usually for a male

hippie lettuce *n American*
marihuana. A jocular term heard on campus since 2000.

hippy, hippie *n*
a proponent and member of the 'alternative society' or counterculture movement which opposed orthodox bourgeois values during the late 1960s. The hippy movement was a much more widely based successor to the **hipster** and **beatnik** tendency, reaching public notice in California in 1966. By the summer of 1967 (known as the 'Summer of Love') manifestations of hippiedom had spread to Britain. True hippies never referred to themselves as such, but rather as **freaks** or **heads**; the term was originally a slightly condescending nickname (based on **hip** or hipster) bestowed by older musicians and other bohemians.

'In punk's style degradation, there is still no worse insult than "hippie".'
(Observer, 24 May 1977)

hipster *n*
a culturally aware person, a **cool** bohemian. Predecessors to the **hippies** of the late 1960s, hipsters were the aficionados of jazz, Oriental philosophy, modernist art-forms, etc., who themselves succeeded the **hepcats** of the 1940s and 1950s. Hipster and **beatnik** are, in a historical perspective, almost identical, although the word hipster, unlike beatnik, was used by those in question to describe themselves. For the etymology of the word, see **hep**.

hissie-fit, hissie *n*
a bout of hysterical anger, agitation, despair, etc. The term is used particularly by women and **gay** males and is obviously derived from the standard term hysterical. **Fanny-fit** is a similar phrase recorded in British speech from the 1990s.

'Julian's having a hissie-fit.'
(*Concierge*, US film, 1993)

hit¹ *n*

1a. a puff on a cigarette or pipe containing marihuana or another illicit drug

Give me a hit on that joint.

'It opens my head, opens my membranes. If you get a good hit, maybe you go comatose for ten minutes.'
(Crack user, *Guardian*, 5 September 1989)

1b. a single dose of a drug, particularly LSD

Both uses date from the late 1960s and are still current.

2. a killing, assassination. An underworld euphemism from the USA since the early 1970s, used or understood all over the English-speaking world. The term invariably refers to a professional murder.

hit² *vb*

1. to assassinate or murder. The verb probably postdates the noun form.

2. *American* to serve a drink to. Usually in a form such as 'hit me again with one of those'.

3. to solicit money from, borrow from. A more robust version of the colloquial 'touch'. A racier and more recent American version is 'hit someone up (for)'.

He hit me for $20.

hit it *vb*

to have sex. In this sense, the term was used among aficionados of London dancefloor culture in the 1990s. It is probably based on the notion of 'scoring a hit' or of 'hitting it off'.

'When they all got together afterwards, I'm sure Max thought he was going to hit it with Lisa.'
(Recorded, club habitué, London, April 1996)

hit-man *n*

a professional killer, a paid assassin. This euphemistic term from the jargon of the American underworld and law enforcers had spread to other English-speaking areas by about 1972.

hit on *vb American*

1a. to 'chat up', attempt to seduce, accost sexually or romantically

1b. to aggress, bully or criticise

1c. to importune or beg for money

All senses of the term became popular in the 1980s, especially among teenagers. The unorthodox verb form probably originates from an immigrants' error, or a deliberate elaboration by black speakers.

hit the bricks *vb American*

a more fashionable version of the colloquial 'hit the road' and later 'hit the street' (to get going or appear in public). Originally the phrase specifically referred to released prisoners.

hit the hay/sack *vb*

to go to bed, lie down to sleep. Both expressions have been widespread in English since the turn of the 20th century and probably originated in tramps' jargon.

hit the toe *vb Australian*

to depart, leave. Although the coinage seems transparent, Partridge records it as rhyming slang for *go* and attributes it to the **surfie** subculture.

hit up *vb*

1. to inject oneself with an illicit drug, particularly heroin. An American addicts' expression of the 1960s, since adopted elsewhere. It may be used intransitively as in 'she's hitting up', or transitively as in 'hit up some smack'.

2. hit (someone) up a racier version of **hit** in the sense of borrow (money) from

hizzle *n American*

a home, residence. A vogue term in **rap** and hip hop parlance since 2000, using the **-izzle** suffix.

ho *n*

1a. a female prostitute, promiscuous and/or immoral woman

1b. a female

The southern US and Afro-Caribbean pronunciation of **whore** became one of the best-known items of hip hop and **rappers'** slang, moving, like many pejorative terms in transgressive subcultures, to take on first ironic, then straightforwardly neutral or appreciative connotations before crossing over into the generalised slang of adolescents in all English-speaking areas.

hobo *n American*

a tramp or vagrant. The word is now a common colloquialism and no longer considered to be slang by most speakers. Authorities disagree on the origin of the term; it may be from a greeting ('Ho! Boy' or 'Ho Bro!') or refer to 'hoe-boys' (agricultural migrant workers).

hobson-jobson *n British*

the linguistic process whereby foreign words or phrases are anglicised for use by English speakers. The practice was particularly noticeable during the colonial era and World War I. Hobson-Jobson is itself a rendering of the Muslim religious cry 'Ya Hasan, Ya Hosain!' (praising or lamenting Hassan and Hussein, grandsons of Mohammed). **Plonk** (an alteration of the French *vin blanc*) and hocuspocus (from the Latin *hoc est corpus*) are examples of this type of pun or folk etymology.

hock *vb*
to pawn. The word comes from the Dutch *hok*, the literal meaning of which is 'hook'. In 19th-century Dutch slang, *hok* meant both debt and the clutches of creditors or the law, whence the English term.

hockey, hockie *n*
1a. an act of (hawking and spitting)
1b. a gob of spit
1c. a piece of any disgusting substance, such as excrement. The term is imitative either of clearing the throat and spitting or of a choking reaction to a disgusting sight.
1d. *American* nonsense, rubbish. A generalisation of the previous senses.

hockshop *n*
a pawnshop, pawnbroker's. An expression (from **hock**) used all over the English-speaking world.

hog *n*
1. a motorcycle. A word popular with American Hell's Angels of the late 1950s and 1960s and their British and Australian imitators. The word originally referred specifically and affectionately to Harley Davidsons, the Hell's Angels' preferred machines. (Hog is the standard American term for pig.)
2. *American* an angry or unpleasant woman. An Americanism which, unlike the similar **pig** or **dog**, has not been adopted in other English-speaking areas.
3. PCP, **angel dust**. This disorienting narcotic, phencyclidine, is an animal tranquilliser used on pigs, among other species.

hogans *n pl American*
female breasts. The word is probably an ignorant or facetious alteration of **ogens**.
'Look at them hogans!'
(*Herman's Head*, US TV comedy, 1993)

hog-tied *adj American*
incapacitated, rendered helpless. Hogs (the standard American term for pigs) were hobbled by having all four legs bound.

hog-whimpering *adj British*
1a. abject, bestial, helpless
1b. abjectly or bestially drunk
Old Ollie was absolutely hog-whimpering last night.
A colourful term popular among **Sloane Rangers** in Britain from the mid-1970s. The word is probably an original public-school or army coinage, but may echo the many now obsolete slang terms containing the word 'hog' that invoke wallowing, snorting and other excessive behaviour: expressions such as **hog-wild**, 'hog-rubber' (a peasant), 'hog-fat' (a slovenly person), etc.

hog-wild *adj, adv*
uncontrolled, unrestrained in behaviour. A folksy Americanism from the turn of the 20th century which is normally heard in the form of 'go hog-wild' or 'run hog-wild'. (Hog is the standard American term for pig.) The term was immortalised as the title of a Laurel and Hardy short film in 1930.

ho-hum *n, adj, vb*
(something) dull, tedious, of mediocre quality or little interest. When used by Americans this expression usually denotes boredom, by British speakers it may rather suggest uncertainty. In American English the adjective occasionally doubles as a noun or, more rarely, a verb (meaning to be bored by or to declare something boring).
a big ho-hum
They ho-hummed the lecture course.

hoick *vb British*
to spit or to clear the throat and spit. The word is a more echoic version of the standard English 'hawk'.
He hoicked over the fence into the garden.

hoist *vb*
1. to steal, particularly by shoplifting or picking a pocket. The term is around 200 years old in underworld jargon, and was still in use in 2004.
He managed to hoist a couple of watches.
2. *American* to raise and down a drink, usually beer. A masculine term with overtones of heroic or hearty drinking sessions. (The word may occasionally refer to eating, as in 'hoist some oysters'.)
What say we go hoist a few?

hoisty *adj British*
stolen, illicit, **bent** or **hot**. The term may have originated in TV scripts (based on

the authentic slang senses of hoist and by analogy with **hooky**), rather than in underworld usage. It was featured in the Simpson and Galton comedy *Over the Rainbow*, 1993.

hoity-toity *adj*
affectedly arrogant, condescendingly superior. A 19th-century term which derives from the earlier 'highty-tighty' (meaning 'high and mighty') and is influenced by haughty.

hokey *adj American*
phoney, counterfeit, of dubious quality, third-rate. A back-formation from 'hokum'.

holding *adj American*
in possession of illicit drugs. A legalistic, officialese term, also adopted by drug-abusers.

> *When they found him he was holding but they had to let him go on a technicality.*

hold it down *vb*
1. *British* to act in a commendably restrained manner, to 'stay **cool**'. The phrase occurs in the language of teenage gangs and was recorded in use among North London schoolboys in 1993 and 1994.
2. to shut up, keep silent. A term used by young street-gang members in London since around 2000.

hole *n*
1a. the anus or vagina. The word is barely a euphemism but a simple description of an orifice, in common use at least since Chaucer's *Canterbury Tales* (begun sometime in the later 1380s).

> *'Dark was the night as pitch or as coal and at the window out she [Alison] put her hole.'*
> ('The Miller's Tale', *Canterbury Tales*, Geoffrey Chaucer)

1b. the mouth. In this sense the word is often used by schoolchildren, especially in the phrase 'shut your hole!'.
2a. an unpleasant place. **Rat-hole** is a more vivid modern embellishment.
2b. a one-person cell, a place of solitary confinement.
3. an abbreviation of **asshole** (in the figurative sense of a foolish/obnoxious individual). This term, originating in North American usage, was adopted by British adolescents in the later 1990s.

holler¹ *n*
a response, telephone call. Probably originating in US speech, the term has

been fashionable since 2000 in all English-speaking areas.

holler², **holler back (at)** *vb American*
to respond to, return a greeting or telephone call. One of the most common slang expressions in adolescent usage as recorded in a number of surveys since 2000.

holler!, holla! *exclamation American*
goodbye. A very fashionable usage among younger speakers since 2000.

hollyhocks *n British*
venereal disease. The word is rhyming slang for **(the) pox**.

home, homes *n*
shortenings of **homeboy**

homeboy *n American*
a street-gang member ready and old enough to defend his area or **turf**. The word, now part of the code of Los Angeles street gangs, was originally an innocuous American term for a good neighbour or good citizen.

> *'And some homeboys looking for trouble down here from the Bronx.'*
> (Lou Reed, 'Halloween Parade', from the album *New York*, 1989)

homegirl *n American*
the female equivalent of the more common **homeboy**, recorded in black American speech as long ago as the 1930s. By the 1990s the term was often abbreviated to **homey**.

home run, homer *n American*
an instance of sexual satisfaction or conquest; full sexual intercourse. This adolescents' expression, inspired by baseball and typically used by males, denotes the successful culmination of a heavy petting session or attempted seduction. Partial success is referred to as reaching **first base**.

> *Danny managed to score a home run.*
> *He made a homer.*

homey, homie *n*
a shortening of **homeboy** or **homegirl**, which became popular in the 1990s and was also adopted by white adolescents to refer to their peers, first in North America and subsequently to a limited extent in the UK When it first appeared approximately fifty years earlier the word was used by black American migrants as an affectionate term of address for anyone originating from the same home town or city

> *'I'm square with my homeys…'*

(17-year-old black female suspected of the murder of another girl, quoted in the *Evening Standard*, 2 March 1997)

homo *n*
a male homosexual. This was probably the most common term in colloquial use among heterosexuals until the popular adoption of the non-discriminatory **gay** and its many pejorative alternatives in the late 1960s.
Compare **stromo**

honcho *n*
a boss, an important person. This word from American English of the late 1950s is not, as is often supposed, Hispanic in origin, but from the Japanese *hancho* meaning squad-leader; the term was adopted by Americans during the Korean War. It is now used typically in a business context, often in the phrase **head honcho**.

> 'He [Reagan] was surrounded in his own White House by the portly honchos of the Democratic Party. The message was unwitting but clear: these are the people who count in Washington today.'
> (*Observer*, 22 November 1987)

honeypot *n*
the vagina. A euphemism which was first recorded in the 17th century and is still employed today, particularly in the USA.

honk[1] *vb*
1. to vomit. The term is echoic and has existed in British slang since the 1950s.
2. to stink. Related to the Liverpudlian **ronk**, this sense of the word is widespread in Australia and not unknown in Britain.
3. to drink (to excess). A middle-class and high-society term of the 1950s in Britain, now rarely heard.
See also **honkers; honking**

honk[2] *n*
1a. a stink, bad smell. A variation of **ronk**, perhaps influenced by **hum** and stink. A usage popular in Australia and, to a lesser extent, in Britain.
1b. an evil-smelling person or animal
2. an act of vomiting, from the verb to **honk**
3. a wild, noisy, drunken party. A British term of the 1950s, probably from **honk**, meaning to drink and **honked**, meaning drunk.

honked *adj British*
drunk. The 'honk' in question may echo the hooting and vomiting of drunkards, or

else the gulping or quaffing. **Honking** and **honkers** are synonyms.

honkers *adj British*
drunk. A middle-class term perhaps originating in armed-services slang, where it has been heard since the 1950s. The **-ers** ending is typical of public-school and army expressions.

honkies *n pl American*
the backside or buttocks. An Americanism of the 1970s, derived from the colloquial verb to 'hunker down' (i.e. to squat), which in turn is related to the word haunches (in mock-rustic English, 'hunkers').

honking *adj British*
drunk. A middle-class usage, heard less often nowadays than in the 1960s, which may have originated in armed-services slang. The 'honk' denotes either drinking in gulps, the braying made by drunken revellers or, more probably, vomiting.

honky, honkey, honkie *n American*
a white person. A pejorative black term which became widely known in the early 1970s. The word's origin is unclear; it is said to be a deformation of 'hunk', meaning an immigrant (ultimately from 'Hungarian'), but may equally be inspired by the honking of pigs.

hooch *n*
alcohol, particularly illicitly produced alcoholic drink. The word originally referred to strong liquor made by the Hoochino Indians of Alaska.

hood[1] *n American*
a neighbourhood. This abbreviation, heard in the argot of black street gangs, was popularised by the title of the 1991 US film *Boyz 'N the Hood*.

hood[2], **hoodlum** *n American*
a criminal, (small-time) gangster. The longer form of the word was in use in the USA by the end of the 19th century; hood became widespread from the 1940s. Many suggestions have been offered as to the origin of the terms. The least unlikely are: a deformation of an Irish surname such as Hoolahan; an altered **backslang** version of Muldoon; a corruption of 'huddle-'em', supposedly the cry of a gang of muggers; and *hodalem* or *hudilump*, respectively Bavarian and Swiss dialect terms for a wretch or naughty boy.

'Go tell your hoodlum friends outside/ you ain't got time to take a ride.'
(Lyrics to 'Yakety-Yak', by The Coasters, 1958)

hoodie *n British*

a young, usually male, hooligan. The term, in vogue in 2005, is the nickname for the hooded tracksuit top worn as a disguise and uniform.

hood-top *n Jamaican*

the tip of the penis. A vulgarism used as the title of a ragga song by Shabba Ranks in 1993; a female singer riposted with a song entitled *Hood Top Flop.*

hoof *n See* **iron**

hoofer *n*

a dancer, particularly a chorus girl, tap-dancer or other hard-working professional dancer

hoof it *vb*

1a. to go on foot, walk. In this sense the term has been used since the 17th century.

1b. to leave, walk away. This sense of the verb dates from the 19th century and enjoyed a vogue in Britain in the late 1980s as a fashionable synonym for **leg it** or **hook it**.

1c. to dance. A usage popularised in the context of pre-World War II Hollywood musicals. The predictable use of hoof (an animal's foot) is probably reinforced by the word's echoing of the panting of hard-working chorus dancers.

hoo-hoos *n pl American*

female breasts. The term, popular from 2003, may be an alteration of **hooters** or an arbitrary coinage.

hook¹ *vb*

1. *British* to steal. This euphemism, which is still in use in London working-class speech, is at least 200 years old. The 'h' is almost invariably dropped.

She managed to hook a few videotapes.
'Barry's been out hookin' again.'
(Recorded, street trader, Islington, London, 1986)

2. *Australian* to 'pick up' (a romantic partner). Unsurprisingly, the word has been used in this sense before, e.g. in 19th century England, where it referred to obtaining a potential marriage partner.

'When you hooked Darcy last night, did you sleep with her?'
(*A Country Practice*, Australian TV series, August 1994)

hook², **hook up** *vb*

to have sex. A term used by young street-gang members in London since around 2000.

hooker *n*

a prostitute (invariably female). This American term has been imported into British and Australian usage since the mid-1970s. The origin of the word is stated authoritatively by many works of reference. However, they disagree. The most popular version cites the Civil War commander, General Hooker, who supposedly encouraged his men to frequent brothels. Another source gives Corlear's Hook, the name of a New York red-light district, as the inspiration for the term. In fact hooker seems to have been in use with its current meaning as early as 1845 (which invalidates the Civil War explanation) and may simply be a figurative use of the literal meaning as 'enticer', 'ensnarer', a sense which it has in Dutch slang (*hoeker* would be known to the large Dutch-American population of New York as meaning 'huckster', for instance). Hooker was obsolescent by the 1920s, but was revived in the late 1960s.

a high-class hooker
down on the strip where the hookers hang out

hook it *vb British*

to leave, run away. The phrase, a variant of 'hook off', an earlier and now obsolescent cockney expression, is over 100 years old and is also heard occasionally in the USA. The origin of the hook reference is obscure but may be related to its use to mean anchor (whence the expression to **sling one's hook**: to weigh anchor, although this etymology is disputed).

hook (someone) one *vb*

to hit, punch

hooks *n pl*

hands. For obvious reasons this metaphorical usage, associated with the images of 'getting one's hooks into' someone or something and to **hook** meaning to steal, has existed for several hundred years.

hook up *vb American*

to kiss, embrace and/or engage in sexual play, especially used of recent acquaintances. The phrase is used particularly by high school and college students.

hooky adj British
stolen, of dubious provenance, **hot**. A London working-class and underworld term from **hook**, meaning to steal. Hooky is often pronounced with a dropped aspirate.

'Last time I saw John 'e was sellin' 'ooky watches out of a suitcase down Brick Lane.'
(Recorded, young male, London, 1988)

hoolie n
a wild, noisy party or celebration. The word is Irish in origin and is probably an anglicisation of the Irish Gaelic term *ceilidh*, meaning an informal gathering for folk music and dance.

hoon n
1a. *Australian* a lout, hooligan or disreputable youth. Originally this word (of unknown etymology) signified a man 'living on immoral earnings'; its meaning has now been generalised to denote, for instance, a member of a gang of ne'er-do-wells.
1b. *British* an obnoxious individual

hoop n British
the anus. The term has been used in this sense in the armed forces since 2000.

hooped adj
tired, exhausted. The reference is to **breathing out of one's hoop**, an expression, evoking a desperate need for extra oxygen, in army and Officer Training Corps usage since around 2000.

hoop out vb American
to play basketball. A high-school and campus term. To 'hoop down' is to play particularly earnestly or dynamically.

hooptie n American
an old and/or dilapidated car. The term is used in black speech and **rap** lyrics.

hooptie ride n American
a drive-by murder, in the jargon of street gangs and **rappers**

Hooray, Hooray Henry n British
a young upper-class male, particularly one who indulges in offensive, rowdy, hearty and/or vacuous behaviour. This pejorative term arose in the late 1960s to describe the more exhibitionist members of a social subgroup which was later anatomised under the name **Sloane Rangers**. Hooray was a later shortening. A version of this epithet first appeared in Damon Runyon's story *Tight Shoes*, in which a young man called Calvin Colby

was described as 'without doubt, strictly a Hooray Henry'. In March 1990 Viscount Linley won libel damages from *Today* newspaper which had, among more serious allegations, referred to him as a Hooray.

'Hooray Henrys sometimes cruise down here just looking for an old codger to beat up. The last time they did it, we smashed up their flashy car.'
(Homeless dosser, *Observer*, 6 August 1987)

hootch n
an alternative spelling of **hooch**

hootchie, hoochie n American
a female, particularly a promiscuous or sexually active female. This term, derived from **hootchie cootchie**, was part of black street slang of the 1990s.
She sure is one hot hootchie.
Compare **coochie**

hootchie cootchie n American
sexual caresses or erotic dancing. A phrase familiar to blues music enthusiasts, from black slang of the early 20th century. A 'hootchie cootchie man' is a lover or **stud**. The phrase hootchie cootchie first appeared in the USA in the 1880s, when it denoted a sort of belly-dance. The words may be a pseudo-exotic invention or a distortion of a now-forgotten foreign term.

hooted adj American
drunk. Although the term, recorded among adolescents, usually describes intoxication by alcohol, it may be influenced by the noun form 'hooter', denoting a **joint**. Alternatively, it may be inspired by the hooting of inebriated celebrants.

hooter n
1. *British* the nose. A common term of the 1950s and 1960s which is still heard. A synonym less widespread on the same lines is **bugle**.
'The doc says the 30-year-old vain singer [Michael Jackson]'s hooter is collapsing after being broken so often in four operations to change his looks.'
(*News of the World*, 7 May 1989)
2. *American* a **joint** (marihuana cigarette). A college and high-school term.

hooters n pl American
female breasts. A favourite term of college boys, reminiscent of **bumpers**, **head-lamps** and other automotive similes. The usage also plays on the supposed simi-

larity in action between pressing a rubber bulb and manipulating and fondling a breast.

hoover (up) vb

to devour, eat or drink rapidly or greedily. A popular use of the vacuum cleaner's household name since the late 1960s. The expression is most common in Britain but is known in the USA. During World War II hoovering was the name given to an airborne mopping-up operation by the RAF.

> 'We laid out a spread and they hoovered it up in minutes.'
> (Recorded, hostess, Weybridge, England, May 1986)

> 'He hoovered up five pints and got pole-axed.'
> (*The Crack: a Belfast Year*, Sally Belfrage, 1987)

hoovered adj British

drunk. An item of student slang in use in London and elsewhere since around 2000.

hophead n American

a narcotics user. Hop was a late-19th-century term for opium, later extended to any 'stupefying' drug including marihuana. Hophead, dating from the 1940s, was one of the first words for a category of drug-users to use the '-head' suffix. By the 1960s the word was used mainly by law enforcers and other disapproving adults. It is now rare.

hop on! exclamation British

a cry of delight or triumph, in use since around 2000. It is synonymous with **get in!** and **result!**

hopped-up adj

under the influence of narcotics. 'Hop' was a late-19th-century term for opium in the USA, later generalised to refer to any intoxicating drug.

hopper n American

a toilet (bowl). A term favoured by 'hardhats' and **jocks** among others. (A hopper is a large metal feeder container in grain silos.) Coincidentally or not, 'the hopper' is also in American usage to refer to the place where schemes are hatched and ideas nurtured. In business jargon or office slang to 'put something in the hopper' is to feed it into the system or to 'put it on file'.

> It's all in danger of going down the hopper.

Horatio n British

fellatio. A usage recorded by *Viz* comic's *Profanisaurus* (glossary of profanities) in 2002.

horizontal dancing n

sexual intercourse, a jocular euphemism typically used by American college students, etc. from the early 1980s. The term probably originated as a joke among middle-class adult sophisticates.

hork vb American

1. to vomit. An echoic term in use among students in 2003.
2. to steal. In this sense it is probably an alteration of **hook**.

horlicks n British

a mess, an unpalatable or confused mixture. The trade name of a bedtime drink has here been appropriated as a euphemism for **bollocks**. The word is used by all social classes and began to appear in print in the late 1980s.

> how to make a total horlicks of it in five easy stages

hormone n

a promiscuous, sexually active or successful person. This term, usually applied to males, was popular among adolescents and younger schoolchildren in Britain and Australia in the 1990s.

> 'He's what we call a raging hormone.'
> (Australian surfer in Biarritz, *Passengers*, Channel 4 TV programme, September 1995)

horn, the n

1a. the penis, particularly when erect. This obvious metaphor has been commonly employed in English for at least 200 years. Prior to that horn more often referred to the cuckold's emblem.
1b. an erection. Usually found in phrases such as to 'have the horn', to **get the horn** or to be **on the horn**.
2. a telephone. In this sense the word usually occurs in the form '(get) on the horn'. This usage is encountered more often in the USA than in Britain.

horny adj

sexually aroused, lustful. Although the **horn** in question is the penis (in an image which dates from the 18th century, if not earlier), the expression is now used by and about both sexes, sometimes in colourful phrases such as 'horny as a hootowl'. It is a 1960s successor of longer phrases such as to **get the horn**, to be **on the horn**, etc.

> 'The total absurdity of it all; seven or eight able bodied policemen keeping 24 hour watch on this horny endomorphic Jewish intellectual.'
> (Bill Levy, *Oz* magazine, February 1970)

horrors, the *n*
1. a bout of terror or fit of existential despair. The term applies especially to the sudden uncontrollable feelings of dread and horror experienced as a result of drug or alcohol abuse (as, e.g., in cases of delirium tremens, heroin withdrawal, amphetamine **comedown**, **acid flashes** or the fits of paranoia associated with over-indulgence in strong cannabis). The expression was used in the 19th century to refer to the effects of alcoholism.
2. menstruation, monthly periods. A rare schoolgirl alternative to **the curse**.

horrorshow *adj, n*
1a. (something) shocking or horrifying
1b. (something) sensational, impressive or excellent
Like **bad**, **creepshow**, **hellacious** and other similar teenage terms of the 1980s, horrorshow has undergone the process (technically known as 'amelioration') whereby a pejorative or negative term acquires a positive meaning. This word, inspired by horror films and comics, has the dual implication of awful and thrilling, the intended meaning apparent only in the tone of voice or context.

horse *n*
1. *British* an unattractive female. In playground usage since 2000, the term is sometimes elaborated to **horse-monkey**.
2. *Trinidad and Tobago* a friend
> He my horse.
> C'mon horse.

3. heroin. A word used by drug addicts and **beatniks** in the 1950s, it was already dated by the late 1960s and was generally supplanted, first by **H**, and subsequently by **smack**, **scag**, etc.

horse's ass *n American*
a fool, especially an annoying or contemptible one. A common folksy phrase among adults. Like other expressions based on 'horse', the term has not spread to British usage.

horseshit *n American*
nonsense, foolish or empty talk. A popular term in the USA where it is similar in meaning to **bullshit**, with perhaps the

suggestion that horseshit is more transparently ludicrous or frivolous. The British apparently still view the horse with more respect or affection; neither horseshit, **horse's ass** or 'horse feathers' have caught on in British English.

> 'You see, there's got to be some respite from the horseshit. And cars give you that. They're primitive.'
> (Paul Newman, *Elle* magazine, May 1989)

horseshoe *n South African*
a hand-rolled cigarette, especially one containing strong tobacco

hose *vb American*
to have sex with. A mainly male vulgarism.

> 'There must be someone here that I could hose...Better get some more sherry to smooth out my brain.'
> (S. Clay Wilson cartoon, *Head Comix*, 1968)

hose-hound *n American*
a promiscuous or sexually active person, usually female. A later coinage based on the verb to **hose** and the noun **hoser 2**.

> 'Look at the fun-bags on that hosehound!'
> (*Dumb and Dumber*, US film, 1994)

hose monster *n American*
an extremely promiscuous and/or sexually active person. The term, which may be used pejoratively or appreciatively, is particularly applied to heterosexual females.
Compare **shag-monster**

hoser *n American*
1. a fraud, deceitful person, cheat
2. a promiscuous person, usually female
Both senses of the term are found in the vocabulary of high-school and college students. The etymology of the word is not certain, but probably derives from **hose** as a noun meaning penis and a verb meaning to copulate or **screw** in the figurative sense of defraud.

ho stroll *n American*
1a. a prostitute's patrolling of her area, streetwalking

> 'I'm on the ho stroll, honey.'
> (Hispanic New York prostitute, Channel 4 TV documentary, October 1994)

1b. a provocative gait, as used by prostitutes looking for customers

hot *adj*
1. stolen, from the image of something 'too hot to handle'. The word was used in

this sense in *The Eustace Diamonds* by Trollope in 1875.

D'you reckon that video is hot?

2. exciting, fashionable. A slang usage (from the language of jazz musicians in which 'hot', frenzied and fast, is contrasted with 'cool', relaxed and slow) which by the mid-1970s had become a common colloquialism.

3. sexually excited or aroused. The adjective has always been used in this sense, both literally and figuratively.

She's hot for him.

Talk dirty to me. You know it gets me hot.

4. provocative, obstreperous. In this sense the word was defined by one of its users as 'acting too obvious' and denotes a transgression of the unwritten codes of behaviour of adolescent gangs. The term was recorded in use among North London schoolboys in 1993 and 1994.

acting hot

hot-dog¹ *vb American*
to perform spectacularly and brilliantly and/or to show off. The term is applied especially in sports' contexts (the sport of stunt skiing, e.g., is known as 'hot-dogging'), or to high-achieving students.

hot-dog², hot-dogger *n, adj American*
(someone or something) outstanding, spectacular and/or successful. The term is used as an exclamation, showing amazement and approval, but when applied to people may often indicate envy or disapproval.

Hot dog! We're havin' a great time here!

hot pants
1. *n* a sexually aroused state; lustfulness, particularly in a woman
2. *n pl* brief shorts as worn by women during a fashion of 1970 and 1971

hot poop *n*
the very latest news, most up-to-date information. An American term of the early 1960s which had spread to Britain, especially in the armed services and in journalistic speech, by the early 1970s. **Poop** is a nursery term and adult euphemism for **shit**.

hot rocks *n pl British*
the glowing embers at the tip of a lit cigarette or **joint**. An expression from school-playground slang. **Cherry** is a synonym.

hots, the *n pl See* **have the hots (for someone)**

hot shit *n, adj*
(something) impressive, exciting, superlative. The common colloquial terms 'hot stuff' and 'hotshot' are in fact euphemisms for hot shit, a term both of contempt and approbation common since the beginning of the 20th century in the USA (still heard more often there than in Britain or Australia).

some hot shit record producer

hotshot *vb, n American*
(to administer) a lethal injection of a narcotic, usually heroin. This term, from the vocabulary of addicts and the underworld, refers particularly to a deliberate lethal dose, either self-administered or as a gangland method of punishment and murder. Sometimes the hotshot is a high-strength overdose, sometimes a normal dose of the drug mixed with a toxic substance.

The guys put him away with a Drano hotshot.

hot tamale *n American*
a sexually arousing or provocative woman. A male expression of admiration or approval first coined by adults but now probably more popular among enthusiastic, if unsophisticated, high-school and college students. A *tamale* is a spicy rolled pancake, a Mexican speciality.

hotting *n British*
the stealing of cars for displays of fast driving and subsequent destruction. An organised criminal adolescent hobby which became a vogue in 1991. Here **Hot** combines the slang senses of 'powerful' and 'stolen'.

hot to trot *adj*
eager and enthusiastic for sex and, by extension, for any activity. A jocular rhyming phrase probably deriving from black American usage in the late 1950s, it was adopted by **hippies** and subsequently enjoyed a vogue in the language of disco dancers, devotees of nightclubs, etc. in the late 1970s, when it usually had the innocuous sense of ready to dance.

Honey, get ready – I'm hot to trot.

hotty, hottie *n American*
an attractive female. This appreciative term, which probably originated in black street slang, became widespread

in campus and high-school speech from the 1990s.

hot-wire *vb*
to start (a car) by tampering with the ignition electrics rather than using the key. A thieves' and law enforcers' term.

hound *n*
1. *British* a reprehensible person. The word is typically used as mild criticism or affectionate disapproval.
2. *See* **brownie-hound**

house *n*
a type of disco music typically played in amateur or impromptu club sessions in the late 1980s. House music is electronically enhanced versions of black and European dance records, growing out of the **rap** and 'scratch' embellishments of 1970s disco. The word house itself refers to the Warehouse club in Chicago where this form of music was pioneered.

housed *adj American*
drunk. An expression used on campus in the USA since around 2000.

house moss *n American*
another term for **dust bunny**

house nigger *n American*
a subservient or deferential black person, a black menial or an 'Uncle Tom'. This old designation, applied originally to slaves and servants, contrasts with the now obsolete expression 'field nigger' for a black estate worker or poor farmer.

He's gonna have to realise that he can't treat me like some house nigger.

howler *n British*
1. a child or baby. An item of middle-class and family slang of the later 1980s and 1990s. **Wowler** is an alternative version. Apart from the obvious reference to a baby's crying, the word might also recall the howler monkey.

'We're going to have to get a sitter for the howler.'
(Recorded, middle-class working mother, London 1994)

2. an ugly person, usually female. An item of student slang in use in London and elsewhere since around 2000.

howling *adj*
1a. *Scottish* smelling offensively. This is one of many synonyms for stinking, such as **minging**, **bowfing**, **honking**.
1b. *British* ugly. The term is usually applied to females by males.

hoy *vb British*
to throw, discard. An item of **Geordie** speech (it originated either as a dialect cognate of 'haul' or as an invention influenced by haul and/or hoist) which became more widely used in the 1990s. The same word occurs in Australian slang.

'Finish your fag and just hoy it.'
(*Away the Lads*, BBC 2 TV documentary, February 1993)

huff *vb*
1. to sniff, **snort** (an illicit drug). A late 1970s alternative to the more common **snort** in connection with cocaine. The term has a more specific relation to solvent and glue abuse. It is American in origin.
2. *British* to **fart**. A schoolchildren's term. **Guff** is a synonym.

hum *vb, n*
(to) **fart**. Especially popular in Australia, this jocular term probably relates to the surreptitious sound rather than the colloquial meaning of hum as 'stink'.

humassive *adj*
enormous. A blend of huge, **humungous** and massive, heard in 2004.

humgrumshious *adj Caribbean*
rough and crude

hum-hole *n*
the mouth. An American high-school word, usually employed as part of an insult or challenge. It appears to date from the early 1980s.

Tell him to shut his hum-hole.

hump¹ *vb*
1. to have sex (with). 'Once a fashionable word for copulation', according to the *Dictionary of the Vulgar Tongue* by Grose, 1785, hump is now scarcely fashionable but is still a widespread vulgarism, often in the form 'humping'.
See also **dry-hump**
2. to carry. This now common informal sense of the word was considered unorthodox in the 1950s.

hump² *n*
1. the hump a feeling of annoyance, resentment or depression. To 'have the hump' or 'get the hump' has meant to be bad-tempered or to take offence since the 18th century. It comes from the notion of a hunchback's burden.

'"I've got the 'ump today!" he told us cheerfully.'

(Security guard, *Evening Standard*, 12 June 1989)

2. *American* a nickname for a Camel cigarette

3. a despicable or contemptible person. This insult may be based on the old term for a hunchback or may derive from the sexual meaning of the verb to **hump**.

humping *adj British*
exciting, dynamic. A synonym of **banging**, **slamming**, etc. heard in South Wales since 2000.

humpty *adj British*
1. having the **hump**, annoyed, resentful
He's a bit humpty this morning.
2. wanting to **hump** someone, priapic, **horny** or sexually aroused
Both senses of the word were current in London working-class usage in the late 1980s. The 'h' is usually silent.

humpty-dumpty *n South African*
a foolish and/or fat person. The mocking or insulting epithet, derived from the children's rhyme, was recorded as an item of Sowetan slang in the *Cape Sunday Times*, 29 January 1995.

humpy *adj*
1. *British* having the **hump**, annoyed, resentful
2. *American* sexually aroused. The term, a more recent synonym for **horny**, is used particularly among American adolescents and can refer to either sex.

humungous, humongous *adj*
enormous, terrifying, tremendous. A popular word among schoolchildren and teenagers since the late 1970s, this is an invention combining elements of huge, tremendous and enormous, on the lines of 'ginormous', 'sponditious', etc. It seems to have originated in the USA.
Man, I got a humungous thirst on me.
'Darlene and I just killed a huge spider – we hadda use a whole can, it was humungous.'
(*Roseanne*, US TV comedy series, 1989)

hung *adj*
1a. sexually endowed (referring to men). A coarse euphemism which is probably Victorian, perhaps older. The word is often part of colourful comparisons such as 'hung like a horse/bull/jack donkey' or, alternatively, 'hung like a fieldmouse'.
'Her opener had a certain showgirl candor: "Is it true what all the girls say – that you're hung like a horse?"'

(Kenneth Anger, *Hollywood Babylon*, 1975)

1b. sexually well endowed, having large genitals. This shortening of **well-hung** has been part of male **gay** jargon since the early 1970s.
Wow, he's really hung.

2. a variation of **hung-up**
'You got me to/ Fall in love with you/ Though I'm not free to/ Fall in love with you/ Oh, why/ Did I/ Have to get so hung on you?'
(The Righteous Brothers, 'Hung on You', written by Spector/King/Goffin, 1965)
'Nothing to get hung about.'
(The Beatles, 'Strawberry Fields Forever', 1967)

hung-up *adj*
1a. suffering from a complex; neurotic, inhibited. A popular **putdown** used by **hippies** to categorise socially or sexually repressed, **uptight** behaviour, especially on the part of **straights**.

1b. hung up on (someone) obsessed with, in love with (someone). A **hippy** usage which persisted into the 1980s and is still heard occasionally.

hunk *n*
a well-built, sexually attractive male

hunky-dory *adj*
fine, in good order, perfect. A well-established colloquialism, adopted in Britain some time after World War I. The phrase arose in the USA in the mid-19th century. The 'hunk' component is from the Dutch *honk*, meaning a post used as a 'home' in a game of tag; 'dory' is probably a meaningless elaboration.

huntley *n British*
karma (personal destiny). An ephemeral and unusual collision between the worlds and concerns of the **hippy** and rhyming slang, this humorous coinage is from Huntley and Palmer, a well-known British biscuit manufacturer.
'Hello love, how's your huntley?"
(Recorded, social worker, London, 1987)

hurl *vb*
to vomit. A usage common in Australia and, to a lesser extent, in Britain.

hurt *adj British*
ugly, unattractive. An item of black street-talk used especially by males referring to females, recorded in 2003.
She's hurt.

hurting *adj*
1. *American* suffering from the lack of a necessity, usually a drug. By the 1990s the term, previously used in a romantic context, almost invariably referred to a narcotics withdrawal.

I was on the street and hurtin' with nothing to cop with and no-one to cop from.

2. unappealing, disappointing

hustle¹ *vb*
1a. to work as a prostitute, solicit sexual clients
1b. to importune, pressurise, take advantage of (someone)
1c. to make great efforts (often selfishly)
All senses of the word (introduced from the USA into other areas in the mid-1960s) derive from its origin in the Dutch *husselen* or *hutseln*, meaning to shake up or jostle. This gave rise to an American version of the word meaning hurry or shove, later used in the specific senses above.

hustle² *n*
1a. a high-pressure scheme, an attempt to obtain money, bully or browbeat someone
1b. a rush, energetic action
The noun forms derive from the earlier verb form.

hustler *n*
1a. a prostitute (of either sex). This specific and euphemistic sense of the word remains exclusively North American.
1b. any intrusive, importunate or over-assertive person
A word which entered world English in the late 1960s, from American usage. Both senses of the word postdate the verb form **hustle**.

hymie, heimie *n*
a Jew. An unaffectionate, if not strongly offensive term inspired by the short form of the Jewish male forename Hyman. The word has been used in British English since the 1950s.

hype¹ *vb, n*
(to create) excessive, overblown or misleading publicity. A term applied first to the activities of the pop music industry in the early 1970s, hype is a shortening of 'hyperbole'. The word was apparently in use in the USA for many years among swindlers and tricksters before becoming part of commercial jargon.

hype², hypo *n*
a hypodermic syringe. This short form was used by drug abusers in the 1950s and early 1960s, but was always rarer than the more colourful alternatives such as **harpoon**, **works**, **artillery**, etc. It persists in the vocabulary of doctors, paramedics, etc., particularly in the USA.

hype³ *adj American*
good, popular, exciting. An expression used on campus in the USA since around 2000.

hyped-up *adj*
1. exaggerated, inflated, overpublicised. From the verb to **hype** (itself from 'hyperbole').
2. excited, over-stimulated, tense. This sense of the word probably originates in hypersensitive, hyperactive or hyperventilate, rather than in hyperbole.

hyper *adj*
an abbreviation of hyperactive and/or hyperventilating. The word, which was especially popular among American devotees of group therapy, 'consciousness-raising', etc., has now taken on a generalised sense of agitated or keyed up.

hyubes *n pl*
female breasts

I

ice[1] *n*
1. diamonds or other jewellery. An underworld term in all English-speaking areas, this word has also been heard in everyday speech.
2. an illicit drug which appeared in Hawaii in 1989 and for a time seemed poised to replace **crack** as a major social scourge in the USA. Ice is a highly synthesised version of methamphetamine (the archetypal **speed** as abused in the 1960s and 1970s under the name of methedrine).

ice[2] *vb*
to kill. An American underworld term which may initially have been a shortened form of 'put someone on ice'. The word has been popularised by its use in crime films and TV series.

> 'Maybe he saw the Hellinger killing go down – they iced him to keep him quiet.'
> (*The Rockford Files*, US TV series, 1978)

ice cold *n*
a beer. An American and Australian term of the 1970s adopted by some British lager drinkers.

> Set up some ice colds, will you.

ice cream *n British*
1. a man. This piece of now obsolete lowlife and demi-monde slang of the 1950s derives from 'ice-cream freezer', rhyming slang for **geezer**.
See also **fridge**
2. a white person. This is a quite separate coinage from sense **1** and is mainly used by black and South Asian schoolchildren to refer dismissively to whites.

iced, iced out *adj American*
1a. wearing jewellery
1b. ornamented by jewels

> 'He [record producer Damon Dash] enjoys Cristal champagne, wears iced out – diamond encrusted – £24,000 watches and likes triple-distilled vodka…'
> (*Sunday Times*, 6 June 2004)

ice man *n American*
1. a jewel thief. From **ice** in the sense of diamonds or other jewellery.
2. a **hit-man**, professional killer. From the verb **ice** meaning to kill.

ice queen *n*
an imperious, haughty and/or aggressive female

icing *n*
1. cocaine
2. jewellery, **bling**

ick *n*
an unpleasant substance. The term is probably a back-formation from **icky**, itself a colloquial description or exclamation of distaste possibly influenced by sticky.

icky (poo) *adj*
1a. distasteful, unpleasant
1b. sickly sentimental, cloying
The word originated as a baby-talk version of 'sticky'. It is now used by adults and particularly by teenagers to refer to something either literally or metaphorically viscous.

iddy, iddy-boy *n British*
a Jew. A London working-class term of disparagement and abuse which is a distortion of **yid**.

idiot box *n*
a television set. A less common alternative to **gogglebox**, dating from around 1960, by which time the mind-numbing effects of TV viewing were attracting critical comment.

> 'An entertaining and salutary study of the tangled, dishonest and sometimes demented relationships our premiers have had with the idiot box.'
> (*Sunday Correspondent*, 13 September 1989)

idiot dancing *n British*
a style of frenzied, abandoned dancing on the spot (invariably consisting of writhing hand and arm movements and shaking of the head) to rock music,

particularly the 'psychedelic' style (a precursor of heavy metal) of the late 1960s. By the mid-1970s it had mutated into the less picturesque **headbanging**.

idren *n*
good friend(s). A version of brethren or children in Caribbean and black British usage.

iffy *adj*
1a. questionable, doubtful or suspicious. In the 1960s this was a slang term heard predominantly in London working-class usage. It enjoyed a vogue among the fashionable in the late 1970s, by which time it was also widespread in the USA. The term is now a common colloquialism.

  'Paid-for lessons at some professional club in Romford; and the use of such iffy stimulants as "Matchroom" aftershave.'
  (*GQ* magazine, August 1989)

1b. *British* (of a person) dishonest, probably criminal or (of a thing) probably stolen. A milder version of **bent** or **moody**.

ikey (mo) *n British*
a Jew. A derogatory term dating from the 19th century. Ikey is a diminutive form of Isaac and Mo (Moses). Ikey Mo was a character in the *Ally Sloper* cartoons at the turn of the 20th century.

ill *adj*
1a. excellent
1b. contented, relaxed
A term used by young street-gang members in London since around 2000.

illin' *adj*
1a. unhealthy, sick. This conversion of the adjective ill has been a feature of many English dialects, particularly black and rural ones, since the 18th century.
1b. stupid, crazy, unbalanced
2. bad, **uncool**. This sense results from the appropriation of the older expression by black youth and later white emulators in the USA in the early 1980s. The word enjoyed a vogue in Britain in 1987 and 1988, having been imported as one of the buzzwords of the **rap** and hip hop cultures.

imbo *n Australian*
an imbecile. A characteristic Australian shortening.

imshi *exclamation, vb*
to go away. An Arabic imperative adopted by members of the armed forces, particularly in Egypt, and imported to Britain where it is still heard occasionally among the older generation.

in a kiddie kingdom *adj Caribbean*
in a state of bliss, very congenial surroundings.
Compare **goat heaven**

in-and-out *n*
a version of **in-out**

in a piss *adj British*
grumpy, bad tempered, angry. An item of student slang in use in London and elsewhere since around 2000.

in a whole world of trouble *adj British*
very intoxicated, a humorous euphemism. An item of student slang in use in London and elsewhere since around 2000.

in bits *adj British*
overcome by strong emotion, devastated, mortified. A common expression since the 1990s.

  'When I heard [of a companion's death] I was in bits.'
  (Teenage gang member, quoted in *Crime Kids*, BBC2, May 2002)

in costume *adj American*
in uniform. Police jargon of the 1980s.

in deep shit *adj*
a later elaboration of 'in the shit', meaning in trouble. This version of the expression became fashionable in the late 1980s.

Indian hemp *n*
cannabis; marihuana or hashish. Very little illegally imported cannabis originates in India, but the potent, smokable strain of the hemp plant has the botanical name *cannabis sativa indica*. Indian hemp was a term employed by official and quasi-scientific authorities in the early 20th century (*The Charms of Indian Hemp* was the title of a 1907 publication). In the 1950s smokers of the drug also used the expression, but by the 1960s it was confined to judicial or journalese usage. The word cannabis largely supplanted the term in the 1970s.

indie *n British*
1a. an independent record label (i.e. one not affiliated to one of the big business conglomerates known as 'the majors'), or a record issued on one of these. The expression and the phenomenon date from the mid-1970s when small-scale record companies, boosted by the advent of **punk** rock with its do-it-yourself ethic,

began to threaten the virtual monopoly of the majors. Indie had previously referred to independent films produced in the USA.

'Apologists for the "indie ghetto", forever championing obscure and unlistenable bands with silly names.'
(*Independent*, 1 December 1989)

1b. the youth subculture coalescing around Indie bands from the late 1980s to the mid-1990s

indijaggers *n British*
indigestion, a stomach upset. A public-school term which perhaps originated as a nursery word in the early years of the 20th century.

'I've got frightful indijaggers!'
(*Guardian*, Posy Simmonds cartoon, 1981)

in Dutch *adj*
in trouble, in a vulnerable condition or delicate situation. This expression is a surviving example of the tendency (dating from the Anglo-Dutch wars of the 17th century) to use Dutch as a pejorative, as in 'Dutch courage', 'Dutch treat' or 'Dutch Uncle'. In Dutch appears to date from the beginning of the 20th century. An alternative etymology would derive the expression from American English in which Dutch refers to the habits of Dutch settlers and indicates peculiarity rather than any more negative qualities.

in effect *adj, adv British*
in action, at large or happening. A black euphemism used particularly by street gangs in the 1980s. The expression has been picked up by black and white schoolchildren.

'Posse in effect.'
(Graffito on wall, Clapham, London, 1988)

in goat heaven *adj See* **goat heaven**

inked, inky *adj*
drunk. These terms, although rare, are not yet obsolete and are common to Britain, Australia and the USA. The origin of the expressions is unclear. They may be humorous parallels to blotto, or perhaps (and more probably) derive from the fact that cheap red wine was, in the early years of the 20th century, referred to as 'ink'.

inky smudge *n British*
a *judge*. An old item of rhyming slang.

in like Flynn *adj*
successful, in a very comfortable or advantageous position. A phrase which originated in the late 1940s and which shows no signs of disappearing despite the death of Errol Flynn, its inspiration. Flynn, the Australian hero of swash-buckling adventure films, was turned, especially in Australia and Britain, into a folk symbol of male sexual prowess by the press coverage of his trial on trumped-up statutory rape charges. The expression originally referred to success in seduction, but is now generalised to mean any impressive achievement, piece of opportunism or stroke of luck.

inna *adj British*
intrusive, 'nosy'. The term was recorded in West London in 1998. It may be related to the notion of 'in one's face'. **Eggs-up** and **extra** were contemporary synonyms.

innit? *question form, exclamation British*
1a. a question tag used to precede or to follow a statement

'"Innit?" has now found its way to the beginning of sentences: "Innit we're going to McDonalds today?"'
(Roy Kerridge writing in the *Evening Standard*, 20 August 1993)

1b. an exclamation of agreement
We should split up and meet back here later.
Innit!

Unlike some languages, English requires many different question phrases (aren't they?, can't we?, don't you?, etc.) instead of one (as in French *n'est-ce pas?*). Indian and Pakistani English has for many years used 'isn't it?' in this way, but in the early 1980s black British speakers appropriated the London working-class 'innit?' to serve as an all-purpose tag. The usage was imitated by white schoolchildren (leading black speakers to adopt 'in't it?', 'an't it?' and 'don't it?' as alternatives) and the word became detached from its context as a catchphrase.

innit-crowd, the *n*
a generic term for Asians or a specific group of Asians, from the colloquial term 'in-crowd' and **innit?** as a question tag characteristic of Asian speakers.
Compare **Asian massive**

in-out *n*
sexual intercourse. A euphemism heard among English speakers everywhere since before World War II. In British

usage it is often part of expressions such as '(a bit of) the old in-out'. An earlier version was 'in-and-out'.

in power *adj American*
successful, enjoying respect. An item of street-gang jargon of the 1990s, which parallels the British **in effect**.

in shtuk/shtook/stook/schtuk *adj British*
in trouble. A very widespread expression which moved from a restricted demimonde and theatrical usage to common currency in the mid-1960s, partly through its use in the entertainment media. *Shtuk* in its various spellings is Yiddish for difficulties. 'In shtuk' often refers to financial difficulties.

inside *adj, adv*
in prison. Formerly a piece of euphemistic underworld slang dating from the 19th century, this word has become so widely known since the late 1950s as to be a colloquialism rather than true slang.

in stir *adj See* **stir**

intense *adj American*
good, positive. This all-purpose term of approval, with overtones of exciting, energetic, vital, etc., has been in vogue, particularly among teenagers, since the late 1970s.
See also **camping**

intercourse *n*
as a shortening of 'sexual intercourse' this term has been used as a humorous euphemism for **fuck** since the late 1970s. It is largely confined to middle- and upper-class speakers. The word is employed in various forms according to the usages of fuck; 'Oh, intercourse!' as an exclamation or 'I'm totally intercoursed', meaning exhausted, for instance.

interfacing *n*
communicating or getting on well. A piece of jargon from the world of computing, transposed by **yuppies** and others into a humorous (or straightforward) synonym for communicating (with) or relating to others.

in the club *adj British*
pregnant. This very common expression is in origin a shortening of 'in the **pudding club**', which dates from the 17th century and is one of many folk expressions using baking metaphors in a sexual context. Pudding is an obsolete euphemism for

semen and, more rarely, for the female sex organs.

in the frame *adj*
identified as a suspect in a crime. This example of police jargon, in use both in Britain and the USA, is derived either from the simple image of a portrait in a frame or from horse-racing parlance, in which it refers to the practice of displaying the numbers of the winning and placed horses in a metal frame at the end of the race.

in the groove *adj, adv*
1a. proceeding smoothly, working well
1b. in harmony with others or with one's surroundings, *au fait* with what is going on
Both terms come from the jargon of pre-World War II jazz musicians.

in the shit *adj*
in trouble. This common expression has been in use since the mid-19th century if not earlier. It is a vulgar version of 'in the soup'.

in your eye, in a pig's eye, in a pig's arse *exclamation*
an all-purpose expression of violent negation; usually denial, refusal or dismissal. The first two versions are euphemistic alternatives to the third.

iona *adj British*
bad. A word used by London schoolchildren in the late 1990s. Its derivation is unclear.

iono! *exclamation American*
a lazy pronunciation or Internet abbreviation of 'I don't know'. In use among adolescents since around 2002.

Irish *n British*
a *wig*. Rhyming slang from 'Irish jig'. Wigs and toupées, which attract much notice and derision in cockney circles, are also known as **syrup (of figs)**, **rugs**, 'mops' or **dogs**.

Irish apricot/apple/plum *n*
a potato. These predictable witticisms have been heard since the 19th century in both Britain and the USA.

Irish confetti *n*
stones, rocks and other debris thrown during riots and demonstrations

> *'The "Irish confetti" was dancing off upraised shields and bouncing and ricocheting all around in the courtyard.'*
> (P. J. O'Rourke, *Holidays in Hell*, 1988)

iron _n_
a pistol or revolver. A slang term of the 19th and early 20th centuries (short for the American 'shooting iron') which survives in the pages of westerns and crime fiction. Iron was revived in the 1990s by members of US street gangs.

iron (hoof) _n British_
a male homosexual. London rhyming slang for **poof**, the expression is an authentic cockney folk term which is still very much in currency.

iron lung _n British_
a bribe or gratuity. The term is rhyming slang for **bung**, and occurs in the speech of criminals, the police, sports promoters and journalists.

Irving _n American_
a boring person, nonentity. The Christian name was thought in the 1950s to be quintessentially mundane, personifying an urban dullard.

issit?, izzit? _question form, exclamation British_
more recent versions of **innit?**, recorded since 2000

ite! _exclamation See_ **aiit!**

item _n_
1. a current (sexual) relationship, a couple. An Americanism of the 1970s which became widespread in the 1980s in expressions such as 'they're an item'. This use of the word began as journalese or jargon of the sort practised by _Variety_ magazine, it then passed into show business, 'society' and, subsequently, teenage usage.
2. an actual or potential sexual partner. A depersonalising reference, like **unit**, heard typically in the context of US singles' bars since the 1970s.

it rocks! _exclamation See_ **rock**²

ixnay _adj, adv, n_
no, not, none. An all-purpose negative formed by the principle of **pig Latin** from the word **nix**, itself derived from the Yiddish and German for not or nothing. Ixnay was heard, particularly in the USA, in the 1950s and 1960s, but is now virtually obsolete apart from in the phrase 'ixnay ofay', meaning no white people allowed. Like **nix** it can also function as a verb.

-izzle _combining form American_
an all-purpose termination, originally in southern US and black speech, which has become emblematic of hip hop and **rap** parlance since 2000. The syllables can be placed after consonants to provide a substitute form of familiar words.

OK, what's the dizzle [deal]?
Fo' shizzle [sure] my nizzle [nigger].

J

j *n*

a **joint** (a cigarette containing cannabis). An abbreviation from the jargon of drug users, dating from the mid-1960s.

I rolled a couple of js for the concert.

jabbering, jabbing *n*

boastful, deliberately confusing or annoyingly incoherent talk. Defined by one user as 'talking bullshit', the standard colloquialism became a vogue word among male adolescents from around 2000.

jabs *n pl Irish*

female breasts. A vulgarism used typically by males, recorded in 2004.

jack¹ *n*

1. nothing. This fairly widespread sense of the word may derive from an earlier and now obsolete sense of jack meaning very little or a small or insignificant amount. (A synonymous expression is 'jack shit'.)

We didn't get jack.

2a. a police officer

2b. an informer

These British and Australian senses of the word have existed at least since the 19th century.

3. meths (methylated spirits) as drunk by tramps, **dossers**, etc.

4. money. A common term in the USA which is also heard in Britain and Australia.

Listen, I just need some jack – in a hurry.

5a. heroin. In the argot of prison inmates and addicts in the 1960s.

5b. a single dose of a narcotic, specifically a tablet of prescribed heroin or heroin substitute

I just scored ten jacks of H.

5c. an injection (of an illicit drug)

Give me a jack of that shit you're banging.

A term from the jargon of addicts since the mid-1960s, probably originating in **Jack-and-Jill**, rhyming slang for *pill*, reinforced by the verb **jack (oneself) up**, meaning to inject.

6. *British* the anus or buttocks. A rarer euphemism than **jacksie**, typically used in provincial working-class speech.

a kick up the jack

7. venereal disease. In this sense the word is common in Australia, although it is also heard in Britain. The origin of this usage is either in archaic rhyming slang, 'jack in the box': **pox**, or from the archaic use of jack to mean the penis or semen.

8. *British* **on one's Jack/Jack Jones**, rhyming slang for *alone*

jack² *vb American*

to steal, rob, mug or hold up. The term, which became widespread in black street-gang jargon in the late 1980s, was probably a shortening of car-jack (itself modelled on hi-jack), describing armed holdups carried out on passing vehicles, a criminal fashion of the time.

'You come down here, you goin' get jacked for sure.'

(Recorded, black youth, New York City, May 1995)

jack³ *adj Australian*

fed up, tired, weary. To be jack of something or someone has been heard in Australian speech since the early years of the 20th century. It is probably not directly related to the more recent near synonym **jacked off**.

Jack-and-Jill *n British*

a *pill*, tablet of an illicit or prescribed drug. A rhyming-slang phrase used by drug abusers since the 1960s.

jacked *adj*

robbed. A back-formation from the earlier **jacking 2**.

jacked-off/out *adj*

annoyed, angry. These 1980s expressions (the first international English, the second primarily North American) are typically used by teenagers and young adults as milder synonyms for **hacked-off** and **pissed-off**.

jacked-up *adj*
excited, agitated, **hyper**. This usage, encountered in all anglophone areas, is perhaps related to the verb **jack up** by (probably false) analogy with **hyped-up**.

jacker *n American*
a thief, robber. The term, from the early 1990s, probably originated as car-jacker.

jacket *n American*
a personal file, record; particularly a police file or prisoner's dossier. A law enforcers' term, from the jargon of office-workers.
Let's take a peek at his jacket.

jacking *n*
1. *British* talking, gossiping. A version of 'yakking' heard particularly in the north of England.
2. *American* a robbery, theft

jack off *vb American*
to masturbate. This phrase may be a euphemistic version of **jerk off**, or may be based on 'ejaculate' or on the archaic meaning of jack as the penis or semen.

jack roll *n South African*
a **gang bang**. Recorded as an item of Sowetan slang in the *Cape Sunday Times*, 29 January 1995, the expression was previously heard in North American slang where it signified a mugging.

jacks *adj, adv British*
alone. The word, used for instance by students in the 1990s, is taken from the cockney rhyming slang expression **on one's jack (jones)**.
'While Kevin was out kicking back somewhere, I was at home, jacks as usual.'
(Recorded, female university student, London, March 1996)

jack shit *n American*
nothing. A dismissive or contemptuous term, originally with folksy southern overtones, but now common.
Man, I worked hard all my life and ended up with jack shit.

jacksie, jacksy *n*
the **arse**, anus, buttocks. A fairly inoffensive working-class word, particularly popular in the north of England, jacksie (the form jaxy has also been recorded) dates from the 19th century. It is probably an affectionate diminutive form of the commoner nickname **jack**. Instances of the word in American speech point to a recent borrowing from British usage.

'The jewel in the jacksie of South London, this place is.'
(*My Beautiful Laundrette*, British film, 1985)

'I've got ten minutes to spare. If you like I can redecorate the front room. A better idea still, why don't we shove a broom up my jacksie and I could sweep the floor at the same time.'
(*Moonlighting*, American TV series, 1989)

Jack-the-lad *n British*
an individual who is cleverer, more successful, more attractive than the rest. Originating in the working-class language of Liverpool and the surrounding area, the phrase had spread to the rest of Britain by the mid-1980s, probably due to the influence of television drama, films, fiction, etc. It can be used to express either approbation or contempt and is a modern example of the coining of male epithets with 'Jack' since medieval times.
He's Jack-the-lad now, but he'll get his comeuppance.

jack up *vb British*
to arrange, organise (especially at short notice). This sense of the phrase, used typically by working-class speakers such as police and gang members, suggests mounting an improvised operation or rigging up a contraption. It is presumably an extension of the specific use of the term as employed by car mechanics.

jack (oneself) up *vb*
to inject (oneself), usually with heroin, but possibly with amphetamines, etc. Apart from **shoot up**, this was probably the most common expression for the practice in the 1960s.

Jacobs (cream crackers) *n pl British*
the testicles, **knackers**. The rhyming slang, employing the name of a brand of savoury biscuits, was used in the film *Snatch* in 2000.

jag *n*
1. a binge, as in a crying jag, cocaine jag, etc. This sense of the word derives from a 17th-century English dialect term originally meaning a burden, later extended to mean a bout (of drunkenness). The word virtually disappeared from British usage in the 19th century, but survived in American slang, whence it was re-imported.
2a. an injection

2b. an inhalation of glue or another solvent. These invented terms are probably influenced by 'jab', **jack**, **jack (oneself) up** and **jagged**, as well as the first and more widespread sense of jag itself. The first sub-sense dates from the early years of the 20th century, the second from the 1950s.

3. a Jaguar car

jagged *adj*
drunk. This predominantly American term (used by **preppies** among others) can be pronounced either as 'jaggid' or, more often, as 'jagg'd'. It derives from **jag** in the sense of a drinking bout.

jailbait *n*
a sexual partner or potential sexual partner under the legal age of consent. The expression is typically used to refer to sexually attractive young girls; it is also part of the **gay** vocabulary. Jailbait (also 'gaol-bait') has been heard in Britain since the 1950s, but has only been in widespread use since the period of sexual liberation in the late 1960s.

> *'Look again, Billy, this is jailbait – could get you into a lot of trouble.'*
> (*Hardcore*, US film, 1979)

jake[1] *n British*
meths, methylated spirits as drunk by tramps, **dossers**, etc. It is also known as **jack**.

jake[2] *adj*
excellent, satisfactory, correct. A word of unknown origin, used since the turn of the 20th century in Canada and the USA, where it is now rare, and subsequently in Australia, where it is still heard. The word has not appeared in British usage.

jakey, jakie *n British*
a tramp, homeless person, particularly one who is a user of alcohol or **jake**

jalopy, jalloppy *n*
an old car. A word which has passed from slang of the 1950s into widespread colloquial use. The word was first used in the USA before World War II and could also refer to an aeroplane. It is of uncertain origin.

jam[1] *vb*
1a. to play music informally, to improvise. The phrase originally referred to loose aggregations of jazz musicians, typically playing 'after hours', later to rock and blues.

1b. to make up an improvised **rap** chant. The word and the practice arose in New York in the late 1970s. Rapping, like the original jazz improvisation, took place in informally composed groups, often competing among themselves.

2. *American* to take part in a wild celebration, to 'party'. An extension of the original musical sense of the word.

3. *American* to have sex (with). This vulgarism usually occurs in the form 'jamming', and is heard typically among adolescents. Slang uses of the word jam as verb or noun play on its standard sense of crush(ed) or wedge(d) together. The additional sense of sweet confection also influences the use of the word in sexual euphemisms.

See also **jooky jam**

4. *American* to move quickly, leave hurriedly. This sense is of uncertain origin, but may refer to jamming the foot on the accelerator.

5. *American* to sniff cocaine. This use of the word presumably refers to jamming the substance up one's nose. It may alternatively refer to jam as something sweet.

jam[2] *n*
1a. a shortening of jam session, meaning a group improvisation or informal performance. The term was originally applied to jazz, and later to rock.

1b. a **rap** session

2. *American* a party (usually a wild, crowded affair)

3a. a sex act

3b. a sexual partner (of either gender)

3c. the vagina

The many sexual sub-senses of jam are based on the two standard meanings of squeeze or wedge and something sweet.

4. a *car*. A shortened version of **jam jar** used by younger speakers since 2000.

jamas *n pl See* **jarmies**; **jammies**; **jim-jams**

James *n British*
a *first* (first-class honours degree). Students' rhyming slang from 'James the First'.

> *'We all expected Penny to get a James but she ended up with a Desmond.'*
> (*Evening Standard*, June 1988)

jam jar *n British*
a *car*. A piece of rhyming slang which dates from the 1920s and is still in use in working-class London speech. An alternative is 'la-di (dah)'.

'He had to blag a jam jar for the getaway.'
(Recorded, petty criminal, Vauxhall, London, 1976)

jammed *adj American*
intoxicated by alcohol or drugs. The standard word in its sense of incapacitated or out of order has predictably been appropriated for slang usage.

jammer *n Jamaican*
the penis. The Caribbean version of the North American terms **jammy** or **jemmy**.

'…how must women feel to hear that "the girls dem want the jammer"?'
(*Sunday Times*, 2 May 1993)

jammies *n pl British*
pyjamas. A nursery term. Alternatives are **jarmies** and **jim-jams**.

jammin' *adj American*
exciting, powerful, impressive. A synonym for **kicking**, **slamming**, etc. heard since 2000.

jammy[1] *adj British*
enviably lucky, very fortunate. This common expression, which is particularly popular among schoolchildren (typically expressed in such phrases as 'jammy dodger', 'jammy bugger', 'jammy sod' or 'jammy bastard') marvelling at a fellow pupil's luck in escaping punishment, derives from the 19th- and early 20th-century colloquial sense of jam as reward, luxury, indulgence, etc.

jammy[2], **jemmy** *n American*
the penis. In its first form the word has been used by **rappers**, including Ice T. The derivation is unclear, but **jam** as verb and noun has been used to mean both 'penetrate' and 'semen' in earlier black street slang.

jam rag *n British*
a sanitary towel. A schoolchildren's term in use since the 1950s. It may also refer to a tampon. (A variant form is **tam rag**.)

jam roll *n British*
parole. A rhyming-slang term from the vocabulary of prison inmates and the underworld.

He's up for his jam roll.

jam sandwich *n British*
a police car, in the argot of schoolchildren, tramps, **dossers** and the homeless

'I'm not going to be moved. The jam sandwiches [police cars] will have to cart me off.'
(Homeless man, *Observer*, 16 August 1987)

jane *n*
1. a women's toilet. A feminine version of a **john**. A term probably coined separately by feminists and humorists of both sexes in the 1970s.
2a. a woman
2b. a female prostitute
Both senses of the word are female counterparts of **john**.

jang *n*
1. *American* the penis. A rare version of **yang** or **whang**.
2. a fight. The word occurs in black British speech and may have originated in Caribbean or black American usage, possibly as a shortened form of 'jangle'.

jangle[1] *vb British*
to gossip, chat. A word which is popular in northern England, particularly in the Liverpool area where jangling describes the working-class ritual or pastime of gossiping over the back fence or front gate.

jangle[2] *n British*
a gossip, chat. The noun postdates the verb form.

jangled *adj*
disturbed, nervous, tense or irritated. A usage first recorded in the 1980s, from the colloquialism 'jangled nerves'. (Jangle is not related to jingle, but is from a Middle English word meaning 'grumble'.)

I'm feeling a big jangled today.

jankers *n British*
military punishment, punishment detail. An army, navy and RAF term heard particularly in the 1950s, when national service was still in force in Britain. The origin of the term is obscure, but it may be related to **jangle**, which had an archaic sense of 'to grumble', hence jankers was either the grumbling servicemen or the punishments which caused them to complain.

janky, jank *adj*
1. unlucky
2. unfashionable, unappealing
The words are of uncertain origin but may be an alteration of 'jinx(ed)'. They have been used in Britain by adherents of the **rave** and dancefloor cultures since the 1990s.

janner *n British*
a synonym of **chav**, in vogue in 2004. The etymology of the term is obscure but it

seems to have originated in the Plymouth area as a local nickname.

JAP *n American*
a young Jewish girl, especially a wealthy or spoilt one. An acronym of 'Jewish American Princess'. A member of a social subgroup supposedly characterised by behaving in a comically spoilt, acquisitive and/or self-indulgent way. Princess here recalls the indulgent term of (usually paternal) affection, and the haughtiness of the subject. Following the *Preppie Handbook*, a *JAP Handbook* was published in 1983 analysing every aspect of the phenomenon.

> *'What does a JAP make for dinner? Reservations.'*
> (*Evening Standard*, 9 May 1988)

jar *n British*
a pint of beer. A pub habitués' term which has been in widespread use since the 1950s. At the turn of the 20th century ale was served in china mugs, known as jars, as well as glasses.

> *'Hey Tom I fancy a bit of lunch. Let's stop at that pub for a few jars.'*
> (*Roger Mellie*, cartoon in *Viz* comic, 1989)

jarmies, jarmas, jamas *n pl British*
pyjamas. Alternative nursery terms to **jammies** and **jim-jams**.

jarred (up) *adj British*
drunk. The term was used of the Irish writer Brendan Behan by his wife.

J Arthur *n British*
an act of masturbation. Rhyming slang from J. Arthur Rank (the British cinema magnate): **wank**. A very popular word in the 1960s, used almost invariably by and about men. (In the 1940s the same phrase was used to refer to a bank.)

> *He was having a J Arthur in the bathroom.*

java *n*
coffee. An Americanism that spread worldwide through the influence of Hollywood and pulp-fiction writers. Coffee was imported from Java in the 19th century.

> *Fancy a cup of java?*

jawache *vb, n British*
(to) kiss

> *He wanted to jawache her.*
> *I got jawache from her.*

jaxy *n See* **jacksie**

jay *n*
1. a **joint**. An alternative rendering of **J**.
2. *American* a dupe, victim, in the language of criminals, gamblers and confidence tricksters. The reference is to the jay bird, popularly supposed to be garrulous and dim-witted.

jazz¹ *vb*
1a. to talk deceitfully, bamboozle, **bullshit**
1b. to tease or provoke
Both sub-senses originated in black American slang and have, since the 1970s, become established in general American colloquial speech. In these meanings, **jive** is a synonym.
2. *American* to have sex with
A black slang term from the early 20th century, jazz is still used, albeit rarely, in this sense. The word jazz is said to be a New Orleans Creole patois term for sex, erotic dancing or music.

jazz² *n*
1a. empty, pretentious or deceitful talk
1b. provocation, obfuscation, nuisance
2a. stuff, unspecified things. Often heard in the dismissive phrase 'all that jazz'.
2b. ornamentation, decoration, showiness
The precise origin of the word jazz is uncertain. It was first used in New Orleans in the early years of the 20th century in the form *jass*, referring to music and dances inspired by African rhythms. The word also had sexual overtones in its Creole origin. It was later applied to improvised music and, later still, to other forms of exciting display.

jeet *vb South African*
to leave, hurry away. The term, recorded since 2000, may be a form of **jet**.

jeeter *n American*
a slovenly male. Jeeter Lester was a quintessentially uncouth rustic character in Erskine Caldwell's 1932 novel *Tobacco Road*; his first name became part of New York slang in the 1940s and subsequently spread to other areas. By the 1990s the term was still used, often as part of domestic slang.

jeez! *exclamation*
a less offensive form of Jesus, originally American, but now heard elsewhere

jeff *n American*
a white person. This sometimes pejorative black term is applied invariably to white males and is inspired by Jefferson Davis, the American president portrayed

on banknotes, seen as a quintessential Caucasian.

Jeffrey n British
£2,000. A probably ephemeral invention by an anonymous wit in the tradition of a **monkey**, a 'pony', etc. It refers to the sum paid by the author and Tory politician Jeffrey Archer to Miss Monica Coughlan, a prostitute, to enable her to go abroad. This figure has also been referred to as an **Archer**.

jekyll adj British
snide. An item of rhyming slang from '(Dr) Jekyll and (Mr) Hyde', recorded among middle-class, middle-aged speakers.

Jekyll and Hyde, Jekyll n British
a guide.
Compare **jekylls**

jekylls n pl British
trousers. The word is rhyming slang – Jekyll and Hydes: **strides**.
  That's a fancy pair of jekylls you've got there.

jellies n pl British
cheap sandals made of brightly coloured transparent plastic as worn by art students, etc. since the early 1980s. The footwear resembled confectionery of the same name.

jellybaby n British
a weak or irresolute person. This item of criminal slang was defined by FHM magazine in April 1996 as 'a slithering disgrace to the profession, one who crumbles under interrogation'.

jelly-belly n
a fat, overweight or paunchy person

jelly roll n American
1a. a woman's sex organs
1b. sexual intercourse
1c. a woman seen as a sexual partner, sex object or sweetheart
1d. a male lover or seducer
All these terms, popularised by their use in jazz, blues and rock music, derive from black American argot of the late 19th century. A jelly roll is literally a jam or Swiss roll. The triple metaphor implied in the first three senses derives from the rolling motion, the supposed resemblance of the cake to the vulva, and the notion of 'sweet reward'. In the case of the fourth sense, which is less common but may historically antedate the others, the word represents the sweet element of 'sweetheart'.

jerk n
a foolish, despicable or obnoxious person. This American term crossed over into limited British usage during and after World War II. It is usually pejorative, although it is sometimes used with pitying or even affectionate connotations in American speech. The word seems to derive from **jerk off**, meaning to masturbate, and was probably originally a rural term for an idle or immature boy.
  'Poor Michael Reagan. As if it weren't bad enough being the son of Ronald Reagan, the guy happens to be a complete jerk as well.'
  (Nigella Lawson, book review, the Sunday Times, April 1989)

jerkin' the gherkin n
male masturbation. A rhyming witticism from around 1960, it replaced other rarer phrases employing the word jerk which had been in use since the mid-19th century, such as 'jerk the turkey', 'jerk the jelly', etc.

jerk off vb
to masturbate. An Americanism which has gained currency throughout the English-speaking world since the late 1960s when it became a **hippy** and student vogue term. The phrase existed in British English in the 19th century but was never widespread.
  'Plus the exhibitionist jerk off fantasia of "let's do it in the road".'
  (Oz magazine, 1970)
See also **jerkoff**

jerkoff n American
a despicable or obnoxious (male) person. The American equivalent of **wanker** (to **jerk off** is to masturbate). A word which became particularly popular in the USA in the late 1960s and which had spread to other English-speaking areas by the end of the **hippy** era.
  The guy turned out to be a complete jerkoff.

jerk someone around, jerk someone's **chain** vb American
to irritate, harass, subject someone to minor humiliations. The image evoked is of an animal on a rope or lead being tugged at the whim of its owner.

jerkwad n American
a term of abuse meaning literally a (male) masturbator, a **jerkoff**. ('Wad' figures in many expressions involving male sexual-

ity and may denote the penis or semen or, more recently, tissue or toilet paper.)

jerkwater *adj American*
remote, insignificant. This expression does not, as is often thought, have any implication of urination or masturbation. It derives from the rural American practice of stopping trains in remote country areas to take on water, by pulling across a connection and sluice or ladling from a trough.

'When you work for a jerkwater [TV] station like this you learn to do everything.'
(*Prime Suspect*, US film, 1982)

Jerry Springer *n British*
a **minger**. The rhyming slang phrase borrows the name of the US talk show host.

jessie *n British*
a weak or effeminate man. A Scottish and northern English term of ridicule which has become widespread since the mid-1970s, partly due to the influence of comics such as the Scot, Billy Connolly. It is synonymous with **nellie** and **big girl's blouse**. There are two proposed derivations for the word; the first is simply a borrowing of the female name as a term of endearment, the second is a Biblical reference to 'a rod out of the stem of Jesse', giving rise to jokes on the subject of masturbation, etc.

Oaw, come on you big soft jessie.
'Peelie [John Peel] blubbed throughout, the big jessie, and before long we all joined in.'
(*Evening Standard*, 31 August 1989)

Jesus *n See* **creeping Jesus**

jet *vb American*
to depart, leave. A vogue term in black street argot and white campus slang since the 1990s. The word has been used figuratively to mean 'run fast' since the 1950s. A variety of euphemisms (like its contemporaries **bail**, **bill**, **book** and **jam**) for 'run away' are essential to the argot of gang members and their playground imitators.

jewels *n pl British See* **family jewels**

Jewish *n, adj South African*
(clothing or accessories considered) fashionable and/or expensive

'Natty dressers are described as Jewish – because members of that community are considered to be stylish.'

(*Johannesburg Sunday Times*, 18 June 1995)

Jewish American Princess *n American*
See **JAP**

Jewish flag *n American*
a dollar bill or other banknote

Jewish lightning *n American*
arson, the deliberate burning of insured property. A type of fraud supposed to be typically perpetuated by Jewish businessmen or landlords.

Jewish typewriter/piano/pianola/joanna
n
a cash register. Supposedly jocular racist terms referring to Jews' presumed love of money. Jewish piano has also been used in Britain for a taxi meter.

jezzy *n British*
a disreputable and/or promiscuous female. Defined as a **slag** by one user in 2002, the term is in use among adolescents in London and elsewhere.

jig *n British*
a black person. A racist term (probably a shortening of **jigaboo**) employed by police officers, among others. It was used in the G. F. Newman TV play, *Black and Blue*, in September 1992.

jigaboo, jiggaboo *n American*
a black person. This was originally a racist epithet used by whites since the early years of the 20th century and later adopted in a gesture of defiance, like **nigger**, by blacks to refer to themselves. The black American author and academic Clarence Major derives the expression from the Bantu word *tshikabo*, meaning 'servile', and dates its adoption to the 17th century. In *School Daze*, a 1988 film by the black director Spike Lee, a fictional all-black southern US campus is riven between the 'jigaboo' faction who want the college authorities to sever links with South Africa, and the **wannabes** who are ambitious and apolitical and ape white pastimes and rituals.

jig-a-jig, jiggy-jig *n*
sexual intercourse. Since at least the 18th century there have been various slang terms for copulation using versions of the word jig. 'Jiggle' and 'jigger', for instance, are now archaic, but jig-a-jig has survived, probably because of its use by non-English speakers and those imitating lewd invitations in broken English.

jigger *n*

the penis. An 18th-century word which is still heard, albeit rarely, mainly in the north of England.

jiggered *adj*

1a. *British* exhausted

1b. nonplussed, astonished. The usual form of words employed is 'I'll be jiggered!' as an exclamation of surprise on the pattern of 'I'll be blowed!' or 'I'll be damned!'.

Jiggered in both the above senses probably originated as a 19th-century euphemism for **buggered**.

jiggy *adj*

happy, contented. A term used by young street-gang members in London since around 2000.

jill *n British*

a policewoman. A term used predominantly in the north of England, particularly in the Liverpool area. It is coined by analogy with **jack**; a policeman (itself usually in the plural form).

jillion *n American*

an almost inexpressibly large number or amount. A teenagers' coinage referring to uncountable figures in excess of millions and billions. Other similar terms are 'trillion' (in fact a real number), **squillion** and **zillion**.

jillock *n British*

a foolish person, buffoon. A variant form of **pillock**, heard since the late 1970s.

Jim Benner *n British*

a £10 note or the sum of ten pounds

jim-dandy *adj American*

excellent, fine. An elaboration of the popular American colloquialism, dandy (jim-, like john- and jack-, was a widespread prefix conferring familiarity). This expression is often used ironically in modern speech.

jim-jams *n pl*

1. pyjamas. A nursery word, especially popular in Britain and Australia.

'A coat that can double as a dressing-gown, nice stripy jim-jams – such are the staples of male Anglo-Saxon sartoria.'
(*Tatler*, November 1985)

2. an attack of nerves, the 'heebie-jeebies'. This expression has been applied to delirium tremens (**the D.T.s**) and to drug-induced terror, as well as more

mundane jitters. It was first recorded in the mid-19th century.

'When the smack begins to flow/ I really don't care any more/ About all the jim-jams in this town/ And all the politicians making crazy sounds.'
('Heroin', written by Lou Reed and recorded by the Velvet Underground, 1967)

jimmies, the *n pl Australian*

1. an attack of nerves; a variant form of the second sense of **jim-jams**

2. an attack of diarrhoea; a variant form of the **Jimmy Brits**

jimmy *n British*

1. an injection of a narcotic, especially heroin. A word from the lexicon of prison inmates and drug addicts.

2. a shortening of **Jimmy Riddle**

'Hang on to me pint for a minute, I've got to go for a jimmy.'
(Recorded, young drinker, London, 1987)

Jimmy Brits, the Jimmy Brits *n pl Australian*

an attack of diarrhoea. Australian rhyming slang for **the shits**, inspired by the name of a British boxer who toured Australia in 1918. (The surname is sometimes spelt Britt.)

Jimmy Durante(s) *n pl Scottish*

female underwear. The name of the jazz pianist of the 1940s has been borrowed as a rhyme for *panties*.
Compare **big jimmies**

jimmy-hat *n*

a condom. The term, common in the USA since the 1970s, also occurs in the form 'jim-hat' and was used by the black comedian Lenny Henry in a televised monologue in November 1993.

Jimmy Hill(s) *n British*

pill(s). The term borrows the name of a TV sports commentator to refer to tablets of illicit narcotics.

Jimmy Riddle *n British*

an act of urination. A childish and jocular term derived from rhyming slang for **piddle**.

Jim Raki *n British*

a Pakistani. The term was in use among London teenagers in 2001.

jingle *n*

1. *British* cash, money, coins. A term used in raffish circles since the 1930s, if not earlier. It has also been recorded in Australian speech.

I'm a bit short of jingle.

2. *American* a telephone call. An American version of the British **bell** or **tinkle**, as in 'give me a jingle'.

jissom, jiss, jizz, jism, jissum, gism *n*
semen. A word of unknown origin, dating from the 19th century in the USA and by the early 1970s in use all over the English-speaking world.

jitter *n, adj British*
(something or someone) unpleasant, obnoxious. In playground usage since the 1990s.

jive¹ *n*
1. deceitful or pretentious talk or behaviour, nonsense.
See also **jive talk**
2. a style of fast dancing to accompany swing music or rock 'n' roll
Both senses of the term originate in black American slang of unknown etymology (it may be from jibe in the sense of change tack, manoeuvre – in conversation or dance – but is more probably derived from a West African dialect term).
3. *American* marihuana. A now obsolete usage.

jive² *vb*
1. to deceive, tease, browbeat. A black American term from the early 20th century which enjoyed a vogue among black and white speakers in the late 1980s. For the possible origins of the word, see the noun form.

'It was always about the man, how they were going to jive the man into giving them a million dollars.'
(*The Switch*, Elmore Leonard, 1978)

2. to dance in a fast energetic style which corresponded in the 1940s to swing music and from the 1950s to rock 'n' roll

jive-ass *adj American*
deceitful, pretentious, worthless. A black expression combining **jive** (worthless or deceitful talk or behaviour) and the suffix **-ass**.
I don't want no jive-ass honky lawyer jerkin' me around.

jive talk *n*
a style of speech using black musicians' slang and picturesque rhythmic phraseology, originally developed to accompany swing music of the 1930s and 1940s. The vocabulary and cadences of jive talk were adopted by American teenagers in

the early 1950s. Jive talk was combined with **bop** talk to influence much of the vocabulary of the later **hipsters** and **beatniks**.

jizz-ball *n American*
an obnoxious, repellent, despicable person. A teenage insult based on the variant form of **jissom** and coined by analogy with earlier terms such as **scuzzball**.

JLD *adj*
'just like dad' in medical shorthand, sometimes added after **FLK**, e.g., on a patient's notes

joanie, joany *adj American*
old-fashioned, boringly outdated. A term from the **Valley Girl** lexicon of the 1970s. Its origins are obscure; it may reflect an original antipathy to an individual such as Joan Crawford or Joni Mitchell or may simply be a choice of Joan as a quintessentially older-generation first-name.

joanna *n British*
a *piano*. A rhyme on the cockney pronunciation of the instrument.
Give us a tune on the old joanna.
See also **Jewish typewriter/piano/pianola/joanna**

Joan of Arc *n Australian*
a *shark*. A piece of native Australian rhyming slang. An alternative is Noah's Ark.

job *n*
1. a crime. This widespread term occurs in expressions such as 'pull a job' and in specific forms such as 'bank-job', 'safe-job', etc. The word was first used in this sense in the 17th century, usually in the context of theft.
2. a person, thing or action. An all-purpose term for a contraption, specimen or piece of handiwork.
a six-cylinder job
Who's the little blonde job by the door?

job (someone) *vb*
1. to hit or beat (someone) up. Job is an old dialect variant of jab which has been preserved in this working-class Australianism. The word was used in the same sense in Britain in the 1950s, by street gangs for instance.
2. *American* to deceive, cheat or ruin (someone). A rare late 1980s usage which is a shortening of 'do a job on (someone)'.

jobbed *adj*
framed, fitted-up, informed upon, deceived, victimised or otherwise taken

advantage of. An item from the vocabulary of the underworld.

jobbie n British
1. *also* **jobbies** an act of defecation,
excrement. A mock nursery word which
is used euphemistically by adults, deriving from expressions such as **big jobs**.
2. an all-purpose word for 'thing'. This
variation of the colloquial **job** may also be
used as a replacement for a forgotten
word or name. The term was defined on
the Internet by *Bodge World* in 1997.

> *Hand me that big jobbie on the top
> there…*

jobbie-jabber n British
a male homosexual. The term was one of
many synonyms denoting 'active' or
'predatory' homosexuality heard since
the 1990s. **Fudge-nudger** and **turd burglar**
are synonyms based on the same supposed association with excrement.

jock n
1a. *British* a Scot. Since the 19th century
this has been the universal nickname for
Scottish males, derived from the northern
diminutive for John.
1b. *British* an unnamed male. The word
is used, sometimes dismissively, either
as a term of address or as a description.

> *Ask jock over there what he's drinking.*

2. a disc jockey. A piece of American
radio jargon adopted in other English-
speaking areas in the 1970s.
3. *American* an athlete or sportsman.
This campus term can now also apply in
some cases to sportswomen, in spite of
its origin as a shortening of jock strap.
Although it can be said affectionately and
is a term used by sportsmen about themselves, the word often has overtones of
excessive heartiness, brawn, aggression
or lack of intelligence.

> *'And the jock shall dwell with the nerd
> and the cheerleader lie down with the
> wimp and there will be peace upon the
> campus.'*
> (*Observer*, 29 May 1988)

jockey vb South African
to help, particularly by a temporary loan
of money. Recorded as an item of
Sowetan slang in the *Cape Sunday
Times*, 29 January 1995.

jocks n pl Australian
underpants, usually male. The word is a
shortening of 'jockey-pants' or 'jockey-
shorts'.

joe n
1. an ordinary man, chap, **bloke**. Originally an Americanism, this use of the
name spread to other English-speaking
areas in World War II.
2. a fool, dupe, victim or weakling. In this
sense the word is used by tricksters,
prostitutes and prison inmates, among
others, and probably derives from the
cockney **joey**, itself short for Joey Hunt,
rhyming slang for **cunt**. (Cunt previously
meant a foolish, unfortunate or pitiable
person, rather than a despicable one.)
3. *American* coffee

> *'I'm not just some kind of machine you
> can turn on. I need a cup of joe, a trip to
> the little boys' room, a glance at the
> sports pages. Then we'll talk.'*
> (*Moonlighting*, American TV series,
> 1988)

Joe Blake n Australian
a *snake*. An item of native Australian
rhyming slang. The eponymous Joe
Blake is probably fictitious.

Joe Blakes, the n Australian
the D.T.s (delirium tremens): a fit of
uncontrolled trembling as a result of alcoholism. Australian rhyming slang for the
shakes.
See also **Joe Blake**

Joe Blow n
an average man, ordinary person. A
rhyming elaboration of **joe**.

Joe Shmo n American
1. an average man
2. a victim, dupe, a simpleton. This
Americanism is a personification of
'schmo', which has also been recorded in
British usage.

Joe Soap n British
1a. an average man, ordinary person.
The equivalent of a **joe** or **Joe Blow**.
1b. a dim-witted male drudge or victim.
This is the original sense of the name,
which is rhyming slang for *dope*.

joey n
1. *British* a fool, dupe, victim or weakling.
The word is from London working-class
usage, deriving from **joe** or Joey Hunt,
rhyming slang for **cunt** which, in cockney
speech until the 1950s, referred to a foolish or unfortunate, rather than a despicable person. Joey is currently used by
teenagers to refer to a timid or unpopular
fellow-pupil or gang member.
2. *Australian* an effeminate man, fop,
hermaphrodite or sodomite. It is uncer-

tain whether this usage is derived from the previous sense or the following one.

3a. *Australian* a young kangaroo. The origin of this term is not the English Christian name but an identical Aboriginal name.

3b. *Australian* a baby

4. *British* a package smuggled in or out of a prison, in the jargon of prison inmates

john *n*

1. a prostitute's customer. John was a 19th-century term for a male sweetheart which was adopted by prostitutes as an all-purpose form of address and later as a synonym for client.

> 'He liked it during the day, the cute ladies sitting around playing music, laughing at things he said. But he didn't care for the white Johns any, their attitude.'
>
> (*The Switch*, Elmore Leonard, 1978)

2. the john a toilet. Originally a more genteel American version of the archaic 'jack' or 'jock' and the almost obsolete **jakes**, all euphemisms for a privy.

3. *British* an arrest. A rare example of police and criminal jargon of the 1960s, from the rhyming slang 'John Bull': **pull**.

4. the penis. A fairly rare but recurring usage. Other personifications, such as **John Thomas**, **willie**, **peter**, **percy**, etc., are much more common.

5. *British* a condom. A shortening of 'johnnie (bag)' or **rubber johnny**.

John Brown *n British*

a £10 note or sum of ten pounds, in street-gang parlance since 2000. The reference is to the colour of the banknote.

John Bull *adj Australian*

drunk. This witticism is a rhyme on **full** in its euphemistic sense of intoxicated.

> He was totally John Bull by three-thirty in the arvo.

johnnie, johnny *n British*

a condom, contraceptive sheath. This is the most widespread slang term in British use since the 1940s, although in the 1960s and 1970s it was more usually in the phrases 'johnnie bag' or **rubber johnny**. John or johnny is, among many other appellations, a 19th-century personification of the penis.

Johnny Cash *n*

1. *Australian* cannabis. An item of native Australian rhyming slang for **hash**, appro-

priating the name of the late American country music star.

2. *British* a **slash**

johnson *n American*

1a. the penis

1b. the backside, buttocks

> 'He can kiss my johnson.'
>
> (*The Boss's Wife*, US film, 1986)

Both senses are personifications used humorously or straightforwardly, especially in black speech. They date from the late 19th century and are elaborations of the use of **john** to designate anything male.

John Thomas *n British*

the penis. A hearty and/or affectionate personification in use since the mid-19th century. It was used by D. H. Lawrence in *Lady Chatterley's Lover*, written in 1928 and first published in an unabridged edition in Britain in 1959. The phrase now seems to be used particularly by women.

joint *n*

1. a marihuana cigarette or a cigarette containing a mix of hashish and tobacco. Joint supplanted **reefer** as the universal term for a cannabis cigarette in the early 1960s. The precise dating and etymology of the word are obscure.

> 'Several large joints passed along the room before someone suggested it was time to go outside and play with the Kalashnikovs.'
>
> (*Tatler*, April 1990)

2. the joint *American* prison. A specialisation of the colloquial sense of 'joint' as a place, building or premises.

3. *American* the penis. A metaphor based on images of meat and (an imaginary) bone.

4. *American* any object or person

joker *n*

1a. a foolish, irritating or unfortunate person

1b. any unnamed individual

jollies *n pl*

gratification. The expression can cover indulgences ranging from innocent enjoyment, through thrills, to more sinister and/or sexual stimulation. The word usually occurs in the phrase **get one's jollies**.

jolly d. *adj British*

'jolly decent'. A public-school or upper-class term of approbation, often used ironically or sarcastically. It is usually an interjection, rather than a description.

jonah n Australian
a *shark*. This is not a reference to the whale but a contracted form of the rhyming slang **Joan of Arc**.

jones n American
1. the penis. Now predominantly a term used by black speakers and their imitators. It may derive from a 19th-century personification of the male member as 'Mr Jones'.
2. a drug habit
They said they had to knock over a couple of stores for money to support their scag jones.

jooky jam vb
to have sex. A phrase originating in black usage: *jook* is said to derive from an African word for jab or poke, used since at least the 19th century in the USA as a euphemism for sex. **Jam** is a slang synonym in its own right.

Jordan n American
an attractive male. The use of the term either refers to Michael Jordan, a US sports star, or to a first name thought to typify a rugged, glamorous male.

josser n British
a foolish or obnoxious person. Used as a less offensive version of **tosser**, the term was heard particularly in the north of England in the 1980s. The word, in fact, has had a separate existence since the 19th century, during which time it has designated a simpleton, a codger, a fop and a parasite, among other senses. Its ultimate origins are obscure, although joss is said to have been a dialect term for bump or jostle.

journo n Australian
a journalist. A characteristic Australian shortening which has been heard among British speakers.

jousting n British
having sex. An item of student slang in use in London and elsewhere since around 2000. A synonym is **lancing**.

joy pop vb
1a. to take illicit drugs on an infrequent and casual, rather than habitual, basis
1b. to inject a drug intramuscularly, to **skin-pop**

joystick n
1. the penis. A pun on the name of the steering control column of aeroplanes, although some authorities claim that the

slang euphemism for the male member actually preceded the aeronautical usage (which may in fact derive ultimately from 'joist').
2. a cannabis cigarette, a **joint**. A fairly rare euphemism.

jub n British
a menial or junior worker, a **gofer**. The word, of uncertain origin, was used in the City of London financial markets from the late 1990s to refer, often dismissively, to messengers and 'back-office' underlings.
Get a jub to do it.

jubbies n pl British
female breasts. This childish-sounding term was used by (predominantly middle-class) teenagers and adults from the 1980s and is probably a blend of **jugs** and **bubbies**.

jubbly n British
money, wealth. The word is used in London working-class speech, especially in the phrase '(lots of) lovely jubbly'. Jubbly was the trade name of an orange drink sold in a triangular carton. Especially when frozen, it was popular with schoolchildren in the 1950s and 1960s. 'Lovely Jubbly!' was its advertising slogan.

jubnuts n pl British
a southern English rural term for **dags** (fragments of dung clinging to the rear of sheep and other shaggy animals)

judy n British
a girl or woman. A very common word in working-class use in the north of England in the 1950s and 1960s. Judy was a popular 19th-century Christian name, seen as typical of common women (as in, e.g., Punch and Judy). The word is also used in Australia as an alternative to **Sheila**.

jug[1] n
prison. This term from the beginning of the 19th century is usually part of the phrases 'in jug' or 'in the jug'. It probably derives from 18th-century dialect *jougs*, meaning stocks or pillory (from the French *joug*, meaning yoke), rather than from jug as a container of liquid. In modern usage the term is jocular.

jug[2] vb
1. also **jug up** British to imprison. From the noun **jug**.
2. also **jug out** or **jug up** American to drink, usually to excess. The phrases are probably influenced by the categorisation 'jug wine', denoting cheap wine bought in

large containers, e.g. by students and other drinkers of modest means.

jugged *adj*
1. imprisoned. From the noun **jug**.
2. drunk. A rare but recurrent term.

jugglin' bone *n*
dealing **crack**. A term used by young street-gang members in London since around 2000.

jug handles *n pl British*
the ears, particularly large prominent ears. The term is used by all ages and social classes for poking fun.

jugs *n pl*
1. female breasts. Originally an Australian vulgarism, inspired by milk jugs and probably influenced by the much older term **dugs**. This expression has also been used in Britain and the USA.
2. the ears, particularly large prominent ears. The word used in this sense, primarily in Britain, is a shortening of 'jug-ears' or **jug handles**.

juice¹ *n*
1. *American* alcohol, **booze**. A pre-World War II American term still in widespread use.
2. *American* electricity, power
  Give it some more juice.
3. *American* gossip, interesting news. A teenage term of the late 1970s and 1980s which is probably a back-formation from 'juicy'.
4. semen

juice², **juice it** *vb*
to have sex. A term used, transitively and intransitively, by young street-gang members in London since around 2000.

juiced, **juiced-up** *adj*
drunk. Unlike other slang terms deriving from **juice**, this is not exclusively American.

  'Howard you never used to talk to me that way.
  I'm just juiced, that's all.'
  (S. Clay Wilson cartoon in *Head Comix*, 1968)

juicer, **juice head/freak** *n American*
an alcoholic, drunkard or habitual heavy drinker. These terms probably originated in black slang of the 1940s.

J.U.L.F. *n British*
an arrogant and/or presumptuous person. The initials stand for 'jumped up little fucker'. The phrase was identified by Salman Rushdie, describing the slang used by his Special Branch bodyguards, in the *Independent*, 11 February 1993.

jumbo *n*
1. *British* a fool, a slow, large and/or dim-witted person. A mainly working-class term, used for instance by the CID to refer to uniformed police officers. (Jumbo as applied to elephants derives from the African word *jamba*, anglicised as a name for P. T. Barnum's famous animal exhibit.) In this case the image of a slow, ponderous person is probably also influenced by **dumbo**.
2. *British* the backside, buttocks
3. **crack**. This is one of many probably ephemeral nicknames used on the American streets for this powerful drug. Jumbo in this sense was recorded in 1986.

jump¹ *vb*
to have sex with. This term implying male assertion, domination or assault has been in use in English since the 17th century. It is paralleled in many other languages (the French equivalent is *sauter*). The word is now often used by street-gang members, etc. to refer to indecent assault, influenced by the term's colloquial meaning of to attack unexpectedly.

jump² *n*
an act of sexual intercourse. This old vulgarism has been revived since 2000, and was defined by one user (a London student) as 'a comedy term for sex used to embarrass mates in innocent situations, i.e. "they're going for a jump" when they are just going for a walk'.

jump in (someone's) face *vb American*
to harass, aggress, criticise (someone). The phrase has been recorded in black street parlance since the 1970s. It is probably based on the earlier imperative 'get out of my face!'.

jump off *vb American*
1a. (of a person) to become aggressive, lose one's temper
1b. (of a situation) to happen or escalate suddenly. The phrase probably arose in black slang where jump was a component in a number of obsolete expressions evoking rapidity and/or violence and the contemporary **jump salty**. **Step off** has similar meanings.

jump salty vb American
to become angry. A well-known item of black argot which was included in so-called **Ebonics**, recognised as a legitimate language variety by school officials in Oakland, California, in late 1996. The phrase, which seems to date from pre-World War II **jive talk** (it was listed in Cal Calloway's famous Hepster's lexicon in 1938), became part of street slang in the 1970s. It is now in widespread use and is sometimes heard among younger white speakers describing a key behaviour pattern, also expressed by **jump off** and **step off** and the British **kick off**.

jump someone's bones vb American
to have sex with someone. The expression, first heard in the 1960s, has rough-and-ready, crass overtones. It invariably refers to the sex act from the male point of view.

I guess she realised I just wanted to jump her bones.

June-July vb South African
to tremble or express fear. The European midsummer months occur in midwinter in the southern hemisphere, hence their association with shivering. The expression was recorded as an item of Sowetan slang in the *Cape Sunday Times*, 29 January 1995.

jungle n South African
a large knife. Recorded as an item of Sowetan slang in the *Cape Sunday Times*, 29 January 1995.

jungle bunny n
a negro or other dark-skinned person. A racist epithet which is usually applied to Afro-Caribbeans, and is also used by Australians to refer to Aboriginals and South Sea Islanders. It has been heard from at least the 1950s.

jungly, jungli adj South Asian
uncultured, uncouth, unsophisticated. An old expression (from 'jungle') in Indian English which is now used by Asians in the UK as part of so-called 'Hinglish' (a variety combining English with words from Hindi and other languages).

junk n
narcotics, hard drugs. The word (originally a Middle English term for nautical paraphernalia and detritus) was applied to opium in American underworld argot in the late 19th century. It was used to designate heroin by the first decade of the 20th century and has remained one of the most widespread synonyms for this and other addictive drugs.

'Fuzz against junk.'
(Title of book by the pseudonymous Akbar del Piombo, 1965)

junker n American
1. a dilapidated car, **banger**
2. an alternative (and rarer) version of **junkie**

junkie, junky n
a drug addict, a habitual user of 'hard' drugs such as heroin or morphine. The term, derived from the word **junk**, became popular in the USA in the 1920s and spread to Britain and Australia in the 1950s.

'When we think of a junkie we picture the reckless youth, squatting in the rubble of his life, a hypodermic in his hand.'
(*Independent*, 17 July 1989)

jupe, juped adj British
shamed, humiliated. One of many terms in the lexicon of teenage gangs which refers to respect or the lack/loss of it. The origin of the term is obscure, but it may be a deformation of the standard 'dupe', 'duped'. It can also be used as an exclamation of triumph or derision. The term was recorded in use among North London schoolboys from the early 1990s.

You're juped!

K

K *n*
1. one thousand. This abbreviation existed in limited slang usage in the 1970s (based on the k of kilo), but it was its use in computer jargon (to mean a storage capacity of 1,024 bytes) which was first transposed to express sums of money when discussing fees or salaries. It then entered general colloquial use in the 1980s.

He's on 60K a year.

2. *British* a knighthood, from the initial letter, or that of KBE, KCMG, etc.

'*Brenda has now let it be known to Downing Street that Milne should be given a "K" in the birthday honours list. Surprisingly enough Thatcher seems to approve.*'
(*Private Eye* magazine, April 1989)

kaffir *n*
a black person. A racist term used initially (and still) in South Africa to refer to indigenous blacks. (Kaffir was one 19th-century name for Bantu-speaking South African tribespeople, originating in the Arabic *kafir*: infidel.) The word is sometimes used, mainly by middle-aged or elderly speakers, in other English-speaking areas.

kahsi *n British*
an alternative spelling of **khazi**

kaifa *n British*
an alternative spelling of **kife**

kalied *adj British*
drunk. A fairly popular word in the north of England (usually pronounced 'kay-lide') which has been used in the long-running TV soap opera *Coronation Street*. Some authorities claim that kay-is a dialect prefix meaning askew or awry; Paul Beale, in Partridge's *Dictionary of Slang and Unconventional English*, derives kalied from 'kali', a children's sherbet dip.

and all he could do was go out and get kalied

kangaroo (it) *vb Australian*
to squat, particularly in order to defecate; from the kangaroo's habit of sitting back on its rear legs, supported by its tail

'*Not wanting to contract any trendy venereal fauna, I kangaroo-ed it.*'
(Kathy Lette, *Girls' Night Out*, 1989)

kangaroos in the top paddock *adj Australian*
crazy, eccentric or deranged. A picturesque coinage, probably based on the colloquial 'bats in the belfry'.

kaplonker *n British*
a crowbar, in the late 1980s jargon of the London Flying Squad. The word is probably in origin a nursery term for any unnamed heavy object.

'*Another funny moment came during a Sweeney raid. The cops use an iron bar nicknamed a "kaplonker" to lever open doors.*'
(*News of the World*, 5 February 1987)

kark *adj British*
suffering a 'hangover' after smoking marihuana. It is not clear whether the word as used by teenagers from the mid-1990s is related to the Australian **cark** recorded in the previous decade.

kark (it) *vb Australian*
an alternative spelling of **cark it**

karma *n*
1a. one's personal destiny, fate
1b. an aura, impression or influence, **vibes**.
See also **huntley**
Both senses of the word are inaccurate borrowings, dating from the **hippy** era, from Hindu and Buddhist writings in which the Sanskrit word denotes actions determining one's future state of incarnation.

karzi *n British*
an alternative spelling of **khazi**

Kate Moss *n British*
since around 2000 the name of the UK supermodel has been borrowed as a rhyme for 'toss' in the vulgar expression **give a toss**

kayf, kafe *n British*
an alternative rendering of **caff** (café), imitating the jocular or unwitting mispronunciation of the original French

kaylied *adj British*
an alternative spelling of **kalied**

kazi *n British*
an alternative spelling of **khazi**

kazoo *n American*
the backside, buttocks. A word of unknown origin (it is probably unconnected with the musical instrument, the name of which imitates its sound). Other jocular terms using the same median sounds include **mazoomas**, **gazungas**, etc. (all synonyms for female breasts).

k.b. *vb, n British*
(to receive) a rejection. An abbreviation of **knockback**, in use in the Liverpool area in 2003.
> I was k.b.'ed.
> She gave me the k.b.

k-cup *adj*
high on drugs or alcohol. The term is a brand name of a coffee container.
See also **lean**; **buzzin'**; **cart**

kecks *n pl British*
trousers. This word is the northern English version of the archaic 'kicks', heard in other parts of the country from the 17th century until the 1940s, but now obsolete. Liverpool **mods** of the mid-1960s used to refer contemptuously to 'half-mast kecks', that is unfashionably short trousers which flap around the lower calves or above the ankles. **Strides** was the slang synonym usually preferred further south. **Underkecks** are, of course, underpants, worn by either sex.

keek *n British*
an alternative form of **cack**

keen *adj*
excellent, great. A teenage vogue word in North America in the late 1950s and 1960s. The enthusiastic term now sounds dated but is still heard, usually said by ingenuous and ironic adults, although there are some signs of a revival among younger speakers both as a description and exclamation ('neato-keeno' was an elaborated version).

keeno, keener *n British*
a keen, enthusiastic person. A schoolchildren's word, usually said scathingly of a **swot** or excessively hearty fellow pupil.
> *'We just sat at the back and let the keenos volunteer.'*
> (Recorded, London schoolgirl, 1987)

keep cave *vb British*
to keep quiet, be wary and/or keep a look out. A schoolboy term of the 1950s from the Latin imperative *cave*: beware. In English the word is pronounced 'kay-vee'.
> *'They asked me to keep cave in case old Goatman came along.'*
> (Recorded, former grammar-school boy, 1986)

keep on trucking *vb*
to carry on, keep going. A black dancers' slogan used as a catchphrase exhortation by American and, later, British **hippies** from about 1970. 'Trucking' has various associated meanings including an exaggerated sauntering stride or simply 'soldiering on', all deriving from jitterbug dance contests of the 1930s and 1940s in which trucking was a dance step.

keester *n American*
an alternative spelling of **keister**

kegged *adj*
drunk. A fairly rare word used typically by college and high-school students in the USA and occasionally by their counterparts in Britain. The British usage may be a separate coinage, also from keg beer.

kegger *n*
1. *American* a beer party. An adolescents' term.
2. a snowboarder

kegs *n pl British*
a variant form of **kecks**

keister, keester *n American*
the backside, buttocks, anus. This fairly common term is from Yiddish *kiste*, in turn deriving from Middle and Old Germanic *Kista* and from the Latin *cista*, meaning a chest. The Yiddish word denoted a portable chest and was adapted by English speakers to mean anything used as a travelling container, including a hawker's display cabinet, a satchel and a trouser pocket. The transition from these senses to a part of the human body is not completely clear; it has been suggested that it became an underworld synonym for the anus as

used to smuggle contraband across borders or into prison. The term is now rather old-fashioned but was used by Ronald Reagan in the late 1980s.

Ken n American
a male dullard, a (clean-cut) bland conformist youth or man. Ken is the name given to the male counterpart of the **Barbie Doll**.

Kensington Gore n British
artificial blood. This expression, which is an elaboration of the literary 'gore', has been in theatrical slang since before World War II and is still heard. It is a pun on the name of the road connecting Kensington and Knightsbridge in London. **Ketchup** is a synonym.

kerflumix vb
an alternative spelling of **kerflummox**

kerflummox, kerflumix vb
to baffle, confuse, bamboozle. A humorous embellishment of the colloquial 'flummox'. Ker- is a prefix indicating force, effort or impulse, reminiscent of Anglo-Saxon and modern German ge-: 'made'.
    'After all their explanations I've got to say I'm totally kerflummoxed.'
    (Recorded, US diplomat's wife, London, 1988)

kermit n
1. British a French person. A jocular nickname used by students since the 1980s. It is inspired by the character 'Kermit the Frog' in the 1970s US television series The Muppet Show.
    'Don't forget to send invitations to the kermits.'
    (Recorded, London student, 1988)
2. **Kermit (the Frog)** an unattractive female. Rhyming slang for **dog**, in use among male adolescents since the late 1990s.
    'We were out on the cotton wool but all we saw were Kermit the Frogs everywhere.'
    (Recorded, agricultural college student, Devon, 1999)

ketch vb British
to criticise, harass. A term used by schoolchildren since the 1990s. The derivation is uncertain, but it may be a northern dialect version of catch.
    I just got ketched for swearing again.

ketchup n
artificial blood, as used in the theatre and broadcast media. **Kensington Gore** is a more colourful(!) synonym.

kettle n British
a watch. This old term, still used particularly among police and criminals, is said to be from the rhyming slang 'kettle and hob', meaning fob.

kettled adj British
drunk. An item of student slang in use in London and elsewhere since around 2000.

Kev n British
a foolish and/or unsophisticated young male. Kev was the name of a truculent uncouth teenager played by the TV comedian Harry Enfield.
    'Blacks and Kevs do cause more fights. U r ignorant for not looking at these stats.'
    (Recorded, contributor to www.wass-up.com, November 2003)

Kevin n British
a common, vulgar or boorish young man. This disparaging term from the 1970s and 1980s is typically used by snobs or wags to designate a working-class or lower-middle-class youth without taste or sophistication. The Christian name supposedly epitomises this social subgroup (the female equivalent of a Kevin is a **Sharon**). **Wayne** is sometimes suggested as an alternative for Kevin.
    That pub's full of Kevins, we never go in there.
Compare **Kev**; **Brian**

Kevinish adj British
common, uncouth and/or vacuous. From the noun form **Kevin**. A disparaging term used by middle-class speakers since the late 1970s.
    'Other schools just can't understand why they look so "Kevin-ish" – a term describing the white socks and footballers' haircuts (long at the back) which are so popular there.'
    (Tatler, March 1987)

kewl adj
a variant spelling and deliberately affected pronunciation of **cool** in its slang sense. In use around 2002, it can indicate irony or self-conscious enthusiasm.
Compare **rawk**

kewpie doll n
an excessively cute and/or overdressed or over made-up girl or woman. The original American Kewpie Doll (a trademark name based on Cupid) is a fairy-like baby. In Australia the name is used as rhyming slang for **moll** in the sense of a prostitute.

key¹ *n American*
a kilo of an illicit drug, typically marihuana, which could be bought by street
dealers in this quantity (in Britain the
standard quantity is the non-metric
weight)

> *He scored a couple of keys and brought
> it across the border.*

See also **church key**

key² *adj*
essential, emblematic or supreme. A
preppie term of approval or endorsement.

> *a pair of real key shoes*
> *Those shoes are key.*

khazi, kharzie *n British*
a toilet. A term dating from the 19th century which has been in widespread use in
working-class speech and in the armed
services. There are many alternative
spellings of this word, which is often
assumed to be of African or Far Eastern
colonial origin, perhaps by analogy with
khaki. In fact it derives from the Latin
word for house and its derivatives, such
as *casa* in Spanish and Italian or *case*
(meaning 'hut') in French. The word
entered working-class speech in **parlyaree**, the latinate jargon of tramps, peddlers and showpeople. Khazi was first
thought suitable for broadcasting in the
late 1960s and was popularised by such
TV comedies as *Till Death Us Do Part*
(written by Johnny Speight).

Khyber *n British*
the anus. From the rhyming slang 'Khyber Pass': **arse**. This London working-
class expression was used in TV comedies of the late 1960s, trading on the fact
that most viewers were only vaguely
aware of its vulgar provenance. The word
appeared in working-class speech after
the Khyber Pass was introduced into the
public perception by the Afghan wars of
the later 19th century.

> *a kick up the Khyber*

khyfer *n British*
an alternative spelling of **kife**

kibble *n American*
food, a meal. Kibble is a word of
unknown origin which literally means
coarse-ground dog food.

> *'OK I've got it, we'll chloroform her
> kibble!'*
> (*M*A*S*H*, US TV comedy, 1981)

kibitz, kibbitz *vb American*
to pass comment on or offer (normally
unwelcome) advice. The verb, which

typically applies to an annoying
onlooker at a card game or sports performance, comes from the Yiddish *kib-
itsen*, which in turn derives from
Kiebitz, the German name for a lap-
wing, a supposedly raucous, insistent
bird. The term is sometimes used to
mean simply spectate without the pejorative overtones.

kibosh *n British See* **put the kybosh/kibosh
on**

kick¹ *vb*
1. to give up (a habit). A piece of drug
addicts' jargon which entered general
currency in the 1950s.
2. *American* to be exciting, successful,
impressive. This is a shortened form of
kick ass in its secondary meaning of
'make a strong impression'.

> *That suit really kicks.*

kick² *n*
1. a sudden sensation of excitement, a
thrill. This Americanism spread to the
rest of the English-speaking world in the
1940s, helped by Cole Porter's song, 'I
get a kick out of you'. The plural form
kicks was a vogue term of the early
1960s.
2. *American* a particular activity or period
of involvement. In the language of **hipsters**, **beatniks**, etc.

> *She's on a health kick.*

kick (over) *vb British*
to subject to a police raid

> *'That information is six months out of
> date, any of these [crack dens] will have
> been kicked by the police.'*
> (*Evening Standard*, 15 September 2003)

kick ass *vb American*
1a. to punish or forcibly restore order,
make trouble or behave aggressively. An
expression used typically of an authority
figure such as an army officer or sports
coach. 'Kick ass and take names' is an
elaborated form of the expression (meaning identify and chastise).
1b. to express oneself or enjoy oneself
boisterously

> *That band really kick ass!*

kickass *adj American*
aggressive, rousing and forceful, tough.
A word usually indicating admiration or
approval (although sometimes grudgingly).

> *I think they kind of appreciate his kickass
> attitude.*

kick back vb American

to relax. A vogue term (sometimes occurring in the tautological phrase 'kick back and relax/chill out') from the lexicon of black street gangs, **rappers** and, subsequently, surfers, skaters, etc., and adopted by British adolescents in the mid-1990s. It may be based on the notion of a motorcyclist 'throttling back' or on the image of kicking away furniture in order to stretch out.

kickback n

money returned or paid as part of an illegal or covert agreement. This term, which is no longer slang, originated in the pre-World War II American underworld, in which to kick back meant to pay a fixed part of one's income, or a fixed commission, in return for favour or protection. (The original image evoked was probably that of kicking back a portion of booty across a floor.)

kicked adj British

ugly. One of a set of synonyms, including **booted** and **busted**, in vogue since 2000 and employing a damage metaphor. The term is also popular in Ireland.

kicker, the kicker n

1a. the 'final straw', clincher

1b. a hidden catch

2a. something exciting or stimulating

2b. a dynamic person

In the last two senses the word is probably a shortened form of the earlier term **shit-kicker** and was in vogue among UK adolescents in the later 1990s.

kickers n pl

shoes, boots. This slang term from the 1950s and 1960s (heard mainly in the USA) was appropriated by the French manufacturers of casual sports boots in the 1970s.

kick in vb

to contribute, subscribe or pay up. The phrase is more popular in the USA than in Britain. It is presumably based on the image of a circle of gang members each kicking a portion of their booty into a central pile. It usually has overtones of illegal, or at least unofficial, activity, such as bribery or a 'whip-round' to buy liquor.

　　If everyone kicks in we should be able to afford to give her a decent sendoff.

Compare **kick on**

kicking adj

excellent, exciting, powerful. A vogue term of approbation of the later 1990s, probably deriving from the phrase (it) **kicks the shit**.

　　'The band was kickin' and Christian was the hottest guy there.'
　　(*Clueless*, US film, 1995)

kicking it adj

enjoying oneself, celebrating or relaxing. A vogue term which, like the adjective **kicking**, is derived from the earlier American expression to **kick the shit**. The phrase was recorded in use among North London schoolboys in the 1990s.

kick it vb

to die. A shortened version of **kick the bucket**.

kick off vb

1. American to die. A later variation of **kick the bucket**, the equivalent of the British and Australian **kick it**.

2. American to leave, go away

3. British to lose one's temper, start to fight. First heard in the speech of the north of England, the phrase became popularised by TV soap operas and became generalised by the mid-1990s.

　　'I'd like to go and see my Dad but only when he retires, we'd just kick off at each other if I went back now.'
　　(Bez of rock group The Happy Mondays, quoted in the *News of the World*, 21 October 1990)

　　'Every time I try and make a go of something, you kick off.'
　　(*Brookside*, Channel 4 TV soap opera, December 1995)

kick on vb Australian

to continue (resolutely). The phrase almost invariably refers to drinkers finding a 'second wind' or a further source of finance for their current drinking session.

kick out the jams vb American

to 'let rip', get rid of all inhibitions and restrictions. A catchphrase in the rock-music world of the late 1960s, to which it was introduced by the rock group the MC5, who were allied to the anarchistic White Panther movement in Detroit. The phrase probably comes originally from an instruction to remove the chocks or wedges restraining a dragster car or aircraft.

kicks *n pl*
1. *British* trousers. An alternative and now archaic form of **kecks**, dating from the 18th century.
2a. *American* sports shoes. A rarer version of **kickers**, used particularly by school and college students.
2b. *American* shoes. The term is used in black street argot and campus slang.
3. thrills. The plural form of **kick**. A usage which became popular in the late 1950s and notorious for its adoption by juvenile delinquents and other nihilists to explain their motives.

'They killed for kicks.'
(Headline in *True Detective* magazine, 1963)

kicksies *n pl*
trousers. A diminutive form of **kicks**, heard since the 19th century, although now rare.

kick someone to the kerb *vb*
1a. to get rid of someone
1b. to beat someone up
Both uses of the phrase were fashionable among devotees of hip hop music around 2000 and were later adopted more widely.

kickstart *vb, n*
(to urge into) sudden action. A metaphor taken from motorcycling and applied to a variety of contexts in both literal and figurative senses.
The chick really had to kickstart the old goat.

kick the bucket *vb*
to die. The phrase dates from the 17th or 18th centuries and the bucket in question may be either a suicide's prop or, more probably, a British dialect word (also in the form 'bucker') for the beam from which slaughtered animals were hung.
'Ches hasn't been the same since his old lady kicked the bucket.'
(Recorded, barman, London, 1988)

kick the shit *vb American*
to succeed, perform powerfully and/or admirably. The image is one of dancing or performing some other frenzied activity in a rustic setting; the phrase itself may be a back-formation from the adjective **shit-kicking**.

kicky, kicksy *adj American*
exciting, stimulating, spirited. From the noun **kick** or **kicks** in the sense of excitement, the word has taken on an extra nuance of up-to-date or modish. (The comparative and superlative forms are *kickier* and *kickiest*.)
that kicky little red sportscar of yours

kiddy-fiddler *n British*
an unpleasant or unfortunate person. The term, literally denoting a child molester, has been adopted as an all-purpose insult in playground parlance since 2000. A synonym is **paedo**.

kidlet *n British*
a small child. A middle-class term employing the otherwise archaic diminutive suffix '-let' (also seen in **quidlet**).

kif, kief *n*
marihuana or hashish. The word, pronounced 'keef', is North African Arabic slang for the cannabis (usually in herbal form) smoked there. More specifically, kif may designate refined powdered hemp plants mixed with powdered tobacco or, as in the Berber stories of Mohammed Mrabet, may refer to uncleaned **grass**. The word's literal meaning is 'pleasure'. Many British drug users of the late 1950s and 1960s had their formative experiences of cannabis in Morocco.

kife, kifer, kyf, kyfer, kaifa, khyfer *n British*
1a. a woman or women as a sexual partner or sex object
1b. sexual activity (invariably heterosexual)
'Bangkok was OK – plenty of kifer.'
(Recorded, petroleum engineer, London, 1987)
This word in its various spellings is now rarely used. It was nearly always restricted to working-class, underworld or armed-services slang, with an area of meaning now more often catered for by words such as **crumpet**, **tottie** or **rumpo**. The exact etymology of the term is obscure; it may be a 19th-century alteration of an Arabic word *keyif*, meaning sensual consolation. As the definition implies, the word is used exclusively by men.

kifer, kyfer *vb British*
to have sex (with). A rare, and now virtually obsolete, derivation of the nouns **kife**, **kifer**, etc. (meaning women or sex). The word was used exclusively by men.

kike *n*
a Jew. An old-fashioned racist term which some authorities derive from diminutives of the name Isaac (see **ikey (mo)**). Others, including the Yiddish expert and humorist, Leo Rosten, ascribe it to the practice of illiterate Jewish immi-

grants signing their names with a circle (*kikel* in Yiddish) on arrival in the USA. The word was adopted by British and Australian speakers and is still occasionally heard.

> 'Take her, kike, she's all yours...a wop whore and a kike fag in a one-room office on the strip should go a long way together.'
> (*Platinum Logic*, Tony Parsons, 1981)

kiki *n, adj American*
1a. (a) bisexual
1b. (a male) homosexual
A fairly rare descriptive term of uncertain origin. It may be a corruption of an Hispanic word or of he/she.

killer, killer-diller *n, adj*
(something) superlative. Killer-diller was an Americanism of the 1940s which was briefly in vogue in Britain in the late 1950s among **teddy boys** and bohemians. Killer was a popular teenage term in the USA, particularly among black youth in the 1960s and 1970s, spreading to Britain and Australia in the 1980s with disco and hip hop music, break dancing, etc.

> That band's a killer.
> Man, that's a killer-diller car.

killfile *n*
a computer program that allows Internet users to discard unwanted messages and exclude unpopular communicators, in the patois of **cyberpunks** and **net-heads**

killing floor *n American*
a place where sexual intercourse takes place. A phrase which figured in the lyrics of many blues and rock songs until the 1970s. The expression may originally refer to an abattoir, in which case the transposition to a sexual context is evoking brutal carnality. Alternatively, the sexual usage may arise via a sense of a place where punishing work or effort takes place. The phrase was used as the title of a Howling Wolf record of the early 1960s.

kimshi, kim'chee *n American*
trouble, difficulties. The origin of the term is uncertain.

> 'You're in deep kimshi, buddy, better have it all in one sock for this one.'
> (*Under Siege*, US film, 1995)

kinetic *adj American*
lively, agitated, busy

> 'Sorry it took so long; it's been kind of kinetic around here.'

(*Hollywood Confidential*, US film, 1997)

king *adj*
superlative, brilliant

> That Usher film is king!

king hit *n Australian*
1a. a hit from behind, stab in the back
1b. a knockout blow

King Lear *n British*
cannabis. The term is rhyming slang for **gear**, and was in use among London students in 1996 and 1997.

kink *n*
1a. a sexual deviant
1b. a sexual perversion or perverse idiosyncrasy, an unhealthy trait
Kinky has been used since the 1920s for deviant, becoming a vogue word of the early 1960s. The noun form (borrowed as the name of the pop group, the Kinks) is a later adaptation, usually used to express mild disapproval. In colloquial speech the word has now acquired an innocent sense of a 'minor problem', flaw or irregularity.

kinky *adj*
perverted or perverse, unorthodox. In Britain in the early 1960s kinky became so widespread a vogue word that its meaning became diluted to denote merely fashionable or interesting. The term began in the 1920s or earlier as an underground euphemism for sexually deviant, and later became an ironic **gay** term of approbation. In spite of its suggestion of perversities such as fetishism, the word was inoffensive enough to be used in 'polite' company, hence its popularity in the first flush of sexual liberalism in the 1960s.

> 'He looks at me like that, at least he's not kinky. That's a relief. He's too fat to be kinky, too fat and forty guineas at least.'
> (*About Town* magazine, June 1962)
> 'Kinky? Kinky is British for weird, you know what I mean?'
> (*Harper*, US film, 1966)

kip¹ *n*
1a. a period of sleep

> I pulled into the lay-by for a quick kip in the back of the van.
> 'If I don't get my full eight hours' kip I'm ratty all day.'
> (Recorded, teacher, Bristol, 1989)

1b. a bed or place to sleep

> a kip for the night

The word *kippe* meant a brothel in 18th-century English, probably deriving from a similar Danish word signifying a low-class inn. In the 19th century the word was extended to denote a **doss house**, and by the early 20th century was acquiring its modern meanings. The word is not unknown in the USA but is much more commonly used in Britain.

kip², kip down vb
to (lie down to) sleep. The verb comes from the noun **kip**.

kipe, kype vb
to steal

Kipling adj British
a term of approval among schoolchildren since the late 1980s. The term is explained by the following elaborate pun:

'If training-shoes provoke an excited exclamation of "Hey, man, they're Kipling!" the wearer can rest assured that their street-credibility is intact. Slur "ruddy hard" into Rudyard, and there you have it.'
(Guardian, 26 September 1989)

kipper n British
the vagina. A vulgarism in use among adolescents in the 1990s and listed in Viz comic in 1994.

kippered adj British
devastated, trounced, **stitched up** or **gutted**. A working-class term which is currently in vogue among the fashionable young in London. The metaphor is 'dead, gutted, skinned and cooked', in the sense of thoroughly humiliated or taken advantage of, and is probably inspired by the earlier 'done up like a kipper'.

'I wouldn't advise you to try doing business with them. I tell you, I was kippered ...'
(Recorded, advertising executive, London, 1988)

kiss n See **French kiss**

kiss ass vb American
to abase oneself, flatter or curry favour. A contemptuous description of obsequious or toadying behaviour.

'You wouldn't like it [working in a large corporation]; the first thing you'd have to do is to learn to kiss ass.'
(Recorded, American female executive, London, 1984)

kiss-ass n American
a sycophantic person, a 'crawler'. This term of contempt can also be employed as an adjective, as in a 'kiss-ass speech', for instance.

kisser n
the mouth. A now rather dated word which probably originated among boxers and their entourages in the mid-19th century. Its meaning is occasionally extended to mean 'face', particularly as part of an expression such as 'a punch/smack in the kisser'.

Wipe that silly expression off your kisser.

kiss-off n
a dismissal. Originally an Americanism, the term has entered international English with the connotations of off-handedness, abrupt thoughtlessness or condescending rejection.

kiss the porcelain god vb
to vomit. A picturesque euphemism which is particularly popular among American college students; an alternative form is 'kneel to the porcelain god' or **drive the porcelain bus**. The image is one of bending over to kiss the feet of an idol. An attack of diarrhoea involves **riding the porcelain Honda**.

kiss up vb American
to behave as a sycophant (towards), 'crawl' to or flatter someone. A rarer version of **kiss ass** or the British suck up.

kissy, kissy-kissy adj
affectionate, sentimental. The words may be applied good-humouredly or pejoratively, suggesting cloying or exaggerated affection.

kit n British
clothes. A working-class expression, typically used by ex-servicemen, which enjoyed a vogue from the late 1980s among working-class speakers and their imitators. It is synonymous with **gear** or **clobber**.

'His idea of romantic chat was to say "get your kit off and come over here".'
(Recorded, female social worker, London, 1987)

kite vb
to pass a worthless cheque

'You wouldn't try to kite a cheque on me, would you?'
(Budgie, TV series, 1971)

kite man/dropper/flyer n
an issuer of worthless cheques. **Kite** has meant a dud cheque or other financial document for the past century. These terms, heard in all anglophone areas, usually refer to professional criminals who specialise in **kiting**.

kiting *n*
passing dud cheques. From the 1980s the term invariably described a deliberate criminal activity, although it could formerly also refer to issuing a cheque in the hope, possibly ill-founded, of finding the funds to support it. The word is part of international English.

kit-kat shuffle *n*
an act of female masturbation. The phrase was explained by the female standup comedian Jo Brand in her 1995 TV show. It occurs in the forms 'have a kit-kat shuffle' or 'do the kit-kat shuffle'.

kitty *n See* **dust kitty**

klangered *adj British*
drunk. An item of student slang in use in London and elsewhere since around 2000. It is probably an arbitrary coinage and unrelated to the Clangers, puppet characters in a children's tv series.

(Calvin) Klein *adj British*
fine. Rhyming slang in use since the later 1990s borrowing the name of the US fashion designer.
   I'm feeling just Calvin Klein.

kludge *n*
a cumbersome, overcomplicated system or situation. A piece of computer jargon, originating in the USA, blending 'clumsy' and 'sludge'.

klutz *n American*
a foolish, clumsy person. The word is from the Yiddish *klots* which literally means lump or block. (It comes from the German *Klotz* with the same meaning, which is related to the English 'clot' and 'clod'.) In the 1980s the word passed from being an Americanism into world English, particularly among adolescents.
   'As the incidents repeated themselves, Ms Reagan told her fellow workers and friends that she was a "klutz" who kept banging into doors and falling down stairs.'
   (*Guardian*, 4 April 1989)

klutzy *adj American*
foolish and/or clumsy. A back-formation from the more common noun **klutz**.

knack *vb British*
to destroy, damage, mess up. This back-formation from **knacker** is common in middle-class and armed-forces usage, often in the form **knack it**.

knacked *adj British*
a variant form of **knackered** in all its senses. The term is heard particularly in the Scottish Lowlands and the north of England.
   She's feeling knacked.
   The motor's totally knacked.

knacker *vb British*
to tire or exhaust. A back-formation from **knackered**.
   'I knacker myself at my job to keep her nice and warm in my house, with my kids and my dog.'
   (Divorced husband in cartoon by Posy Simmonds, *Guardian*, 1981)

knackered *adj British*
exhausted. This is not, strictly speaking, a slang word as it derives from 'knacker', denoting a worn-out horse or a slaughterer of horses, but has come to be seen as slang because of confusion with **knackers**, in the sense of testicles. The ultimate origin of the word is probably a dialect word meaning saddle-maker and based on a version of the word knock.
   'That washing machine's about knackered, gel, and we ain't even finished payin' for it yet!'
   (*Biff* cartoon, *Guardian*, 1986)

knackers *n pl British*
the testicles. Originally a dialect or rustic pronunciation of knockers (with the sense of 'clappers'), this is the form of the word which has predominated. In the 1950s and 1960s the word was often used in the form of an exclamation on the lines of the now more widespread **balls**, **bollocks** and **cobblers**, expressing defiance or contempt.
   'Your boyfriend burned his jacket
   his ticket expired
   his tyres are knackered
   his knackers are tired.'
   (*Pyscle sluts*, poem by John Cooper Clarke, 1978)

knee-jerk *n, adj*
(a person) displaying a reflex action, an unthinking, automatic reaction. This piece of American slang of the early 1970s has passed into general colloquial use since its adoption as part of disparaging descriptions such as 'knee-jerk liberal' or 'knee-jerk reactionary'. The expression of course derives from the doctors' testing of the patellar reflex, featured in cartoons and situation comedies since the mid-1950s.

knees-up n British

a boisterous party, celebration and/or sing-song. The popular cockney song 'Knees up, Mother Brown' probably produced the expression.

kneetrembler, knee-tremble n British

an act of sexual intercourse while standing up. A popular term in the 1960s, when furtive assignations outdoors were perforce more prevalent. The word was used in TV comedies such as *The Likely Lads*; it originated in the 19th century and is still heard.

> 'Lugged their possessions from one digs to another in a cardboard suitcase, and, by way of recreation, enjoyed a quick "knee-trembler" up against a tree in a twilit local park.'
> (*Sunday Times* book review, 18 March 1990)

knickers! exclamation British

a cry of dismissal, defiance or contempt. This primary and junior schoolchildren's rude word has been adopted for humorous use by adults since the early 1970s. Some authorities claim that it was originally a euphemism for the more offensive **knackers**, but this seems unlikely in that underwear in itself is a favourite subject of prurient interest in pre-pubescent children. (Knickers is in origin a shortening of 'knickerbockers', meaning baggy knee-length trousers as worn in 19th-century Holland.)

knob[1] vb British

to have sex (with). This is a variant of **nob**, and is said by users of the word to be the incorrect spelling, in spite of the derivation.

> 'If you were in with the Royal Family and you were a girl, you'd definitely want to knob Prince Andrew or someone.'
> (Boy George, *NME*, 4 June 1988)

knob[2] n

the penis. The word has been in use with this sense since the 19th century and was the most common vulgar synonym in Britain and Australia in the 1950s and 1960s, since when such words as **dick** and **prick** have increased in popularity.

knobbo n British

a fool, contemptible person. The expression, probably based on **knob-head**, was heard in the 1990s and quoted in the *NME*, a music paper.

knob-end n British

a stupid, unfortunate or unpleasant person. A fashionable term of adolescent abuse since the late 1980s. (There are no sexual connotations, in spite of the word's provenance.)

knob-head n British

a stupid and/or contemptible person. A common insult or term of disapproval recorded since the 1970s.

knob job n

an act of (male) masturbation or fellatio. A vulgarism in use since the 1960s, **knob** being one of the commonest terms for the penis in Britain and Australia. Although knob alone is rare in this sense in the USA, 'knob job' is commonly heard there.

knob-jockey n British

a male masturbator. The phrase itself is invariably used by male speakers.

knobrash n British

a foolish, irritating and/or unpleasant (male) individual

knob-rot adj See **nob-rot**

knock vb British

1. to kill. A recent, racier variant of **knock off** or **hit**.

> 'I've never spoken to anyone I'm going to knock.'
> (Hit-man quoted in the *Observer*, 31 May 1987)

2. to have sex (with). A 300-year-old usage which has been rare since the early 1960s. It now survives mainly in variations such as **knock off**, **knocked up** or **knocking shop**.

3. to criticise, disparage. The use of knock to mean deprecate is no longer, strictly speaking, slang; it has been employed in this sense since the 19th century.

4. to cheat. An item of underworld slang.

> They tried to convince her it was a fair deal, but she definitely got knocked.

5. to steal. The term is heard particularly in the Scottish Lowlands and the north of England.

> Willie and Andy knocked a couple of videos from out the flats.

knock, the n British

1. stolen goods, criminal booty. A police and underworld term derived from **knock off** in the sense of to steal.

2a. credit, hire purchase. This meaning is usually expressed by the phrase to buy something 'on the knock'.

2b. a loss or bad debt (a **knocker** is a debtor or **welcher**). The phrase usually forms part of a longer expression such as 'take the knock' or 'get the knock'. Knock here may originally refer to 'financial damage' or to the rapping of the table by a player who cannot take his or her turn in cards or dominoes.

3. the arrival of the police at one's home, or of a summons to appear in court. From the ominous knock at the door.

> *Charlie got the knock last night.*

See also **knocker**; **on the knock**

knock (someone) back *vb*
to rebuff, reject, disappoint

> *'Maybe you could give her some coaching?'*
> *'I offered: she knocked me back.'*
> (*Blackjack*, Australian tv crime drama, 2004)

knockback *n British*
1a. a rejection of an application for parole

> *Jacky's hopeful but if you ask me he's going to get a knockback.*

1b. a rejection of sexual advances

> *Don't worry about it Jane. I was expecting a knockback anyway.*

These terms are specific instances of the more general colloquial sense of knockback as any type of disappointment or rebuff.

knock boots *vb American*
to have sex (with). An expression (also rendered as **get boots**) which was popular among black street gangs from the early 1990s.

knocked *adj British*
rebuffed, rejected, disappointed. In this sense the term is a shortening of the colloquial 'knocked back'. It was in use among teenagers from the late 1990s. **Bumped** is a synonym.

knocked out *adj*
bowled over, very impressed. Now a fairly widespread colloquial expression, this was considered both an American-ism and slang until the late 1970s.
See also **knockout**

knocked up *adj, vb*
1. *American* (to be) made pregnant. Amateur lexicologists never tire of pointing out the possibility of confusion between the American sense and the innocently colloquial British sense of waken (someone) up.

> *'Garp? My daughter got knocked up by a goddam fish?'*

(*The World According to Garp*, US film, 1982)

2. *Australian* (to be) exhausted

knocker *n British*
1. a borrower of money, debtor, defaulter. The word is used to refer to personal debtors, those reneging on hire purchase agreements or, by prisoners in particular, to those who **welch** on a bet – a sense in which the word was used in sporting circles before World War II. The origin of this use of knock is not completely clear; it may simply have the sense of to damage (financially), come from an obsolete word meaning to borrow, or may refer to some more specific practice such as rapping on a table to indicate one's inability to continue in a card game.

2a. a door-to-door salesperson

2b. a door-to-door tout for an antiques dealer, hoping either to trick the gullible into parting with valuables or, occasionally, to identify items for later theft.
See also **on the knocker**

3. a breast. A rarely heard singular form of **knockers**.

knockers *n pl*
1. female breasts. A widespread usage which seems to have arisen as recently as the 1940s. It has been suggested, but not convincingly demonstrated, that the word comes from **norks** and was first coined in Australia, whence it spread to the USA and Britain.

2. the testicles. This usage is rare. **Knackers** is the usual term.

knockie(-knockie) *n British*
an act of sexual intercourse. A humorous euphemism heard since the early 1980s. It derives from the sexual connotations of the verb to **knock** and is probably also influenced by **nookie**. The expression is sometimes in the form 'play knockie(-knockie)'.

knocking shop *n British*
a brothel. A popular light-hearted term now used to refer to a seducer's lair or any scene of promiscuity, as well as to a genuine bordello. The euphemism was recorded with the latter meaning in the mid-19th century.

> *'Life here was hell with that girl. We thought she was running a knocking shop and it drove us all mad.'*

(Resident of block of flats, *News of the World*, 19 February 1989)

knock off *vb British*
1. to kill
2. to steal or rob

They knocked off a lorry load of antiques.
The boys tried to knock off a bank.

See also **knock over**

3. to have sex with, succeed in seducing. In American English to 'knock off a piece' is a depersonalising description of a sexual conquest.

'the 18-year-old he had been knocking off since she was 14'
(*Daily Mirror*, 11 May 1989)

All these uses of the phrase are variations of the underlying meaning of 'to account for' or 'accomplish hurriedly'.

knock one on *vb British*
to have sex (with). A vulgar euphemism reported as being in use in the London area in *City Limits* magazine in May 1992.

Compare **knock one out**

knock one out *vb British*
to masturbate. The term is used by and of males in the slang of prison or hospital inmates.

Compare **knock one on**

knock out *vb British*
to sell or distribute. In this sense the phrase probably originates in illegal auctions where the apportioning of the (usually stolen) goods was accompanied by the rap of a gavel. The term is now typically used by or of street traders.

We've been knocking out over a hundred of those every week.

knockout *adj*
wonderful, impressive, first-rate. Originally an Americanism, deriving from the noun form meaning something stunning, the word was introduced to Britain and Australia in the **hippy** era and by the mid-1970s sounded somewhat dated. It was often used in the form of an exclamation of (over)enthusiasm.

I met this knockout chick.

knock over *vb*
to rob. A racier euphemism than **knock off**, this American underworld expression was picked up by British speakers in the early 1980s.

Willis is suspected of knocking over a bank in Oregon.

knuckle¹ *vb*
to hit, beat someone up. A word used in Britain by street gangs and other 'toughs'.

He knuckled the geezer.

knuckle², knuckle-up *n British*
a brawl, fistfight

knucklehead *n*
an idiot. A variation of the older **bonehead**, the term originated as a folksy Americanism, entering world English in the 1950s.

'The most startling language occurs on a thing called "Bob George", which features a monologue from some knuckle-head having it out with his lady.'
(*Independent*, 26 February 1988)

knuckle sandwich *n*
a blow from a fist, punch in the mouth or face. A humorous phrase which is often used in unfunny situations in all English-speaking countries. The expression dates from before World War II when it probably originated in a euphemism such as 'feed someone a knuckle sandwich'.

kode *n*
the complex system of language and signals used by **gays** in order to secretly communicate with one another, particularly about their sexual proclivities or preferences. This includes the wearing of key rings, chains and specific colours of handkerchiefs in specific pockets, etc. The language is literally code in that it takes terms from standard English such as **straight**, **clone**, **boystown**, etc. and uses them ironically. The alternative spelling of code is an example of the use of K to render English words more Germanic or Slavonic and thus lend them totalitarian overtones, as in 'Amerika' or 'klan'.

kong *n American*
1a. strong alcoholic drink
1b. a strong narcotic
Both senses derive from the celebrated fictional giant gorilla 'King Kong' as a symbol of potency.

konk *n*
an alternative spelling of **conk** (in its sense of a hairstyle)

kook *n American*
an eccentric, quirky or crazy person. This word is an alteration of 'cuckoo' which has been popular in the USA since the 1950s. It has spread to Aus-

tralia but, although understood in Britain, is rarely used there.

kooky *adj American*
eccentric, quirky, crazy. This adjective probably postdates the noun **kook**.

kopacetic *adj American*
an alternative spelling of **copacetic**

kosher *adj*
correct, proper, above-board. This Yiddish term (usually referring to food prepared according to Talmudic law) is originally from the Hebrew *kasher*, meaning fitting or proper. The word was adopted in the late 19th century by non-Jewish speakers, particularly in the underworld, market trading or other raffish contexts. By the 1970s kosher was generally understood and used by speakers from a wide variety of backgrounds.

Don't worry, it's quite kosher.
Let's check out his so-called company and see if it's a kosher set-up.

kraut *n*
a German. The word, which originated in the USA, has supplanted 'hun' and, later, **Jerry** in British slang usage. It is a shortening of *sauerkraut*, a popular German food consisting of thin-cut cabbage pickled in brine.

kron(z) *n American*
an alternative spelling of **cron(z)**

ku *n*
inside knowledge, the latest news, 'score'. In Jamaican patois *ku* means 'look', while in Mandarin Chinese slang it is a rendering of the English **cool**.

They know the ku.

kugel *n South African*
a spoilt young female. The term, which is derived from Yiddish, has a male counterpart, which is **baigel**. Kugel has been defined by users of the word as 'a superficial and indulged young adult girl from a Jewish family'.

kuri, koorie *n*
1a. *New Zealand* a Maori
1b. *New Zealand* an unpleasant or unpopular person
1c. *Australian* an Aborigine
This racist epithet is the Maori word for mongrel.

kushti *adj British*
an alternative spelling of **cushdy**

kvetch[1] *vb*
to complain, whine, **whinge**. An Americanism that has been adopted by fashionable and literary sectors of British and Australian society. It is a Yiddish verb meaning to squeeze or press.

kvetch[2] *n*
a person who complains constantly, a whiner or **whinger**. The word comes via the USA from the Yiddish verb meaning to squeeze or press.

kweef *n American*
a vaginal **fart**

kybosh *n See* **put the kybosh/kibosh on**

kyf *n British*
an alternative spelling of **kife**

kyfer *vb British*
1. an alternative spelling of **kife**
2. an alternative spelling of **kifer**

L

L7 *n, adj American*
(a person who is) conformist, (a dull) reactionary. The term is a synonym for **square** and is based on the square made by the two symbols. It was adopted as the name of a **rriot-grrrl** band of the early 1990s.

labonza *n American*
1a. the belly or paunch
  a punch in the labonza
1b. the backside, buttocks
A word used particularly by pugilists, criminals and working-class speakers. It is mock-Italian or Spanish, probably based on *la pancia* or *la panza*, both related to the English 'paunch'. The second sense referring to the posterior is rarer.

lace curtain *n*
a foreskin. A term from the homosexual lexicon, punning on a symbol of coy respectability which pre-dates **gay** emancipation.

laced *adj*
1. *American* intoxicated by drugs or drink. The term usually refers to a mild intoxication by, e.g., marihuana.
  It's OK to get laced at a party but not to get fried all on your own.
2. physically attractive. An item of youth slang heard in the USA and UK since around 2000.

laced up *adj British*
1a. (of a person) fully occupied, obligated, embroiled
1b. (of a thing) completed, accomplished, 'in the bag'
Both senses are variant forms of standard metaphorical meanings of tied up.
1c. repressed, inhibited. In this sense the phrase is influenced by strait-laced.
  She's a bit laced up isn't she?
Compare **laced**

laddish *adj British*
boisterous, uncouth and **macho**. The word, which appeared in the late 1970s, refers to the typical behaviour of adolescent males in groups. It is inspired by 'male-bonding' expressions such as 'one of the lads' and the **Geordie** battle cry 'howay the lads!', but is more often used disparagingly or dismissively by women or more mature males. The term took on greater significance when it was applied to a social tendency among young adult males in the second half of the 1990s which involved celebrating, rather than disguising hedonistic excess, love of sport/cars/hardware, socialising in male groups, etc. The new 'laddishness' was celebrated in publications such as *Loaded* magazine and TV comedies such as *Men Behaving Badly*.

ladette *n British*
a female who behaves laddishly. The term became popular at the end of the 1990s and was the title of a reality TV 'makeover' series, *Ladette to Lady*, in 2005, in which ladettes were taught to be ladylike.

ladies who lunch *n pl*
self-indulgent and/or pampered females. The expression originated in the late 1980s as a New York characterisation of wealthy, leisured wives of rich (working) husbands. Since 2000 it has been generalised to refer jocularly to any females thought to be indulging themselves.

Lady (Godiva) *n British*
1a. a £5 note, a sum of £5. London rhyming slang for *fiver*. The phrase is still heard, although alternatives such as **deep sea diver** are now probably more popular.
Compare **commodore**
1b. £5 million, in the slang of city traders since the 1990s. In this sense the word is usually shortened to **Lady**.

ladybumps *n pl*
female breasts. A jocular euphemism heard since 2000.

Lady Muck n British
a woman thought to be 'putting on airs' or behaving high-handedly. The female equivalent of **Lord Muck**.

Who does she think she is, carrying on like Lady Muck?

laff n
a source or occasion of amusement. A jocular, ironic or journalese form of 'laugh'. When said by southern British speakers it is distinguished by a pronunciation rhyming with 'chaff'.

lag[1] n
1a. a convict or former convict or recidivist. In non-criminal circles the word is usually heard only in the phrase **old lag**.
1b. a term of imprisonment. At different times in different areas the term has denoted specific periods. **Lagging** is now the more usual form of the word.

lag[2], **lag up** vb British
1a. also **lag up** to send to prison
1b. to arrest
Both words, which are now rare, date from the beginning of the 19th century, when lag meant specifically 'to transport to a penal colony'. (An archaic meaning of the word was 'to carry away'.)

lag[3], **lag on** vb Australian
to inform (on someone), to tell tales. A prisoners' and schoolchildren's word, this was British slang of the 19th century with the meaning of 'betray to the authorities'. It has survived in Australia but has not been heard in the UK since the turn of the 20th century. Its frequent use in Australian TV soap operas during the 1990s may result in the reintroduction of the term.

'Don't worry – 'e won't go laggin' on us.'
(*Prisoner: Cell Block H*, Australian TV series, 1985)

lagged, laggered adj British
drunk. The words may have originated as a deformation of 'lager(ed)' or may be an invention like the synonymous **langered**.

lagging[1] n British
a period of imprisonment. The word has sometimes had the specific sense of a term of three years or more.

lagging[2] adj British
very attractive, gorgeous. An item of student slang in use in London and elsewhere since around 2000.

lah-di n British
a motor car. Rhyming slang from 'la-di-dah'. An alternative cockney term to **jam-jar**.

laid n See **lay**[2]

laid out adj American
1a. drunk. Another synonym for inebriated. Although the original metaphor is of someone knocked unconscious (or placed in a mortuary), the use of the phrase does not necessarily indicate intoxication to the point of stupefaction.
1b. under the influence of drugs. This sense of the term, deriving from the previous one, is most commonly used by teenagers.

lainie adj
an alternative form for **laney**

lair, lare n Australian
a layabout, flashy young tough. This modern usage postdates an earlier sense of the word denoting an over-dressed, showy or beautiful man. Since the 1940s the term has been identified specifically with delinquent or disreputable young males. It forms the basis of many combinations such as 'come the lair', 'lair it up' or 'ten-cent lair'. Lair is based on a variant form of older British words such as **leery**, **leary**, etc.

lairy adj
1a. flashy, showy, especially in an ostentatious, provocative or vulgar way. This term is especially popular in Australia but was also in use among British youth from the late 1980s.

'Wow, Ches's got a really lairy T-shirt.'
(Recorded, youth, Portobello Road, London, 1986)

1b. vain, presumptuous or boastful. This sense of the term was in use among working-class speakers, particularly **teddy boys**, in Britain in the 1950s and early 1960s.
Both sub-senses of the word come from the earlier **leary** or **leery**.

la-la n American
a ladies toilet. The term is used by female college students.

la-la-land n
a state of drugged or drunken euphoria. An expression usually used disparagingly by abstainers.

'Cameraman Gerry McGough, who snapped these shots, said "She was completely in la-la land".'

(Caption to pictures of drunken celebrity, *Daily Mirror*, 9 February 1989)

lallies *n pl British*
legs. A word used in theatrical circles and by dancers, art students, etc. in the 1960s. Lallies was given exposure in the radio comedy shows *Beyond our Ken* and *Round the Horne* in the exchanges between Kenneth Horne and the **camp** characters Julian and Sandy, played by Kenneth Williams and Hugh Paddick. The word, of unknown origin, is still in limited use.

lam *vb*
1. to run away or escape from prison. The verb form is probably a back-formation from the phrase 'on the lam', although 'lam' originates in the verb 'lambaste', meaning to hit or beat.
2. *Australian* to have sex with. Like many of its synonyms (**boff**, **biff**, **bonk**, etc.), the term uses the notion of striking in evoking sex from the male perspective. Lam in its earlier colloquial sense derives from the Old Norse *lemja*, meaning to thrash.

lamb chop *vb British*
to inject a drug (e.g. heroin). The phrase is rhyming slang for **pop**.

lame *adj*
1a. poor quality, disappointing, bad. The common colloquialism was adopted as an all-purpose teenage vogue word from the late 1980s.
1b. unfortunate, unfair
Based either on the colloquial sense of lame meaning poor (as in 'lame excuse'), or on the image of a lame person who is unable to keep pace, the term has been generalised and intensified in the fashionable speech of adolescents since the 1990s.

lame-arse *n, adj British*
(a person who is) unpleasant, unfair, obnoxious. A vogue term from the language of adolescents in the late 1990s, probably adopted from the following American usage.

lame-ass *n, adj American*
(a person who is) feeble, disappointing, unconvincing. An embellishment of the colloquial 'lame'.
    another lame-ass excuse

lamebrain *n, adj*
(a person who is) dim-witted. Lame has been used to mean feeble or weak in colloquial speech throughout the anglophone community. This compound form

was coined in the 1960s in the USA, whence it spread in the 1970s.
    '"English people don't expect high standards because they don't know how to go out and eat in restaurants", scolds Payton. "We're also lamebrains when it comes to going to the cinema".'
    (*Evening Standard* magazine, May 1989)

lamer *n*
an inadequate person. An item of Internet slang, used for instance by **hackers** since the 1990s.

lamp *vb*
1. to look (at), to eye. The term, currently in vogue among fashionable adolescents in Britain, comes from a now archaic three-hundred-year-old use of lamp as a slang synonym for an eye.
2. *British* to hit, beat up or attack. A now dated usage perhaps combining elements of 'lam', in the sense of beat, and lump. The word was frequently used with this meaning in the 1950s.
3. *Australian* to have sex with. A synonym of **lam**, **slam**.
4. to relax. A contemporary synonym of **chill**.

lancing *n British*
having sex. A synonym is **jousting**. An item of student slang in use in London and elsewhere since around 2000.

laney, lany, lani, lainie *adj*
inferior, worthless. These recent vogue terms are probably deformations of the obsolescent American slang 'lane', which signified unsophisticated, provincial or naïve, and which was said to derive from the notion of a rustic living on a country lane. Originating in American adolescent speech in the 1980s, these variants were adopted by young British speakers in the 1990s.

langered *adj British*
extremely drunk. A vogue term in the adolescent drinkers' lexicon since the mid-1990s.

lani *n South African*
a white person. Recorded as an item of Sowetan slang in the *Cape Sunday Times*, 29 January 1995.

lard *n American*
a police officer or the police. The usage is derived from the earlier **bacon** and **pig**.

lard-ass, lard-bucket *n American*
a fat person. The American equivalents of the British 'tub of lard'.

lard-head *n*
a stupid or slow-witted person. An expression used in Australia and the USA.

lardo *n*
a fat person. An innocuous variant of **lard-ass**.

'Apart from being a congenital lardo, [Clive] James has a further hurdle before he can reasonably take part in the pro-celeb car chase: he can't drive.'
(*Independent*, 23 December 1988)

lare *n Australian*
an alternative spelling of **lair**

large¹ *n British*
one thousand, a **grand**. A shortening of 'large one(s)', used typically by criminals, market traders, gamblers, etc.
I give him five large and asked him to get hold of some gear for me.

large² *adj British*
excellent, powerful, exciting. A vogue term of approbation among devotees of **rave**, techno and **indie** subcultures since the 1990s. This usage also occurs in North American adolescent speech.

large it *vb British*
to enjoy oneself, behave boisterously. Together with **large** and **give it large**, this was a vogue term among devotees of **rave** and **indie** culture in 1994, although it had been recorded in London usage in 1991 and may originally have been adopted from black American speech.

large portions *n British*
enjoyment. Recorded in the Midlands in 2005, usually in the phrase 'get large portions', this is an elaboration of the earlier slang sense of **large**.

larrikin *n Australian*
a ruffian, ne'er-do-well. The word has been in use in Australia since the mid-19th century and may be a native coinage or an imported British dialect term based on 'lark'. It is not usually strongly pejorative, having the sense of (fairly harmlessly) rowdy and cheeky.

larrup *vb*
to beat, spank, thrash. A word used by toughs in Australia but mainly by parents to children in Britain, where it now sounds rather dated. The term may be a blend of 'leather' and 'wallop' or may be an attempt to imitate the sound of blows landing.

Larry the loner *n British*
an outcast, misfit, lonely person. In playground usage since 2000. The term is a less common synonym of **Billy no-mates**.

larupped *adj British*
drunk. An item of student slang in use in London and elsewhere since around 2000.

lary *adj*
an alternative form of **lairy** or **leery**

lash¹ *n Australian*
1. a rampage, bout of wild behaviour
to go on a lash/have a bit of a lash
2. an attempt, try. A variant of 'bash' as in 'have a bash (at)'.

lash² *vb*
to have sex. A term used by young street-gang members in London since around 2000.

lashed, lash *adj British*
drunk. The terms, recorded in South Wales in 2000, probably postdate the phrase **on the lash**.

lash it *vb British*
to keep quiet, restrain oneself. The expression, from provincial rather than London speech, often occurs as an imperative.
Just lash it, will you!

later(s) *exclamation*
1. an all-purpose farewell. An abbreviation of the standard 'see you/catch you later', probably originating in US speech but heard among UK teenagers in the 1990s.
2. a threat to be carried out in future, as implied by statements such as 'I'll see you/deal with you/get you later'
These terms, from code employed among adolescent gang members, were adopted as fashionable expressions among adolescents in general from the mid-1990s.

lathered *adj British*
drunk. The word may suggest the image of beer froth or saliva on the face of the drinker or may, like many similar terms, be based on the notion of beating/punishment as conveyed by the colloquial sense of 'lather', meaning to thrash. An item of student slang in use in London and elsewhere since around 2000.

'...topics that might appear unrelated to those not pleasantly lathered at this comfortably indecent hour.'
(*Q* magazine, March 1997)

lattie *n British*
a flat, home. This item of **parlyaree** originated as 'lettie' (from the Italian *letto*), denoting a bed. Most recently it has occurred in **gay** and theatrical speech.

laughing boy *n British*
1a. a morose, grumbling, sullen or excessively serious-looking person. The phrase is used with heavy irony to deride or provoke someone thought to be unnecessarily grumpy, stern or self-pitying.

Why don't you go and ask laughing boy over there.

1b. someone who is smirking or offensively cheerful. A less common subsense of the term.

laughing gear *n British*
the mouth. A joky euphemism playing on the notion of body parts as equipment on the lines of **wedding tackle**. It probably dates from the 1970s.

'Get your laughing gear around this!'
(Dialogue in TV advertisement for Heineken beer, 1988)

laughing soup/water/juice *n*
alcohol. These are middle-class witticisms applied particularly to champagne or gin. Laughing water also recalls the Indian princess in Longfellow's long narrative poem *Hiawatha*. Similar terms still in use are **giggle water**, **electric soup** or **lunatic soup**.

launch lunch *vb American*
to vomit

'He looked like he was into it, but she looked like she was going to launch lunch over Mr Jurgen.'
(*Things To Do In Denver When You're Dead*, US film, 1996)

lavender *adj*
(of a male) homosexual, **gay**. A facetious term appropriated from the vocabulary of heterosexual mockers for use by the gay community itself; the colour and scent of lavender being thought of as quintessentially feminine and old-maidish respectively.

lay[1] *n*
1a. a person viewed or evaluated as a sexual partner
1b. an act of sexual intercourse

He's not interested in her, he's just looking for a lay.

These uses of the word spread to British English from the USA with the verb form during the 1950s and 1960s, becoming established by the early 1970s. In the first

sense the word is nearly always used in combinations such as 'a good lay' or 'an easy lay'.

lay[2] *vb*
to have sex (with). The verb was absorbed into British English gradually during the 1950s and 1960s from the USA, where it had been current since the turn of the 20th century. The term implies sex from the male viewpoint but during the **hippy** era began to be used by women. The word is a development of the literal sense of to lay someone down and of the euphemistic 'lie with', meaning to copulate with, well known from its use in the King James translation of the Bible.

'One time I thought she was trying to make me come lay her – flirting to herself at the sink – lay back on huge bed that filled most of the room, dress up round her hips.'
(*Kaddish*, poem by Allen Ginsberg, 1958)

lay an egg *vb*
1. *American* to fail, to be responsible for a dismal or disappointing performance. This expression comes from the Victorian British saying 'lay a duck's egg', meaning to score zero (now extinct in British speech).
2. *Australian* to behave in an agitated, over-excited way. One of many farmyard metaphors in Australian use.

lay down *vb See* **lie down**

lay (someone) down *vb American*
to kill. A euphemism used among black street gangs in the late 1980s.

laylay *adj Caribbean*
long

lay (something) on (someone) *vb*
to inflict or impose on. This is one of many expressions, originating in black speech, which were disseminated during the **hippy** era, often in the form e.g. 'lay a (heavy) trip on'.

lay one on someone *vb*
to hit, punch someone. A euphemistic expression on the same lines as 'stick one on', **put/hang one on someone**.

If that joker doesn't stop mouthing off I'm going to be forced to lay one on him.

lay rubber *vb American*
to drive very fast, especially from a standing start, in a car or on a motorcycle. The phrase is inspired by the shedding of tyre rubber when spinning the wheels at

speed, a technique used in **drag** racing to ensure good road adhesion at the beginning of a race.

lay some on *vb British*
to acquire illicit drugs. The term usually applies to **scoring** for personal use and was in currency among aficionados of dancefloor culture in the 1990s.

lay the smack-down (on someone) *vb American*
to defeat, beat. The term has been part of the lexicon of street gangs and **rap** aficionados since 2000.

Lazy Y *n See* **lunching at the Lazy Y**

leaf *n*
marihuana. A predictable nickname for herbal cannabis.
We blew some leaf and mellowed out.

leak *n*
an act of urination. Usually in the expressions 'have a leak' or 'take a leak'. The origin of this predictable usage may be nautical.

lean *adj British*
under the influence of illicit drugs. The usage, which appeared in the late 1990s, is possibly related to the American **laney**.
'Nowadays lean in youth parlance has less to do with slim and healthy than spaced and out. It is the consequence of indulging in untold quantities of unspecified substances.'
(*Sunday Telegraph* magazine, 15 December 1996)
See also **blazed 1a**; **mash¹ 2b**

leary *adj*
an alternative spelling of **leery** or **lairy**

least, the *n, adj American*
(something) very bad, disappointing, of the worst quality. This term, which is popular especially with teenagers, was probably coined in the 1970s as a humorous complement to the older **hip** expression **the most** (meaning superlative). 'The very least' is a stronger term.
Boy, that movie was the least.

leather *n British*
1. a middle-aged male jet-setter, an ageing sun-tanned playboy. This term was coined by the upper-class young and their imitators in the late 1970s to refer disparagingly to the more prominent members of the international **white trash** frequenting ski resorts, yacht basins, etc. The word could occasionally be extended to apply to women too. Leather refers to

the skin texture of the subgroup in question (perhaps compounded by their characteristic wearing of expensive leather clothes in the period in question).
2. a wallet or purse. A long established item from the underworld lexicon.

leatherboy *n*
1a. a motorcycle enthusiast, **rocker** or **biker**. A word popular with parents and journalists in the early 1960s.
'The mean and moody leatherboy on a thundering bike is the strongest image of pop culture.'
(Johnny Stuart, *Rockers*, 1987)
1b. a young male homosexual, male prostitute or androgynous youth wearing leather
'A faggy little leatherboy with a smaller piece of stick.'
(Lyrics to 'Memo from Turner', by Mick Jagger, 1969)

leathered *adj British*
drunk. An item of student slang in use in London and elsewhere since around 2000.

lech, letch *n British*
1a. a carnal desire, brief sexual infatuation. This word, often used by women, was particularly popular in the 1960s and early 1970s in upper- or middle-class speech. It was often (and sometimes is still) used in the form 'letch, letch!' as a jocular or coyly prurient exclamation (although this more probably refers to the verb form to **lech after** or **lech for**).
'Leched over by managers, stitched up by agents, girls in the music biz have traditionally paid a high price for succumbing to the lure of lurex.'
(*Ms London* magazine, 4 September 1989)
1b. a lecherous person, usually male. A word expressing attitudes ranging from light mockery to angry rejection.
He's nothing but a boring old lech.

lech/letch after/for/over/on *vb British*
to nurse or exhibit a carnal desire for, to behave lecherously towards (someone). A back-formation from the adjective 'lecherous'.
He's always letching after young girls.

ledge *n British*
a person of note and/or outstanding qualities. The abbreviation of 'legend' is used ironically and scathingly about a conceited person, usually male.
'He thinks he's a bit of a ledge.'

(Recorded, secondary school pupil, London, October 2004)

leech off (someone) *vb*
to behave as a parasite. An extension of the colloquial use of the noun form.

leery, leary *adj*
1a. wary, suspicious, shy, cautious. This sense of the word is standard in all English-speaking areas.
1b. *British* alert, clever, cheeky. This sense of leery is related to **lairy**, meaning both flashy and conceited.
1c. *British* bad-tempered, sour
1d. *British* untrustworthy, devious, cunning

These nuances of meaning within the same term are difficult to disentangle, given that modern usage is probably derived from two originally separate words: the archaic *leer*, from an Anglo-Saxon word meaning 'face' or 'cheek', and the obsolete dialect term *lere*, related to 'learn' and 'lore' and similar in meaning to 'know-how'.

left field *n, adj*
(something) unorthodox, bizarre, unexpected. An American usage which was picked up by British journalists, musicians, etc. in the mid-1970s. The term arises from an earlier colloquial expression 'out of left field', used to describe something startling or totally unexpected coming from an improbable source. The field in question is the baseball field and the left field, the area to the batter's left and beyond third base, is an area of the park which sees little action and from which the ball rarely arrives. The same thing can be said of the right field, however, and the choice of left field perhaps has something to do with the overtones of unorthodoxy and radicalism inherent in 'left' in its political context, or simply by analogy with left-handed.

left-footer *n*
1. a Catholic
2. a homosexual

Both uses of the term have been heard since the 1960s and are derived from the notion of abnormality associated with left-handed/footedness.

leg-biter *n*
a small child, a toddler or baby. A less common alternative to **ankle-biter**, heard since the 1980s.

legged over *adj British*
a phrase from the jargon of City of London financial traders which is a euphemism for **shagged** or **fucked** in the sense of having lost money (and perhaps been humiliated) in a failed transaction. It is based on the verb to **get one's leg over**.

leg it *vb British*
to run away, escape or leave. A working-class expression, formerly popular with police and criminals, which became fashionable in middle-class circles in the later 1980s in keeping with a tendency among **yuppies**, students and those in the media, among others, to affect cockney styles of speech.

'His pals sprang him by blowing a hole in the wall. He then legged it to Amsterdam, where he changed his name.'
(Charles Catchpole, *News of the World*, 5 February 1989)

legless *adj*
drunk. The word originally denoted someone who was helplessly or falling-down drunk; nowadays 'getting legless' can simply mean getting drunk. It has moved from being a raffish slang term to a common colloquialism over the last 25 years.

'Same old story really: by 7pm she was wide-eyed and legless.'
(Recorded, Financial Secretary, London, May 2005)

legover *n British*
an act of sexual intercourse (usually from a male perspective). The term originates in the expression **get one's leg over**, one of many 18th- and 19th-century phrases in which leg is meant both literally and as a euphemism for the parts of the lower body ('leg-business' is one archaic example). From the 1980s the satirical magazine *Private Eye* has regularly referred to a 'legover situation', a supposed middle-class code for copulation.

lem, lemmo *n*
a variant form of **lemon 2b**

lemon *n*
1. something substandard, useless or worthless. The word is used, particularly in the USA, to apply particularly to cars which are unsaleable. It may also denote any 'dud', from an unattractive woman to a badly-performing share in the stock exchange. This negative sense of the name of a fairly popular fruit derives from the unavoidably sour taste.

2a. a fool, embarrassed or discomfited person. To 'feel a lemon' is to be put in an uncomfortable or humiliating situation.

2b. also **lem**, **lemmo** an outcast, misfit, lonely person. In playground usage, from the earlier colloquial sense of an unfortunate person.

3. the penis. In black American slang the word has been used in this sense which, although no longer common, is immortalized in the lyrics of many blues songs.

Squeeze my lemon, baby / 'till the juice runs down my leg.

4. *American* a Quaalude tablet, **'lude** (a hypnotic tranquillising drug, the equivalent of the British Mandrax or **mandie**)

5. a lesbian

6. *See* **lemons**

lemons *n pl*
female breasts. Another image of fruitfulness and rotundity on the lines of **melons**, **cantaloupes**, **apples**, etc. The term is probably most widespread in Australian speech.

lemon-squeezer *n British*
a man. This phrase, rhyming slang for **geezer**, occurs in anthologies of such expressions but is rarely actually heard in everyday speech. **Ice cream** is a synonym.

lend *n Australian See* **have a lend (of someone)**

length *n British*
1. a six-month prison sentence
2. the penis. The word is almost invariably used in the phrase **slip someone a length**.

lergi, lerghi *n British*
an unspecified disease, a mysterious infection or illness. An invented word (the 'g' is hard) in imitation of exotic or tropical complaints, much used by schoolchildren in the 1950s and still heard today, often in the phrase 'the dreaded lergi'.

'Hilary was supposed to come but she's gone down with the lergi.'
(Recorded, housewife, London suburbs, 1986)

les, lez, lezz, lezzie, lesbo *n*
a lesbian. Shortened forms of the word in use throughout the English-speaking community.

lesbian *n British*
a fruit-based alcoholic drink, such as a Bacardi Breezer or alcopop. The term has been in use since around 2000

among students and clubbers, presumably playing on the ideas of (alcoholic) strength and ideas and tastes associated with females.

Lester *n American*
a supposed molester of females. An expression used on campus in the USA since around 2000.

letch *n, vb British*
an alternative spelling of **lech**

let it all hang out *vb, exclamation*
to express oneself or otherwise behave without inhibitions, act without restraint. This euphemism became a catchphrase of the late 1960s counterculture, spreading with it from the USA to other English-speaking areas.

let off, let one off *vb British*
to **fart**. The first variant is a common schoolchildren's term, the other forms tend to be used by adults. **Blow off** is one synonym among many.

let one go *vb British*
1a. to fire a shot from a gun. An East End gangland euphemism from the 1960s quoted by Albert Donaghue, a former Kray brothers' associate in an ITV interview, March 1994.
1b. to **fart**

lettuce *n*
1. money. Another term like **long green**, **cabbage**, etc. that makes the connection between green banknotes and succulent vegetation. The word was probably first heard in raffish use in the USA, where banknotes of all denominations are, and were, predominantly green.
2. the female genitals, from the supposed resemblance

lez, lezz, lezzie, lezzo *n*
an alternative spelling of **les**

lick[1]
1. *vb American* to smoke **crack** by sucking the smoke from a burning pellet of the drug through a glass pipe or tube. The term is from the users' own jargon.
2. *vb* to beat up. Probably a back-formation from the earlier colloquial noun form '(to give someone) a licking'.
3. *n* **the lick** a superlative person, thing or situation. This term, meaning 'the (very) best', probably originated in black American speech but by the mid-1990s was in use among adolescents in Britain, too. It may be related to **lickin' stick**.

lick[2] *n American*
an illicit drug, particularly cocaine

licker n British

a **swot**, sycophant. This abbreviated form of **arse-licker** is in use among schoolchildren together with its synonym, **boff**.

'"Licker", says Jonathon Angel, 13. "That's what you get called if you have your hand up all the time; licker or swot".'
(*Independent*, 17 October 1996)

lickin' stick n American

a sweetheart, favourite friend. This item of black slang (the item referred to is a licorice-stick or popsicle) was used by the feminist writer Mtozke Shange.

lick it vb British

to steal. A term used by young street-gang members in London since around 2000.

licks n pl

plangent sequences of notes played on the electric guitar, short improvised musical solos. The term was adopted by rock guitarists from earlier jazz musicians who had adapted the colloquial 'lick', meaning both a stroke or hit and an attempt. The word is part of the terminology which includes **chops** and **riff**.

'Jimi [Hendrix] has got some licks that none of us can match.'
(Eric Clapton, speaking in 1970)

lid n

1. *American* a measure of marihuana (about one ounce), so called because it is approximately the amount which can be held on the lid of a beer can or tobacco tin

2. a military or motorcyclist's helmet

liddy adj American

crazy, eccentric. A term deriving from the expression 'to flip one's lid'. **Wiggy** is a word of similar provenance.

lie, lye n British

marihuana. Lye is a strong alkaline liquid, but the association if any with this cannabis-smoker's term is unclear.

lie down, lay down vb

to surrender, abase oneself. A fashionable euphemism in the late 1980s, particularly in the contexts of business and politics. It normally had the sense of giving up without a struggle in an adversarial situation. **Sit down** and **bend over** are used similarly.

I'm damned if I'm going to lie down for them.

Liffey water n Irish and British

Guinness. The Liffey is the river flowing through Dublin, where Guinness is brewed, and Liffey water is an archaic rhyming-term for porter, of which Guinness is an example.

lift vb

1. to arrest or capture, in police jargon and a sanitised euphemism of Vietnam-era military parlance

2. to steal. Lift has been used euphemistically in this sense since the 16th century.

3. to drink (alcohol). A beer-drinkers' euphemism inspired by the raising of glasses; **hoist** is an American synonym.

What say we go and lift a few?

lifted adj British

intoxicated by drugs or alcohol, **high**. A term used by young street-gang members in London since around 2000.

lift-off n American

an erection

'She doesn't give you a boner? – because I definitely have lift-off.'
(*Disclosure*, US film, 1995)

lig[1] vb British

to freeload, enjoy oneself at someone else's expense. The word, coined in Britain in the early 1970s, refers to the activities of hangers-on, **groupies**, music journalists, etc., who attend receptions, parties, concerts, and other functions, usually financed by record companies. The origin of the word is obscure, it has been suggested that it is made up of the initials of 'least important guest' or is a blend of 'linger' and **gig**. Alternatively it may be an obscure vagrants' term from a dialect survival of the Anglo-Saxon *liegan*, meaning 'to lie'.

lig[2] n British

an opportunity for freeloading, a party, reception or other occasion when it is possible to enjoy oneself at someone else's expense. The word refers to the rock and pop-music world, and probably postdates the verb form **lig** and the noun **ligger**.

ligger n British

a freeloader, hanger-on or gatecrasher at concerts, receptions, parties, etc., in the rock and pop-music milieus. The word is part of rock music's jargon and was adopted enthusiastically by journalists in such publications as *New Musical Express* in the 1970s to describe those enjoying themselves at the expense of record companies.

'Julia Riddiough, 27 "going on 180", is a world-class ligger who could club for Britain.'
(*Observer*, Section 5 magazine, 7 May 1989)

liggeratti *n British*
a journalese blend of **ligger** and 'glitteratti'

'"The club animals" own Johnny Morris, Caris Davis, who wrote about clubland's scenestealers, wimp-bods and ligeratti in his novel, "Stealth".'
(*Observer*, Section 5 magazine, 7 May 1989)

Compare **digerati**

lighten up *vb*
to relax or take things less seriously, calm down and/or cheer up. This expression moved from US parlance into the rest of the English-speaking world in the early 1980s.

'Lighten up will ya – do you have to take the fun out of everything?'
(*Cheers*, US TV comedy series, 1985)

lightning *n American*
1. another name for the drug **crack**
2. *See* **white lightning**

lightweight *adj British*
insufficiently daring, outrageous, excessive. In the fashionable adolescent vocabulary of the late 1990s this was the opposite of **hardcore**.

like a big dog *adj, adv American*
extremely, excessively. The phrase, heard on campus since the 1990s, is a euphemism for **like a bitch**.

'He's been prepping for these tests like a big dog.'
(Recorded, US student, London, April 2005)

like a bitch *adj, adv*
extremely, excessively. The term is in use in the USA and the UK.

Man, I was sweating like a bitch.

likely lad *n British*
an alert, smart and/or cheeky youth. A colloquial working-class phrase used particularly in the north of England to describe a young man who shows promise or self-confidence. The expression was adopted as the title of a popular Newcastle-based TV comedy series in the 1960s.

like the pies *vb British*
to be greedy and/or obese. A humorous euphemism favoured by students among others since 2000.

That Monica Lewinsky likes the pies these days, doesn't she?

lilac *adj*
(of a male) homosexual or effeminate. A rarer synonym for **lavender**.

Lillian Gish *n British*
(a) *fish*. This old item of cockney slang, borrowing the name of the silent film star and used, e.g., by the Great Train Robber, Ronnie Biggs, in an interview, was still heard in the late 1990s.

lils *n pl British*
female breasts. A vulgar schoolchildren's word of the 1950s and 1960s, which may be a shortening of an earlier term, 'lily-whites', or an invention, possibly influenced by 'loll' and 'spill'. The term was still in use in 2004.

lime *n*
a casual gathering of friends and family. A Caribbean usage later adopted by black speakers in the USA. The term is probably a back-formation from the noun **limer** and verb lime.

This lime has no juice! [This gathering is dull.]

limer *n Caribbean*
a hanger-on. A back-formed verb, 'to lime', is also heard. Both are inspired by the adhesive qualities of birdlime or quicklime. The word was adopted by some white speakers in London from the later 1980s.

limey *n, adj*
(an) English (person). The word, used mostly in North America, is a shortening of 'lime-juicer', a usually pejorative term applied originally to British sailors who were issued with rations of lime juice as a protection against scurvy. The word limey is now rather dated; 'Brit' is increasingly taking its place.

limo *n*
a limousine, luxury car. An American abbreviation, employed by chauffeurs, then showbiz journalists among others, in the early 1970s and now widely used.

limp-dick *n, adj*
(someone who is) weak, ineffectual, irresolute. The metaphor is one of impotence, but the term is invariably used to express generalised rather than sexual

contempt. The phrase probably originated in the USA as a harsher version of 'limp-wristed'.

line *n*
a portion of cocaine, amphetamine or other drug ready for **snorting**. The powdered crystals of the drug are scraped into a strip (quite literally 'a line of coke/speed'), typically on a mirror, tile or similar surface, so that they can be sniffed through a straw, rolled banknote, or any other improvised tube.

> 'We had dinner at 192 and then I went back to Sophie's place to do a few lines.'
> (Recorded, record company executive, London, 1983)

line (up/out) *vb*
to sniff **lines** of cocaine or amphetamine. A drug users' euphemism of the 1980s.

linen *n British*
a newspaper. This old item of London rhyming slang (from 'linen draper', meaning *paper*) was still in use in the 1990s.

> '… although she does not know much about rhyming slang, it is good to see that she reads a good "linen" on Sunday.'
> (Reader's letter to the *Sunday Times*, 13 September 1992)

lingo *n*
a language, jargon or way of speaking. The word, which often indicates puzzlement, amusement or xenophobia on the part of the speaker, obviously derives ultimately from the Latin word *lingua*, meaning tongue and language. The question as to which romance language inspired the modern slang word is difficult to resolve; it may be a corruption of the Latin word itself, or of Italian, Spanish (*lengua*), or Portuguese (*lingoa*). Provençal is the only modern language in which the correct form of the word is *lingo*.

> 'Oxford University aristocrats disguise themselves with lingo like: "It's wicked, guy".'
> (*Evening Standard*, 16 June 1988)

lint-brain, lint-head *n American*
a dim-witted or foolish person. This adolescent term of abuse draws on the American use of lint to denote fluff, particularly that lodged in the navel.

Lionel Blairs, Lionels *n pl British*
flared trousers. This item of rhyming slang, using the name of a celebrity dancer, replaced the earlier **Grosvenor**

Squares, and was itself supplanted by **Tony Blairs** in the late 1990s.

lip¹ *n*
cheek, back-chat. The expression dates to at least 1818 and is typically used by authority figures to characterise the utterances of unruly subordinates. It is a common usage in Britain and Australia, but less so in the USA.

> 'Lesson number one: learn to give less lip and do more work.'
> (*Neighbours*, Australian TV soap opera, 1987)

lip² *vb*
1. to cheek, speak insolently (to)
2. to play a wind instrument, blow. A jazz musicians' term.

> *cool lipping*
> *Lip that thing.*

lippy *adj*
cheeky, insolent. This usage comes from the noun form **lip**, which was first recorded in 1818.

> *He's a bit too lippy for his own good.*

lip service *n*
fellatio. A humorous euphemism from the professional jargon of prostitution and pornography (punning on the standard idiom 'to pay lip service to').

lipsin' *n*
1. kissing. Originating in Afro-Caribbean usage, the term has been adopted by slang speakers of other ethnic origins in the UK since 2000.
2. *British* insulting, quarrelling. Used transitively or intransitively, the word was popular among London adolescents in 2004.

lipstick *n American*
a lesbian interested in high-fashion, a 'feminine' lesbian. A Yale University term of the 1970s. Lipsticks are contrasted in this setting with the more aggressive or 'masculine' **crunchies**. The word lipstick has subsequently entered the **gay** female lexicon.

liquid cosh *n British*
a heavy tranquilliser or sedative. In the jargon of prison inmates the phrase has been used to describe substances such as Largactil, Paraldehyde, etc.

liquid laugh *n*
a bout of vomiting. The term probably originated in Australia. It is now heard in Britain (where it was part of the vocabulary of the influential late 1960s cartoon character Barry McKenzie, the

Australian boor and ingénu) and, especially on campus, in the USA.

liquid lunch n
a lunchtime session of alcoholic drinking (usually as an alternative, rather than an accompaniment, to eating)

liquored up/out adj American
drunk. The same phrase was in use in Britain in the 19th century.

listerine n British
a person holding anti-American views. The term surfaced in 2004 in connection with the US invasion of Iraq. Listerine is the brand name of an antiseptic mouthwash; **septic** (tank) is rhyming slang for **Yank**.

little boy's room, the little boys' room n
a gentlemen's toilet. Originally a coy euphemism, used by some Americans in all seriousness, this expression has come to be used facetiously all over the English-speaking world.

> 'I'm not just some kind of machine you can turn on. I need a cup of joe, a trip to the little boys' room, a glance at the sports' pages. Then we'll talk.'

(*Moonlighting*, American TV series, 1989)

little girl's room, the little girls' room n
a ladies' toilet. A coy euphemism now almost always used humorously, but originally (in the USA in the late 1940s) used to spare the blushes of the speaker and audience.

little jobs n British
an act of urination, as opposed to **big jobs** (defecation), in the now rather dated euphemistic language of the middle-class nursery.

little man/boy in the boat n
the clitoris. So-called because of a supposed resemblance, though it is unclear why the pilot of this particular craft is invariably male. In the 19th century the same phrase referred to the navel.

little number n See **number**

lit up, lit adj
1a. drunk. Originally an American expression, this phrase derives from the visible effects of alcohol (a 'glow', red nose, etc.) as well as the sensation of heat and the notion of alcohol as firewater or fuel. Embellishments of this usage are 'lit up like a Christmas tree' and 'lit up like a dime-store window'. The shorter form, lit, often signifies tipsy or merry rather than thoroughly inebriated.

> 'As a whiskey salesman … I'm often lit up by elevenses, loop-legged by luncheon and totally schnockered by 6.'

(Cartoon by Posy Simmonds, *Guardian*, 1979)

1b. American under the influence of marihuana, **high**

live adj British
excellent, exciting. A vogue term since 2000, probably from the notion of the superiority of live music or from the urgency of live broadcasts.

live at one's aunt's vb Caribbean
to live in dire circumstances

livener n British
a strong alcoholic drink

live phat adj
excellent, exciting, very attractive. An elaborated form of **live** in its slang sense, heard since 2000.

living, the n British
a superlative thing, person or situation. A vogue term from the vocabulary of adolescents in the later 1990s, it is probably a shortening of 'the living end'.

lizards n pl
snakeskin, crocodile-skin or iguana-hide footwear. Part of the sartorial repertoire of many social subgroups including cowboys, pimps, street gangs, etc., lizards are also known as **reptiles**.

load[1] vb Australian
to plant (someone) with illicit drugs or stolen goods, or to **frame** by manufacturing evidence. A term from the Australian criminal milieu which was first recorded in the 1930s and is still in use. The noun form is occasionally used to mean either an act of framing or the supposed evidence used.

load[2] n
nonsense, something worthless or unpleasant. In this sense the word is a shortening of the colloquial vulgarism 'a load of **shit**'.

> '… academic electronic music – what a load!'

(*Vivisect*, Australian fanzine, July 1994)

loaded adj
1a. drunk. An Americanism in use since the turn of the 20th century, now heard elsewhere in the English-speaking world. The original metaphor may refer to a burden or a large quantity being imbibed or, more dramatically, to the person being charged like a firearm.

'Dropped into a tavern/ Saw some friends of mine./ Party was gettin' under way/ And the juice was really flyin' and I got loaded.'

('I Got Loaded', song recorded by Peppermint Harris, 1957)

1b. intoxicated by illicit drugs. An American term popular in the late 1960s and early 1970s. It was this sense that inspired the title of the fourth LP by the seminal New York rock group The Velvet Underground in 1970.

2. rich. This term, formerly slang, is now a common colloquialism.

3. *British* in the mood for sex or sexually aroused. The term, which refers to males only, is part of the language of adolescents in use in the later 1990s and was included in *Just Seventeen* magazine's 'lingo of lurve' in August 1996.

I can tell he's loaded/feeling loaded.

loadsamoney *n British*

(someone flaunting) excessive wealth; vulgar, conspicuous consumption. The eponymous comedy character Loadsamoney, created by Harry Enfield in 1987, was based on observation of a specific social group. This group comprises bumptious and philistine skilled and semi-skilled working-class young people from southeastern England, who use their comparative wealth – often gained as part of the black economy – to taunt and provoke those worse off than themselves.

'Singer Mike Rivers has vowed never again to work for the Hooray Henry set – "I hate those loadsamoney thugs", he declared.'

(*News of the World*, 29 May 1988)

The catchphrase 'loadsamoney!' was seized upon by journalists and by the leader of the Labour opposition, Neil Kinnock, who in May 1988 accused the Thatcher administration of fostering an uncaring 'loadsamoney mentality'. In journalese 'loadsa-' was a vogue prefix in 1988 and 1989.

load up *vb American*

to take illicit drugs. A campus and high-school term of the late 1970s.

Listen, if you're loading up, that's it between us.

loaf *n British*

1a. the *head*. The shortening of the cockney rhyming-slang phrase 'loaf of bread'

is now more a colloquialism than slang. Since the late 1950s, it has largely been confined to the phrase 'use your loaf!'.

1b. life. The more common sense of 'head' and the word 'life' itself are blended in the cockney oath 'on my mother's loaf'.

lob[1] *vb British*

to throw away, dispose of. A fashionable narrowing of the standard English meaning of the word, heard, particularly in the London area, since the beginning of the 1980s. A near-synonym to **bin**.

It's no use any more – just lob it.

lob[2] *vb, n British*

(to give) a bribe. A more recent synonym for **bung**.

If we want him to keep quiet we'll have to lob him.

lob (in) *vb Australian*

to arrive unexpectedly, drop in

You'd better get home right away; the rellos have lobbed.

lobe *n British*

a dull, conformist person. This word, used typically by schoolchildren of a tedious or unpopular fellow pupil is a shortening of 'earlobe', itself probably inspired by the long established working-class **ear'ole**.

lob-on *n British*

(of a male) a partial erection. A term popularised by *Viz* comic since the 1990s. A synonym is **semi**.

'Can I put my lob-on in your mouth?'

(*Bo Selecta!*, UK TV comedy, July 2004)

loc *n, adj American*

(a person who is) crazy. This abbreviated form of **loco** (pronounced to rhyme with 'poke') became a vogue term among devotees of **rap** and hip hop culture in the late 1990s. The word could be used either pejoratively or with admiration for a fanatical individual.

local *n, adj British*

(someone who is) provincial, unsophisticated, boorish. The usage was further popularised by its adoption as a catchphrase for the tv comedy series *The League of Gentleman*.

lock *n American*

1. a certainty, usually heard in the teenagers' phrase 'it's a lock'. This sense of the word is an adaptation of the colloquial phrase to 'have (the situation) all locked up'.

2. a person of Polish origin or descent. The racist term heard in the US is supposedly a corruption of **polack**.

locked adj

drunk. The term was recorded in Ireland in this sense in 1970 and was in use among London clubbers in 2002. It may be a short form of **bollocksed** or **airlocked**.

lock-in n British

a drinking session taking place in a pub after official closing time. The practice, which usually involves locking out late arrivals, hence locking in the existing clientele, is illegal but sometimes unofficially condoned by local police. A more fashionable term is **afters**.

They have a lock-in every Friday night.

locko adj

angry. In use since 2000, the term probably originates in Caribbean speech. **Loops** is a contemporary synonym.

loco adj

mad, crazy. This word, popularised worldwide by its use in western movies and cowboy fiction, is the standard informal Spanish word for crazy, deriving from the Latin *ulucus*: owl (which is incidentally related to the English 'ululate').

lodge (someone) vb British

to reject or eject a person, especially a partner. This item of London working-class speech was recorded in the BBC documentary *Forty Minutes* on 30 November 1993.

He was taken completely by surprise when Debbie lodged him.

log n

1. *Australian* a lazy, inert person

2. a piece of excrement, a **turd**

3. a surfboard. The term was defined in *Just Seventeen* magazine in January 1994.

log-rolling n

unofficial or dubious collaboration for mutual advantage, especially in the word of politics. This expression has been in use since the 19th century when it referred to lumberjacking, where pioneer neighbours would help each other move the timber required for building by physically rolling the logs to their destination before cutting them up; it has recently become popular in British journalistic circles under American influence.

loke n American

an unattractive thing and/or unattractive person. An expression used on campus in the USA since around 2000. The origin of the word is uncertain. It might conceivably be related to **local** as used in black British speech to denote a slovenly or promiscuous person.

lollapalooza, lolapaloosa n American

something wonderful, outstanding, enormous and/or spectacular. This invented term is a synonym for words like 'whopper', **lulu** or **humdinger**, depending on the context. (Like 'whopper' it can sometimes refer to an outrageous lie.) The word is used in particular by schoolchildren and parents.

lollipop vb British

to inform on someone, betray (to the police). This is London rhyming slang for the term to **shop**. It is sometimes shortened to **lolly**.

It wouldn't be like Smoky to lollipop his mates.

If you ask me they were lollied.

lolly n British

money. A well-established, light-hearted word which was popular in the 1950s and 1960s and enjoyed a revival, significantly, in the 'Thatcher years' (the mid- and late 1980s), when many obsolescent euphemisms for money had received a new lease of life. It is said to originate in the Romany word *loli*, meaning red, used by gypsies to mean copper coins, and hence money in general. It is perhaps easier to derive the word from lolly, meaning sweet or candy, which itself originated in dialect with the meaning of tongue. (The sense of lollipop is later.)

Lots of lovely lolly – that's what we want.

lombard n British

a wealthy but stupid and/or unpleasant person. A late 1980s acronym from 'loads of money but a real dickhead', coined by **yuppies** to refer particularly to young moneymakers in the City of London, on the lines of expressions such as **dinky**, **nimby**, etc. The word's resonance is enhanced by the role of London's Lombard Street as the home of banking and insurance companies. (The historical Lombards were incidentally a 6th-century Germanic people who invaded northern Italy and became known as money-lenders.)

> 'If they were not Sloanes or yuppies they had to be dinkies (dual income no kids), lombards (lots of money but a real dick-head) or even swells (single women earning lots of lolly).'
>
> (*Evening Standard* magazine, May 1988)

long *adj British*
tedious, time-consuming, oppressive. The word has long been generalised in youth slang since to 2000 to denote anything distasteful.

longbeard *n*
an old person. A quasi-folksy term from science or fantasy fiction adopted face-tiously by rock-music journalists to describe members of the older genera-tion (or themselves when reminiscing). **Greybeard** is a slightly more widespread alternative.

long green *n American*
money (dollar bills of all denominations in America are coloured green). The euphemism is old, dating from the turn of the 20th century, and is still in use.

> 'We'll soon have enough of that long green to choke a horse.'
>
> (*Knight Rider*, US TV series, 1981)

long streak of misery *n British*
a tall, thin person who may or may not be morose, gloomy or habitually pessimistic. This expression, like the less common 'long drink of water' and the more vulgar **long streak of piss**, is normally part of the working-class catchphrase announce-ment 'here he comes again – the long streak of misery!' which may indicate affectionate recognition or genuine dis-like. The phrase can refer to women as well as men.

long streak of piss *n British*
a tall, thin person. An expression of con-tempt or dismissiveness, usually imply-ing weakness or insignificance as well as an ectomorphic body shape. The expression is almost always applied to males.

long ting *n Caribbean*
something or someone who wastes time
> *ain't no long ting*

loo *n British*
a toilet. The most widespread and socially acceptable euphemism for lav-atory, privy, etc. This word, which became firmly established in the mid-1960s, is a favourite of amateur etymol-ogists who derive it variously from *lieu* ('place', as in the French euphemism *lieu d'aisance*, 'place of ease'); from *l'eau* (water) or *gardez l'eau* (mock-French for 'watch out for water', said to be the cry of someone emptying a chamber-pot from an upstairs window into the street below in 17th-century British cities); from *bordalou*, a type of travellers' chamber-pot; from an abbre-viation of the name of Lady Louis Ham-ilton (apparently affixed to a lavatory door) in Dublin in 1870; or, least con-vincingly of all, from leeward (the side of a boat from which one would logically urinate). It may be significant, however, that this rather refined euphemism for water-closet was not recorded until well after the battle of Waterloo and the naming of the London railway station.

> 'And a bit about doing up the loo in chintz is sure to do the trick.'
>
> (*About Town* magazine, June 1962)

looka(h) *n See* **luka**

looker *n*
an attractive person. The word can now be applied to either sex; formerly it was invariably used appreciatively (if some-times patronisingly) by men of women. It originated as a truncated form of 'good-looker'.

looking for Europe *n British*
vomiting. The word Europe is thought to echo the sound of violent regurgitation. The term was posted on the b3ta web-site in 2004.

loon[1] *n British*
1a. a bout of uninhibited and eccentric behaviour. In this sense the noun is derived from the following verb.

1b. a crazy, eccentric or silly person. This word is, in its modern usage, a con-vergence of three sources. It is both a shortening of lunatic and the name of an American diving bird with a cry like a demented laugh. In addition, it prob-ably also recalls an archaic Middle Eng-lish and later Scottish dialect word, *loun*, meaning a rogue. The late Keith Moon, drummer with the English rock group The Who, who was notorious for his wild and outrageous behaviour, was dubbed 'Moon the loon' in the late 1960s by acquaintances and the press.

loon[2], **loon about**, **loon out** *vb British*
to behave in an uninhibited, light-hearted and/or outrageous manner. The

expression was coined at the end of the 1960s to describe a bout of high-spirited, anarchic play typical of those liberated from convention by drug use and/or progressive ideas.

> *'Gone is the rampaging looner of old, the very sight of whom would strike fear into the hearts of publicans and club owners throughout the land.'*
> (*Record Mirror*, 26 August 1967)

loony, looney *adj*

crazy. An adaptation of 'lunatic' (see the noun **loon** for other influences) which is now a common colloquialism.

loony bin *n*

a hospital for the insane or mentally subnormal, an 'insane asylum'. The most common slang expression for such an institution in the English-speaking world since the end of the 19th century. In modern British parlance it is usually shortened to **the bin**.

loony tune/tunes/toons *n, adj*

(a person who is) mad or eccentric. Originally an Americanism derived from *Looney Tunes*, the name of a series of cinema cartoon comedies in the 1940s, the term has become fashionable since the 1980s in Britain and Australia.

> *'I've been hit twice in the face this morning and now some loony tune is breaking up my aircraft.'*
> (*The Flying Doctors*, Australian TV series, 1987)

> *'That is it, Mork! He's got to go, or I'll end up as loony-tunes as he is.'*
> (*Mork and Mindy*, US TV series, 1979)

looped *adj American*

1a. exhausted

1b. intoxicated

> *'It was just crazy. We were all so looped by the time we left.'*
> (*Valentine*, US film, 2001)

loops *adj British*

angry. A term used by young street-gang members in London since around 2000.

loopy *adj*

1a. crazy, eccentric, silly

1b. illogical, out of control

A fairly mild pejorative, often said in bemusement or disbelief rather than disapproval. The word has been in use since the early years of the 20th century, but its origin is obscure.

loose cannon *n American*

a dangerously uncontrolled ally or associate; a member of one's team who is liable to run amok or cause havoc. This piece of political and journalistic jargon has become fashionable in the late 1980s. It continues the nautical image evoked by such vogue clichés as 'take on board'. In this case the person in question is seen as an unsecured cannon careering unpredictably and dangerously across a deck with the pitching of a ship. The phrase was used of General Haig during the Nixon administration and of Colonel Oliver North under the Reagan administration.

> *'Danko is the perfect weapon Charlie – a loose cannon. If he helps us find Victor Rosla, great. If he screws up, breaks rules ... he's a Russian.'*
> (*Red Heat*, US film, 1988)

loot *n*

money. A predictable extension of the standard English sense of booty. The word is an anglicised spelling of the Hindi word *lut* which sounds and means the same as the English derivation.

> *'I tell you what though, Zackerman can recruit the very best because he's got the loot.'*
> (*Serious Money*, play by Caryl Churchill, 1987)

Lord Muck *n British*

a man thought to be 'putting on airs' or behaving high-handedly. This expression from the turn of the 20th century is now probably less prevalent than the female equivalent, **Lady Muck**.

> *Well, won't you just look at them – Lord and Lady Muck.*

lorg *n American*

a foolish, clumsy person. The word is probably a deformation of **log**, as used to denote an inert individual.

lose it *vb*

1. to lose one's temper or control over oneself

2. *See* **lose the plot**

lose one's bottle *vb British*

to lose one's nerve, have one's courage desert one. A vogue term of the late 1970s, when it crossed from the jargon of marginals, criminals and the lower working-class into general currency. (For the origins of the expression see **bottle**.)

lose one's cool *vb*

to lose one's composure or one's temper. A phrase from the 1950s American **hip** vocabulary, usually heard in the form of an admonition. It was adopted in Britain, first by jazz fans and then **beatniks**, in the late 1950s.

> *Try not to lose your cool even if the guy provokes you.*

lose one's lunch/doughnuts/pizza *vb* *American*

to vomit. Hearty, jocular high-school and college terms.

lose one's marbles *vb*

to become deranged or feeble-minded, go crazy. **Marbles**, when referring to male faculties, usually refers to testicles, but in this case one's wits or intelligence are in question. The origin of this phrase is uncertain, in spite of many attempts to clarify the choice of words (marbles have been seen as a synonym for the bearings which allow a machine to operate or as part of a catchphrase based on a story in which a monkey steals a boy's marbles). What is undisputed is that the expression originated in the USA.

lose one's rag *vb British*

to lose one's temper, lose control of oneself. This mainly working-class expression is of obscure origin; the word rag has meant variously one's tongue, a flag, to tease and to bluster or rage, but none of these senses can be definitively linked to the modern phrase.

> *'Don't you go losing your rag – stay cool.'*
> (*EastEnders*, British TV soap opera, July 1988)

lose the plot, lose it *vb*

vogue terms since the later 1990s which probably originated in references to, e.g., a film director whose work became incoherent after an auspicious beginning

> *'Here are Claudia [Schiffer] and Boris [Becker] losing the plot in the name of fashion.'*
> (*Evening Standard*, 2 August 2004)

lotion *n British*

an alcoholic drink. A now dated middle-class term with the implications of the soothing medicinal effects of (strong) liquor. The word can be countable ('a lotion') or uncountable ('some lotion').

louie *n American See* **hang a louie**

Lou Reed *n British*

the drug **speed**. Rhyming slang using the name of the New York rock star.

lousy *adj Australian*

ill, under the weather. A local synonym for **crook**.

love *adj American*

excellent. An expression used on campus in the USA since around 2000.

love bumps *n pl British*

female breasts. A schoolboyish euphemism of the 1970s. 'Love bubbles' was a pre-World War II synonym. **Love lumps** is an alternative form.

loved-up *adj*

1. high on drugs, especially **ecstasy**
2. amorous or enamoured

An item of student slang in use in London and elsewhere since around 2000.

love handles *n pl*

folds of flesh at the waist or paunch. An affectionate, joky, reassuring or polite euphemism usually applied to the male body by women or by the person himself.

> *'The love handles of Jonathan Ross are no strangers to this column, but news reaches us that they are shrinking by the hour.'*
> (*Time Out* magazine, July 1989)

love-in *n*

a gathering involving displays of mutual affection and/or ecstatic 'one-ness'. An ephemeral phenomenon and term from the early **hippy** era, seized upon by the press.

love lumps *n pl British*

female breasts. A jocular term used by university students and teenagers in the mid- to late 1980s in keeping with the trend to coin childishly coy expressions as alternatives to established or taboo terms. **Love bumps** is an alternative form.

love sausage *n*

the penis. Probably American in origin, the usage was adopted in the UK from around 2000.

love-truncheon *n British*

the penis. This joky euphemism was employed by the comedians Rik Mayall and Ade Edmondson in the stage performance of their TV comedy *Bottom* and subsequently occurred in student slang from the later 1990s.

love-tunnel *n British*
the vagina. A vulgarism in use among adolescents in the 1990s and listed in *Viz* comic in 1994.

low-flyer *n British*
a *liar*. An item of rhyming slang heard in the 1990s.

low-heel, low-wheel *n Australian*
a prostitute. The term refers to someone who is literally down at heel from walking the streets. The second form of the expression is based on a mis-hearing of the true phrase.

lowlife *n American*
a disreputable and/or contemptible person. A fashionable term of the 1970s which was adopted by some British speakers to refer to those considered socially unacceptable.
Jesus, Katy, what are you doing with this lowlife?

low rent *adj American*
shabby, sordid, inferior. A phrase referring to lodgings, extended first to denote a poor district, then to signify anything or anyone considered distasteful or third-rate. 'Low budget' is a near-synonym in British English.

low rider *n American*
1a. a devotee of customised cars with lowered suspension, characteristic of Chicano or Hispanic youth gangs in Los Angeles and elsewhere during the 1970s. The term low rider (the fashion was still in evidence at the end of the 1980s) can also be applied to the car itself. Low riding involves (contrary to raising suspension for road racing or rallying) driving very slowly in convoys for display.
1b. an obnoxious or disreputable youth. This pejorative use of the word is an extension of the original sense, probably influenced also by standard terms such as 'low'.

lubricated *adj*
drunk. A politely jocular euphemism on the same lines as **well-oiled**.

luck out *vb American*
1a. to 'strike it lucky'
1b. to have bad luck
This term with its contrary senses is occasionally used by British speakers.

lucoddy *n British*
the body. Part of the **parlyaree** lexicon used, e.g., by the **gay** and theatrical community in the 1960s. The precise derivation of the term is unclear, apart from the obvious rhyme.

'lude *n American*
a Quaalude (pronounced 'kway-lood') tablet. A widely prescribed and misused Methaqualone (hypnotic sleeping pill), equivalent to the British Mandrax or **mandie**. The drug was taken, particularly in the 1970s, for its relaxing and disinhibiting effects and to mitigate the after- and side-effects of other drugs.

lug *n British*
an inhalation of smoke, a **drag**. The term is used in this sense in British and Irish speech.
'Didn't any of them enjoy a lug on the herbals?'
(*Q* magazine, March 1997)

lughole, lug'ole *n British*
ear. A common term of the 1950s and 1960s which now sounds folksy or dated, although the comedian Frankie Howerd employed 'pin back your lugholes' as one of his catchphrases. Lug has been the commonest colloquialism for 'ear' outside London since the 16th century. It originated in Middle English meaning flap or ear-cover, from an older Scandinavian word *lugga*, meaning to pull.

luka, lookah *n British*
money, wealth. This word, spelled in a variety of ways and which was recorded among London schoolchildren in the mid-1990s, is in fact from the much older term '(filthy) lucre' and has been adopted as a vogue term, probably in ignorance of its origin. (*Lucre* is Middle English from the Latin *lucrum*, meaning reward or booty.) In American slang **ducats** is another archaism which has been revived in a similar context.

lulu *n*
1. something spectacular, impressive, exceptional. This word was originally an Americanism, in use since the mid-19th century. Many attempts have been made to explain its etymology, which remains obscure. (It is almost certainly unconnected with the female nickname.)
2. *British* an elaboration of **loo**

lumber[1] *n British*
1a. trouble, burdensome difficulties. This sense of the word is usually expressed by the cockney phrases 'in lumber' or 'in dead lumber'.

1b. a fight or struggle. A word which in working-class, particularly northern, usage is often in the form of an exclamation to signal the start of a street or playground brawl, and is another sense of lumber as trouble.

> '*Tables flew, bottles broke, the bouncers shouted lumber/ the dummy got too chummy in a Bing Crosby number.*'
> (*Salome Maloney the Sweetheart of the Ritz*, poem by John Cooper Clarke, 1980)

lumber² *vb, n British*
(to pick up) a partner of the opposite sex. The usage probably originated in the Lowlands of Scotland but is now heard in other parts of Britain, employed as a synonym for 'get off with' or **pull**.

lummock, lummox *n*
a large, clumsy and/or stupid person. The word is used in the USA and Australia as well as in Britain, but is originally a rural British dialect form of 'lump', in the same way as 'hummock' is a diminutive form of 'hump'.

> '*The awkward lummox of a kid who, though only ten years old, was almost as big as his fifth grade teacher.*'
> (*Wild Town*, Jim Thompson, 1957)

lumpy-jumper *n British*
a female. The term is used by males.

lunatic soup *n*
alcoholic drink. A humorous expression on the lines of **electric soup**, **giggle water** and **laughing soup**.

lunch *adj Australian*
defeated, confounded, destroyed. Defined by one surfer in 2002 as 'what you become after a wipe-out' (i.e. shark food).

lunchbox *n*
1. the stomach, belly or abdomen. A jocular euphemism, used particularly in the context of fighting.

> *a kick/punch in the lunchbox*

2. the male genitals as visible through tight clothing. The term, an elaboration of the earlier **box**, was applied by the *Sun* newspaper to the athlete Linford Christie in a number of headlines in the mid-1990s and the stand-up comedian Ben Elton drew attention to the usage at the Montreal Comedy Festival in 1992. Synonyms are **packet** and **basket**.

> '*Gym bans a big boys' lunchbox.*'
> (Headline in the *News of the World*, August 1994)

luncheon truncheon *n British*
the penis. The luncheon component of the phrase probably refers to 'luncheon meat', a product similar to the 'spam' in the synonymous **spam javelin**. Luncheon truncheon was recorded on the Royal Marines website in 2004.

lunching at the Lazy Y *n, phrase*
engaging in oral sex, particularly cunnilingus. A humorous expression playing on the shape of a reclining person with their legs spread and a famous cattle brand from the American Wild West. (A 'lazy' letter in a brand was one lying on its side.) An alternative form is 'dining at the Y'.

lunch out *vb British*
to back out of an appointment or arrangement

> '*I think I'm going to have to lunch out this afternoon; I've got an essay to write.*'
> (Recorded, student, Devon, 2002)

lunchy, lunchie *adj*
1a. crazy, eccentric, deviant. From the colloquialism 'out to lunch', this became a vogue term of the 1990s, originating among American adolescents.

> '*I knew the kid was lunchie, but not this fuckin' lunchie!*'
> (*Things To Do In Denver When You're Dead*, US film, 1996)

1b. inferior, unacceptable, unpleasant. This generalisation of the original sense of the term was adopted by British adolescents as a vogue term in the mid-1990s.

lundy *n British*
a collaborator, traitor. A Northern Irish term derived from the name of the governor of Londonderry in the 18th century, Lieutenant Colonel Robert Lundy, who was suspected of Catholic sympathies by the Protestant community.

lunk, lunkhead *n American*
a slow-witted person, dullard. The term originated in the USA in the 19th century. It usually evokes a large, clumsy, ungainly person of low intelligence and/or slow reactions. It is a blend of lump and hunk.

lurgi, lurghi *n*
alternative spellings of **lerg(h)i**

lurk *n Australian*
a dodge, shady scheme, clever and/or disreputable trick. The word is now used in these senses mainly by middle-aged and elderly speakers.

lurker *n*

1a. *British* a disreputable, suspicious, unwholesome person. A word often used by disaffected youth ironically of themselves, it was adopted as a name by a suburban London **punk** rock group in 1977.

1b. *British* a fly-by-night or unlicensed street trader

1c. *Australian* a petty criminal, fraudster or cardsharp

All these senses are variations on the standard English meaning of lurk which comes from the Middle English *lurken*, meaning to lie in wait.

2. a market stallholder who simply waits for customers without attempting to attract them.

Compare **rorter**; **pitcher**

3. an Internet user who observes communications without participating, in the patois of **cyberpunks** and **net-heads**

'[Lurkers] are invisible unless you run a roll call command and see how many voyeuristic weazels [sic] there actually are.'

(*Surfing on the Internet* by J. C. Herz, 1994)

lurk off *vb British*

to leave, go away. The verb often, but not invariably, suggests slinking away. It can also be employed as a euphemism for the imperative **fuck off** as in the 1995 BBC 2 TV comedy *Game On*.

lush¹ *n*

an alcoholic, habitual drunkard or heavy drinker. This is an American term, adopted by British speakers in the 1960s, which derived from an earlier British usage which had fallen into desuetude; from at least the 18th century until the early 20th century lush had been used to mean alcoholic drink.

lush² *adj British*

1a. very attractive and/or desirable

A lush bird.

'I love your ski pants, Tray.

Nice aren't they! £12.99. You want to get some. You'll look lush.'

(*The Fat Slags*, cartoon in *Viz* comic, 1989)

1b. delicious

Well, how was it?

Lush.

This British colloquialism, heard especially in the 1960s among schoolchildren, young people and unsophisticated adults, is a short form of 'luscious' rather than the standard adjective (as in 'lush vegetation', for example). It has enjoyed a revival since the late 1980s and is still popular, especially among pre-teens.

lushed *adj*

drunk. This is probably a recent coinage inspired by **lush** meaning a heavy drinker. In fact lush as a verb, and lushed as a past participle, had existed in English slang and dialect since the early 19th century, but had fallen out of use in most areas before World War II. The renewed use of the term is mainly confined to teenagers and students.

lye *n*

an alternative spelling of **lie**

M

M *n*

morphine. A drug users' abbreviation.

mac *n*

1. *American* a term of address to a male stranger. The word often conveys a hint of provocation rather than straightforward friendliness.

2. *British* a mackintosh, raincoat

machismo *n*

assertive maleness, overt masculinity. The word evokes virility, supremacism, etc. It is not strictly speaking slang but a direct borrowing from the Spanish (and as such should be pronounced as in 'match' not 'mack').

macho *adj*

assertively male, aggressively masculine. The word is a direct borrowing from Spanish in which it means male, particularly in an animal context, hence virile.

> 'Her experience among women rappers trying to cut it in the macho world of Hip Hop led Charlotte to look again at the girl groups from the Seventies she'd always loved.'
>
> (*Ms London* magazine, 4 September 1989)

macho up *vb*

an alternative form of **butch up** (to behave more assertively, courageously or to show more masculine characteristics). **Macho** is Spanish for male in the assertive or dominant sense of the word.

mack *n British*

the penis. The word, of uncertain origin, was reported in *Loaded* magazine in October 1994.

macker *n British*

a black person. An item of racist rhyming slang based on 'macaroon': **coon**, heard in London working-class circles in the early 1990s and reported in the London *Evening Standard*, 9 September 1991.

mack on (someone) *vb*

to flirt with, try to impress. The term probably originated in the USA but by 2004 was in use among UK teenagers.

mad *adj American*

a large amount or great number of. In this sense the word is a key item of black American speech. Since 2000 it has been in use also among younger speakers from other ethnic backgrounds.

> *Mad love to all my peeps.*

made-in *n British*

a 'two-one' honours degree. A students' jocularism based on 'made-in-Taiwan'. An alternative form is a **draw**: 'two won'.

made-up *adj British*

content, satisfied. This regional term from the Merseyside area became widespread in the 1990s, following its use in TV soap operas such as *Brookside* and *Coronation Street* and reports such as that of the London *Evening Standard*, 25 November 1993, regarding the James Bulger murder case.

mad for it *adj British*

enthusiastic, unrestrained. The phrase was popular in Manchester during the mid- to late 1990s and was a favourite expression of Liam Gallagher of the Britpop band Oasis.

> 'Everyone's going, oh you're splitting up, but we're not splitting up. 'Cos we're mad for it.'
>
> (Liam Gallagher quoted in the *NME*, 30 September 1995)

madhead *n British*

a crazy, unrestrained person

> 'The majority of the press we've had makes us out to be these madheads who only appeal to dickheads who'd stick a bottle over your head.'
>
> (Liam Gallagher of Oasis quoted in the *NME*, 30 September 1995)

mad money *n American*
1a. money set aside by a girl or woman in case she is abandoned or offended by her date. In this sense of the word mad signifies anger (on the part of the girl or her escort).
1b. money set aside for frivolous, impulsive or self-indulgent purposes. In this version the sense of mad is the British 'crazy'.
Both uses of the phrase date from before World War II. They are now dated but not quite obsolete.

mad props *n American*
congratulations, respect. A catchphrase since 2000, originating in hip hop parlance.

mad-up *adj British*
annoyed. An item of black British slang.

mady *n South African*
a sweetheart or wife. Recorded as an item of Sowetan slang in the *Cape Sunday Times*, 29 January 1995.

mag *n Australian*
a conversation, chat. Usually heard in the phrase to 'have a mag with someone'. This sense of the word was first recorded in England in the 18th century and is said to be derived from 'magpie' as a synonym for or an evocation of chatter.

maga *adj*
an alternative spelling of **margar**

ma-gent, amagent *n South African*
a young male, particularly one considered dapper, alert, aware, etc. Recorded as an item of Sowetan slang in the *Cape Sunday Times*, 29 January 1995.

maggot *n*
1. a despicable, dirty and/or insignificant person. In British use, the predominant idea is usually 'beneath contempt', whereas in Australia maggot is a generalised term of abuse.
2. *British* money. A rare usage, heard among petty criminals or their imitators among others. Like many obscure synonyms for money, it has been rehabilitated since the late 1980s.
I've got to get hold of some maggot in a hurry.

maggoted *adj Australian*
drunk. One of many synonyms evoking low, despicable behaviour and/or impaired movement.

magic[1] *adj British*
superlative, excellent. An over-used colloquialism since the late 1970s which is characteristic of garrulous or over-enthusiastic lower-middle-class and working-class speech. It is often heard in the context of sports such as football or darts.
'Belfast is "magic" – local demotic for "super" or "marvellous" or whatever high superlative leaps instinctively off the tongue.'
(*The Crack: a Belfast Year*, Sally Belfrage, 1987)

magic[2]**, magic dust, magic mist** *n American*
the drug **PCP** (also known as **angel dust**)

magic mushrooms *n pl*
any hallucinogenic mushrooms such as psilocybin or the native British 'liberty caps'. In the later 1980s users began to refer to them as **shrooms**.
Compare **rooms**

Mahatma (Gandhi) *adj British*
randy. The rhyming slang term, borrowing the name and title of the late Indian spiritual and political leader, was first recorded in 1998 but may be older.
feeling a bit Mahatma tonight

maiden *n*
an unattractive woman. This pejorative use of the word has been recorded among US college students and London teenagers since 2000.

main drag *n*
the main or central street. An American phrase from the early years of the 20th century, heard elsewhere since the 1970s. (**Drag** was also used to mean street in Victorian cockney speech.)

mainline *vb*
to inject (an illicit drug) directly into a vein. The term is one of the most persistent pieces of addicts' jargon, contrasted with **skin-popping** (injecting subcutaneously or intramuscularly). The meaning is sometimes extended to denote the regular ingestion of anything in large quantities.

main man *n American*
1a. a boss, leader
He's the main man around here.
1b. (a woman's) partner, boyfriend, husband or protector
He's my main man.
1c. one's best friend, **buddy**, bosom pal
Yo, Billy, my main man! How're they hanging?

main squeeze *n American*
1a. (one's) boyfriend or girlfriend, sweetheart
1b. the most important person, a boss, leader

major *adj*
excellent, exceptional, admirable. A vogue adjective in adolescent usage in the 1990s. The appropriation of the standard term probably occurred first in American speech. Like **mega** and **totally** it was initially used to qualify another word before being allowed to stand alone.

> '… the sixties were mega, the seventies were major, and what you are going to see now is going to be totally massive!'
> (*Scratchy & Co.*, children's TV show, 8 March 1997)

make[1] *n*
1a. *American* an identification or instance of recognition (of a suspect)
1b. *American* a check in official records on the identity of a suspect or on another piece of evidence

> *Run a make on this guy, will you?*
> *Can we have a make on the license number?*

2. a sex partner. The term is a back-formation from the sexual sense of the verb **make**, on the same principle as **lay**.

make[2] *vb American*
1. to identify, recognise (a suspect or adversary). A piece of police and criminal jargon well known from its use in fiction, TV and films.

> '*Can you make him?*'
> (*The French Connection*, US film, 1971)

2. to have sex with, seduce. This euphemism from the turn of the 20th century, although understood, has never caught on in Britain or Australia. It has occasionally been adopted by individuals, including the philosopher Bertrand Russell.

make babies *vb*
to have sex, make love. A coy or jocular euphemism used by adults.

make ends *vb American*
to win, achieve success. The term, used by **rappers** and hip hop aficionados, is a triple pun: in slang **ends** denotes money, to 'make ends' is, in the game of dominoes, to win, and the colloquial to 'make ends meet' is sometimes a euphemism for to become wealthy.

make out *vb American*
1a. to indulge in **necking** or heavy petting

1b. to succeed in having sex.
See also **make-out artist**
Both are teenagers' extensions of the colloquial sense of the phrase; to be successful. The usage is probably influenced by the verb **make** as a euphemism for seduce or have sex with.

make-out artist *n American*
a successful seducer, **stud**. The term is invariably applied to males. It is from the verb **make out**, meaning to achieve sexual satisfaction or success.

malco *n British*
an unpleasant and/or obnoxious person. In playground usage since 2000 and also used by adults in the Liverpool area. It derives from 'mal-coordinated'.

mallie, mall rat *n American*
a (usually female) teenager who hangs around shopping malls in order to meet friends, misbehave and/or otherwise have a 'good time'. A phenomenon and expression in existence since the early 1980s.

malteser *n*
1. an old or middle-aged male. This item of rhyming slang for **geezer** was quoted in *Private Eye* magazine, 6 May 1994, ascribed to Essex girls at Tramp nightclub who were referring derisively to the newspaper editor Andrew Neil.
2. a black person who adopts or accepts white culture

> '*What's wrong? This one's a racist and this one's a malteser.*'
> (*Grange Hill*, BBC TV series, February 1997)

mampy[1]**, manpy** *adj*
1. *British* ugly. This term, originating in black usage, was adopted as a vogue word by London schoolchildren from the 1990s, along with near-synonyms **mash-up**, **bruck(ers)** and **uggers**. Its precise etymology is uncertain.
2. ruined, destroyed

mampy[2] *n British*
defined by a user in 2002 as 'a **mashed(-up)** or fat person'

mams *n pl British*
female breasts. A shortening of mammaries. The word has been used by adolescents of both sexes since 2000.

Man, the *n American*
1a. the police, the government, the (white) establishment or any other authority, or person in authority. A usage coined by underdogs which was taken up

by the black power and **hippy** movements of the late 1960s.

> *'Looking for a job in the city/ Working for the Man ev'ry night and day.'*

('Proud Mary' by John Fogerty, recorded by Creedence Clearwater Revival, 1969)

1b. a sports champion, pop singer, etc. considered by the speaker to be the top practitioner of his craft

> *There were a lot of good heavyweights around in the '60s, but Ali was the Man.*

2. a supplier of illicit drugs, a **pusher**, **dealer** or **connection**

> *'I'm waiting for my man/ Twenty-six dollars in my hand.'*

('I'm Waiting for my Man' written by Lou Reed, recorded by The Velvet Underground, 1967)

man at C&A *n British*
a male wearing embarrassingly unfashionable clothes. The derisive phrase borrows the name of a range of mass-market casual wear from the C&A clothing chain. An item of student slang in use in London and elsewhere since around 2000.

mandie, mandy *n British*
a tablet of Mandrax (the British trademark name of methaqualone, a potentially addictive 'hypnotic' sleeping preparation). These drugs, like their American counterparts, Quaaludes or **'ludes**, were taken by drug abusers for their relaxant, disinhibiting and supposedly aphrodisiac effects.

> *'The staff and editors of Oz wish to protest against the flippant attitude of our art director towards Mandrax in the caption above ['Mandies make you randy']. Mandies are both addictive and dangerous.'*

(*Oz* magazine, July 1972)

M and M's *n pl British*
tedious and/or unpleasant people. The disguised term of abuse (the letters stand for '**muppets** and morons') has been used in office slang and in call centres, etc. since 2003. M and Ms are chocolate-covered sweets.

Mandy *n British*
an alternative for **Sharon**

> *Did you see all the Mandies vamping around their handbags?*

mangled *adj British, Irish*
drunk

mangoes *n pl American*
female breasts. One of many terms employing the metaphor of round fruit.

man in the boat *n See* **little man/boy in the boat**

mank *n, adj British*
(something) unpleasant. In playground usage since 2000, the term is probably a shortening of the earlier adjective **manky**.

manky *adj British*
grotty, disgusting or distasteful. A 1960s vogue word, mainly in middle-class usage. The word had existed previously in working-class speech: it may be an invention influenced by 'mangy', 'cranky', 'wonky', etc., or a corruption of the French *manqué* (lacking, failed). It is still used in northern England where its usual sense is naughty or spoilt.

man-like ... *combining form British*
in the fashionable language of teenage gangs of the mid-1990s, the phrase is affixed to a proper name, e.g., 'man-like Toby', when addressing or referring to a friend. The term was recorded in use among North London schoolboys in the 1990s.

manners *n pl Caribbean*
situation, moral ambience. Usually heard in the phrase **under heavy manners**, meaning oppressed, behaving under the threat of discipline. The term was employed in the context of the Rastafarian and reggae subculture in the early 1970s and was briefly adopted by young whites, especially in the world of rock music.

mano-a-mano *adj, adv, n American*
(engaged in) a physical confrontation or face-to-face encounter. The term, which refers literally to grappling or wrestling, is the Spanish for 'hand to hand'.

> *He remembered his mano-a-mano with Palma.*

manor *n British*
one's own district or area of jurisdiction. A word used by both police and criminals since before World War II.

mans *n Caribbean*
a group of men. The term has been adopted by some UK teenagers since 2000.

mansdem *n Caribbean*
a group of close friends. The term has been adopted by some UK teenagers since 2000.

man upstairs, the *n*
a humorous euphemism for God

map of France/Ireland/America/etc. *n*
1a. a stain on a sheet
1b. a patch of vomit
The use of the phrase map of Ireland to describe semen stains on bedsheets is said to originate among chambermaids, many of whom were themselves Irish.

mapping *n British*
tracing the contours of a partner's body with the fingers. The term is usually heard among adolescents describing petting, and was included in *Just Seventeen* magazine's 'lingo of lurve' in August 1996.

maps *n pl British*
male breasts. The word, heard since 2000, was probably coined by analogy with **baps**.

maracas *n pl*
1a. female breasts. A mainly American usage.
1b. the testicles. In British speech the (rare) term is reinforced by the rhyme with **knackers**.

maratata *n South African*
a gun

marbles *n pl*
1. the testicles. A predictable drawing of a literal parallel (rather than, as some have claimed, an example of rhyming slang on 'marble halls'). **Pills**, **balls**, **stones** and **nuts** are similar metaphors.
2. common sense, sanity, mental faculties. This use of the word was originally American, perhaps deriving from a folk tale.
See also **lose one's marbles**

mardarse, mardie *n British*
a 'softie', a weak person. A schoolchildren's word heard from the 1930s onwards, particularly in the north of England. It is now rare, but not quite archaic, and comes from a dialect form of 'marred' which has the specific sense of spoilt or sulky. Anthony Burgess mentions that the word was used of him by tormentors during his childhood. Mardie has also been heard in use as an adjective.
   'Go out with your Dad. Don't be such a bloody mardie.'
   (Recorded, Leicester, 1990)

mare *n British*
1. a woman. A derogatory working-class usage on the lines of **cow**, **bitch** or **sow**.

Mare usually has overtones of 'nag' in both its senses and hence denotes a drab, wearisome woman. The word was given a wider currency by its use as a strong but acceptable term of abuse in TV comedies.
   'It was a mare of a game.'
   (Comedian Bob Mills in ITV *Heroes and Villains*, 1994)
2. *See* **have a mare**

margar¹, maga *adj*
skinny, slender. An item of Caribbean patois, also heard in the UK.

margar² *n*
a thin man or woman. A term from Caribbean speech, also heard in the UK since 2000, especially among younger speakers.

marinate *vb American*
1. to hang out
2. to relax, **chill out**

mark *n*
a dupe or target chosen by a conman, pickpocket, etc. An old term, recorded as long ago as 1885 and still in use all over the English-speaking world.
   'She is drawn into an underworld of cons, scams, "marks" (suckers) and "tells" (their involuntary give-away gestures).'
   (Review of David Mamet's US film, *House of Games, Independent*, 19 November 1987)

mark someone's card *vb British*
to tip someone off, give someone a warning. This phrase from the jargon of horse-racing has been adopted by London working-class speakers, in particular in police and underworld circles. The usual implication is a firm but gentle (or menacing) taking aside and 'putting in the picture'.
   You can leave it to me, I'll mark his card for him.

marmalize, marmelise *vb British*
to destroy, utterly defeat. This invented word, suggesting, like **spifflicate**, some unspecified but comprehensive punishment, is probably a children's invention, perhaps based on marmalade. It has been used by adults for comic effect, particularly on radio and television (by Ken Dodd's 'Diddymen' and the scriptwriters of *Coronation Street* among others).
   I'll marmalize you!

marmite-driller *n British*
a male homosexual. The term, one of a set of synonyms including **chutney-ferret**, **fudge-nudger** and **turd burglar**, was used, e.g., by the British stand-up comedian Ben Elton in a monologue in January 1994. The reference is to contact with excrement in the course of sodomy.

Marmite motorway *n British*
the anus. A synonym is **Bourneville boulevard**; the American equivalent is **Hershey highway**.

marp *n British*
an erection. The usage was recorded among middle class adolescent males in 2000.

married alive *adj British*
in a steady or long-term relationship. The pun, on 'buried alive', evokes a person trapped in a sterile partnership. The phrase was popularised by the UK journalist Julie Burchill.

mary ann *n British*
a male homosexual, effeminate man. One of several usages of common Victorian or Edwardian female forenames (Nancy, as part of **nancy boy**, and **jessie** are others which have survived) to refer derisively to effeminate men.

Mary Jane, Mary Warner, Mary Jane Warner *n*
marihuana. These are English puns or **hobson-jobson** versions of the Spanish name for cannabis. One spelling of the word, *marijuana*, is a literal translation of Mary-Jane, although the original Mexican form, *marihuana*, is a familiarising prefix (from 'Maria') added to a native Amerindian word meaning something like 'herbal substance'.

Marzipan set, the *n British*
a **yuppie** coinage, defined by George Pitcher in the *Observer* as 'Those city flyers who are above the rich cake but below the icing'

mash¹, mash-up, mashed(-up) *adj British*
1a. destroyed or damaged
1b. ugly
2a. exhausted, worn out
2b. intoxicated by drugs, **high**

'After secretly munching her pills my mates watched in confusion as I sweated my way through lasers and flame-throwers. I was totally mashed; Christmas had definitely come early.'
(*Independent*, 24 January 1995)

2c. extremely drunk
'Let's go and get mash-up.'
(Recorded, Kent schoolgirl, 2003)

All the senses of the words arose in black speech and derive from the image of destruction and damage. In the later 1990s the expression crossed over into the fashionable slang of white teenagers and young adults.

mash² *n, vb British*
(to make) tea. From the use of the term in the beer-brewing process.

mash-up *n British*
a disaster, mess. From the earlier adjectival usage.
a real total mash-up

mass *n British*
a gang or group of friends. A fashionable synonym for **crew**, **set** and **posse** in the mid-1990s. The term was recorded in use among North London schoolboys in 1993 and 1994.

massive¹ *adj*
excellent. This sense of the word probably arose from its use in the music and film industries in such formulations as 'massive hit', extended to 'this band are going to be massive'.

'... the sixties were mega, the seventies were major, and what you are going to see now is going to be totally massive!'
(*Scratchy & Co.*, children's TV show, 8 March 1997)
'We had a really good time. the whole experience was massive.'
(*Celebrity Love Island* contestant, *The Sun*, 21 June 2005)

massive² *n*
a group, clique or gang. The vogue term, heard since the end of the 1990s and popularised by the comedian Ali G among others, may be in origin an elaborated form of **mass**, or influenced by **massive** in the sense of overwhelming, impressive, etc.
Shout goin' out to the Dundee massive.

Masters of the Universe *n pl American*
yuppies, high-fliers, senior or influential figures. In the early 1990s the phrase was adopted from video games and children's toys to refer only partly ironically to the most successful Wall Street traders, brokers, etc.

matelot *n British*
1a. a sailor, referred to patronisingly by soldiers, policemen, etc.

1b. a member of the river police, as referred to by other sections of the police force

The word *matelot* is French for sailor.

mattress-muncher *n Australian*
a (passive) male homosexual. A rarer and probably later version of **pillow-biter**.

maulers *n pl British*
hands. A mainly middle-class school-children's usage, popular in the 1950s and early 1960s.

Keep your maulers off my things, will you.

maungy *adj*
miserable, grumpy, disaffected

MAW *n American*
a glamorous and/or idle woman of uncertain profession. An abbreviation of 'model, actress, whatever ...', it was an ironic social categorisation originating in the later 1980s and heard in show-business and media circles. (It is pronounced as a word rather than letter by letter.)

max *adv*
at most, to the maximum extent

I swear he only earns £25k, max.

See also **to the max**

mazooma, mazuma *n*
money. An American term heard since the early years of the 20th century. Like many other picturesque but dated synonyms it was revived in British speech in the late 1980s. The word is originally Hebrew, entering American slang via Yiddish.

McDonald *n British*
the sum of £250 or, more usually, £250,000 in the argot of City of London financial traders in the 1990s. The reference is to the McDonald's 'quarter-pounder' hamburger.

McJob *n American*
a menial and/or temporary job. The term arose in connection with the **slacker** generation/**Generation X** and was based on the notion of educated middle-class youngsters taking temporary jobs at, e.g., McDonald's burger restaurants.

'People with short attention spans and no work ethic ... barely surviving in ... low status, short-term McJobs.'
(*Independent*, 24 April 1997)

MCP *n*
a sexist man. An abbreviation of 'male chauvinist pig', a feminist vogue term which appeared in 1970. It was often used in this shortened form both in writing and, less often, in speech. If used, the expression is now usually truncated to 'chauvinist' or even 'chauve'.

'He'd ordered a Heineken from a waitress who was a real throwback, an MCP's delight.'
(*The Serial*, Cyra McFadden, 1976)

MDA *n*
methyldiamphetamine, a synthetic drug which is chemically related to the stimulant amphetamines, but which in some users elicits hallucinogenic experiences supposedly similar to those associated with LSD. The drug was first popular in the early 1970s in the USA, and came once again into vogue in the late 1980s in the UK, where it was known as **adam** or, more usually, **ecstasy**, and became the drug of choice among young club-goers and dancers.

mean *adj*
wonderful, impressive, excellent. A typical reversal of the standard (American) meaning in black code and later teenage usage, like the more recent **bad** and **wicked**.

meat and two veg *n British*
the male genitals. A working-class vulgarism dating from the days when these components constituted the standard British meal, as advertised in cafés, boarding houses, etc. (Veg is short for vegetables and is spoken with a soft 'g'.) Meat has been a slang synonym for the penis, as well as for human sexuality in general, since at least the 16th century.

meatball *n*
a clod or fool; a brawny but unintelligent male. The word may be used as a variation of **meathead**, or less pejoratively to denote an attractive male, a **hunk** (albeit patronisingly).

'My Swedish Meatball.'
(Title of an American softcore movie)

meathead, meat head *n*
a stupid person, dullard. This word was first popularised in the USA. The image evoked is either based on meat signifying solid muscle (instead of brains) or perhaps on the sexual sense of **meat** as the penis, in which case the expression is a precursor of the popular term **dickhead**.

'A man of patient indulgence, apparently capable of putting up with every bozo and meathead who comes his way.'

(Jonathan Keates reviewing Malcolm Bradbury's *Unsent Letter*, *Observer*, 5 June 1988)

meat injection *n British*
an act of sexual intercourse. The vulgar euphemism is invariably used by male speakers.

meat market *n*
a place where people congregate in the search for sexual partners; a singles bar. The phrase is usually used dismissively of dance halls, clubs, etc. by non-participants or ex-participants.

meat rack *n*
a place where, or occasion when available sexual partners are on display. The phrase is specifically used in a **gay** context to describe public places and events such as bars, discos, parties, etc. at which homosexuals gather.

meat wagon *n*
1a. a police van, **black maria**
1b. an ambulance
1c. a hearse
All the senses of the phrase were first heard between the world wars.

mega *adj*
enormous, hugely successful, great, wonderful. A popular teenage buzzword since the mid-1980s, by the end of the decade mega had penetrated adult speech, in particular journalese. In origin it was an adaptation by black American youth of the fashionable late-1970s prefix 'mega-' into an independent adjective.
This band is going to be mega, mark my words!
We had this real mega thrash.

megabucks *n*
an enormous amount of money. An Americanism of the 1970s which is now heard elsewhere, including Britain, where '-bucks' remains the suffix although not strictly appropriate. ('Mega-' was a fashionable prefix of the late 1970s.)
He's making megabucks in the City.

mellow out *vb*
to become relaxed, serene; to free oneself from tension and inhibition. The phrase is a cliché of the **hippy** era, taken from the jargon of jazz and, later, rock musicians. It is still heard, largely in American speech.

melon *n American*
the head. The humorous usage featured in the cult 1992 film, *Wayne's World*.
Use your melon, guy!

melon(-head) *n British*
a stupid person. The word was recorded in use among younger teenagers in the late 1980s.

melons *n pl*
female breasts. An obvious metaphor which exists in other languages, notably Spanish. The word was employed as a nickname by the British tabloid press in 1986 to refer to the supposedly buxom figure of Lady Helen Windsor.

melvin *vb American*
to grab by the testicles
'I don't believe we just melvined death.'
(*Bill and Ted's Bogus Journey*, US comedy film, 1991)

Melvin *n American*
a boring person, nonentity. The Christian name was thought in the 1950s to be quintessentially mundane, personifying a suburban dullard. More recently it has been a term of abuse among college students.

Melvyn (Bragg) *n*
1. a sexual encounter, **shag**
2. a cigarette, **fag**
The rhyming slang uses the name of the British TV arts programme presenter and novelist.

memsahib *n British*
1a. one's wife
1b. a dignified, domineering or redoubtable woman
The word, now usually employed facetiously, is a form of madame-sahib (*sahib* is Hindi for master or lord), a form of address used by Indian servants in the colonial era. (The usual pronunciation is 'memsaab'.)

meneer *n South African*
a teacher. The term is Afrikaans for 'sir'. Recorded as an item of Sowetan slang in the *Cape Sunday Times*, 29 January 1995.

mensch, mensh *n*
1a. a reputable, admirable or dependable person (usually, but not invariably, a male). An approving term from Yiddish and German in which its literal meaning is man, woman, person or humankind.
1b. an exclamation of surprise or alarm from Yiddish or German

mental¹ *n See* **throw a mental**

mental² *adj*

1. *British* mentally ill, subnormal or deranged, crazy. A widespread colloquialism which showed signs of losing popularity in the 1970s, perhaps due to increased sensitivity; this tendency was reversed by **punks**, fans of heavy metal and others who enthusiastically adopted the term to refer to their characteristic frenzies, **headbanging**, etc. In these circles the word may be used to express admiration.

See also **chicken oriental**; **radio rentals**

2a. exciting, dynamic

2b. excellent, good

mentalist *n British*

a crazy, eccentric or obsessive person. A common pejorative term among younger speakers since the late 1990s. In standard English the word denotes a mind-reader.

me 'n' you *n*

a menu. A time-honoured pun heard in all English-speaking areas.

merchant banker *n British*

a contemptible person, a **wanker**. This rhyming slang, coined in the late 1980s like its synonym 'Kuwaiti tanker', highlights a contemporary concern (in this case the spectacular mid-1980s developments in the financial centres of the City of London) to revitalise a familiar epithet.

mereng *n South African*

money

merkin *n*

1a. the female pubic area or female sex organs

1b. an artificial vagina, used as a sex aid

Merkin is a late medieval word for a wig designed to be worn on the female pubis, usually in order to disguise the effects of syphilis. It probably originates as an affectionate diminutive form of Mary. From the 1960s the word was better known in the USA than Britain.

mersh *adj*

commercial. A word used in the 1980s in fashionable youth circles and rock journalism, usually at least slightly pejoratively.

mersh tendencies.

Meryl (Streep) *adj British*

cheap. The rhyming slang term, in use since around 2000, uses the name of the Hollywood actress.

messed up *adj*

intoxicated by or suffering the aftereffects of alcohol or drugs

messy *adj*

excellent. A term from the lexicon of dance music and hip hop.

mestern *n South African*

fashionable clothing. Recorded as an item of Sowetan slang in the *Cape Sunday Times*, 29 January 1995.

Met, the *n British*

the London Metropolitan Police force. The abbreviation by which they refer both to themselves and their district or area of jurisdiction (which covers most of central and suburban London but excludes the City).

meth *n*

Methedrine (the trademark name for methamphetamine). A drug user's abbreviation for the powerful amphetamine-based stimulant (**speed**) which has been widely abused, particularly in the mid- and late 1960s.

meths *n British*

methylated spirits, as drunk for its intoxicating effects by alcoholics, vagrants, etc.

metrosexual *n*

a stylish, narcissistic male. The term combines metropolitan and heterosexual and denotes a **straight** man with **gay** tastes or attitudes. It was coined in the USA in 2002 and became a vogue term in most English-speaking areas in 2003.

Compare **stray**; **stromo**

Mexican breakfast *n*

a cigarette and a glass of water. A witticism originating in the USA, where the Mexican reference is supposed to evoke poverty and lack of sophistication or competence. There have been other, probably later, variations on this pattern, among which are **dingo's breakfast** and 'pelican's breakfast' (a glass of water).

mezoomas *n pl*

female breasts. One of many similar invented terms probably based on the archaic **bazumas**, a corruption of bosom.

Michael Jackson *n British*

an amount or quantity under ten. The term was used by City of London financial traders in the 1990s and the reference was to the celebrity singer's supposed attachments to young children.

mick n
1a. an Irish person. This shortening of one of the most common Irish Christian names (along with Patrick or **Paddy**) was first used in the USA and Australia to personify the Irishman or a person of Irish descent. The usage had spread to Britain by the early years of the 20th century.
1b. a Roman Catholic, by extension from the first sense
In both senses, the word is usually used unaffectionately or pejoratively.
2. See **take the mick/mickey/michael**

mickey (finn) n
a soporific or stupefying drug administered to a person without their knowledge. The word was first recorded in the USA in the early 20th century. It may derive from the name of a real individual or from a generic (probably seafarers') term for a cudgel or thug.

Mickey (Bliss) n See **take the mick/mickey/michael**

Mickey Mouse adj
amateurish, unworthy of consideration or respect. A contemptuous description beloved of the business world in the 1970s and 1980s, Mickey Mouse has in fact been used in this way since before World War II when the phrase was applied for instance to childish or simplistic music or the bands which played it. It subsequently denoted any institution or venture which did not deserve to be taken seriously.
    It's strictly a Mickey Mouse operation they're running there.

middle leg n
the penis. **Third leg** is an alternative form of the euphemism.

mighty greens n South African
dagga. The term, referring to the colour of the herbal cannabis, was recorded as an item of Sowetan slang in the Cape Sunday Times, 29 January 1995.

milf n American
a desirable older female. The designation, typically used by young males in conversation or Internet chats, derives from the phrase '(A) Mom I'd like to fuck'.

militant adj
1. an all-purpose term of approval. A usage originating in Jamaican **yardie**

speech, which has now been taken up by adolescents in the US and Britain.
2. violent or 'known as being hard'
3. angry
A term used by young street-gang members in London since around 2000.

milkshake n American
female allure, sexiness. The quality, referred to in a song by Kelis, is the feminine counterpart of **pimp-juice**.
    She got milkshake.

milly n British
1a. a disreputable young female
1b. a **chav** of either gender
The term, of uncertain origin, was recorded in 2005.

milned-up adj British
incarcerated. The term, from the jargon of prisoners, now often refers to temporary imprisonment in, e.g., an observation cell. In the form 'milned-in' the phrase dates back at least to the 1940s: Milne were the makers of door-locks used in prisons.

milquetoast, milktoast n American
an un-macho, meek man; a **wimp**. Reminiscent of the food given to invalids, milquetoast derives from the name of the fictional character Caspar Milquetoast, created by the American cartoonist H. T. Webster. Zsa Zsa Gabor used the term, to the puzzlement of many British viewers, when interviewed during her trial for assault in California in 1989.
    'Asked why she resisted, she said: "I'm a Hungarian woman … not a milquetoast".'
(Agency report on Zsa Zsa Gabor during trial)

mincer n British
a male homosexual, effeminate or effete male. In armed-forces' usage, from the notion of a 'mincing gait'.

minces n pl British
the eyes. From the cockney rhyming phrase, 'mince pies'. The expression is still used today by working-class Londoners; it is now invariably heard in the shortened, one-word form.
    OK then, feast your minces on this!

minder n
a bodyguard. A word which emerged from the obscurity of working-class and criminal slang into general usage in the early 1970s, mainly due to the fashion for quasi-realist crime drama on British television. This trend culminated in the

later, gentler television series of the same name, starring Dennis Waterman and George Cole.

mindfuck *n*
a disorienting experience, a manipulation of or interference with one's mind, a staggering idea or event. A **hippy** expression which has lingered on into post-hippy usage. It has been used approvingly to describe a particularly strong drug.

minge *n British*
the female pudenda. A taboo word which was particularly prevalent in working-class speech of the 1950s. It originated in late 19th-century country dialect and may be from Romany.

'Minge is one of the assortment of words for the sexual bits that people think should keep him [Chubby Brown] off television because some viewers would not understand him anyway.'
(*Independent*, 31 July 1989)

minger *n British*
an unattractive person, particularly a promiscuous woman. A vogue term among adolescents since the later 1990s. The term comes from the verb 'to ming', originally a Scottish dialect synonym for stink.

minghawk *n Scottish*
a foolish and/or annoying person. The term has been adopted in other parts of Britain since around 2000.

minging *adj*
1a. *Scottish* stinking
1b. *British* unpleasant, unattractive. A vogue term in adolescent speech since around 2000.

mingy *adj British*
a term of childish criticism or abuse which is a blend of 'mean' and 'stingy' with which it rhymes, rather than an adaptation of the taboo word **minge**

mini-me *n*
a diminutive and/or irritating person, imitator, epigone. The term can also be used as a combining form, as in 'he's a mini-me Hayward', i.e. an inferior imitator of Hayward. From US usage from the Mike Myers *Austen Powers* comedy movies.

mink[1] *n*
1a. *American* a woman, particularly a provocative, spirited and/or sexually attractive or active woman

1b. *American* the female sex organs, female sexuality
We gotta get us some mink.
2. *Irish* a gypsy. The word is used by Romany travellers to refer to themselves, presumably evoking the fast-moving and alert animal and perhaps reflecting the irony that the mink is considered both valuable and vermin.

mink[2], minky *adj British*
excellent. A term of approbation recorded among art students in the south of England in 2002.

mint *adj British*
excellent, fashionable. A vogue term of approbation used by adolescents since the 1990s. Synonyms are **fit** and **top**.

minted *adj British*
wealthy, solvent. A term widespread in all age-groups since around 2000.

miraculous *adj Scottish*
drunk. The humorous and ironic usage may derive from the word's resemblance to **ridiculous**, which is used in the same sense or, as Eric Partridge suggests, may be a mocking adaptation of a 19th-century euphemism such as '(in) miraculous high spirits'.

mish *n British*
a journey or task. This abbreviated term for 'mission' was popular among adolescents in the later 1990s, and can probably be considered as a new coinage, although the same word was recorded in public-school slang as early as 1913.

Miss Brown *n British*
(a cup of) coffee. A code term from the slang of medical staff.
'If ever your doctor is asked, "Would you like to see Miss Brown after this patient?" he or she is being offered a cup of coffee.'
(*Sunday Times*, 6 October 1996)

Mister Nice-guy *n*
a paragon of kindness, friendliness, tolerance, etc. This American expression has become international mainly in the form of the catchphrase 'No more Mr Nice-guy!', expressing exasperation.

mitch *vb British*
to play truant, **bunk off**. Partridge dates this usage to the mid-19th century. It is still heard (**ditch** is a current synonym).

mither *vb British*
to complain, nag, bother or prevaricate. A northern English dialect word which is now widely known due to its use by comics such as Jasper Carrot and in the

soap opera *Coronation Street*. It is a variant form of 'moither' or 'moider', words first recorded in the 17th century and meaning both to babble and to baffle or bewilder.

> *I can't stand his endless mithering about what he's going to do and how he's going to afford it.*

mithered *adj British*
shivering with cold. Used by adolescents since 2000, the word originates in provincial English dialects.

mitt, mit *n*
the hand. A shortening of 'mitten', first used to mean glove (particularly in boxing and baseball) and, later, the hand. This American slang term, popular among pugilists and underworld 'tough guys', crossed the Atlantic in the early 20th century. 'Mitten' itself is from an old French word (*mitain(e)*) which was either a pet name for a cat or a corruption of the Latin *media*; half(-fingered).

> *'He started with a cartwheel/finished in the splits/leaving Salome with his toupee in her mits.'*
> (*Salome Maloney, the Sweetheart of the Ritz*, poem by John Cooper Clarke, 1980)

mixin' *n British*
fighting, from black speech. Synonyms are **tanglin'**, **startin'**.

mix-up *n British*
an argument. In this sense the term is used by black British speakers and teenagers of other backgrounds.

mob, the *n American*
organised crime, the mafia. Mob was used to refer to gangster syndicates from the 1930s onwards, in underworld and police jargon and subsequently in journalese. The term is now standard. It has produced derivatives such as 'mobster' and 'mobbed-up' (involved with the mob).

moby¹ *adj*
1a. *American* huge
> *A moby truck.*

1b. *American* overweight
> *Getting/going moby.*

Both terms derive from the fictional whale *Moby Dick* as a symbol of enormity. The first sense may be appreciative or neutral, the second usually pejorative.

2. *British* nauseous, *sick*. An item of rhyming slang from Moby Dick.

moby², moby dick *n British*
a mobile phone. A term used by teenagers since 2000. **Brick** was an earlier synonym.

mockers *n British*
misfortune, curse, frustration. An expression which is used by schoolchildren as an exclamation, sometimes of defiance, more usually in an attempt to put off or jinx an opponent in sports or games. Mockers probably derives via the Yiddish *makeh*, from Hebrew *makah*, meaning 'plague' or 'wound', reinforced by the English words 'mock' and 'muck (up)'. In adult usage the word normally appears in the phrase **put the mockers on**, meaning to ruin, thwart or jinx.

mockie *n American*
a Jew. A pejorative term of uncertain etymology; it may be related to the British **mockers**, but this cannot be demonstrated conclusively.

mockney *n British*
(a person) affecting a quasi-proletarian accent. The term arose in theatrical circles and was picked up by the media in the late 1980s to refer to attempts by upper- and middle-class speakers to modify their accents in order to render them more stylish and 'streetwise'.

mod *n British*
a member of a 1960s youth cult characterised by an obsessive interest in fashionable clothing, in the riding of motor-scooters and in listening and dancing to soul and ska music. The first mods, who began to gain prominence in 1962, referred to themselves as modernists, whence the more lasting epithet. The intention behind the word at this time was to distinguish these style-conscious, mainly working-class young people from the parochial or traditional appearance and attitudes then prevalent in Britain.

> *'When we found out that mods were just as conformist and reactionary as anyone else, we moved on from that phase too.'*
> (Pete Townshend, *Rave* magazine, February 1966)

mode *adj British*
affectedly fashionable, pretentious. A deliberate mispronunciation of **mod**, heard in the 1960s and used to express derision.

> *Oh yes, get a load of that gear, very mode!*

MoFo n American

a disguised form of **motherfucker**, used in conversation and in journalese in the 1990s

moggy, moggie, mog n British

a cat. Moggy was originally a term of endearment or familiarity for any animal. In northern English dialect it was used to designate e.g. a mouse, calf or cat. The exact etymology of the word is uncertain; it may be from the Norse *magi*, meaning stomach, or from the use of 'Maggie' as a name for a pet.

'Can I just inform you that in South Lancashire a moggy is not a cat, it is a mouse or a small insect. When will the rest of the country learn this?'

(Reader's letter to the *Independent*, 4 September 1992)

mojo n

1a. a magic charm, spell or influence. A black American concept, popularised elsewhere by its use in blues and rhythm-and-blues records of the 1950s and early 1960s. The word's origin is thought to be West African, but no specific source has been identified.

1b. any un-named object; thingummy. The word can be used as a euphemism for anything, but is characteristically employed for sex organs or drugs.

moll n

1a. *Australian* a prostitute. Moll, a short form of 'Molly' (itself a familiar version of 'Mary'), has been used to denote a woman of 'easy virtue' since at least the time of *Moll Flanders* by Daniel Defoe, published in 1722. This sense has survived in Australia, where a 'band moll', for instance, is a **groupie**.

1b. *American* a woman, specifically a female companion. This sense of the word, familiar from its use in crime fiction as 'gun moll' or 'gangster's moll', is now outdated.

molly exclamation British

the term, recorded in 2000, was defined as '…used to alert someone to the fact that their inability to act seriously or stop laughing is starting to irritate you'

momma n

a female adherent to a Hell's Angels chapter. The momma is a sort of unattached member of the entourage; steady girlfriends are usually known as 'old ladies'.

'We've got a few mommas so they get passed around.'

(London Hell's Angel, *Oz* magazine, April 1969)

momser, momzer n

1a. a contemptible person, particularly a cadger or sponger

1b. a cheeky, enterprising or self-willed person

The term, which is most often heard in American speech and applied to males, is the Hebrew word for 'bastard'.

mondo adj British

excellent, admirable. The American combining form was adopted as a synonym for such vogue terms of approbation as **top** in around 1991.

That new video-game is mega-mondo.

mondo- combining form American

an all-purpose combining word which in Italian and Spanish means 'world (of)' and in American English means 'a situation of…' or 'a state of affairs characterised by…'. The word is then followed by the defining word, usually with a mock-Latin 'o' ending as in 'mondo-sleazo', 'mondo-bozo' or 'mondo-cheapo'. This pattern derives from the 1963 Italian documentary film *Mondo Cane* (translated as 'A Dog's Life') which acquired cult status and inspired first intellectual wits and later college students and **Valley Girls** to coin similar phrases.

Monet adj American

attractive at a distance but not when seen at close quarters. This vogue pejorative term from the language of Californian high-school girls in the 1990s (it features in the 1994 US film *Clueless*) is applied to the appearance of persons and occasionally objects. It is based on the notion of Impressionist paintings.

'To her character Cher Silverstone would have therefore been a "Monet" – which means OK from a distance but a mess close up.'

(*Sunday Times 'Style'* magazine, 22 October 1995)

money adj American

cool. A fashionable term since the **yuppie** era.

You're so money and you don't even know it.

mong n British

an idiot, clumsy fool. A shortened form of 'mongol', itself a term (for those suffering from Down's syndrome) now considered offensive. Mong was a vogue term of abuse among London school-children in the early 1970s and was still in use in 2004.

mong'd, monged, monged out adj British
1a. intoxicated and incapacitated by drugs. The words, fashionable in 1990s **rave** culture, are based on 'mongol(oid)'. **Gurning** and **sledgied** are similar terms.
1b. hung-over or suffering from a drugs **comedown**. A term used by young street-gang members in London since around 2000.

mongie, mongy adj British
(of a person) stupid, dull-witted, slow and clumsy. A 1970s derivation from **mong**, itself short for the pejorative 'mongol'. Both spellings of the word are pro-nounced with a hard 'g'. Like the noun, the adjective was mainly heard among schoolchildren.

mongrel n
1a. a despicable person. This use of the standard word dates from the 1700s. It is now particularly prevalent in Australia and New Zealand.

> 'They call themselves journalists but they're a bunch of bloody mongrels.'
> (Recorded, Australian reporter, London, November 2004)

1b. Australian a person of mixed race. A racist term of abuse since the 18th cen-tury.

moniker, monniker, monicker n
a name, nickname or alias. No defini-tive history of this word has been estab-lished. What is known is that it has existed in various spellings since the mid-19th century and that it was first used by tramps, vagrants and other 'marginals'. The three most likely deri-vations are from 'monarch', 'monk' or 'monogram', but none of these is prova-ble nor is there any clear connection with the (Saint's) name 'Monica'.

> 'Christened by his father – a heavy duty John Wayne and Cowboy fan – with the name WAYNE WANG. Would this split-cultural, cartoon moniker destine the baby to grow up, leave Hong Kong and end up in California directing an all-American film ... and a violent one at that?'
> (I-D magazine, November 1987)

monkey n British
1. £500. A raffish term in use among gamblers, street traders, **spivs**, etc. The origin of the term is obscure; it has been in use since at least the early 19th cen-tury and, confusingly, is also used to refer to sums of £50 or, on occasion, £50,000.

> 'My client is not the kind of man to be satisfied with a mere monkey for his serv-ices.'
> (Arthur Daley in Minder, British TV se-ries, 1987)

2. an inferior or menial. Inspired by such images as the organ grinder and his monkey, the word is used to refer dis-missively or contemptuously to under-lings or errand-runners, etc.

> 'I'll deal with this myself; the monkeys downstairs can take care of the calcula-tions.'
> (Recorded, accountant, London, 1986)

monkey run/walk/parade n British
a teenagers' promenade, a ritual parade of courting couples or hopeful 'singles'. This dated term was used particularly before World War II to describe both the location and the practice. The expres-sion continued to be used by older speakers until the 1960s.

monkey's n British
a damn. A word invariably heard as part of the dismissive or defiant expressions 'don't give/care a monkey's'. The term is an abbreviated form of undefined but presumably offensive phrases such as 'monkey's **fart/fuck/balls**'.

> 'I'm sure they'll be saying terrible things about us, but quite frankly I couldn't give a monkey's.'
> (Recorded, university lecturer, London, June 2005)

monkey suit n
a uniform, particularly one which is thought to demean the wearer. Typically applied to bellboys, doormen, etc. dressed in absurd or confining outfits, the term derives from the practice of dressing monkeys in such clothing for carnival displays.

monniker n
an alternative spelling of **moniker**

monster n British
an unattractive and/or unpleasant per-son. Defined as 'someone who looks disgusting and smells', this is an item of student slang in use in London and elsewhere since around 2000.

monster! exclamation British
excellent. A popular expression of enthusiasm or admiration, mostly heard

among middle-aged speakers in the 1990s.

-monster *combining form*
1a. *American* a personification of a threat or irritation, as in 'rack-monster' (exhaustion) or 'pavement monster' (bumps or holes in a road surface)
1b. an epitome or outstanding example, as in 'beer monster', **shag-monster**

monstering *n British*
(a) chastisement, 'dressing-down' or harangue. A word which occurs predominantly in middle-aged usage in a professional context and among members of the armed forces.

> *'In one confrontation, Montgomery, the group's chief executive, delivered such a "Hitlerian monstering" to a senior executive that she was reduced to tears.'*
> (*Sunday Times*, 30 March 1995)

Montezuma's revenge *n*
an attack of diarrhoea. Heard all over the English-speaking world, this jocular expression is the American equivalent of **Delhi belly** or **gyppy tummy**. In Mexico, Montezuma (spelt 'Moctezuma' locally and by many academics), the 16th-century Aztec emperor, is a national hero.

monty *n See* **full monty, the**

moo *n British*
a woman, particularly a stupid or unpleasant woman. It has been claimed that the comedy script-writer Johnny Speight invented this abusive term for his 1960s television series *Till Death do us Part* to avoid the BBC ban, in force at that time, on the use of the word **cow**. In fact the word already existed in London working-class vocabulary from at least the 1950s.

moobs *n pl*
male breasts. The term, recorded in 2004, is formed from man or male and **boobs**. **Maps** is a contemporary synonym.

mooch¹ *vb*
1a. to hang around, linger aimlessly, idle
1b. to cadge, sponge, take advantage of (one's friends)

> *'I've been mooching off you for years and it's never been a problem until she showed up.'*
> (*School of Rock*, US film, 2003)

The word has been in use since the 19th century in both senses and has formed part of the lexicons of tramps, criminals, **beatniks** and the fashionable young of the 1980s in both Britain and the USA. Its ori-

gin is uncertain.

mooch² *n American*
a cadger, sponger, scrounger. A back-formation from the verb.

moody¹ *n British*
1a. a sulk, fit of bad temper or sullenness. A popular working-class expression of the late 1970s, usually in the form 'throw a moody'. Moody was a popular all-purpose cockney term for negative, fake or false in the earlier 20th century and 'doing a moody' used to mean acting suspiciously. Later, a moody signified a simulated fight or quarrel.
1b. a lie. A word which usually occurs in criminal or police usage, sometimes in the form 'old moody'.

> *Listen we don't need old moody, give us the names.*

moody² *adj British*
illegal, counterfeit, of dubious value, quality or provenance. A London working-class term which, from the late 1980s, began to spread into fashionable youth parlance.

> *They accused him of selling moody gear off his stall in the market.*

mook *n American*
a term of abuse of uncertain meaning and unknown origin. It may be a variant form of **mooch** or even **mug**.

> *'It's very nasty to call a person a honky mook.'*
> (Steve Martin, *All of Me*, US film, 1984)

moolah, moola *n*
money. A humorous word imported into Britain from the USA before World War II. It is an invented term, probably in imitation of Amerindian, African or other foreign languages, as is the more recent British synonym, **womba**. Like most slang terms for money, moolah underwent something of a revival in the late 1980s.

> *'Many congressmen arrive in Washington expecting to get rich – if not quick, at least before they leave. The art is in finding ways to get the moolah without contravening the various laws and rules of ethics.'*
> (*Observer*, 12 June 1989)

moon¹ *vb*
to exhibit the buttocks publically, typically from the window of a moving car. A term and practice popular with American teenagers since the 1950s. It has been a common practice among young male students in Britain from at least

the late 1970s. (Moon refers to the white globes on display.)

> *'And it's hard not to warm to Panic's bare-faced nerve – mooning in discos, lifting a wallet and rifling through it insolently in full view of the impotent owner.'*
> (*Independent*, 12 January 1988)

moon[2] *n British*
a foolish, irritating or obnoxious person. The word has been used in this sense by young schoolchildren (perhaps by analogy with 'loon' or 'buffoon') for many years. Since 2000 it has been adopted by some adolescents, sometimes evoking strong dislike.

moonrock *n American*
a mixture of **crack** and heroin

moose[1] *n*
an ugly or unattractive female. A vogue term, in use among British adolescents in the later 1990s, which has been defined as 'someone who looks disgusting and smells'.

moose[2] *adj British*
1. unpleasant, boring, ugly. The adjectival usage postdates the noun.
2. excellent. In this sense the word was recorded in South Wales in 2000.

moose-knuckles *n Canadian*
a synonym for **camel toes**

moosh *n*
an alternative spelling of **mush**

moreish, morish *adj British*
appetizing, tempting. This predominantly middle-class colloquialism, applied to anything edible, is a pun on 'moorish' (as in architecture), dating surprisingly from the 18th century.

more-time *exclamation*
'see you later'. The expression, which was used by London teenagers in the 1990s, may originate in black speech. **Later(s)** is a synonym.

moriarty *n British*
a *party*. A fairly rare item of rhyming slang employing the name of the arch enemy of Sherlock Holmes, later reinvented as a dastardly villain in the BBC radio comedy show *The Goons* in the 1950s, from when this usage dates.

Mork and Mindy *adj British*
windy. The rhyming slang term, still heard after 2000, uses the title of a US comedy TV series of the late 1970s and early 1980s.

> *It's a bit Mork and Mindy out this morning.*

morning lager *n British*
tea. Used invariably by males, in army and Officer Training Corps usage.

mortal, mortalled *adj Scottish*
drunk. The expression 'mortal drunk' (i.e. hopelessly or dangerously) was in use from the early 19th century.

Moses *vb, n British*
(to go to) sleep. From the name of the Kenyan athlete, Moses Kiptanui, and the slang term **kip**.

> *get some Moses*
> *I've got to Moses.*

moshing *n British*
dancing in a packed scrimmage to heavy metal, **hardcore** or any other fast, loud rock music. This activity, which is more a form of energetic communal writhing than dancing, was adopted by fans of hard rock during the late 1980s as a successor to **slam dancing**, **headbanging** or the characteristic playing of imaginary guitars ('air guitar').

moss-back *n American*
an elderly person. The term is often applied affectionately in family slang to an older relative. Synonyms are **cotton-top** and **frost-top**.

most, the *n*
something superlative, the very best. A well-known item from the vocabulary of **hipsters**, **beatniks**, etc. of the 1950s. (A later jocular coinage by analogy is **the least**.)

mother *n American*
1. an abbreviated and euphemistic version of **motherfucker**. This version, more common than the full form, is often used appreciatively rather than pejoratively. It is sometimes spelled **muthah** in imitation of black or southern pronunciation. The word is probably used to refer to objects and animals as often as humans.

> *Man, that was some big mother.*
> *Did you get a look at that mother?*

2. a male homosexual, particularly a man in a dominant, protective or influential relation to younger males

motherfucker *n American*
1a. a despicable person. The most common term of strong abuse in the American vocabulary. (Euphemistic forms such as 'mother-raper', 'mother-jumper' or just **mother** are sometimes substituted.) The expression, naming the ultimate in degeneracy, originated among poor blacks.

'Oedipus was a motherfucker.'
(Graffito, Euston station, London, 1972)

1b. an awesome or appalling thing, situation, etc.

one motherfucker of a mess

mother's ruin *n*
gin. A late 19th-century nickname which refers to the widespread effects of cheap gin on the working class (of both sexes); to the later supposed predilection of women for the drink; and to its long-lived reputation as an abortifacient.

motoring *n British*
making good progress, performing well. A driver's expression of the 1970s (meaning moving at speed) which became generalised in the 1980s to mean roughly the same as the American **cooking**.

OK, great, now we're motoring!

motormouth *n American*
a person who talks excessively, a 'fast-talker'. A popular term from the mid-1970s, it originated in black ghetto slang. The word was later applied to amphetamine users, disc jockeys, comics and **rap** artists.

mott *n British*
the female sex organs. A vulgarism still widely used (by men) in the 1960s, but now rare. It is from the French *motte*, meaning mound, used by 19th-century pornographers among others.

motzer, motza *n*
(an instance of) good fortune, surprising luck. The words, heard in British and Australian speech, are versions of the Yiddish name for an outsize cookie, itself related to *mazel*: good luck.

mousetrap *n British*
a Japanese person. An item of cockney rhyming slang (for *Jap*) which probably originated during World War II, but is still heard, for instance, among City financial traders in London.

mouth-breather *n*
a primitive, brutish person. The phrase is used contemptuously for those considered thuggish and/or moronic, evoking the image of a shambling, open-mouthed, slack-jawed creature, invariably male.

mouth down *vb American*
to keep quiet, shut up

mouthpiece *n*
a lawyer, specifically one's defence counsel or legal representative. A term used, particularly by the underworld, since the mid-19th century. The word is sometimes extended to refer to any spokesperson.

'A deliberate slip of the tongue gets a laugh. A sergeant begins a question: "When a defendant has got a mouthpiece – sorry, I mean solicitor…".'
(*Inside the British Police*, Simon Holdaway, 1983)

mouthy *adj British*
talkative, boastful or verbose. A pejorative working-class term.

moxie *n American*
spirit, vim, courage, enterprise. Moxie was the trade name of a soft drink on sale in the USA in the 19th century (probably based on a local Amerindian place name). The drinks company used the advertising slogan: 'What this country needs is plenty of Moxie!'.

Mozart *adj Australian*
drunk. The word is one half of the rhyming-slang phrase 'Mozart and Liszt': **pissed**. The British equivalent is **Brahms (and Liszt)**.

mozzer, mozza *n*
luck, good fortune. This seems to be the main surviving variant among many words ('mozz', 'mozzle', 'mozzy') deriving from the Yiddish *mazel*: a cookie blessing the consumer with good luck. The words have existed in British working-class speech since at least the 1880s and later became part of Australian usage, usually in the forms **motzer** or **motza**.

'That was a bit of mozzer – all six at one stall.'
(Recorded, Newbury, 1989)

Mr/Mister Sausage *n*
the penis. An adults' imitation nursery-word of the sort which has enjoyed a vogue since the mid-1980s, particularly in middle-class British usage. The playwright Mike Leigh used the term in dialogue ascribed to a **yuppie** couple in his 1988 feature film, *High Hopes*.

Mr/Mister Whippy *n British*
flagellation. A code term from the argot and repertoire of prostitutes. The light hearted euphemism is from the name of a brand of ice cream displayed on vans.

muckamuck, (high) mucky-muck *n American*
a person in authority or a VIP, especially a self-important one. The term originated in the 19th century and apparently derives from an Amerindian phrase meaning 'plenty to eat'.

'Fuck you. It [a concealed gun]'s in Mr Chancellor's name. He got it okayed by the muckamucks.'
(Jonathan Kellerman, *Over the Edge*, 1987)

mucker *n*
a friend, 'mate', pal. The term is said to have originated in armed-service usage as a longer expression, 'mucking-in pal' or 'mucking-in spud', soon shortened to mucker. The word survives mainly in the speech of hearty males.

There you are, Keith, me old mucker.

mucky duck *n British*
an unattractive female, defined on the Student World website in 2001 as 'an ageing slapper'

mucky pint *n British*
a combination of Bailey's Irish Cream liqueur and other alcoholic drinks. The reference is to the muddy colour and slightly viscous consistency as compared with a pint of ale or lager. The term has been in use among students and younger drinkers since 2000.

mudfish *n*
an ugly or unattractive female. One of many pejorative synonyms in use among UK students since 2000. **Mutt**, **munter** and **swamp-donkey** are contemporary alternatives.

mudskipper *n*
a synonym for **mudfish**

mudsucker *n American*
an unpleasant or despicable person. A term of abuse coined to echo the syllables of the more offensive **motherfucker**.

muff *n*
the female sex organs and/or the female pubic hair. This euphemistic use of the standard word for an enveloping hand- or ear-warmer made of fur (deriving ultimately from the mediaeval Latin for mitten, *muffula*) originated in the 17th century and is still current, although less common than in the 1950s and early 1960s.

muff-diving *n*
cunnilingus. A jocular coinage based on the long-established use of **muff** to denote the female genitals.

muffin *n*
the female genitals. An elaboration on the older 'muff', used singularly or generically. The term is heard in Britain and Australia. In the USA the plural form is occasionally used to denote the breasts.

muffins *n pl American*
female breasts. **Baps** is a British synonym.

mug *n*
1. the face. The word has had this meaning since the early 1700s; it derived from the practice of making china drinking-mugs decorated with grotesque human faces.
2. a fool, dupe. This use of the word was inspired by the image of the victim as an open-mouthed receptacle.

muggins *n British*
a victim, dupe or 'loser', especially when referring to oneself. The word is an embellishment of **mug** (and is also an authentic, if comic-sounding, surname). It is now so common as to be an innocent colloquialism rather than true slang.

And muggins here was left holding the bill.

mug (someone) off *vb British*
to make a fool of, take advantage of. An item of London working-class speech dating from the 1950s.

'She's taken the mickey and mugged me right off.'
(Gangster Ronnie Kray, quoted in the *Sun*, 5 October 1993)

mugwump *n American*
an important, powerful person. This now rather dated word is invariably used facetiously or pejoratively and is especially applied to someone who has power and influence but is a maverick or unreliable. It is from the Algonquin Indian *mugquamp*, meaning a chief.

mule *n*
a carrier of illicit drugs across frontiers and/or through customs, a transporter of contraband; someone hired to do this rather than the owner of the drugs. The term was first used by smugglers, then later by law enforcers.

'He used to go over and buy the stuff, then pack it, but it was always brought in by mules.'
(Recorded, London, 1989)

mulga *n Australian*
an unpleasant situation, experience, etc. *Mulga* is a native Australian synonym for acacia and originally denoted an inhospitable or deserted region of bush. 'Mulga-madness' is an archaic term for the mental disorientation experienced by outbackers.

mulled *adj British*
drunk. An inoffensive term heard predominantly outside the London area.

muller *vb British*
to destroy, ruin, confound. The term is said to derive from the German surname 'Muller', perhaps referring to a footballer who scored against England in 1970, or to a manufacturer of armaments. The word became very widespread from the later 1990s in all areas and age groups.

They absolutely mullered us.
We were mullered big time.

mullered *adj British*
1a. destroyed
1b. intoxicated by drink or drugs. A popular term among adolescents from the 1990s, it is an elaboration of the earlier **mulled**.
1c. exhausted
The term is said to derive from the German surname 'Muller', but pronounced as if English.

mum *n British*
a homely female. The term is one of a set of (mainly unflattering) categorisations applied by young males, such as City of London financial traders, to female colleagues in the 1990s. Others include **Nora**, **oof**, **dragon**. A mum is not necessarily motherly, but benevolent and sexually irrelevant.
See also **mumsy**

mumblefucker *n British*
an irritatingly clumsy, inept or fastidious person. A term heard in the early 1970s. There have been other invented terms, with a similar lack of meaning, playing on the comical overtones of the syllables employed; **fucknuckle** is an example.

mumbler *n British*
a UK synonym for the earlier Americanism **camel toes**. The word refers to the

notion that 'lips are visibly moving but no sound is heard'.

mumping *adj British*
scrounging, soliciting favours, begging. A word dating from the 17th century which survives in police and underworld argot. It used to refer to the activities of beggars and vagabonds; it is now often applied to the reciprocal favours encouraged by police officers in contact with local people. The word is descended from the Dutch *mompen*, meaning to cheat.

mumsy *adj British*
the older generation's colloquialism to describe a woman who is unglamorous and 'motherly' has become a fashionable categorisation for a younger generation for whom the maternal aspect is probably less important than the suggestion of fussiness, unfashionable appearance, asexuality, etc.

munch *n British*
food. A recent usage posted on the Internet by *Bodge World* in February 1997.

munchied *adj*
hungry. The term is derived from the older notion of **(the) munchies**, but does not necessarily refer to peckishness induced by cannabis consumption. It was recorded among middle-class London students in 2002.

munchies, the *n*
hunger, especially a craving for food brought on by the lowering of blood-sugar levels that is a well-known side-effect of smoking cannabis. The word was a children's synonym for snacks which was adopted by **hippy**-era smokers of hashish and marihuana.
'Those smug, stupid hippies, who thought it so cool to be comatose called that post-smoke famished feeling "the munchies", and for once they were right.'
(*Platinum Logic*, Tony Parsons, 1981)

munchkin *n*
a cute small child, a dwarf, underling. An American expression taken from the name of the little people in the musical, *The Wizard of Oz*; the word is used affectionately or condescendingly. (A low-level munchkin is an employee near or at the bottom of a hierarchy.)

mung *n*
dirt, muck. A term that encompasses everything filthy or distasteful, used

particularly by teenagers or students since the late 1970s.

munged adj South African
intoxicated by drink or drugs

munt n South African
a black person. A highly offensive term used by white racists. The word is Afrikaans slang deriving from the Bantu *umuntu*, meaning a person.

munter n British
defined in 2001 as 'someone who looks disgusting and smells', the term has been in vogue among adolescents and young adults since 2000

muntered adj British
drunk. An item of student slang in use in London and elsewhere since around 2000.

munter-hunter n British
a male who seeks out ugly females 'looking for an easy lay', as reported on the Student World website in 2001

munting toad n British
a very ugly or unattractive female. The phrase is an elaboration of the more widespread **munter**.

muppet n British
a retarded, incapacitated or grotesque person. A word usually used with none of the affection or humour that its innocent source (the American TV puppet show of the 1970s) might suggest. The term has been applied to hospital inmates, mentally deranged prisoners or simply to unattractive teenagers by their peers. According to a UK student in 2002, 'when many muppets are gathered in one place, the expanded phrases *The Muppet Show* or *Muppets Take Manhattan* may be used'.

murphies n pl American
female breasts. The word 'murphy' is adapted from its use (since the 19th century) as a nickname for a potato.

murphy¹, the murphy n
1. *British* a potato. The Irish surname has been used as a joky synonym since the early 19th century.
2. the murphy *American* a confidence trick whereby valuables lodged for safekeeping are stolen or substituted by worthless goods

murphy² vb American
to subject (someone) to **the murphy** (a term denoting various forms of a simple confidence trick)

mush, moosh n British
1. the face. A word which has been in use since the 19th century, when it often referred specifically to the mouth. Mush is nearly always used in connection with fisticuffs and may have originated as pugilists' slang. The precise etymology of the word is uncertain, but it has obvious connotations of softness and mastication.
2a. an all-purpose term of address to a stranger (invariably used by men to other men). A working-class, mainly London, usage which was common in the 1950s and 1960s but is now rarely used. The word is not particularly friendly and is quite often used provocatively. It comes from the Romany word for man, *moosh*.

'I suggest you buy better shirts in future. Are you asking for a punch up the faghole, mush?'
(*Hancock's Half Hour*, BBC TV comedy, 6 November 1959)

2b. a man, unnamed person. The derivation for this usage is as for the previous sense. The word has rarely been used thus (rather than as a term of address) since the 1950s.

mushroom n
an innocent bystander caught in the crossfire of a gunfight. This term, from the jargon of the Jamaican yardie 'Shower Posse', was reported in the *Sunday Times*, 14 November 1993.

muso n
1a. a musician, player of rock music with real technical expertise
1b. a rock or progressive music fan who displays a pedantic or obsessive interest in his or her favourite music and/or musicians

mutant n
a clumsy, foolish or otherwise unpopular individual. A term used by adolescents to refer to unpopular or despised fellow-students or other contemporaries. The same word is used with the opposite connotations in the form **mutie**.

muthah n
an alternative spelling of **mother** (in its slang or euphemistic sense), particularly used by fans of heavy metal music to refer appreciatively to each other or their heroes

mutie n British
a daring exponent, devotee. A word used by skateboarders and some surfers and rock-music fans to refer to themselves

and their fellows. The word is a diminutive form of **mutant** which itself is usually employed with negative connotations.

mutt n

an ugly or unattractive female. The term, originally denoting a dog, has been popular among younger speakers since 2000.

mutton, Mutt 'n' Jeff adj British

deaf. Rhyming slang, from the cartoon figures created by Bud Fischer, which were popular before World War II. The slang expression has been heard in London from the late 1940s to the present day. It was spread further afield by its use by the character of Albert in the popular 1960s television comedy series *Steptoe and Son*.

> '*I'm sorry, love, you'll have to speak up. I'm a bit mutton in my old age.*'
> (Recorded, London, 1988)

mutton dagger n

the penis. A joky euphemism on the lines of **pork sword** and **beef bayonet**.

muttonhead n

a variation of **meathead**

mutt's nuts, the n, adj

(something) excellent. In playground and student usage since 2000. Like **the dog's dangly bits** it is a version of the earlier **the dog's bollocks**.

> *Dave's new stereo is the mutt's nuts.*

mwah exclamation

an imitation of a kissing sound, originally often suggesting insincerity or affectation, now often sincere affection and sometimes written down, as in e.g. closing a text message

my bad! exclamation American See **bad²**

mystery n British

a runaway person, vulnerable minor. A term from the language of pimps, paedophiles, the homeless and police, referring to someone of uncertain origin or identity.

mystery bags n pl Australian

sausages. The term is influenced by the name of a children's lucky dip sweet packet and is both a rhyming slang term for **snags** (another slang term for sausages) and an ironic comment on the dubious contents of some sausages. Often thought to be a native Australian coinage, mystery bags is another example of British slang of the 19th century which seems to have died out in the country of origin but has survived among the emigrant population; it was recorded in 1889 in this form; previously occurring simply as 'mystery' or 'bag of mystery'.

> '*What's for dinner?*
> *Mystery bags ... snags ... sausages.*'
> (*Razorback*, Australian film, 1984)

N

nabe n American
1a. a neighbourhood
A new guy in the nabe.
1b. a neighbour
The nabes are acting up again.
A shortening of the sort popularised by *Variety* magazine and perpetuated in teenage speech. (**Mersh** and **the burbs** are other examples of this trend which enjoyed a particular vogue in the late 1980s.)

nack vb British See **knack**

NAD adj British
'not actually done' in medical shorthand, e.g. as added facetiously to a patient's notes

nada n
nothing. The Spanish word is used in English slang, especially in the USA.

nadgered adj British
a middle-class alternative of **knackered** in all its senses
'By the time I got home I was feeling pretty nadgered.'
(Recorded, 15-year-old boy, Horsham, England, October 1995)

nadgers n pl British
1. the testicles. The word was probably used in this sense merely due to the resemblance to **knackers**. It has not been widely used since the 1960s.
a kick in the nadgers
2. the nadgers a state of nervous agitation, irritation, distress or unhealthiness, as in such phrases as 'he's got the nadgers' or 'it gives me the nadgers'. The word could also be used to describe a curse or jinx in the same way as **mockers**. This humorous nonsense term of the 1950s (popularised in broadcast comedies such as *Hancock's Half Hour*) is now virtually obsolete.

nads n pl American
the testicles. An abbreviated form of 'gonads' used jocularly by teenagers since the 1980s.

naff adj
tasteless, inferior, shoddy and unappealing. Naff had existed in working-class slang for at least 40 years by the time it became a vogue word in the later 1970s. It had been used in the jargon of prostitutes to mean nothing or negligible. In the theatrical, criminal and street-trading milieus it meant third-rate or poor quality. The word's sudden popularity occurred probably because it was seized upon by TV scriptwriters (particularly Dick Clement and Ian La Frenais in the comedy series *Porridge*) as an acceptable euphemism for **fuck** in such forms as 'naff-all' (meaning **fuck-all**), **naffing** and **naff off**. Naff's ultimate origin, which seems to be 19th century, is nonetheless obscure. It has been claimed that it is a **backslang** form of **fan(ny)** (in the sense of female sex organs) or an acronym or alteration of a phrase involving the word fuck (such as 'not a fucking fart' or similar). Neither etymology is attested (or particularly convincing), and the similarity to NAAFI is probably coincidental.
'To be naff is to be unstylish, whatever that may mean.'
(*The Complete Naff Guide*, Bryson et al., 1983)

naffing adj British
an all-purpose intensifying adjective used as a euphemism for **fucking**

naff off vb British
to leave, go away. The expression is usually in the form of a dismissive exclamation or instruction synonymous with **fuck off**. First used in the TV series *Porridge* in the mid-1970s, the phrase was given great prominence in 1982 when Princess Anne told reporters who were pestering her to naff off.

nag n
a horse. The well-known term is used particularly by horse-racing enthusiasts. It was first recorded in 1400 when it

was paralleled by the Dutch *negge*, meaning a small horse.

nail (someone) *vb*

to identify, catch, punish or defeat (or any combination of these). This common term, which can now also by extension (and by analogy with **screw**) refer to the sexual conquest of a woman by a male, has been heard since at least the 18th century.

nailed-up *adj British*

arrested, imprisoned. An item of police and underworld slang.

> *'I used to shift cars, but I'm telling you that there's more money and less hassle in this. I don't know anyone who's been nailed-up for shifting spares.'*
> (Car thief, quoted in the *AA Magazine*, 1995)

namby *n British*

1. a weak, cowardly person, a **wimp**. A schoolchildren's word of the late 1980s which is a shortening of the standard English adjective 'namby-pamby'.

> *'Him? He's a fucking namby.'*
> (Recorded, teenage schoolgirl, London, 1988)

2. a committed opponent of a controversial environmental policy (such as nuclear power). This journalistic quasi-acronym of 'not in anyone's backyard' was coined in imitation of the more common **nimby** ('not in my backyard') in the USA in the mid-1980s.

nana *n British*

a silly fool. This word was very popular among children from the 1950s to the early 1970s and is still sometimes revived; adults, too, used the term in the late 1950s and early 1960s. It is a nursery shortening of 'banana', a meaning it still retains in post-colonial nurseries in areas such as India and the Caribbean.

nanana *n South African*

a small car. Recorded as an item of Sowetan slang in the *Cape Sunday Times*, 29 January 1995.

nancy boy, nance *n British*

an effeminate man, a male homosexual. This term seems to have originated in the late 19th century, when the name Nancy, a diminutive form of Ann or Agnes, was applied indiscriminately to women as a term of affection and famil-

iarity. The echoes of 'nice' and 'mince' in the rather prissy sound of the word probably went toward reinforcing its derogatory use for men. There was a vogue in the East End of London in the 1930s for male street-dancers in women's clothing who were known as nancy boys.

> *'See the nancy boys do their dance.'*
> (Poster in satirical illustration of decadent England, *Private Eye* magazine, 1963)

nang *adj British*

excellent. A vogue term among London schoolchildren since the late 1990s. **Bare nang** is an intensified form.

nanny (goat) *n British*

a *quote*. An item of journalistic rhyming slang of the 1990s.

nanty, nanti, nants *adj British*

no, none, nothing. The word was in use in London working-class and theatrical slang from the early 19th century until the 1960s; this is an example of **parl-yaree**, the Italian-inspired patois of actors, showmen and circus workers. Nanty originates in the Italian *niente*, meaning nothing. The last recorded instance of its use was in the radio comedy *Round the Horne*, in which the effeminate characters Julian and Sandy referred to Kenneth Horne's having 'nanty **riah**' (no hair).

narc, narco *n American*

a narcotics investigator or member of a police drug-squad. The word is particularly heard among drug users referring to undercover agents. It may be influenced by, but is not directly related to, the British **nark**.

nards *n pl American*

the testicles. A distorted pronunciation of **nads**, itself an abbreviation of gonads. The word is heard among pubescent and adolescent males.

narg *n British*

a tediously or offensively hard-working and/or socially inept individual. The term was first recorded as part of Oxbridge student slang in the 1960s and is invariably applied to males who are typically unattractive and badly dressed. It may derive from an imitation of the drawling nasal speech seen as typical of such students.

nark[1] *vb British*
1. to inform on, betray. From the noun **nark**.
2. to stop or to keep quiet. This cockney usage invariably occurred in the command 'nark it!'.
3. to annoy or affront; to needle. This expression, which was particularly popular in the 1950s and which is also heard in Australia, is derived ultimately from the Romany word *nak*, meaning nose. Nark in its modern sense is semantically related to such expressions as 'to have one's nose put out of joint', **to get up one's nose**, or 'poke one's nose in'. It is often heard in the form of its past participle, **narked**, meaning annoyed or affronted.

> 'The trouble is, many people today they won't do anything. I got a very poor opinion of my fellow creatures, a very poor opinion. So I nark them whenever I can. I like narking people.'
> (82-year-old Ted Bosley, quoted in the *Independent*, 18 May 1989)

nark[2] *n British*
1a. an informer. The expression originated in the 19th century as 'copper's nark', meaning a police spy or **grass**, nark being an alteration of the Romany (gypsy) word *nak*, meaning nose.
1b. a spoilsport, teacher's pet, nuisance or toady. This more generalised usage, deriving from the previous sense, was fairly widespread in the 1950s in working-class circles and is still heard among schoolchildren.
1c. a policeman. In underworld, prison and tramp's jargon.

narked *adj British*
irritated, annoyed, affronted. For the derivation of the word see the verb **nark**.

narky *adj British*
irritable, upset. A working-class term used principally in the north of England.

> She's been a bit narky all morning.
> He's feeling narky.

narly *adj American*
an alternative spelling of **gnarly**

narr *exclamation British*
a synonym for or alteration of 'no'. The fashionable usage was posted on the Internet in February 1997 by *Bodge World*.

nash *n British*
the vagina. An item of black street-talk used especially by males, recorded in 2003.

nasties *n pl British*
nursery slang for (old and dirty) underwear or swimming trunks. A narrowing of a general notion of 'offensive objects'.

> 'Don't forget to pack some nasties if we're going anywhere near a beach.'
> (Recorded, social worker, London, 1986)

nasty[1] *n*
1. a sex organ, the genitals. A childish word used humorously by adults in phrases such as 'as dry as a nun's nasty': thirsty.
2. a sexual act. A synonym of the coy or euphemistic **naughty**.

nasty[2] *adj American*
excellent, impressive, skilled. An expression used on campus in the USA since around 2000.

> That guy is nasty on the handball court.

natch *adv*
naturally. A shortening used in **hip** talk.

nathan *n American*
nothing. The name is substituted in black street slang and campus usage.

natty *adj*
impressive, admirable, **cool**. A vogue term in Jamaican youth patois, particularly in the phrase 'natty dread', but usable as an all-purpose term of approval. It derives from a shortening of 'natural', referring in Rastafarian terms to someone following the laws of God and nature, perhaps influenced by the standard English adjective meaning trim or smartly-dressed (which itself is probably a variation of neat).

naughty[1] *n*
an illicit act, usually referring to sex and typically occurring in phrases such as 'have a (quick) naughty'. The coy expression, which sometimes also refers to a crime, is heard in both British and Australian speech.

naughty[2] *adj British*
1a. criminal, corrupt. A typical piece of understatement from the argot of police and the underworld. This tendency is characteristic of London working-class speech (**spanking**, meaning a (severe) beating-up, would be another instance).
1b. impressive, daring. A fashionable usage in working-class speech, generally

among adults, from the late 1980s; the word is used to indicate admiration or approval as in 'That's a well-naughty looking bird'.

nause n British

1a. a nauseatingly unpleasant person. A middle-class term popular in the mid-1960s and now very rarely heard. It has been suggested that this word is in fact a variation of 'Noah's', short for 'Noah's Ark', 1950s underworld rhyming slang for **nark**. As nauseate and nauseous were both fashionable terms in middle-class British and American use in the early 1960s, they would seem more likely origins.

'She was going out with a policeman; God, he was a real nause.'

(Recorded, student teacher, London, 1965)

1b. a nuisance, an unpleasant situation or task. 'Nauseate' had a (now obsolete) slang sense of bother, irritate or infuriate in the 1950s, whence this usage. The concept is rendered in modern speech by the colloquial expression to **get up one's nose**.

nause (someone) out vb

to disgust, nauseate. The term is used by adolescents on both sides of the Atlantic, although often in Britain minus the 'out' component.

nauticals n pl British

haemorrhoids, *piles*. An item of jocular rhyming slang (on 'nautical miles') used in *Viz* comic in the 1990s.

Ooh, me nauticals!

navvy n British

a manual labourer, unskilled construction worker or road digger. Navvy is a shortening of 'navigator', which was a nickname given to open-air construction workers engaged in building roads, canals and railways in the late 18th and early 19th centuries. Canals in England were often built by navigation companies, hence the nickname of their employees.

nearly-wife n

a live-in girlfriend, not a fiancée. An item of student slang in use in London and elsewhere since around 2000.

neat adj American

an all-purpose term of approval which became popular among teenagers in the mid-1960s and has survived. It is often ridiculed by sophisticates as evidence

of naïve or gushing enthusiasm. The word occurred with this sense in the slang of jazz musicians, the 'smart set' and adolescents as long ago as the early 1920s.

'You're a neat girl.

So are you – I mean … you're a neat guy.'

(*Blue Velvet*, US film, 1986)

nebbish, nebesh, nebech n

a fool, an ineffectual, clumsy or pathetic person. The word entered English speech from Yiddish in which one of its meanings is a pitiful nonentity or 'loser'. The ultimate origin of the word is the Czech adjective *nebohy*, meaning unhappy, unfortunate or diseased.

'A nebech is more to be pitied than a shlemiel. You feel sorry for a nebech; you can dislike a shlemiel.'

(*The Joys of Yiddish*, Leo Rosten, 1970)

neck[1] n

cheek, impudence, daring, **chutzpah**. This sense of the word is at least 100 years old, originating in rustic northern English speech. It survives principally in the form **brass neck**, a synonym for 'barefaced cheek'.

'I tell you, she's got plenty of neck: she walked out [on her husband] and then told him to move out.'

(Recorded, housewife, London, 1988)

neck[2] vb

1. to kiss, embrace and pet. An American euphemism dating from the early years of the 20th century.

2. *British* to drink, ingest. The raffish verb, probably a back-formation from the drinkers' catchphrase-injunction 'Get this down your neck!', became fashionable from the early 1990s. It was adopted by members of the **acid house** and **rave** subcultures who referred to 'necking E's' (swallowing tablets of **ecstasy**).

neck-oil n

alcohol. Drink thought of as a physical and social lubricant by (usually hearty) drinkers.

necro n British

an unpleasant and/or obnoxious person. In playground usage since 2000. It is a shortening of 'necrophiliac'.

ned n Scottish

a hooligan. The word has been in use since the 1960s: it may be related to **ted(dy) boy**. In 2004 it was a synonym for **chav**.

neddy n British
a horse, **gee-gee**. A children's pet name appropriated by adults, particularly in the context of betting and horse-racing.

need it! exclamation British
an all-purpose cry of provocation, defiance or solidarity, used by schoolchildren in the 1970s

needle, the n British
irritation, resentment, provocation. The word has been used in expressions such as 'take the needle' (take offence), 'give someone the needle' and **get the (dead) needle** since the late 19th century.

needle-dick n
(someone with) a small penis. This expression (usually heard in the USA) is also sometimes used as a non-specific term of abuse.

nellie[1], **nelly** n British
1. an ineffectual, weak, effete or sentimental person. Often given more emphasis by phrases like 'big soft nellie' or 'great wet nellie'. Nellie was used until the late 1940s in the USA and Britain as a humorous or contemptuous appellation for a male homosexual.
2. in the phrase 'not on your nellie', the word was originally from Nelly Duff, an invented name providing a rhyme for **puff** in the sense of breath, hence life
3. a fat and/or dowdy female. The pejorative term, used by adolescents, may derive from the 1950s children's song Nellie the Elephant.

nellie[2], **nelly** adj American
effeminate. The adjective, based on the earlier noun form, became fairly widespread in the late 1990s.

Nelson (Mandela) n British
(a drink of) Stella Artois lager, playing on the name of the former President of South Africa and leader of the anti-apartheid movement. **David (Mellor)**, **Paul (Weller)** and **Uri (Geller)** are synonyms, all popular with students since the late 1990s.
OK, set up the Nelsons.

nerd n
a gormless, vacuous, tedious and/or ineffectual person. Since the later 1970s this has been a vogue term, particularly among adolescents. It was coined in the USA in the late 1960s or early 1970s by members of surfing and hot-rodding cliques to refer to outsiders considered feeble or conformist. The word was then taken up on student campuses and by **hippies**. (An underground cartoon strip of the early 1970s portrayed nerds as a sub-species of suburban dullards.) The word nerd itself (**nurd** was an earlier alternative spelling) is of uncertain origin, but may be influenced by **turd**.
'And the jock shall dwell with the nerd and the cheerleader lie down with the wimp and there will be peace upon the campus.'
(Observer, 29 May 1988)
'"Being a nerd is chic these days", proclaimed the tediously Teutonic Britta Hoffner from Frankfurt, Germany. "I am a nerd and proud of it".'
(Sunday Express, 27 February 1994)

nerdling n British
performing devious financial manoeuvres, 'massaging the figures'. The word was used by City financial traders in London from the 1990s. It is a technical term from the game of Tiddlywinks, in which it means to execute a clever move that confounds one's opponents.

nerdy adj
gormless, ineffectual, characteristic of a **nerd**. The adjective postdates the noun.
'He favoured dark business suits, dark ties that hung straight down against his white shirts, and a short nerdy Afro.'
(Where Did Our Love Go?, Nelson George, 1985)

nerk n British
a fool. An invented, mainly middle-class term which predates the (probably unrelated) American **nerd**. 'Fred Nerk' was a fictitious personification of idiocy or small-mindedness in the 1950s.

nerts n American
a polite alteration of **nuts**

net-head n
an enthusiastic user of the Internet. This phrase, using the component **head** in the sense of aficionado (as in, e.g., **petrolhead**), moved in the 1990s from being an obscure item of American jargon to being a widespread and fairly respectable designation.
'A net-head's adventures online.'
(Subtitle to Surfing on the Internet by J. C. Herz, 1994)

never-never n British See **on the never-never**

newbie n
a newcomer or new user on the Internet, in the patois of **cyberpunks** and **net-**

heads. **Noob** is a more recent variant from.

> 'Depending on where they show up or on how they behave, newbies are either patiently tolerated or mercilessly hazed.'
> (*Surfing on the Internet* by J. C. Herz, 1994)

Newquayed, newkied *adj*
drunk. The expression, used by young males, may derive from **nuke** or from 'newky' as a nickname for strong Newcastle Brown beer.

newted *adj British*
drunk. A term based on the vulgar expression 'as **pissed** as a newt'.

N.F.A. *adj British*
a homeless person in the jargon of the police and representatives of other authorities. The term is based on the official designation of 'no fixed abode'.

N.F.N. *adj British*
unintelligent and/or unsophisticated. An item of medical slang (reported in the *Sunday Times* 'Style' magazine, 6 October 1996) which can facetiously be written on case notes in front of patients without their understanding. It is an abbreviation of 'normal for Norwich/Norfolk', based on the supposition that inhabitants are characteristically slow-witted and provincial.

niagaras *n pl*
the testicles, **balls**. Rhyming slang from 'Niagara Falls'. A word heard in Britain and Australia, where it has been adopted especially by students, rock journalists, etc. from the original 1950s working-class usage.

> She kicked him in the niagaras.

nice guy *n See* **Mister Nice-guy**

nick[1] *vb British*
1. to steal. The word has been used in this sense since at least the 1820s. The word is rare in the USA, but has been recorded in the sense of rob.

> 'The doctor's had his bike nicked and his place turned over, and the only time we see the Old Bill is when they're in here getting legless.'
> (*Biff* cartoon, 1986)

2. to arrest. Nick was a colloquial term for catch from the 16th century. By the early 19th century it had also acquired this specific meaning.

nick[2], **the nick** *n British*
a prison or police station. This common expression dates from before World War

II and postdates the verb form **nick**, meaning to arrest.

> I think you'd better come down the nick and explain yourself.
> He's been in nick on and off all his life.

See also **nick-bent**

nick-bent *adj British*
temporarily or expediently homosexual because incarcerated. A prisoners' term mentioned by the upper-middle-class former prisoner Rosie Johnston in 1989. **Nick** is a well-established slang synonym for prison, **bent** for homosexual.

nickel-and-dime *adj American*
trifling, cheap, petty. Nickels and dimes (five and ten cent coins) constitute small change.

nicker *n British*
£1, one pound (sterling). This common term has been in use since about the turn of the 20th century (when it also denoted a sovereign). Nicker was the name given to pieces of metal thrown down in a game and later applied, in racing, to flinging down a sovereign bet on a horse.

> I made about fifty nicker on the deal, didn't I?

nick off *vb British*
1a. to play truant. A synonym of **bunk off**, **wag it** or **wag off**.
1b. to skive off, do a runner

> She gone and nick'd off.

niff *vb, n British*
(to give off) a bad smell. Originally an Eastern English dialect version of 'sniff'.

> There's a terrible niff in here.
> 'I wouldn't get too near to that dog; he niffs a bit.'
> (Recorded, editor, London, 1988)

nifty *n British*
a sum of £50. This old rhyme was revived among City traders and subsequently adolescents in general during the 1990s.

> Bung him a nifty and he'll probably come across.

Nigel *n British*
an upper-middle-class or upper-class male. A pejorative term since the 1960s, Nigel is thought to epitomise ostentatious young men who drive sports cars and wear flat caps and tweed jackets.

'Naff causes of death: ... racing a right Nigel from Oxford to Cambridge in a silly sports car.'
(*The Complete Naff Guide*, Bryson et al., 1983)

Nigerian lager n British
Guinness beer, stout. A witticism inspired by the black colour of the brew. **African lager** is a synonym.

nigger n
a black person. This word has been in use since the late 18th century. It is now a term of racist abuse when used by white speakers, although it can be used affectionately or sardonically between black speakers. The word is derived from *niger*, the Latin word for the colour black, via Spanish (*negro*), French (*nègre*) and the archaic English *neger*.

nightmare adj
awful. In adjectival form the word has been in vogue among teenagers and young adults in all English-speaking areas since the 1990s, possibly influenced by the cliché 'nightmare scenario'.
nightmare homework

nimby n
an opponent of controversial legislation (typically on environmental issues), only so long as he or she is directly affected. The word is an acronym for the slogan or catchphrase 'not in my back yard', coined in the United States (where a 'yard' is a garden) in the 1980s to describe a syndrome whereby a person supports a potentially harmful move or policy in principle but opposes it for selfish reasons. The American expression entered common currency in Britain around 1986. (An unqualified opponent to the same issues is a **namby**.)

> *'He thinks working motherhood is a jolly good thing, but he's also a nimby ("by all means let mothers work, so long as it's not in my office").'*
> (Sarah Jane Evans, *Sunday Times*, 18 March 1989)

nimrod n
a foolish, unattractive or unfortunate person. The term was recorded on US campuses in the early 1990s and subsequently in UK school playground parlance.

nine-ball n American
an outsider, misfit, socially inept person, from the billiard ball

nine-bob note n British
1a. a homosexual, sexual deviant
1b. something false, obviously counterfeit or crooked
Both senses are usually expressed in the phrase 'bent as a nine-bob note', a surviving example of many expressions using comparisons beginning '**queer** as–' or '**bent** as–'. In pre-decimalisation UK currency there was a ten-shilling banknote but not a nine-shilling one.

ning-nong n Australian
a fool. A now dated, but not altogether obsolete word inspired by **nig-nog** (in the earlier non-racist sense) and nincompoop. It may be unrelated to the synonymous **nong**.

ninny n British
the vagina. The term was recorded among adolescent girls in 2002.

nip, Nip n
1. a Japanese person. (*Nippon* is the Japanese word for Japan.) 'Jap' has been the preferred term among British speakers, but nip has made headway since the mid-1970s. This term is largely pejorative.
2. a computer microchip

nipply adj American
cold, chilly. The term is derived from the colloquial 'nippy' and the phenomenon of erect, painful nipples caused by cold. An expression used on campus in the USA since around 2000.

nish n British
nothing. An old alternative form of **nix**, first heard among working class Londoners and in showbiz circles and **polari**. It was recorded in use by adolescents in 2000.

> *'How much did you ask her for?'*
> *'£25 a week.'*
> *'How much did you get?'*
> *'Nish.'*
> (Recorded, secondary pupils, London, March 2005)

nit n
1. *British* a foolish person. A contraction of nitwit which was popular in the 1950s, especially among radio comedians, but is now almost obsolete.
2. *American* nothing. A variant form of **nix**.

nitso, nitto n British
nothing. British alternative forms of **nix**, in working-class London usage.

nitty-gritty, the *n*
the essentials, small details. This now
common phrase was adopted in Britain
from American speech in the second
half of the 1960s. The expression originated in black slang, in which nitty-
gritty referred to the scalp in the context
of grooming.

nix¹ *n*
no, nothing, none. One of very few German words to enter the thieves' and low-
life cant of the early 19th century and
remain in occasional use. *Nichts* is the
standard German for nothing or not, *nix*
being a colloquial version.

nix² *vb*
to forbid, veto. This form of the word is
predominantly American, its brevity rec-
ommending it to journalese usage.
The governor nixed the proposals.

nizzle *n See* **-izzle**

Noah, Noah's *n*
1a. *Australian* a shark
1b. *British* a park
1c. *British* a **nark** (informer)
All the senses of the word are examples of
rhyming slang, from 'Noah's ark'. The two
British instances are now rare if not obsolete.

nob¹ *vb British*
to copulate. A working-class usage which
became fashionable in the 1970s and
early 1980s. It derives from the use of
(k)nob to mean the penis, and as such is
usually, but not invariably, used by and
about men.
'We ate your food and nobbed your tarts.'
(Jools Holland, of the pop group
Squeeze, at the end of a tour of Venezue-
la, 1980)

nob² *n British*
1. the head. This now old-fashioned
usage dates from the 17th century or earlier and is a form of archaic words which
survive as 'napper', 'nape' and 'knob'.
2. an aristocrat or VIP. Nob in this sense
may derive from sense 1 (by way of the
notion of a famous, prominent or swollen-
headed personage), from the use of nob
to designate the head on the Jack card in
cribbage or, more straightforwardly, as a
shortening of 'noble' or 'nobility'.
*'A second battle between the nobs and
the yobs was a slice of real life, as filmed
by BBC2's new documentary series,
"Enterprise Culture". A builder named
Ken King has bought Avebury Manor.'*

(Kate Saunders, TV review, *Evening
Standard*, 17 May 1989)
3. the penis. In this sense the spelling
knob is usually preferred.

nobber, nobba *n British*
a fool. Often used as a term of endearment, usually by and between males.

nobble¹ *n British*
1. an act of dishonestly interfering with a
process, such as by bribing a member of
a jury or drugging a racehorse. From the
verb.
2. a trick, a devious scheme or clever way
of doing things
*'I said, look, the nobble is to give me
some money and I'll get you some
[drugs]. It's just a bit of a nobble really.'*
(Rockstars' **minder**, *Guardian*, August
1987)

nobble² *vb British*
to incapacitate or subvert. The term
applies specifically to drugging or otherwise distressing a racehorse in order to
adversely affect its performance, or to
suborning or threatening members of a
jury. The word probably originated in rustic use with the meaning 'knock on the
head', perhaps influenced by **nob**, and
hobble.

nobbo *n See* **knobbo**

nob-rot *adj British*
bad. A term popular among schoolchildren since the 1990s.
They're a nob-rot band.

noddy *n British*
a buffoon, simpleton, clumsy or
ungainly person. In modern usage the
term has been specifically applied to
low-ranking police officers by members
of the CID and public. Noddy is an
archaic rustic term for a simple-minded
or cloddish individual, inspired by such
a person's inadvertent head movements. The use of the word for the
famous children's storybook character
created by Enid Blyton reinforced the
image evoked.

noddy bike *n British*
a Velocette motorcycle, as used by police
patrolmen until the end of the 1960s.
The ungainly, inelegant motorbikes were
derided by professional police motorcyclists, motorbike enthusiasts, **rockers**,
etc. **Noddy** is a nickname applied to low-
ranking police officers, reinforced by
identification with the children's storybook character created by Enid Blyton.

no diggety *exclamation*
'no doubt', 'no question'. An expression from the lexicon of **rap** and hip hop.

nod out *vb*
to become unconscious or fall asleep. This racier version of the standard 'nod off' is used especially in connection with drug-induced somnolence or stupor.

noggin *n British*
1a. a drink. The word of unknown origin may designate a measure of a quarter pint or simply an alcoholic drink of any size or type.
1b. the head

noid *n*
a paranoid person. The clipped form, typical of adolescent slang since the late 1980s, was popular among students in Britain in the late 1990s.

> *Don't be such a noid, no one's getting at you.*

no-mark *n British*
an insignificant person, a 'nobody'. An item of Merseyside slang popularised by the TV soap opera *Brookside*.

nonce, nonse *n British*
a prisoner found guilty of sexual offences against children or other acts against the pale of prison morality. Short for 'nonsense boy' or 'nonsense case'.

> *'Nonce meaning nothing, a non-sense, a no one, a non-thing, a phenomenon existing somewhere between noun and verb, between the most terrible acts and the dreadful word for them: pervert, child molester, sex offender, monster, beast ... The nonce is the game in an open season.'*
> (Ken Smith, *Inside Time*, 1988)

noncey *adj British*
affected, pretentious, overly respectable. The word is probably an alteration of **ponc(e)y**, perhaps influenced by **nancy boy** or **nonce**.

> *'There was a time in my life when this sort of noncey Robert Robertson thing would have made me puke, but I must be getting old or something.'*
> (Zoë Heller, *Sunday Times* magazine, 12 November 1995)

nong *n Australian*
a fool. The word is of obscure origin; it may originate in an Aboriginal word or as a corruption of *non compos mentis* (meaning 'not of sound mind'). It is prob-

ably unrelated to the synonymous **ning-nong**.

non-linear *adj*
upset, agitated, anxious. In this sense the term arose in the language of computer specialists in the 1990s.

no-no *n*
something forbidden, impossible, unwelcome, inadvisable, etc. An American slang term which, since the early 1970s, has become a common colloquialism in all English-speaking countries.

non-swimmer *n British*
an Afro-Caribbean person. A euphemism, usually used with mildly racist connotations by younger middle-class white speakers since the 1990s.

non-trivial *adj*
important and/or demanding. A usage originating in the jargon of computer specialists.

noob *n*
a more recent form of **newbie** used in Internet communication since around 2002

noodle *n*
1. the head. In this sense the word is a variant form of **noddle**.
2. a fool or simpleton. This sense of the word is probably inspired by the notion of softness.

noodling *n*
behaving in an aimless and/or unhurried manner. This use of the word is variously explained as being inspired by the length and consistency of noodles, or as an alteration of 'nodules' – the object apparently of leisurely 'fossicking' by Australian miners.

> *'The Dead would crank up an old standard ... and zone off into extended soloing and noodling as their LSD trips unfurled.'*
> (*Q* magazine, March 1997)

noogie, nuggy *n American*
1a. a kiss or hug
1b. petting or other sexual activity
This Americanism, which may possibly be distantly related to the British **nookie**, is a survival of an archaic British dialect term 'nug', which is itself related to the verb 'nudge', and which meant to fondle.

nookie *n British*
sexual intercourse or sex in general. This coy term became popular in the late 1970s and 1980s, probably due to its

use in the media in place of more offensive synonyms. (Nookie also occurs, albeit rarely, in American usage.) The etymology of the word is uncertain. It may be a form of the archaic British dialect verb 'nug' (which has survived in American speech in the form **noogie**: kiss or hug), or it may alternatively be an alteration of an older euphemism for the female pudenda as a 'shady nook'. It has been defined recently as '70's style slang for sex, now making a bit of a comeback'.

noonie *n*
an alternative spelling of **nunnie**

noov, noovo *n, adj British*
(a person who is) nouveau riche. A dismissive term employed by upper-class and public-school speakers and pseudo-intellectuals. Etonian schoolboys applied the term to Harrovians in the late 1980s.

Nora *n British*
a drab or unattractive woman. The phrase 'a right Nora' was used in the 1990s by students and other adolescents to condemn any female thought to be frumpy, unattractive or shrewish. The term is inspired by the character of Nora Batty in the TV comedy *Last of the Summer Wine*.

norks *n pl Australian*
female breasts. This word is said to be inspired by the wrapper design for butter produced in the 1950s by the Norco Co-operative Dairy Company, which showed a cow with a full udder. The word was introduced to British speakers by the *Barry McKenzie* cartoon series, running in *Private Eye* magazine in the 1960s. 'Norkers' and 'norgs' were earlier forms.

Norman no-mates *n British*
a rarer version of **Billy no-mates**

Norman Normal *n British*
a very conventional, conformist person. The mythical Norman (supposedly an especially dull, typically bourgeois or petit bourgeois Christian name as well as resembling 'normal') was invoked by the last **beatniks** and, after them, the **hippies** as a term of light-hearted contempt.

Norris *n American*
a misfit, outsider, clumsy and inept person, usually male. An expression used on campus in the USA since around 2000.

north and south *n British*
the *mouth*. A piece of Victorian London working-class rhyming slang that is still heard, always in the full form.

'What a mouth, what a mouth/ What a north and south/ Blimey what a mouth he's got!'
(Lyrics to 'What a Mouth', recorded by Tommy Steele, 1960)

nosebleed *n American*
an obnoxious person

nose candy *n American*
cocaine. Another euphemistic use of **candy** in particular and sweet imagery in general to describe drugs. This term was widespread among users following the adoption of cocaine as a middle-class fashion in the late 1970s.

nosh¹ *n British*
1. food. In Yiddish, the noun (deriving from the verb form, itself from the German *naschen*) signifies a snack or tidbit eaten between meals. In English usage it has been generalised to encompass all sizes of meal.

'Hey look at all that lovely nosh going to waste.'
(*Biff* cartoon, 1986)

2. a promiscuous and/or disreputable female. A term used by young streetgang members in London since around 2000.

nosh² *vb*
to eat. The word is a later alteration of *nashn*, a Yiddish version of the German word *naschen*, meaning to snack or eat surreptitiously.

After he'd noshed everything on the table, he started in on the fridge.

no shit, Sherlock! *exclamation*
an ironic riposte to a statement of the obvious. Probably originating in American speech, it is also an item of student slang in use in London and elsewhere since around 2000.

nosh (someone) off *vb British*
to have oral sex with someone, perform fellatio or cunnilingus. A 1980s invention in self-conscious imitation of cockney forms of the 1950s.

nosser *n British*
a homeless person, vagrant

not(!) *exclamation*
a contradiction of the previous statement. The usage, which some linguists claim to have originated in Celtic languages, was popularised by the cult US

film *Wayne's World* in 1992 and the comedy sketches on the US TV programme, *Saturday Night Live*, on which it was based. It neatly replaces the older mechanism whereby the phrase 'I don't think!' was appended.

She's my favourite person. Not!

no-tail *n British*
a female. The term, used typically by males, is probably inspired by its usage in the black comedy TV series *The League of Gentlemen*, but may be earlier in origin.

not bill *n British*
the vagina. Based on **bill** in the sense of the penis, this term was in use among middle-class adolescent males in 2000.

not bill mice *n British*
tampons. A jocular term in use among middle-class adolescent males in 2000.

notch *n American*
the female sex organs

not many! *exclamation British*
an all-purpose term of dismissal, derision, etc., in London working-class speech. Its precise derivation is unclear, but it may be a replacement for the earlier use of 'not much!' as an ironic riposte to a statement of the obvious.

not shy *adj British*
sexually forward, promiscuous. A jocular euphemism heard e.g. on British campuses since 2000.

not the full shillin' *adj British*
slow-witted and/or distracted, eccentric. A folksy expression dating from the pre-decimalisation era, still heard in 2004, perhaps due to its use in the TV soap *Coronation Street*.

nouve, nouveau *n, adj British*
alternative renderings of **noov, noovo**

novel *adj British*
pretentious, unoriginal, unappealing. The standard term has been used ironically in this way by students and others since 2000.

nowhere *adj*
worthless, inferior, hopeless, uninteresting. A dismissive term which formed part of the **beatnik** vocabulary in the USA in the 1950s and later in Britain. When the Beatles recorded *Nowhere Man* in 1965, the word was in vogue in very limited circles; it was subsequently heard among **hippies**, particularly in the USA.

nowherian *n*
a vagrant or feckless person

nowt *n British*
nothing. A northern English dialect version of the archaic or literary 'naught'. The word is sometimes appropriated by southern speakers for emphasis, irony or familiarity.

N.T.D. *adj British*
an abbreviation of 'not top-drawer'; a code term of snobbish disapproval sometimes used in all seriousness by **Sloane Rangers** or would-be members of the upper classes

nuddy, nuddie *adj British*
nude, naked. A schoolchildren's humorous or coy mispronunciation of the standard English term, usually in the phrase 'in the nuddie'.

nudger *n*
a **gay** male. This pejorative term is a shortened form of **fudge-nudger**.

nudnik, noodnik *n American*
an irritating, boring or stupid person. This Yiddish word is derived from the Czech adjective *nudny*, meaning tiresome or boring.

'nuff *n*
a humorous rendering of 'enough' reflecting its pronunciation in rapid or childish speech. The word is usually seen in this form in the cliché "nuff said". Vogue expressions also employing the word were 'nuff-tuff', meaning bold or daring, and 'nuff carn', meaning enough money, both used by teenagers from the late 1980s.

nuff! *exclamation American*
possibly a contraction of the phrase 'enough said'

nug *n American*
a girl(friend). The term is probably a shortening of the word **nuggy** which is equivalent to the British **nookie**.

nugget *n British*
a one pound coin. From its gold colour and thickness.

nuggets *n pl American*
the testicles
    Man, it was so cold my nuggets nearly froze off.

nuggy *n American*
an alternative spelling of **noogie**

nuke *vb*
1a. to attack with nuclear weapons. The verb was coined by 'hawks' in the USA in

the early 1970s. During the Falklands War of 1981, T-shirts and car stickers were produced in Britain with the exhortation 'Nuke Buenos Aires!'.

1b. to devastate, defeat, overwhelm. By extension the verb is now used with this general meaning, particularly by teenagers and students.

We nuked them in the inter-college play-off.

1c. to cook in a microwave oven. The colloquial verb for a nuclear attack has been used in this sense throughout the English-speaking world.

nukes *n pl*
nuclear weapons. An abbreviated form first seen in the USA in the 1970s, especially in the disarmament slogan 'no nukes!'.

number *n*
1. a marihuana cigarette, **joint**. A vogue term of the late 1960s originating in the USA and deriving from the use of number to mean item, piece or unit. The word remains in use among cannabis smokers.

'Roll another number for the road.'
(Song title, the Holy Modal Rounders, 1969)

2. an act of betrayal, a confidence trick, a scam. Most often heard in the phrase **do a number on (someone)**: make a dupe of someone. Related is the phrase 'to get someone's number': to see through someone's deception.

3. a sexual partner. An unromantic term of the 1970s and 1980s denoting a casual or anonymous pick-up. (American author John Rechy published a novel with the title *Numbers*, dealing with **gay** liaisons, in 1970.)

'She goes to singles bars to pick up what she calls "numbers".'
(Recorded, London, 1986)

number (someone) *vb*
to identify, single out, denounce someone

They numbered him as a prime suspect.
I got numbered.

number-cruncher *n*
a (human or mechanical) calculator, handler or manipulator of (usually large) numbers. This light-hearted phrase evoking a mill or grinding mechanism fed with figures has become a standard item of business jargon.

number-crunching *n*
the activity or practice of handling complex calculations and large quantities.
See also **number-cruncher**

number one(s) *n*
urination. A nursery term dating from the Victorian concept of personal hygiene as a drill. The idea is usually expressed in the form 'do number ones'. In the USA it is occasionally a verb, in the form 'to number one'.
See also **number two(s)**

number two(s) *n*
defecation. A children's term often used humorously by adults. It occurs in both British and American speech.
See also **number one(s)**

numb-nuts *n*
an ineffectual, stupid or contemptible person, invariably male. A term of abuse popular for instance with college students in the USA; since the mid-1980s it has been heard in other English-speaking areas. (Nuts refers to the testicles, although the epithet has no sexual connotations.)

numero uno *n, adj American*
(something or someone considered) superlative or supreme. A borrowing, from Hispanic American speech, of the Spanish for 'number one'.

numptie, numbty, numshie *n British*
a fool, buffoon. This Scottish term became more widespread from the early 1990s. It has been derived from the unfortunate children's character Humpty-Dumpty, but is equally likely to be based on 'numb(-skull)'.

nunnie, noonie *n American*
the backside, **butt**, **ass**. An invented inoffensive euphemism.

'You're gonna freeze your nunnie.'
(*M*A*S*H*, US TV comedy series, 1981)

nurd *n*
an alternative spelling of **nerd**

nurk *n*
an alternative spelling of **nerk**

nut[1] *n*
1. the head. A predictable metaphor which had become established slang by the mid-19th century (see the verb form).
2a. a crazy, eccentric person. The word was used in this sense in the USA for about thirty years before its adoption by British speakers in the late 1940s, from **nut-case**.

2b. a devotee, fan(atic) or **buff**. The word is used, particularly in American English, as a combining form or suffix, as in 'health-nut'.

nut² vb British
to butt someone with one's head, usually in the face, a common form of assault among street fighters and practised brawlers. The concept is also expressed by phrases such as 'stick the nut on (someone)' or 'give someone the nut'. **Gorbals kiss**, **Glasgow kiss** and 'Glasgow handshake' are colourful alternatives.

> 'Millions of TV viewers ... saw the Wimbledon wildman nut Everton skipper Kevin Ratcliffe.'
> (News of the World, 12 February 1989)

nut-case n
a crazy person. A slang version of 'mental case' which spread from American speech into British usage at the end of the 1950s. It is now a fairly mild term, usually denoting harmless eccentricity. A racier, more modern version is **headcase**.

nut-house n
a psychiatric hospital, mental home. The phrase has been in use since the 1920s.

nut-job n American
a more recent variation of **nut-case**

nut out/up vb
to go crazy, lose control of oneself, run amok. A recent teenagers' and college students' term.

nuts¹ adj
1a. crazy, absurd, insane. An Americanism from the turn of the 20th century, adopted elsewhere before World War II, it derives ultimately from the 19th-century notion of 'off one's nut', a slang version of the colloquial 'off one's head'.
1b. extremely enthusiastic or enamoured
> He's nuts about her!

2. British good. As heard since 2000, the word is probably a shortening of **the mutt's nuts** rather than the colloquial term for crazy.

nuts² n pl
the testicles. A metaphorical use of the word which serves as a more acceptable euphemism for **balls**.

nuts! exclamation
an exclamation of defiance which may be used without offence, unlike the synonymous **balls**. The most famous instance of this (typically American) expression was General McAuliffe's one-word riposte to the German army's request for surrender at Bastogne in World War II.

nutter n British
a maniacal, unrestrained, unpredictable person. Often said in awe or grudging admiration of the subject's energy and capabilities.

> 'He then began saying I would get into trouble. "That boy of yours looks a nutter to me!"'
> (Joe Orton's diary, 12 May 1967)

nutty adj
1. crazy, absurd, eccentric. A usage which slightly pre-dates the almost synonymous **nuts**. By the 1960s it was considered a well-established colloquialism.
2. Jamaican **natty** (in the standard and patois senses), smart and spirited. Caribbean English has retained the 19th-century British sense of dandified. The word was applied by the white British pop group, Madness to themselves in a punning reference to their 'craziness' and the inspiration they gained from black music.
3. British excellent, exciting. An all-purpose term of approval in use among schoolchildren, clubbers and **fashionistas** from the late 1990s.

nyaff n Scottish
an irritating or obnoxious person. The term is supposed to be echoic in origin, and is based on the irritating sound of a dog or a small child.

nyam (up) vb British
to eat. The term was heard in black British speech in the early 1990s. It was thought to be echoic, but possibly originates from a West African language.

nympho n
a promiscuous woman. The word is a shortening of 'nymphomaniac'. The word has often been used by schoolchildren since the 1950s.

O

O *n*
opium, in the jargon of drug users

oats *n pl See* **get one's oats**

oatsy *adj*
spirited, assertive, restive or **feisty**. A coinage derived from the earlier phrase to 'feel one's oats'.

obbo *n British*
observation by police officers, surveillance. An item of police slang recorded by the *Evening Standard* magazine, February 1993, and popularised by its use in the many TV dramas based on police work broadcast in the later 1990s.

obv *adj, adv British*
short for 'obvious(ly)'. An abbreviated form in use among middle-class speakers from around 2000.
Compare **unforch**

ocean-going *combining form British*
an all-purpose intensifier used to prefix nouns, as in 'an ocean-going shit' (an extremely obnoxious person). The usage is inspired by such terms as 'ocean-going yacht', denoting a larger and more powerful version of the thing in question. **Born-again** is used in a similar way.

ocker *n Australian*
a working-class male, especially one epitomising the more boorish Australian attributes. This word, which seems to be related to the British **oik** by an unrecorded process, has a resonance beyond its simple definition. It has overtones of the American 'good ole boy'. 'Ockerism' and 'ockerdom' describe the cult or syndrome of male comradeship, beer-drinking and lack of refinement embodied in such cultural icons as the comedian Paul Hogan's 'Hoag' character and the Test cricketer Merv Hughes. (**Alf** is a less well-known synonym for ocker.)

'Paul Hogan ...the archetypal Aussie Ocker.'

(Photo caption, *Southern Cross* magazine, July 1989)

ockerina, ocarina *n Australian*
a female **ocker**. A play on words heard occasionally.

octopus *n British*
a *bus*. An item of rhyming slang from the Merseyside area, given exposure by its use in the TV soap opera *Brookside*.

O.D., o.d. *n, vb*
(to) overdose. The abbreviation replaced the full form in the 1960s among 'counterculture' and street drug users. It is still in use and is sometimes extended to refer to a surfeit of something innocuous.

Oh God, I've completely o.d.'d on those chocolates.
'Billy O.D'd on Drano on the night that he was wed.'

('People Who Died', written and recorded by Jim Carroll, 1981)

oddball *n, adj*
(a person who is) eccentric, nonconformist or an outsider. An Americanism which has been established in British and American speech since the 1950s. The origin of the expression probably lies in pool playing or another sport.

She's a bit of an oddball.
That's thoroughly oddball behaviour.

odds and sods *n pl British*
a rhyming vulgarisation of 'odds and ends'

odds it *vb British*
to 'play the odds', take a risk or chance. A piece of London working-class terminology, used particularly by police officers and members of the underworld.

You're oddsin' it a bit, aren't you?
I can't be sure, we'll just have to odds it.

ofay *n American*
a white person. The word is said to be a **backslang** version of 'foe' in black American slang of the late 1960s. Another proposed etymology is the Yoruba word *ofé*,

meaning a ju-ju or charm. The word probably originated earlier in the 20th century in the immigrant underworld as a code reference to the police and other authority figures. It is sometimes encountered in the phrase 'ixnay ofay(s)', meaning 'no whites'.

> *'Nice integrated neighbourhood, ofays, Arabs, Chaldeans, a few colored folks. Ethnic, man.'*
> (*The Switch*, Elmore Leonard, 1978)

off[1] *vb American*
to kill. A word popular at the time of the Vietnam War when 'off the pigs' was a slogan much chanted by militant protesters. The term, possibly derived from **bump off**, was picked up by British speakers and enjoyed a brief vogue in the early 1970s. It is still heard occasionally, especially in the verb form 'off oneself' (to commit suicide).

> *'Isn't he the dude on trial for offing the undercover cop?'*
> (*The Last Innocent Man*, US film, 1987)

off[2] *n British*
a fight. A playground term also used by teenage gangs.

> *Quick, there's going to be an off.*

offie *n British*
an off-licence, liquor store

off-key *adj British*
ugly, unattractive, badly dressed. One of a number of terms, including **bungled**, **cake-up**, **cruttess**, in vogue among street-gang members, hip hop aficionados and students in the UK since 2000.

off one's block/chump/crust/head/nut/ onion *adj*
mad, crazy. These phrases are all elaborations of the well-established colloquialism, 'off one's head' (heard since the mid-19th century). The terms are sometimes extended to mean intoxicated by drugs or drink, more usually denoted by phrases beginning with 'out of', such as **out of one's head**.

off one's face *adj*
completely drunk or under the influence of drugs. A variant of 'off one's head'. The usage arose in Australian speech, but by the mid-1990s was in common use in Britain among younger speakers. The variant 'off one's case' is also used by prison inmates in the UK.

> *'"I went high at university!" he said reasonably. "Used to get really on my face in fact …'"*

> *'"Off! Off! Dad, it's off your face", Mouche screeched from the bed.'*
> (*Girls' Night Out*, Kathy Lette, 1989)

> *'… inside, we were buzzing nicely … I was off my face: 1995 had come early.'*
> (*Independent*, 24 January 1995)

off one's jaw *adj British*
drunk. A variant form of the earlier **off one's head/face** recorded in 2002.

off one's pickle *adj British*
drunk. A variant form of the earlier **off one's head/face** recorded in 2002.

off one's trolley *adj British*
deranged, unstable, crazy. A variation on the **off one's block** theme, which has been popular in British speech since the 1970s. The original image evoked may be of a child losing control of a cart or scooter, or of a patient falling from a mobile stretcher or frame.

off-side *adj British*
unfair, improper behaviour. An upper-and middle-class term of disapproval, deriving from various field sports.

off the hook *adj American*
1a. excellent
1b. terrible
The expression, heard since 2000, probably originated in black speech. It is sometimes altered to 'off the **hizzle**'.

off the wall *adj American*
eccentric, unusual, **way-out**. A phrase (possibly inspired by the unpredictable trajectory of a ball or an ice-hockey puck rebounding from a wall) which has been adopted outside the USA, usually in connection with zany and/or creatively original ideas or behaviour.

O.G. *n American*
'original gangster': an older and respected gang member. A term from the code of the Los Angeles street gangs of the 1980s.

ogens *n pl American*
female breasts. The name of the small spherical variety of melons is used figuratively, sometimes altered to **Hogans**.

oggie, oggy *n British*
a Cornish pasty. A term of uncertain origin heard in the west of England. It more usually occurs in the form 'tiddy oggie'.

oggle *vb British*
a humorous or simply mispronounced version of the verb to 'ogle', usually in the sense of 'eye lasciviously'. A middle-class colloquialism.

oggle-rye *n British*
1a. an eye
1b. an eyelash
1c. an eyebrow

A **parlyaree** term recorded since the 1960s, in use particularly among London **gays** and transvestites. It combines the verb **oggle** (a deformation of 'ogle') and a nonsense syllable to provide the rhyme.

ohno-second *n*
a realisation of error, sudden panic, in e.g. medical slang. The expression mimics technical terms such as nanosecond. It describes '…the moment you realise you've dropped that blood sample it took six stabs to get'. (Recorded, *British Medical Journal* online, 2002).

-oid *suffix*
the suffix, seen in slang since the late 1960s, confers a sense of the pseudoscientific or pathological on the preceding word or part of a word. It is invariably also pejorative, and as such performs as a negative version of the neutral '-ish' or '-esque'. Examples are 'Ramboid', 'bozoid' (from **bozo**), 'trendoid' and **zomboid**.

oik *n British*
1. a vulgar, coarse, boorish or socially inferior person. This term was, and still is, applied by public schoolboys (rarely by girls) to local children or those attending state schools. It is also sometimes used self-effacingly or ironically by working-class males to refer to themselves. The word's origin is obscure (one suggestion is that it was an imitation of the sound of unsophisticated speech), but seems to lie in the 19th century; it is almost certainly cognate with the 20th-century Australian term **ocker**, also denoting a working-class male. Evelyn Waugh used the word, in his diary entry of 7 January 1920, when referring to his host as a 'wizened, pleasant little oik'.

  'I'm constantly amazed that a couple of oiks like me and Gray have managed to make it.'
  (Recorded, advertising executive, London, 1986)

2. a person with 'one income and kids'. An acronym in **yuppie** use in the late 1980s. Similar coinages are **dinky** and **oink**.

oiler *n*
1. *British* a sycophant. The *Sunday Times*, 16 October 1994, reported that Princess Diana had used the term in reference to Prince Charles's entourage.
2. *American* a synonym for **greaser** in the sense of a Hispanic person

oily *n British*
a stupid, unsophisticated or unfortunate person. This derogatory term, heard among black teenagers in the late 1980s, is probably a blend of **oik** and **wally**, rather than a specialised use of the standard English adjective.

  'I don't want to walk down the street and have them shout, "Hey, oily" because of how I look.'
  (Recorded, black youth, London, 1989)

oily rag *n British*
1. a disparaging term applied to inexperienced or incompetent motor mechanics who are assigned menial jobs such as wiping away grease
2. a cigarette. This piece of rhyming slang, from **fag**, was common in the 1950s but is now rarely heard.

oink *n*
a person with 'one income and no kids'. An acronym characterising one type of worker in the **yuppie** milieu from the late 1980s. Similar coinages are **dinky** and **oik**.

oinker *n American*
a vulgar, obnoxious or greedy person. A young person's euphemism for **pig**. The term was, and is, predictably, applied to police officers.

OK, O.K., okay *exclamation*
all right, correct. The term is no longer thought to be slang, but its origins are frequently debated by amateur and professional etymologists. The first recorded use was in the Boston *Morning Post* of 23 March 1839 by C. G. Greene, who used OK as a facetious abbreviation of a mis-spelled 'Orl Korrect'. This novelty, possibly reinforced by the Scottish phrase 'Och, aye', which has the same meaning and an almost identical pronunciation, was imitated by other comic writers and taken as the title of a Democratic political club in 1840; this last example was also probably a pun on 'Old Kinderhook', the nickname of the politician Martin van Buren. The several other proposed sources for the word, including a posited cry in French *au quai!* ('to or on the quayside'), are probably spurious. By

the end of the 19th century OK was in use in Britain.

okey-dokey, artichokey! *exclamation*
a joky expression of agreement on the lines of **aye-aye, shepherd's pie**. Apparently the okey-dokey version was a favourite of First Lady Hillary Clinton.

-ola *suffix*
this word ending has been appropriated from Spanish where it signifies large and negative. It is added to standard terms and slang terms (as in **payola** and **boffola**) to convey the notion of outrageous, excessive or 'super-'. The usage arose in the USA in the 1950s.

Old Bill, the Old Bill *n British See* **Bill**

old cheese *n Australian*
a mother or matriarch. An affectionate epithet used principally by males.

old Dutch, my old Dutch *n British See* **Dutch¹ 1**

old fellow *n*
the penis. An affectionate euphemism used by hearty males.

old lady *n*
one's mother, wife or sweetheart. The term was notably adopted by **hippies** in Britain in the late 1960s, not from local working-class usage, but in imitation of American **bikers**, etc.

old lag *n British*
a recidivist, habitual offender or former prisoner. **Lag** is an elastic term which, since the early 19th century, has encompassed imprisonment, sentencing, a notion of transportation or simply a convict.

old man *n*
one's father, husband or sweetheart. *See also* **old lady**

old moody *n British See* **moody¹ 1b**

old trout *n British*
a middle-aged or elderly woman, especially one who is frumpish or short-tempered. This expression has been used as a mild pejorative (very occasionally even affectionately) since the 19th century.

> 'Here's what's coming up for you; two old trouts and a man who should be in the army.'
> (Victoria Wood, *As Seen on TV*, BBC comedy series, April 1988)

See also **out trouting**

Oliver (Twist) *adj British*
drunk. An item of rhyming slang for **pissed**. Unlike many similar multi-word

examples, it invariably occurs in its full form, rather than being abbreviated to 'Oliver'.

ollie *n British*
a marble, in the literal sense of the children's plaything (which is probably a variant form of **allie**), and in the figurative sense, as in the expression to **lose one's marbles**

> 'Another few days with those dozy gobshites and I'd have lost me ollies.'
> (Alexei Sayle, *Great Bus Journeys of the World*, 1988)

omi, omee *n British*
a man. A **parlyaree** word which survived into the modern era, omi is a corruption of the Italian *uomo*, meaning man. The term featured in the language of the theatre and among street traders and vagrants among others.

omipolone, omipoloni *n British*
a male homosexual. This now-dated form has survived in theatrical and film usage from more widespread earlier currency in the argot of the underworld, tramps, tinkers, etc. It is a portmanteau comprising **omi** (man) and **polone** (woman). The word was used as a euphemism in the radio comedy series *Round the Horne* during the 1960s.

on a mish *vb See* **mish**

on blocks *adj, adv See* **up on blocks**

on canvas *adj, adv British*
in solitary confinement, in prison. The phrase derives from the fact that prisoners in solitary confinement are issued with canvas mattresses and nightshirts.

oncer *n British*
an alternative spelling of **oneser**

on crack *adj American*
behaving in an eccentric, crazy way. An expression used on campus in the USA since around 2000.

one-er *n British*
a £100 note or sum of one hundred pounds. In the parlance of street gangs, recorded in London in 2002.

one-eyed trouser snake *n*
the penis. A colourful metaphor which probably originated in Australia in the 1950s. The word has spread to Britain and the United States and is nowadays generally truncated to **trouser snake**, which has developed further connotations.

oneser n British
a one-pound note or pound coin
All I got on me is a oneser.

one time n
the police (referred to as such because you have one time or one chance to get out of the situation alive). An expression from the lexicon of **rap**.
See also **Babylon**; **Feds, the**; **pig**

on holiday adj British
in prison (temporarily), in the argot of tramps and the homeless

on one adj British
1a. under the influence of (a tablet of) **MDA** or **ecstasy**. An expression from the jargon of **acid house** club habitués.
Are you on one, matey?
1b. in the know, *au fait* or *au courant*
In both senses this is an adolescent vogue phrase of the late 1980s.

on one's Jack/Jack Jones adj
alone, on one's own. Rhyming slang from the name of the American singer.

on one's tod adj
alone, on one's own. The phrase is rhyming slang from 'Tod Sloan', the name of an American jockey active at the turn of the 20th century.

on the arm adj British
bribed, corrupted. An instance of police and criminal slang.
Don't worry, we've got a prison officer on the arm.

on the batter vb British
engaged in prostitution and soliciting. An item of working-class slang heard throughout the UK since the 1960s, deriving from a more generalised 19th-century sense of the phrase as signifying 'engaged in a violent debauch'.

on the blob adj
menstruating. The expression, which seems to be used mainly by males, is heard in many English-speaking communities. **Blob** has also been used in several sexually related contexts. **On the rag** is an older synonym.

on the brew adj, phrase British
on the dole, unemployed. The sense of 'brew' in this phrase, which was heard in the 1980s, especially in the north of England, is unclear.

on the bum adj, adv
1a. on the road. Leading the life of a hobo or tramp.

'Just about a year ago I took off on the bum.'
(Lyrics from 'Lodi', written by John Fogerty and recorded by Creedence Clearwater Revival, 1968)
1b. engaged in cadging or begging. From the verb to **bum**.
2. malfunctioning, out of order. A less common synonym of 'on the blink', **bum** here meaning dud or useless.

on the bung adj Australian
out of order, broken down

on the cotton wool adv, adj British
a rhyming-slang version of **on the pull**, recorded in 1999

on the creep adj, adv
in search of a sexual partner. The term, heard in the Lowlands of Scotland and the north of England, usually refers to male behaviour. Contemporary synonyms include **on the sniff** and **out trouting**.

on the drip adv, adj British
on hire purchase, by instalments. One of many synonyms (including **on the knock**, **on the never-never**, **on the strap** and 'on the lay-by') in use since the 1950s.

on the earhole/ear'ole adj, adv British
cadging, trying to borrow money. An old London working-class expression which was still heard in the 1980s. For the etymology see **ear'ole**.

on the elbow adv British
engaged in cadging, borrowing money or scrounging. A London working-class expression. The elbow reference may evoke literal nudging or figurative barging or pushing.

on the floor adj British
rhyming slang for *poor*

on the fritz adj, adv American
malfunctioning, out of order. A synonym of the colloquial 'on the blink'. Fritz here may be the German nickname, probably alluding to imported German goods, thought by Americans in the 1930s to be shoddy. It may alternatively echo the sound of a short circuit, a buzzing in electrical equipment.
'We're thinking about getting a doberman since the alarm system went on the fritz.'
(*Hart to Hart*, US TV series, 1981)

on the heavy bevvie adv
engaged in heavy drinking. The term is heard particularly in the Scottish Lowlands and the north of England.

on the hot cross (bun) *adj, adv British*
on the *run*. An item of rhyming slang used, and possibly coined, by the crime novelist Ruth Rendell.

on the hurry-up *adv British*
at full speed. An item of London police jargon.

on the job *adj, adv British*
engaged in sexual intercourse. An unromantic euphemistic phrase which has been used increasingly in 'polite' company in Britain and Australia since the 1960s.

on the knock *adj, adv British*
1. on credit or hire purchase, by instalments
2. *See* **knock**
3. engaged in selling or canvassing door to door. An alternative form of **on the knocker**.

on the knocker *adj, adv British*
going from door to door. Typically to sell something of dubious worth or to persuade the gullible to part with items such as antiques for less than their true value. A non-regional working-class term.

on the lash *adj British*
engaged in drinking or otherwise having fun. An item of student slang in use in London and elsewhere since around 2000.

on the money *adj*
correct, accurate. The phrase, which probably originated in the US in gambling circles, is usually heard among middle-class speakers.

  'It's good when the band's on the money.'
  (UK TV documentary on the band Status Quo, 18 June 1993)

on the needle *adj*
habitually injecting heroin or another narcotic

  She finally admitted she was back on the needle.

on the nest *adj, adv Australian*
having sex

on the never-never *adj, adv British*
on hire purchase, on credit, by instalments. One of many such phrases originating in the 1950s; this one ruefully reflects on the impossibility of ever getting out of debt once enmeshed.

on the nose *adj Australian*
stinking, smelly, rank. The expression is either a shortening of a phrase such as 'heavy on the nose' or an inversion of an earlier expression 'to have a nose on (someone or something)', meaning to dislike.

on the (h)orn *adj British*
(of a male) having an erection. A very common working-class and schoolboy vulgarism of the 1950s and early 1960s, now somewhat dated. 'Horn' has been a synonym for the penis since at least the 18th century.

on the other bus *adj British*
homosexual. Used typically by males, usually of other males, the pejorative or mocking phrase is a synonym for **batting for the other side**.

on the piss *adj, adv British*
engaged in a drinking bout or habitual heavy drinking

on the pull *adv, adj British*
looking for a sexual partner, hoping to pick up a member of the opposite sex. A working-class term in use since the late 1960s from **pull**; its predatory overtones mean that it is usually applied to males.

  'Don't bother asking – those two are out on the pull again.'
  (Recorded, adolescent girl, London, 1987)

on the q.t. *adv*
discreetly, secretly. A version of 'on the quiet', first recorded in 1870.

on the rag *adj British*
menstruating. 'Rag' was, until the 1970s, a common slang synonym for a sanitary towel.

on the razz/razzle *adj, adv British*
engaged in boisterous celebration, on a binge. The old colloquialism (razzle dazzle') probably originated as a rhyme for 'dazzle') has been adopted by adolescents since 2000.

on the reg *adv American*
frequently, regularly. An expression used on campus in the USA since around 2000.

  I smoke weed on the reg.

on the salmon *adj British*
(of a male) having an erection. The phrase is a shortened form of the rhyming slang 'on the salmon and prawn', meaning **on the (h)orn**. The phrase was used as the title of an art exhibition in the East End of London by the young artist Sarah Lucas in 1995.

on the sniff adj, adv
looking for a sexual partner. This more obscure synonym of **on the pull**, **out trouting**, etc., was used by the Scottish comic character Rab C. Nesbitt in the BBC comedy of the same name, 18 November 1993.

on the square adj British
belonging to a Masonic lodge. A term from the code of freemasons themselves. (The square is a Masonic symbol.)

  'Three Crown witnesses were themselves "on the square".'

  (Former detective quoted in Inside the Brotherhood, Martin Short, 1989)

on the up-and-up adj, adv
above board, bona fide. Originally an Americanism of uncertain derivation (perhaps an intensification of upright), the term is now widely used in Britain, especially in London working-class speech.

  No it's OK: he finally convinced me that the deal was on the up-and-up.

on tilt adj, adv American
unsteady, unbalanced. The phrase comes from the light flashed on a pintable to say that the game has been curtailed because the machine has been forced out of alignment by overenthusiastic play. It often refers to a person who is behaving uncharacteristically or eccentrically.

on top adj, adv British
(caught) in the act, red-handed. A criminal and police expression evoking the image of, e.g., a burglar on a roof, i.e. exposed.

oof n British
a promiscuous or sexually willing female. One of a set of terms in use among male City traders, recorded by psychologist Belinda Brookes in the Independent on Sunday, 9 July 1995. Others included **mum** and **dragon**. The word may imitate a gasp of desire, like its 1920s' predecessor, 'oomph' (an archaic term for sex-appeal).

oof key adj British
a variant form or mishearing of **off key**, heard among teenage Londoners since around 2000

open the kimono vb American
to reveal one's secrets, disclose normally confidential information. A piece of corporate slang popular in the US and elsewhere since the 1990s.

oppo n British
1. an opposite number, a partner. A military abbreviation used in police, underworld and more general contexts. Most users assume, understandably (and probably correctly), that this is based on 'opposite'. A more fanciful suggestion is that it is in fact a corruption of 'hop o' my thumb', rhyming slang for chum.
2. an operation, particularly a military operation (a surgical operation is simply an 'op')

optic (nerve) n Australian
a sexually perverted or lecherous individual. The phrase rhymes with **perve**.

oracle n See **work the oracle**

oral n
oral sex, fellatio, cunnilingus

orange squash n British
money. Rhyming slang for **dosh**, in use among City traders and others in 2003. **Rogan (josh)** is a contemporary synonym.

orbital, orbital rave n British
an **acid house** party. In 1989 there was a vogue for large-scale gatherings of adolescent party goers, usually paying to attend clandestine dance celebrations which often ended in confrontations with the police. The practice was part of the acid-house cult in which the drug **ecstasy** played an integral part. The parties in question revived the dated term **rave** and were held within reach of the London orbital motorway, the M25, hence the names.

orchestras n pl British
the testicles. The word is late 19th- and early 20th-century rhyming slang from 'orchestra stalls' (a category of theatre seating): **balls**. It is invariably used literally rather than figuratively.

order of the boot, the n British
(notice of) rejection, dismissal or refusal. The humorous expression, based on the more exalted Order of the Bath, Order of the Garter, etc., is normally employed in the context of a sacking or a rejection by a lover. This form of words has largely supplanted the earlier 'order of the push'.

original adj British
excellent, acceptable. A vogue word of approval first used among black British gangs and later adopted by schoolchildren in the mid-1990s.

original gangster n American See **O.G.**

ornamental n British
an Oriental person, in student parlance. The term is usually descriptive rather than derogatory or racist.

O.S. adv Australian
overseas
> Charlene's gone O.S.

oscar adj British
unrestrained, out of control, wild. This pun on the name of the writer Oscar Wilde was in use among commune dwellers and **hippies** in the late 1970s in such phrases as to 'go completely Oscar'. (In archaic slang in both Britain and Australia an oscar was a male homosexual.)

ossifer n
a police officer. A facetious and/or provocative deformation of the standard word, often said in imitation of the slurred speech of a drunk. It occurs all over the English-speaking world.

O.T.F. adj British Jewish
the initials stand for 'of the faith'. The phrase is used euphemistically by Jews and non-Jews and is also occasionally used by other users in the London area to mean 'one of us'.

other, the n
sexual intercourse or other sexual misbehaviour. A common euphemism probably deriving from the phrase 'this, that and the other', coyly referring, like 'hanky-panky', to unnameable activities. Until the late 1950s the other often signified homosexual activity as opposed to orthodox sex. Nowadays phrases such as 'a bit of the other' are usually heard in a heterosexual context.
> 'He asked me if I fancied a bit of the other, so I told him yes, but only if the bit belonged to some other bloke.'
> (Recorded, London, 1965)

O.T.T. adj British
outrageous, wild and uncontrolled. A shortening of the late 1970s catchphrase **over the top**, given wider currency by its adoption as the title of an anarchic TV comedy show in the early 1980s. It often occurs in phrases such as 'go (completely) O.T.T'.

out[1] adj
living or behaving openly as a homosexual. The result of having **come out** (of the closet). A term from the **gay** lexicon.
> Bruce is out.
> She's been out for some time now.

out[2] vb
1. to reveal or denounce as being a homosexual. The term, originally an obscure item of **gay** jargon, became famous in the 1980s as the practice of public naming of **closet cases** gathered momentum.
2. to knock unconscious, beat up. A term from the lexicon of **teddy boys** and **mods**.

outasight adj
superlative, excellent, sensational. The phrase 'out of sight' was probably used first in this sense by jazz musicians and their **beatnik** imitators in the late 1950s in the USA. Outasight, like the earlier **way-out** and the coeval **far-out**, used the image of something far from the ordinary or far outdistancing its rivals. The expression was popular among the **hippies** of the late 1960s and in the jargon of soul music.

outfit n See **fit**[2] 1

outlaw[1] n
a gang member. The word has been adopted by gangs in many different milieus, including the American **biker** gangs of the 1950s and, more recently, the black street gangs of the USA and urban Britain.

outlaw[2] adj American
exceptional, outstanding. A teenage expression, originally a term of approbation from the street, where outlaw is a term used of gang members by themselves.
> 'Outlaw dress.'
> (Broadcast News, US film, 1987)

out of it adj
euphoric and/or semi-conscious after ingesting drink or drugs. A fashionable shortened version of **out of one's head/skull/box** which spread from the USA to other English-speaking areas around 1971.
> 'Her main hobby these days seems to be getting out of it as often as possible.'
> (Recorded, female rock singer, Devon, 1986)

out of one's head/skull/box adj
1a. crazy, deranged
1b. intoxicated by drugs or drink
These terms became widespread in the mid-1960s, before which synonymous phrases (with the exception of 'out of one's mind') usually began with 'off'. When the Rolling Stones called their 1965 album Out of Our Heads the phrase was still a lit-

tle-known Americanism. The 'box' version has been fashionable in Britain since the mid-1970s.

out of one's pram *adj British*
out of control, crazy. An alternative form of **off one's trolley**, the term has overtones of a childish tantrum or loss of temper rather than true insanity.

out of one's tree *adj*
1a. crazy, deranged
1b. intoxicated by drugs or drink
A colourful variation on **out of one's head** that is typically American and Australian. The implication is of someone volubly or energetically crazy or **high** and chattering like a monkey.

out of order *adj British*
1. transgressing, beyond the pale
> *'"I think you're well out of order", he said. Apparently he had been waiting for seven years to see Grace [Jones] again, and was peeved about the extra four hours standing around.'*
> (*Independent*, 30 March 1990)

2. incapacitated, particularly by drink or illicit drugs. These extensions of the standard sense of the phrase became fashionable in raffish speech in the early 1970s. The first sense is more often heard in working-class speech, the second, predictably, in the drug-using subcultures.

out sharking *n See* **sharking**

out to lunch *adj*
1a. crazy, deranged
> *'The second most out-to-lunch politburo in the north of England.'*
> (*Private Eye* magazine, 27 October 1989)

1b. unconscious, incapacitated by drink or drugs. A usage which was particularly popular in Britain around 1975.

out trouting *n British*
looking for a sexual partner. A vogue term of the mid-1990s heard in raffish usage, particularly among young adults in the advertising industry, journalism and city financial circles. It is based on the derogatory **old trout**, meaning a woman.

over the top *adj, adv British*
outrageous, bizarre, beyond the bounds of normal behaviour or decorum. The expression equally describes fury, extraordinary generosity or simple bad taste. It derives from the general idea of going 'off the scale', of being beyond measurable or acceptable limits, reinforced perhaps by the use of the phrase in World War I to describe troops climbing out of the trenches to go into battle, hence throwing caution to the winds. Often abbreviated to **O.T.T.**, the phrase was a vogue term in 1979.
> *There's no point in going over the top about someone like that.*
> *Wearing that dress with those shoes is really over the top.*

own goal *n British*
a suicide. An unsentimental item of police jargon since the 1970s.

Oxo (cube) *n British*
the *Tube*, the London Underground railway. The rhyming slang uses the brand name of a concentrated meat-stock product.
> *He disappeared down the Oxo.*

oy-oy, saveloy! *exclamation British*
a synonym for **aye-aye, shepherd's pie!**

oyster *n British*
a shoplifter. Recorded in 1999 among petty criminals in London, the word may be a cockney pronunciation of 'hoister'.

Oz *n*
Australia

P

packed *adj*
well-hung. The term was used by the British comedian Dawn French in January 1994.

packet *n*
the male genitals. A term from the **gay** lexicon, usually referring to the crotch as it appears clothed.

pad[1] *n*
a home. The word now invariably refers to a room, apartment or house. In 17th-century Britain pad was used by peasants and poor travellers to designate a bed made of straw or rags, while in American slang before 1950 it designated a pallet or couch on which opium smokers or other drug takers reclined; this sense was later extended to encompass any room or place in which drug users gathered, or the beds on which they slept. The dissemination of **beatnik**-related jargon introduced the word to a wider audience, as did its adoption by the **hippy** generation.

'Drop-out pads for the large numbers of people hitting London at the moment looking for the mythical beautiful dream-boat.'
(*International Times*, April 1968)

pad[2] *vb, n British*
(to go for) a walk

paddle *vb*
to hit, beat, thrash. This synonym of 'wallop' probably derives from the archaic use of the noun paddle to mean both hand and, more rarely, foot. Long before signifying a bat, paddle also denoted a small spade.

Paddy *n*
an Irish person. A nickname derived from the short form of Patrick, the most common male Christian name in Ireland. It has been used since at least the 18th century. Although the term can be used as an epithet, it may be used descriptively and is also heard among the Irish

themselves, where it is usually a personification of a typical rustic Irishman. An alternative, usually with a slightly more pejorative emphasis, is **mick**.

'We Import More Paddies Every Year.'
(Joke acronym for Wimpey, British construction and civil engineering firm)

paddywaggon *n*
a secure police van, a **black maria** or a police car. This term was introduced into Britain and Australia from the United States at the end of the 19th century. The reference to paddy reflects the importance of the Irish population of New York and other northern cities in providing police officers at the time, rather than to the number of Irishmen arrested. **Meat wagon** is a racier, more modern alternative.

paedo, pedo *n British*
an unpleasant or unfortunate person. This contraction of the term 'paedophile' has been adopted as an all-purpose insult in playground parlance since 2000. A synonym is **kiddy-fiddler**.

pain in the arse/ass *n*
a nuisance, irritation or source of problems. A vulgar version of 'pain in the neck', an expression in use since the early 20th century. (**Arse** may be substituted by any synonym or **balls**, etc.)

'A few drinks and respectable family men, dads, became lecherous pains in the ass.'
(*The Switch*, Elmore Leonard, 1978)

painters *n pl See* **have the decorators in**

paki *n British*
1a. a Pakistani. The abbreviation, invariably used in a racist context, began to be heard in the later 1960s.

'Paki scum go home.'
(Racist graffito, Whitechapel, London, 1980)

1b. a shop, usually a supermarket or general store, operated by a Pakistani or other South Asian

'I'm just off down the paki for a can of beans.'

(Recorded, housewife, London, 1987)

The simple shortening is used, in the first sense, as an offensive racial epithet and in the second sense as a simple descriptive term for the many independent corner stores owned and run by immigrant families. In both senses the word is often applied, loosely, to any immigrant from the subcontinent, including those of Bengali, Indian or Sri Lankan origin.

paladic, palatic *adj British*
drunk, a light-hearted term of uncertain origin; it may be a corruption of **paralytic**

palari *n British*
speech, talk, particularly in **camp** and theatrical circles. It is a corruption of the Italian *parlare* or of **parlyaree**.

palatic *adj See* **paladic**

palooka *n American*
a large, clumsy and/or slow-witted male. Before World War II the word was usually employed to describe a third-rate prizefighter. It was apparently coined by Jack Conway, an ex-baseball player and sports writer. The resemblance to *peluca*, Spanish for wig, may be coincidental.

'This big palooka has been trying to get me pregnant every which way but lopsided.'

(*The Boss's Wife*, US film, 1986)

palookaville *n American*
1a. an out-of-the-way, slow, rustic town, the **boondocks**. The expression describes the kind of town popularly supposed to be inhabited by **palookas**.
1b. oblivion, ignominy. A metaphorical use, describing the state of mind characteristic of washed-up, punch-drunk prizefighters.

You keep on fighting out of your class, you're buying a one-way ticket to palookaville.

pan-handle *n British*
an erection. The term probably dates back to the 1950s, but was popularised in the late 1980s by *Viz* comic.

panned *adj*
drunk. An expression used on campus in the USA since around 2000.

pansy *n*
a male homosexual or an effeminate, effete or weak male. A word first used in this context in the 1920s and well-established until the late 1960s. It sur-

vives mainly in the speech of the middle-aged and elderly.

pant- *combining form British*
an affix without specific meaning but used jocularly or for the purposes of ridicule. It can be prefixed to word parts in exclamations (**pantlo!** [hello], **pantbye!**), especially by middle-class schoolchildren and students.

pant off *exclamation British*
go away! An item of student slang in use in London and elsewhere since around 2000

pants *n, exclamation, adj British*
this all-purpose term of disapproval was a vogue word of 1995 and 1996 among adolescents. (Under)pants had long been a subject for pubescent children's jokes, a tradition reinforced when the word was picked up by disc-jockeys and comedians, e.g. on the children's TV programme *Alive and Kicking*.

'Pants, said Tom, pants, pants … I'm afraid I think this pants is a very silly word. I must go, I've a book to read.'

(*Independent*, 9 October 1996)

pantsgan *n, adj British*
a meaningless term (the -gan element is obscure, although one informant claimed that it derives from the female name Megan) employed as an intensifier or sometimes as an exclamation. It was in use among middle-class adolescents in 2001 and 2002.

pants man *n Australian*
a promiscuous male, seducer or **stud**

panty *adj British*
fortunate, lucky and/or attractive. An item of student slang in use in London and elsewhere since around 2000.

Panty him!

panty-man *n*
a male homosexual. The term, usually pejorative, originates in Caribbean usage. **Antiman** is a contemporary synonym.

pantywaist *adj American*
an effete person, sissy or weakling. The term comes from the image of a male wearing women's underwear or a type of toddler's one-piece garment of the same name.

paper bag job *n*
an ugly or unattractive person. The image is of a person who could only be considered as a sexual partner if his or her face were covered. The expression, first heard in the 1960s, probably orig-

inated in US high-school or campus usage; it enjoyed a vogue among schoolboys in Britain in 1968 and 1969.
Compare **bag one's face/head**

paper-hanger *n American*
a passer of dud cheques and/or counterfeit money in the jargon of the underworld and police

papers *n American*
money

papes *n*
money, especially to buy drugs. The short form of **papers** was probably first used by gang members but by around 2002 was heard on campuses and in financial circles in the USA and UK.

pappy *n British*
bread. An item of student slang in use in London and elsewhere since around 2000.

para *adj British See* **paro**

paracat *n British*
a person under the influence of drugs, especially when rendered agitated, anxious and/or suspicious. A blend of para(noid) and **cat** in the sense of an individual. More recently, the term is sometimes re-shortened to **cat**. It is typically heard in black street-talk and club culture since 2000.

paraffin lamp *n British*
a tramp. This rhyming-slang expression was recorded in the Merseyside area in the early 1990s, although it is presumably much older. **Penny stamp** and **Harold Ramp** are synonyms.

parallel parking *n American*
sexual intercourse. A popular euphemism since the 1970s among high-school students and **preppies**. (The phrase is displayed on car park notices to remind drivers of parking discipline.)

paralytic, paralysed *adj*
(extremely) drunk. A very common expression in Britain (but less so in the USA, where **paralysed** is probably more prevalent) since the first decade of the 20th century.

paraphernalia *n*
the apparatus and equipment (pipes, cigarette papers, scales, etc.) accompanying the taking of illicit drugs. A euphemism popularised by its use in 'head shops' from the late 1960s, paraphernalia there refers to the soft-drug culture of cannabis and hallucinogens. The same term is used, especially by

law enforcers, to describe the equipment used by hard-drug addicts and users.

parental units *n pl American*
parents, a rarer form of **units** or **rents**

parentectomy *n British*
the removal of a patient's (presumably troublesome) parents, in medical slang

park a custard/tiger *vb British*
to vomit. The chosen words are intended to suggest consistency or colour. The first version was said by Eric Partridge to be in use in the Royal Navy in the 1930s.

> 'People … were actually trying to park a custard after eating something they had only identified after swallowing and didn't want to digest.'
> (*Love it or Shove it*, Julie Burchill, 1985)

park and ride *vb British*
to have sex. From the phrase indicating public transport arrangements for some greenfield and (sub)urban campuses. The expression was recorded by the Student World website in 2001.

parking *n American*
necking and petting in cars. A teenage euphemism of the 1950s which is still in limited use.

park one's arse/bum/carcass *vb*
to seat oneself, position oneself

park one's bus *vb*
(of a male) to have sex. An item of student slang in use in London and elsewhere since around 2000.

parky *adj British*
cold. A word of obscure origin dating from at least before World War II and still in use. Among middle- and upper-class speakers the term is occasionally altered to parquet (as in 'parquet flooring').

> 'It's a bit parky in here – mind if I close this window?'
> (Recorded, teacher, London, 1987)

parlyaree, parliari *n British*
the strong Italian influence on the theatre, dance, music and the humbler entertainments of the streets from the late 17th to the late 19th centuries gave rise to an Italianate jargon. This terminology was adopted by English speakers (including vagabonds, street traders and the like), with resulting deformation of the original Italian words. This code, later known as parlyaree or parliari (itself a corruption of the Italian *parlare*, meaning

to speak), died out slowly during the 20th century. Certain terms remain in limited use, among them **nanty**, **omi**, **khazi** and **bona**.

parni n See **pawnee**

paro, parro, para, parra adj British
paranoid, in the popular sense of nervous or suspicious. These short forms were in use among schoolchildren from the end of the 1980s.
Compare **noid**

parquet adj British See **parky**

parra, parro adj British See **paro**

party down vb American
to let oneself go, to enjoy oneself to the full. A later embellishment of the colloquial verb to party, with overtones of dedicated involvement or application.

party-hat n American
a condom. Synonyms are **hat**, **jim(my)-hat**.

party pooper n
a spoilsport, 'wet blanket'. This expression (see **poop** for the probable origin) was introduced to Britain from the United States in the early 1960s. It originally referred to adults interfering in teenagers' activities, but was later generalised to describe any morose or unconvivial person.

pash¹ n British
1. a teenage 'crush', an infatuation; especially a young girl's feelings towards an older girl or teacher. A shortening of 'passion' still heard in public schools.
Amanda has a pash on Miss.
2. a girlfriend or lover. In armed-forces usage.
3. rubbish. An item of student slang in use in London and elsewhere since around 2000.

pash² adj British
passionate
feeling pash

passion wagon n
a car or van used for purposes of dating and/or seduction. The word was probably first used in armed-services slang during World War II, describing buses used to transport female personnel. **Draggin' wagon** and **shaggin' wagon** are later, racier alternatives.

paste (someone), paste one on (someone) vb British
to hit, beat up, 'thrash' or defeat someone. This use of the word paste, perhaps inspired by the slapping of paste on walls, posters, etc., or from 'baste' or 'lambaste', arose in the 19th century and was popular in colloquial speech until the late 1950s. 'Paste one on (someone)' was then an alternative version; 'give someone a (good) **pasting**' survives.

pasting n
a beating or resounding defeat. From the verb to **paste (someone)**.

patch n
one's territory, area of jurisdiction. A designation used by street gangs, drug dealers and law enforcers.

patna n American
a friend. The word, heard since 2000 and typically used by African Americans, is an 'Afro' pronunciation of 'partner'. It is generally used in situations where solidarity or affiliation are being emphasised.

patootie n American
1. the backside, buttocks. An inoffensive term which may be an invention or a deformation of 'potato'.
She fell flat on her patootie.
You can bet your sweet patootie I will!
2. a girlfriend or boyfriend, a sweetheart. In this (now obsolescent) sense the word is almost certainly a jocular alteration of (sweet) potato.

patsy n
a dupe. The term dates from the early years of the 20th century but its original significance is lost. Robert L. Chapman's New Dictionary of American Slang tentatively derives it from pasqualino, Italian for a scapegoat or loser.

Patsy Cline n British
a line (of cocaine). The term uses the name of the late US country music star and has been heard since the later 1990s.

Pattie n British
a first (first-class honours degree). A student pun (rhyming slang on Pattie Hearst) on the pattern of **Desmond**, etc. A set of nicknames of this sort was coined in 1987 and 1988.

Paul (Weller) n British
(a drink of) Stella Artois lager, playing on the name of the former neo-mod musician. **David (Mellor)**, **Nelson (Mandela)** and **Uri (Geller)** are synonyms, all popular with students since the late 1990s.

Paula n British
the female genitals as visible through clothing, **camel toes**. The term refers to the late TV celebrity Paula Yates. **Bob** is the male counterpart. 'To have a Paula' means to be wearing very tight leggings or trousers which, because of their tightness, cause the female labia to be very pronounced.

Pavarotti n British
a £10 note or sum of ten pounds. A pun on the name of the famous Italian tenor and 'tenner'. Synonyms are **Ayrton (Senna)** and **Tony Benner**.

pavement pizza n
a patch of vomit in the street. A drinkers' term from the 1980s which forms part of a set of terms such as **road pizza**, **road apple**, etc. as supposedly humorous euphemisms for distasteful discoveries.

paw n
a hand

pawnee n British
1a. a body of water; a lake, pond, the sea
 'Two ducks on the pawnee.'
(Bingo callers' code for the number 22)
1b. water in any form (such as rain, tears, etc.) The word, now very rarely heard but not extinct, is a corruption of the Hindi *pani*, entering English through colonial slang, Romany, or both.

pax exclamation British
a request for a truce, usually heard in the course of children's games. The word is Latin for peace and was formerly used by public-school masters as well as boys to appeal for calm or silence. Non-public schoolchildren usually employed the word **faynits**.

paydirt n
profit, reward, success. A mining metaphor originating in the USA.

payola n
bribery or extortion. This underworld term achieved prominence in the 1960s in the USA when it was applied to a scandal involving illicit payment to disc jockeys in return for airplays. It is the word pay combined with the Spanish suffix **-ola** (big, grandiose or outrageous).

P.C.P. n
angel dust. The initials are from phencyclidine, an animal tranquilliser that was abused (and manufactured in home laboratories), particularly in the USA in the 1970s, for its disorienting effects.

P.D.A. n American
a 'public display of affection'. A **preppie** code term for overt kissing, hugging, etc., usually said in a disapproving tone.

P.D.Q. adj, adv
'pretty damn quick'. A middle-class adults' expression often used in issuing commands or instructions. The term was recorded in Britain in 1900 and may be earlier.

pea-brain(ed) n, adj
(someone who is) stupid

peace, peace out! exclamation American
goodbye. A term from the lexicon of **rap** and hip hop aficionados which was adopted by some white speakers, particularly on university campuses in the 1990s.

peach n British
a foolish person. A less common synonym of **plum** and **pear**, used by schoolchildren since the 1990s.

peach (on someone) vb
to inform upon someone. This term originated in the 15th century as a shortening of the archaic term *apeach* (related to 'impeach') and has yet to be adopted into orthodox usage. It was commonly used as late as the 1960s but is now rare, except in the speech of an older generation.

peachy adj American
wonderful, excellent. The term, now often used ironically, is based on the earlier noun 'peach', meaning someone or something delectable. 'Peachy-keen' is an intensive form of the word.

peaky adj American
producing euphoria. This appreciative term formed from 'peaking' (i.e. achieving a maximum **high**) refers to the enjoyable effects of drugs.
 We managed to get hold of some peaky shit.

peanut-smuggling n See **smuggling peanuts**

Pearl (Harbour) adj British
cold, chilly. The witticism, referring to the weather, is based on the notion that there 'is a Nip in the air'.

pearler n Australian
an excellent, exceptional person or object. From the notion of a pearl as a peerless example.
 She's a little pearler. I don't know what I'd do without her.

pears n pl Australian
female breasts. Another example of the tendency for any vaguely rounded fruit to be used to symbolise the breasts, such as the synonymous **apples**, **melons**, etc.

pear-shaped adj British
awry, faulty, inadequate. This increasingly common adult colloquialism is usually heard in the phrase to 'go pear-shaped', presumably from the image of a balloon or football losing its spherical shape after puncturing.

> 'Things were OK until Christine left and then within a short time it all started to go pear-shaped.'
> (Recorded, London schoolteacher, February 1996)

pecker n American
the penis. The term may originate as a rural shortening of woodpecker, as a euphemism for **cock**, or simply as a metaphor for an importunate member.

> 'When I told him to get a-hold of himself I didn't mean for him to get his pecker out.'
> (Recorded, US oilman, Norway, 1982)

peckerhead n American
a fool, slow-witted or clumsy person. Originally used by country people, now a favourite term of abuse among college students and others. The British and Australian equivalent is **dickhead**.

peckerwood n American
a white person. This derogatory term has been used by black and white alike and uses the southern American name for the red-headed woodpecker (the link is the reference to that bird's red neck). The term is sometimes abbreviated to 'wood' and is often thought wrongly to be a synonym for **peckerhead**.

> 'Selective breeding in the good-old-boy peckerwood, white-sheet, lynch-mob states has brought about a monster ... a dog that is auditioning for the apocalypse ...'
> (Lights Out for the Territory by Iain Sinclair, 1997)

pecs n pl American
the pectoral muscles. A word used particularly by body builders and by women admiring (or disparaging) the male physique. The shortening became widespread in the 1970s.

> 'The guys there [California] all have great pecs, but I guess that's not the only thing.'

(Recorded, American female executive, London, 1986)

pedigree chum n British
an upper-class girl's escort or boyfriend. A witticism inspired by **debs' delight** punning on the brand name of a dog food. The phrase arose in the 1980s.

pedo n See **paedo**

pee[1], **pee-pee** n
urine or an act of urination. The word is probably in origin a euphemistic form of the more onomatopoeic **piss**, but is reinforced by being the initial sound of **piddle** and a cognate of other European forms (such as the French pipi). It was not recorded before the 18th century.

pee[2], **pee-pee** vb
to urinate
(For the origins of the word see the noun form.)

pee'd adj British
a more polite version of **pissed**

pee'd off adj
a less offensive version of **pissed-off**

peek n British
an observation cell in a prison, in the jargon of prisoners recorded in the 1990s. (The verb 'peek' itself is not slang, being a direct descendant from the Middle English piken.)

peely-wally adj British
wan, ailing. The phrase is heard particularly in the Scottish Lowlands and the north of England, but is also sometimes used by Jamaican and black British speakers. The expression may be an elaboration of 'pale' or derive from a personal nickname.

> feeling/looking a bit peely-wally

peepers n pl
the eyes. A humorous euphemism.

peeps n pl
people. The term occurs in American slang, in which it may refer to one's fellow gang members or one's friends and family, and in British, where it is often a plural term of address, probably inspired by its use in the comic monologues delivered by the comedian Harry Enfield in the character of Stavros the kebab-shop owner in the 1980s.

peeve n British
an alcoholic drink, alcohol. The term, used by teenagers in particular since around 2000, is often in the phrase **sconned on peeve**, that is, drunk.

peg it, peg out vb
to die. The first version of the phrase is currently more fashionable than the earlier peg out, which appeared in the USA in the mid-19th century, inspired by the use of pegs in the game of cribbage ('pegging-out' was finishing the game). The form peg out may also mean to collapse exhausted or fail in one's efforts.

pegs n pl
legs. From the 19th century the word peg has denoted a wooden leg.

pelf n British
money. An old term, like many others (**rhino**, **spondulicks**, etc.) revived in the money-conscious environment of the later 1980s. Pelf is from the Middle English pelfre, related to 'pilfer' and meaning loot.

> 'Miss Smith … Cold as the Ice itself; She admires nought but Pelf.'
> (List of Covent Garden Ladies, or the New Atlantis, pamphlet, 1773)

pen-and-ink n, vb British
(to) stink. An early 20th-century cockney rhyming-slang term which has survived to the present. It can be used as a noun phrase, as in 'there's a real pen-and-ink in here!' or as a verb, normally in a form such as 'it don't half pen-and-ink in here!'.

pencil-dick n American
a vulgar alternative of **pencil-neck** and **pencil geek**

pencil geek n American
a tediously studious person, a **swot**. One of many high-school and campus categorisations of fellow students; **grind** and **conch** are synonymous.
See also **geek**[1] 1

pencil-neck n American
an earnest, unattractive, excessively studious male. A derogatory term, suggesting the appearance of a scrawny individual, which has been used as a synonym for **nerd**, **grind**, etc. **Pencil geek** is an alternative form.

penguin suit n
formal male evening dress; a dinner suit

penny stamp n British
a tramp. This old example of London rhyming slang was still in use in the 1990s, now referring to homeless persons in general. **Paraffin lamp** is an alternative.

pep pill n
a tablet of amphetamine or a similar drug. This term was used in the 1940s when stimulant drugs such as caffeine and benzedrine were taken to combat fatigue and sleep. The expression was used by illicit drug takers until the early 1960s when it was appropriated by spokesmen for the anti-drug establishment and the media.

percussive maintenance n
striking something in an attempt to make it work. A jocular term used especially in the medical and other technical fields.

percy n
the penis. One of a number of personifications of the male member which include **peter**, **dick**, **willie**, **John Thomas**, etc. The word principally functions as part of the phrase **point percy at the porcelain**.

perk vb Australian
to vomit. A variant of **puke**, perhaps influenced by the phrase 'to perk up' or the word 'percolate'.

perp n American
a wrongdoer, felon. An abbreviation of 'perpetrator' used by law enforcers.

> 'They've ID'd the perp, but they can't touch him.'
> (Recorded, journalist, Pocatello USA, November 2004)

perpetrate vb American
1a. to put on a show of confidence, self-assurance
1b. to dissimulate, pretend
Both usages of the word probably originated in black speech.

personals n pl Australian
lingerie, (female) underwear. An adult euphemism used both facetiously and seriously.

> I wouldn't hang your personals out here in full view.

Peruvian marching powder n
cocaine. A jocular middle-class American euphemism of the mid- to late 1970s which was probably too long and unwieldy to gain a wider currency.

perve[1], **perv** n
a lascivious or perverted person, a 'dirty old man'. A shortening of 'pervert' heard since the 1960s.
See also **optic (nerve)**

perve², **perv** *vb Australian*
to behave lasciviously. From the noun form.

pervy *adj*
perverted or lascivious

pesterous *adj Caribbean*
irritating, troublesome

peter *n*
1. the penis. A personification and pre-dictable euphemism dating from the 19th century (if not earlier) and mainly used by adults.

> *'Absence makes the peter fonda.'*
> (Caption to nude photograph of Peter Fonda, *Oz* magazine, 1969)

2. a safe. In the jargon of the underworld peter originally meant a trunk or strong-box, later a safe. The word was being used with this sense as early as the 17th century, perhaps inspired by some sort of biblical pun, now lost.

peter-man *n British*
a safecracker. An underworld and police term in use for the last few decades or so. Peter is an old word for a safe or strongbox.

Pete Tong *adj British*
wrong. The rhyming slang expression, using the name of a star club DJ, has been in use since around 1998 and was used in the title of a 2004 film.

> *Oh God, it's all gone Pete Tong!*

petrified *adj American*
intoxicated by alcohol or drugs. The term has no connection with the colloquial sense of 'terrified' but is a pun on the more common **stoned**.

petrol-head *n*
a car enthusiast. The term is heard both in Britain and Australia and was given wider currency in Britain from the 1990s by its usage in motoring maga-zines and such television programmes as BBC TV's *Top Gear*.

pew *n British*
a chair. A colloquialism usually heard in the verb form 'take a pew': sit down. This humorously elevated version of chair arose around the turn of the 20th century.

pezzie, pessy *n British*
an unsophisticated, gormless individ-ual. A derivation of 'peasant' used by schoolchildren since the 1990s.

P.F.O. *adj British*
injured as a result of drunkenness. Joc-ular medical shorthand for 'pissed, fell over', e.g. as recorded as a mock diag-nosis in a patient's notes.
Compare **P.G.T.**

P.G.T. *adj British*
assaulted while drunk. Jocular medical shorthand for 'pissed, got thumped', e.g. as recorded as a mock diagnosis in a patient's notes.

phat *adj*
excellent, **hip**. The re-spelling of **fat** (itself alternatively derived from its use in the phrase **fat-city** or from the fat tyres favoured by **low-riders**, etc.) was an emblematic term first in hip hop and **rap** circles and then in other youth subcul-tures such as surfers, skateboarders and skaters, etc. (A magazine named *Phat* catering for rollerbladers and computer-game fans was briefly published in Brit-ain in 1994.) In this spelling the word, which some authorities claimed was actually based on 'emphatically', had no comparative or superlative forms to com-pare with 'fattier' or 'fattiest'.

> *phat garms*

phat-free *adj British*
unpleasant, **uncool**. The term was used by schoolchildren in 2004.

phreak *vb*
to hack into a telephone, telecommuni-cations or computer system, in the patois of **cyberpunks** and **net-heads**. The term is a later back-formation from 'phreaker', the designation for the first hackers who interfered with the US telephone system for fun, in search of knowledge or for profit.

phudi, phudu *n*
female sex organs, in British Asian usage

piano *adj British*
faint, delicate, 'under the weather' or indisposed. This upper-class expression derives from the Italian musical term *piano*, which is an instruction to play or sing softly. The British speaker's pro-nunciation, in imitation of the original Italian, is 'pee-aah-no'.

> *'Please don't disturb her, she seems to be feeling a little piano today.'*
> (Recorded, hostess, Dorset, 1974)

pickled *adj*
drunk. A fairly inoffensive term, usually heard in the speech of the middle-aged or elderly.

> *'I sat next to Pat Collins who is a very intelligent and delightful woman. I felt sorry that she had George Brown, completely pickled, on the other side of her.'*
> (Tony Benn's Diaries, 14 October 1969)

picni, pickney *n*
a child. The term is Caribbean dialect, a more recent variant form of the often racist 'picaninny', itself from the Portuguese *pequenino*, meaning tiny.

piddle¹ *vb British*
to urinate. A childish or humoroussounding word, this is nonetheless one of Britain's oldest 'non-respectable' words in current use.

piddle² *n British*
urine or an act of urination. Piddle is etymologically related to puddle and to piddling meaning insignificant or trifling. It has been used as the name of small rivers in county districts and seems to have had a colloquial meaning of 'small water' or 'insignificant scrap' before its narrowing to the modern sense during the 18th and 19th centuries.

> *'Piddles were done out of the back window last night, standing on the bed.'*
> (Spike Milligan, Adolf Hitler; My Part in His Downfall, 1971)

piece¹ *n*
1. *American* a gun. An underworld euphemism.
2. a graffiti artist's *oeuvre*. A shortening of 'piece of work' or 'masterpiece' and forming part of the graffiti subculture lexicon of the 1980s.

> *'Kids do it mainly for the clothes – jeans or trainers, or to buy cans of spray paint to do pieces (graffiti).'*
> (Teenage mugger, Observer, 22 May 1988)

3. *British* a girlfriend, female. An item of black street-talk used especially by males, recorded in 2003.
> *my piece*
4. *British* the penis. In black street-talk.

piece², **piece of ass** *n American*
a woman (or, less often, a man) considered as a sexual object. Piece has been employed in a similar sexual context, invariably referring unromantically to a woman, since the 15th century. The various phrases such as 'piece of ass', **piece of tail**, etc. are probably more recent, arising, like **bit of fluff**, in the 19th century.

piece of piss/pudding *n British*
something easy to accomplish, presenting no problems, a pushover. Both terms are variants on the common colloquialism 'a piece of cake'.

piece of tail *n*
an alternative form of **piece of ass**

pieces *n pl British See* **do one's nut/block/crust/pieces/taters**

pie-eater *n*
a fat and/or greedy person. The derisive terms, used by adolescents in particular, coincided with national concerns over obesity in the US and UK since 2002. **Pie-wagon** was a synonym heard in the US in 2004.

pie-hole *n American*
the mouth. A humorous usage heard among adolescents and featured in the US film, *Sleepwalkers*, 1992. **Hum-hole** and the earlier British **cakehole** are synonyms.

pie-wagon *n American*
a **pie-eater**
> *Joe's scored himself a real pie-wagon this time.*

piff *n British*
nonsense. A 1980s shortening of the colloquial 'piffle', heard among adolescents.
> *a load of piff*

piffy *adj British*
dubious, doubtful, suspect. A middleclass usage, often said disdainfully or superciliously. Its origin is obscure; it does not appear to be related to piffling in the sense of insignificant, but may be influenced by 'iffy' or 'piffle'.

pig *n*
1. a policeman or woman. An offensive term that gained its greatest currency in the 1960s in the USA whence it was reimported into Britain. (It was used in the same sense in the late Victorian underworld.)
> *'Today's pig is tomorrow's bacon.'*
> (Anti-war protestors' and demonstrators' slogan of the 1960s)

2a. a girl. A usage from the argot of street gangs, **beatniks**, etc. since the 1950s. Surprisingly, in these contexts the word is not necessarily pejorative.

2b. *American* an ugly, repellent girl. A term current in the late 1980s in US colleges, where 'Pig of the Year/Week' contests took place and the unwitting winner was presented with a prize.

3. a sexist male, as characterised by feminists. A shortening of the catchphrase 'male chauvinist pig' (also rendered as **MCP**).

4. a segment of an orange

These sub-senses evoke the familiar images of the pig as gluttonous and disgusting or round and chubby.

pigeon *n American*
a worthless female. In hip hop and **rap** parlance since the 1990s.

pigfucker *n*
a despicable, disgusting and/or unpleasant person. An all-purpose term of strong abuse, usually applied to males. This version of the insult is probably more prevalent in the USA; **fuckpig** is a British synonym.

pigging *adj British*
an intensifying adjective used as a milder substitute for **fucking**. Pigging has the merit of being able to be broadcast. It is used, often with vehemence, by both men and, particularly, women.

> *I told him to take his pigging 'peace offering' and get lost.*

pig it *vb British*
to behave in a disgusting manner. The expression may apply to living in filthy surroundings, acting in a slovenly way or 'slumming'.

pig Latin *n*
a synonym for **backslang**, or a means of coining slang terms by the rearranging of syllables. **Ixnay** is an example.

piglet *n Australian*
1. an unattractive teenage girl
2. *See* **pig**

pig off *vb*
to leave, go away. A euphemism for more offensive terms such as **piss off**, etc., usually heard in the form of an imperative. It is often used by women who wish to express themselves forcefully without obscenity.

> *'I finally got fed up and told him to pig off.'*
> (Recorded, female teacher, London, 1989)

pig out *vb*
to eat excessively and/or messily, to behave in an outrageous or obsessive way. This racier version of the colloquial

'pig (oneself)', meaning to overindulge, probably originated in the USA and was established in Britain during the later 1960s.

pig's, pig's ear *n British*
1. beer. A London rhyming-slang term that is still heard. (The dismissive exclamatory phrase 'in a pig's ear!' is unconnected, being a euphemism for 'in a pig's arse!').

> *I'll have a pint of pig's.*

2. an alternative version of **pig's breakfast/arse**

pig's breakfast/arse/ear *n British*
a mess, an outrageous failure, a complete disaster. Most often heard in statements such as 'you've made a right pig's breakfast of that!'.

piker *n American*
a mean, tightfisted person; a **welcher** on a bet or a shirker. A now obsolescent word, related distantly to the British **pikey**, or from an abbreviation of 'turnpike', piker occurred in the writings of Raymond Chandler in the 1940s. It originally referred to the unreliability of vagrants or itinerants.

pikey, pikie *n British*
a gypsy or vagrant. The term properly denotes one of the travelling people who lives in a settlement, such as a member of a family of hop-pickers. The precise origins of these terms (and the American **piker**) are unclear because of the convergence of two similar senses of 'pike'; the first is a toll road as in turnpike, the second is an archaic British verb meaning to depart or travel. In 2004 pikey was one of the terms used as a synonym for **chav**.

pikeys' wedding *n British*
a brawl. The term was posted on the b3ta website in 2004.

pill *n*
1. *British* a ball. A schoolboy term of the 1950s.

> *'If I pla there is dead silence becos i never hit the pill at all they are all air shots chiz.'*
> (Geoffrey Willans and Ronald Searle, *Back in the Jug Agane*, 1959)

2. pills *British* the testicles; by extension from the above sense

3. *British* a foolish or stupid, annoying person. A shortening of **pillock**.

4. *South African* a **joint**. Recorded as an item of Sowetan slang in the *Cape Sunday Times*, 29 January 1995.

pill-head *n*
an amphetamine user or addict

pilling *adj*
under the influence of an illicit drug or drugs, not necessarily in pill form

pillock *n British*
a foolish or stupid, annoying person. A vulgar but not taboo term of abuse which had existed in British slang usage since the 1950s (its exact date of origin is undetermined), coming into vogue in the mid-1970s. Various etymologies have been proposed for the word; 'pillicock' was a late medieval term for the penis, sometimes used as an expression of endearment or affectionate abuse; pill-ocks has also been explained as a rural term for rabbit droppings, or as a synonym for the testicles (**pills**) employing the diminutive or affectionate suffix '-ocks' (as in the case of **balls** and **bollocks**).

pillow-biter *n*
a male homosexual, particularly a passive partner in sodomy. This expression probably originated in Australia, where it is common. It was introduced to the British public during the trial of Jeremy Thorpe (accused of plotting the murder of a male model, Norman Scott, in 1974) by the satirical magazine *Private Eye*.

pill-popper *n*
a user of amphetamines or tranquillisers

pimp, pimped (out) *adj*
exciting, fashionable, admirable. Vogue terms among hip hop aficionados and US teenagers since 2000, from black street culture's elevation of the pimp as a style icon.

pimp (someone) (over) *vb American*
to deceive, cheat someone

Man. I got pimped that time.
He pimped us over good.

pimp-juice *n American*
1. masculine allure. An imaginary or intangible quality possessed by some males. The term has become popular since 2000. The female equivalent is **milkshake**.

Damn, that boy got pimp-juice.
2. semen

pimps *n, adj British*
(something) very easy, a pushover. A word used by young schoolchildren from the late 1980s, particularly when showing off or boasting. The word is usually

used in an exclamation such as 'that's pimps!' or 'it's pimps!', meaning 'there's nothing to it'. There seems to be no relation between this term and the standard English word for a procurer or the archaic use of pimp to mean sneak or inform upon.

pimpsy, pipsy *adj British*
easily accomplished, no trouble. A variant of **pimps** used typically by middle-class schoolchildren.

pinch *vb, n*
(to make) an arrest. An underworld and police term on both sides of the Atlantic.

pinch a loaf, pinch one off *vb American*
to defecate. The phrases are part of male **toilet-talk**.

pineapple *n Australian See* **rough end of the pineapple, the**

ping *vb British*
to shoot or wound by shooting. An item of underworld slang from the early 1990s, the word is echoic, imitating the sound of a small-calibre gunshot or a ricochet.

pinhead *n*
1a. a fool, idiot
1b. a person with a small head and a (proportionately) large body

pink¹ *adj*
a code or facetious term for **gay** adopted from the heterosexual lexicon by the male homosexual community for ironic or semi-ironic self-reference. (The Nazis affixed pink triangles to homosexuals.) **Lavender** is a similar usage.

pink² *n American*
the female genitals. This term, which arose in the language of pornographers, prostitutes, etc., was picked up in show-business jargon in such phrases as 'surrender the pink' (the title of a book by the actress Carrie Fisher) and the name *Kissing the Pink* adopted by an early 1990s rock band.

pinkie *n*
1. a white person. A term of mild racist abuse used by black speakers in London in the mid-1970s. A more accurate and less flattering version of **whitey**.
2. the little finger. An American term now generally understood in Britain and Australia.
3. *British* a fifty-pound note or the amount of £50, from the colour of the banknote

pinko[1] *n, adj American*
(someone with) liberal or left-of-centre politics or ideas. The image is of a watered-down 'red' (someone with extreme left-wing beliefs).

pinko[2] *adj, n Australian*
(intoxicated by) methylated spirits, which are often dyed pink

pink oboe *n British*
the penis

pins *n pl*
legs. The word was first recorded in this sense in 1530 when pin was synonymous with (wooden) peg.

I'm a bit unsteady on my pins.

pint-man *n British*
a boorish male. The pejorative term is used by college students and others to denote an aggressive and/or unsophisticated male, whether or not that person is drinking beer at the time of speaking.

'People should not take being bounced [menaced or aggressed] by pint-man.'
(Recorded, 17-year-old male, North London, 1999)

pipe *n*
1. *American* a gun. An item of street jargon used especially by adolescent criminals in the 1990s.

'Teachers report that teenagers talk about "packing a barrel" or "chilling someone with a pipe".'
(*Sunday Times*, 31 August 1992)

2. *British* a telephone, particularly a mobile telephone, in the jargon of truck-drivers and rescue services
3. *American* a very easy task, programme of study, etc. This usage is probably based on the earlier phrase 'pipe course', used on campuses to describe an undemanding study option. The relationship to the standard sense of the word is unclear.

pipe one's eye *vb*
to weep. This phrase is now almost obsolete, except in self-consciously fanciful speech. Although 'pipe your eye' has been interpreted as cockney rhyming slang for *cry*, the expression had been recorded as early as the beginning of the 19th century (before either cockney rhyming slang or the use of the word cry to mean weep were widespread). Connections have been drawn with plaintive, tear-provoking pipe music or the more prosaic image of waterworks,

but the precise origins of the term remain uncertain.

piper *n American*
a **crack** smoker. A term of the late 1980s.

piss *n*
1. urine or an act of urination. An echoic word with cognates in other European languages (*pisser* is the French verb) which has been in use since the Middle English period. Its level of respectability has varied; originally it was a generally acceptable term, by the 18th century a vulgarism, and by the mid-19th century virtually taboo. Since the 1960s it has been possible to use the word in public, although **pee** is preferred in polite company.
2. *British* alcoholic drink. In this sense the term usually occurs in the phrase **on the piss**.
3. weak beer
4. nonsense
5. *See* **take the piss (out of someone)**

piss about/around *vb*
a vulgar version of 'mess about'

piss all over (someone) *vb*
to thoroughly defeat, humiliate or overwhelm. The image is taken from the literal behaviour of animals or humans ritually signalling victory.

piss and wind *n See* **all piss and wind**

piss-ant, pissant *adj American*
trifling, paltry, insignificant. Although a fairly strong indicator of contempt or dismissal, this word is not treated as a taboo item in the same way as other compounds containing **piss**. The word is originally a rustic noun (also rendered 'pissmire') meaning an ant. The piss element refers to formic acid.

piss-artist *n British*
an habitual or accomplished heavy drinker, a drunkard. A term used sometimes with contempt, sometimes with admiration.

pissed *adj*
1. *British* drunk. This usage came into the language at some unrecorded date early in the 20th century. It presumably originally referred to the incontinence of a helpless inebriate, or else to the equation of alcohol itself with urine. This sense of the word is rare in American English, but was encountered e.g. in the 1980s parlance of East Coast sophisticates.

'If you look at all the slang words for 'drunk', you'd think we were permanently pissed.'

(Recorded, London student, February 2002)

2. *American* upset, angry, **pissed-off**

When I told him to go he got really pissed. I was pissed at her for making me go through all that grief.

pissed-off *adj*

angry, irritated, disappointed, upset. Like the verb to **piss (someone) off**, this usage emerged at the time of World War II.

'Well … people who bought from our competitors are probably pretty pissed off. The plastic should be worn through just about now!'

(Record bootlegger, *Oz* magazine, February 1970)

piss-elegant *adj American*

smart, refined or fashionable. This (fairly mild) vulgarism implies either that the elegance in question is excessive or pretentious or simply that the speaker is envious or disapproving.

pisser *n*

1. something annoying or disappointing. Originally an Americanism, the term spread to Britain in the mid-1970s.

'Living in a world where nothing boring ever happens is a real pisser.'

(*The Young Ones*, BBC TV comedy, 1982)

2. a toilet

pisshead *n*

1. *British* a habitual drunkard, **piss-artist**

2. *American* an unpleasant person, **shit-head**

pissing-match, pissing contest *n American*

a competitive display, especially a futile one. The term, inspired by the common male pastime of competing to urinate farthest or highest, is used typically to describe displays of masculine aggression or rivalry.

'Look sister, I don't want to get into a pissing contest with you, just tell me where the command bunker is.'

(*Screamers*, US film, 1996)

piss in someone's pool *vb American*

a vulgar alternative to **rain on someone's parade**

piss in the wind *vb*

to do something futile, make a doomed attempt. A vulgar version of such colloquialisms as 'whistle in the wind/dark'.

piss it *vb British*

to succeed effortlessly. A term probably deriving from **piece of piss**: a ridiculously easy task.

'They told Sophie the entrance exam would be a bugger, but she absolutely pissed it.'

(Recorded, personal assistant, London, 1989)

piss off *vb*

to leave, go away. This vulgarism was in use throughout the 20th century, particularly in British speech. The word piss has no specific significance, but adds intensity and often overtones of exasperation, both where used descriptively and as an instruction.

'You got a couple of options: piss off out of town, or take him out, mate.'

(*Blackjack*, Australian TV crime drama, 2004)

piss (someone) off *vb*

to irritate, anger, annoy or provoke someone. This phrase entered the English slang lexicon around the time of World War II and was probably more prevalent in American speech than British until the 1970s.

It really pisses me off the way she just assumes I'm going to pick up the pieces.

piss on someone's chips/sandwiches *vb British*

more vulgar synonyms for the American phrase **rain on someone's parade**. The latter version was used by the standup comedian Jo Brand in 1994.

piss-poor *adj*

dreadfully bad. Piss is used here as an intensifying addition. The phrase was earlier used to mean destitute. Since the late 1970s it is in fairly widespread use, particularly in journalistic circles where it denotes 'of miserable quality', pitiful.

piss pot *n*

a chamber-pot, potty

piss-take *n British*

an act of mockery, parody. A common back-formation from the phrase to **take the piss (out of someone)**.

piss-up *n British*

a drinking bout, drunken celebration. A vulgarism generally used neutrally or with cheerful overtones rather than disapprovingly.

'Bob Bee, for Hawkhead Productions, has secured the ultimate television

commission: to organise a piss-up in a brewery.'
(*Independent on Sunday*, 1 April 1990)

pissy *adj*
insignificant, trivial, inferior

pistol *n American*
an attractive, active or powerful person. Used of and by both sexes as a term of admiration, the word need not have sexual connotations, but in modern usage often does.

Isn't she a pistol?

pit *n*
1. a bed. A popular word in the armed services since before World War II, now in general use.
2. any dirty, sordid or unpleasant place. A more recent alternative to dump, a synonym for **tip**.
See also **pits, the**; **throttle pit**

pitcher *n British*
a market trader who sells his or her wares by way of an ostentatious performance.
Compare **lurker**; **rorter**

pits, the *n*
an unpleasant, disgusting and/or unbearable place, situation or person; the worst place, situation or state of affairs imaginable. This Americanism has become widely used throughout the English-speaking world. It is, in origin, said to be a shortening of armpits.

'You are the pits of the world!'
(John McEnroe characterising an umpire, Wimbledon Lawn Tennis Championship, 1981)

'This review has nothing to do with the world of mountaineering and in a sport where there is a wealth of first-rate literature, this "offering" can only be regarded as the pits.'
(Reader's letter, *Sunday Times* Books supplement, October 1989)

pit stop *n*
1a. a pause in a drinking bout in order to visit the toilet
1b. a pause in a journey or other activity for alcoholic refreshment
Both senses are humorous adaptations of the pit stops made by racing drivers in order to undergo refuelling, a change of tyres or running repairs.

Placido *n British*
a £10 note or the amount of ten pounds, a pun on 'tenner' using the name of the

tenor Placido Domingo. Synonyms are **Pavarotti**, **Ayrton (Senna)**.

plank *n*
1. *British* a dull-witted person, someone who is as 'thick as two short planks'. The term was used by the late Princess Diana, referring to herself.
2. a solid-bodied electric guitar. A musician's term of the 1980s; playing such a guitar is known as **spanking the plank**.

plant *n American*
marihuana. The term was recorded in 2001.

plastic *adj*
(usually of a person) artificial, shallow, insincere. A **hippy** buzzword of the 1960s, borrowed from **beatnik** usage to castigate the conformist and materialist world of the **straights** as well as the legions of 'weekend' hippy imitators. The word submerged during the 1970s, but by 1990 was back in use in British playground slang.

plat *n Australian*
a stupid person. The word's origin is uncertain (Eric Partridge derives it from the French *plat*: flat), but the resemblance to **prat** may not be fortuitous.

plate *vb*
to perform fellatio. A term from the 1960s, now dated, which was part of the jargon of rock-music **groupies**. Conflicting etymologies cite the rhyming slang 'plate of ham' for **gam** (a synonym for fellatio), or simply the image of licking a plate.

plate-face *n Australian*
someone of Oriental origin. A derogatory racist term referring to the supposedly wide, flat, round faces of the Mongoloid racial type.

plates (of meat) *n pl British*
the *feet*. A well-known example of cockney rhyming slang which is actually still used, although almost always in the shortened form, by working-class Londoners.

I've got to sit down – I've been on me plates all day.

platter *n*
a phonograph record. The term dates back to the era of 78 r.p.m. records; it does not seem to have been transferred to apply to CDs.

player, playa *n*
a person who has multiple and simultaneous sexual partners, 'a smooth talker

who cheats, is stylish'. This vogue term, heard among younger speakers since 2000, probably derives from the notion of 'playing around' or 'playing the field'. It probably originated in black US speech.

play footsie vb
1a. to indulge in amorous or flirtatious caresses with the feet, typically covertly under a table
1b. to flirt with or toy with in a general sense; often in the context of business and commercial relationships

play gooseberry vb British
to be the unwanted third person present at a romantic assignation, as a chaperone, uninvited guest or unwitting intruder. The expression dates from the 19th century: in the language of parents and children 'gooseberry' then, as now, denoted a buffoon or figure of fun, possibly from the supposedly comic appearance of the fruit or its sour taste.

play hardball vb American
to behave in a tough, unrelenting or uncompromising way. A phrase used for instance among business people, politicians, sportsmen, etc. from the 1960s, and now heard outside the United States. A metaphor taken from baseball, where a hard ball is used by professionals and a soft one by juniors and amateurs.

play hooky vb American
to play truant. Hooky (or 'hookey') is related to the cockney **hook it**: 'to take to one's heels', escape.

playing away n British
indulging in extra-marital or illicit sex. The use of the phrase was particularly apposite when referring to sports celebrities such as David Beckham, Wayne Rooney and Sven Goran Eriksson in 2004.

'Unlucky in love, Kylie was furious last night after lover Olivier Martinez was caught playing away with Hollywood babe Michelle Rodriguez.'
(*Daily Star*, 29 July 2004)

play the arse vb British
1a. to behave foolishly
1b. to behave in a truculent, **arsey** manner

play the whale vb Australian
to vomit. The image is of a whale spouting.

pleb n
a plebeian, member of the lower classes. A fashionable term in Britain in the early 1960s when class-consciousness preceded 'consciousness-expanding' among the educated young.

plod, the plod n British
the police force or a uniformed policeman. From 'P.C. Plod', a character from the popular children's stories featuring Noddy, written by Enid Blyton in the 1950s. The term additionally evokes a slow-witted, literal and figurative plodder in a civilian context.

plonk n British
1. wine, especially cheap wine. The word usually refers to red wine, although it was originally a corruption of *vin blanc* coined by British soldiers in France during World War I.
2. a woman police officer. An item of derogatory police slang (from **plonker**) recorded in the *Evening Standard* magazine, February 1993.

plonker n British
1. the penis. A term probably influenced by 'plonk (down)' in the sense of place down heavily or present defiantly. The word has been in use since early in the 20th century. It was rarely heard during the 1960s and 1970s but was revived during the 1980s vogue for 'schoolboy' vulgarity.

'If she's game and wants your plonker wear a Jiffi so you can bonk her.'
(Promotion slogan for *Jiffi* condoms, 1988)

2. a **dickhead**. Inspired by the previous sense of the word and by the suggestion in 'plonk' of ponderous or clumsy movement, this usage became a vogue term of the late 1980s.

'You end up shouting at the people who care about yer, not to the plonkers who treat you like dirt.'
(*EastEnders*, British TV soap opera, 1989)

3. a gaffe or blunder
4. a kiss, particularly a heavy **smacker**

plook, pluke n Scottish
a spot or pimple on the skin, **zit**. The etymology of the word is obscure.

plop(s) n British
excreta. A humorous nursery term sometimes used facetiously by adults.

ploughed, plowed adj American
drunk. One of many terms evoking an image of laid low, crushed or destroyed. **Blitzed, smashed, legless**, etc. are others on this theme.

p.l.u. n British
'people like us'. An old upper-class code term of approbation and social discrimination, still used occasionally.
I'm afraid they're not really quite p.l.u.

plum n British
a foolish person. Synonyms are the less common **pear** and **peach**. The widespread term was recorded in use amongst junior schoolchildren in the 1980s and among teenage North London schoolboys in the 1990s.

plums n pl
the testicles. One of many examples of fruit as a sexual metaphor.

plunker n American
a condom

po n British
a chamber-pot, potty, toilet. Now a dated nursery word, po was used by adults until the 1960s. The word is an imitation of the French pronunciation of *pot (de chambre)*.

pocket billiards/pool n
(of a man) manipulation of one's genitals through the trouser pockets. The first phrase is British, the second the American version.

pod n American
marihuana. A dated term derived from the seedheads found in herbal cannabis.

podger n British
an act of sexual intercourse. The humorous vulgarism was used, e.g., in the British TV comedy *Absolutely Fabulous* in 1991. It is perhaps influenced by **roger** and the many sexually related terms beginning with p-, or could be a hitherto unrecorded term for an erection based on the colloquial 'podgy'.
a swift podger

pods n pl British
the testicles. This use of the word has been popularised by *Viz* comic.

pog n British
a synonym for **chav** recorded in 2004

pogie, pogey, pogy n American
the female sex organs. The word is probably derived from the obsolete 'pogie' or

'pogue', which denoted a male homosexual, hence sexual activity in general.

point percy at the porcelain vb
to urinate. An expression invented by Barry Humphries which, via the comic strip *The Wonderful World of Barry McKenzie*, has passed into common currency in Britain as well as Australia. **Percy** is one of many common personifications of the male member.

pointy-head n American
an intellectual or person of excessive refinement. The expression has been used in the USA since the late 1960s by the self-consciously philistine or genuinely uncultured in expressing contempt for political or social pundits, artists, academics, etc.

poke n
1. an act of sexual intercourse. Poke shares this sexual sense with **bang, boff, knock**, etc., which are all synonyms for strike.
2. a punch, blow. A specialised sense of the standard English word poke meaning to prod (having the same meaning as the Middle Dutch *poken*).

polack n
a Polish person. The slang term, often pejorative in American usage, is, minus the e, the word for Pole in the Polish language.

polari n
a variant form of **parlyaree** widely used, e.g. on the Internet, since the 1990s. **Palari** is an alternative form.

polisher n
a toady, ingratiating person, obsequious flatterer. A London working-class term also briefly in vogue in the media in the early 1980s. It is a truncated form of the (originally American) **apple-polisher** (from the image of a schoolchild presenting an apple to a teacher in order to curry favour).

Polish fire drill n American
a chaotic situation, bungled operation, mess. A supposedly jocular expression heard in adult speech since the 1970s. (Polish may, in US slang, play the part that Irish or Egyptian have traditionally played in British racist jokes.)

polluted adj American
drunk. A probably ephemeral campus and **preppie** term.

polone, poloni *n British*
a woman, female. A near-obsolete term of theatrical and showman's slang, dating from the 19th century. The word is an example of non-Italian **parlyaree**, ultimately derived from *beluñi*, a Spanish gypsy term for an (immoral) woman.
See also **omipolone**

Pom *n Australian*
a native of Britain, especially an Englishman. The word is a shortening of the earlier term **Pommy**.

Pomgolia *n*
an alternative form of **Pongolia**

Pommy, Pommie *n, adj Australian*
(a person who is) British. The standard, and usually derogatory, slang term for natives of or immigrants from the British Isles, Pommy is probably a corruption of 'pomegranate', chanted as a humorous semi-rhyme for 'immigrant'. The epithet has been in use since the first decade of the 20th century. The noun is now probably more common in the form **Pom**.

pom-pom *n Jamaican*
the vagina. The word was used in the lyrics to ragga music.

ponce *n British*
1. a pimp, procurer. This sense of the word was first recorded in the late 19th century.
2a. an ostentatious, effeminate male
2b. a parasite, 'sponger', idler
Ponce derives either from the standard English 'pounce', or possibly from the French *pensionnaire*, in the sense of a non-paying guest. In its first and literal sense, ponce is virtually standard English (used by the police force among others). The following senses are terms of contempt directed at individuals thought to be showy, smugly idle or parasitic.

ponce (off someone) *vb British*
to take advantage (of someone), borrow or cadge (from someone). A widespread usage derived from the noun.
    Can I ponce a fag off you?

ponce around/about *vb British*
to behave in a showy and/or irresponsible manner. A usage based on the noun, **ponce**.

ponced-up *adj British*
smartly dressed or overdressed. From the noun **ponce** (a pimp, idler or show-off).

pond scum, pond life *n*
a contemptible, worthless person or people. Originating in American usage in the 1980s, this more colourful rendering of the colloquial 'low-life' became widespread in all English-speaking areas in the 1990s.
Compare **bottom-feeder**

pong[1] *vb, n British*
(to) stink. The word is of uncertain origin but may derive from a similar Romany (gypsy) verb.

pong[2] *n Australian*
an Oriental. A racist epithet, either based on **Pongo**, or imitating the sound of Oriental speech.

Pongo *n*
1. a black man, a coloured person, a foreigner. A patronisingly derogatory middle-class term used, e.g., in public-school and army speech.
2. an English person. An Australian and New Zealand slang term derived from the previous sense of the word.

Pongolia, Pomgolia *n Australian and New Zealand*
the UK, Britain. Jocular terms based on **Pom** and **Pongo** and punning on Mongolia (evoking the notion of a distant and barbaric country).

ponies, the *n pl British*
horses, in the context of horseracing and betting
    I lost it all on the ponies.

pony[1] *n*
1. *British* the sum of £25 or, more recently, £25,000, in the jargon of the racetrack, underworld, market traders, etc. In its traditional sense the word was probably adopted to reflect the small size of a £25 bet.
2. *American* a promiscuous female. Equivalent to the male **player**, it is probably from the euphemism/song lyric 'ride the pony'.

pony[2] *adj British*
of poor quality, disappointing, worthless. In this sense the word is a shortening of the rhyme 'pony and trap': **crap**.
    'If we don't take our time, it risks being utterly pony.'
    (Recorded, theatre director, London, July 2003)

pony up *vb American*
to pay. A synonym for 'pay up' or 'fork out', the phrase was first recorded in the early 19th century and was said to

derive from the earlier British use of the Latin form *pone*, meaning put (money down or forward).

> '*At 100,000 tax dollars a pop the American people ponied up for one reason; it was the future.*'
> (*Philadelphia Project*, US film, 1993)

poo[1] *n British*
1. a nursery term for excrement that has passed into standard colloquial English
2. champagne. A **yuppie** and **Sloane ranger** abbreviation of **shampoo**.

> '*You're getting good at this. Extra poo tonight.*'
> (*Serious Money*, play by Caryl Churchill, 1987)

poo[2] *adj British*
bad. The adjectival use of the word has been recorded since 2000.

> *a completely poo bike*
> *That film was so poo!*

pooch *n*
a dog. This well-known term, particularly well-established in the USA, is of mysterious origin. Possible etymologies are from a dialect version of pouch (alluding to a dog's insatiable desire to 'tuck away' food) or from a term of endearment, possibly the German *putzi*.

> '*Podgy Chas Clark, son of ex-Chancellor Nigel Lawson's financial guru Sir William Clark, called his pooch Charlie – a nickname for cocaine.*'
> (*News of the World*, 29 October 1989)

poodle-faker *n*
an effete, over-refined or offensively genteel young man, specifically a young man in attendance on older ladies. Faker here implies insincerity and poodle the attitude or appearance of a lapdog. The word appeared in Britain in the second decade of the 20th century.

poof, pouff, poove, poofter, pooftah, puff *n*
a male homosexual. The most common slang term in Britain and Australia. The variations of the word go in and out of fashion. Poof and poove were popular in the 1960s, poofter in the 1970s. The origin of the epithet is obscure and the subject of argument. Possibilities include 'pouff!' as a supposedly affected exclamation of disdain, or a northern English pronunciation of 'puff', which itself could be a dialect exclamation of disgust, a reference to puffed-up with pride, or a Victorian term for a sodomite. It might equally be inspired by the 'puff' of 'powder puff', or the French words *pouffe*: a stuffed seat and *pouffer (de rire)*: giggle.

poofer *n*
an unspecified or unnameable thing. An item of middle-class slang recorded in 2002.

pool *See* **pocket billiards/pool**

poon, poontang *n American*
1. the female pudenda
2. women in general, seen as sexual objects. The word is from Louisiana French in which it is a corruption of *putain* (the standard French term for **whore**), first applied to black women.

> '*I guess this means my poon days are over.*'
> (Remark widely attributed to John F. Kennedy following his inauguration as US president, 1960)

poona *n American*
marihuana or hashish. A word of uncertain origin (Poona is an Indian city but is not renowned as a source of narcotics) recorded in adolescent usage in the 1990s.

poonanie, punany, punani *n*
1a. the vagina
1b. females, when considered as sex partners

This formerly obscure item of Caribbean patois was popularised by the comedian Ali G at the end of the 1990s. It is variously derived from the Ashanti *oponaani*, meaning keyhole or the Hawaiian *punani*, meaning heavenly flower.

poonanny *n See* **poonanie**

poop[1] *n, vb*
excrement, (to) **crap**. A nursery word used humorously by adults and in the phrases 'poop-scoop', a small lidded shovel used to clear up dog-droppings, and **hot poop**, the latest news or gossip, the newest fashion. Poop is heard all over the anglophone community but is particularly prevalent in the USA. It has existed since the time of Middle English and the same word has been used with the same meaning in Dutch. **Poo-poo** is a synonym.

poop[2] *adj*
bad. Since the later 1990s the noun has been used adjectivally, e.g. by UK schoolchildren, in the same way as **poo**.

poop-chute *n*
the anus

pooped, pooped out *adj*
exhausted, out of breath. The word is probably an imitation of the sound of puffing and blowing, although there is a theory that it derives from British sailors' slang for a ship being swamped by a 'poop' wave. In its current sense it was originally a North American term, spreading to Australia and Britain in the 1960s.

too pooped to pop

pooper *n See* **party pooper**

poo-poo *n, vb See* **poop¹**

poor *adj*
1. bad
2. good
The standard word has been adopted into adolescent slang in the same way as **bad**, **tragic**, etc. since 2000.

poot¹ *vb, n*
(to) **fart**. Originally an echoic nursery word, probably originating in the USA, poot has achieved prominence in the vogue for references to flatulence in adolescent humour since the late 1980s (epitomised by *Viz* comic). In American usage poot may also mean excrement.

poot² *n See* **get some poot**

poove *n British*
a version of **poof** which was current in the early 1960s

pop *vb*
1. *British* to pawn. The word has had this meaning since the 18th century.
2. *See* **pop one's clogs**
3a. to take (an illicit drug) orally. The expression refers particularly to amphetamines or barbiturates rather than hallucinogenics such as LSD or hard drugs such as heroin.
3b. to inject a narcotic. The word is used more often in connection with intramuscular than intravenous injection, often in the specific forms **skin-pop** and **joy pop**.
4. to hit, punch
   He popped him one in the eye.
5. to give birth
   Has she popped yet?
6. to have sex with or to achieve orgasm. This usage of the word is long-established, pre-dating for instance **pop one's rocks**.
7a. to shoot
7b. to kill. An underworld euphemism.

pop a chubby *vb See* **chubby**

pop a vein *vb American*
to become apoplectic with anger. A children's equivalent of 'burst a blood vessel', applied to and about furious adults.

pop it *vb*
to die. The phrase is heard in Britain and Australia.

po-po, po *n American*
1a. a police officer
1b. the police force in general
An expression used on campus in the USA since around 2000.

pop one's clogs *vb British*
to die. A humorous, sometimes incongruously light-hearted phrase popular e.g. with TV presenters, disc jockeys and other entertainers. 'Pop' here is probably the old slang word for pawn, the suggestion being that when the family member dies, his or her clogs are sold.

pop one's rocks *vb*
to achieve orgasm, ejaculate. A version of **get one's rocks off** which was briefly a vogue expression in the early 1970s. Pop has been used in a sexual sense at least since the 19th century. (An American synonym is 'pop one's cookies'.)

popper *n American*
a gun. In this sense the word was first recorded (referring to a revolver) in the 1940s and was still in use among street gangs in the 1990s.

poppers *n pl*
amyl nitrite capsules. This strong stimulant drug, prescribed to relieve angina pectoris, comes in glass phials which are broken under the nose and sniffed. The drug was taken for pleasure in the 1960s and 1970s and later specifically for its supposed effects as an enhancer of sexual pleasure by the **gay** community in the 1970s and 1980s.

porcelain *n See* **point percy at the porcelain**; **pray to the porcelain god**

porch monkey *n*
a black person. The racist phrase, adopted by some adolescents in the 1990s from their elders, is intended to evoke a slave or child asleep on a porch or ministering to its white superiors.

porg *n British*
a small person. From the initials of the euphemistic 'person of restricted

growth', this is usually a term of abuse, e.g. in playground usage.

pork *vb American*
to have sex with. A college students' word that was widely used in films in the 1980s. It probably derives from the earlier **pork sword** and **dork**.

He claims to be porking her.

porker *n*
1. a fat person. From the use of **pig** to mean glutton.
2. a police officer. This is a later development from **pig**, used for instance by anarchists, squatters and late-1980s **hippies**.

pork out *vb*
to eat to excess. A variant form of the colloquial **pig out**, recorded since the early 1980s.

pork pie, porky-pie, porky *n British*
a *lie*, an untruth. A piece of rhyming slang from London working-class speech that surfaced suddenly in the playground and the media and became widely popular at the end of the 1970s.

'I think you'll be finding that William's been telling porky-pies again.'
(Recorded, secretary, London, 1986)

'You wouldn't be tellin' me porkies would you, son?'
(*Minder*, British TV series, 1987)

pork sword *n*
the penis. A term used particularly by American college students on the same lines as **mutton dagger** or **beef bayonet**.

porridge *n British*
a term of imprisonment. Leaden, grey, institutional porridge is evoked as an image of the general deprivations of prison life, but is probably in origin a pun on **stir**. This underworld term was given wider currency by its use as the title of a BBC TV comedy series, starring Ronnie Barker.

portion *n British See* **give (someone) a portion**

portion of yes *n British*
sex. An item of student slang in use in London and elsewhere since around 2000.

Posh and Becks *n British*
sex. A rhyming slang term in use in 2003, derived from the nicknames of celebrity couple singer Victoria ('Posh Spice') and footballer David Beckham.

posho *n, adj British*
(a person who is) snobbish and/or from a privileged background. This elaboration of the colloquial 'posh' was used by students from the mid-1990s.

a posho restaurant

'King's College is full of poshos.'
(Recorded, London student, March 1996)

posse *n*
1a. *Jamaican* a criminal gang or secret society. The self-dramatising term, from western movies, was adopted in the 1970s to describe **yardies**. It became known through their overseas activities in Britain and the USA in the 1980s.
1b. a youth gang. The word was adopted in urban Britain by teenagers in the late 1980s.

postal *adj American*
uncontrollable, irrational, disoriented. This vogue term among Californian adolescents was popularised by the 1994 US film *Clueless*. It often occurs in the form **go postal**. The term is derived from the image of deranged postal workers who embark on a shooting spree before committing suicide.

By the time I got home Dad was, like, totally postal.

postie *n*
1. a postman, mailman. A shortening that is heard in Britain and Australia.
2. a postgraduate student

pot *n*
1. cannabis. This 1950s term was considered old-fashioned by drug users by the early 1960s, but was adopted by critics and commentators in the press to refer to hashish and marihuana. This use of the word originated in North America in the early years of the 20th century but its etymology is unknown. Some authorities claim a derivation from an obscure Mexican term for the drug (*potiguaya* or *potaguaya*), others that there is a connection with the use of **tea** as a nickname for marihuana, or that it is a deformation of **pod**, an attested synonym.

'I do not advocate legislation of pot, merely because I dread the inevitable hassle of commercialism.'
(Letter to *Oz* magazine, June 1969)

2. a pot belly

He's got a bit of a pot on him.

potatoes n British
money. In armed-service slang during World War II '(big) potatoes' denoted both great wealth and the possessor thereof. The use of the same word since the 1990s may be a separate coinage.

'Oh where are those potatoes? Tell me about those potatoes because I can't eat, I can't eat.'

(Sarah Ferguson, Duchess of York, in conversation with her psychic, Madame Vasso, reported in 1996)

potato-head n
1a. a person with coarse or indistinct features
1b. a stupid person. 'Mr Potato-head' was a children's toy popular during the 1970s. It consisted of a set of plastic parts to stick into a potato.

pothead n
an habitual smoker of cannabis (hashish or marihuana). An early 1960s term which was out of fashion by the late 1960s, save in whimsical or ironic usage.

potless adj
destitute, 'broke'. This use of the word is probably from the vulgar colloquialism 'without a pot to piss in', or may simply refer to the pot of money required for a gambling session.

potty-mouth n American
a user of obscene language, a 'foul-mouth'. This jocular middle-aged colloquialism was adopted by adolescents in the 1990s, including the **rriot grrrl** band Bratmobile who used it as an album title in 1993. It was still in use in 2005.

pouff n
an alternative spelling of **poof**

pound one's pork/pudding/meat/weenie, etc. vb
(of a male) to masturbate

pov n British
a synonym for **chav**, recorded in 2005. It derives from poverty (-stricken).

pox, the pox n
venereal disease. Originally referring to syphilis, pox is a variant form of 'pocks' (as in pock-marks) meaning pustules and itself related to 'pocket'.

poxy adj British
very bad, worthless, inferior. Originally signifying diseased, from the use of **pox** to mean syphilis, poxy is now a fairly strong (mainly working-class) term of contempt.

P.R. n American
a Puerto Rican. The abbreviation is usually heard in a derogatory context.

prairie-fairy n American
an environmentalist, green activist. A derogatory term which featured in the 1992 Montana State Election debate. Synonyms are **tree-hugger**, **eagle freak**, etc.

pram n See **out of one's pram**

pramface n British
a disreputable, vulgar or shabby-looking female. A term of abuse for supposed social inferiors ('they look as if they should be pushing a pram on a council estate') such as **chavs**. The term was posted on the b3ta website in 2004.

prang[1] vb, n British
(to) crash. A word, used in the context of motoring, which moved from echoic air-force slang of the 1940s to become a common colloquialism of the 1970s and 1980s.

prang[2] adj British
scared. An item of student slang in use in London and elsewhere since around 2000.

prank n British
a foolish and/or unpleasant person. The term, used by schoolchildren and students since 2000, is a blend of **prick**, **prat** or **prannet** and **wank(er)**.

He's a complete prank, that one.

prannet n British
a fool. A term which enjoyed a vogue in the late 1970s. Prannet looks like a blend of **prat** and **gannet**, both widespread terms of mild abuse. However, it is probably a form of a much earlier word (also seen in the form **pranny**) denoting buttocks and the female pudenda.

pranny, prannie n British
a fool. Variant (and possibly earlier) forms of **prannet**.

prat, pratt n British
1a. the backside, buttocks. A word dating from the 16th century or earlier which is currently an inoffensive, if rare synonym for **bum**, etc. (encountered in the compound 'pratfall').
1b. the vagina. This sense of the term is an extension of the preceding, it has been rare since the 1960s.
2. a fool, idiot, buffoon. A sharp, but not obscene term of criticism or abuse, in vogue in the 1980s. The word denotes extreme foolishness and is derived, in the

same way as the synonymous **arse** or **twat**, from the previous senses of the term.

> 'Anyone who bought a futon from the Nagasaki Futon Company should return this to the shop immediately as a serious design fault could result in the owner looking like a stupid prat.'
> (*Great Bus Journeys of the World*, Alexei Sayle, 1988)

prat about *vb British*
to behave stupidly or irresponsibly, to do things in a disorganised, messy way. From the noun **prat**.

prawn *n See* **come the raw prawn**

pray to the porcelain god *vb*
to vomit in a toilet

preggers *adj*
pregnant. Originally an upper- or middle-class expression using the Oxbridge and public-school termination **-ers**.

preppie, preppy *n American*
1a. a student or ex-student of an American preparatory school. The term was popularised by Erich Segal in his best-selling novel *Love Story*. American prep schools (as opposed to the British version which educates boys from 8 to 13) prepare teenage boys for higher education.
1b. a young person embodying the values, manners and dress of upper-class America. The preppy is roughly the equivalent of the British **Sloane Ranger**.

> 'He is variously described as "Ivy League" or "preppy" and he is instantly recognizable by his blue button-down Oxford cloth shirt, navy blazer, club tie and penny loafers. He might be viewed as an American Hooray Henry, except that he is quietly-spoken, excessively polite and never throws muffins.'
> (*Independent*, 12 March 1988)

presh *n, adj British*
a vogue term of endearment based on 'precious' and used both straightforwardly and ironically in London **parlyaree** since the 1960s. 'Presh-bag' is an elaborated form often used teasingly to a loved one or acquaintance.

press *vb*
to have sex (with), penetrate. A term used by young street-gang members in London since around 2000.

previous[1] *adj British*
premature, impetuous, presumptuous. A term of mild disapproval favoured by London working-class speakers and members of the police force, usually in the phrase 'a bit previous'.

previous[2] *n British*
a criminal record, previous convictions. A shortening adopted by police officers and the underworld, usually in the phrase 'has he/she got any previous?'.

prick *n*
1. the penis. The Oxford English Dictionary records the first use of the term in 1592; it was probably extant in the spoken language for some time before. Prick was probably coined with the image of a thorn in mind, from the shape and the image of penetration evoked. In the 20th century while it is, in 'polite company', the least acceptable of the many terms (**cock, tool,** etc.) for the male member, it is nevertheless commonly used, together with **dick**, by women in preference to those alternatives.
2. a fool, obnoxious or contemptible male

> 'He's something like a financial management consultant, in other words a complete prick.'
> (Recorded, homeless male, London 2002)

prick-tease, prick-teaser *n*
a potential sex partner who excites sexual arousal without allowing consummation. This phenomenon, usually in the context of male-female encounters, is paralleled by the French *chauffe-cul* and the synonymous **cock-tease, cock-teaser** in English.

primo *adj*
first class. (From the Spanish for first.) **El primo** is an alternative version.

privates *n pl*
the genitals, 'private parts'. A euphemistic or humorous term.

pro *n*
a prostitute

proctoheliosis *n British*
arrogance, overweening self-assurance. From the Greek *helio*, sun, and *procto-* meaning rectal, a condition in which somebody thinks that the sun shines out of their **arse**. Also known as **helioproctosis**.

Prod *n British*
a Protestant. **Prot** is an Australian alternative version.

profiling *n American*
behaving ostentatiously, 'posing'. A term from the post-1990s black lexi-

con, often denoting ritual showing-off within a group.
Compare **styling**; **vogu(e)ing**

prole *n British*
a proletarian, member of the 'lower' classes. A contemptuous term employed by overt snobs or, ironically or self-deprecatingly, by the 'proles' themselves.

prong *n*
the penis

proper! *exclamation American*
a general cry of appreciation, approval, etc., in use among adolescents on the West Coast in the 1990s. The term was also heard among middle-class youth in London as reported by the *Evening Standard* magazine, July 1994.
Compare **proper job**

proper job *n, exclamation British*
an all-purpose term of approbation often used as an exclamation, particularly in the speech of the West Country

props *n American*
respect. An item of black street-talk (a shortening of 'pay/show proper respect') which was included in so-called **Ebonics**, recognised as a legitimate language variety by school officials in Oakland, California, in late 1996.

Prot *n See* **Prod**

prune *n British*
a foolish person. A mild term of childish abuse, employing one of the less appetizing elements on the typical family and/or school-dinner menus of the 1950s and 1960s.

pseud *n British*
a pseudo-intellectual, pretentious or 'bogus' individual. A buzzword of 1962 and 1963, largely because of its frequent use in *Private Eye* magazine. *Pseud's Corner* in *Private Eye* is a long-running column, reprinting instances of pretentiousness.

psych (someone) out *vb*
to unnerve, outmanoeuvre or overwhelm. An Americanism which has spread to other areas, psych out originally meant to use psychology to gauge an opponent's weakness.

psych (oneself) up *vb*
to work oneself into a state of mental alertness, aggression, intensity. The phrase originated in the USA (probably in the context of self-expression or therapy groups) in the early 1970s.

'In fact his [the footballer Vinny Jones] disturbing habit of psyching himself up before a game by screaming, kicking doors and head-butting dressing-room walls is causing team-mates increasing concern.'
(*News of the World*, 12 February 1989)

P.T. *n British*
1. a **prick-tease**. A pun on the school subject 'physical-training'.
2. *See* **Egyptian PT**

pud *n American*
1. the penis. The word is a clipped form of 'pudding' which has denoted both the male member and semen in earlier slang usage.
2. a worthless, contemptible or obnoxious person. This term of adolescent abuse may be a shortened version of **pud-w(h)apper**.

pudding *n See* **pull one's pud/pudding**

pudding club *n See* **in the club**

puddled *adj British*
drunk. The term was recorded in 2003.

pud-w(h)apper *n American*
an obnoxious or contemptible person. One of many synonyms in use among young adolescents employing the notion of male masturbation. Here it combines **whap**, meaning beat or thrash, with **pud**, meaning the penis.
'That little pud-whapper just trod on my foot.'
(*Heathers*, US film, 1986)

puff[1] *n*
1. an alternative spelling of **poof**
2. *British* life. In humorous working-class speech the notion of 'breath of life' has given rise to this usage. It is probably most prevalent in northern English conversation.
'Never in all my born puff.'
(*Coronation Street*, British TV series, 1989)
3. marihuana, cannabis

puff[2] *vb British*
to smoke cannabis. A usage appearing in the 1990s.

puff-bucket *n American*
a braggart or 'wind-bag'. A mild term of abuse denoting a loquacious or pompous individual.

puffy *n British*
cannabis. This innocent-sounding nursery term, playing upon puffs of smoke, is used typically as a code word by users and dealers.

'There's no news on the puffy front – my friend's friend is still out in Morocco.'
(Recorded, drug dealer, London, 1987)

puggy n Scottish
1a. a monkey
1b. an unnamed object, animal or person. This old nickname is thought to derive from 'pog', a dialect term for hobgoblin or puck-figure.

puke vb
to vomit. An echoic expression pre-dating Shakespeare's reference to 'an infant mewling and puking'.

pukka adj British
1a. authentic, first-rate. A word adopted from the Hindi *pakka* (meaning substantial) for use in the Anglo-Indian speech of the colonial era.
1b. excellent, admirable. The earlier term was adopted as an adolescent vogue word from the 1990s, often used by those who were ignorant of its provenance and longevity. It was popularised by the TV chef Jamie Oliver.
Well pukka shoes.
A pukka geezer.

puky, pukey adj
disgusting, sickening, awful. An adolescent usage based on the ancient verb to **puke**.

pull vb British
1. to 'pick up' a member of the opposite sex. A common term applied to males searching for sexual partners since the late 1960s, when it was usually part of a phrase such as 'pull a bird' or 'pull a chick'. In current working-class usage predatory males are said to be **on the pull**. (Pull is now part of the homosexual as well as heterosexual lexicon and women also use the expression.)
2. to arrest or take into custody. A police jargon usage.

pull a stroke vb British
to succeed in a clever manoeuvre, effect a trick or deception. 'Stroke' is a common colloquialism for move, ploy or action.

pull a whitey vb British
to experience confusion, nausea, etc., especially after combining cannabis and alcohol. The term has been in use among adolescents since around 2000.

pull finger vb New Zealand
to get a move on, stop dawdling, increase efficiency. A brusque shortening of the colloquial 'pull one's finger out'.
OK, it's time to pull finger and get moving.

pulling power n British
sexual attraction, the ability to attract and/or 'pick up' members of the opposite sex. The term, from the verb to **pull**, is usually applied to males.

pull (oneself/someone) off vb
to masturbate oneself or someone else. A term used invariably of men, now dated.

pull one's pud/pudding vb British
(of a man) to masturbate. The word pudding has been used with various connotations in a sexual context (denoting the penis, semen, pregnancy, etc.) since the 16th century.

pull the plug vb
to commit suicide. An unsentimental euphemism, from the colloquial sense of the phrase meaning to abort (a venture).
'Kathy was eleven when she pulled the plug, on 26 reds and a bottle of wine.'
(Lyrics to 'People who died', Jim Carrol, 1981)

pump[1] vb
1. *British* to **fart**. A children's term adopted by adults and now appearing in print in such publications as *Viz* comic.
2. *American* to have sex (with). A vulgarism usually heard in the catchphrase 'pump 'em and dump 'em', a male expression of the late 1980s.

pump[2] n
1. *American* the heart. The predictable usage occurs in the language of prizefighters and street gangs, etc.
He got it right in the pump.
2. *See* **town bike/pump**

pumped (up) adj
excited. An Americanism now in use elsewhere.

pumps n pl British
tennis shoes, trainers. Like **daps** and **bumpers**, this is typically a schoolchildren's term.

pum-pum, pum n British
the vagina. An item of black street-talk used especially by males, recorded in 2003. It is pronounced to rhyme with 'room'.

punani, punany, punash *n British See* **poonanie**

punch deck *vb*
to type on a computer keyboard. This item of **net-head** slang was employed in interviews, perhaps partly ironically, by the **cyberpunk** author, William Gibson, in 1995.

pung *n South African*
trash. Recorded as an item of Sowetan slang in the *Cape Sunday Times*, 29 January 1995.

punk *n*
1. a bumptious but insignificant or contemptible person. This sense of the word has been well-established in American English since the 19th century referring typically to a youth, particularly a presumptuous or irritating one, or to a petty criminal or gangster. The word originated in British slang around the end of the 17th century when it was used to denote a **whore** and later was a precursor of the modern **rent boy**. In the 20th century the term punk fell out of use in Britain, being reintroduced via the American media and later by way of the punk rock phenomenon of 1976 and 1977.

> '*The play-house Puncks, who in a loose undress*
>
> *Each night receive some Cullie's soft address…*'
>
> (*Poor Pensive Punk*, poem by John Dryden, 1691)

2. an adherent of a youth subculture first coalescing in 1976 around punk rock music. Punk rock was so called because of the callow, defiant poses and amateurish musicianship of its proponents. Led by American groups such as the Ramones and the British band the Sex Pistols, punk rock became the musical vogue of 1977, accompanied by a self-consciously nihilistic and pessimist attitude and imagery, spikey and mohican hairstyles, safety pins and chains, etc.
3. *British* **skunk** marihuana

punk (someone) *vb American*
to humiliate, belittle. 'Punked!' has been used as an exclamation of malicious triumph since around 2000, and as the title of a TV show in which victims are duped.

punkette *n*
a young female **punk** (rocker)

punk out *vb American*
to behave in a cowardly manner. An item of street-gang argot, deriving from the sense of **punk** as a weakling. **Wimp out** is a slightly milder version.

punter *n British*
1a. a gambler, speculator. Coming from the terminology of card games, 'punt' was transferred to the context of horseracing, then to betting in general in the 19th century. In the late 1980s it was used e.g. of small investors or share purchasers. The term enjoys continuing popularity.
1b. a customer or client. The sense of punter as a gambler was extended to refer to anyone paying money for a service or item. First specifically applied to prostitutes and street-trader's customers, punter became a key word in the market-oriented 1980s.
See also **Billy (Bunter)**

punting *n British*
engaged in prostitution. An item of police slang (from the idea of looking for **punters**).

puppy's privates, the *n*
a jocular version of **the dog's bollocks**, recorded in Dublin in 2004

purple *n British*
a twenty-pound note or the amount of £20, from the colour of the banknote

purple hearts *n pl*
amphetamine tablets. The phrase referred to purple or blue coloured tablets of amphetamines, barbiturate or a mixture of the two as prescribed and abused in the USA in the late 1950s. (The 'purple heart' was a medal awarded for bravery.) In Britain the word was adopted in the early 1960s as a generic term for **pep pills** or **speed**.

push *vb*
to sell illegal drugs, especially when the sale involves coercion

pusher *n*
a supplier of illicit drugs, especially addictive drugs. The word implies that the seller uses coercion or tries to lead people into addiction in order to profit from them (if this is not the case, **dealer** is the alternative). The term is now used by police, journalists, parents, etc. and only rarely by drug users or sellers.

push the envelope *vb American*
to test or extend limits, go too far. The term, used in fiction by Tom Wolfe and

John Grisham, derives from the jargon of test pilots: the envelope is the ultimate technical capability as expressed on a graph.

puss *n*
1. *American* the face, mouth. A word often used in compounds such as 'sour puss' and 'glamour-puss', puss was a favourite word of pugilists and 'tough guys' in the earlier 20th century. It derives from the Irish Gaelic *pus*, meaning mouth.

> *He told her if she didn't shut up he'd give her a sock in the puss.*

2. a variant form of **pussy** (in all its senses)

puss boots *n Caribbean*
soft-soled shoes

puss-weed *n American*
a variant form of **pussy** in the sense of **wimp**, heard among US adolescents since the late 1980s

pussy¹ *n*
1. the female genitals. A cause of many double entendres and minor embarrassments, this usage of the word derives from the resemblance of pubic hair to fur, perhaps reinforced by male notions of affection. (The French equivalent is *chatte*, virtually a literal translation.) Pussy or **puss** was first recorded in the sexual sense in the 16th century.
2. women viewed as sex objects. An unromantic male term used in the same indiscriminate manner as **tail**, **ass**, etc. In this generic sense, the term may be expressed as pussy, 'some pussy' or, occasionally, 'a piece of pussy'.

> *'I hate to say it but I understand in London there's a lot of pussy over there.'*
> (US police officer, *Sunday Times* colour supplement, 1 January 1967)

3. a weak, harmless male, a timid person. A word which probably originated in the boxers' lexicon to describe the feeble, patting punches of a loser.

> *'He's a pussy, Frank.*
> *Yeah, but he's our pussy.'*
> (*Blue Velvet*, US film, 1986)

4. furs, in the jargon of criminals and the police. This example of the jargon of cat burglars was recorded in *FHM* magazine in April 1996.
5. a coquettish or 'kittenish' female, in lesbian parlance

pussy² *adj British*
unpleasant, execrable. This use of the word in the late 1990s was probably inspired by the noun sense of the female pudenda, rather than that of a weak, ineffectual person and reflects a distaste for female sexuality on the part of male adolescent gang members, its first users.

pussy-whipped *adj*
'hen-pecked'. An American vulgarism probably inspired by the western cliché 'pistol-whipped'. **Pussy** is a long-established term for the female genitals or women in general.

put (someone) down *vb*
to snub, humiliate or belittle. A vogue term among British **beatniks** in the early 1960s, adopted from American street slang.

> *'Evil hearted you, you always try to put me down, with the things you do and the words you spread around …'*
> (Lyrics to 'Evil-hearted You', the Yardbirds, 1965)

putdown *n*
a snub or humiliation. A back-formation from the verb to **put (someone) down**.

> *Being left off the guest list was the ultimate putdown.*

put in the fix, put the fix in *vb American*
to bribe, suborn, or corrupt (in order to resolve a problem)

put-on *n*
a deception, fraud, cheat. A back-formation (with slightly changed emphasis) from the verb to **put someone on** (although Partridge cites instances of the expression in Victorian use).

put one on someone *vb*
to hit, punch someone. An aggressive euphemism which is also rendered by **lay/hang one on someone**.

> *'One of my colleagues said that he felt like "putting one on" the attendant for the way he treated the child.'*
> (*Inside the British Police*, Simon Holdaway, 1983)

put one's hands up *vb*
to surrender, give in, confess. A euphemism popular among the British police and underworld.

> *'It was brilliant. He couldn't believe it. He had to put his hands up. Yes I did that one by subterfuge.'*
> (Police officer quoted in *Inside the British Police*, Simon Holdaway, 1983)

put someone away *vb British*
to kill. A euphemism employed by underworld or would-be underworld figures.

> *When I told him he went spare – he threatened to put the guy away.*

put the acid on *n Australian*
to demand money or information (from someone)

put the bite on *vb*
to pressurise someone, especially for a loan or repayment of money owed, or as part of a campaign of intimidation. This expression seems to have originated in North American usage early in the 20th century.

put the boot in *vb British*
1a. to kick (someone). An expression used by **skinheads** of the late 1960s as part of their repertoire (along with **aggro**, **bother** and **put the nut on**).
1b. to attack someone figuratively, particularly when they are already under attack, vulnerable or incapacitated

put the frighteners on (someone) *vb British*
to menace, threaten or intimidate (someone). An underworld and police expression employing a familiar form of words (as in **put the bite/kybosh/mockers on**).

put the hammer on (someone) *vb*
to bully, oppress, extort (someone). This phrase is heard throughout the English-speaking world, particularly in Scotland, meaning to pressurise someone for a loan, gift, etc., and in the US,

where it commonly denotes bullying or menacing.

> *Every time we go near a pub one of you guys puts the hammer on me.*
> *As soon as he starts to put the hammer on, let me know.*

put the kybosh/kibosh on *vb*
to frustrate, ruin, prevent, jeopardise. Many conflicting and often far-fetched etymologies have been suggested for this phrase, first recorded in the 1830s meaning to defeat. Its ultimate origin remains obscure.

put the mockers on *vb British*
to frustrate or jeopardise (someone's plans), to curse with bad luck. This old phrase was last popular in the 1960s, but is still heard occasionally. It almost certainly originates in the Yiddish *mockers*, meaning a curse or bad luck, from the Hebrew *maches*, meaning plague.

put the moves on (someone) *vb American*
to menace, oppress, cheat (someone). An item of street slang also heard among adolescents and featured in the US film, *The Sandlot Kids*, 1994.

putz *n American*
a foolish, clumsy or unfortunate person. The word is the Yiddish for 'ornament' used as a synonym for the male member, hence **prick**. Despite its (little-known) origin, putz is a relatively mild term of abuse in English; in Yiddish it still carries more pejorative overtones.

p.w.t. *n American*
an abbreviation of 'poor **white trash**'

Q

Q *n*

1a. a geriatric person

1b. a hospital patient

1c. a corpse

2. All senses of the term are based on the image of the capital letter Q as representing an open mouth with lolling tongue and seem to have originated in the slang of North American health carers. The letter may be written (in notes, on charts, etc.) or pronounced by medical staff.

Q.T., q.t. *n See* **on the q.t.**

quack *n*

a doctor. This usually lightheartedly pejorative term originated in the 17th century when it referred to a peddler of spurious cures. It is a shortening of 'quacksalver' which is composed of 'quack' (give one's verbal 'patter') and 'salve' (save, soothe or cure), and is a pun on 'quicksilver'.

quad, quod *n American*

a clumsy or unfortunate person, misfit. The word, used by high school and college students from the 1990s, is probably a shortening of 'quadriplegic' (disabled in all four limbs), although some users derive it from 'quadrilateral' as a version of **square**.

quail *n*

a girl, young woman, or females viewed as sex objects. This equating of the female with the game bird is approximately three hundred years old, surviving in the language of American high-school and college students, where predatory males also talk of going out 'loaded for quail' (ready or equipped for seduction).

quakin' *adj American*

excellent, impressive, exciting and/or excessive. A synonym, heard since 2000, for **slamming**, **jamming**, etc.

quality *adj*

good. As an appreciative description or exclamation of approval the word is used by British schoolchildren among others.

quandong *n Australian*

a woman. The quandong fruit (*santalum acuminatus*) is fleshy with a hard seed centre; the word has thus been appropriated to refer to women with supposedly similar qualities – either prostitutes or friendly females who refuse to be seduced.

quean *n British*

the earlier spelling of **queen**, meaning an effeminate homosexual. This spelling coexisted with queen until the early 1960s when it virtually disappeared. Quean was a descendant of Old and Middle English words related to (but not derived from) 'queen', stemming ultimately from an Indo-European ancestor, *gwena*, meaning woman. Over 1,000 years the senses of quean shifted from 'woman' to 'wanton', before being transferred to a male context.

queef *n American*

an alternative spelling of **kweef**

queen *n*

an effeminate homosexual. The word **quean** signified a **whore** in early 19th-century slang. This appellation was transferred to male prostitutes (often transvestite) and thence to male homosexuals in general. The use of the word is obviously reinforced by its colloquial use to mean an imperious or ostentatious (older) woman. In the **gay** environment of the 1970s and 1980s queen was used to refer specifically to individuals who are affected in manner, elderly and/or consciously effeminate.

'And he's just a go-getting queen. He's interested in you purely because of your plays.'

(Kenneth Halliwell, quoted in Joe Orton's Diary, 2 May 1967, 1986)

queer *n, adj*
(a person who is) homosexual. Until the 19th century queer denoted odd or curious, as it still does in standard English. Its use as first a euphemism, then a slang synonym for homosexual arose between the world wars, probably first in the USA. Queer ultimately derives from *quer*, a German word meaning crooked or awry. In the mid-1980s **gay** activists began to use the term to refer to themselves, in keeping with the trend among 'transgressive' minorities to appropriate the language of their oppressors (as in the earlier case of **nigger**).

> *'You can't expect to pick up a young post-office worker and his middle-aged keeper, and burst into tears because the keeper is queer.'*
> (Joe Orton's Diary, 2 May 1967)

queer-bashing *n British*
the attacking, intimidation or mugging of male homosexuals. A practice indulged in by **teddy boys**, and later **skinheads**, among others. The term has been extended to denote verbal aggression or prejudice against **gays**.

quiche out *vb*
1. *British* to eat very greedily or to excess. A **Sloane ranger** and **yuppie** version of **pig out**, which was later adopted by university students.
2. to behave in a weak, irresolute, cowardly way; to **wimp out**. In this sense the term has been used in Oxbridge student slang, sometimes shortened to 'quiche'.

quickie *n*
a hurried or short-lived sex act

quid *n*
a pound sterling. The word was first used to refer to a guinea, then a sovereign, later to the sum of one pound. The origin of the word (it arose in the 17th century) is obscure. Partridge suggests 'what' (*quid* in Latin) as a synonym for 'wherewithal'. An equally plausible derivation is from *quid pro quo*, alluding to the words on older banknotes, 'I promise to pay the bearer the sum of...'.

quidlets *n pl British*
money, pounds sterling. A humorous version of **quid** using the diminutive suffix '-let'.

quiff *n*
1. *British* a pompadour hairstyle, kiss-curl or backcombed fringe. The quiff was fashionable with **teddy boys** and **rockers** among others.
2. *British* a male homosexual or effeminate male. The usage is probably influenced by the words **queer** and **poof**.
3. a **fart**
4a. *American* a prostitute or promiscuous woman
4b. *American* a woman or women as (a) sex object(s). A term used invariably by males.

> *I'm going to get me some quiff.*

quim *n British*
the female sex organs. A taboo term featuring in 19th-century pornography and the 20th-century lexicon of obscenity. The word has probably lost popularity since the 1950s, although it remains in use, invariably among males, particularly outside the southeast of the country. The exact origin of quim is unclear. It may be related to the Chaucerian *queynte* (the vagina) or the Welsh *cwm* (a valley or crevice).

quince *n Australian*
a male homosexual or effeminate male. The word is probably a blend of **queen** and 'mince'. It may also be derived from the Asian fruit of the same name.

quoit *n Australian*
the anus. A coinage inspired by the earlier **ring**.

R

raar *adj British*
good. The word, recorded among teenagers in Kent in 2003, may be a form of **rare**, which in black speech can mean both good and bad. The word often occurs in the combination 'bare raar', meaning very good.

raas *n Jamaican*
an all-purpose term of abuse or exclamation of anger or contempt. A version of (up) (your) **arse** or a short form of **raasclat**.
Compare **yass**

raasclat, rassclaat *n Jamaican*
a term of strong abuse used as an insult or as an exclamation. The word literally means a rag for wiping the backside, the equivalent of the later American insult **ass-wipe**, **raas** being a patois version of (your) **arse** and 'clat', a cloth.

rabbit *vb, n*
(to) talk, gossip, (have a) conversation. The term is cockney rhyming slang, from 'rabbit and pork': *talk*. The word gained widespread currency through TV comedies of the 1970s and the soundtrack to a 1980s advertisement for Courage Best beer. Rabbit (or 'rabbit on') is now often used by middle-class speakers unaware of its rhyming provenance. Genuine cockneys often prefer the derivation **bunny**.

race off, race *vb American*
to seduce. A common term in the 1960s. The original image evoked is that of sweeping a victim off her feet and away.

rack *n American*
1. a bed. This use of the word is probably of armed-service origin.
2. female breasts
    'She's attractive – great rack, nipples like pencil erasers...'
    (*Disclosure*, US film, 1995)

rack (out) *vb American*
to lie down and/or go to sleep. An expression now used principally by teenagers and college students, but which originates in the armed-service slang noun **rack**, meaning bed.

rack attack *n American*
a bout of extreme laziness, a period spent in bed. A campus witticism (other rhyming compounds are **snack attack** and **tack attack**) based on the use of **rack** to mean bed.

racked *adj American*
1. ruined, defeated, disabled. The term referred originally to being kicked or struck in the **rack** or male genital area.
2. intoxicated by drugs or alcohol. The adolescent usage is probably a borrowing of the standard term as it occurs in phrases such as 'racked with pain', although it may be based on the preceding sense or be an alteration of **wrecked**.
    I was racked by 9 p.m.

racked-off *adj Australian*
irritated, disgruntled. An expression ranking in vehemence somewhere between 'cheesed-off' and **pissed-off**.

racked-up *adj American*
tense, stressed, **strung up**. An expression heard occasionally since the 1970s.
    'I remember my first shoot. You know I was really racked-up but the lieutenant was there for me.'
    (*Miami Vice*, US TV series, 1988)

rack off *vb Australian*
to go away, leave. A brusque, but less offensive alternative to **piss off**, **fuck off**, etc. The phrase, usually in the form of an admonition, has been introduced to a British audience via Australian soap operas of the late 1980s, such as *Neighbours*.

rack up *vb*
to prepare a line of cocaine for **snort**ing
    'Rack up the line and get her face in it.'

(Former pop star Brian Harvey quoted in *News of the World*, 15 June 2003)

rad *adj American*
excellent, outstanding, admirable. A shortening of **radical**, used as a term of great approbation by school and college children in the late 1970s. It is also heard in the UK and Australia since the 1980s where it has become a vogue term, especially among the subcultures of surfers and skateboarders.

  'But the really rad word is still to be had from the skater/authors themselves…'
  (*Mail on Sunday*, *'Biz'* magazine, June 1987)

radical *adj*
excellent. In the 1980s the word moved from its political sense, via 'radical chic', to a generalised meaning of admirable in adolescent speech. It is now usually shortened to **rad**.

  'That radio station is well radical.'
  (Recorded, teenage male, London, May 2003)

radio rentals *adj British*
crazy, deranged, **mental**. A humorous expression recorded in 1988, employing an approximate rhyme using the name of a television hire chain.

  If you ask me, she's completely radio rentals.

rads *n British*
the police. A term used by young street-gang members in London since around 2000.

raf *vb Caribbean*
to steal or borrow without permission. The term was recorded in Trinidad and Tobago in 2003. Synonyms are **bandit** and **sprang**.

rag (on) (someone) *vb American*
to criticise, denigrate, nag. This usage dates back to the 19th century when 'ragging' was also employed in British slang to mean teasing or provoking. In black American slang from the 1990s rag was often used synonymously with **diss**.

rag doll *n American*
a gullible or compliant female. The term is used by street-gang members, hip hop aficionados and college students.

rage *n Australian*
a wild party or celebration. A 1960s expression which is the equivalent of the British **rave-up** and, like that term, underwent a revival in the late 1980s.

ragged out, ragged up *adj American*
1. dressed or dressed up. Since the 19th century this term has been used colloquially like 'dolled up' or 'in one's glad rags'. **2.** distasteful, unpleasant. A teenage and **Valley Girl** expression of the late 1970s.

raggedy-ass, ragged-ass *adj American*
unkempt, uncouth, disorganised. An elaboration of ragged.

raggo *adj*
berserk, uncontrolled or uncontrollable. Possibly originating in black speech and probably derived from **lose one's rag**, this is a term used by young street-gang members in London since around 2000.

rag-head *n*
an Arab. A pejorative term inspired by the headdress worn particularly by Gulf Arab males. The term is occasionally applied to turban-wearers too. An alternative is **towel-head**.

raging *n British*
a *first* (first-class honours degree). Students' rhyming slang (on 'raging thirst') of the late 1980s. **James** and **Pattie** are alternative versions.

  He was tipped for a raging, but he ended up with a Desmond.
Compare **Douglas**; **made-in**; **Richard**; **Taiwan**

rag it *vb*
to have sex

  'Listen man, you rag it…if you want.'
  (Former pop star Brian Harvey quoted in *News of the World*, 15 June 2003)

rags *n pl American*
clothes. Heard in the speech of black Americans since the 1960s (**threads** and **vines** were contemporary synonyms) and later elsewhere, the word has more recently been supplanted to some extent by **garms**.

  Where d'you get them cool rags?

rag-top *n*
a convertible car. The Americanism has also occasionally been heard in Britain as an alternative for soft-top or the earlier drop-head.

rag week *n British*
the time during which a woman is menstruating, a 'period'. The expression is a play on both **on the rag** and rag week as signifying a student carnival.

rah *n, adj British*
(someone who is) 'posh', a synonym is **yah**: both terms imitate the drawling or braying speech supposedly characteristic of such individuals

rail n American

a line of cocaine

'I smoked my first joint at 12, did my first rail at 13…'

(Corey Taylor of US rock band Slipknot, speaking in 2002)

rain on someone's parade vb American

to spoil someone's enjoyment, frustrate someone's efforts, etc. A colloquial phrase which gave rise to many more vulgar synonyms such as **piss in someone's pool** or **on someone's chips**.

rally vb American

to behave outrageously, indulge in wild activity. A **preppie** term, used invariably by and about males.

Come on, let's rally!

They were really rallying.

ralph¹ vb

1. to vomit. One of many echoic terms for the activity, ralph is typically heard among students in all English-speaking areas. 'Call (for) Ralph' is an alternative version.

2. *American* to take a right turn

ralph² n

a right turn. The word is usually part of the phrase **hang a ralph** (as opposed to **hang a louie**).

rambunctious adj

lively, troublesome, loud. A facetious invention elaborated from rumbustious. The term has been in use since the early 19th century and is probably Irish or American in origin, although the invention of such jocularities (as in the 19th-century 'obstrepalous' and the recent 'spondicious') was paralleled in Britain.

'This is a lullaby my mother used to play when I'd get rambunctious. It always seemed to calm me down.'

(*Kindred*, US film, 1987)

rammed adj British

very crowded, full

'Coming back on Eurostar, it was rammed.'

(Recorded, female traveller, London, June 2003)

ramp vb

to provoke, annoy. A term used by young street-gang members in London since around 2000.

Don't ramp with me.

She's been ramping him.

ramp up vb British

to organise or arrange. The phrase presumably comes from the terminology of

car mechanics whence it has been extended in working-class usage (by police officers among others) to mean mounting any sort of operation.

ranch vb American

to ejaculate. The slang usage, heard among adolescents, seems to be unconnected to the standard sense of the word.

random¹ n, adj American

(a person who is) unfashionable, unattractive, mediocre, unwanted or excluded from fashionable circles. The term was popular among adolescents, particularly female, on college and high-school campuses in the US during the 1990s.

'There's no getting round the style question. If you want to be "do-able" … you cannot afford to dress "random".'

(*Sunday Times 'Style'* magazine, 22 October 1995)

random² vb British

to **pull** or **score** with a stranger. An item of student slang in use in London and elsewhere since around 2000.

R and R n

1. relaxation. A piece of armed-services shorthand (for 'rest and recreation') now used by civilians.

2. rock 'n' roll. A short form used by aficionados and the record industry.

randy adj British

sexually aroused, lecherous. A word which was formerly considered unsuitable for normal use but which, since the 1960s, has been used in the media and in 'respectable' conversation. (Mickey Dolenz of the pop group The Monkees heard the phrase 'randy Scouse git' on the British TV comedy series 'Till death us do part' and used it as the title of a single in 1967. This was deemed too offensive for radio and in Britain the song title was changed.) Randy is of uncertain origin. It was first recorded at the end of the 18th century. Two suggested etymologies for the word are: a dialect verb meaning to behave in a wild or wanton manner, and a Hindi word meaning lustful. Of these, the first (the rarely recorded word was related to 'rant' and 'random') is the more likely.

'Girls…showing their arms in thin, thin frocks (good luck to randy grandfathers).'

(*About Town* magazine, June 1962)

rang-a-tang *n Caribbean*
a belligerent or troublesome person

rang(e)y *adj American*
aggressive, oppressive. The term (which rhymes with 'tangy') is of uncertain origin.

rank¹ *adj*
1. unpleasant. The standard adjective (its original meaning was overbearing or excessively strong) has been adopted as an all-purpose vogue term of disapproval by teenagers in the USA and in Britain, where it probably originated in black usage.

> *'This health-drink stuff is just so rank!'*
> (Recorded, teenage schoolboy, London, 1994)

2. excellent, admirable. A term of approbation originating, it is said, in the 1960s *pachuco* (Hispanic street-)culture of the USA.

rank², **rank out**, **rank on (someone)** *vb American*
to insult, taunt or provoke. The terms, which occur in adolescent speech, probably originated in black street slang.

rap¹ *n*
1a. a conversation, especially an earnest and/or lengthy discussion. A word which became an important part of the counterculture lexicon at the end of the 1960s, rap was originally used by blacks and **beatniks**, deriving from the verb form.

1b. a rhythmic spoken chant, often to a musical background. This form of (originally) improvised delivery became a vogue first among young blacks in New York and other eastern American cities (inspired by Jamaican 'toasting'), and then a worldwide pop phenomenon in the 1980s.

2. an accusation or charge, blame or punishment. An 18th-century British use of the verb 'rap' was to denote swearing an oath against, accusing of, or charging (with a crime). This sense survives, via American English, in the phrases 'take the rap' and 'beat the rap' and the term **rap sheet**.

rap² *vb*
1a. to talk, converse or discuss. A key term from the **hippy** era which usually denoted an earnest or communal exchange of ideas. The word was first heard in this sense in black American speech; it was subsequently adopted by

white **hipsters**, **beatniks** and hippies in turn. (Rap was in use in Britain in the late 1960s but in its original sense is now confined to the remnants of hippy culture.) The exact origin of this use of the word is not at all clear; possible etymologies include a shortening of 'rapid' (speech), 'rapport' or 'repartee'. The term might come simply from the similarity between talking and tapping ('rapping') on a drum or other surface; this might fit an origin among jazz musicians. Alternatively, in archaic slang a 'rapper' was someone who 'talked' to the authorities (see the noun form) and this notion may have become generalised in black argot into 'talk'.

1b. to deliver an (originally improvised) monologue to a musical backing; to perform rap music. This musical form of the 1980s originated as a street phenomenon among black youth in American cities in the 1970s.

rapid *adj British, Irish*
clever, stylish, attractive. In 2000 the term was defined as 'dead cool, as used by Ronan and Shane from Boyzone'. In Leicester in 2004 the same word was being used as an all-purpose term of appreciation.

> *He thinks he's rapid, doesn't he?*

rapper *n*
a practitioner or devotee of **rap** music

rap session *n American*
a conversation or discussion. A phrase first used in the 1950s by black Americans, **hipsters** and **beatniks**, later taken up by **hippies**, alternative therapists and teenagers.

rap sheet *n American*
(documentary evidence of) a person's criminal record. The expression has been in use since World War II and derives from the underworld slang noun-form **rap**, meaning an arrest or arraignment.

rapt *adj*
delighted. A vogue term of the late 1980s which seems to have spread from Australia to both Britain and the USA in the **hip** parlance of adolescents. The word is the standard (literary) English term meaning enraptured.

> *She wasn't exactly rapt when I told her, I can tell you.*

rare *adj British*
1. an all-purpose term of approbation, often employed as an exclamation by

schoolchildren since the 1980s, especially in the north of England and Scotland. This sense of the word probably originated in black youth-culture in the USA and was transmitted via **rap**, skateboarding terminology, etc. Rare was previously used as a generalised vogue term in this way by **mods** briefly in 1966. It was used as long ago as the 16th century, with sporadic examples in between.

2. unpleasant, unattractive, inappropriate. Probably a deliberate reversal of the earlier slang usage, since around 2000 this has been a vogue term of disapproval among UK teenagers.

See also **raar**

rash *adj*
wonderful. A term of high appreciation among American teenagers and aficionados of hip hop in the 1980s. It is nearly always expressed as 'totally rash' and was coined on the lines of **wild**, **bad**, **wicked**, etc.

raspberry *n*
a farting sound made by blowing through the lips, a **Bronx cheer**. Now an innocent colloquialism heard all over the English-speaking world, it derives from the late 19th-century London rhyming-slang phrase, 'raspberry tart': **fart**.

rasta *n*
a Rastafarian. The word is a shortening of the name of the devotees of Ras Tafari (one of the titles of the late emperor of Ethiopia, Haile Selassie) whose sacrament is **ganja** and who wear **dreadlocks**. The language of the Jamaican movement has influenced English slang mainly via reggae music.

rat (on) *vb*
to inform on or betray (someone). An Americanism employing the familiar identification of a rat with treachery or spite. The phrase was imported into Britain and Australia before World War II.

> *Rule number one is you don't rat on your friends.*

rat-arsed *adj*
drunk. The terms rat-arsed, **rat-faced** and the milder **ratted** enjoyed a vogue among adolescents and young adults (particularly those from middle- and upper-class backgrounds) from the mid-1980s. Terms employing rat- as a prefix evoking disgust were heard throughout the English-speaking community in the

1980s (**rathole**, **ratshit**, etc.), particularly in Australia and the USA.

ratbag *n Australian*
a despicable, disreputable or obnoxious person. This term of abuse originated in Australia where it derived either literally from a bag used by a rat-catcher or from the notion of a bag full of rats as the epitome of obnoxiousness. The word became popular in Britain in the early 1960s (helped in no small part by its frequent use in the popular radio comedy-series *Hancock's Half Hour*) and is now often used with a degree of affection. In Australia it often denotes an eccentric.

> *'She's a total ratbag – I don't want to have anything more to do with her.'*
> (*Neighbours*, Australian TV soap opera, 1987)

rated *adj British*
excellent, admirable. A vogue term of approbation heard among adolescents from the later 1990s, which began as an abbreviated form of 'A-rated' or 'highly-rated'.

rat-faced *adj*
drunk. A vogue term of the late 1980s among all social classes in Britain (particularly heard among **Sloane Rangers** and **yuppies**).

ratfink *n American*
a treacherous, despicable person. The word is a combination of 'rat' (traitor) and **fink** (informer) and was first used to refer to union blacklegs or **scabs**. It enjoyed a vogue in the 1960s in its more generalised sense and is still used, albeit less widely.

See also **fink**

rathole, rat-hole *n*
a disgusting, squalid place. A fashionable expression of distaste in the later 1980s. In 1987 the college lecturers' union NATFHE condemned 'Thatcher's rathole Britain' in a press handout.

rat out *vb*
to abandon, betray, cravenly withdraw. An Americanism which is also heard in Australia and, to a lesser extent, in Britain. Usages involving the 'rat' components have been in vogue since the 1980s.

> *She ratted out at the last minute.*
> *They ratted out on us.*
> *Don't rat me out.*

rat-run n British
a side street used for fast commuter traffic. A phrase and phenomenon of the late 1980s.

ratshit adj Australian
worthless, inferior, utterly disappointing. The word (pronounced like 'ratchet') usually expresses bitter disapproval or disillusion.

ratted adj British
drunk. A more polite version of **rat-faced** or **rat-arsed**. All three terms were in vogue in the second half of the 1980s.

> 'When we were looking for the personification of the Kentucky face, we got so ratted, so drunk … for an entire week.'
> (Ralph Steadman, I-D magazine, November 1987)

rattle (someone) vb
a word mainly heard in Scotland meaning to have sex with someone

rattler n
1. a surface or underground train. The word has been used in Britain and the USA (where travelling hobos referred to 'hopping a rattler') since the 19th century. Until the late 1950s the London underground system was sometimes known to workmen as the Rattler.
2. British a womaniser, seducer. It derives from the verb form **rattle (someone)**, meaning to have sex with and, like that term, is heard mainly in Scotland.

rattle someone's cage vb
to provoke, disturb, rouse. A phrase in mainly working-class usage which, like others ('drop off the perch', 'sick as a parrot', etc.), uses the imagery of a caged bird or animal. The expression usually forms part of a provocative rhetorical question 'who rattled your cage?', addressed to someone suddenly roused to anger or indignation. **Yank (someone around/someone's chain)** is an American alternative.

rattly n
a female. The word was used by British adolescents in 2001.

raunchy adj
sexually provocative, earthy, risqué; lustful or lust-inducing. The word probably took one of its original meanings, 'ripe' or over-ripe in the metaphorical sense, from the Italian rancio, meaning rank or rotten, although a British dialect origin has also been posited. Until the late 1960s raunchy was mainly in American usage.

rave, rave-up n British
a wild party, dance or occasion of abandoned behaviour. A usage originating in bohemian circles in the late 1950s. In the early 1960s the word was taken up by **mods** and shortly thereafter by the media and the older generation, who still employ the term. More recently still the **acid house** youth cult adopted the word to refer to their (typically large-scale and movable) celebrations, sometimes specified as **orbital raves** (those within reach of the M25 motorway). By 1990 schoolchildren were also using the word as a synonym for a party.

raver n British
an unrestrained, hedonistic person. An archetypal 1960s term which originated in the 1950s among bohemians and **beatniks**, when it was applied to frequent attenders of all-night parties and jazz clubs, etc. In the later 1960s the already slightly dated word epitomised **hippy** abandonment to euphoria. Since 1986 the term has referred to devotees of **rave** culture.

raw adj British
1a. crazy
1b. angry
A term used by young street-gang members in London since around 2000.

rawk n British
a variant spelling of rock (music), heard from 2004 and intended to suggest self-conscious enthusiasm or mockery thereof

> 'I guess I'm really into rawk.'
> (Recorded, student, Reading, UK, June 2005)

raw meat n
a euphemism for the sex organs or sexual activity, heard in the late 1960s and 1970s

razoo n Australian
a very small sum of money, 'a brass farthing'. A word said to be of Maori origin, used in negative phrases such as 'I haven't got a brass razoo' or 'without a razoo'.

razorblade n British
a black person. An unaffectionate rhyming-slang term (based on **spade**) used by police officers among others in the 1970s and 1980s.

razz *vb*

to tease or deride. A word which is currently more popular in Australia and the USA than Britain (although it features in British public-school argot). Razz was originally a theatrical shortening of **raspberry** and the verb is still used in theatrical parlance to mean jeer. In modern usage it often appears to have overtones common to 'rag', 'rouse' and **roust**.

readies *n pl*

cash, banknotes, money. A shorter and racier version of the phrases 'ready cash' or 'ready money'.

> *'It was always the same old story. "I've no money on me. Have you any readies, Al?" They must think we're a bit daft up North.'*
> (*Guardian*, 12 December 1987)

ready, the ready *n*

money, cash. This is currently a less common form (except in the USA) of the plural **readies**. Ready or the ready was in fact probably the original form of the term, first recorded in the 17th century.

rear-end *vb*

to ruin, damage. The figurative use of the phrase probably derives from the colloquialism referring to a car collision, with possible suggestions also of sexual activity.

> *'The guys upstairs rear-ended him good.'*
> (Reported, New York office worker, September 1995)

rear-gunner *n British*

a male homosexual. One of many pejorative synonyms in use among heterosexuals since the 1980s. The phrase was used on more than one occasion in interviews by the **punk** singer John 'Johnnie Rotten' Lydon.

recce *n British*

a reconnaissance or reconnoitring. An armed-service shortening (pronounced 'reckie'), which has been generalised in civilian usage to mean a preliminary check or look around.

recco *n Australian*

recognition, peer-group respect. An abbreviation heard among young adults and adolescents.

rectum rider *n*

a male homosexual

red *adj British*

suffering the after-effects of smoking marihuana or of another drug. A term

used by young street-gang members in London since around 2000.

red-arse *n British*

a new army recruit. In the early 20th century the term referred specifically to a Guardsman (whose jacket was red).

red-assed *adj American*

furious, irate

red biddy *n British*

cheap red wine or methylated spirits as drunk by tramps or derelicts. Biddy, originally a diminutive of Bridget, was an affectionate name for a woman, preserved in the colloquial term 'old biddy'.

red bumpies *n American*

a venereal infection. An expression used on campus in the USA since around 2000.

red-eye, the *n*

an early-morning or overnight flight or train service. The expression, which refers to the tired appearance of the passengers, originated in the USA where it was a nickname given to coast-to-coast flights.

red-heat *vb American*

to harass, importune, pursue

red-high *adj British*

delighted, ecstatic. The term was recorded in use among North London schoolboys in 1993 and 1994.

red-inker *n British*

a recorded arrest. A 'score' in the tally of arrests for a particular officer or police station, in the jargon of the police force.

redneck *n American*

a rustic bigot or boor. This now familiar expression became well known in the late 1960s when it was extended from the original sense of a rural white southern farmer (with a neck red from being bent to the sun or from anger) to include all opponents of liberation or the counterculture.

red Ned *n Australian*

cheap red wine. The Australian version of **red biddy**.

reds, red devils *n pl American*

capsules of Seconal, a barbiturate used by drug abusers, from the colour of the capsules

> *'The use of "reds" or barbiturates for highs (lows would be more descriptive) seems to be increasing again.'*

(*Dr Hip Pocrates* (Eugene Schoenfeld), 1969)

red sails in the sunset *adj*

menstruating. A phrase, taken from the title of a popular song, which has been used (almost invariably by men) since the 1960s.

Looks as if she's red sails in the sunset.

reeb *n British*

beer in **backslang**. A word which was heard in the 1950s and which survives in limited use (among young market-workers for instance).

reefer, reef *n*

1a. a marihuana cigarette, an earlier term for a **joint**. A word which fell out of favour with cannabis smokers in the late 1950s but which was perpetuated by the media and law enforcement agencies.

1b. marihuana. A famous and risible American anti-drug film of 1936 was entitled *Reefer Madness*. In origin the word is a corruption of *grifa*, the Spanish slang for marihuana.

reek *vb American*

to be repellent, inferior or worthless. A vogue term of disparagement or denigration among American adolescents since the 1990s. It is a synonym for **suck**, 'stink' and **wipe**.

Like it totally reeks!

re-entry *n American*

in the parlance of LSD users, the return to normality after the effects of an LSD **trip** have worn off. A term briefly popular in the mid- and late 1960s, derived from the jargon of space exploration.

reestie *adj American*

unpleasant, obnoxious. The word can be applied to persons or objects and is characteristically used by adolescents. It is probably a blend of **reek** and **beasty**.

regulatin' *n British*

fighting, from black speech. Synonyms are **mixin'**, **startin'**, **tanglin'**.

reject *n*

a term of abuse popular among British schoolchildren since the 1980s

rello *n Australian*

a relative, relation

We're having the rellos over.

remmy, remmie, rem *n British*

a fool. This item of schoolchildren's slang was reported in the 1990 publication *Bad Language* by the sociolinguist

Peter Trudgill. It may derive from the designation 'remedial (pupil/lesson)'.

renk *vb*

1. to become furious

2. to be repellent

The word, of uncertain derivation, has been used in both senses by UK adolescents since around 2000.

rentacop *n*

a hired security guard. A term generally used disapprovingly or derisively, particularly in the era of student unrest when US campus authorities frequently called on such personnel for assistance.

rentals *n pl American*

parents. A version of **parental unit(s)**, also rendered as **rents** or **units**. The expressions became fairly well known from the later 1980s.

I'm going to be in deep doodoo when the rentals see this.

rent boy *n British*

a young male prostitute. A **gay** slang term of the later 1960s that moved into common currency following press revelations of scandals in the 1980s. Young, sometimes homeless (and often heterosexual) rent boys frequented the Piccadilly area of London from at least the 1970s.

rents *n pl*

parents. Originally a term in use among American teenagers, this clipping, typical of youth slang of the late 1980s and early 1990s, was adopted by other English-speaking adolescents in the 1990s. A synonym is **units**.

The rents are away for the weekend.

rep¹ *n*

a shortening of 'reputation', used especially to denote (appreciatively) a reputation for violence or sexual prowess or (pejoratively) promiscuity. The word, typical of the clippings popularised first by American adolescents from the late 1970s, has moved from the language of street gangs and **rappers** into schoolchildren's usage since the late 1990s.

He's gotta protect his rep.

If she goes on like this she's going to get a rep for skeezing.

rep² *vb*

to impute a reputation to someone

'Yea there are Asians that rep us bad, but other than that we're nice good-hearted peepz.'

(Recorded, contributor to www.wass-up.com, November 2003)

represent *vb*
to perform or behave creditably. It is often in the form of an exhortation on the lines of 'well done', 'keep up the good work'. It is said to be inspired by phrases such as 'you are a fine representative of your family/group/race'. The term was popular in UK hip hop and R 'n' B circles from 1999.

reptiles *n pl*
1. shoes or boots, particularly those made of alligator, lizard or snakeskin. This footwear, favoured by American pimps for instance, is also referred to as **lizards** or **alligator shoes/boots** (which also ironically denotes old, open-toed shoes).

> *'I wanted to wear the silk suits, wear the reptiles on my feet.'*
> (Washington DC drug dealer, *World in Action*, British TV documentary, 10 April 1989)

2. journalists, reporters, the press in general, especially those from the gutter press. A usage popularised by its appearance in the *Dear Bill* letters featured in *Private Eye* magazine in the 1980s.

respect *n American*
an all-purpose exclamation of greeting and acknowledgment and an essential concept in peer-group relationships. 'Respect' was a key term from the rituals of street-based black subcultures of the late 1970s and early 1980s.

> *He didn't give me no respect.*

See also **touch-respect**

result, a result *n British*
1a. an outcome in one's favour, what is due, a good result. The term originated in football jargon where to 'get a result' means not to lose. Since 2000 it has often been used as an exclamation of delight, surprise and/or triumph.

> *'He owes me money. He's not ill – it's just a ploy to stop me getting a result!'*
> (*Minder*, British TV series, 1982)

1b. an arrest and/or conviction. A specialised use of the above sense among members of the police force.

retard *n*
a term of abuse among schoolchildren in the UK and the USA (where it is more fashionably shortened to **tard**) since the 1970s

retarded *adj American*
tedious, disappointing, of poor quality. An expression used on campus in the USA since around 2000. It is a synonym of **lame**. **Tardy** is a more recent variant form.

retrosexual *n*
a man who is unconcerned with his appearance; a slovenly male. The jocular social categorisation was invented in 2004 on the lines of the earlier **metrosexual**.

See also **contrasexual**

rettes *n pl American*
cigarettes. A shortening fashionable among **preppies** in the late 1970s.

revved *adj American*
excited. An expression used on campus in the USA since around 2000.

> *By the time the band came on everyone was totally revved.*

rhino *n British*
money. A raffish term which seemed obsolescent until its revival, along with synonyms such as **pelf**, **dosh**, **moolah**, etc., during the glamorising of finance and commerce in the mid-1980s. The word has had this meaning since the end of the 17th century, perhaps because of the value of the (supposedly aphrodisiac) rhinoceros horn or simply because the animal was at that time a fabulous symbol of wealth and exoticism.

rhubarb *n British*
meaningless babble, nonsense, empty talk. The theatrical term for background mumbling or hubbub has been adopted by London working-class users as a contemptuous or dismissive term for rubbish of all sorts.

> *He gave me a load of old rhubarb.*

riah, riach *n British*
hair, head of hair. One of the few instances of **backslang** to escape from a very restricted milieu. The word, usually pronounced to rhyme with 'fire', was used in the 1950s and early 1960s by actors, dressmakers, hairdressers, etc.

rice-queen *n*
a **gay** male who is attracted to Oriental partners.

Compare **curry-queen**

Richard *n British*
a third-class university degree. Like **Desmond**, **Pattie**, **Taiwan** and **made-in**, it is a student witticism, based on 'Richard the Third'. A **Douglas** (Hurd) is a more recent and fashionable version.

Richard (Gere) n British
(a glass of) *beer*. An item of rhyming
slang using the name of the Hollywood
star, heard amongst students from the
early 1990s.

Richard the Third n British
1a. a *bird* (in the literal sense or as slang
for a woman)
1b. a *turd*
The phrase has two senses in cockney
rhyming slang; the first is now dated
whereas the second achieved limited currency among non-cockneys in the 1970s
and 1980s.
2. the longer (rarely used) form of a **Richard**

Ricky n American
a foolish, unfortunate and/or unpleasant
male. An expression used on campus in
the USA since around 2000. The original reference is uncertain.

riddle n See **Jimmy Riddle**

ride¹ vb
to copulate (with). A metaphorical
usage which has been in evidence since
at least the 16th century, when it was a
standard synonym or euphemism in the
same way as 'mount'. Ride is still heard
in this sexual sense, albeit rarely,
whereas the noun form is still fairly
widespread.

ride² n
1. an act of sexual intercourse or a sex
partner. This is a later derivation of the
(now less common) verb form of the
word.
2. a car. This sense of the word probably
originated in US usage.
 *'His most "ghetto fabulous" ride is his
 GM van in New York.'*
 (*Sunday Times*, 6 June 2004)

ride someone's ass vb American
to nag, harass. The phrase is a pun on
'ass' as a donkey, as well as evoking an
image of driving or urging from behind.
 Quit riding his ass over this, will you?

ride the baloney-pony vb
1a. to have sex (with)
1b. (of a male) to masturbate. This adolescent witticism is inspired by the American name for the Bologna sausage.

ride the porcelain Honda/bus vb
American
to suffer from diarrhoea, sit on the toilet.
A **preppie** witticism on the pattern of **kiss
the porcelain god** (to vomit).

ridgy-didge, ridgy-didgy adj Australian
truthful, reliable, honest, authentic.
This phrase, which is still heard in Australian speech, has been derived from
'rigid digger', meaning an upstanding,
honest Australian. Alternatively it may
be based on the archaic English 'ridge',
meaning gold.

ridiculous adj British
drunk. The term is particularly heard in
Glaswegian speech. **Miraculous** is a synonym.

riffed adj American
intoxicated by drugs or alcohol. The
word 'riff' has had several slang senses,
but it is not clear which, if any, gave rise
to this usage.

riffing n American
behaving in a provocative or obstreperous manner. The term, heard in black
slang of the 1990s, covers a number of
meanings related to the earlier use of the
word 'riff' in **jive talk**, including provoking, complaining and boasting, but the
logic of the connection is unclear.

riff-raff n
a 'street-smart' individual. Often appreciative, e.g. in the parlance of British
Asian youth.

rift¹ n See **get a rift/rush/hustle on**

rift² vb British
(to emit) a belch. The term, which imitates the sound of the eructation, is
heard particularly in the Scottish Lowlands and the north of England.

rig n American
1. the male sex organs. A word used,
especially by women, in the **hippy** era,
although the word is older.
 *'I got this cute little pendant in the form of
 a flying rig.'*
 (*Groupies*, US film, 1973)
2. a truck, large van or bus
3. a heroin user's syringe, ligature, etc.
 *'I remember saying to the guy I was with
 "Don't fill the rig up. Don't put too much
 coke in it".'*
 (*Q* magazine, March 1997)

righteous adj American
1a. good, admirable
 A righteous dude.
1b. large or excessive
 A righteous mess.
Both senses are originally black adaptations of the standard English term, influenced by religious jargon. The terms are
now also used, sometimes ironically, by

white speakers.

right-on¹ *adj American*
admirable, thoroughgoing, authentic. A term of approval from the late 1970s which derives from 'right on!', the 1960s exclamation of enthusiasm, support, agreement or solidarity (itself originally from black American speech). The phrase is increasingly used ironically to mean **gung-ho** or self-righteous.

a right-on guy
She was right-on.

right-on² *n British*
an endorser of radical, liberal or leftist opinion. The invariably pejorative usage is based on 'right on!', the catchphrase supposedly characteristic of fashionable leftists of the 1960s.

She comes across as a bit of a right-on, unfortunately.

rigid *adj*
drunk. The term often (but not necessarily) refers to someone helplessly drunk.

rim *vb*
1a. to lick the anus as part of sexual stimulation
1b. to sodomise

rimmer *n British*
a despicable and/or obnoxious person. An all-purpose playground insult, probably from the more specific senses of **rim**. This usage was reinforced by the fact that an un-likeable character in the cult TV comedy *Red Dwarf* was given the name.

ring *n*
the anus. A common vulgarism in all English-speaking communities. The word has also occasionally been used for the vagina.

ringburner *n British*
a hot curry, or the condition following its digestion and excretion. An expression used typically among males for whom a hot curry is a test of **machismo** and/or a natural adjunct to drinking. (The ring in question is the anus and the word is a pun on a designation of a stove or cooking hob.)

ringer *n*
1a. something such as a stolen or defective car, a racehorse or greyhound, which has been tampered with or doctored in order to deceive

1b. a person who alters the appearance of a car, racehorse, antique, etc., in order to deceive
2. *American* a substitute introduced by subterfuge into a game or race in order to gain an unfair advantage

ringing *adj British*
excellent, exciting. A contemporary synonym of **banging**, **kicking**, etc.

ring-piece *n British*
the anus. An elaboration of **ring** popularised by its constant appearance in *Viz* comic.

ring someone's bell *vb*
to bring to a sexual climax. A euphemistic phrase which appears in the lyrics of several soul and disco records of the 1970s, also sometimes meaning simply to 'catch someone's eye' or 'strike a chord'.

ring-sting *n British*
a painful act of defecation or the resultant feeling. The term was defined on the Student World website in 2001 as 'the result of bad food and cheap toilet paper'.

rinky-dink *adj*
1. *British* cute, neat, smart. This fairly rare sense of the phrase may be based on a misunderstanding of the American usage, or a separate coinage influenced by **dinky**.
2. *American* shoddy, makeshift, meretricious. The phrase probably originated as an imitation of the sound of fairground music, evoking gaudiness and kitsch.

rinse *vb*
to perform, play or use to excess. A vogue term since 2000 among DJs and club aficionados.

'That Destiny's Child song has been rinsed on the radio.'
(Recorded, London student, March 2002)

rinsin' *adj*
exciting. A vogue term, especially in dancefloor culture, from black speech heard since the late 1990s. It probably derives from DJ jargon in which 'rinsin' out the plates' denotes spinning the records.

a rinsin' tune

ripe *adj American*
physically attractive. An expression used on campus in the USA since around 2000.

rip off *vb*
to cheat, steal (from) or take advantage (of). A raffish black street euphemism for steal or rob, in the mid-1960s rip off passed quickly via **hippy** jargon into popular currency all over the English-speaking world.

'Well, just about everyone in the music business has been ripped off, financially speaking. That's Entertainment!'
(*Ms London* magazine, 4 September 1989)

rip-off[1] *n*
an instance of theft, deception or unfair appropriation. It is now used in fairly mundane contexts, such as overcharging or plagiarism. The noun, like the verb, is from 1960s black argot in which it meant a robbery or a fraud.

rip-off[2] *adj*
(of goods) overpriced; (of people) grasping; and (of financial arrangements) crooked

ripoff artist *n*
a practitioner of **rip-offs**, fraudster or thief. The late 1960s **-artist** suffix does not denote expertise, but merely habitual involvement.

ripped *adj*
1. stoned on marihuana or a similar drug. The word is occasionally also used to mean drunk and is often elaborated into 'ripped to the gills' or 'ripped to the tits'.

'We're just sitting around getting ripped and listening to records.'
(*IT* magazine, July 1972)

2. *American* killed. A 'tough guy' euphemism of the 1970s and 1980s.
He just got ripped.
3. *American* unhappy, disappointed
4. *American* muscular, physically attractive

ripper[1] *adj Australian*
excellent, first-rate. A word which goes in and out of vogue, ripper was a British term of admiration, probably originating in the sports world (it has denoted a well-bowled cricket ball or a devastating punch in boxing) in the mid-19th century.

ripper[2] *n British*
a promiscuous female, **slag**. A term used by young street-gang members in London since around 2000.

rippy *adj British*
excellent, thrilling. A late 1980s version of the archaic 'ripping' (equivalent to the

Australian term **ripper**), heard among middle-class teenagers, for instance.

ripshit *adj American*
angry, enraged, frenzied

rivets *n American*
money, dollars. The term was recorded in British speech from the early 1800s but is now rare.

rizzer *n British*
a candidate for student office whose chances are 'risible'. A probably ephemeral term employed by Oxford University students in 1988.

roach *n*
1a. the butt of a **joint** (a marihuana cigarette). An American term adopted elsewhere in the late 1960s; this use of the word arose before World War II and is probably simply a borrowing of 'cockroach'. (Some authorities have suggested a connection with 'to roach', i.e. to clip a horse's mane.)

1b. a marihuana cigarette, **joint**. A US teenage usage, probably derived from the first, more widespread sense of the word.

2a. *American* a despicable or contemptible person
2b. *American* an unattached girl

road apple *n*
a piece of horse manure on the highway. In the USA, where the term probably originated, the synonym **alley apple** also exists.

road brew, road sauce *n American*
beer. A college-students' term. The significance of the 'road' component is unclear; **brew** and **sauce** are both slang terms for alcohol in their own rights.

roadie *n*
1. a rock group's assistant, responsible for handling equipment and general tasks. The word is a short form of the portentous official title 'road manager'.
2. *American* beer. A shortened version of **road brew** or **road sauce** in **preppie** jargon. It is usually in the plural form.
Let's grab some roadies.
3. *American* an unattractive female. An expression used on campus in the USA since around 2000. It may be a shortened form of 'road-kill'.

road pizza *n American*
any small creature that has been run over and flattened by a car. A sardonic witticism of the late 1980s.
Compare **pavement pizza**

roarer n British
a male homosexual, especially one who
is actually or supposedly flagrant. This
alternative form of 'roaring **pouff/queen**',
etc. is a heterosexual term of abuse of the
1970s and 1980s.

roasting[1] n British
a (usually consensual) sexual practice in
which a female is penetrated by two or
more males simultaneously. The term,
which is a contraction of the earlier metaphorical **spit-roasting**, was popularised
by media reporting of the activities of the
former UK TV presenter John Leslie in
2003.

roasting[2] adj
feeling sexually frustrated. Usually
referring to males, the term has been in
use in the UK since 2000.

rob-dog n British
a dishonest and/or despicable individual. The epithet, often expressing
strong dislike, was first widely heard in
the north of England in 2003 and
2004.

robobabe n American
an overwhelmingly attractive female. An
item of invented slang from the cult
1992 US film, *Wayne's World*. The prefix is adopted from the earlier cult film,
Robocop.
Compare **babia-majora**

robot n South African
a set of traffic lights

rock[1] n
1. a gem, diamond
2. **crack**, cocaine. The term has been
used for many years by dealers and users
to denote any crystalline preparation of a
narcotic. In the USA in the late 1980s,
rock is the most widespread generic term
for crack among law-enforcers and
breakers.

> 'A $15 "rock" – costing about the same
> as two cinema tickets – contains six
> "hits", enough to keep two people high
> for 90 minutes.'

(*Independent*, 24 July 1989)

3a. the Rock Gibraltar
3b. the Rock Alcatraz, the escape-proof
island prison (now closed) in San Francisco Bay, USA

rock[2] vb
to be exciting, **cool**. The usage began as
an Americanism but is now heard in all

English-speaking areas. In the USA it
sometimes occurs in the form 'rock out'.

Their new single rocks.

rocker n British
a member of a youth cult of the early
1960s, characterised by the wearing of
black leather jackets and enthusiasm for
motorcycles and 1950s rock 'n' roll
music. These mainly working-class teenagers and young adults were the successors to the **ton-up boys** and coevals of the
self-consciously 'progressive' **mods**, who
despised them for their adherence to
1950s American fashions and music.
Mods and rockers fought each other spo-
radically until the late 1960s, when each
group metamorphosed; rockers into
greasers and subsequent anonymity, or
into **bikers**.

> 'Rockers' hard-wearing clothes were of
> the type worn out of doors. Mods on the
> other hand were recruited in the main
> from the forum of office juniors and shop
> assistants.'

(Johnny Stuart, *Rockers*, 1987)

rockets n pl
female breasts, particularly when prominent or 'jutting'

rock-head n American
a stupid person. Like its later derivative
rubblehead, rock-head is based on the
uniquely North American notion of having rocks in one's head instead of brains.

rock house n American
premises where **crack** (also known as
rock) is processed and/or sold

> 'In the depressed inner-city areas of Los
> Angeles or New York, crack is frequently
> consumed in "crack houses" or "rock
> houses" – derelict buildings, often occu-
> pied by squatters, where addicts can buy
> and consume the drug.'

(*Sunday Times*, 10 September 1989)

rocking adj
excellent, exciting, **cool**

rock 'n' roll, the n British
the *dole* or a dole office (the term is
extended to cover Social Security payments and offices). A piece of recent
rhyming slang.

on the rock 'n' roll again
I'm going down the rock 'n' roll.

rocks n pl
the testicles. An American version of
the archaic British 'stones', rocks is

now in limited use elsewhere in the English-speaking world.

See also **get one's rocks off**

rod *n*

1. *American* a gun, particularly a pistol or revolver

2. the penis

3. a short form of hot rod

roddy, rodder *n British*

1a. a male masturbator

1b. a foolish or obnoxious individual

This playground term, usually used by males of males, probably derives from the earlier **rod-walloper**, a rarer synonym of **wanker**.

Rodney *n British*

a foolish or stupid person. This use of the name (by schoolchildren since the 1980s) is inspired by the character of Rodney in the long-running British TV comedy *Only Fools and Horses*.

rod-walloper *n*

a male masturbator. **Rod** is an occasional slang synonym for the penis.

rogan (josh) *n British*

money. An item of rhyming slang heard since the 1990s, borrowing the name of a popular curry dish to rhyme with **dosh**.

'By the look of them they're not short of a bit of the old rogan josh.'

(Recorded, musician, London, August 1994)

roger *vb British*

to copulate with (a woman). First recorded in 1711, the term is probably older. Roger, like **dick**, **peter**, **willie**, etc., has been used in the past as a nickname for the penis. It was also frequently given as a name to bulls and rams. In modern British middle-class use it is often employed as an 'acceptable' alternative to taboo synonyms. Roger has also been employed to denote buggery (in a homosexual context).

'Should not a Half-pay Officer roger for sixpence?'

(James Boswell, writing in his *London Journal*, 1762)

roll[1] *vb*

1. to rob or mug (someone). Originally the term referred to robbing someone who was dead drunk or asleep, hence literally rolling over an inert body in order to rifle pockets.

2. to have sex with. The verb form is much rarer than the noun in this sense.

3. *American* to leave. The word was used in this sense in the 1960s and has again become fashionable since the mid-1990s.

roll[2] *n*

1. an act of sexual intercourse. Usually heard in a fairly light-hearted context, particularly in the cliché 'a roll in the hay'.

2. a wad of banknotes, a bankroll

3. an act of mugging or robbing, particularly of an already unconscious person. A rare noun form of the verb sense.

rolling *adj British*

rich. A middle-class colloquial shortening of 'rolling in it', which is itself based on the image of a pig, horse or other animal rolling in manure.

She's absolutely rolling.

rollocking *n British*

a severe dressing-down, an angry and pointed tirade. The word is a euphemism for **bollocking**.

'Though Dad gave me a real rollocking, in the end I won. I just fluttered my eyelids at him and promised I wouldn't be seeing Josh again.'

(Jade Jagger, quoted in the *News of the World*, 29 March 1989)

ronk *vb British*

to stink. An invented word probably combining 'stink' and 'rotten'. **Honk** is a synonym. Ronk is a popular word in Liverpool and elsewhere in the north of England, though its use is not restricted to this area.

God, it doesn't half ronk in here.

roof-rack *n British*

a Pakistani. A partially rhyming phrase in use among working class adults since 2000. **Jim Raki** is a contemporary synonym.

rookie *n*

a learner, neophyte or newcomer, particularly to a job or a sports team. The term originated in Britain in the armed forces of the late 19th century, but more recently rookie has been in more widespread use in the USA. The word is said to be a deformation of 'recruit', perhaps influenced by the noisy chattering of rooks.

'Are you crazy? You're just a rookie. I've been on night patrol for years.'

(*Night Patrol*, US film, 1984)

rooms *n pl American*
mushrooms. This abbreviation refers to innocuous mushrooms as eaten on pizzas rather than **magic mushrooms**, which are known as **shrooms**.

rooster *n*
a male homosexual, particularly a predatory prison inmate who dominates or victimises younger fellow prisoners. In **gay** and prison jargon, roosters or **chickenhawks** prey upon **chickens**. Rooster is American for 'cock' in the sense of a male chicken.

root¹ *vb*
to have sex (with). A vulgar euphemism which occurs in working-class English speech and which is common in Australia. It derives from the archaic use of root to mean the penis and from 'root/rootle around' in the sense of searching in crevices. The term, first recorded in the 19th century but probably older, is hardly ever used in a homosexual context or by women.

root² *n*
1a. an act of sexual intercourse
1b. a sexual partner or available 'sex object'
The noun senses postdate the verb and are widespread in British and Australian usage.
2. *American* a cigarette or **joint**. A rare term which may originate in 'cheroot'.
3. *British* the penis, in playground parlance

rooted *adj Australian*
1a. ruined, destroyed, broken. Used in the same way as the more offensive **fucked** and **buggered**, this expression derives from the verb to **root**.
Christ, now the engine's rooted!
1b. exhausted

root-faced *adj Australian*
humourless-looking, having a morose expression. A phrase known in Britain mainly through the writing and performances of the Melbourne satirist, Barry Humphries, it is inspired by the wooden, knotted appearance of an old root.

roots! *exclamation*
goodbye. In use among UK adolescents since 2000.

rope *n*
1a. *American* a cigar

1b. tobacco
1c. marihuana
The connection and resemblance between tobacco, hemp and rope has given rise to these usages.
2. *American* a decorative metal chain, especially a heavy golden chain as worn by males. This item of hip hop regalia dates from the early 1980s. A synonym is **cable**.

ropeable *adj Australian*
furious or berserk. A slang interpretation of the notion contained in the colloquial expression 'fit to be tied'.
Well when we broke the news to her – I tell you, she was ropeable.

rort¹ *n Australian*
1. a swindle, a small-time confidence trick. This term of uncertain origin, until recently used mainly by people over 40 years of age, is undergoing something of a revival in media circles.
2. a noisy, riotous and wild party or celebration. In this sense the noun is probably a back-formation from the adjective **rorty**.
See also **rorter**

rort² *vb Australian*
to cheat, manipulate or bamboozle
'The Federal Government is to crack down on abuse of English language courses to rort the migrant selection system following examination of an inter-departmental submission to Cabinet.'
(*LAW* [*London Australasian Weekly*] magazine, 4 September 1989)

rorter *n*
1. *Australian* a swindler, a small-time confidence trickster or cheat. The origin of the Australian terms based on the word **rort** is unclear; one suggestion is that they are in fact based on 'wrought(er)', an archaic British term for trick(ster).
2. *British* a market trader who shouts his or her wares. This category, like the **lurker** and the **pitcher**, was defined in a Channel 4 TV documentary, 28 July 1994.

rory *adj*
flat broke. The word is from the rhyming slang for '(on) the floor': 'Rory O'Moore'. 'On the floor' is itself rhyming slang for *poor*. The Rory O'Moore in question is probably a fictional Scots/Irish personification from the 19th century.

rosie, Rosie Lee *n British*
tea. A genuine example of cockney rhyming slang which has been adopted for light-hearted use by non-cockneys. The term seems to have originated at the turn of the 20th century, from a common proper name, and was reinforced by the later fame of the American striptease artist Gypsy Rose Lee.

A nice cup of rosie should do the trick.

rot-gut *adj, n*
low quality alcoholic drink. A four-hundred-year-old term which was applied formerly to weak beer, but which more recently has usually denoted inferior spirits or wine.

rotten *adj*
very drunk. A euphemism in British and Australian usage.

rough *adj British*
1. unpleasant, distasteful, disgusting. The standard term became an all-purpose pejorative in working-class speech and then a vogue word among adolescents and then younger schoolchildren from the mid-1990s.

That girlfriend of his is well rough if you ask me.

2. excellent. The process whereby negative becomes positive operated particularly rapidly in the case of rough, which by the late 1990s was being used appreciatively.

'... "wicked" (for good) has vanished, replaced by the new term of high praise, "rough", invariably accompanied by a jerky wave of the right hand at shoulder level.'
(*Guardian*, 19 October 1996)

rough end of the pineapple, the *n Australian*
a disadvantageous position, the worst of a deal. A colourful alternative to such phrases as 'the sharp end of the stick' or 'the shitty end of the stick'.

roughneck, ruff-neck *n British*
a youth, especially a tough, admirable male. A 1990s synonym for **rude boy** or **bad-boy** first used by black gang members before being adopted by other schoolchildren and teenagers. Like those terms, it is typical of the tendency by transgressive subcultures to adopt, for the purpose of irony and bravado, the pejorative language of their critics (as in **bad**, **wicked**, etc.)

rough trade *n British*
1a. a homosexual lover (usually a casual pick-up) considered to be lower class, uncouth and/or violent. From the homosexual underground slang of the 1950s, used for instance by male prostitutes about their customers. The phrase was later used to characterise a stereotypical homosexual icon, i.e. the muscular, aggressively masculine 'working man'.
1b. an uncouth or violent client of a heterosexual prostitute

'Behind the throat-level peep-holes eyes took in the body swathed in Ralph Lauren finery trailing after her piece of rough trade.'
(*Platinum Logic*, Tony Parsons, 1981)

roundeye *n*
1. a white person. The term, used originally by Orientals as an opposite of 'slit-eyed', is also used by blacks.
2. *American* the anus, especially as a focus of sexual attention

roundhead *n British*
(a male with) a circumcised penis. A schoolboy counterpart to **cavalier**.

round the houses *adv British*
1a. on a (long and) futile mission
1b. all over the body. The phrase is prostitutes' and pornographers' code for all-over sexual stimulation.

round the twist *adj, adv British*
crazy, deranged. A racier version of the colloquial 'round the bend', this phrase moved from limited working-class usage to general currency in the 1960s.

roust *vb American*
to disturb, harass and/or arrest. The word is usually used to describe the actions of police against suspects. Roust was first used by criminals or street-frequenters in the early 20th century, later by the law-enforcers themselves; it is from the noun 'rouster', a version of 'roustabout', employing a strong form of 'rouse'.

rozzer *n British*
a police officer. This word originated in the 19th century and is still in limited use. The standard derivations offered by reference sources (Romany *roozlo*, meaning strong, or 'roosher', a supposed corruption of 'rusher') are not entirely convincing.

rriot-grrrl *n American*
a member or devotee of a neo-punk movement organised by various all-girl

rock bands, including Bratmobile and L7 in 1992 and 1993

rub-a-dub, rubbidy *n*
a public house. These rhyming-slang phrases (with *pub*) are heard in both Britain and Australia. Rub-a-dub(-dub) has also been used in Britain, especially in underworld circles, as rhyming slang for *club*.

rubber, rubber johnny *n*
a condom. The first version is international English, the second British. **Johnnie**, **johnny** and 'johnnie bag' are synonyms.

rubbish *vb*
to deride, condemn, tease. Originally Australian, the expression has established itself in British English since the early 1970s.

rubblehead *n American*
an idiot. A term, like **rock-head**, which evokes the notion of having rocks rather than brains in one's head. This version was popular among teenagers and college students in the late 1980s.

rube *n American*
a yokel or rustic simpleton. A short form of the male Christian name Reuben.

rub off *vb*
(of a female) to masturbate

rub out *vb*
to kill, murder. A euphemism from the language of the American underworld of the 1920s and 1930s, enthusiastically adopted by crime novelists. In modern street parlance the phrase is often shortened to 'rub'.

Ruby (Murray) *n British*
a *curry*. This item of rhyming slang comes from the name of an Irish-born popular singer of the 1950s. The word or phrase is perpetuated by some speakers too young to be familiar with its inspiration.

ruck *n British*
an undisciplined brawl, a gang fight. A characteristic London working-class use of a mild-sounding term (from 'ruckus') to denote something often involving extreme violence. (**Bother** and **aggro** are examples of the same tendency.) The word is an important element in the football hooligan and **skinhead** vocabulary.

> 'He [a hooligan] brags about his "rucks" with Millwall's notorious F troop.'
> (*News of the World*, 17 July 1988)

rucking, ruck-up *n British*
a brawl, row or dressing-down. These are variant forms of **ruck**.

ruddy *adj British*
an inoffensive intensifying adjective, now dated but used extensively from the turn of the 20th century until the mid-1960s as a milder euphemism for **bloody**

rude *adj*
1. excellent. In this sense the term, probably adapted from or imitating black speech, was used by Californian adolescents in the mid-1990s, often in the form 'totally rude'.
2. shockingly bad, horrible. In this generalised sense a vogue term among younger British teenagers since 2000. It probably represents an ironic borrowing of an older generation's term of prissy disapproval.
3. belonging to someone who thinks they're hard
> *a rude car*
> *rude clothes*

rude bits *n pl British*
the breasts and/or genitals. A coy quasi-nursery term in middle-class use.

rude boy, rudie *n*
1a. *Jamaican* a gangster, gang member
> 'Interestingly, there is a theory that the word "reggae" was originally derived from its Kingston rude boy exponents being derided as "ragamuffin men".'
> (*Independent*, 1 September 1989)

1b. *British* a would-be tough and/or fashionable youth

ruff *adj See* **rough**

rug *n*
1a. a toupee, wig. A predictable pre-World War II jocularism which probably originated in theatrical slang.
1b. the female pubic hair
2. *See* **cut a rug**

rug bug *n*
an alternative form of **rug rat**

rugged *adj*
1. *Australian* suffering from bad luck
2. *British* excellent, powerful. An item of student slang in use in London and elsewhere since around 2000.

rugger bugger *n British*
a hearty (usually boorish) sportsman. The expression became popular from the 1960s primarily to denote the stereotypical rugby-club mentality.

rug-muncher *n American*
a lesbian. **Carpet-muncher** is an alternative version of the pejorative term as used by males.

rug rat *n*
a child. A phrase which, like the synonymous **ankle-biter**, has become popular, especially in young middle-class families, since the 1980s. **Rug bug** and 'carpet rat' are alternative forms. The phrase was popularised by its adoption as the title of a US TV cartoon in the mid-1990s.

ruined *adj American*
drunk, often pronounced 'ruint'. An expression used on campus in the USA since around 2000.

ruler, the *n British*
an impressive, admirable individual. A key term in the adolescent language of status since the late 1980s. 'The boss' and 'the man' were earlier colloquial synonyms.

  'Chris Evans is the ruler, seriously he is so rad, totally funny, he knows what's up (nice shirts) and when he is not presenting the show, it sucks.'
  (*Phat* magazine, 1993)

rumble[1] *n*
a fight, especially a planned streetfight or brawl involving gangs. An American expression used by teenage neighbourhood gangs since the 1950s, the word has subsequently been picked up in other English-speaking areas.

rumble[2] *vb*
1. to fight. The word, like the noun form, originated in the slang of American urban gangs of the 1950s. It has since been appropriated and generalised by other adolescents in the USA, UK and Australia.

  'If you wanna stop us then you'll have to come and rumble us.'
  (*The Firm*, British TV play, 1989)

2. *British* to uncover (a deception), to be disabused. Now a fairly widespread colloquialism, rumble, like 'tumble', in this sense originated in the 19th century. Rumble probably derives from the archaic 'romboyle', meaning to search for a wanted fugitive or suspect (a 17th-century term of unknown origin).

  We better get out of here – we've been rumbled.

rummage[1] *vb British*
to raid and/or search (premises). The specialised sense, deriving from the standard colloquialism, has been used by police and criminals since the 1990s.

  'It's going to be rummaged tomorrow.'
  (*River Police*, ITV documentary, 15 September 1995)

rummage[2] *n British*
a sexual act. The word is pronounced with a long 'a', perhaps in imitation of French. An item of student slang in use in London and elsewhere since around 2000.

rummaging *adj British*
having sex. The word is pronounced with a long 'a', perhaps in imitation of French. An item of student slang in use in London and elsewhere since around 2000.

rumpo *n British*
an act of sexual intercourse. A 'smutty' euphemism first popularised by the fictitious folksinger and specialist in innuendo, 'Rambling Sid Rumpo', played by Kenneth Williams in the Kenneth Horne radio comedies of the 1960s. In the 1980s the term was seen as an acceptable suggestive euphemism. It derives from 'rump' as an archaic verb meaning to copulate and from the noun as a synonym for **tail**, **arse**, etc. **Rumpty-tumpty** and **rumpy-pumpy** are elaborated forms.

  'Susannah Hoffs is writing a "steamy" romance novel. Packed with intrigue and rumpo, it will, she claims "put Jackie Collins in the shade".'
  (*Smash Hits* magazine, November 1989)

rump-ranger *n American*
a male homosexual. A pejorative term used by (invariably male) heterosexuals.

  'That old Greek rump-ranger just saw me knocking on the fuckin' door.'
  (*Sketch Artist*, US film, 1993)

rumpty-tumpty, rumpy-pumpy *n British*
an act of sexual intercourse or sexually related 'naughtiness'. Quasi-nursery elaborations of **rumpo**, used typically by disc jockeys, TV comedians and tabloid journalists since the 1980s.

  'And if they were to temporarily stray from marital fidelity, where would they turn for a bit of royal rumpy pumpy?'
  (*Viz* comic, May 1989)

run[1] n

1. *American* a rally by Hell's Angels, usually involving a lengthy mobile debauch

2. an initial euphoric sensation following the ingestion or injection of a narcotic, particularly heroin; a **rush**

'When I'm rushing, on my run/And I feel just like Jesus's son.'

('Heroin', the Velvet Underground, 1967)

run[2] vb British

to denigrate, humiliate. A term reflecting the ritualistic status games of adolescent gangs, it is probably an abbreviated form of the colloquial meaning of 'run down'. The term was recorded in use among North London schoolboys in 1993 and 1994.

run game vb British

to work as a prostitute or behave promiscuously. An item of black street-talk used especially by males, recorded in 2003.

She runnin' game.

runner n British

1a. an escapee. The word is thus used in police jargon.

1b. an escape, a disappearance, unauthorised departure. A usage well known in the form **do a runner**.

runners n pl British

trainers, sports shoes, in playground parlance. The word is also used in this sense in the Republic of Ireland.

running adj

intoxicated by drugs. The term, coined by analogy with **buzzing** and **rushing**, particularly applied to those under the effects of amphetamines, **crack** or, later, **ecstasy**.

run off at the mouth vb American

to talk excessively, to say more than one should. Usually used in an accusatory way, for instance to someone who betrays secrets.

runs, the n British

an attack of diarrhoea. The expression is based on both the notion of runniness and running to a place of relief. A more sedate alternative is **the trots**.

Rupert n British

an officer or officer cadet. A pejorative term in armed-forces' usage. The proper name was chosen as supposedly being quintessentially upper-class.

rush n

1. the initial heady or euphoric sensation consequent on taking a mind-altering drug. The word is used especially, and most literally, of stimulant drugs such as cocaine and amphetamines; it generally refers to the sudden effects of a drug injected intravenously or taken through the mucous membranes rather than the more gradual onset attendant upon smoking or swallowing. The term is sometimes extended to refer to any exciting or stimulating action or situation.

'When you inhale real hard, even before you exhale you're starting to feel the rush. It just goes straight to your head quicker than any other drug, and a better rush than any other drug.'

(Crack smoker, *Independent*, 24 July 1989)

2. defined by a London schoolboy as 'when lots of people beat up one person'

There was a rush down there.

rust-bucket n

an old dilapidated or shoddily manufactured car. The term was earlier applied to ships and aeroplanes.

rusty sheriff's badge n British

the anus

S

sabbing *n British*
an act of sabotage. A word used by animal-rights activists and hunt saboteurs in the 1980s.

> *'Meeting to discuss sabbing tactics.'*
> (Campus announcement, Essex University, 1986)

sack¹ *vb British*
to discard or reject. Used in this sense and generalised from the colloquial meaning of dismissal from one's job, the term was popular in adolescent slang of the 1990s, often in reference to 'dumping' a partner.

> *I think we should sack the whole idea.*
> *Tina's planning to sack Martin, but she won't admit it if you ask her.*

sack² *n*
1. a bed. The word was probably first used of hammocks in the 19th century.
See also **sad sack**
2. the scrotum

sack artist *n*
a womaniser, seducer, Lothario. In the *Literary Review*, June 1987, in a review of *Intercourse* by Andrea Dworkin, Jane Ellison attributed this to Martin Amis. She was wrong. It is North American in origin, in common with other formulations such as 'con artist', spreading to Britain in the 1980s. Sack artist started life with the quite different meaning of a lazy person or idler (who spent most of their time in the **sack**).

sack it, sack it off *vb British*
to forget, disregard (something or someone). As used by adolescents since 2000, the term may be inspired by the colloquial 'sack' as dismiss, or the image of disposal in a bag.

sackless *adj*
1. (of a female) flat-chested
2. incompetent, vacuous. The word is used in this sense particularly in the north east of England. It is said to derive from a Norse word meaning innocent or

naïve. An annoyingly inefficient person is often described as a 'sackless wonder'. The term is also used in the USA.

> *'R– C– is a gutless, sackless pansy who has never failed to shy away from a challenge in his life.'*
> (Recorded, US Internet sports chat room, 9 July 2004)

sack out *vb American*
to go to bed, (lie down and) sleep. A colloquialism based on the long-established use of **sack** to mean bed.

sack time *n*
1a. bed time. An armed forces and prison usage, carried over into civilian colloquialism.

> *'Lift that weight drag that woodbine/ lights out mate sackarooni time/ lights out sack time.'*
> ('36 Hours', poem by John Cooper Clarke, 1980)

1b. time spent sleeping

sad *adj British*
unfortunate, unattractive, unexciting. This standard word was appropriated as an all-purpose vogue term of dismissal, disapproval, etc. among adolescents and younger children in the early 1990s, shortly afterwards crossing over into adult speech. (The bouffanted Tory minister Michael Portillo, for instance, was said to have 'sad hair'.)

> *'I hate myself when I find myself using "sad" in all its repulsively contemporary glory … basically it's no more than the latest linguistic expression of the bullying, teasing ways of school – it refers to kids with glasses, trainspotters, slow learners …'*
> (Paul Stump, *Guardian*, 8 November 1992)

saddo *n British*
a pitiable, contemptible or unfortunate individual. An elaborated form of the fashionable adjective **sad** in adolescent usage throughout the 1990s.

'What sort of chronic saddo really believes that the best days of his life were spent in the mud at Woodstock or fighting on Brighton beach.'
(Julie Burchill, *Sunday Times* magazine, 28 November 1993)

sad sack *n American*
an unfortunate, characteristically depressed or confused individual. This term originated before World War II and was subsequently widespread in armed service slang to describe a misfit or pitiable person (normally male). The name was given to a popular cartoon character of the 1950s.

safe[1] *adj British*
good, fine. The standard meaning was extended in schoolchildren's slang at the end of the 1980s to encompass anything positive. The word is thus used as an all-purpose term of approbation, often as an exclamation. 'Safe' in this generalised sense probably derives from its over-use by petty criminals and gang members.

safe[2] *n Canadian*
a short form of **French safe**

sag (off) *vb British*
to play truant. The verb, which can be used transitively or intransitively, became well known after reports of the abduction and murder of the toddler James Bulger by truanting boys in 1993. Partridge dates 'sag' in the sense of absenting oneself from work to the 19th century, and in the sense of truancy to the Merseyside of the 1930s.

'In the first interview child A admitted "sagging off" school with B and going to the Strand precinct, but denied taking James.'
(*Evening Standard*, 2 November 1993)

salad-dodger *n British*
an overweight, obese and/or greedy person. The term of mockery or abuse evokes an individual who is avoiding healthy food.

How could he go for a salad-dodger like Monica Lewinsky?

salami, salam' *n American*
1. the penis. A teenagers' term almost always heard in the phrase 'hide the salami' (a euphemism for sexual intercourse).
2. a fool. A high-school and campus term.

salamite *n British*
a male homosexual. Part of the language of teenage London schoolchildren in the 1990s, this term, usually used derogatively, is probably a deformation or misunderstanding of 'sodomite', perhaps blended with 'catamite'.

'Kayleigh said Keith was a salamite and he completely lost it.'
(Recorded, London schoolgirl, May 1995)

salmon *n British*
1. a cigarette. This usage, which is probably from the older rhyming slang phrase 'salmon and trout', meaning **snout**, was popular among London schoolchildren from the mid-1990s and was featured in the Shamen's controversial 1995 hit *Ebenezer Goode*. **Biff** was a contemporary synonym.
2. *See* **on the salmon**

salty *adj American See* **jump salty**

sambo *n*
a black person (usually male). This derogatory racist term comes from *zambo*, the Spanish American designation of those (slaves) with three-quarters negro and one-quarter Amerindian or European blood. The word was picked up by English speakers in the early 18th century and its use was reinforced by the 19th-century children's storybook character, 'Little Black Sambo'. The term has fallen out of use in the USA since the 1950s but is heard in Britain and Australia.

sandbag *vb American*
1a. to attack unexpectedly, stop (someone) dead, incapacitate or thwart. A sand-filled bag was formerly used as an improvised cosh or blackjack. The word was taken up into business jargon in the 1980s. (**Handbag** has been coined as a feminine counterpart.)

'You sandbagged me on Blue Star!'
(*Wall Street*, US film, 1987)

1b. to obstruct or outmanoeuvre, especially by feigning weakness. The word is a gambling term now extended to other contexts.
2. to drive at full speed, in the jargon of 'hotrodders'

S. and M. *n*
sado-masochistic practices, in the code of pornographers and prostitutes

sanga, sanger n British
a sandwich. The term is popular in the north of England and the Midlands.

sap n American
1. a fool, simpleton or dupe. Originally a British term, the word is now more often heard in the USA. It was in origin a shortening of the word 'sapskull', meaning wooden-head, dating from the late 17th century. In the 19th century schoolboy **swots** were known as 'saps', from the Latin *sapiens* (wise or knowledgeable), and this meaning applied ironically may have converged with the older sense of the word.
2. a blackjack, cosh. This sense of the word is probably based on sap meaning a hoe or shovel in archaic speech.

saphead n American
a fool, simpleton or dupe. A version of **sap**.

sarnie n British
a sandwich. A diminutive form which has spread from the north of England.

sashay vb
to walk proudly, stride, flounce or 'mince'. Sashay originated as an Americanisation of the French *chassé* (in this case a rapid, gliding movement; a term used in square dancing).

She sashayed up to the bar and ordered a daiquiri.

sass[1] vb American
to speak or behave irreverently or insolently (towards), to cheek (someone). The verb is from the earlier, but now rarer, noun form.

Don't you sass me, boy.

sass[2] n American
impudence, insolence. Sass is a folksy or dialect form of 'sauce', in the sense of sauciness. It is now rare in the noun form, although the verb is still used.

I don't need none of your sass.

sauce n
alcoholic drink. In Britain this is a mainly middle-class euphemism employed particularly by heavy drinkers; the implication is that alcohol is liberally dispensed. There may also be a subconscious identification with **soused**.

'I couldn't stop – I got on the sauce real good.'
(*The Dancer's Touch*, US film, 1989)

sauced (out) adj
drunk. A usage based on **sauce** as a slang term for alcoholic drink (and influ-

enced by **soused**). The '-out' version is a racier modern variant.

saucepan lids n pl British See **dustbin lids**

sauny n, adj British
(someone) insincere, untrustworthy, 'slimy'. The term was used by teenage girls in 2001.

sausage grappler n Australian
a male masturbator. One of many synonymous vulgarisms (**rod-walloper**, etc.) heard since the 1960s.

sausage jockey n American
a **gay** male. A pejorative term used by heterosexuals in the 1990s. The British equivalent is **sausage-rider**.

sausage-rider n British
a male homosexual. The term was one of many supposedly comic synonyms in use among heterosexuals in the 1990s.

savage adj
excellent. Like many similar terms (**brutal**, **evil**, **tough**, etc.), the standard word has been appropriated for use in adolescent slang in both Britain and the US.

sawbuck n American
a ten dollar bill. The Latin X for ten was thought to recall the wooden cross-struts of a saw horse.

sawn-off, sawed-off n American
a person of restricted stature, a 'runt'

saying! exclamation British
a synonym of **safe** and **seen** heard among adolescents in the late 1990s

saymara See **sianara**

say uncle vb American See **uncle**[1] 2

scads[1] n pl British
underpants. The term, often referring to male underwear, was recorded in 2005.

scads[2], scad n American
a great deal, large quantity (particularly of money). This colloquialism is of uncertain origin; it probably derives from a British dialect form of 'shed(full)' or from a dialect word 'scald', meaning multitude.

scaffer, scuffer n British
a homeless person, beggar or tramp. The term is heard in Scotland and the north of England. It is probably a version of the archaic dialect word *scaff*, related to 'shuffle' and denoting a vagabond or idler.

scag, skag n
heroin. This word entered American usage in the later 1960s, probably from black street slang in which skag and

skank were used to refer to anything inferior or unpleasant. The word presumably first referred to low-quality narcotics.

> 'The ladies kept a couple of grams [of cocaine] in the refrigerator. Ordell said he would not tolerate any scag, though.'
> (*The Switch*, Elmore Leonard, 1978)

scally *n British*

1a. a young man, lad

1b. a criminal, delinquent or hooligan, **chav**

1c. a male inhabitant of the Liverpool area

The word has overtones of 'cheeky', 'smart' and 'one of the boys'; it is a regional shortening of 'scallywag', a word meaning reprobate or rascal first used abusively in the USA before the Civil War. Scallywag itself is probably a form of an older expression from English or Scottish dialect meaning something like 'scurvy wretch'.

scallywag *n American*

the penis. The standard colloquial term for a rascal (which dates from the 19th century but is of unknown origin) has been appropriated by older teenagers and young adults for facetious use.

scalper *n*

a ticket tout or other form of ruthless (though small-scale) profiteer. The term comes from the verb to scalp, which was 19th-century stock-exchange jargon for buying cheap and selling at an exaggerated price (from the notion of 'taking a cut off the top').

scalping *n*

profiteering, particularly by re-selling tickets at an inflated price

> 'This is a shrewd and practised Londoner trading in what the Americans call "scalping". We call the business "touting", and this summer ticket touts are set for a final beano.'
> (*Evening Standard*, 9 May 1988)

scam[1] *n*

a deception, fraud, swindle or confidence trick. This Americanism entered fashionable British usage around 1977, subsequently becoming fairly widespread, particularly in business parlance. 'Scampery' was British slang for a highway robbery in the 18th century, a word later used by vagrants, showmen, etc. This, via American adoption, may explain the modern term (the similarity with 'scheme' is probably fortuitous). By the late 1980s scam had

come sometimes to be used to mean merely a 'dubious scheme or display'.

> '"You know, I think there are a million people running scams out there", said Suzanne McGuire, the tournament's director of corporate marketing. "But what can you do? This is New York".'
> (*Sunday Times*, 10 September 1989)

scam[2] *vb American*

to perpetrate a fraud, deception or devious scheme. The verb is derived from the noun.

scan *vb British*

to be vigilant, watch out. The standard term has been appropriated for the language of adolescent gangs. It was recorded in use among North London schoolboys in 1993 and 1994. 'Scan out' is a variant heard in black American speech since the 1990s.

> You stay here and scan while we check out the shop.

scangey *adj American*

unpleasant, squalid, disreputable. A term of unknown origin (it is pronounced to rhyme with 'mangy') which first became fashionable in adolescent speech at the beginning of the **grunge** era around 1992.

scarf (up/down) *vb*

to devour greedily and completely, eat and/or drink voraciously. Perhaps a humorous alternative, tinged with onomatopoeia, of **scoff**, the term originated in the USA where it was adopted by adolescents from 'low-life' milieus in the 1960s. ('Scarf out' is another derivative; a synonym of **pig out**.)

> 'Harvey watched Joan scarfing down Milanos, biting them in half with her even teeth.'
> (*The Serial*, Cyra McFadden, 1976)

scarfing *n British*

practising auto-asphyxiation as sexual stimulus. The term came to prominence after the death of Conservative MP Stephen Milligan in 1994. Practitioners are known as **gaspers**.

scarper *vb*

to leave hurriedly, run away. The word was adopted by cockneys at the turn of the 20th century, from **parlyaree**, the Italianate pidgin used by peddlars, showmen, actors, etc. *Scappare* (to escape) is the original Italian term. Since World War I many have assumed that the word is rhyming slang from 'Scapa flow': *go*.

scatty *n South African*
a weak or irresolute person

scene *n*
1. the scene the fashionable, **hip** or currently favoured milieu. A favourite word from the **beatnik** and later **hippy** vocabularies, often used in such phrases as 'make the scene' (to be present or active in the currently hip environment) and 'on the scene'. 'It's not my scene' was a common dismissal of an undesirable activity or place. In colloquial usage the word simply means environment or 'world', as in 'the music scene'. The word is now dated but is still used by some journalists and, self-consciously or ironically, by the fashionable young.
2. a state of affairs, situation. In this generalised sense the word is now dated.

> '"It was a very emotional time, a lot of yelling and screaming, a really bad scene", Bolker remembered.'
> (*Sunday Times*, 24 September 1989)

3. *See* **have a scene (with someone)**

sch- *prefix*
many slang words of Yiddish origin may be spelled with these initial letters, but 'sch' is the standard German form and, as such, is not employed in this dictionary, except for words which have been specifically recorded in this form. The alternative spelling **sh-** is used in writing by most Yiddish speakers and writers in English-speaking countries and is therefore preferred here.

schemie *n British*
a synonym for **chav**, recorded in 2005. Like **ned** the term originated in lowland Scotland and refers to (low-rent) housing schemes.

schizzed-out *adj American*
1a. deranged, uncontrolled
1b. drunk
The term is an elaboration of 'schizophrenic' or 'schizoid'. In fashionable slang of the early 1970s, schizzed-out was used in the same way as the more common 'flipped out' or 'freaked out'. The sense of drunk was an adaptation by high-school and **preppie** speakers.

schlemiel *n*
a fool, clumsy unfortunate, loser. A Yiddish word (pronounced 'shler-meal') used with a mixture of pity and contempt. In 1813 von Chamisso wrote *Peter Schlemihl's Wunderbare*

Geschlichte; a parable describing a man selling his shadow and his soul. The author probably took the name from Schlumiel, a biblical general notorious for losing battles.

> 'I've never been able to stand Woody Allen – he's such a schlemiel.'
> (Recorded, antiquarist, London, 1986)

schlong[1] *n American*
the penis. A Yiddish word (meaning 'snake') which has entered the mainstream of American slang since the 1960s. It has been used in the novels of Elmore Leonard, Philip Roth's *Portnoy's Complaint* and the film *Sophie's Choice*, among other instances. In the late 1980s wits coined an alternative form: 'schlort'.

schlong[2] *vb*
to have sex (with). The word was in use among UK university students in 2001 according to the Student World website.

schlub, schlob *n American*
alternative or earlier forms of **slob**

schmaltz *n*
sickly sentimentality. The word is Yiddish, from the German for cooking fat or dripping. The word was used in the New York Jewish community to describe what Leo Rosten in *The Joys of Yiddish* (1970) defines as 'corn, pathos, maudlin and mawkish substance; excessive sentimentality, overly emotional mush, sugary banality'.

> 'With chapter headings such as "I'm in love with a dishwasher", "I love you too, Mommy", "I love you, Michael", and "We all love each other", On the Outside Looking In has more schmaltz than a New York deli.'
> (Book review by Nigella Lawson, *Sunday Times*, April 1989)

schmeck *n American*
1. a sniff or taste (in Yiddish from German)
2. heroin. It is this second sense which is the origin of the more recent **smack**.

schmeckle *n American*
an unnamed object, substance, etc. The Yiddish word actually denotes the penis, but in adolescent usage since the late 1990s has been generalised to an all-purpose designation.

> She's got some schmeckle down the front of her shirt.
> Pass me the schmeckle on the shelf there.

schmendrick *n American*
a foolish or clumsy nonentity. A Yiddish word which is used by Jews and non-Jews alike in American speech. Shmendrik was a character in an operetta by Abraham Goldfaden.

schmooze, schmoose *vb See* **shmooze**

schmuck *n American*
a pitiful, foolish or obnoxious person, usually male. Schmuck is from the Yiddish word *shmok*, itself from the German *schmuck*, meaning ornament. In Yiddish the word was used first as a euphemism for the male member, it then became a synonym for the English **prick**, figuratively as well as literally. As employed today, especially by non-Jewish speakers, schmuck is a fairly mild term of abuse, often used ruefully, despairingly or affectionately. It was perceived as an obscenity in the USA for many years with the result that the euphemism **shmo** was invented in the 1940s.

> 'He gave his small son a gun and taught him how to shoot all God's little creatures … and called him "his little schmuck", giving Mike a nice warm glow, until he finds out what it means.'
> (Nigella Lawson, *Sunday Times*, April 1989)

schmutter *n*
clothing. The word is Yiddish, deriving from the Polish *szmata*, meaning rag. Schmutter was popularised in Britain by its use in the tailoring trade.

> *a nice bit of schmutter if you ask me*
> *They used to be in the schmutter business.*

schnockered *adj*
drunk. The word is probably not Yiddish or German, despite its most usual spelling, but may derive from an archaic dialect term 'snock', meaning to hit. Schnockered, also spelled **snockered**, is encountered more often in American speech than British.

> 'As a whiskey salesman … I'm often lit up by elevenses, loop-legged by luncheon and totally schnockered by 6.'
> (Posy Simmonds cartoon, *Guardian*, 1979)

schnook *n American*
an unfortunate, timid or pathetic person. The word is Yiddish, but apparently was coined in the USA. It is probably related to the German *schnucki*: darling, or *schnuck*: a small sheep.

schnozzle, schnozz *n*
the nose. The word is Yiddish, from German, in which *schnauze* is the translation of 'snout'. The comedian Jimmy 'Schnozzle' Durante (named for his large nose) introduced the word to non-Americans.

schwing! *exclamation American*
an expression of male delight at the sight of an attractive female. The word is a mock-Yiddish alteration of 'swing' and probably refers to an erection. It originated in the ersatz slang of the cult 1992 film, *Wayne's World*, and was subsequently adopted by high-school and college students in the US.

scoff *n British*
food. A noun formed from the colloquial verb (itself probably from an imitative dialect word) and used, particularly by young people, as a more fashionable synonym for **grub**. In fact this use of scoff dates from the 19th century.

> 'What I've got my eye on is all that lovely scoff.'
> (Recorded, student, London, 1987)

sconned (on peeve) *adj British*
drunk. A term used by teenagers since the mid-1990s.

scooby[1] *adj*
1a. excellent, attractive
1b. delicious
A vogue term among adolescents in the 1990s, the word was also used by adults, particularly women. It is part of the nonsense phrase 'scooby-doo', which was used as the name of a cartoon character in the 1970s and of a plastic swatch used in children's games in the 1960s (then in the French form *scoubidou*).

scooby[2] *n British*
a treat, enjoyable experience. The noun derives from the adjective, which itself derives from the earlier **scooby-doo**. Since around 2000 the term has been popular among adults as well as teenagers.

scooby(-doo) *n British*
1. a clue. Invariably as part of a phrase in utterances such as 'Don't ask me, I haven't got a scooby-doo'.
2. a **screw** (prison warden)

scoop *n*
1. *American* the latest news, information, gossip. The term has been in use since at least the later 1970s and is often used in

the phrase 'have the scoop on something/someone' or 'give me the scoop'.

2. *British* an alcoholic drink, especially a pint of beer. Often in the plural.

Let's pop out for a few scoops.

scoots *n pl American*
dollars. A word of unknown origin used mainly by adolescent speakers.

scope¹ *vb American*
to look at, examine. A vogue term among adolescents since the 1980s, it is heard on college campuses and is in use among the neo-**Valley Girls** featured in the 1995 US film, *Clueless*. In black speech 'scope on (something/someone)' is a common variant.

We're going to scope the betties in the park.

scope², scoper *n British*
a clumsy, inept and/or foolish person. A synonym for **spanner**, **spack**, etc. in use among adolescents and by *Viz* comic in 2001. The word was coined as a result of the UK Spastics Society changing its name to Scope.

scope out *vb American*
to explore, investigate, evaluate

score¹ *n*
1. *British* £20. The word has been particularly popular in underworld and police usage since before World War II.

I thought it was worth at least a hundred, but I only got a score for it.

2. a success or coup, especially a successful crime, seduction or arrest

'Shaft's Big Score!'
(Title of US film, 1972)

3. a drug purchase. From the verb form.
They set up a score downtown.

score² *vb*
1a. to buy (illicit drugs). An Americanism that became the standard term worldwide in the late 1960s.

1b. to obtain. This is a young person's generalisation of the previous raffish usage.

Look on the bright side – you may not have got the job, but at least you scored a free lunch.

2. to succeed in gaining sexual satisfaction

I saw you leaving the pub with that red-head – did you score?
Chas scored with Emma.

score³ *exclamation American*
an expression of joy, triumph or relief

scorf *n, vb British*
1a. a variant form of **scoff**
1b. a variant form of to **scarf**

scouse¹ *adj British*
of or from Liverpool. The word is derived from 'lobscouse', a stew traditionally containing vegetables, hard-tack or ship's biscuit, and sometimes meat. Lobscouse was eaten by sailors and was popular in the Liverpool area.

scouse² *n British*
the accent and speech of the Liverpool area

scouser *n British*
a Liverpudlian. From **scouse**.

scrag¹ *vb*
1. *British* to torment, tease, attack, beat up. A schoolboy term dating from the 19th century.

2. *American* to kill, destroy. An underworld term adopted by black street gangs in the 1980s. In 18th- and 19th-century British slang scrag was used to mean 'execute by hanging', strangle or grab by the neck. The word is originally a Scottish dialect term for neck and is related to 'crag'.

3. *American* to copulate (with)

scrag² *n British*
a foolish and/or annoying person. The word, an archaic term for a thin or bony person or animal, has been used in this way since around 2000 by adolescents.

scram *vb*
to leave quickly, go away. Nearly always heard in the form of a brusque dismissal, the word is a shortening of 'scramble', first used in the USA at the turn of the 20th century. (The **pig Latin** version of the term is **amscray**.)

scran *n British*
food. The word is used throughout the armed services and by some civilians, particularly public schoolchildren and students. It comes originally from Romany and has been employed since the 18th century to mean victuals, scraps or leftovers.

All we want to know is where we can get some decent scran in a hurry.

scrapaloids, scrapoids, scrappers *n pl British*
underpants. An item of student slang in use in London and elsewhere since around 2000.

scrat n

an ugly or unattractive female. A term used by young street-gang members in London since around 2000.

scratch n

cash, ready money. This sense of the word has been in use since the end of the 19th century. It is either derived from the notion of 'scratching a living' or of banknotes which are 'up to scratch', i.e. genuine.

> 'What about you Charlie; why don't you try to come up with some scratch for a change.'
>
> (The Late Show, US film, 1977)

scratcher n British

a match, in the jargon of prisoners since the early years of the 20th century

scratchy adj

irritable or bad-tempered and over-sensitive. Predominantly American with rustic overtones, the word is a synonym for 'prickly' or 'tetchy'.

scratter n British

a synonym for **chav** recorded in 2004

scream n American

ice cream. A conflated form heard among adolescents.

screamer n

a flagrant homosexual. A derogatory term used typically by flagrant heterosexuals, derived from 'screaming queen/nancy', etc. The word is heard in Britain and Australia.

screaming (h)abdabs n pl British

a state of mental agitation bordering on hysteria. Usually heard in the phrase 'It gives me (a case of) the screaming abdabs': it makes me extremely irritated, agitated.

screw[1] vb

1. to have sex (with). This use of the word was recorded in Grose's Dictionary of the Vulgar Tongue in 1785. It may be a direct metaphor or may be influenced by the archaic use of screw to mean a key (turning in a lock). Since the late 1960s the verb can refer to the sexual act from the woman's point of view as well as the man's. The word owed much of its popularity to the fact that it is a synonym for **fuck** which is nevertheless acceptable in the media and what used to be referred to as 'mixed company'.

2a. to take advantage of, defraud, cheat or treat unfairly

2b. to ruin or spoil. An extension of the previous sense paralleled by **fuck**, **bugger**, etc.

3. British to stare (at). In working-class London speech, especially among **skinheads** of the late 1960s, the question 'Who're you screwin'?' was often the prelude to violence. It has been suggested that this use of the word is in origin a shortening of scrutinise, but this seems hard to credit. Screwing up one's eyes or metaphorically boring a hole into someone are other possibilities.

> 'Villains call it clocking in Leeds, eyeballing in Manchester and screwing in London's East End ... It came as a shock: juries can be intimidated by a stare.'
>
> (Sunday Times, 5 June 1988)

4. British to rob, in the argot of the underworld

screw[2] n

1a. an act of sexual intercourse

1b. a sexual partner

Both usages derive from the verb form.

2. British a prison guard. This is the standard term applied to prison officers by inmates since the 19th century. It derives from the archaic use of the same word to mean key. Thus 'turnscrew', later shortened to screw, was a synonym for 'turnkey'.

> 'A banner was draped from the cell windows reading: Support the screws – Old Bill out.'
>
> (Guardian, 31 January 1989)

3. an income, wage or salary. In this sense, first recorded in the mid-19th century, the word almost invariably occurs as part of the common phrase '(on) a good screw'.

screw around vb

1. to 'mess about', behave clumsily, irresponsibly or irresolutely. The phrase, which is particularly popular in the USA, is a milder form of **fuck around/about**.

2. to behave in a sexually promiscuous way. A more brusque version of 'sleep around'.

> 'Even pre-teens are screwing around these days.'
>
> (Recorded, London student, March 2002)

screwing n

to be annoyed, angry. A term used by young street-gang members in London since around 2000.

screw up *vb*

1a. to make a mess or mistake, perform ineptly, fail, ruin. This phrase was in predominantly American currency until the late 1960s.

1b. to traumatize, render maladjusted

She claims she's been screwed up by her upbringing.

scrinchy *adj British*

grumpy, bad tempered, angry. An item of student slang in use in London and elsewhere since around 2000.

scripaloids, scripoids, scrippers *n pl British*

underpants. An item of student slang in use in London and elsewhere since around 2000.

script *n*

a drug prescription. The word has been used since the 1950s by drug users and by the police and some doctors.

I got him to give me a script for methadone.

They were trying to sell some stolen blank scripts.

scrog *vb*

to grope. The word can refer to a mock-sexual attack or to consensual petting. It has been recorded among UK armed forces personnel and US adolescents.

'Did you see them scrogging outside the dorm last night?'

(Recorded, student, North Carolina, 2000)

scrote *n British*

1a. a non-specific term of abuse used, and perhaps invented by Clement and la Frenais in their 1970s TV comedy *Porridge* (set in a prison). It is presumably inspired by scrotum.

'One man in the West Belfast area said they (British paratroopers) had a nickname for us – it was scrotes ... they were young guys and aggressive.'

(*Sunday Times*, 29 January 1995)

1b. a synonym for **crustie** or **smellie**, in use among the homeless, travellers, etc.

scrub *n*

defined in 2000 as 'a useless and worthless male who has huge misconceptions of his own brilliance', the word is part of the hip hop and **rap** lexicon. **Busta** is a synonym.

We don't want no scrubs hittin' on us!

He ain't nothing but a scrub.

scrubber *n British*

a coarse, vulgar and/or promiscuous female. This now common term was first heard in the 1920s. 'Scrub' had been used to mean a shabby or seedy person or a prostitute since the 18th century. Scrubber, like 'scrub', derives from the notion of having to scrape and forage for food or money, rather than to scrub floors, etc.

scrud *n British*

an unpleasant and/or obnoxious person. In playground usage since 2000.

scrumming *n British*

eating. The word (as a transitive verb 'scrum' is rare), which is typically used by middle- or upper-class speakers, often denotes voracious or exuberant feeding and is probably inspired by 'scrumptious'.

As far as I can tell, he's been scrumming non-stop all day.

scrummy *adj British*

attractive, delectable, excellent. A blend of 'scrumptious' and 'yummy', used particularly by middle-class speakers.

'Actually, I thought he was rather scrummy really.'

(Recorded, female public relations consultant, London, 1994)

scrump *vb American*

to have sex. The verb, which in slang is usually intransitive or in the form 'scrumping', is inspired by the old term for stealing apples (itself British dialect related to 'scrounge' and 'scrimp'), and is perhaps also influenced by other words such as **screw** and 'rump'.

scrut *n*

an ugly or unattractive female. Defined on the Student World website in 2001 as 'a dirty fat girl'.

scuds *n pl British*

underpants. The term has been recorded in use among younger speakers since 2000, and used in cartoons in *Viz* comic.

scuff *vb British*

to attack, beat up. A term used by young street-gang members in London since around 2000.

They scuffed him.

She got scuffed.

scuffer *n British*

a police officer. This word (more often heard in the plural) originated in the

Liverpool area. It derives from dialect terms associated with 'shuffle', 'scuff' and 'cuff' (in the sense of a blow).

scumbag n American

a despicable person. This term of abuse is now widespread and is permitted in the broadcast media, in spite of the fact that its origin, unknown to many of its users, is as an obscene euphemism for condom; 'scum' being an obsolescent American term for semen. The word was adopted by British speakers around 1985.

'Even scumbags have rights here in the USA.'

(Red Heat, US film, 1988)

scummer n British

a synonym for **chav**. The term was posted on the b3ta website in 2004.

scum-sucker n American

a despicable, contemptible or degenerate person. This word, originally synonymous with **cocksucker** in that 'scum' is an obsolescent American slang term for semen, is now often used as if it were a milder, euphemistic epithet.

scum-sucking adj American

disgusting, contemptible. The word is usually employed as a meaningless intensifier in longer terms of abuse. (For the original sense see **scum-sucker**.)

This scum-sucking low-life deserves to die!

scungy adj Australian

dirty, messy, unkempt or sordid. The word is probably a coinage blending the sounds and connotations of such words as 'scurvy', 'mangy' and **gunge**. It may alternatively be influenced by **scunner**.

scunner n British

a despicable, traitorous or devious person. This unusual word has spread beyond its origins in Scottish dialect and is occasionally heard throughout the north and Midlands of England.

scutting n British

having sex. The term was recorded in the Midlands and north of England in 2004, usually in the noun form although occasionally as the transitive or intransitive verb **scut**. It may be an arbitrary coinage, or a dialect term perhaps related to scut meaning the short tail of a rabbit or deer.

All she thinks about is shopping and scutting.

scuttlebutt n American

gossip or rumour. The scuttlebutt was a cask or fountain of drinking water on board naval ships, around which news was exchanged.

'I hear some scuttlebutt says he likes to kick the ladies around.'

(Night Game, US film, 1988)

scuzz n American

1a. dirt, seediness, anything distasteful. The word has been widely used since the late 1960s and probably postdates the adjective form **scuzzy**. The word had been picked up by some British speakers by the 1980s.

'Foul-mouthed critics and their lairs – Old Compton St, the Coach and Horses, Private Eye, The Spectator, Fleet Street Freelancer – the whole scuzz world of journalism is here in black and white (albeit seen through the bottom of a glass).'

(I-D magazine, November 1987)

1a. also **scuzzball** or **scuzzbag** or **scuzzo** a disreputable, unpleasant, unattractive or worthless person. A derivative of **scuzzy** which has been popular since the early 1970s.

'Impeachment: how much of a scuzzball is Hastert?'

(Posted on Daily Kos website, 19 June 2005)

scuzzed out adj

disgusted. A more recent synonym of **grossed out**, based on **scuzzy** and **scuzz**.

scuzz-hole n

a dirty, unpleasant place

'K- F- Hotel, Reading. What a scuzz-hole!'

(Online review, November 2004)

scuzzy adj American

dirty, unpleasant, distasteful, shabby and disreputable. This word, which is used particularly by young people, may be a nursery version of 'disgusting' or an invention influenced by 'scum' and 'fuzz'. Scuzzy has been heard in North America since the late 1960s but to date has not been adopted elsewhere, except by a handful of journalists.

seeing-to n British

1a. a beating-up, an assault. A typically understated, hence menacing euphemism in working-class, police and criminal usage.

He's asking for a seeing-to.

1b. a sexual act; specifically the sexual 'possession' of a woman by a man. The word has simultaneous and revealing overtones of brusque, no-nonsense domination, of a duty accomplished and of an unaffectionate resolution.

Well, I gave her a good seeing-to, didn't I.

seeking action *n British*
looking for sexual contact. An item of student slang in use in London and elsewhere since around 2000.

seen *exclamation British*
an all-purpose expression of agreement, thanks, approval, solidarity, etc. The word began as part of the code of street gangs in the early 1990s (like **safe**), probably meaning something like 'observed and noted' or 'under surveillance'. It was still in use as a vogue term among teenagers in 2004. **Skeen** is a later version.

seized *adj British*
drunk. An item of black street-talk used especially by males, recorded in 2003.

semi *n British*
a partial erection. **Lob-on** is a contemporary synonym.

send *vb*
to transport emotionally or intellectually. This supposed **beatnik** term of the late 1950s (originating among US jazz musicians in the 1940s) was used to characterise **hip** youth in various unhip media.

I just love Elvis. He sends me!

sent down *adj British*
sentenced to imprisonment, imprisoned. This euphemism, also used to mean expelled from university, has been in currency since the 19th century. The phrase may originate in the image of the convict descending the steps from the dock.

sent up *adj American*
imprisoned. The American version of **sent down**. Sent up has been in use since the late 19th century; it may be derived from the archaic slang sense of 'upriver' as imprisoned. In Britain, to be 'sent up' is to be imitated in a parodic manner.

septic *n*
an American. A piece of rhyming slang, from 'septic tank': **Yank**. The word was first recorded being applied by Australians to visiting American servicemen during World War II. It is in continued currency among the younger generation in Australia and the UK (**Sherman (tank)** is a British synonym.)

serving up *n British*
dealing drugs. An item of black streettalk used especially by males, recorded in 2003. Synonyms are **cutting**, **shotting**.

sesh *n British*
1. a drinking bout. A shortening of '(drinking) session' used typically by middle-class youths in Britain from the late 1980s.

We had a good sesh last night.

2. romantic play or sexual petting. In this sense the abbreviation is typically used by teenage girls.

set *n*
the fashionable word for gang in the 1990s argot of the Los Angeles **rap** and street-gang subcultures

'I ain't nothing without my set. They the only ones who care.'
(*Grand Canyon*, US film, 1991)

severe *adj*
impressive, excellent. An all-purpose vogue term of approval used first by British **mods** in 1963 and 1964 and later by American teenagers and their British imitators in the 1970s and 1980s.

'How did she look?' 'Severe, man!'
That's a really severe shirt.

sexing *vb British*
having sex. A term used by young children.

'Fraser said he saw someone in a car sexing.'
(Recorded, 8-year-old, London, 1988)

sex up *vb*
1a. to increase the sexual content (of a publication, broadcast, etc.)
1b. to modify in order to render more exciting, compelling, dramatic
A term probably originating in US media or showbiz circles, given prominence by its use in connection with the pre-invasion Iraq dossier compiled for the UK government in 2004.

sh- *prefix*
this form is generally preferred in this dictionary for the many words of Yiddish origin which exist in modern English slang. Certain terms are recorded under the alternative (German) **sch-** when there is evidence of their prevalence in that form.

shabby *adj*
1. bad
2. good
The Kaiser Chiefs did a well shabby set.
The standard term has been used in these senses by adolescents in the UK and USA

since around 2000.

shack *vb American*
to stab (someone). The word was used by prison inmates and members of the underworld.

shackout *vb British*
to run away, escape, leave hurriedly. A term used by young street-gang members in London since around 2000.

shack up *vb*
to live with someone in a sexual relationship outside marriage. Such a relationship is sometimes known as a 'shack-up'. The term was an Americanism first used by itinerants and marginals between the World Wars; it was adopted into World English during the 1960s.

shade *n American*
a receiver of stolen goods, **fence**. The word, an item of slang from the police and underworld lexicon, in use since the 1920s may be derived from 'shady' (dealing).

shades *n pl*
sunglasses. The word was first used in this sense in the USA in the 1940s. (Shades are blinds in American English.)

shady *adj American*
of dubious quality, potentially dangerous. A synonym of **sketch(y)** and **dodgy**.

shaft[1] *n*
1. the penis. A predictable but rare use of the standard term.
2a. a sex partner
   A good shaft.
These usages are back-formations from the verb.
2b. an act of sexual intercourse
   a quick shaft
3. the shaft an alternative form of a **shafting**. It usually occurs in the form 'get the shaft'.

shaft[2] *vb*
1. to have sex with, penetrate. From the noun **shaft**, denoting the penis.
2. to ruin, damage, destroy (someone). Most often heard in the form of the past participle 'shafted', this term is another example of a slang word literally meaning to have sex with someone used metaphorically to mean humiliate or abase.
   I tell you, we were well and truly shafted over that Abco deal.
Compare **fuck**; **bugger**; **roger**; **screw**

shafting *n*
an instance of extremely harsh, ruinous and/or unfair treatment. The term derives from the sexual senses of the verb to **shaft**.

shag[1] *vb*
1. to have sex (with). A common vulgarism in Britain and Australia which is unknown in this sense in the USA. The word is an archaic relative of 'shake', which was used in a sexual sense from at least the 16th century. In Britain shag took over the taboo role in the 18th century. In modern usage the word is considered less offensive than **fuck** in male company, but more vulgar than other synonyms. Like 'fuck' it occurs in other forms, such as the noun **shag**, the intensifying adjective 'shagging' and phrases such as 'shag off'.
   'When I was 17 I was obsessively in love with a girl who only liked me. It blighted my adolescence. I would have given anything to shag her.'
   (Ben Elton, quoted in *NME*, March 1989)
2. *American* to depart, leave. The 1990s use of the term, which may be related to earlier uses of the word to denote a fast jitterbug-style dance or later a reluctant, shuffling walk, also occurs in the phrase 'shag off/out'. By the 18th century shag had come to mean 'move quickly' in American speech.

shag[2] *n British*
1. a sexual act or a sexual partner. See the verb form for origins.
2. a term of endearment in use among London financial traders in 2000, probably from earlier public-school usage

shagadelic *adj*
excellent. A jocular coinage from the sexual sense of **shag** and 'psychedelic' used, usually ironically, by US and UK teenagers since around 2000.

shagged out, shagged *adj British*
exhausted, worn out. The vulgar origin of the phrase (tired out from sexual activity) is partially forgotten in the modern usage wherein the expression serves as a more robust version of **knackered**.
   Listen. I really can't make it, I'm feeling absolutely shagged.

shaggin' wagon, shag-wagon *n*
a more vulgar term for **passion wagon** or 'draggin' wagon'. This form of the expression is heard in Britain and Australia.

> *Old Gregory turned up in a brand new shaggin' wagon.*

shag-monster *n British*
a promiscuous or sexually active person. The term can be used either pejoratively or appreciatively.

> *'Lyrics like "We should both go to bed until we make each other sore"... have seen [singer Louise Wener] labelled a "sluttish shag-monster"...'*
> (*The Big Issue*, 6 March 1995)

shake *vb*
1. *British* to alert, rouse, summon. This use of the word, obviously deriving from the literal shaking of someone to wake them, is now employed as part of police, underworld and working-class jargon.

> *'The solicitors ... We'll shake them for you.'*
> (*Flying Squad*, British TV documentary, March 1989)

2. *American* to search or stop and harass (a suspect). The word, used by police and criminals, is a shortening of the more familiar **shake down**.

shake down *vb American*
1. to extort money from (someone), either face-to-face (usually by threats) or by blackmail
2. to search a person or premises. The phrase usually refers to an official search by police officers which may involve a degree of harassment or force.

shakedown *n American*
1. an act of extortion or blackmail
2. a search of a person or premises, usually by police officers

shamed-up *adj British*
humiliated, shamed. A 'buzz-term' among teenagers in the 1980s, from the admonitory catchphrase 'take the shame!'. This playground phrase is from black slang.

shampoo *n*
champagne. A **Sloane ranger** and **yuppie** witticism of the 1980s. The word is often abbreviated to **poo**. In the USA **preppies** and others also use the terms.

shandy *n British*
a weakling, person unable or unwilling to take strong drink. Not to be confused with **hand shandy**.

shank *n American*
a homemade knife. A term used in prisons and by the members of street gangs since the 1950s. In standard English shank denotes the shaft or connecting rod of a tool or instrument.

sharking *n British*
pursuing members of the opposite sex. This item of Oxbridge slang of the 1990s often denotes aggressive or devious attempts at seduction, usually on the part of males. By 2004 it was heard across the UK.

Sharon *n British*
the female equivalent of a **Kevin** or **Wayne**. The name is used to designate a supposedly typical (and by implication uncultured) working-class young woman. These generic epithets were coined in the 1970s for the purpose of social stereotyping. (In 1965 Sharon was the tenth most popular Christian name for new-born girls in Britain.) A quintessential 'common' female, invariably with a cockney estuary English accent, typified by white trainers, loud clothing and much gold jewellery.

> *'A thousand slavish Sharons copied Diana's wedding look, as they did her flicked 'n' sprayed hairstyle.'*
> (Judy Rumbold, *Guardian*, 11 December 1989)

sharpies *n pl Australian*
members of a short-lived teenage youth movement of the 1950s who were contemporaries of the **bodgies** and **widgies**. Sharpies were short-haired, aggressive and less flamboyant than the **teddy boy**-like bodgies.

shatter *n British See* **top shatter**

shat upon *adj*
humiliated, slighted, victimised or punished. Shat is a past tense of the verb to **shit**.

shedloads *n British*
a disguised version of the more vulgar **shitloads**, meaning a large quantity. The expression was popular among City of London traders in the late 1990s.

> *'... how can a T & G sponsored prime minister break it to the union which gives his party shedloads of money that the marriage is over?'*
> (*Private Eye*, 11 July 1997)

sheeny *n*
a Jew. The term appeared in Britain in the early 19th century when it did not

necessarily have the offensive racist overtones it acquired in the 20th century. Many possible etymologies have been proposed for sheeny: the three most plausible are the German word *schön* (beautiful) as applied either to their children or to merchandise by Jews, the 'sheen' of dark hair or skin as perceived by Anglo-Saxons, or the Yiddish phrase *a miesse meshina* ('an ugly fate or death'), a phrase supposedly common among Jews.

sheep-dip *n*
low-quality alcoholic drink

sheepdog *n Australian*
a brassière. The jocular usage, invariably heard in male speech, is based on the notion that, like the bra, the dog 'rounds them up and keeps them together'.

sheepshagger *n British*
a rustic, bumpkin or primitive. A vulgarism heard since the 19th century.

> 'Uni is over and I'll never see you pathological sheepshaggers again!'
> (Posted on online student blog, December 2004)

sheet *n British*
an official report. An item of prison jargon recorded in the 1990s in Brixton and Wandsworth prisons.

Sheila *n Australian*
a woman. This well-known Australianism, although old-fashioned, is still heard. It is an alteration of an earlier word *shaler* (meaning 'young woman'), of Gaelic origin, which was used by Irish immigrants. The word became a generic term for females, the feminine counterpart of **Paddy**, and was altered to coincide with the female Christian name.

> 'Cripes! I was nearly up shit creek that time. Now I'm stuck with this po-faced Sheila!'
> (Barry Humphries and Nicholas Garland, *The Wonderful World of Barry McKenzie*, 1988)

shell *n American*
1. a dollar. This usage may recall the use of cowries and other sea shells as currency, or come from the verb to 'shell out' (in which shell refers to the shell or pod containing seeds). **Clams** is a synonym.
2. a beer, beercan. This rare sense of the word may conceivably draw a comparison between empty beer cans and discarded (ammunition) shell cases.

shellacked *adj*
drunk. A term originating in the USA in the 1920s; 'shellack' (its standard meaning being to apply varnish) first meant to beat or punish; this was then extended to denote the effects of alcohol.

shellacking *n*
a beating, defeat. A humorous borrowing of the standard term meaning to slap on shellac, a resin used for varnishing and insulation. The slang sense arose in the USA where it is still heard; it is not unknown in British speech.

sherbert *n British*
an alcoholic drink. A term first heard in the raffish or jocular speech of the colonial era, since the late 1990s in use among adolescents.

sheriff *n British*
a fifty-pence coin. The nickname comes from the supposed resemblance to a western sheriff's star.

Sherman (tank) *n British*
1. a native of the USA, **Yank**. A piece of rhyming slang playing on the name of the World War II vehicle.
2. an act of masturbation, a **wank**. A probably ephemeral piece of rhyming slang of the late 1980s, quoted for instance in Steve Bell's *If* comic strip in the *Guardian*.

shibby¹ *adj American*
excellent, attractive. A vogue term since 2000 when it featured in the US comedy film *Dude, Where's My Car?* It is probably inspired by the noun form.

shibby² *n American*
cannabis. The word is of uncertain origin but may be an alteration of the earlier **chiba**.

shickered, shikkered, shicker *adj*
drunk. The word is used primarily in the USA and Australia. It is from *shikker*, the Yiddish word for inebriated, which itself is from the Hebrew *shikor*.

> 'You're stoned, Bazza!
> Come off it – just a bit shicker.'
> (*Bazza Comes into His Own*, cartoon by Barry Humphries and Nicholas Garland, 1988)

shif(t) *vb British*
to run for it

shift *vb, n Irish*
(to have) sexual intercourse. The usage was explained to a British audience by

the stand-up comedian Jo Brand in her 1995 TV show.

shikse, shiksa *n American*
a non-Jewish female. A Yiddish term used by Jews of gentiles often, but nowadays not always, pejoratively.

shill *n*
a con-man's accomplice. The word has been used since the 19th century to denote a decoy or agent planted in a crowd to stimulate trade or encourage spending. Nowadays it usually refers to a participant in a rigged card game or other fraud. The origin of the term is unclear; it is said to be based either on a proper name such as Shillibeer or on an archaic dialect form of 'skill'.

shinaton *n*
a girl who gives a lot of oral sex. The term is probably an Afro-Caribbean pronunciation of 'shinathon', an imaginary event combining shiner(s), fellator(s) and marathon.

shine[1] *n American*
a black person. This now dated, usually pejorative term from the early 20th century (used by Raymond Chandler among others when describing the Los Angeles low-life of the 1940s) is still occasionally heard. The origin of this usage is obscure; it may be inspired by the appearance of black skin or contrasting white teeth, or may even be a shortening of 'shoe-shine'.

shine[2] *vb American*
to snub, reject. The term is probably a back-formation of the earlier **shined-on**.

'Let's face it, she shined you.'
(*California Man*, US film, 1992)

shined-on *adj American*
ignored, disregarded. Its origin may be by analogy with **mooning** (showing one's buttocks as a gesture of contempt) or connected with the noun **shine**, meaning a black person, hence a social inferior, or more poetically may derive from the image of the moon shining down with cold indifference.

I'm not going to be shined-on! I think I deserve some attention.

shiners *n*
1a. fellatio
1b. a girl giving oral sex
The term, heard among gang members, hip hop aficionados and schoolchildren in London since 2000, is probably in origin a shortening of 'knob-shiner'.

shine the fireman's helmet *vb British*
to masturbate (a male) or fellate

'I was having my fireman's helmet shined.'
(Posted on Alaskan 'flirting' website, June 2005)

shirt-lifter *n*
a male homosexual. An Australian euphemism used pejoratively but usually humorously. The phrase originated in the 1960s and had been adopted by some British speakers by the late 1970s. (The Melbourne satirist Barry Humphries has frequently used the term and has coined 'chemise-lifter' as a lesbian counterpart.)

shit[1] *n*
1a. excrement. This word of Anglo-Saxon origin has parallels in other Germanic languages (e.g. in modern German *Scheisse*). It derives from an ancient common verb, imitative of the sound of defecation. In English shit is now a mild vulgarism, although in rustic speech it has been the standard term for centuries.
1b. an act of defecation, usually in phrases such as 'have/take a shit'
1c. a contemptible person. This usage conveys real dislike or disapproval and has been common, particularly in upper- and middle-class speech in Britain since the 1920s.

'Tiny 19-year-old Mark Aldrich beat up two youths who called him "a little shit" – but the comment "could be appropriate" a judge said yesterday.'
(*Daily Mirror*, 10 September 1988)

1d. an illicit drug, especially hashish. In the 1950s heroin users referred to their drug as shit; by the mid-1960s the word usually designated hashish (which is characteristically brown) or marihuana. When used in this context the word is synonymous with 'stuff' and carries virtually no pejorative overtones.

Hey, this is excellent shit, man.

'P.S. I cannot get any shit, my friends have split to other lands, they are free.'
(Reader's letter in *Oz* magazine, February 1970)

1e. rubbish, something worthless or inferior
1f. nonsense, lies or deceitful talk. This is a specific use of shit as something worthless, or simply a shortening of **bullshit**.

Come on, don't give me that shit, I wasn't born yesterday.

1g. unnecessarily hostile behaviour or ill-treatment

'I'm definitely not going to take any more shit from any of them.'

(Recorded, disgruntled office worker, London, 2005)

shit² *vb*

1. to defecate. The verb probably pre-dates the noun form. Both seem to have existed in Old English, deriving from a common Germanic ancestor, itself cognate with the Greek *skat-* (later giving 'scatological'). Used intransitively the verb is now probably rarer than phrases such as 'have a shit'. (The usual past form in British English is 'shat', in American 'shit'.)

2a. to deceive, bamboozle, confuse (someone)

2b. to browbeat or annoy (someone)

These transitive usages may originate as short forms of the verb **bullshit**, but have taken on separate identities as a designation, usually in American speech, of time-wasting or harassment by lies or deceit.

shit³ *adj*

1. awful, inferior. A simple transference of the noun form, popular especially in British youth parlance of the 1980s.

a shit record

2. *American* excellent, admirable. In the **hip** language of the street, of **rap** and hip hop practitioners and their teenage imitators, shit has been used with this unexpected sense. The probable explanation is that it is a shortening of **shit-hot**.

shit a brick, shit bricks *vb*

to panic, be in a state of nervous apprehension. 'Shit a brick!' is sometimes used as an exclamation of surprise or irritation.

shit and derision *n British*

a terrible state of affairs, confusion, mess. A mainly middle-class term typically used ruefully or humorously.

shit-ass *adj American*

very unpleasant, worthless, contemptible. Used especially in Canadian English, in much the same way as **shithouse** in Australia.

shitbag *n British*

an obnoxious or unpleasant person. A term which was widespread in the 1960s but is now less common.

shitcan *vb*

1a. *Australian* to denigrate, to **rubbish**. The word is used to signify the upbraid-

ing or insulting of someone who deserves to be humiliated.

1b. *American* to throw away, reject

Both senses derive from the noun shitcan as a toilet receptacle or rubbish bin.

shite *n British*

a variant form of **shit**, heard particularly in northern English speech

shit-eating grin *n*

a facial expression showing extreme (usually malicious) satisfaction. Originally an Americanism, the expression is now also heard elsewhere.

'I didn't want to see the shit-eating grins on the cozzers' faces.'

(Jimmy Robinson, released prisoner speaking on the BBC TV programme *Panorama*, 24 February 1997)

shitfaced *adj American*

drunk, helplessly or squalidly intoxicated. The term was particularly in vogue in the mid-1970s.

She was totally shitfaced.

Let's get shitfaced.

shit-fit *n*

a bout of anger or intense irritation, etc. The term probably originated in the US, but by the mid-1990s was common throughout the English-speaking world.

'Look at this mess! Lloyd is going to have a shit-fit.'

(*A Passion for Murder*, US film, 1993)

shit-for-brains *n*

a very stupid person. This term of abuse, deriving from an earlier rustic expression on the lines of 'he/she must have shit-for-brains', has been widespread in the USA and Australia since the 1970s. It is now sometimes used adjectivally, as in 'a shit-for-brains idea'.

shithead *n*

1a. a despicably unpleasant or unfriendly person. This sense of the word has been predominant since the 1970s.

1b. a stupid or foolish person

2. a hashish smoker. This sense of the word was briefly current from the mid-1960s, before being replaced by synonyms such as **doper**, etc. (**Pothead** was a less contentious or ambiguous synonym.)

shitheel *n American*

an unpleasant or obnoxious person. An embellished form of the milder and more common 'heel'.

'I suffer no such illusion, having had first-hand experience at the hands of that world-class misogynistic shitheel.'
(Posting on a Canadian blog, November 2004)

shit-hot *adj*
1a. first-rate, excellent, powerful or dynamic
1b. very keen, enthusiastic or punctilious. Shit here is used as an intensifier rather than a metaphor.

shithouse¹ *n*
1a. a toilet
1b. a dirty or untidy place

shithouse² *adj*
terrible, inferior, worthless. This elaboration of **shit** or **shitty** is particularly common in Australian speech.

shit-kicker *n*
1. a lowly menial, humble worker or rustic. An alternative to 'shit-shoveller' heard particularly in the USA and Australia.
2. a dynamic or energetic person

shit-kicking *adj*
wild, earthy, primitive. The word is used especially in the context of country or rock music and signals approval rather than criticism.
some stomping, howling, shit-kicking rhythm 'n' blues

shit-licked *adj*
drunk. A variant form of the earlier **shit-faced**.

shit-list *n American*
a real or imaginary black list; either as kept by organisations or individuals
Jerry's top of my shit-list this week.
I think I'm on the shit-list of every bar in town.

shit-load, shitloads *n*
an enormous amount or quantity. The term originated in US speech, but by the mid-1990s was heard throughout the English-speaking world. **Shedloads** is a British euphemism.
We're in shitloads of trouble here.
'What about the Mets? I bet you won a shit-load of money!'
(*Bad Lieutenant*, US film, 1994)

shit oneself *vb*
to be overcome with fear or panic

shit on one's own doorstep *vb British*
to do something damaging or unpardonable which will rebound upon oneself or one's friends; to ruin one's own environment. This expression, like the politer

'foul the nest', has equivalents in most European languages (normally involving beds rather than doorsteps).

shit on wheels *n American*
an extremely adept or adroit person. The phrase is based on the notion of 'a slippery customer'.

shit-parade *n American*
an alternative form of **shit-list**

shits, the *n*
1a. diarrhoea
1b. a feeling of annoyance, disgust or bitter resentment. This figurative sense of the preceding vulgarism seems to be acquiring a separate identity, usually in the form 'it/he/she gives me the shits'.

shit-scared *adj British*
terrified. An intensive form of the standard adjective.

shit-sheet *n American*
a police file (recording criminal activity) or school report (particularly one recording poor results)

shit-storm *n American*
a spectacular fuss and/or mess

shitter, the *n*
1. a toilet
2. the anus

shitty *adj*
1a. unpleasant, unfair. The word may mean merely bad or nasty, but usually carries overtones of resentment on the part of the speaker.
That was a really shitty thing to do.
1b. inferior, poor quality
That cassette machine's got shitty sound.

shiv *n*
a knife. An alternative rendering of **chiv**, a Romany word used in British underworld and low-life milieus since the 17th century. In the 20th century the word was used (also in the USA) to mean any bladed weapon, including homemade knives and razors. Shiv was also used as a verb, particularly in the argot of street gangs of the 1950s and early 1960s.

shizit *n, vb American*
a disguised or playfully altered form of **shit**

shizzle my nizzle, shizza my nizza *exclamation*
an expression of strong agreement, an alteration or disguising of 'for sure, my nigga', using the vogue combining form **-izzle**, recorded in 2004

shlemiel *n See* **schlemiel**

shlep[1], schlepp *vb*

1a. to drag, haul, pull or carry

1b. to drag oneself, move or travel with difficulty. This is the Yiddish version of the German verb *schleppen*, meaning to drag. It has entered English slang via the American underworld and entertainment industry.

    'I don't want to shlep all the way down there.'
    (*Budgie*, British TV series, 1971)

shlep[2], schlepp *n*

1. a long, tedious or tiring journey or burdensome task. The noun form is based on the verb.

    I hate having to go there – it's a real shlep up that hill.

2. *American* a tedious, feeble or irritating person. This sense of the term is inspired by the notion of burden and drag (literally and metaphorically) in the verb to **shlep**.

shlepper, schlepper *n*

1. a clumsy, inept and/or irritating person

2. *American* a cadger, scrounger or hustler

3. a sluttish, slovenly and/or immoral person

All the senses of shlepper, which encompass a number of nuances and connotations, derive ultimately from the verb **shlep** with its suggestions of burdensome activity. In British English sense 3 has been extended to denote a prostitute in London slang.

shlock *n*

anything shoddy, inferior or meretricious. The word is Yiddish from German (either *schlacke*: dregs, or *schlagen*: slap or knock, in the sense of jacking up prices or damaged goods). The main application of shlock in American, and later British, slang has been to the products of the entertainment industry, particularly films and television.

shlong *n See* **schlong[1]**

shlub *n See* **schlub**

shm- *prefix*

this is the spelling representing the initial sound of many slang terms of Yiddish origin (also **sch-** and **sh-**). Jewish wits and their emulators substitute these letters for the standard beginnings of English words to indicate mockery or negation.

    'Revolution; Shmevolution.'
    (Headline in *Wall Street Journal*, January 1968)

    'It's not the season for beagling. Season shmeason!'
    (*Ticket to Ride*, British TV series, 1988)

shmarmy *adj British*

smarmy, offensively ingratiating or smug. This new pronunciation of the common colloquialism represents a late 1980s phenomenon in fashionable and youth circles whereby certain words are altered to resemble the many words of Yiddish origin beginning with **sh-**.

    'That shmarmy man in the coffee advert.'
    (Interview, *Making the Break*, British TV documentary about advertising, 1989)

shmear *n*

a term of Yiddish origin literally meaning a smear or spreading-out, but now also denoting a complete state of affairs, situation or scenario

    'The Goldmark Gallery, in the person of the friendly and efficient greeter, Sally Jones, demystifies the whole, schmear.'
    (*Lights Out for the Territory*, Iain Sinclair, 1997)

shmeg *n British*

an idiot. A schoolchildren's term, fashionable from the 1980s, which is a variant form of **smeg** or **smeggy** (from smegma), a word popular among young males in the **punk** era. The altered pronunciation is influenced by Yiddish words such as **schmock**, **schmuck**, **schmendrick**, etc.

shmegegge, shmegeggy *n American*

a contemptible or foolish person. The word is Yiddish, but seems to have been an American coinage, often heard in show-business circles. It does not appear to derive from any older term.

shmendrik *n See* **schmendrick**

shmo, shmoe *n*

a fool, 'sucker' or **jerk**. The word was invented in the USA as an acceptable euphemism for the Yiddish **schmuck** in the late 1940s when the latter term was understood in its literal and obscene sense. Shmo, like 'shmuck', has been heard in Britain in Jewish and non-Jewish circles since the 1950s.

    She seems to like him but the guy's a bit of a shmo if you ask me.

shmooze, shmoose *vb American*

to chat or gossip at length, to have a heart-to-heart talk. This American Yiddish word comes from the Hebrew *shmous*, meaning 'things heard'. The word, spoken with a hard or soft final 's', has overtones of intimacy and affection rather than malicious gossip.

shmuck *n See* **schmuck**

shmutter *n See* **schmutter**

shnide *adj British*

snide (in both its standard sense of sneering and its slang sense of counterfeit). This quasi-Yiddish pronunciation has been popular with the **hip** young and some working-class speakers since the 1950s; other words are having their pronunciation altered in a similar fashion (**shmarmy** and **shmeg**, for instance). In this case the speakers may be reproducing the original pronunciation (*see* **snide** for the origins of the word).
See also **jekyll**

shnorrer *n*
a cadger, scrounger or hustler. This is a Yiddish word occasionally used by non-Jewish speakers, particularly in the USA, to refer to a sponger or parasite. It derives from the German verb *schnorren*, meaning to beg (itself from *schnurren*, meaning to purr or whirr – the sound of a beggar's entreaties or their musical accompaniment).

shocking out *n*
dancing. The term has been used in hip hop and clubbing milieus since 2000.

shoddy *adj British*
excellent, admirable. A reversal of the standard use of the term, shoddy in this sense was a fashionable item of schoolchildren's slang in 2002 and 2003.

shoeing *n British*
fighting, brawling, attacking. In playground usage in 2003.

shonk, shonker *n British*
1. the nose, especially a large and prominent one. A synonym of **conk**, this is derived from the following sense.
2. a Jew. An offensive, racist term dating from the 19th century, when *shonniker* was a Yiddish word denoting a pedlar or small-time tradesperson.

shonkie, shonky *n, adj*
1. (a) Jew(ish). Like **shonk** and **shonker**, these words derive from *shonniker*, an archaic Yiddish term for a peddler or small-time tradesperson.
2. *American* (a person who is) mean or grasping

shoo-in *n American*
a certainty; a candidate or contestant who is certain to win. The term is inspired by the idea of a horse which

merely has to be ushered across the finishing line. The phrase is a common colloquialism in the USA which was picked up by some British journalists in the second half of the 1980s.

shoomers *n pl British*
patrons of clubs playing **acid house** music. *Shoom* was the name of one such club in London in 1988 when the cult was at its height (and before the **orbital raves** of 1989 became established). The word probably evokes the rush of euphoria experienced by users of the drug **ecstasy**.

shoot *vb*
1. *also* **shoot off** to ejaculate. The word has been used in this sense since the 19th century.
2. *also* **shoot up** to inject. A drug user's term, widespread since the late 1950s.
3. to leave hurriedly. A word used in Britain mainly by young people since the 1970s. It is probably a shortening of 'shoot off'.
I've got to shoot, I'll see you later.

shoot! *exclamation American*
an inoffensive euphemism for **shit** used as an exclamation since the 19th century

shooter *n British*
a gun. Neither a colourful nor particularly imaginative piece of slang, but the only term with any real currency, as opposed to the inventions of crime fiction.

'Standing over two corpses with a hot shooter in your hand.'
(*Twinkle, Twinkle Little Spy*, Len Deighton, 1976)

shooting gallery *n*
a place where drug users gather to inject themselves. The word has been applied to open spaces, pubs and communal flats for instance. It is an addict's pun which the police have also adopted both in Britain and the USA.

'Sam got his leg broken recently in some mysterious street-corner dispute – heading for the shooting gallery they call the Chateau Luzerne.'
(*Sunday Times*, 10 September 1989)

shoot one's bolt/load/wad *vb*
to ejaculate. These terms for the male orgasm have been in use since the 19th century.

shoot one's cookies *vb American*
an alternative form of **toss one's cookies/ tacos**

shoot the breeze/bull *vb*
to chat inconsequentially

> *'They were just standing around shooting the breeze when it all went off.'*
> (Recorded, US student, Palo Alto, October 2003)

shoot the shit *vb American*
to talk, gossip. A vulgarisation of **shoot the breeze/bull**.

shoot through *vb Australian*
1a. to die. An expression probably first introduced to an English audience via the lyrics of Rolf Harris's hit record 'Tie Me Kangaroo Down, Sport'.
1b. to leave, depart. The phrase has been in use in Australia since before World War II and is still heard.

shoot up *vb*
to inject (a narcotic)

shootzie *adj British*
fashionable, chic. This item of 1960s London **parlyaree**, recorded in the TV documentary *Out* in July 1992, is of uncertain origin. It may derive from **chutzpah**.

shop *vb British*
to inform on (someone). The noun shop meant prison in 16th-century British underworld parlance. The verb form was first used to mean imprison, then (since the first decades of the 19th century) to cause to be imprisoned. The word has become a well-known colloquialism since the 1960s; in school and prison slang it has largely been overtaken by the synonymous **grass**.

short-and-curlies, the *n pl British*
the pubic hair(s). The expressions 'got/grabbed/caught by the short-and-curlies', meaning to be rendered helpless or vulnerable, are common vulgarisms.

short arm *n*
the penis. A euphemism heard especially in the armed services; short arm is an archaic variation of 'small arm' in the sense of a handgun. 'Arm' also reflects the common notion of the penis as a limb. 'Short-arm inspection' was the medical examination for symptoms of venereal disease.

shortarse *n*
a small person. A contemptuous term heard particularly in London working-class speech and in Australia since the early years of the 20th century.

short-eyes *n American*
an underworld and prisoners' term for a child molester; the equivalent of the British **nonce**. The exact significance of the words is unclear; the phrase may be related to 'shut-eyes', an archaic term for a sex offender.

short hairs *n pl*
the pubic hair(s). A euphemism in use since the 19th century. It is most often heard figuratively in phrases such as 'they've got us by the short hairs' (i.e. at their mercy, rendered helpless).

short out *vb American*
to lose control of oneself, lose one's temper, 'blow a fuse'. The image is of an electrical system developing a short circuit.

> *He tries to keep his cool, but every now and again he shorts out.*

short-stuff *n American*
a small person. An affectionate or condescending form of address almost invariably said to a child by an adult.

shorty *n*
a girlfriend. The word is often used as a term of endearment by males, especially in black speech since 2000.

shot *n*
an injection.
See also **hotshot**

shottie *n British*
a gun. A term used by young street-gang members in London since around 2000.

shotting *n British*
dealing drugs. An item of black street-talk used especially by males, recorded in 2003. Synonyms are **cutting**, **serving up**.

shout[1] *n British*
1. a round of drinks or the ordering thereof

> *It's my shout.*

2. a message indicating an emergency, request for help, etc. (usually by radio). A piece of jargon used by police and the emergency services.

shout[2] *vb Australian*
1. *also* **shout at the floor** to vomit
2. to buy (someone) a drink, to treat someone to something

> *'Real generous…like giving me a job when I was stoney and shouting me all them chilled stubbies the other day.'*

(*The Adventures of Barry McKenzie*, cartoon strip by Barry Humphries and Nicholas Garland, 1988)

shrapnel *n British*
small change, coins. A vogue term among adolescents in the later 1990s. Unsurprisingly, the term may have come from the armed forces. Partridge has recorded that New Zealand soldiers used the word to refer to tattered banknotes in World War I. **Smash** is a synonym from the same period.

shreddies *n pl British*
revolting, tattered (shredded) underwear. A mainly middle-class usage among students and schoolchildren, punning on the name of a popular breakfast cereal. The term has been heard since the 1960s. It may possibly derive from the British rugby players' practice of 'shredding'. This involves an attempt to remove a pair of underpants from a male victim by pulling them upwards rather than downwards.

shrimping *n American*
sucking someone's toes for the purposes of sexual gratification, a jargon term among pornographers, prostitutes, etc.

shrink *n*
a psychiatrist, psychoanalyst. Shrink is a shortening of the earlier **headshrinker**, which was imported from America to Britain and Australia in the 1960s.

> *'We called in a consultant, a psychiatrist. A shrink?*
> *A highly respected doctor.'*
> (*The Dancer's Touch*, US film, 1989)

shrooms *n pl*
magic mushrooms. This abbreviated form describing hallucinogenic mushrooms probably originated in British adolescent slang in the 1990s.
Compare **rooms**

shtenkie *n, adj British*
(a person considered) obnoxious, contemptible. The term is a quasi-Yiddish deformation of 'stink(y)' and was popular among **acid house** aficionados and **ravers** from the 1990s.

shtick *n*
1a. a performance, term, act or routine, in the context of the entertainment business
1b. a piece of (repeated) behaviour characteristic of a particular person
1c. a gimmick, trick or ruse

The Yiddish word *shtik*, from Middle German *stücke*: piece, was passed via American showbiz slang into fashionable speech and journalese in the 1980s.

shtum *adj*
silent, unspeaking. Most often heard in the phrase 'keep/stay shtum': be quiet. A Yiddish term from the German *stumm*: dumb, which entered London working-class slang via Jewish influence in the East End.

shtup *vb*
to have sex (with). This Yiddish word meaning press or push (oneself) is from the German *stupsen* (push). In American slang it has come to mean copulate, in which sense it is occasionally heard in fashionable British speech since the 1980s.

> *'As any regular reader of Marie Claire magazine knows, some four out of five young French women would rather shop than shtup.'*
> (Julie Burchill, *Elle* magazine, December 1987)

> *'The big question is, did they shtup or didn't they?'*
> (Posted on online messageboard, 15 February 2005)

shubbs *n British*
a party, dance, **rave**. A term from Caribbean speech, also heard in the UK since 2000, especially among younger speakers.

shufti *n British*
a look, glance. The word is Arabic and was imported by armed service personnel before World War II.

shutzie *adj British See* **shootzie**

shway, shwey *adj American*
nice, elegant, attractive. The term has been popular among younger speakers since 2000.

shyster *n*
a dishonest, avaricious, contemptible person. The term is usually applied to unscrupulous professionals, particularly lawyers, who were the original subjects of the epithet in the USA in the mid-19th century. The etymology of shyster is open to several interpretations; *shicer* was a 19th-century anglicisation of the German *scheisser* (literally 'shitter'); 'shy' was used in the 19th century colloquially to mean disreputable. In addition there is a historical record of a lawyer named Scheuster who was offi-

cially reprimanded in New York courtrooms for obstructive and unprofessional behaviour.

shysty *adj British*
good. Of uncertain derivation, the word was used by adolescents in the southeast of England in 2002.

sianara *exclamation*
goodbye and/or 'good riddance'. The Japanese word (more properly *sayonara*) was popularised by its use in the catchphrase 'sianara, sushi boy!' in the 2001 film *Tomb Raider*.

> *'I am so out of here! Sianara, suckers!'*
> (Posting at www.livejournal.com, March 2004)

sick *adj*
1. *American* amusing, funny. An item of black street-talk which was included in so-called **Ebonics**, recognised as a legitimate language variety by school officials in Oakland, California, in late 1996.

> *He's such a sick dude when he's tellin' all those stories!*
> *That's so sick!*

2. excellent. Used as a vogue expression of enthusiasm by e.g. skateboarders, and usually self-consciously or ironically by students since the 1990s.

sicko *n*
a pervert or mentally disturbed person. The word generally denotes a sexual deviant and is now heard in Britain as well as the USA, where it originated.

siff, the siff *n*
an alternative spelling of **(the) syph**

sighted! *exclamation British*
an all-purpose exclamation of solidarity which ranges in meaning from 'thank you' to 'beware'. Synonyms from the same period are **seen** and **safe**. The term, which probably originated as a warning or shout of recognition by a gang lookout, was recorded in use among North London schoolboys in 1993 and 1994.

simoleons *n American*
coins, cash, dollars, money. This archaic term (a blend of 'Simon': obsolete slang for dollar. and 'Napoleon': a 20 franc gold coin) is occasionally revived in the same way as similar British words such as **rhino** or **pelf**.

simp *n*
a dim-witted individual. The word, originating in the USA early in the 20th century, was a shortening of 'simpleton'. More recently it has sometimes acquired connotations suggested by 'simper' and **wimp**.

> *'Some guest and some employer – the simp and the blimp.'*
> (*Honeymooners*, US TV comedy series, 1951)

simpatico *adj*
agreeable, pleasant, friendly. The Spanish and Italian word has been adopted by certain English speakers.

sin bin *n British*
a place to which difficult or 'hopeless' cases are consigned. The term is applied particularly to schools or other educational or correctional institutions. It is derived from ice hockey, where the sin bin is the rinkside area where transgressing players serve out time penalties.

sing *vb*
to inform, confess, give information to the authorities. This underworld term, originating in the USA before World War II, is often embellished as 'sing like a bird' or 'sing like a canary'.

> *'Last month the alleged cocaine importer from America was driven north to a secure house where he is said by detectives to be "singing like a bird".'*
> (*Observer*, 16 August 1987)

sink *vb*
to drink, down (alcohol). This drinkers' euphemism usually occurs in such phrases as the invitation to 'sink a few (jars)'.

sink the sausage *vb Australian*
a version of **hide the sausage**

siphon/syphon the python *vb*
to urinate. A humorous vulgarism introduced to a British audience via the Australian character *Barry McKenzie* in Barry Humphries' and Nicholas Garland's cartoon strip in *Private Eye* magazine in the late 1960s. **Drain the lizard/dragon/snake** are alternatives.

> *'Hang on a jiff, though, will you? I've just got to nip into the dunnee to syphon the python.'*
> (*Bazza Pulls It Off*, cartoon strip by Barry Humphries and Nicholas Garland, 1988)

sitch *n American*
a situation. An abbreviated form of the word in use in adolescent speech.

> *So what's the latest sitch?*

sit down *vb*
to acquiesce, submit or suffer in silence. The opposite to 'standing up for oneself',

sit down is a synonym for the probably more widespread **lie down**. The phrase has become a vogue term and a business-jargon expression rather than a mere metaphor.

There's no way I'm going to sit down for this one. We've taken enough!

sit off *vb British*
1a. to relax
1b. to act in a lazy, disinterested way
The term was in use among adolescents, especially in the Liverpool area, in 2003. The noun 'sit-off' denotes a party or gathering at which participants are inert, e.g. after drug use.

six-pack *n*
1a. the male abdomen showing the stomach muscles
He's got a great six-pack.
1b. a powerful and/or attractive male
The beach was covered with six-packs.
These uses of the term, based on a comparison with a row of beer cans, arose in the US in the early 1990s and by the end of the decade were also heard (especially in the second sense) in the UK

sixteen-valve *n South African*
an attractive female. The designation is that as applied to a powerful car. **Spoilers** and **hatchback** are other automotive images that were used in the same context in the late 1990s.

sixty-nine *n*
simultaneous and mutual oral sex. The term, originating in the French *soixante-neuf* (suggested by the shape of bodies engaged in cunnilingus and fellatio), is from the jargon of pornography and prostitution. The expression also occurs as a verb.

size queen *n*
a male homosexual who favours sexual partners according to the size of their genitals. The expression is part of the post-1960s **gay** lexicon and is generally used to indicate disapproval. The term is occasionally applied to women adopting the same criterion.

skag *n*
an alternative spelling of **scag**

skagger *n British*
a handicapped or slow-witted person. The term has been in playground usage since 2000.

skanger *n British*
a synonym of **chav**, in vogue in 2004. It is probably related to **skagger** and/or **skank**.

skangey *adj American*
an alternative spelling of **scangey**

skank[1] *n*
a trick, neat manoeuvre. An item of jargon originating in Nintendo *Game Boy* usage.

skank[2] *n, adj American*
(something or someone) unpleasant or disgusting. The word seems to have arisen in black speech, but its etymology is uncertain. Skank is sometimes used specifically to denote an immoral woman or a prostitute.

skank[3] *vb*
1a. to abandon, betray
Skank your mates to go out with your girl.
1b. to cheat or rob

skanker *n*
1. *British* a synonym for **chav**, recorded in 2005
2. an unpleasant, untrustworthy individual. A variant form of **skank** recorded in 2004.

skanking *n*
a swinging and jerking style of dancing characteristic of reggae and the 'two-tone' music of 1977 to 1980. The word originally means stealing, and hence behaving disreputably or moving stealthily, in Jamaican patois.

skanky *adj*
1a. unpleasant, disreputable, dishonest, repellent
That was a skanky trick to pull.
1b. inelegant, unfashionable, vulgar
Did you clock those skanky shorts she was half-wearing?
A vogue term in hip hop and R 'n' B milieus since the 1990s, the word originated in Jamaican speech in the 1970s or earlier.

skat *adj*
fashionable. A vogue word from 1985 and 1986, of unknown origin. The word was used by adolescents in the fashion, music and club milieus of New York and London.

skate *n American*
a pushover, an easy task, a 'smooth ride'. A 1980s usage, from the image of skating across a surface or between obstacles.
Relax, it's going to be a skate.

skate it *vb British*
to succeed easily or effortlessly. The term is heard particularly in the Scottish Lowlands and the north of England.

skattie *n*

1a. *South African* a girlfriend

1b. *British* a promiscuous woman or prostitute. The term, of obscure origin, was in use among young adult and teenage black males in the late 1990s.

skeen *exclamation, adj British*

an all-purpose term of approval, agreement, solidarity, etc. This version of the earlier **seen** was described on the Internet in 2003 as 'used by junior wannabe gangstas' and 'the proper hardcore way to say **seen**'.

skeet *vb American*

to achieve male orgasm, **come**. This item of black slang is of uncertain provenance but is presumably related to **skeeze**.

skeeze *vb American*

to have sex. The word has been common in black speech since the late 1980s, but its exact etymology is unknown.

skeezer, skeeze *n American*

1a. a promiscuous and/or disreputable person. The term is almost invariably pejorative.

1b. a **groupie** or ardent fan of hip hop or **rap** performers

The words appeared in the 1980s.

skeezy *adj American*

dissolute, disreputable. The term of disapproval is typically used of a promiscuous person.

> *'I'm a crack-whore who should have made my skeezy boyfriend wear a condom.'*
> (*10 Things I Hate About You*, US film, 1999)

skeg *n*

an unfashionable, badly-dressed and/or irritating person. The term, heard in the UK and Australia, is typically used disapprovingly of members of skateboarding subcultures.

skell *n American*

a homeless person. The origin of the term, heard in the 1990s, is uncertain.

sket(s) *n British*

a promiscuous and/or disreputable female. A term used by young streetgang members in London since around 2000. It may also designate a **chav** of either gender.

sketch, sketchy *adj American*

of dubious quality, potentially dangerous. A synonym of **shady** and **dodgy** in widespread use among younger speakers since around 2000. The terms were defined by one user as 'shady, illicit, weird'.

sketchmaster, sketchmeister *n American*

a male who is socially inept, off-putting. An elaboration from the adjective **sketch(y)**.

skettle *n*

an alternative spelling of **skittel**

-ski, -sky *suffix American*

a humorous ending added, usually to slang terms, by teenagers and students. Examples are **finski** and **buttinsky**. The termination indicates friendship, respect, acceptance into the group when attached to a proper name, e.g. 'Normski' (a black UK TV presenter). When terminating the name of an object, e.g. **brewski**, it denotes affectionate familiarity. The suffix occurs in Slavonic languages and in many Yiddish surnames.

skid[1] *vb*

1. to leave, go away. A usage which was fashionable among adolescents in Britain in the late 1980s.

2. *British* to 'slum', make do with little money, secondhand clothes, etc. This student term of the 1980s is probably inspired by 'skid row'.

skid[2] *n American*

a scruffy, disreputable individual. The term, used in the USA and Canada since the 1990s, is probably based on 'skid row'.

skid-lid *n British*

a crash helmet

skid-marks *n pl*

traces of excrement on underwear

> *'Hand-me downs – me first nappy had your skid-marks on it!'*
> (*Birds of a Feather*, British TV comedy series, October 1989)

skidoo, skiddoo *vb*

a version of **skedaddle**

skids *n pl Australian*

the fortunes of fate, hard luck, the 'breaks'. An encapsulation of the philosophy of the young and callously indifferent, most often heard in the shrug-off sentence 'them's the skids': 'that's the breaks'.

> *'"Them's the skids", as the young fry say.'*
> (Peter Corris, *The Greenwich Apartments*, 1986)

skill *n British*

a younger schoolchildren's exclamation of admiration, appreciation or approval, heard in the late 1980s. The word has been extended from its original literal sense to become an all purpose vogue word, sometimes in the phrase 'skill and brill'.

skimming *n*

taking money illegally (e.g. before declaring it for tax purposes, or to defraud the eventual recipients) from income or profits, especially in casinos. The word is part of underworld jargon as used by organised crime in the USA. 'Skim' was used to mean money or profit in both Britain and the USA in the 19th century, the image evoked being that of taking the cream off the top of the milk.

skimpies *n pl*

underwear. The term has been recorded in the UK, US and Australasia.

skin¹ *n*

1. *British* a **skinhead**

2. *British* a cigarette rolling paper, as part of the makings of a **joint**. A word from the lexicon of drug users since the 1960s, now occasionally heard to describe cigarette papers put to more legitimate use.

See also **skin up**

3. *American* a dollar bill

skin² *vb*

to rob or defraud, **rip off** or 'fleece' someone. The word implies comprehensive and efficient removal of wealth.

He thought he was pretty smart but those guys skinned him.

We got skinned in that deal.

skinflick *n*

a pornographic or semi-pornographic film. The skin element of the phrase refers to nudity; **flick** has been a slang term for film since the days of the silent movie. Skinflick is an Americanism which has been understood, albeit not widely used, in other English-speaking areas since the early 1970s.

skinful *n*

an excess of alcohol. The word dates from the 18th century and evokes a distended belly or bladder.

We'd better get him home, he's had a skinful.

skinhead *n*

1. a bald person or someone with close-cropped hair. (**Chrome-dome** is a more recent synonym.)

2. a member of a working-class youth cult originating in the late 1960s. The skinheads (the term was applied scornfully by longer-haired contemporaries, particularly **hippies**) mutated from the **mods** and 'tickets' of the mid-1960s. They dressed in a functional uniform of American shirts, jeans and, often, **bovver-boots** and espoused soul music and gang violence.

skin it *vb*

to shake or slap hands as a greeting and gesture of solidarity. The term, like the action itself (which is sometimes accompanied by the cry 'give me some skin!' or 'skin me!'), was part of 1990s youth culture throughout the English-speaking world.

skinny *n American*

news, information, gossip. A vogue term among adolescents in the 1980s. This use of the word is said to have originated in the armed forces in the 1940s and might be jocularly based on 'the naked truth'.

These guys've got the skinny on what's going on after hours.

skin-pop *vb*

to inject (an illicit drug) intramuscularly or into flesh, rather than into a vein. An addicts' term.

skins *n pl*

1. drums, in the jargon of jazz and rock musicians

2. car or motorcycle tyres in the jargon of racers, bikers, etc.

3. *British* **skinheads**

skin up *vb*

to roll a **joint**. From **skin**; a cigarette rolling paper.

skip *n*

1. *British* an escape or an instance of jumping bail. This specialised use of the common colloquialism for 'avoid' is part of underworld jargon.

2. *American* a person who fails to answer a bail bond, an escapee

3. *British* a boss, **guvnor**. A shortening of **skipper**, used typically by police officers in familiar address to a superior or, in sports, by team-members to their captain.

4. *British* a place to sleep or shelter. A shortened form of the tramps' term **skipper**.

5. *British* a dilapidated, old or cheap vehicle, particularly a car. The name of the common large metal refuse containers has been appropriated as a vogue term among schoolchildren since around 1988.

skipper¹ *n British*

1. a captain of a ship or a team. Skipper in this sense is not, strictly speaking, slang, although it is considered to be so by some. The word has been in use since it was anglicised from the Middle Dutch *schipper* (from *schip*: a ship).

2. a rough shelter, place to sleep for the night, typically in a derelict building. The word, which may describe no more than a patch of rough ground, is now a near-synonym for **doss house** or **derry**. It is part of the vocabulary of tramps, **dossers** and other down-and-outs, and originated in Celtic words for barn (rendered as *ysgubor* in Welsh, *sciber* in Old Cornish).

> *'When you're drunk and face-down in some skipper you just don't think there's much future in it.'*

> (Recorded, vagrant, Waterloo, London, 1987)

3. a friend, 'mate'. A friendly term of address between males, now rarely used except by vagrants.

skipper² *vb British*

to sleep rough, be homeless. From the noun.

> *'I tell you, I was forced to skipper. I never had any choice.'*

> (Recorded, vagrant, Waterloo, London, 1987)

skippering *n British*

sleeping rough, living in derelict buildings or improvised or makeshift shelters. From the second sense of the noun **skipper**.

skippy *n*

1. *American* a male homosexual, particularly an effeminate or affected one. the word was previously used to· refer to female prostitutes by the US army in the Pacific. 'Skibby' was an earlier form of the word, the derivation of which is

obscure: some relation to 'skivvy' looks possible, but there is no proof of this.

2. *British* a **chav**. The term was posted on the b3ta website in 2004.

skirt *n*

a woman or girl, or females in general. A depersonalising term as used by males in the 20th century. The usage is much older, probably originating in the 1500s.

skite¹ *vb Australian*

to boast. The word is a shortened form of **blatherskite**.

skite² *n, adj*

1a. (something or someone that is) disgusting, worthless, inferior. A dialect or disguised form of **shit** or **shite**.

1b. (a male who is) fashionable, admirable, **cool**. A term used by young street-gang members in London since around 2000.

skit out *vb*

to behave in an erratic, unpredictable, excessive fashion. The phrase, recorded in London in 2001, may be based on the earlier **schizzed-out**, or on skittish.

> *Every time things get a bit heavy she just skits out.*

skittel, skittle, skettle *n*

a promiscuous and/or disreputable female

skive, skive off *vb British*

to avoid work or duty, malinger. Skive is either from the obscure verb in standard English meaning to shave off (pieces of leather), from the Old Norse *skifa*, meaning to slice, or from another unrecorded dialect term. It has been heard in the sense of shirk since the early 20th century.

skivvies *n pl American*

male underwear. The origin of the word is not known.

> *'Ordell looked over at Louis Gara having his morning coffee in his skivvies, his bare feet up on the coffee table.'*

> (*The Switch*, Elmore Leonard, 1978)

skrag *vb*

a variant spelling of **scrag**.

skull¹ *n American*

1. a synonym for 'head' in racy speech or **hip** talk. The word most usually occurs in the phrase **out of one's skull** (intoxicated or crazy) or in the following extended specialised sense.

2. oral sex, especially fellatio. This term, popular among college students since the late 1970s, is either derived from, or an imitation of black street slang; a racier version of **head** in its sexual context. It is usually used as part of the parodic exhortation 'whip some skull on me baby!'.

skull² *vb Australian*
to drink (alcohol)

skulled *adj*
drunk or **stoned** on drugs. The term is a shorter form of **out of one's skull** (although when used by Australian speakers the verb **skull** meaning to drink may also come into play).

skull-fuck *vb, n American*
(to perform) an act of fellatio

skunk *n British*
marihuana, cannabis. Originally referring to 'skunk-weed', a hydroponically grown and extra-strong strain of **grass**, the term became generalised to refer to other marihuana in the 1990s.

sky pilot *n*
a priest, particularly a naval or military chaplain. The phrase dates from the later 19th century.

slack¹ *n See* **cut (someone) a little slack**

slack² *adj Caribbean*
immoral, particularly in a sexual context. This use of the word is archaic in Britain (although it was probably the origin of **slag**) but survives in 'Jamaica talk'.

> *'The spurned wife of Tessa Sanderson's lover called the Olympic athlete "slack" – Jamaican slang for promiscuous.'*
> (*Guardian*, February 1990)

slackass *adj*
lazy, incompetent. An Americanism also heard in the Caribbean.

slacker *n American*
a disaffected, apathetic middle-class young person; a member of **Generation X**. 'Slacker-culture' was promoted as a significant youth movement (supposedly a reaction against **yuppie** materialism and ambition) for a brief period in the early to mid-1990s on the USA's West Coast.

slackness *n Jamaican*
immoral behaviour, speech, etc.; obscenity. The term was picked up by devotees of hip hop and **rap** culture in the US during the 1990s.

> *'... not all black women take slackness lying down ... Rasheda Ashanti ... says; we don't want to continually hear explicit details about our anatomy ...'*
> (*Sunday Times*, 2 May 1993)

slag¹ *n British*
1a. a (supposedly) promiscuous woman. A derogatory word used mainly by working-class men and women which often carries overtones of slovenliness and coarseness.

> *'Self-conscious and self-adoring parodists of slagdom, such as Madonna and Samantha Fox, understand this; that a man who calls a woman a slag isn't saying anything about her, but a lot about his condom size.'*
> (Julie Burchill, *Elle* magazine, December 1987)

1b. a despicable male. The word conveys real contempt and distaste; it is now generally heard in London working-class or criminal usage. Slag has been used since the 18th century to convey notions of moral laxity and worthlessness. The ultimate source of the word is probably in 'slack' rather than 'slag', meaning mining or smelting residue.

slag² *vb See* **slag off**

slagging *n British*
a bout of criticism, denigration or abuse, a serious dressing-down. The noun comes from the verb to **slag** or **slag off**.

> *'Jo Brand gives Chris Moyles a slagging.'*
> (Headline on *Grassroots Media* website, June 2005)

slag it *vb British*
(especially of females) to behave promiscuously or in a dissolute manner, to 'sleep around'. A term used by young street-gang members in London since around 2000.

slag off, slag *vb British*
to denigrate, criticise bitterly or insult. This working-class term probably derives from the dialect 'slag', meaning to smear, or from the standard English noun 'slag', meaning refuse or waste material. In the form 'slag' the modern expression occurs in American speech. US authorities cite the German verb *schlagen* (to beat or lash), but this is an unlikely source for the British usage.

> *'We get slagged off something chronic by a lot of people.'*
> (Recorded, telephone engineer, London, May 1989)

slam *vb British*
to have sex with, penetrate. The term, like its synonyms **lam** and **lamp**, invariably refers to male sexual activity. It can be used both transitively and intransitively.

An item of black street-talk used especially by males, recorded in 2001.

Drew's been hoping to slam her for weeks.

I slammed her.

slammed *adj British*
drunk. A mainly middle- and upper-class term of the 1980s. (Certain cocktails are known as 'slammers'; both words evoke the sudden and stunning effect of strong alcohol.)

slammer *n*
a prison. An Americanism used in Britain and Australia since the early 1960s, it was originally a 1930s slang word for door, hence cell door and, since World War II, now denotes a jail.

'You're consortin' with a criminal, so when he goes to the slammer, you go, too!'

(*Smokey and the Bandit III*, US film, 1983)

slammered *adj British*
drunk. The term does not necessarily refer to the result of ingesting Tequila slammers (neat shots). An item of student slang in use in London and elsewhere since around 2000.

slamming¹ *n American*
injecting heroin, **shooting up**. An item of police and underworld slang which is interchangeable in addicts' parlance with **geezing**.

slamming² *adj British*
excellent, exciting. Like its synonyms **banging** and **kicking**, it is a vogue term of approbation in use among adolescents since the early 1990s.

slanging *n American*
selling illicit drugs, usually on the street. This usage, from black American street argot in the 1990s, is found in the phrase 'slangin' and bangin'' (banging here is **gang banging**) to describe the typical behaviour of gang members and devotees of drug subcultures. The word is almost certainly a deformation of **slinging**, which has also been used with the same meaning.

slant *n*
an Oriental person. A shortening of 'slant-eyed', used in the United States and Australia since the 1960s and now heard among young Londoners, e.g. young city businessmen referring disparagingly to the Japanese.

slap¹ *n British*
1. make-up, face-paint. A piece of theatrical slang which Partridge's *Dictionary of Slang and Unconventional English* dates to 1860 and claims to be obsolete by 1930. In fact the term was still in common currency in the theatre in the late 1980s.

We're going to need some more slap on here.

2. a meal, feast. Derived from 'slap-up (meal)', the term was recorded among bohemians and students in the late 1950s and early 1960s.

a good slap

slap² *vb, n British*
(to have) sex. In Jamaican slang the word is a contemporary synonym for **slam**. The word has also been used in this sense in the UK since around 2000.

slap-and-tickle *n British*
petting, kissing and caressing. A joky and innocuous euphemism for love-play of various degrees of intensity. The phrase dates from the Edwardian era but was most popular in the late 1950s, usually in the form 'a bit of slap-and-tickle'.

slaphead *n British*
a bald person. A vogue term among adolescents from the early 1990s. The phrase may have been inspired by the comedian Benny Hill slapping the bald head of his diminutive assistant in his TV comedy shows of the 1980s.

slapper *n British*
a prostitute or slut. This working-class term from East London and Essex is probably a corruption of **shlepper**, a word of Yiddish origin, one of whose meanings is a slovenly or immoral woman.

'…it was either Posh's fault for being too thin and failing to follow her husband when he moved to Madrid; or it was Rebecca Loos's fault for being a slapper.'
(*Guardian*, 13 April 2004)

slash¹ *n British*
an act of urination. A vulgar term, used generally by males. The word came into use in this sense sometime before the 1950s, but was not recorded in writing until recently. The word usually occurs in phrases such as 'have a slash' or 'take a slash'. Slash may be echoic (as 'slosh' or 'slush') or may be inspired by the standard use of the word to refer to rain driving obliquely.

slash² vb British
to urinate. The verb form is less common than the noun.

slate vb
to insult, denigrate. As used by adolescents since 2000, the standard colloquialism (originally a northern English dialect word meaning to harass or hurt) has stronger, more personal overtones.

slaughter n British
a place where stolen goods are hidden and/or shared out. This example of the jargon of cat burglars was recorded in *FHM* magazine in April 1996. It probably originated in underworld argot as 'slaughterhouse' or 'slaughter-yard', but the exact significance is unclear.

slaughtered adj British
extremely drunk. A fashionable item from the adolescent drinkers' lexicon of the 1990s.

'They [a convention of "nerds"] crammed the hotel to get slaughtered on non-alcoholic wines and beers.'
(*Sunday Express*, 27 February 1994)

sleazeball, sleaze-bag, sleaze-bucket n American
a very unpleasant person. A socially acceptable alternative to terms such as **shitbag**, etc., popular in the late 1970s and 1980s.

sleazo, sleazoid n
a 'sleazy' person; a disreputable, immoral or otherwise repellent individual. These Americanisms are now heard elsewhere.

'There were a bunch of sleazo bars on or near the Sunset Strip.'
(*www.badmags.com*, June 2005)

sledgied adj British
intoxicated by drugs or drink. A vogue term among devotees of **rave** culture since the early 1990s and subsequently among students, it is probably based on the notion of being suddenly struck as with a sledgehammer.

sleighride n American
1. a smooth or easy passage, the easy achievement of a task
2. a bout of cocaine intoxication. A witticism inspired by the exhilaration resulting from ingestion of **snow**.

slewed adj
drunk. The word (formerly sometimes spelled 'slued') has been used in this sense since the mid-19th century.

slice vb American
to harass, oppress, criticise. A piece of adolescent and teenage slang of the early 1990s, almost always referring to parents or teachers.

I sure wish the rents would quit slicing me.

slick up vb
to make oneself look attractive, elegant, prepare oneself to impress. From the earlier colloquial sense of slick as smart or glib.

slide vb American
to leave, depart. A vogue term, like **jam**, **jet**, **bail**, etc., probably originating among street gangs and subsequently in use among adolescents on high-school and college campuses.

It's time to slide.

slider n British
a shirker, idler. Probably a clipped form of the word 'backslider', this late-1990s usage was defined on the Internet by *Bodge World* in February 1997 as 'someone who manages to get out of doing work'.

slime¹ vb
1. to behave in a devious, sycophantic or ingratiating way. A usage popular among adolescents and young adults from the 1980s.
2. *Australian* to ejaculate

slime², **slimeball, slimebucket, slimebag** n
a despicable person; popular terms of abuse or distaste in the 1980s

sling vb, n
(to pay) a bribe. The Australasian term is the equivalent of the British **bung**.

slinging n See **slanging**

sling off vb Australian
to denigrate, criticise

sling one's hook vb British
to leave, go away. This term, which originated and largely survives in working-class speech, is either of nautical or mining origin. It dates from the second half of the 19th century. **Hook it** is a racier alternative.

We don't want you here. Go on, sling your 'ook!

slip it to someone vb British
to have sex with someone. A version of the more common vulgar euphemism, **slip someone a length**. The phrase is generally employed by men and usually implies a casual and surreptitious coupling.

slip someone a length *vb*
to have sex with someone (from the male point of view). A euphemism originating in the 19th century.

slit *n*
1a. the vagina

> *'A vagina indeed! Admittedly, some people did call it a slit sometimes.'*
> (*Nice Work* by David Lodge, 1988)

1b. a female. The word in the plural was adopted as the name of a British all-girl **punk** group in 1977.

Sloane Ranger, Sloane *n British*
a young upper-middle or upper-class person, educated at a public school and affecting certain well defined modes of dress and behaviour. The phrase was applied to a recognisable sub-category of British youth displaying characteristics of what used to be known as the 'county set'. The equivalent of the American **preppies** and the French *B.C.B.G.s* (for 'bon chic, bon genre'), Sloane Rangers were defined and described by the journalists Peter York and later Ann Barr in articles in *Harpers and Queen* magazine and publications such as *The Official Sloane Ranger's Handbook* (1982). The first time the words appeared in print was in October 1975, but Peter York was not the originator of the expression. It was used by bar-room wits of the early 1970s to refer to would-be 'men about town' frequenting Chelsea pubs, only some of whom were the upper-class youths (then known solely as **Hooray Henrys**) later so described. The source of the pun, the Lone Ranger, was the dashing cowboy hero of a 1950s TV series; Sloane Square is in Chelsea.

> *'The appalling Sloane Ranger look. Worn by strapping, horsey girls aged 20 going on 53. Other components: striped shirts, a tame string of pearls, impenetrable pleated skirt, blue tights and prissy shoes. Printed headscarves optional. Thick ankles mandatory.'*
> (Description of female Sloane Ranger, Judy Rumbold, *Guardian*, 11 December 1989)

slob *n*
a coarse, slovenly and/or lazy individual. This word had existed for many years in Anglo-Irish speech where it denoted a fat, slow child (probably from *slab*, Irish Gaelic for mud). Coincidentally a similar word, apparently of Slavonic origin and rendered as *zhlub* or *shlub*, exists in Yiddish. It means an uncouth person, but is probably derived from a root form related to the Czech *zlobit*, meaning to get angry.

slob out *vb*
to relax, behave in a lazy or disinterested way. An item of student slang in use in London and elsewhere since around 2000.

slope *n*
an Oriental person, especially a Vietnamese. This derogatory term, deriving from 'slope-eyed', moved from the US to Australia in the 1970s.

> *'The newest "new Australians", as anyone who looks foreign is called, are the Lebanese and the Vietnamese, the "slopes".'*
> (*Observer* magazine, 13 December 1987)

Compare **slant**

slope off *vb*
to leave, depart surreptitiously. This colloquialism derives from the 19th-century slang use of 'slope' to mean decamp or sneak away. The term originated in the USA. It is either from the Dutch *sloop*, meaning to steal away, or from the standard verb.

sloshed *adj*
drunk. One of the most common and least offensive terms in British usage since the late 19th century. It is also heard in the USA.

slosher, slusher *n*
a promiscuous and/or disreputable female. A term used by young street-gang members in London since around 2000.

slot *n*
1a. the anus. In **gay** parlance.
1b. the vagina

sly *adj British*
an all-purpose term of disapproval fashionable in the later 1990s. It was defined on the Internet by *Bodge World* in March 1997.

smack *n*
heroin. Originally an American term, the word spread to Britain and Australia at the time of the Vietnam War. It is derived from the Yiddish *shmek*, meaning a sniff, whiff or taste, reinforced by the English word's suggestion of a sudden, violent effect.

> *'I don't think Jimmy Hendrix was on smack 'cos I was with him last Saturday*

*night and I know when a man's on smack
and he wasn't.'*
(Murray Roman, quoted in *Oz* magazine,
June 1969)

smacked-out *adj*
addicted to or under the influence of heroin (**smack**)

*'Nathan had staked everything he had
ever worked for on this loser who was too
smacked out to worry about taking MOM
Records into the bankruptcy court.'*
(*Platinum Logic*, Tony Parsons, 1981)

smacker *n*
1. a kiss
2. *British* an active or potential sexual
partner. In this sense, the term was used
by aficionados of London dancefloor culture in the early 1990s.

smackers *n pl*
pounds or dollars. Like **smacker** in the
sense of a kiss, this lighthearted term is
often embellished to give 'smackeroos' or
'smackeroonies'. The original word probably refers to the slapping of coins or
notes onto a table or counter or into the
palm of an outstretched hand.

*'Do you wanna take the thousand
smackers or try for the sensational bathroom suite?'*
(*Biff* cartoon, 1986)

smack-head *n.*
a heroin addict, a **junkie**. A combining of
smack with the '-head' suffix meaning a
habitué. ('Smack-freak' was a synonymous term of the late 1960s and early
1970s, subsequently yielding to smack-
head in popularity.)

*'If a smack-head tries to chat you up,
what's he really after?'*
(UK Government anti-heroin advertisement, 1986)

smack it, smacked it *exclamation*
a cry of triumph or congratulation. It
may be accompanied by, or inspired by
the victorious slapping of hands.

smams *n pl British*
female breasts. A term used by younger
speakers of both sexes since 2000.

*'Jackie was being all oily, but he just
wanted to touch her smams.'*
(Recorded, male teenager, Richmond,
UK, April 2005)

smartarse, smartass *n, adj*
(a person who is a) know-all, smug or
insolent. The word describes someone
whose display of real or supposed clev-

erness renders them obnoxious. 'Smart
alec' or 'wise-guy' are politer synonyms.

*'If she felt like giving them a smartass
answer, why didn't she? Because she
couldn't think of a smartass answer fast
enough.'*
(*The Switch*, Elmore Leonard, 1978)

smartmouth *vb American*
to cheek, speak disrespectfully or insolently (of someone)

smarts *n*
intelligence, wits. A coinage inspired by
the word wits itself and/or 'brains'. The
word is American, but is occasionally
heard in Britain.

She's got more than her share of smarts.

smash[1] *n British*
small change, money in the form of
coins. The term is heard particularly in
the Scottish Lowlands and the north of
England. **Shrapnel** is a southern equivalent.

smash[2] *vb British*
to have sex with, penetrate. An item of
black street-talk used especially by
males, recorded in 2003.

I smashed her.

smashed *adj*
drunk or intoxicated by drugs

*'Having discovered that it is possible to
be smashed, keep on the stereo headphones AND read, I have managed to …
get through … several books.'*
(Jim Anderson in *Oz* magazine, February
1970)

smashed it! *exclamation*
a cry of triumph

smashing *adj British*
excellent. The colloquialism of the
1950s was revived, often with ironic
overtones, after 2000.

smash mouth *vb American*
to kiss. A humorous equivalent to the
better known 'chew face' in use among
adolescents.

smeg, smeggy *n British*
a foolish and/or dirty person. These
terms, deriving from smegma, are vulgarisms which have been popular with
schoolboys, students, **punks** and other
youths since the mid-1970s. Despite
their origin the words do not usually indicate great distaste but rather mild contempt or even affection. Smeg and
various derivatives such as 'smeg-head'
were used in the cult British TV comedy
series of the late 1980s *Red Dwarf* as an

all-purpose swearword, a euphemism for **fuck** or **shit**.

smellie *n British*
a beggar or homeless person, a **crustie**

smok *n South African*
a flirtatious or unconventional female. Recorded as an item of Sowetan slang in the *Cape Sunday Times*, 29 January 1995. In 19th-century British slang 'smock' could be used to denote a 'loose woman'.

smoke¹ *vb American*
1a. to kill. A euphemism in underworld and police usage since the 1940s, this unsentimental term was fashionable in teenage speech and crime fiction in the 1980s.
1b. also **smoke out**, **smoke off** to defeat or to better (someone). In the **hip** jargon of the rock music business since the 1970s.
'Out-playing the headliner is known in the trade as "smoking"…Thin Lizzy were notorious for smoking their superiors – and consequently for being mysteriously removed from bills.'
(*Independent*, 27 January 1989)

smoke² *n*
1a. tobacco
1b. hashish or marihuana
2. the Smoke, the big Smoke London or any large town or city (in British and Australian usage). The word was first recorded in this sense in 1864 referring to London. It usually evokes the city as seen by those who are not native to it or are in temporary exile from it.
'This is one of the things they have come for – an escape from the Smoke and a whiff of the sea.'
(*Town* magazine, September 1963)

smoke out *vb American*
to smoke cannabis. A West Coast expression in contemporary use.

smoker *n British*
1. an old, worn-out or mechanically unsound motor-car. A piece of jargon from the vocabulary of second-hand car dealers and enthusiasts.
2. a cannabis smoker

smoke up *vb American*
to smoke cannabis. An East Coast expression in contemporary use.

smokey, smoky *n American*
a police officer. The term derives from 'Smokey the Bear', a cartoon character wearing the hat of a Forest Ranger, who issued warnings against careless behaviour that could cause forest fires; it was then applied, jocularly at first, to any uniformed authority figure. Smokey became the CB (Citizens' Band) radio code word for a highway patrol officer in the 1970s.

smoodge *vb Australian*
a variant form of **shmooze** in the sense of ingratiate oneself or flatter
Don't try and smoodge me, it won't work.

smooth *adj*
good. An all-purpose term of approbation used by adolescents.

smudger *n British*
1. a friend, 'mate'
All right me old smudger?
2a. a photographer. A jocular reference to inept developing and printing.
2b. also **smudge** a photograph. This old item of press slang came, in the 1990s, to refer specifically to an illicit paparazzi snap of, e.g., a star *en déshabille.*
3. a flatulent person
All three sense of the word are from working-class speech; the first and third are specific to the London area. All are now dated but not obsolete.

smuggling peanuts *n*
(of a female) displaying the nipples through clothing

smurf¹ *n*
1a. *British* a black person. A racist pejorative.
1b. *British* an unfortunate, contemptible person or misfit, in working-class and schoolchildren's usage
1c. a smuggler of drugs, specifically a lowly courier or dupe
1d. *British* another term for **jub**
The Smurfs were ugly, plump, gnome-like cartoon creatures marketed as a children's craze in the early 1970s and revived in the late 1990s.

smurf² *vb*
1a. to transport illicit narcotics
1b. to launder money
Both terms are from underworld usage, probably originating in North America.

smutty *adj British*
1a. excellent, good
a smutty time
1b. serious
a smutty fracas
1c. 'deep'
well smutty music
A vogue synonym for **heavy**, **diesel**, **sick**.

An item of black street-talk used especially by males, recorded in 2003.

snack attack *n*
a bout of compulsive eating, **(the) munchies**. A late 1980s vogue term, still in limited circulation (as is its contemporary, **tack attack**).

I'm afraid in the middle of the night I had a snack attack.

snafu *n*
an impossible situation, a foul-up, a labyrinth of incompetence. The expression, from 'Situation Normal, All Fucked Up' was developed in the US army in World War II (in imitation of that institution's passion for acronyms) to describe the quotidian effects of bureaucratic stupidity.

'I tell you, its been snafu after bloody snafu here.'
(Recorded, businessman, London, 1987)

snag *vb American*
to steal, appropriate. A term from street slang that was adopted by middle-class adolescents during the 1990s, often to describe the seduction of another's partner.

snags *n pl Australian*
sausages. A word in use since the 1940s and still heard, particularly at **barbies**.

snake[1] *n South African*
an unfaithful female. Recorded as an item of Sowetan slang in the *Cape Sunday Times*, 29 January 1995.

snake[2] *vb American*
to seduce and/or have sex with. The term's recent usage may have originated in black slang, but the same word was employed with the sense of 'steal surreptitiously' in British slang of the 19th century.

'He goddam tried to snake my old lady.'
(Recorded, Californian male, September 1995)

snakes *n Australian*
1a. urine or an act of urination. The word is native Australian rhyming slang from 'snake's hiss': **piss**.
1b. a toilet

snakey *adj Australian*
angry. The usage may derive from the old phrase 'as mad as a cut snake'.

snanny *n, adj British*
(someone) insincere, untrustworthy, 'slimy'. The term was used by teenage girls in 2001.

snap *n British*
food. Formerly a dialect term for a packed lunch or snack, since 2000 the word has been generalised in teenage parlance to refer to any food.

snap one's gums *vb American*
to talk. An alternative form of **bump/flap one's gums**.

snapper *n*
1. *British, Irish* a child. The term, popularised by the Irish writer Roddy Doyle's story and 1993 film of the same name, may have originated as a shortening of 'whippersnapper' or 'bread-snapper'.
2. a male homosexual, in armed-forces' usage

snarf *vb*
1a. to eat, devour
1b. to appropriate, adopt wholesale. In the language of **cyberpunks** and **netheads**, the term refers to incorporating information from elsewhere into one's own documents and files, etc. It is probably a blend of 'snort' or **snag** and **scarf (up/down)**.

snart *vb, n British*
1a. (to) snigger or snort (with derision)
1b. (to) sniff or inhale. (In the latter sense, 'snart up' is an alternative form.)
1c. (to) sneeze
A rare expression heard among students and others since the early 1970s. It is a humorous corruption of **snort** in both its standard and slang senses.

snash *n British*
money. The usage has been recorded among schoolchildren, students and army cadets since 2000. **Smash** is a contemporary synonym.

snatch *n*
1a. the vagina
1b. women in general. In the 16th century this word was used to denote an impromptu and/or hasty ('snatched') sexual encounter. The meaning was transferred to the female pudenda, and in the 20th century extended to refer to females as sex objects. The use of snatch in these senses has never been common but enjoyed a brief vogue in the late 1960s and early 1970s, first in the US and Canada, subsequently in Britain.
2. *British* an instance of bag-snatching, in the argot of teenage muggers

'The child muggers told with chilling frankness how and why they resorted to

*muggings or "snatches" as they are
sometimes called.'*
(*Observer*, 22 May 1988)

3. a kidnap or abduction, in underworld
jargon

snazz *n*
elegance, smart showiness, élan. The
noun, most commonly encountered in
American speech, is a back-formation
from the adjective snazzy.

snazzed-up *adj*
smart, elegant, dressed-up, embellished or enhanced. A more recent derivation of snazzy.

sneaks *n pl American*
trainers, sneakers. A teenage abbreviation heard in the 1990s.

sneeze *n*
cocaine. A term used by **yuppies** in the
late 1980s.

snide *adj British*
illegal, counterfeit, dishonest or unacceptable. The word's exact origins are
obscure but it is related to the German
schneiden (or its Dutch or Yiddish equivalent), meaning clip, and was used in the
context both of coin-cutting and of cutting remarks. The former sense gives rise
to the modern slang usage and the latter
to the standard English meaning. Snide
was first heard in Britain in the mid-19th
century. Interestingly, young speakers
have begun to revert to a Yiddish or Germanic pronunciation of the word as
shnide.

*'Are you accusing me of selling snide
gear?'*
(Recorded, street trader, Portobello
Road, London, 1986)

snip *n*
a small, insignificant and/or irritating
person. The word usually implies
aggression and pettiness. It is derived
from the notion of snip meaning to cut.

*some little snip throwing her weight
around*

snippy *adj*
irritatingly critical, brusque or presumptuous. Snippy is a dialect word for 'cutting' in origin.

She struck me as a little snippy snitch.

snit *n*
1a. a small, obnoxious or devious person.
The term is typically used of a smug or
devious child.

1b. an insignificant person. The word is
an invention influenced by **snip**, **snitch**
and possibly **snot**.

2. a fit of irritation, a tantrum

snitch¹ *vb*
to inform on (someone). Snitch was originally a slang term for the nose, which
was itself used to signify a police spy or
grass in the 18th century (as was **nark**).
Snitch began to be used in the verb form
in the 19th century and is still in use in
the USA, although in Britain it survives
mainly in children's speech, meaning to
'tell tales'.

snitch² *n*
an informer. The word (like **nark**, originally meaning nose) was first used in this
sense in the 18th century. It is still used
in the USA to mean a paid police
informer, whereas in Britain it is largely
confined to the language of children, in
which it denotes a 'tell-tale'.

snockered *adj*
1. an alternative form of **schnockered**
2. *American* completed, finalized, solved.
A term heard particularly among schoolchildren, students and parents.

snog¹ *vb*
to kiss ('snog up', used transitively, is a
racier late 1980s version). This light-
hearted word, used typically by children
and adolescents, first appeared in Britain before World War II. It is probably a
variant of 'snug' and 'snuggle (up)'. In
the 1950s, particularly in the USA,
snog took on a more general sense of
flirt. It retains its specific sense in Britain.

*'And I expect she's seen you walking out
with Dolly Clackett, and snogging on the
front porch.'*
(*Hancock's Half-hour*, BBC radio comedy, May 1960)

snog² *n British*
a kissing session. (For the origin of the
term, see the verb form.)

*They were having a quick snog while the
lights were out.*

snoot¹ *n*
1. the nose. A humorous variant form of
'snout'. (In Middle English 'snout' was
written as *snute* and pronounced
'snooter'.)

a punch on the snoot

2. a snooty person

snoot[2] *adj British*

showy, expensive, luxurious. The word is a shortening of the colloquial 'snooty'. An item of student slang in use in London and elsewhere since around 2000.

Look at all his snoot gear, I bet that guy doesn't do Byrite.

snooze *n*

something boring or tedious. A synonym of **yawn**.

'I must admit that last Tuesday's board meeting was a bit of a snooze.'
(*Maid to Order*, US film, 1987)

snore *n*

a boring experience. A synonym of **snooze** and **yawn**, typically used by adolescents.

A three hour talk on the EU; God, what a snore!

snork[1] *n Australian*

1. a baby or immature person. The word is said to be a distortion of 'stork', but may also be influenced by such words as 'snort', 'snicker', 'snit', 'snot' and the following sense of the word.

2. a sausage. This rare use of the word may be related to the synonymous **snag**.

snork[2] *vb*

to kiss. An imitative term from adolescent usage.

snorker *n Australian*

1a. a sausage

1b. the penis

The term is obviously related to the Australian **snork**, and perhaps to **snag**, but the exact origin of all of these terms is obscure.

snort *vb*

to sniff or inhale (illicit drugs such as heroin, cocaine, amphetamines, etc.) An Americanism which spread to Britain and Australia in the 1960s. The word supplanted the more sedate 'sniff', used previously.

'And am I dreary if I think that showing someone snorting coke on the telly is not such a great idea?'
(Janet Street-Porter, *Today*, 19 March 1988)

snot *n*

1. mucus from the nose. The word is from the Middle English *snotte*, itself from the Old English *gesnot*, variant forms of which existed in all Germanic languages. These terms are related either to 'snout' or to an Indo-European root

meaning to flow. Snot is a widespread term but, because of its distasteful context, is considered a vulgarism.

Wipe the snot off your face and cheer up.

2. an obnoxious person, usually a young or diminutive and self-important individual

That little snot.

snot-nosed, snotty-nose(d) *adj*

obnoxious and immature; young and over-confident

I'm not letting some snot-nosed kid tell me what to do!

snot-rag *n British*

a handkerchief

snotted *adj American*

intoxicated, drunk

snotty *adj*

1. suffering from catarrh, afflicted with a runny nose

2. obnoxious, self-important, snooty

snout[1] *n British*

1. the nose

2. a paid police informer. 'Nose' was used to denote a police spy or informer and so were slang synonyms such as **nark**, **snitch** and **snout**. Snout is of more recent origin than the other terms, dating from between the world wars.

3. tobacco, a cigarette. The use of snout to mean tobacco dates from the end of the 19th century when it originated among prison inmates. It was inspired by convicts touching their noses, either while cupping a surreptitious smoke or as a silent sign requesting tobacco. (The explanations are not mutually exclusive, one may have given rise to the other.) In the 1950s the use of 'a snout' for a cigarette became widespread in working-class speech.

snout[2] *vb British*

to inform, especially regularly in return for pay. The verb is derived from the earlier noun form.

'Naff ways of making money – snouting for a gossip columnist (esp. Nigel Dempster).'
(*The Complete Naff Guide*, Bryson et al, 1983)

snow[1] *n*

1. cocaine. The white crystalline drug resembles snow and its anaesthetic effect numbs like cold. The slang term dates from the turn of the 20th century. ('Snowbird' and 'snowball' were elaborations used in some circles.)

'A little snow at Christmas never did anyone any harm.'

(Legend on a 1969 Christmas card sent out by the record producer Phil Spector, featuring a still from the film *Easy Rider*, in which he had a cameo role as a cocaine dealer)

2. a **snow job**

3. *Australian* a nickname for a blond male, usually used pejoratively

snow² *vb*

to fool, cheat, bamboozle, especially by overloading someone with information. This Americanism (now occasionally heard in Britain) is based on the notion of 'snowing someone under' in order to deceive or manipulate them. It may also have originally evoked a 'snowstorm' of documentation.

'When you go into town on a false pass who do you think you're snowing?'

(*Battle Cry*, US film, 1954)

snowdrop *vb*

to steal clothes, typically underwear, from a clothes line. The underworld and police term may refer to a fetishistic practice or the actions of vagrants.

'We busked on street corners and snowdropped clothes from the backyard Hills Hoists of trendy Paddington.'

(*Girls' Night Out*, Kathy Lette, 1989)

snowdropper *n British*

someone who steals clothing, usually lingerie from washing lines, in the language of vagrants, police and prisoners. The term first referred (in the early 19th century) to the theft of clothes due to poverty; it now often denotes the act of a fetishist.

snow job *n American*

a case of deceit, browbeating or manipulation, particularly by means of glib or overwhelming persuasion or flattery. The phrase has been common since World War II.

Snow White *n American*

a white female or the personification of white womanhood. A black term almost always used pejoratively or facetiously.

snuff¹ *vb*

1. to kill. An old term, derived from the notion of extinguishing a candle. The curt 'tough guy' use of the word remains pop-

ular in street slang and crime fiction, particularly in the USA.

See also **snuff movie**

2. to sniff cocaine. An item from the drug user's vocabulary.

snuff² *n*

cocaine

snuff it *vb British*

to die. Inspired by the snuffing out of a candle, this expression has been heard in British English, particularly in working-class usage, since the turn of the 20th century.

snuff movie *n*

a violent, **hardcore** pornographic film supposedly featuring the actual death of one of the actors. Rumoured to have been made in the early 1970s, the actual existence of such a movie has never been proved. In the 1980s the term began to be applied to **splatter movies**, where the death and mayhem is indisputably faked.

snufty *n British*

an individual who derives sexual excitement from sniffing (clothing, bicycle saddles, etc.)

snyster *n British*

a snack. A dialect term from Lowland Scotland occasionally heard in other parts of the country.

soap-dodger *n British*

a dirty, unkempt or smelly person, a 'scruffbag' or **dosser**. An expression of disapproval among adults. **Bath-dodger** is a synonym.

soap (someone) up *vb American*

to flatter, cajole. A phrase used especially by adolescents since 2000. It may derive from the earlier phrase 'to soft-soap someone'.

S.O.B., s.o.b. *n American*

son of a bitch. The initial letters are often used in order to moderate the strength of the phrase, which is highly offensive in American usage.

Some S.O.B. walked off with her purse.

social handbag *n British*

an escort for a social occasion, **arm candy**. An item of student slang in use in London and elsewhere since around 2000.

sock (someone) *vb British*

to have sex with. An item of black street-talk used especially by males, recorded in 2003, often in the form of the taboo insult or provocation 'sock yer mom!'.

sod[1] *n British*

1a. an unpleasant person (of either sex, but more often male). The word often implies unfair or cruel behaviour on the part of the person described.

I'm sorry I was such a sod to you.

1b. an individual. Like **bugger**, the term is used when referring to someone with pity, irony or mild contempt.

'And that was another coincidence because he was the bloke I'd met earlier in the boozer, so I gave him my last £20 note because I thought, poor sod, he'll soon be dead.'

(William Donaldson, *Independent*, 26 August 1989)

1c. a nuisance or annoyance

That lid's a real sod to get off.

2. a sodomite. The original sense of the word is almost never heard in current English, it was last used in this way in the early 1960s. (The inhabitants of Sodom were, according to the book of Genesis, guilty of unnatural sexual practices.)

sod[2] *vb British*

the verb usually occurs as part of expletives such as 'sod you!' (indicating indifference, rejection, etc.) or 'sod it!' (indicating irritation or anger). Unlike its synonym **bugger**, the word is not used to mean sodomise.

soda *n American*

cocaine or **crack**. A term current among police and drug users in the late 1980s. From the resemblance and volatile effects of the drug(s).

sod-all *n British*

nothing, **bugger-all**

He got the profit and I got sod-all.

sodding *adj British*

an intensifying adjective like **bloody**, **bleeding**, etc. Sodding usually carries overtones of extreme irritation, impatience, etc.

sod off *vb British*

to leave, go away. The phrase is almost always an imperative, sometimes conveying only mild annoyance or aggression.

I told them to sod off and leave me alone.

sofa spud *n American*

a lazy, inert person. The term is a jocular variant of **couch potato**.

soft boy *n Jamaican*

a male homosexual or an effete or effeminate man. This phrase from Jamaican patois was adopted ironically as a name by the Soft Boys, a London rock group of the 1970s.

softshoe *vb*

to move or behave surreptitiously or in a manner both cautious and devious. Like **tap-dance** the metaphor is applied in raffish or **hip** talk to someone manoeuvring cleverly in social or professional situations. The expression is of course from the 'softshoe shuffle' dance step.

The guy managed to softshoe his way out of trouble again.

soggies *n British*

breakfast cereal. A middle- and upper-class term of the late 1970s and early 1980s inspired by the trademark names of cereals such as *Shreddies* and *Frosties* and their eventual consistency.

soixante-neuf *n See* **sixty-nine**

soldier *n See* **dead soldier**

solid[1] *n British*

hashish (as opposed to loose-leaf marihuana)

solid[2] *adj*

excellent, exciting. The slang term, still used by younger speakers in 2004, originated as part of pre-World War II **jive talk**, based on the colloquial sense of solid as denoting dependable, satisfactory.

something else *n*

something or someone outstanding, excellent, exceptional. An enduring phrase from the **hip** lexicon of the 1950s.

'She goes with all the guys from out of my class

But that can't stop me from thinking to myself,

"She's sure fine looking, man, she's something else".'

('Something Else', written by Sharon Sheeley and Eddie Cochran, recorded by Eddie Cochran, 1959)

sometimeish *adj Caribbean*

moody and unreliable

son of a bitch, sonofabitch *n American*

an unpleasant, obnoxious or despicable person. The expression is roughly the equivalent of the British **bastard** or **sod**, and often implies active nastiness, although it may be used with pity ('poor son of a bitch') or annoyance ('that engine's a son of a bitch!'). The epithet fell out of use in British speech around the middle of the 19th century. (The British Reverend Benjamin Newton records in his diary for 1818 how a wealthy fellow clergyman who had two sons called the one born out of wedlock 'son of a whore' and the one born within 'son of a bitch'.) In American speech the phrase son of a bitch was until recently considered too offensive for 'polite company' or broadcasting and would often be reduced to **S.O.B.**

> 'Wherever he went, Andy would have to be the nice guy and I had to be the sonofabitch.'
> (Fred Hughes on Andy Warhol, *Observer* magazine, March 1988)

sook, sooky *n Australian*
a 'cry-baby'. The noun probably postdates the adjective **sooky**, but the origins of both forms are uncertain.

sooky *adj Australian*
1a. sulky, sullen
1b. sentimental, 'soft' or 'unmanly'
The word may be a corruption or nursery version of 'sulky' itself, but the etymology is obscure. It has been suggested that it may derive from an archaic diminutive of 'Susan'.

sooty *n British*
a black or coloured person, an Arab. The racist epithet is derived from the colour of soot and the name of a glove puppet of a yellow bear, a popular figure in children's entertainment, especially television, since the 1950s. Although sooty does not sound unaffectionate, in actuality it is often used highly offensively. (In 1745 Henry Fielding referred to Jews as 'the Sooty Tribe' in his *Covent Garden Tragedy*.)

> 'We're pretty liberal really, we've only got one rule: no sooties.'
> (Recorded, proprietor of **Sloane Rangers**' nightclub, 1986)

soppo *adj British*
fashionable, exciting. This term of unknown origin, recorded among London's schoolchildren in the early 1990s, was defined by one user as **'funky** or **groovy'**. It is unlikely to be related to the negative 'soppy', but might be an alteration of 'sophisticated'.

sort *n*
a girl or woman. This specific sense of the word as used in working-class British and Australian speech may derive from the archaic 'salt'.

sort (out) *vb British*
1. to beat up. An innocuous euphemism describing a brutal reality, in keeping with a tendency of London working-class slang toward menacing understatement.

> 'I'll go and sort this Daley geezer.'
> · (*Minder*, British TV series, 1987)

See also **bother**; **seeing-to**
2. to have sex with. A masculine vulgarism with overtones of depersonalisation and brusqueness.

sorted *adj British*
1a. in a satisfactory situation, comfortable and content

> I reckon if you've got a girl, a car and a few bob, you're sorted.
> 'Sorted for E's and Whizz.'
> (Title of song by Pulp, 1995)

1b. excellent

> 'Let's finish up and get going.'
> 'Sorted.'

This use of the word (a clipping of the phrase 'sorted out'), which originated in criminal circles, meaning 'safely arranged' or 'adequately supplied', became one of the most popular vogue terms of the 1990s, beginning as a catchphrase among drug-dealers and eventually finding its way into the colloquial speech of middle-class adults.

sound *adj British*
excellent. A vogue term of approbation, generalised from the standard sense of 'reliable' for use among adolescents from the early 1990s. The word was particularly popular in the speech of the Merseyside area and often used as an exclamation.

soup (someone) up *vb American*
to flatter, cajole. The phrase, which probably derives from a mis-hearing or alteration of **soap (someone) up**, was used in the US film *Glitters*, a 2001 vehicle for the singer Mariah Carey.

soused *adj*
drunk, from the standard use of the word to mean soaked or drenched

> 'The Case of The Soused Superintendent'
> (Headline of online article at *www.ethics scoreboard.com*, 2 May 2004)

sov *n British*
one pound. The word is a shortening of 'sovereign' and was used to designate that gold coin (worth one pound) until its discontinuance in 1914. Sov was popularised by its copious use in the popular TV series *Minder*, set among

the working-class and criminal population of London.

> 'Eric Idle sounds as though he might just have relieved a punter of 500 sovs for a second-hand motor.'
> (*Independent*, 17 March 1989)

sow *n British*
an unpleasant woman. The (fairly rare) term of abuse usually implies real distaste or bitter recrimination.

S.P. *n British*
starting price, the odds on a horse. Hence essential information, a basis for judgment, the known form. A term fashionable in working-class and raffish circles since the later 1980s. It has been in underworld and gambling use since the 1950s.

> 'What's the S.P. on Murphy? Dead from the neck up!'
> ('Arthur Daley' in *Minder*, British TV series, 1984)

spa *n British*
a good friend. The term has been in use among London teenagers since the 1990s and before that was heard in Wales. It may derive from 'sparring-partner'. **Star-spa** is a variant form.

space *vb American*
to daydream, lose concentration or enter a euphoric state. An adolescents' expression based on the earlier **spaced out** and **spacy**.

> She puts on the headphones and just starts to space.

space cadet *n American*
an eccentric, mad or **spaced out** person. A popular expression since the later 1970s, which has entered British and Australian usage. The term is inspired by the expression 'spaced out' and the 1950s science fiction TV series, *Tom Corbett, Space Cadet*. 'Space-case' is a synonymous term.

space-case *n American See* **space cadet**

spaced out *adj*
under the influence of drugs or behaving in an eccentric or insane fashion. A term that originated in America and spread to Britain with the drug-culture of the 1960s. The term is based on the notion of being extremely **high** and disconnected from earthly realities.

spack[1] *adj Australian*
an all-purpose term of disapproval or doubt, in use among schoolchildren in the late 1980s. The word, of uncertain

origin, is used as an adjective or exclamation.

spack[2], spac *n British*
an unfortunate, weak or slow-witted person. A more recent synonym of **spanner**.

spacy, spacey *adj*
1a. producing euphoria or evoking a dream-like state

> Spacy music.
> This is spacy dope.

1b. behaving in a distracted, euphoric or **spaced out** way

spade *n*
1. a black person. The term comes from the expression 'as black as the ace of spades' and originated sometime before the 1920s. Spade has almost never been used with racist connotations; it was the word used by white devotees of West Indian culture and music in Britain in the 1950s and 1960s, notably in the title of Colin Wilson's landmark novel, *City of Spades*, published in 1959.

> 'A constable said to me, as he left the canteen, "I'm going to get a spade now, sarge". He punched a fist in the palm of his hand.'
> (Simon Holdaway, *Inside the British Police*, 1983)

2. *South African* a gun, in particular an AK-47 rifle

spaghetti-eater, spaghetti-bender, spag *n*
an Italian. These are derogatory terms heard predominantly in Australia, referring to immigrants. The equivalent American term is usually simply 'spaghetti'.

spakker *n British*
a handicapped or slow-witted person. A variant form of **spack**.

spam *vb*
to flood another's computing system with redundant or meaningless information. The practice is indulged in as a prank or punishment by **cyberpunks** or **net-heads**.

> 'Spamming is often doled out as punishment for behaviour that runs against the grain of net culture – corporate advertising say – or posting a chain letter ...'
> (*Surfing on the Internet* by J. C. Herz, 1994)

spam! *exclamation British*
an all-purpose exclamation of defiance, rejection, irritation. The word was defined on the Internet in February 1997 by *Bodge World*.

spam javelin, spam baton n British
the penis. The second version was
recorded on the website of the Royal
Marines in 2004. **Beef bayonet** is a synonym.

spangled adj British
intoxicated by drink or drugs

> 'I got absolutely spangled on vodka the
> night before and had a really great time.'
> (Johnny Borrell of Razorlight, NME 28
> March 2005)

spank, spanking n British
a beating, usually a severe one. An
example of menacing understatement
in working-class slang, as used by
police officers and criminals. The term
is used only slightly more lightheartedly
as a euphemism for sadistic games or
flagellation.

> taking part in spanking sessions
> 'D'you want your spankin' now?'
> (The Firm, British TV play, 1989)

spankin' adj American
excellent, exciting, powerful, impressive.
A vogue term since around 2000, synonymous with **jammin'**, **quakin'**.

spank the plank vb
to play the guitar. A piece of musicians'
jargon.

spank your very crotch exclamation
British
thank you very much. A jocular alteration recorded on the Student World
website in 2001.

spanner n British
an unfortunate, weak individual, a misfit.
The term became a popular phrase
among adolescents in the early 1990s
following its use on the BBC TV comedy,
The Mary Whitehouse Experience. It
probably originated as a schoolboy variation of **spastic** and **spasmo**, perhaps
blended with **prannet** or **pranny**.

spannered adj British
intoxicated by drugs or alcohol. The
term was in use among young British
holidaymakers on Ibiza in 1999.

spare[1] n British
an unattached and presumably available female or females. A condescending, slightly archaic term, usually
forming part of a phrase such as 'a bit
of spare'.

> What's it like down the dancehall? Plenty
> of spare?

spare[2] adj British
out of control, furious. The word, usually in the form 'go spare', has been in
use since before World War II. It derives
from the notion of excess.

spark vb British
1. to incite someone to anger or violence.
A vogue term among British adolescents
since the 1990s.

> It's easy to spark him, but I wouldn't do it
> if I were you.

2. to hit (someone). The term may be
based on the phrase **spark out**, meaning
(knocked) unconscious.
3. to take drugs, become **stoned**

> We was sparkin'.

sparkler n British
a lie, especially a welcome or helpful
lie. A working-class Londoner's expression.

> 'So he wouldn't say the old sparkler?'
> (Simon Holdaway, Inside the British Po-
> lice, 1983)

sparklers n pl
jewels, gems. A long established term
from the lexicon of thieves, counterfeit-
ers, **spivs**, etc.

spark out, sparko adj, adv British
fast asleep or completely unconscious.
The expression is now a mainly working-
class colloquialism; it was formerly a
rustic expression evoking a dead fire or
extinguished candle. Sparko was a variant form heard in the 1980s.

> He had three or four drinks and went
> spark out.
> She's been sparko for the last hour or so.

sparkplug n American
a tampon. An expression used on campus in the USA since around 2000.

spark up vb
to light a cigarette or **joint**. The phrase,
which became widespread in the 1990s,
also occurs as a request or demand to
'spark me up'.

sparrowfart n
dawn. A joky euphemism inspired by
'cock-crow'. The phrase became obsolete in Britain in the 1930s but
remained in use in Australia, and was
revived in Britain in the late 1960s by
the cartoon strip The Adventures of
Barry McKenzie, published in the satirical magazine Private Eye.

spasmo n British
a variant form of **spastic** or **spazz**

spastic adj, n
(behaving like or reminiscent of) a clumsy, unfortunate, feeble, foolish or unpopular individual. A schoolchildren's vogue word in Britain from the early 1960s onwards, prompted by the publicity given to charities and other schemes to aid spastic children. The same word was used in the 1950s by adults, particularly in the armed services, and in the 1960s by schoolchildren and adolescents in the USA. The noun form is frequently shortened to 'spas' or **spazz**; the adjective altered to 'spazzy'.
   That's an utterly spastic idea.
   You can't fancy him! He looks an utter spastic.

spazz, spaz n, adj
(a person who is) foolish, clumsy, incapable. A version of **spastic** used by schoolchildren in Britain and the USA.

spazzmobile n British
1a. an invalid car
1b. an old, decrepit or (supposedly) ludicrous vehicle
The word has been used by schoolchildren since the 1960s.

spazz out vb American
to lose control of oneself; become hysterical or agitated, go berserk. A teenage phrase of the 1970s and 1980s, from **spastic**.

spec adj British
excellent. In playground usage since 2000. It may derive from the appreciative use of 'special'.

special adj British
slow-witted, foolish. A playground term of abuse from the notion of children 'with special needs'.

special K n
the drug ketamine. The nickname borrows the brand name of a breakfast cereal.

specky adj Australian
neat, clever. The fairly common term has been defined by Internet slang enthusiasts as 'nifty'. 'Specking' was an old term for mining for gold, but the connection is not proven.

spee n British
a friend, comrade. In an article in the *New Statesman and Society*, Maria Manning reports this word, of unknown origin, as being used in school playgrounds in the UK in February 1990.

speech vb British
1a. to 'chat up' a potential partner
   He was speeching her all evening.
1b. to attempt to persuade, cajole
   Don't try speeching me.

speed n
an amphetamine drug. The word was first applied in the 1960s to methedrine, a powerful stimulant. By 1968 it was becoming the generic term for all amphetamines (which literally 'speed up' the nervous system).
   'Someone suffering (and they do!) from speed hang-ups and come-downs really drags the whole scene down.'
   (Letter to *Oz* magazine, June 1968)

speedball n
a combination of stimulant and depressant (e.g. heroin and cocaine) for injection. The word arose among hard-drug users of the 1940s in the USA. By the 1980s it was also used to designate various other concoctions including those taken orally or by inhalation.

speedfreak n
1a. a user of **speed** (amphetamines)
1b. a person who behaves as if over-stimulated, by extension from the first subsense

speeding adj
under the influence of **speed**

spencer n South African
an attractive young female

spesh adj British
exceptional, excellent. A characteristic clipping of the standard sense in adolescent usage from the 1990s.
   They were hoping for something really spesh.
   You're my spesh mate.

spewing adj Australian
extremely irritated, agitated, flustered, etc.

spewsome adj British
nauseating, repellent. A middle-class usage, blending 'spew' and 'gruesome'.

spick, spic n, adj
(a person) of Latin origin, (an) Italian or Hispanic. This highly offensive racist term parodies the speech of such people in the catchphrase 'no spick da Inglish'.

spide n British
a synonym for **chav**, in vogue in 2004. It is said to originate in Belfast slang.

spidge n British
chewing gum. The term was posted on the b3ta website in 2004.

spiel vb, n
(to give) a speech or talk, particularly a glib or persuasive patter. The expression may also encompass hard luck stories or lengthy excuses. The word originated in the 19th century, deriving from the German *spieler* (a player) or *spielen* (to play), as applied to card-sharps, hence hucksters, fast-talkers, etc.

> He gave me this long spiel about how he was so overworked he wouldn't have time to help.

spiffed, spiffed-up, spiffed out adj
dressed smartly. These expressions, now popular among American teenagers, are, like the British **spiffy**, 'spiffing' and **spiv**, a derivation of the early-19th-century British dialect term 'spiff', meaning dandy. Spiffed itself was heard in British speech until the 1930s and spiffed-up until the 1960s.

spifflicate vb British
to beat up, thoroughly defeat. A nursery word of the 1950s, spifflicate was coined in the 18th century (the first recorded use was in 1785 meaning to confound). It does not derive directly from any standard or dialect term, but is an invention imitating Latinate multi-syllabics.

spiffy adj
smart, dapper, impressive. A word which, since it is in mainly middle- and upper-class use, is generally considered colloquial rather than slang. It derives from the archaic 19th-century dialect word 'spiff' (noun and adjective), meaning (a person who is) dandy or smartly dressed, which is also the origin of spiffing and **spiv**.

> 'You're the best looking cop in the place. Well, you look pretty spiffy yourself.'
> (*Legwork*, US TV series, 1987)

spike n
a hypodermic syringe. An item of drug addicts' jargon dating from the 1950s. The word was used to denote an ordinary needle for many years before that.

> 'When I put a spike into my vein,
> Then I tell you things aren't quite the same.'
> (Lyrics to 'Heroin', written by Lou Reed and recorded by the Velvet Underground, 1967)

spike up vb
to inject onself (with a narcotic)

spill vb
to confess, own up or reveal a secret. A racier version of the colloquial 'spill the beans', the term is typically used in an underworld context, often involving informing on associates or otherwise betraying a confidence.

> I couldn't get him to spill.

spill one's guts vb
to confess or reveal information. An elaboration of **spill** or 'spill the beans' used particularly by or about criminals.

> They put a little pressure on him and the creep spilled his guts.

spin n British
a search (of a home or other premises), typically by police officers. A derivation of **spin (someone's) drum**.

> I think we'd better give their gaff a spin.
> He's about due for a spin.

spin (someone's) drum vb British
to make an official search of someone's house, in the jargon of the police force. **Drum** is one's home and spin provides the play on words, referring to the spinning of a drum in a fairground lottery. In the 1990s 'spin this' was used as an expression synonymous with 'up yours', and was accompanied by a one-fingered gesture.

spin out vb
to become confused or disorientated

> 'I was totally spun out when I found out James was cheating on me.'
> (Recorded, teenager, Devon, 2002)

spit[1] n American
1a. rubbish, nonsense, **shit**
1b. nothing at all, **zip**, **zilch**

> 'What did he tell me? – He told me spit.'
> (*Macgruder and Loud*, US film, 1985)

In both cases spit is a euphemism for **shit**, usable in fairly polite company or in the mass media.

spit[2] n See **big spit, the**

spit-spot adj
fine, excellent, as it should be. A euphemistic version of **shit-hot**. (The expression is used by the fictional Mary Poppins in the film of the same name, as a synonym for 'chop-chop'.)

spit the dummy vb Australian
to lose one's temper, express one's anger. The image is presumably that of a baby expelling its pacifier in a fit of rage.

spitting feathers n British
exhibiting extreme enthusiasm or agitation. The colourful phrase is heard particularly in armed-forces' usage and probably evokes the squawking of a frantic bird. It is one of many bird-related images in colloquial speech, such as **drop off the twig**/perch and 'sick as a parrot'.

spiv n British
a disreputable, flashy male, typically one who lives by shady dealing rather than orthodox work. This word had existed in the jargon of race-track habitués and petty criminals since the late 19th century, but came into its own after World War II, when it was adopted by the press and public to designate the touts, black marketeers and 'wide boys' who flourished in the late 1940s and early 1950s. Spiv is an alteration of 'spiff', an archaic dialect word for a dandy which also gave rise to the adjectives **spiffy** and 'spiffing'.

'Max Kidd was an ex-plumber made good; a total spiv down to the last camel hair in his coat.'
(TV review by Kate Saunders, *Evening Standard*, 17 May 1989)

splash the boots vb
to urinate. A euphemism heard, particularly among drinkers, in Australia and Britain since the 1960s.

'Excuse I, but could you direct me to the bathroom. I've got to splash the boots.'
(*The Wonderful World of Barry McKenzie*, cartoon strip by Barry Humphries and Nicholas Garland, 1966)

splatted adj British
stabbed. An item of black street-talk used especially by males, recorded in 2003.

splay[1] n American
marihuana. A word of obscure origin used by schoolchildren and students.

splay[2] vb American
to have sex (with). The vulgarism invariably applies to male sexual activity. It has been recorded in use among Californian pornographers and prostitutes and may have originated as photographers' jargon, from 'splay-shot', employing the standard word (itself a Middle English clipping of 'display').

splend adj British
excellent, admirable, very satisfactory. A shortening of **splendid** favoured by middle-class adolescents and young adults since 2000.

splendid adj British
excellent. The standard word was borrowed as a vogue term of approbation by British teenagers in the early 1990s.

splib n American
an Afro-Caribbean person. A racist epithet heard since the 1980s, of uncertain origin although it is claimed unconvincingly to be a blend of **spade** and 'liberal'. It is more likely to be a nonsense bebop or **jive talk** coinage.

splice vb British
to have sex (with)

'I spliced his woman while he was on bar duty downstairs.'
(*Harry's Kingdom*, British TV film, 1986)

spliff n
1. a cannabis cigarette, **joint**. The word, which is of uncertain derivation, originated in Britain or the Caribbean in the 1960s. In the USA it designates a joint containing both cannabis and tobacco, in the 'English style'.
2. a stupid person. The word is used in this way by teenagers.

split[1] vb
to leave. A piece of American slang that came to Britain in the **hippy** era, it is a shortening of the earlier **beatnik** term 'split the scene' (from the notion of separating oneself from a group or gathering).

split[2] n British
a female. This highly derogatory term is short for 'split arse' and was popularised by the comedian Roy 'Chubby' Brown.

'Lesley Morris, 23, said sailors called the WRENS sluts, slags, splits and turtles.'
(*Daily Mirror*, 4 February 1997)

splosh n British
1a. a woman or women in general
1b. an act of sexual intercourse
Both these related uses are vulgarisms popular in London working-class parlance since the late 1970s, often in the form 'a bit of splosh'.
2. money. This sense of the word is now almost obsolete, but existed in the vocabularies of cockneys, **spivs** and their upper-class imitators in the 1950s.

splurt vb British
to leave, run away. The term, whose etymology is uncertain, may be an altered form of **split**. It has been used by gang

members and schoolchildren since the late 1990s.

spod¹ *n British*

1a. smegma

1b. seminal fluid

A vulgarism which was in use among adolescents in the 1990s.

2. a clumsy, dimwitted or socially unacceptable person. The term is applied to school misfits by fellow pupils and was reported to be in current use at Eton in the September 1989 issue of *Tatler*. In the 1990s it was defined as a synonym for **narg** in Oxbridge student slang.

spod² *vb British*

to engage in meaningless activities when supposedly doing a job. Posted on the Internet by *Bodge World* in 1997.

spoilers *n pl South African*

the buttocks. An appreciative term applied to females by males by analogy with the rear of a sports car. **Hatchback** and **sixteen-valve** are other automotive terms applied to females.

spon *n British*

1. money. A clipped form of **spondulicks**, fashionable in certain circles since the late 1980s.

'We're going to have to go round to Bill's to pick up some spon.'

(Recorded, self-employed decorator, London, 1988)

2. a fool. This childish term of abuse or disparagement has been obsolete since the early 1960s. It was almost certainly a survival of the early 19th century use of spoon to mean a simpleton.

spondulicks, spondoolicks *n*

money, wealth. A lighthearted term which was obsolescent by the 1960s (having originated in the USA in the 1850s), but which, like other synonyms for money, was revived in the 1980s (compare **rhino**, **pelf**, etc.) It originated as a learned witticism, borrowing the Greek term *spondylikos*; pertaining to the *spondylos*, a seashell used as currency.

spoof *vb Australian*

to ejaculate. **Spuff** is a variant form.

spooge *n American*

sperm. The word is an invention based on the standard term and used by children and adolescents.

spook *n American*

1. a black person. The reference is either an ironic one to the subjects' black colour (as opposed to the white of spectres) or to their 'haunting' of certain locations.

2. a spy, secret agent. This usage may be a simple reference to unseen 'ghosts' or may derive from the fact that many World War II agents were recruited from the Yale secret society, the 'Skull and Bones'.

'In 30 beautifully crafted novels during the past 16 years, he [Ted Allbeury] has revealed details from the real world of spooks that have been struck from others' memoirs.'

(*Sunday Times*, 17 December 1989)

spooky *adj British*

eccentric, crazy. An item of youth slang recorded in the 1990s which may have originated in black usage.

That Linda's well spooky.

spoon *n British*

1. a person from a privileged and/or wealthy background. The word became fashionable among young City financial traders in the early 1990s, used either contemptuously or teasingly by working-class speakers of their upper- (or sometimes middle-)class fellows. It derives from the expression 'born with a silver spoon in one's mouth'.

2. a stupid, 'thick' person.

See also **mong**; **minghawk**; **scrag²**; **spliff**

spooner *n British*

an unpleasant and/or obnoxious person. In playground usage since 2000.

sport girl *n Caribbean*

a prostitute or promiscuous female

spot (someone) *vb*

1a. *American* to pay for, lend or advance money to. This usage of spot probably derives from gambling or sports jargon in which it means to specify odds or conditions.

Spot me a twenty will you?

1b. to lend or give. The older adult colloquialism has become a vogue term among British adolescents since 2000.

Can you spot me a cig?

spout off *vb British*

to talk volubly, pompously or out of turn. A post-1970 version of the earlier 'spout' or the more literary 'spout forth', suggesting the outpouring of words. Spout off, like 'mouth off', is usually used intransitively and is more disparaging than the earlier forms.

sprang vb Caribbean
to steal or borrow without permission. Recorded in Trinidad and Tobago in 2003. Synonyms are **bandit** and **raf**.

sprankious, sprankshious adj Caribbean
lively, attractive

sprat vb British
to look for a sexual partner, attempt to seduce. Often in the form 'out spratting', the equivalent of **out trouting** which may have inspired it. It may also be based on the phrase 'a handful of sprats' (a variant of the more recent **bit of fish**), meaning successful sexual contact with a female.

sprayed adj British
shot. An item of black street-talk used especially by males, recorded in 2003. Said to be from the resultant spraying of blood rather than bullets.

spree-boy n Caribbean
a roisterer

spring (someone) vb
to obtain someone's release from captivity or prison, either as a result of a legal manoeuvre or, more commonly, by assisting their escape

spring for vb British
to pay for. A raffish expression, used typically by working-class speakers, indicating willingness or alacrity.

   OK, keep your hand in your pocket, I'll spring for the grub.

sprog n British
1a. a child, offspring
1b. a novice, new recruit
The first sense of the word has become widespread in colloquial speech since the mid-1970s, the second is limited to the context of institutions, including the armed services. The exact origin of the word is obscure, but it is reasonable to assume that it is a blend of **sprout** and 'sprig'. Sprog also means 'head' in Australia.

sprog some dosh vb British
to withdraw money from a cash-dispenser or bank. A phrase used by students from the late 1990s. The **sprog** element may denote 'give birth to'.

   'I need to sprog some dosh before we get to the pub...'
   (Recorded, London student, 1999)

sprout n British
a child. The word is a middle-class 1990s' alternative to the earlier **sprog** and the more recent **howler** and **wowler**.

sprung adj American
infatuated. An item of teenage slang applied to someone who 'has a crush' on another.

   I could tell she was totally sprung on me.

spuck n American
semen

spud n
1. a potato. This universal slang term has been recorded since the 1840s. A 'spud' was a small narrow spade (from the Middle English spudde, meaning a dagger, itself from the Italian spada, meaning a sword) of the sort used to dig up potatoes.
2. a stupid person. This use of the word, recorded among schoolchildren, may be an alteration of **spod** rather than a reference to the potato.

spud-bashing n British
potato-peeling, especially as a punishment

spuff vb Australian
to ejaculate. A variant form of **spoof**, the term was used in the Australian movie The Hard Word in 2003.

spunk n
1a. spirit, vim. The word has been recorded in this sense since the 18th century. Most authorities derive it from spong, a Gaelic word for tinder (itself from the Latin spongia, meaning sponge), hence 'spark'.
1b. semen. The idea of a life-force, 'vital spark' or spirit in the male context led to spunk being used in this sense (as was 'mettle' in archaic speech) from the 19th century onwards.
2. Australian a **spunk rat**. The shorter form, usually referring to males only, has become increasingly widespread since about 1987.

spunk rat n Australian
a sexually attractive young person. The phrase is based on **spunky** in the sense of spirited, and is influenced also by **spunk** in the sexual sense.

   'But it's all right for her, she's got a whole smorgasbord selection of classic spunk rats.'
   (Kathy Lette, Girl's Night Out, 1989)

spunky adj
spirited. The adjective is derived from the noun **spunk**.

squaddie n British
an army private. The word is either from
'squad' or from the archaic swaddy,
meaning a bumpkin.

square adj, n
(a person who is) conventional, conservative or unfashionable. Since the 17th
century square has been used to mean
honest, reputable or straightforward. The
modern sense of the word dates from the
1930s **jive talk** of black jazz musicians in
Harlem, New York. (Cab Calloway's 1938
lexicon defines a square as an 'unhip
person'.)

> 'To be square is to be dull, middle aged,
> old fashioned. To be square is to be not
> with it.'
> (About Town magazine, June 1962)

squat n American
(a) **shit**. From the action of squatting
down to defecate. By extension, squat, a
word used typically in country areas of
the USA, is also used to mean nothing or
a worthless thing. **Doodly squat** is an elaboration.

> It ain't worth squat.

squawk¹ vb
1. to complain noisily or raucously
2. to inform (on someone). A rarer synonym of **squeal**.

squawk² n
a radio message. A term used especially
by police officers or military personnel
for a short burst of information coming
into a walkie-talkie radio or field telephone.

squawker n British
1a. a walkie-talkie as used by police officers or security guards
1b. a mobile telephone
Both terms were commonly used from the
early 1990s.

squeak n British
a young naive teenager. A term applied
by older adolescents to would-be members of the fashionable circles of London
in the late 1980s. The term usually
referred to a girl of the sort previously
designated as a **teenybopper**.

> 'The bouncer gets a bit heavy demanding
> ID from a group of squeaks who look like
> they have given their babysitter the slip.'
> (Evening Standard magazine, May 1989)

squeal vb
to inform (on someone). The usage
arose in early 19th century dialect,

spreading to underworld argot first in
Britain and subsequently in the USA.

squeeze n
1. American a girlfriend or boyfriend, a
sweetheart. The word is inspired by the
squeeze of an embrace and is often
heard in the form **main squeeze** (which
has the added meaning of 'most important person').
2. British money, cash. The word often
has overtones of hard-earned or reluctantly paid money.

squid n American
a **swot**. A high school and campus term,
perhaps suggesting oiliness or the emis-
sion of quantities of ink.

squidgy n British
an amateur windscreen cleaner.
'Squeegee' is an alternative form.

squidlet n British
1. a child
2. a pound coin or other amount of
money

squids n British
money. A term of middle-class slang
common since the later 1990s. It is an
alteration of **quid**.

squiff n Australian
1a. a drunkard
1b. a drinking bout
Both terms are back formations from the
adjective **squiffy**.

squiffy adj
(slightly) drunk, merry or inebriated. An
inoffensive, lighthearted word suggesting slight disorientation, squiffy has
been in use since the 19th century.

squiffy doo adj British
dubious, doubtful, suspect. A middle-
class expression heard in the 1980s. It
derives from the notion of 'askew' and
'out of true' expressed by the adjective
squiffy.

squillion n British
a hyperbolically huge number. A
pseudo-nursery word, typically used by
condescending or ingratiating journalists in teenage magazines, that became
a teenage vogue term of the 1980s.

> 'Last week we got thirteen squillion letters
> asking which video company brought out
> Star Trek IV, our fab giveaway. Well it was
> CIC. So there.'
> (Just Seventeen, teenage girls' magazine,
> December 1987)

squirly adj American
restless, agitated. A word with rustic overtones which is probably a form of 'squirrely' (which itself was not only a metaphor, but formerly a punning synonym for **nuts**).

'We can't afford to let him go and get squirly on us.'
(Recorded, US executive, London 2002)

squirt n
1. an insignificant, diminutive and/or impudent and annoying individual (usually male). This figurative use of the standard word dates from the mid-19th century. It is not certain whether it originated in British or American speech.
2. British money, cash, funds. The term is probably based on the idea of a squirt of oil lubricating the system, or a squirt of spirit igniting a fire or engine.

We just need a bit more squirt and we can go ahead with our plans.

squirts, the n
a case of diarrhoea. An alternative form of **the squits**.

squit n British
an insignificant, small and/or irritating person. The word is a variant form of the synonymous **squirt** and has been heard since the 1880s.

'There are 5 squits, 9 snekes, 19 cribbers, 2 maniaks, 4 swots.'
(Back in the Jug Agane, Geoffrey Willans and Ronald Searle, 1959)

squits, the n
a case of diarrhoea. Both words are onomatopoeic.

'No thanks, love, olive oil doesn't agree with me.
Gives you the squits, does it, Grandad?'
(Nice Work, David Lodge, 1988)

squiz, squizz n
a look, glance. Perhaps influenced by squint and/or quiz(zical), the term is heard in Australasia and the UK.

'Let's take a squizz at the new place.'
(Brain Dead, New Zealand film, 1993)
'Have a squiz at the back pages of a society magazine...'
(Daily Telegraph magazine, 9 November 2002)

stabber n British
a male homosexual. The term was applied to supposedly active **gay** males as opposed to the passive **stooper**. The

pejorative, supposedly humorous designations were in use among heterosexual Fleet Street/Wapping journalists in the early 1990s. Stabber is said to be a shortening of 'suit-stabber'.

stack[1] adj
1. excellent, fantastic. A teenage vogue word of the late 1980s, used as an exclamation of approval or delight. The term spread from the language of hip hop in New York to London aficionados.

'Just forget about using the word mega to express your delight. The latest expression is stack!'
(Daily Mirror, September 1987)
2. inferior, negative, 'no way', etc. The word, like many similar vogue terms, is also used to mean its virtual opposite.

'Stack (meaning: not at all, i.e. Samantha Fox is immensely talented ... STACK!) is now the only logo to be seen with (we know, we invented it).'
(Advertisement in I-D magazine, November 1987)

stack[2] vb
to crash (a vehicle), destroy. The word is used in this sense throughout the English-speaking world. For skateboarders and schoolchildren since the late 1990s it refers to falling over or tripping up.

stacked adj
(of a woman) having large breasts, 'well-endowed'. A male term of approbation which is now offensive to most women. The expression, first popular in the USA, is a shortening of 'well-stacked'.

'When one person is important and the other person is stacked and/or well-hung.'
(Sub-heading in P. J. O'Rourke's Modern Manners, 1983)

stack some zees/zeds vb
to sleep. The phrase, originating in the USA, is synonymous with the more common **cop/bag some zees**.

stain[1] n British
an unfashionable, tedious individual or a **swot**. This term of contempt was in use among university students in the late 1980s. It is usually a synonym of **anorak**; unbeknown to most users it is short for **wank stain**, i.e. a despicable nonentity.

'"Stains" are "replete with acne and anoraks".'
(Evening Standard, 16 June 1988)

stain² *adj British*
bad, unpleasant, disappointing. The adjectival usage dates from around 2000.

stalk *n*
1a. an erection or the penis. This British and Australian sense of the word principally survives in the phrases 'stalk fever' and **stalk-on**.
1b. effrontery (in a male), cheek, **bottle**. A rare working-class usage (recorded in *The Signs of Crime, A Field Manual for Police* by Deputy Assistant Commissioner David Powis, 1977).

stalk-on *n*
an erection. A vulgarism heard since the 1950s.

stallion *n*
a **stud**. The term has been used figuratively in this way since the 14th century.

stan *n British*
1. a Pakistani. The 'a' is long, the term is usually neutral not pejorative.
2. a curry

stand, stand-on *n*
an erection

standard *adj British*
1a. excellent
1b. an all-purpose exclamation of approval or agreement

> *'Standard in East London means like definitely, for sure.'*
> (Posting on www.blackchat.co.uk, March 2004)

The term has acquired these specialised senses in black British speech since 2000, and in 2004 was reported as a vogue term among **chavs**.

stand-up *adj American*
honourable, reliable, steadfast. A term of (mainly male) approbation or admiration in such clichés as 'a stand-up guy'. It derives from the notion of 'standing up for someone' or being willing to 'stand up and be counted'.

> *'It's funny that priest going AWOL. I always thought he was a real standup guy.'*
> (*V*, US TV film, 1983)

stank *adj American*
1a. unpleasant
1b. in poor taste, inappropriate
> *That girlfriend's outfit is stank.*

An expression used on campus in the USA since around 2000.

stanky *n American*
an unstylish person. A more recent variation of **skank(y)** and **scangey**.

star *exclamation British*
an all-purpose intensifier placed at the end of an utterance

> *'Hey, I'm the king at table tennis – star!'*
> (Recorded, London student, 2000)

starkers *adj British*
naked. A characteristic public-school or Oxbridge version of 'stark naked' which has become a common colloquialism. (It is sometimes elaborated to **harry-starkers**.)

star-spa *n British*
a friend, fellow gang member. The term was used as an indicator of solidarity by adolescent gang members and as a term of address. It was recorded in use among North London schoolboys in the 1990s.

startin' *n British*
fighting. From black speech. Synonyms are **mixin'**, **regulatin'**, **tanglin'**.

stash *vb*
to hide, put away. The word, which spread from America to the rest of the English-speaking world at the turn of the 20th century, was probably originally a blend of 'stow', 'store' and 'cache'. It was formerly often spelled 'stache'.

state *n British*
a mess, disaster. This word became an all-purpose vogue term in London working-class speech of the early 1970s. The original notion of 'to be in a (bit of a) state' was transformed so that state (**two and eight** in rhyming slang) came to refer to the individual rather than the situation.

> *He looks a right old state, doesn't he?*

static *n American*
criticism or hostile interference. A respectable slang term inspired by the standard sense of an electrical disturbance or interference. The suggestion is typically of opposition from various quarters that threatens to frustrate a scheme.

> *We're getting a lot of static from higher up now that the powers that be have been informed.*

staunch *adj South African*
tough, strong, attractively fit. A vogue term in youth slang.

stay loose *vb American*
an alternative version of **hang loose**

steamboats adj British
drunk. A lighthearted term of uncertain derivation. It may have something to do with the use of a name such as 'Steamboat Bill', possibly in a lost rhyming-slang expression.
  He was completely steamboats by mid-day.

steamed adj American
furious. A 1980s variation on the more generalised 'steamed-up'.

steamer n British
a bout of heavy drinking. Often heard in the phrase 'on/in a steamer'.

steamers n pl British
gangs of muggers who enter a shop, train compartment, etc. en masse and overwhelm their victims with some force. From the colloquial 'steam (in)', meaning to move forcefully and quickly. The term arose in London in 1985 among black street gangs.

steaming[1] n British
the activity of **steamers**
  'Steaming is very modern, a term for mob-handed theft often by joeys, young criminals.'
  (James Morten, Independent, 23 December 1988)

steaming[2] adj British
1. an otherwise meaningless intensifying adjective, almost invariably used in the now dated expression '(a) steaming nit', which was briefly popular in the early 1960s
2. drunk
  'You've only had two cans and you're steaming.'
  (Red Dwarf IV, BBC comedy, 1994)

steek n British
a synonym of **chav**, in vogue in 2004. It may be an altered form of **stig**.

stem n
a knife, particularly when carried or used for criminal purposes. An item of New York street slang that spread to other English-speaking areas in the early 1990s.

step! exclamation
don't try it!

stepford adj American
dully conformist, android-like. The term is inspired by the 1975 cult film The Stepford Wives, depicting a suburb in which women are turned by men into placid robot hausfraus. **Devo** carries the same connotations.

step off, step vb American
1. to opt out, desist, stop
2. to lose one's temper, become aggressive
Both usages originated in black street slang and may refer to the figurative sense of stepping off the straight and narrow, or the physical sense of leaving a path, sidewalk, escalator, etc., in order to launch an attack.

step on adj
to adulterate, cut (a drug). The term has been used by drug users and dealers since the end of the 1960s, particularly in reference to cocaine or heroin; occasionally it is used of amphetamines, but not of cannabis or other organic substances.
  'You expect a cut at this level, but this stuff has been stepped on by a gang of navvies in hob-nailed boots.'
  (Recorded, cocaine user, London, 1982)

step on one's dick vb American
to make a blunder. A term used particularly in the context of the workplace or the armed forces.
  Just give those guys some slack and pretty soon one of them will step on his dick.

Steve McQueens n British
jeans. Rhyming slang using the name of the late Hollywood star.

stick n
1. a **joint**, **reefer** (cannabis cigarette). A term which was fairly widespread among smokers of the drug (**beatniks**, prisoners, etc.) until the mid-1960s, when joint and **spliff** largely supplanted it.
2. British chastisement, physical or verbal punishment. Originally implying a literal thrashing with a stick or cane, then generalised to any violent assault, the expression is now used, especially by middle-class speakers, to encompass verbal abuse, denigration or nagging.
  You've done nothing but snipe at me since I got home – what have I done to deserve all this stick?
3. British a police truncheon
  'His trousers weren't done up and his shirt tails were flapping and he had a stick in his hand.'
  (Police officer, Inside the British Police, Simon Holdaway, 1983)
4. an excessively serious, dull or repressed person
From the notions of rigidity, woodeness

and chastisement.

5. a pickpocket's associate or decoy.
See also **sticksing**

sticker *n British*
an unsolved crime, a case left open, in the jargon of the police

sticks, the *n*
the countryside, a rural or provincial place, the 'backwoods'. Originally, in the USA and Canada, a humorous reference to trees, the term had spread to other English-speaking areas by the 1950s.

> *He lives way out in the sticks somewhere – Ongar I believe.*

sticksing *n British*
pickpocketing. A term used in black criminal circles.

stick the nut on (someone) *vb British See* **nut²**

sticky *n British*
a liqueur. The word (like 'liqueur' itself in middle-class and 'society' usage) is occasionally extended to refer to sweet wines.

sticky beak *n Australian*
a 'nosy parker', an interfering or inquisitive person. The common phrase evokes a bird poking its bill into something viscous.

> *'If he hasn't told you … it's certainly not my place.*
> *And what is your place? Head chook in the sticky beak brigade?'*

(*Neighbours*, Australian TV series, 1988)

sticky-beak *vb Australian*
to poke one's nose into other people's affairs. A back-formation from the noun.

stiff¹ *vb*
1a. to kill. An Americanism based on the noun form of the word (denoting a corpse). Since the 1960s the term has been heard in raffish or underworld parlance in Britain.
1b. *British* to attack physically, trounce
2. to take financial advantage of (someone); to cheat, rob or extort from

> *She tried to stiff me for the fare.*

3. to 'stand someone up', snub (someone)

> *I don't like getting stiffed like this.*

4. to flop, fail. A term used typically in the context of the entertainment business or sports.

> *Their last single stiffed.*

The first four senses of stiff are related to

the noun form denoting a corpse.

5. *American* to aggress, treat harshly. The term is from 'stiff-arm', a version of 'strong-arm'.

6. *British* to have sex with. A working-class vulgarism.

stiff² *n*
1a. a corpse. An unsentimental term inspired by rigor mortis and originating in American slang in the 19th century.
1b. a rigidly conventional, dull or serious person
1c. an individual, particularly one to be pitied

> *I'm just a poor working stiff.*

1d. *American* a hobo, vagrant
1e. a drunk
1f. a flop or failure

Most of the many sub-senses of stiff are related to the idea of corpse-like rigidity or absence of life. The notion of 'stiff-necked' also plays a part in the case of sub-sense **b**.

stiffie *n British*
1. an erection. A jocular term heard principally among middle-class males, although women also employ the word.

> *'Got a stiffie? Wear a Jiffi!'*
> (Promotional T-shirt logo for Jiffi condoms, 1985)

2. an invitation card. The term describes the engraved social missives exchanged in traditional, **Sloane ranger** and **yuppie** circles.

stig *n*
an outsider, misfit, provincial bumpkin. The term became popular in 2003 and 2004 together with other terms synonymous with **chav**. It had been used in this disparaging sense previously, possibly after the publication of Clive King's children's novel *Stig of the Dump* (1963) about a caveman, but it may be an older dialect word. (It is also a Scandinavian first name.)

stikkie *n South African*
a sweetheart, girlfriend. Recorded as an item of Sowetan slang in the *Cape Sunday Times*, 29 January 1995.

sting *n American*
1a. a confidence trick, fraud or act of extortion
1b. a scheme devised in order to trap or entrap criminals

Both senses of the word (popularised by the film of the same name released in 1973) imply an elaborate arrangement with a sudden 'pay-off'.

stinking adj British
1. a short form of 'stinking rich'
2. extremely drunk. An alternative for **stinko**.

stinko adj
drunk. This word (an abbreviation from 'stinking drunk', with the addition of the lighthearted adjectival suffix '-o') is almost obsolete in British speech except in upper-class usage.

stinky finger, stink-finger, stinky pinky n
manual stimulation of a woman's genitals. The phrases are typically used by adolescent males.

stir n
prison. Various Romany (gypsy) words such as *stardo* and *steripen*, dealing with the concept of imprisonment, gave rise to 'start', an 18th-century British slang term for prison, and later, in the mid-19th century, to stir, which has remained one of the most widespread words for jail or imprisonment in all English-speaking areas, particularly in the phrase 'in stir'.

stir crazy/happy adj
psychologically disturbed as a result of confinement in prison (**stir**). The notion is sometimes extended to encompass a sense of frustration or hysteria felt in any institutional surroundings. (The less common form 'stir happy' is now dated.)

stitch n American
something funny, a source of hilarity. A typically middle-class and **preppie** term derived from the expression 'to be in stitches'.

  'Oh Jean-Marie, you're a stitch!'
  (*Planes, Trains and Automobiles*, US film, 1987)

stitch this! exclamation British
an exclamation of defiance said while hitting someone, particularly when butting them in the face. The phrase is used by 'toughs'.

stitch (someone) up vb British
1a. to concoct false evidence against someone, to 'frame'. A piece of underworld and police jargon from the 1950s which penetrated popular speech in the 1980s.

  'Openshaw, 41, allegedly said on his arrest: "I'm being stitched up". The trial goes on.'
  (Court report, *Daily Mirror*, 14 July 1989)

1b. to outmanoeuvre comprehensively, defeat by devious means, render helpless. This extension of the previous sense of the phrase became a vogue term of the early 1980s.

  'Leched over by managers, stitched up by agents, girls in the music biz have traditionally paid a high price for succumbing to the lure of lurex.'
  (*Ms London* magazine, 4 September 1989)

stoat n British
the vagina. A vulgarism in use among adolescents in the 1990s and listed in *Viz* comic in 1994.

stocious adj
an alternative spelling of **stoshious**

stogie n American
a cigar. An old but surviving nickname which is from Conestoga, Pennsylvania, where covered wagons were manufactured. The driver of the wagons smoked cheap cigars which became known as stogies.

stoked adj
excited, thrilled, stimulated. The usage probably arose in the surfing community in the US, whence it spread to other English-speaking areas. It is now popular, particularly in Australian speech. It derives from the image of a furnace being 'stoked up' or perhaps from the words 'stunned' or 'choked'.

  'Beth's really stoked you're going to give her away.'
  (*Neighbours*, Australian TV soap opera, 1993)

stomp vb
to beat up, attack and/or defeat. A usage which was part of the Hells Angels' lexicon, referring to the ritual punishing of enemies. The word was adopted by **hippies** in the USA and Britain in about 1968.

stompers n pl American
1a. the American term for **brothel creepers**, the thick-soled shoes worn by teenagers in the 1950s
1b. heavy workboots or cowboy boots

stomp it vb British
to hurry, go quickly. The term is used by devotees of dancefloor and **rave** culture.

  On Tuesday we stomped it down to the Limelight.

stone n British
the drug **crack**. A synonym, recorded in 2002, of the earlier **rock**.

stoned *adj*
intoxicated by narcotics or alcohol. In the 1960s stoned proved the most popular of a number of synonyms employing the metaphor of punishment or damage (**wrecked**, **destroyed**, **blitzed**, etc.) It became the standard term to describe the effects of cannabis in particular. This use of the word originated in the argot of jazz musicians and bohemians in the USA in the 1940s.

> *'[Richard Neville] suggesting making love when stoned with stereo headphones on both partners, playing the first Blind Faith album.'*
> (*Oz* magazine, February 1970)

stoner *n*
a drug user, especially a habitual user of cannabis. Originally an Americanism, the word has become more widespread since 2000.

> *'This is a stoners' western for crystal-dangling deadheads.'*
> (*Evening Standard* film review, 22 July 2004)

stonker *n British*
something stunning, devastating or powerful. This invented word should logically be derived from a verb 'to stonk' which is, however, unrecorded in modern slang, although **stonkered** and **stonking** are. In origin the term is probably influenced by words such as 'stun', 'clunk' and 'bonk'. *See also* **stonkered**

stonkered *adj*
1a. drunk

1b. destroyed, out of action, devastated or exhausted. (For the probable derivation see **stonker**.)

stonking *adj British*
extremely. The word is an all-purpose intensifying adjective, usually used in place of more offensive terms. Mainly in working class and armed service usage, stonking was in vogue in the late 1980s. It probably postdates **stonker** and **stonkered**.

stony, stoney *adj*
penniless. A shortened form of 'stony broke', heard especially in Australia.

stooge *n British*
an innocent stand-in at an identity parade. A term from the jargon of police officers, deriving from the standard colloquial senses of menial, dupe, etc. (The word stooge, which appeared in

the USA in the 19th century, is said to be a corruption of 'studious' or 'students'.)

> *'They don't think they can get the I.D. parade off the ground. I don't know if there are problems with the stooges, or what.'*
> (*Flying Squad*, British TV documentary, March 1985)

stoolie *n*
an informer. A shortening of **stool pigeon**.

stool pigeon *n*
an informer. In North America in the 19th century pigeons were tied to wooden frames (known as stools) as decoys to lure game birds. The expression was later applied to a cardsharp's human decoy, and later still to a police informer or spy. By World War I the use of the phrase had spread to Britain where it was adopted by crime fiction and the real underworld. The term is commonly shortened to **stoolie**.

stooper *n British*
a male homosexual. The word is applied to a supposedly 'passive' **gay** male. The pejorative term (its counterpart is **stabber**) was reportedly in use by Wapping journalists in 1990.

stoosh *adj*
1a. costly

1b. wealthy

1c. offensively ostentatious or snobbish

The word, heard in London speech since 2000, occurs in Jamaican slang but its exact origins are obscure.

stormer *n British*
an impressive, admirable thing, person, etc.

storming *adj British*
excellent, exciting. One of many vogue terms in adolescent usage, particularly among devotees of dancefloor, techno and jungle music since the 1990s.

stoshious, stotious, stocious, stoshers *adj British*
1a. drunk

1b. silent, tight-lipped, discreet

This mysterious word can be traced to the 19th century and was thought by some authorities to be extinct by the 1930s. It survives, however, in jocular usage. The term is either a mock-Latinate invention or a corruption of a dialect word for water-logged or muddy.

stote *vb*
to go for a walk. The term, of uncertain origin, was in use among UK adolescents in 2003.

stouch, stoush, stoosh *adj British*
presumptuous, arrogant, overbearing. The fashionable term, recorded among adolescents in the 1990s, was defined by *Touch* magazine in September 1993 as 'acting like your shit don't stink'. The origin of the expression is uncertain.

stoush *n Australian*
a brawl. The word is probably a descendant of lost dialect terms for 'uproar' or 'strike'.

straight¹ *n*
1. a heterosexual, particularly heard in the language of homosexuals
2. a conventional person, someone who does not take drugs or ascribe to 'counterculture' values. A term from the language of drug abusers and counterculture members which was a buzzword of the later 1960s.
> 'Would you say Hunter Thompson was afraid of anything in particular? "Ah ... Straights".'
> (Ralph Steadman, *I-D* magazine, November 1987)

3. a cigarette (as opposed to a **joint**). A now dated cannabis users' term in wide currency in the 1960s.
> If you give me a straight I'll roll us something for the journey.

4. *South African* a bottle of alcoholic liquor. Recorded as an item of Sowetan slang in the *Cape Sunday Times*, 29 January 1995.

straight² *adj*
1a. honest, not criminal or corrupt
> 'You couldn't bribe or compromise him because he was straight. However, he was also naive.'
> (Former detective, *Inside the Brotherhood*, Martin Short, 1989)

1b. heterosexual
In the first two sub-senses, the opposing slang term in British English is **bent**.

1c. not under the influence of drugs or a drug-user
> I've been straight for three days.
> Don't offer her any, she's straight.

The word has been used to mean 'upright' or honest, fair, scrupulous, etc. for more than a century. The sub-senses above, not always used approvingly, were established in the 1950s and 1960s. The following

sense is in ironic contrast.
2. restored to one's desired state of drunkenness or drugged euphoria
> Just one shot and I'll be straight again.

straightened-out *adj*
bribed, suborned or otherwise corrupted. A euphemism in underworld and police usage.
> 'Their tip-off was supported by a tape recording of a bugged conversation involving an American criminal, referring to "a top man" who had been "straightened out in Scotland Yard".'
> (*Observer*, 16 August 1987)

straighten (someone) out *vb British*
to bribe or corrupt (someone). A euphemistic term in use among criminals and police officers.
> We wanted to straighten out a magistrate, but we couldn't get to any of them in time.

straight-up *adj*
honest, reliable. This usage is an extension of the use of the phrase as an exclamation meaning 'It's the truth'. or 'Honestly'.
> He's a straight-up guy.

strain the potatoes *vb Australian*
to urinate. The phrase is a survival of a 19th-century British euphemism inspired by the resemblance to the resulting colour of water. In Britain, the phrase 'strain the greens' was heard before the 1950s.

strap *n American*
1. a gun, in the argot of street gangs and other criminals. By 2005 the term was in use in London, too.
> 'I'm hoping to hook up with some more straps ...'
> (*Gang War*, Channel 4 TV documentary, August 1995)

2. a humorous synonym for **jock**

strapped *adj*
1. short of money, broke. A short version of the phrase 'strapped for cash'.
2. armed with a gun. In this form the word crossed the Atlantic eastwards, so that by the early 1990s criminals in the UK were referring to 'going strapped'.
3. good-looking, physically fit. In this sense the word has been used appreciatively by UK adolescents, especially females, since around 2000.

strapping *n American*
carrying a firearm

strawberry n American
a prostitute who sells sex for drugs

'All the vice girl victims [of a Los Angeles serial killer] were known as strawberries – American slang for hookers who trade sex for drugs.'
(*Sunday Mirror,* 3 March 1989)

stray n British
a heterosexual who associates with **gays**. The term was defined in the *Modern Review,* June 1994 and was still in media use a decade later.
Compare **metrosexual; stromo**

streak n
1. a run through a public place while naked. From the verb.
Some guy did a streak at the Test Match.
2. British a person of ectomorphic build. A mildly pejorative term, sometimes expressed more brutally as **long streak of piss**, invariably said of males. **Long streak of misery** denotes a tall, thin and morose or excessively serious individual.

street adj American
'streetwise' or having 'street credibility'. A term of approbation originating in black argot of the 1970s.
She's OK, she's street.

street apple n See **road apple**

street pizza n See **road pizza**

stressed-out, stressy, stressin' adj British
1a. unwell, uncomfortable, discontented. In secondary school playground slang this use of the colloquialism is generalised from its normal sense to incorporate almost any negative feeling.
1b. inferior, inadequate. A further generalisation of the original sense of the word, used as a vogue term by teenage gang members from the late 1990s.

stretch n
1. American a tall, thin person. A term of cheerful mockery. The equivalent of the British **streak**, or rather the nickname 'Lofty', since stretch is often a term of address.
How're y' keeping, Stretch?
2. a period of imprisonment. This underworld term originally referred specifically to one year's incarceration; it has now been generalised to mean a term of indeterminate length.
He did a four-year stretch.

strides n
trousers. The word has existed in raffish usage since the turn of the 20th cen-

tury. Originally an Americanism, it is now heard in Britain and Australia.

'Fair crack of the whip! Lady, I'm not taking me strides off for anyone.'
(*Bazza Pulls it Off,* cartoon by Barry Humphries and Nicholas Garland, *Private Eye,* 1970)

stripe n
a scar, especially as the result of a knife or razor slash

stroke book n American
a pornographic or semi-pornographic publication. 'Stroke' in this context refers to male masturbation.

stroll on! exclamation British
a cry of dismissal or disbelief. The phrase usually conveys indignation.

stromo n
a **gay** male who behaves like or appears to be a heterosexual. The term is a blend of **straight** and **homo**.

strong it vb British
to behave aggressively, presumptuously or excessively. A working-class expression heard particularly in the London area in the 1980s. It is a variation on the colloquial phrases 'come on strong', 'come it strong' and 'go it strong'.
You been strongin' it again down our boozer?

strop n British
a bout of bad temper. A back-formation from the earlier adjective **stroppy**.
put on/throw a strop
'She got herself into a strop about it, d'you know what I mean?'
(*Big Brother,* UK TV show, 23 July 2004)

stroppy adj British
obstreperous, aggressive, uncooperative. The word is an alteration of obstreperous, perhaps via a fanciful deformation of this word, such as 'obstropalous'. Stroppy appeared in the 1940s. Various deformations of obstreperous have been recorded since the 18th century.

strumping n British
promiscuous behaviour (on the part of a female). This back-formation from 'strumpet' was used in the 1990s TV comedy *Birds of a Feather.*

strung out adj
1a. tense, nervous and upset
She was strung out inside, nibbling on her lower lip and smoking one cigarette after another.

1b. suffering from the effects of an illicit drug or from withdrawal

strung out on morphine

The first, now widespread, usage derives from the second, which is a drug user's slang expression dating from the 1950s.

strung up *adj*
a less common variant of **strung out**

stubbies *n pl Australian*
short trousers, as worn by men

stubby, stubbie *n Australian*
a small bottle of lager

stud *n*
a sexually active, powerful, potent male. Only slang when applied to men as opposed to (real) animals, the term often indicates a degree of approval or admiration, even if grudgingly. In black American street parlance the word was sometimes used in the 1960s and 1970s simply to mean a 'guy'. There seems to be no female equivalent that stresses sexual power rather than degeneracy.

> *'The eternal teenage sexual paradox is that boys who "put it about" are called "studs" by their admiring friends but girls who do the same are "slags".'*
> (17-year-old public-school pupil, *Harpers and Queen* magazine, August 1978)

studly *adj American*
cool. The term is typically applied to people, particularly males.

stud-muffin *n American*
1a. an attractive male
1b. a male seducer (of females)
In both senses this elaboration of **stud** was heard from the early 1990s, first among adolescents and later among adult speakers.

studsley *n American*
a smart, dapper or sophisticated male. A term of address between males which seems to have originated as a black elaboration of **stud** in the sense of a 'fine fellow'.

stuff *vb*
1. to have sex (with). The verb has very seldom been used in the active or transitive form since the 19th century (and it was never common). The abusive exclamation 'get stuffed' is its main legacy.
2. to dismiss, throw away, destroy. This adaptation of the sexual sense of the word, or of the expression 'stuff it up your arse!', has proved useful as a non-taboo means of conveying strong rejection,

impatience, etc. It often occurs in the all-purpose exclamation 'stuff it!'.

> *'Stuff the wedding!'*
> (Anti-royal-wedding slogan written on walls and reproduced on badges in Britain in 1981)

Stuff is currently fashionable in media, sporting and raffish circles with the sense of to defeat or humiliate.

stuffed *adj British*
ruined, abandoned, 'kaput'. A brusque but fairly inoffensive derivation of the verb **stuff**.

stuff up *vb Australian*
to blunder or fail. A euphemistic version of **screw up**.

> *'I really stuffed up, didn't I?*
> *You sure did.'*
> (*Flying Doctors*, Australian TV series, 1995)

stumblebum *n American*
a vagrant or derelict, literally a stumbling, helpless tramp. The word is now usually generalised to denote an inept, incompetent or clumsy person.

stumpy *n British*
a small person. The word is generally a term of abuse, e.g. in playground usage.

stunned mullet *n Australian*
(the facial expression of) a gormless, slow-witted or stupid person. The phrase is common in Australian speech and was used in Parliament by the Premier Paul Keating, among others, when describing the supposedly vacuous expression of political opponents.

styler *n British*
a person who attempts to be stylish and fashionable, a 'trendy'. This vogue term of the later 1990s is invariably used by adolescents to indicate derision or disapproval. It is probably influenced by the black American concept of **styling**.

styling *n American*
showing off, behaving ostentatiously. A vogue term in the 1990s in hip hop and dancefloor culture which originated more than thirty years earlier in black American speech.
Compare **profiling**; **vogu(e)ing**

substance *n British*
cannabis, hashish or marihuana. A euphemism adopted by users of the drug from the legalistic description (employed particularly in sentences

such as 'Certain substances were taken away for analysis.').

Got any substance?

suck *vb American*
to be repellent, inferior or worthless. An extremely common term of strong disparagement or denigration in American English, suck is both a euphemism for **fuck** and an amalgam of notions contained in words such as 'sucker', **cocksucker**, etc.

> 'To say something or someone "sucks" is to use America's most common term of disparagement … The term suck originally had as its prefix the word for a male hen.'
>
> (Simon Hoggart, *Observer* magazine, 1989)

> 'Is it me, or does the party all of a sudden suck?'
>
> (*10 Things I Hate About You*, US film, 1999)

sucked in *adj Australian*
fooled, duped, 'conned'. A racier version of 'taken in'.

sucker-punch *vb American*
to attack from behind or without warning, to land an unfair or surprise blow. From the colloquialism 'sucker', denoting a dupe or easy victim.

> 'You're a witness, Alex. I just came here to talk to you and Fruitfly sucker-punched me.'
>
> (Jonathon Kellerman, *Over the Edge*, 1987)

suck face *vb American*
to kiss. An adolescent euphemism on the lines of **swap spit**.

suck-hole, suck-holer *n Australian*
a sycophant, toady or other contemptible person. A more recent variant on the ancient notion expressed by 'bum-sucker', **arse-licker**, etc.

suck off *vb*
to perform fellatio (on someone)

sucky *adj American*
tasty, sweet

suds *n American*
beer; a 'college-boy' word

suffer! *exclamation Australian*
a cry of defiance, challenge or contempt, as used by schoolchildren and adolescents from at least the late 1970s

sugar daddy *n*
a wealthy older protector and lover of a young woman. Judith S. Neaman and Carole G. Silver, in their *Dictionary of Euphemisms* (1983), date this expression to the 1920s and derive it from the American rhyming slang phrase 'sugar and honey': *money.* While this is possible, sugar had been a term of endearment or a metaphor for affection or luxury for many years before.

> 'I see Natalie's managed to find herself another sugar daddy.'
>
> (Recorded, magazine editor, London, 1986)

suit *n*
a bureaucratic functionary, *apparatchik*, corporation man. The term appeared in the 1980s and is used contemptuously or dismissively by working people and, especially, the fashionable young. In 1989 and 1990 the elaboration 'empty suit' was heard, underlining the notion of anonymity.

> 'What the hell is that?
>
> Some suit from the mayor's office.'
>
> Just in time for the evening news.'
>
> (*Cagney and Lacey*, US TV series, 1982)

suit-stabber *n British See* **stabber**

sunnies *n pl Australian*
female breasts

supersonic *n British*
tonic (water). The rhyming slang term was used by bar staff and drinkers in the 1990s sometimes in conjunction with **Vera Lynn**.

surfboard *n*
1. a flat-chested girl. An expression popular among pubescent schoolgirls.
2. a promiscuous girl or woman. From the image of supine acquiescence and the sexual connotations of **ride**.

surfie *n Australian*
a member of a 1960s subculture based only partly on surfing. They were the contemporaries of the British **mods** and contributed (like their American surfer counterparts) many colourful expressions to modern Australian slang.

surf the crimson wave *vb American*
to menstruate. The phrase occurs in adolescent speech and was featured in the 1995 US film *Clueless*, where it may have originated.

suss[1] *adj British*
suspect or suspicious

> I thought it was a bit suss when they offered it to me for nothing.

suss² n British
1. 'knowhow', 'savvy'. A usage in currency since the 1970s, based on **suss (out)**.

 I wouldn't worry about her, she's got a lot of suss.

2. suspicion. The much criticised Vagrancy Act, under whose provisions (young) people could be arrested for 'loitering with intent (to commit an arrestable offence)', was known as 'the sus law'. 'On sus(s)' refers to being taken into custody on suspicion of committing an offence.

suss (out) vb British
to discern, discover, deduce or realise. A vogue expression among **beatniks** of the early 1960s (in the longer form); it had probably been in sporadic use before that. At first the phrase usually meant to perceive someone's true nature or intentions, it is now a fairly common colloquialism, often meaning no more than to 'work out'.

 I think I've managed to suss out a way round this.
 She sussed him out in five minutes.

sussed, sussed out adj British
(of a person) well-adjusted, adapted to the circumstances, self-aware or self-reliant. This more recent derivation of the verb **suss (out)** is based on the notion of **suss** in the sense of 'knowhow'. Since the 1980s it is often in the form 'well-sussed'.

 'This time, man, we've got it all sussed … all the albums gonna be made here, first class jobs.'
 (Record bootlegger, *Oz* magazine, February 1970)

 'A post punk skatezine that's aggressive, sussed and caustic about skating UK'
 (*Mail on Sunday*, 'Biz' magazine, June 1987)

swag¹ n
loot, booty, stolen goods. In this sense the word originated among itinerants and thieves in the early 19th century. It had earlier denoted goods or possessions when carried. The word is ultimately related, via dialect, to 'sway' and 'swing'. In modern usage swag is usually used humorously.

swag² adj British
bad. The word was in vogue among London schoolchildren in the late 1990s.

swallow n British
a drink of alcohol
 Shall we go for a quick swallow?

swamp n
a poor housing estate. The term was recorded in West London in 1998.

swamp-donkey n
an extremely ugly or unattractive female. A vogue term among university students since around 2000. A British origin has been claimed for the phrase, but it may be a rural North American slang word for a **moose**.

swap spit vb American
to kiss, used particularly when referring to **French kissing**, in the jargon of teenagers and students

swayve n, adj
(the quality of being) sophisticated, elegant, refined. The word is a mock-affected mispronunciation of 'suave' (along the lines of the earlier British **fabe** and **mode**).

 He's got loads of swayve, hasn't he?
 She's très swayve.

sweat¹ vb American
to put pressure on (someone)
 'No-one's sweating you to join a gang.'
 (Los Angeles policeman to street-gang member, ITV documentary, August 1989)

sweat² n British
a brutish, unsophisticated individual. The term sometimes denotes someone engaged in menial tasks and was heard in working-class speech in the 1990s.
 'No you don't ya dozy sweat!'
 (*Blonde Fist*, UK film, 1994)

sweated adj British
angry or annoyed. An item of black street-talk used especially by males, recorded in 2003.

sweat-hog n American
a physically repugnant person. A term of contempt or abuse typically applied by males, such as college students, to females.

sweaty n British
a disco, dance or frenetic party, in the 1990s jargon of Oxbridge students

swedge vb British
to have sex with, penetrate. An item of black street-talk used especially by males, recorded in 2003.
 I swedged her.

sweet *adj British*
excellent, acceptable. A vogue term of approval among adolescents in the later 1990s.

sweet F.A./Fanny Adams *n British*
1a. nothing at all, **fuck-all**
1b. a pitifully small amount. In 19th-century naval slang 'Fanny Adams' was tinned or cooked meat, a sardonic reference to a girl of the same name who was murdered and dismembered in 1867. The name was later matched with the initials of **fuck-all** and used euphemistically in its place.

swell *n British*
a well-off single woman, in **yuppie** argot of the late 1980s. An acronym ('single woman earning lots of lolly') also recalling the dated description of a fashionable 'person-about-town'.

swift¹ *vb British*
to give false evidence, 'bend' the evidence. A piece of police slang. A police officer who is adept at this practice is known as 'a (bit of a) swifter'. 'Swift it' is another form of the verb.

swift² *adj*
1a. *American* alert, clever. Now heard among various social groups, the word has been used in this sense in black adult speech since before World War II.
The kid's not too swift.
1b. *British* devious, cunning, deceitful. This usage has occurred in London working-class and underworld speech since the 1950s.
I thought it was a bit swift when they left me standing holding the gear.

swifty *n*
an alcoholic drink, usually beer. The term has been recorded in the USA since 2000, as well as in the UK where it is probably a short form of the established phrases 'a swift one' or 'a swift half'.

swing *vb*
1a. to behave in an uninhibitedly hedonistic way. This use of the word, originating in jazz and rock music circles, was popular in the 1960s; by the early 1970s it had been narrowed to its current sense (*see* sub-sense **b**).
1b. to engage in 'liberated' and/or sophisticated sexual practices, particularly wife-swapping and group sex. The word is a catch-all euphemism for promiscuity,

originating and still mainly heard in the USA.

swing both ways *vb*
to engage in sexual relations with both men and women. A euphemism heard in the USA since the later 1960s.

swinger *n*
1a. a sophisticated hedonist, a fashionable pleasure lover. This quintessential 1960s term evolved quickly into its current sense (*see* sub-sense **b**).
1b. a euphemism for a practitioner of wife-swapping, group sex or other types of sexual 'liberation'. This American term was adopted by 'adult' magazines, contact agencies, etc. in the 1970s as an acceptable designation for adultery and/or promiscuity, etc.

swinging dick *n American*
a variant form of **Big Swinging Dick**
'I ain't no swinging dick. I know better than to fuck with the wrong people.'
(*Heaven's Prisoners*, US film, 1995)

swish *n American*
a **gay** or effeminate male. A mildly pejorative term, inspired by the actual or supposed flouncing of the individuals in question. It is used by gay as well as heterosexual commentators.

Swiss *adj*
1. *American* of good quality, like a Swiss watch. An expression used on campus in the USA since around 2000.
2. *British* inferior, useless. *Viz* comic's *Profanisaurus* records this usage in 1999. It may be an irony, or just possibly related to a Victorian use of Swiss to mean bogus or exaggerated, as in a 'Swiss Admiral'.

switched-on *adj British*
1a. fashionable, alert. A vogue term of the 1960s equating with **turned-on**.
1b. excited either sexually or by drugs. A short-lived sense of the phrase, current in the mid- to late 1960s.

switch-hitter *n*
a bisexual person. The phrase is used in the USA and Australia; it is from baseball jargon, in which it denotes an ambidextrous batter.

switz *n*
sweat marks on clothing. An item of office slang, probably American in origin, recorded in the London *Evening Standard* in March 2004. The term is usually used derisively for referring to a harassed or anxious person whose arm-

pit sweat is seeping through their cloth-ing.

sword *n See* **pork sword**

swot *n*
a diligent, hard-working student. A pejo-rative term which has survived from the mid-19th century into modern usage. It is an alteration of 'sweat' and, like that word, may be used as a noun or a verb. In the USA there are many terms used enviously or contemptuously of conscien-tious fellow-students, among them **grind**, **pencil-geek**, **squid** and **wonk**.

> '*But finally armed with a baseball bat, he intervenes when a bullying sports-star humiliates a kindly swot, preaching a sermon that converts the whole institu-tion.*'
> (*Observer,* 29 May 1988)

syph, the syph *n*
syphilis

syphon the python *vb See* **siphon/syphon the python**

syrup (of figs) *n British*
a *wig*. A piece of approximate rhyming slang invoking a laxative remedy.

> '*That is not a syrup.*
> *I've got a tenner here says that's a syrup.*'
> (*Only Fools and Horses,* British TV com-edy series, 1989)

T

T *n*

marihuana. An alternative form of **tea**.

tab *n*

1. a tablet, specifically a tablet or dose of the drug LSD, from the jargon of users in the late 1960s and 1970s

> 'Well, the one that stopped me from doing acid forever was when I dropped seven tabs. I completely lost my mind and went to Muppetland – the whole trip lasted for about six months.'

(Zodiac Mindwarp, *I-D* magazine, November 1987)

2. *British* a cigarette. The word, probably from 'tab-end', appeared in northern British usage before World War II but, since its use in *Viz* comic from the 1980s, has been used in other regions, mainly by adolescents.

> 'He pulls out the tab ... he's trying to get the packet into his top pocket ...'

(Jack Docherty's talk show, Channel 4 TV, March 1997)

tabby *n*

a female, especially an attractive and/or lively girl

table-ender *n*

a sexual act, especially when impromptu and/or in a public place, but not necessarily on, against or under a table

tache, tash *n British*

a moustache

tack *n*

1. squalor, shabbiness, seediness, bad taste. A back-formation from the earlier Americanism, **tacky**. 'Tackiness' is an alternative noun form. (Very often 'tackiness' refers to the quality, 'tack' to the evidence thereof.)

2. *British* cannabis. A term used by adolescents, particularly in the northeast of England, during the 1990s. It may be a shortening of 'tackle' as used to mean equipment or heroin.

tack attack *n British*

a fit or bout of bad taste. A witticism based on **tack** and **tacky** heard among fashionable 'young professionals' and media circles in London in 1988 and 1989. (**Rack attack** and **snack attack** are other rhyming phrases.)

> Judging by the décor of his flat, I'd say he'd had a tack attack.

tacker *n British*

a child. A northern English dialect word of obscure origin but possibly related to 'thumb(tack)'. It is occasionally heard in other parts of Britain.

tackies *n pl Irish*

sports shoes, trainers

tackle *n British*

1. a short form of the humorous euphemism **wedding tackle** (the male genitals). Tackle alone was used in this sense from the 18th century, if not earlier.

2. heroin. An item of prison slang.

tacky *adj*

shabby, seedy, inferior, vulgar. An American term which had existed in southern speech in the USA since the late 19th century, before being understood (in the early 1970s) and partially adopted (in the late 1970s) in Britain. The origin is not in 'tacky', meaning sticky or viscous, but in a dialect word for an inferior horse, hence a shabby yokel. 'Tack-e-e-e' is the last word and final verdict in the main text of Kenneth Anger's *Hollywood Babylon* (1975), an exposé of show-business scandal.

taco-bender *n American*

a Mexican or other person of Hispanic origin. A derogatory term coined on the lines of **spaghetti-bender** or **bagel-bender**. (A taco is a Mexican fried bread pancake.)

tacos *n pl American See* **toss one's cookies/tacos**

tad *n, adj, adv*
a small or slight amount, a little, slightly. An American expression now fairly widespread in British use, especially in phrases such as 'a tad hungry'. In American English tad has been used to mean a small boy since the late 19th century. It is probably from earlier British dialect, in which it is related to 'toad' or 'tadpole'.

tadger *n British*
the penis. A vulgarism of unknown origin (probably from a lost dialect verb) used for many years in the north of England and revived by students, alternative comedians, etc. in the 1980s. **Todger** is an alternative modern version.

tag
1. *vb, n* (to spray) a graffiti artist's personalised signature or motif. The word has been a colloquialism for a person's name for many years. It was adopted by teenage graffiti artists in the 1970s in the USA, whence it spread with the craze.

> *'If you go to one of the big guys of hip hop art and they have not heard of your tag, you are nothing. But if they've seen it and like it then you are bad.'*
> (15-year-old graffiti artist, *Evening Standard*, 11 November 1987)

2. *vb*
2a. *American* to hit or knock out
2b. *American* to kill, especially by shooting. In the latter sense the term was used in the cult US 1993 film *Reservoir Dogs*.

tagger *n*
a graffiti artist. From the use of **tag** to mean one's name or pictorial signature.

tail *n*
1a. a woman or women seen as (a) sexual object(s). The word usually occurs in phrases such as 'a bit/piece of tail', tail being a euphemism dating from the 14th century for the less polite **arse** or **ass**.
1b. (particularly in Caribbean or **gay** usage) a man or men seen as (a) sexual object(s)

> *'She spend all her time chasin' tail!'*
> (Recorded, Trinidadian student, London, 1988)

tail-end *n British*
the penis. Confusingly, since the term usually denotes the backside, it may also, particularly in the northeast of England, refer to the male member.

tailpipe *n American*
the anus. A US teenagers' term. This predictable use of the word ('exhaust-pipe' in British English) is possibly influenced by the car driver's experience of having another driver 'up one's tailpipe', i.e. driving too close.

Taiwan *n British*
an upper second or 2.1 ('two-one') honours degree. A student nickname on the lines of **Desmond**, **Pattie**, **Douglas**, etc. coined in the mid-1980s. A **made-in** is a synonym from the same source.

take a bath *vb*
to suffer a financial loss or commercial setback. A piece of business jargon that has become fairly widespread. The image evoked seems to be of a drenching rather than just washing.

take a dive/tumble/fall *vb*
to deliberately lose a boxing match or other contest. Expressions in use since the inter-war years, originating in the USA.

take a dump *vb See* **dump**

take a leak *vb See* **leak**

take a pill *vb American*
to relax, luxuriate. The phrase was popularised by the 1992 US film *Wayne's World*.

take a pop (at) *vb*
to attack, hit, lash out at. A phrase popular in working-class London speech in the late 1980s.

> *'Now you're taking a pop at my business partners.'*
> (*EastEnders*, British TV soap opera, 1988)

take a powder *vb*
to leave (quickly), go away. A now dated expression originating in the USA in the 1920s. The powder in question refers to a laxative or stimulant medicine.

take a raincheck *vb*
to accept a postponement, put something off to a future date. An Americanism which entered international English in the mid-1970s. The raincheck in question was originally a ticket stub entitling the holder to entry to a ball game at some future date if the fixture is rained off.

take berties *vb British*
1a. to behave in a presumptuous or intrusive way

1b. to take advantage (of someone)
You can stay but just don't go taking berties.

The jocular phrase, used by university students from the later 1990s, is a shortening of the colloquial 'take liberties'.

take down *vb American*
to kill or immobilise. A 'tough-guy' euphemism.

take it in the shorts *vb American*
to suffer a direct hit, literally or metaphorically. A phrase used typically in sports, business or military contexts.

take names *vb American*
to act resolutely and/or primitively, chastise. The image evoked is that of an authority figure noting the names of miscreants. The phrase is often placed after **kick ass**.
Listen, you're going to have to go in there and kick ass and take names!

take one's lumps *vb American*
to suffer misfortune or harsh treatment

take out *vb*
to kill or destroy. A military euphemism which came to public notice in the USA during the Vietnam War. The term was subsequently appropriated for use in the context of crime and law enforcement.
'I thought, if I could get my hands around his throat... I'd just take him out right now.'
(Female contestant in US TV series *The Apprentice*, 2004)
'You got a couple of options: piss off out of town, or take him out, mate.'
(*Blackjack*, Australian TV crime drama, 2004)

take the mick/mickey/michael *vb British*
to mock, deride, poke fun at. These expressions are milder versions of **take the piss**. Unbeknownst to most users, they employ rhyming slang; Mickey is short for a mythical 'Mickey Bliss', providing the rhyme for **piss**. 'Michael' is a humorous variant. The phrases, like their more vulgar counterpart, have been in use since the 1940s.

take the piss (out of someone) *vb British*
to mock, deride, poke fun at. This vulgarism has been in widespread use since the late 1940s. The original idea evoked by the expression was that of deflating someone, recalling the description of a

self-important blusterer as **all piss and wind**.

take the shame *vb British*
to accept the blame (publicly and/or wholeheartedly) or face the criticism of one's peers. A key phrase in the playground vocabulary of London teenagers since the later 1970s. The concept is from black speech; 'shamed-up' is another derivation from the same source.

talent[1] *n British*
attractive potential sexual partners. A generic term first applied before World War II to women and men. Since the mid-1960s female speakers have also applied the word (sometimes ironically) to desirable males.
Let's check out the local talent.

talent[2] *adj British*
excellent. An adjectival use of the noun, heard among schoolchildren since the 1990s.

talk dicks *vb*
to speak in an elegant way, talk 'posh'. Dicks may be an alteration of diction.

talking-brooch *n British*
a police-officer's personal radio, also known as a **squawker** and **batphone**. An item of police slang recorded by the London *Evening Standard* magazine, February 1993.

talk on the big white telephone *vb*
to vomit in a toilet. This colourful expression probably originated among US college students, like the synonymous kneel/**pray to the porcelain god**.

talk turkey *vb*
to perform oral sex. A 1980s pun on the slang usage **gobble** and the well-known colloquial American expression meaning to discuss openly (it is also perhaps influenced in US usage by **turkey-neck**: the penis).

tall poppies *n pl Australian*
'over-achievers', persons of prominence. The expression originates in the 1930s when the Lang government threatened to enforce tax laws which would 'cut off the heads of the tall poppies'.

tamale *n American See* **hot tamale**

tam rag *n British*
a sanitary towel or tampon. A variant of **jam rag** influenced by 'tampon' and the trademark 'Tampax'.

T and A *n American*
tits and **ass**. The American equivalent of the British 'B and T', a phrase describing a visual or tactile experience of a naked woman or women. The abbreviation and the expression in full probably originated in the jargon of journalists and/or showmen.

tanglin' *n British*
fighting, from black speech. Synonyms recorded since 2000 are **mixin'**, **regulatin'**, **startin'**.

tank[1] *n*
1. *American* a firearm, handgun. A hyperbolic term occasionally used by criminals and law enforcers.
2. *British* a police car or van. The word is used in this way by ironic or self-dramatising police officers.

tank[2] *vb British*
1a. to crush, overwhelm
'They'd all tank Tyson.'
(Headline in the *Sun*, 28 February 1989)
1b. to defeat, trounce
'England are going to tank Monaco tomorrow!'
(TV sports trailer, February 1997)
1c. to move forcefully and powerfully
'Tanking up and down the motorway all holiday … but Christmas itself was very quiet … very pleasant…'
(*Biff* cartoon, *Guardian*, December 1987)
All senses of the word became popular in the later 1980s.

tanked, tanked-up *adj*
drunk. A common term since the turn of the 20th century; the shorter form is more recent. Tank up evokes the filling of a container or fuelling of a vehicle and parallels such expressions as **loaded** and **canned**.
Man, she was, like, totally tanked last night.
'I'll do the washing-up tomorrow if I don't get too tanked-up tonight.'
(*Biff* cartoon, *Guardian*, 1986)

tap[1]**, tap up** *vb*
to borrow or seek to borrow from (someone). To tap meant to spend liberally in archaic slang; by the early 20th century it had acquired the second sense of to solicit, borrow or obtain. The origin of the term is in the tapping of liquid from a container, reinforced by tapping someone on the shoulder to gain their attention and the later slang sense of

'hitting' someone for a loan. Tap is in international English, while the full form tap up is in British usage.

tap[2] *adj American*
physically attractive, handsome, usually of a male. An expression used on campus in the USA since around 2000. The same term was recorded in Nigeria in 2003.
That guy is just totally tap.

tap city *n, adj American*
(the condition of being) penniless, broke. A humorous version of **tapped-out**.
It's no good asking me. I'm in tap city.
It's tap city the rest of this month.

tap-dance *n*
a clever evasion, devious manoeuvre. The term, which is used all over the English-speaking world, recalls a dancer either **busking it** or improvising in a difficult situation, or merely executing an elegant sequence of steps.
'That was not an opinion – that was a tap-dance worthy of Fred Astaire.'
(*Hooperman*, US TV series, 1987)

tap-dancer *n*
a person who can avoid danger by a combination of clever, if devious or dishonest actions and luck; someone able to talk themselves out of difficult situations
'That man's a born tap-dancer; he's always out the back door five minutes before the front door's kicked in.'
(Recorded, drug dealer, London, 1988)

tapped-out *adj American*
1a. penniless, broke. A term used especially by gamblers and, more recently, by adolescents. It is inspired by the very old slang use of the word to **tap**, meaning both to spend and later to obtain money from another person.
Man, I'd like to help you but I'm all tapped-out.
'Wall Street's Trust Fund's tapped-out.'
(Headline in *Fortune* magazine, 18 April 2005)
1b. exhausted. From the idea of being 'drained'.

tapped up *adj British See* **get tapped up**

tapper *n British*
an obnoxious or disreputable person. A vogue term recorded in junior schools from 1991. The origin is obscure but may relate to a sexual sense such as **get tapped up**.

tarbrush *n See* **a touch of the tarbrush**

tard *n American*
a fool, simpleton. A teenagers' shortening of the popular term of contempt, **retard**. The word was adopted by British adolescents in the late 1980s.

tardy *adj*
foolish, irritating. The adjective, from the earlier noun form **tard**, has been in use, especially in the USA, since around 2000.

tart *n*
a promiscuous, vulgar or sexually provocative woman. This modern sense of the word has gradually supplanted the older meaning which was simply a woman or sweetheart. As a term of affection (inspired by the pastry sweetmeat and reinforced by 'sweetheart'), tart was applied to women of all ages from the mid-19th century. By the early years of the 20th century it was more often used of the flighty or immoral and by the inter-war years often referred to prostitutes. In modern theatrical, **gay** (where it is often used of men), cockney and Australian speech, tart is still used affectionately.

tart about *vb British*
1a. to flounce about, behave archly or flamboyantly
1b. to mess about, behave in a disorganised or irresolute way

Many derogatory or vulgar terms (**arse**, **dick**, **fanny**, etc.) have been converted to verbs on the same pattern.

tash *n British*
an alternative spelling of **tache**

tassel, tassle *n*
the penis. An inoffensive term often used by parents and children and referring particularly to the member of an immature male. In older (pre-1950s) British usage, 'pencil-and-tassle' was a euphemism for a boy's genitals.

tasty¹ *adj British*
attractive, desirable, smart. An all-purpose term of approbation, used in working-class London speech for many years and, more specifically, as a fashionable word among the young in the late 1970s and 1980s.
a tasty geezer
Love the threads. Really tasty.

tasty² *n British*
an alcoholic drink. A specific application of the wider notion of something

desirable, from the popular cockney adjective.
'I know a pub that does late tasties.'
(*Only Fools and Horses*, British TV comedy series, 1989)

tat *n British*
shoddy, cheap or low-quality material. A colloquialism, originally meaning specifically rags or cloth remnants, which is derived from 'tatter(s)' and 'tatty' (both of which are ultimately descended from an old Germanic term meaning tuft).
'Liverpool comprehensive pupils would not be seen dead in "second-hand tat", however grand the previous incumbent.'
(*Sunday Times* magazine, 30 July 1989)

taters *n*
1. *British* potatoes. A short form most often heard in London and the south of England.
2. *See* **do one's nut/block/crust/pieces/taters**
3. *American* the buttocks

taters (in the mould) *adj British*
cold. This authentic cockney rhyming-slang expression has survived in its shortened form to the present day. It is now common in 'respectable' jocular speech and is usually thought by users to be merely a shortening of 'cold potatoes'.
It's a bit taters out there, I can tell you.

taties *n pl British*
potatoes. A variant form of **taters** more often heard in Scotland and the north of England.

tats¹, tatts *n pl*
1a. *Australian* the teeth, especially false teeth
1b. *British* dice

Both senses of the word are now rare; the first probably postdating the second. The origin of the term is obscure but may imitate the clattering of the objects in question.
2. tattoos

tats² *n pl*
female breasts. A variant form of **tits**, heard since 2000.

tatters *n pl*
female breasts. Used in the UK TV comedy *Absolutely Fabulous* in 2001.

tax *vb*
to mug or steal from someone, leaving them with a proportion of their money. A miscreants' jargon term for partial

robbery, recorded among street gangs in London and Liverpool since the late 1970s.

t.b. *adj American*
loyal, faithful. This abbreviation of 'true blue' was in use among adolescents in the 1990s and was featured in the 1994 US film *Clueless*.

　　a t.b. buddy
　　You don't have to worry about her, she's t.b.

T.B.A. *n, adj American*
'to be avoided'. An item of **preppie** code similar to the British **Sloane ranger** term N.S.I.T. ('not safe in taxis'), but extended to refer to things and situations as well as people.

tea *n*
marihuana. Tea has been a nickname for herbal cannabis since the early years of the 20th century. Originally an Americanism, the term derives from the close resemblance in all but colour between the two substances. By the mid-1960s tea was a dated word restricted to older speakers, having been supplanted by such synonyms as **pot**, **charge**, **shit**, etc. **Teaed-up**, in the sense of intoxicated by marihuana, survives in teenage use.
See also **T**

teaed-up, tea'd-up *adj American*
high on marihuana. A (mainly middle-class) teenagers' term which preserves the otherwise obsolescent **tea** as a euphemism for cannabis.

tea-leaf *n British*
a *thief*. A well-known item of rhyming slang in use since the end of the 19th century. It also occurs in Australian speech and is occasionally heard as a verb.

team *n*
a street gang. Like **firm** and **crew**, the usage evokes the notion of camaraderie and united effort.

tear-arse (around/about) *vb British*
to rush about or otherwise behave hastily and recklessly. The image evoked is of activity so violent that it would tear the bottom out of a vehicle or of one's clothing.

tearaway *n British*
a wild, reckless (usually young) person. This previously obscure term, which had referred to a 'tough-guy' or mugger since the turn of the 19th century, was popularised as a useful epithet for unruly youths or 'juvenile delinquents' in the early 1960s. It is still heard in colloquial usage.

tear off a piece *vb*
to have sex (with). A phrase denoting seduction or sexual achievement from the male point of view. The expression is American or Australian in origin and dates from the end of the 19th century. (The use of 'tear off a strip' with this sexual sense has been recorded in Britain.) The unromantic image evoked is that of tearing a piece of meat off a carcass for consumption.

tear one off *vb*
to succeed in seduction, have sex (with). A less common version of **tear off a piece** and, like that expression, used mostly in the USA and Australia.

tea-towel holder *n British*
the anus. From the resemblance to the plastic press-in kitchen attachment.

technicolour yawn *n*
an act of vomiting. An Australian expression of the early 1960s, popularised in Britain by the *Barry McKenzie* comic strip by Barry Humphries and Nicholas Garland.

ted[1]**, teddy boy** *n British*
a member of a youth cult of the 1950s characterised by a particular style of dress (a long drape or waisted jacket worn with **drainpipe** trousers and thick crepe-soled **brothel-creeper** shoes) and music (jitterbug from about 1948, rock 'n' roll from 1956). Teddy boys, mainly working class in origin, combined a rough simulacrum of Edwardian dress (hence their name: they were sometimes jocularly referred to as **Edwardians**) with the adoption of American teenage hairstyles and music.

ted[2]**, teddy** *n British*
the penis. Rhyming slang from Teddington Lock: **cock**, recorded by *Viz* comic in 2002. It is a synonym for **Hampton Wick** (the next-door Thames-side community).

teef *vb*
to steal, rob. A term from Caribbean speech, also heard in the UK since 2000, especially among younger speakers.

teenybopper *n*
a lively, fashionable teenager or pre-teenager. The word, originating in the USA sometime in the mid-1960s, began to be used in a condescending or derogatory

sense in the 1970s and 1980s. (When used approvingly or neutrally in the 1970s, the term was often shortened to **bopper**.) The expression is composed of a diminutive form of teen(ager) and **bop**, meaning to dance or behave enthusiastically.

> 'The Doors are a chance for all the little teenyboppers in the States to think they're digging something avant garde.'
> (Mike Ratledge of the Soft Machine, *Oz* magazine, February 1969)

T.E.E.T.H. *phrase British*
an item of doctors' slang, as written facetiously on a patients' notes. The letters stand for 'tried everything else, try homeopathy' and imply a hopeless case or a specialist bereft of ideas.

teethe *vb American*
to fellate. An expression used on campus in the USA since around 2000.

telephone *n See* **talk on the big white telephone**; **trombone**; **dog (and bone)**

ten-pinter *n See* **five-pinter**

tent-pole *n*
an erection

Terry Waite *adj British*
late. The rhyming slang phrase borrows the name of the hostage held for 5 years in the Lebanon. In schoolchildren's usage the expression was first recorded in 1998.

> It's a bit bloody Terry Waite to tell me that now!

thick, tick, tik *adj*
attractive, physically well formed. A key term of appreciation in black speech, adopted by other speakers since 2000.

thicko, thickie *n British*
an unintelligent, slow-witted person. Common terms, especially among children and adolescents, derived from the colloquial use of 'thick' to denote someone cloddish and 'dense'.

> 'I'm not some blinkin' thickie, I'm Billericay Dickie and I'm doin' very well.'
> ('Billericay Dickie', recorded by Ian Dury, 1977)

thing *n*
a synonym for **scene**, **kick**, **vibe** or **trip** in the sense of main activity or preferred ambience. This item of raffish or **hip** usage (originating in the USA, probably in the 1940s) has become a well-established colloquialism in such phrases as 'it's not really my thing'.

third leg *n*
the penis. A variant of **middle leg**.

third peanut *n*
the clitoris. The first two peanuts are the nipples. The term was posted on the b3ta website in 2004.

this is me! *exclamation British*
defined by a London student as 'used by people to ridicule someone who is extremely self-centred'

thrape *vb British*
1a. to perform energetically and at full capacity
1b. to defeat (an opponent). The word seems to have originated in Midland and East Anglian dialect and is now used predominantly by middle-aged speakers.

thrash *n*
1. a wild celebration, dance or party. In this sense the word has been used since before World War II.
2. a variety of very fast heavy metal music of the late 1980s, in the jargon of rock journalists and aficionados

threads *n*
clothes. A usage which originated in the black-influenced **jive talk** of the 1930s in the USA. Like many similar Americanisms, it was imported into Britain and Australia with the youth culture of the 1960s. If used today the term is generally self-consciously **hip**, humorous or ironic.

> 'Wide-boy or spiv, personified in Oliver Schmitz' film by Panic, an unprivileged South African black in loud threads and two-tone shoes.'
> (*Independent*, 12 January 1988)

threepenny bits, the *n*
an attack of diarrhoea. A rhyming expression for **the shits**. 'The tray-bits' and 'the tom-tits' are alternative versions; all are especially popular in Australian speech.

throat *n American*
a **swot**, in **preppie** jargon. This is one of many synonyms used by US adolescents for a tedious, conscientious and/or unpopular fellow-student; **grind**, **squid** and **pencil geek** are others. This term probably derives from 'cut-throat (competitor)'.

throne *n*
a lavatory, toilet pedestal. A humorous synonym widely heard since before World War II and still in use. (A 'potty

throne' was a device formerly used for toilet training.)

He can't come to the phone right now – he's on the throne.

throne room *n*
a lavatory, toilet. A humorous pun playing on the euphemism **throne** for a toilet pedestal and the room used by a sovereign for receiving formal audiences.

throttle pit *n Australian*
a toilet. A vulgarism inspired by several expressions using the verb to 'throttle' as a synonym for defecation.

throw, throw up *n, vb*
(to) vomit. Throw is a short form of synonyms such as throw up, **throw one's voice**, etc.

throw a Bennie *vb British*
to lose control of oneself, become flustered or furious. The phrase, heard in the late 1990s, employs **Bennie** in the sense of a slow-witted or confused individual.

throw a flaky *vb British*
to lose control of oneself, lose one's temper. This phrase has been heard since the 1960s, particularly in Scotland and the north of England.

throw a mental *vb American*
to lose control of oneself, lose one's temper. A teenage and **Valley Girl** term of the early 1980s, the phrase with its variant form, **chuck a mental**, has become popular among British and Australian schoolchildren.

I totalled the car and Mom threw a mental.

throw a wobbly/wobbler *vb British*
to suddenly behave irrationally or to have a temper tantrum. This phrase has become popular in Britain since the end of the 1970s, but dates from the 1950s. Its exact derivation is unclear, but may reflect simply an attack of shaking or quivering, or alternatively refer to throwing or bowling a ball in an erratic and confusing arc, or may refer to the loss of control when a wobbling wheel comes off e.g. a wagon or a bicycle.

'Caroline's much calmer these days. She hasn't thrown a wobbly for ages.'

(Recorded, suburban housewife, London, 2003)

See also **wobbler**

throwin' it down *n*
moving in an attractively energetic way on the dancefloor. An emblematic term in the lexicon of club culture since 2000.

throwin' shapes *n*
moving on the dancefloor in an angular fashion. An emblematic term in the lexicon of club culture since 2000.

throw one's voice *vb Australian*
to vomit. One of many colourful synonyms originating in Australia in the late 1950s. Since the 1970s the expression is often shortened simply to **throw**.

throw wood *vb British*
to have an erection, from black speech. The verb is typically pronounced 'trow'.

thug[1] *n, adj American*
(someone who is) attractively uncouth. The word can also be used as a term of address or friendship towards males. It probably originated in gang usage around 2000.

thug[2] *vb American*
to cultivate a scruffy appearance and/or nonchalant attitude. An expression used on campus in the USA since around 2000.

thumbsucker *n British*
an immature weakling, a baby

'I ain't followin' a bunch of thumbsuckers – you want to run a national firm, friend, you put your arse in gear behind us.'
(*The Firm*, British TV play, 1989)

thumper *n Scottish*
an erection

thunder-bags *n pl Australian*
male underpants. A jocularism drawing on the analogy with explosive flatulence or defecation, more often encountered in the expression **thunderbox**.

thunder-bowl *n British*
a toilet. A variant of **thunderbox** used predominantly by middle-class speakers.

thunderbox *n British*
a toilet. The word was originally applied particularly to a commode in the colonial period. It was later extended, especially in middle- and upper-class usage, to denote a small privy, and later any lavatory.

thwoppage *n*
a sexual act. The word is pronounced with a long 'a', perhaps in imitation of French. An item of student slang in use in London and elsewhere since around 2000.

thwopping *n*
having sex. An item of student slang in use in London and elsewhere since around 2000.

tick[1] *adj British*
excellent, attractive. This all-purpose vogue term, heard especially among young black speakers in the late 1990s, usually indicates admiration of someone's appearance or physique. Although it is the Afro-Caribbean pronunciation of **thick**, the word more probably refers to a tick as a mark of approval.

tick[2] *n British*
1. a smaller, and often younger, school pupil, usually one considered insignificant and irritating. A traditional public-school term which is still heard today, it likens the person to the parasitic insect.
2. hire purchase, short-term credit. Tick meant 'credit' in post-17th-century slang. It has survived mainly in the phrase 'on tick'.

ticked off *adj*
annoyed, irritated, angry or resentful. A politer form or euphemism for **pissed-off**, heard especially in the USA.

> *'Thank you guys, but Mork's not here and I'm too ticked off to go anywhere.'*
> (*Mork and Mindy*, US TV comedy series, 1981)

ticker *n*
one's heart. Ticker was first slang for a clock or fob-watch then, by analogy, the heart.

> *'Oh my dicky ticker!'*
> (Catchphrase from the British TV comedy, *'Allo 'Allo!*)

tickle *n British*
1a. a hint
1b. an inkling
1c. a minor success or sign of future success
1d. a mild expression of interest
All these closely-related sub-senses of the word are well established in working-class speech and commercial jargon. They derive from the use of tickle to denote the sensation felt when a fish nibbles at a bait.

tickle the ivories *vb*
to play the piano

tickle the pickle *vb*
(of a male) to masturbate. A humorous coinage in imitation of the more widespread **jerkin' the gherkin**, mainly heard in Britain and Australia.

tiddly-dum *adj British*
tedious, dull, boring. An imitation of bored humming, synonymous with, but rarer than **ho-hum**.

tie off *vb*
to bind one's limb in order to raise a vein in which to inject narcotics. An addicts' term.

tie one on *vb*
to get drunk. Like its synonym, **hang one on**, this phrase was a 1930s Americanism, now heard in other English-speaking areas. The precise etymology of these expressions is not clear, but both probably convey the image of attacking a quantity of liquor or the burden resulting from its ingestion.

tight *adj*
1. mean, stingy, miserly. Now a common colloquialism rather than slang, this usage originated in the USA in the early 19th century. The image evoked is of someone who is 'tight-fisted'. A modern elaboration is **tight-arsed**.
2. tipsy or drunk. The word was first used in this sense in the USA in 1843, being adopted almost immediately in Britain. The word evokes someone full of or bulging with alcoholic liquid.
3. *American* very friendly, close
> *Me and Harry been tight since we were kids.*
4. *American* excellent, skilful. A generalisation of the use of the term from musicians' jargon, in which it signifies closely co-ordinated. In this sense tight has become a vogue word since 2000.
5. unfair, harsh. A fashionable usage among some adolescents since 2000.

tight-arse, tight-ass *n*
1. a mean, miserly person. This sense of the word is more common in British usage than the following sense. The term has existed, mainly in working-class speech, since the early part of the 20th century. 'Tight' alone has had this meaning since the mid-19th century.
2. a repressed, prudish or **uptight** person; an 'anal retentive'. This use of the expression is probably more widespread in American speech. In the 19th century it usually meant specifically sexually repressed, puritanical or chaste.

tight-arsed *adj British*
miserly, mean, stingy. This is an elaboration of **tight** (itself used to mean stingy

since the 1820s), heard since the early years of the 20th century.

tighten one's face *vb American*
to shut up, keep quiet. A teenagers' and **Valley Girl** expression, usually heard in the form of an instruction.

Aw, come on, you, like tighten your face!

tightwad *n*
a miserly, ungenerous person. A pre-World War I Americanism, later adopted elsewhere. The **wad** in question is a role of banknotes.

Tijuana bible *n American*
a pornographic magazine or book. Just across the US-Mexico border, the town of Tijuana has long been a centre of uncontrolled sexual amenities for visitors from the north.

tik *adj*
a South Asian version of **thick**, in the sense of physically attractive

tin *n*
money; cash, coins. A fairly rare expression.

tincture *n British*
1. an alcoholic drink. An adult male middle-class term, popularised by the fictional Denis Thatcher in the satirical 'Dear Bill' letters in *Private Eye* magazine in the 1980s.
2. a tincture of cannabis; hashish in liquid form as legally prescribed to some drug users for a period in the 1960s

tin-cupping *n*
cadging or begging for money. The phrase has become part of business jargon where it refers to approaching a series of companies for loans.

tings *n*
the penis. A term from Caribbean speech, also heard in the UK since 2000, especially among younger speakers. It is probably a borrowing from the adult euphemism 'things' to denote genitals.

tinkle[1] *n British*
1. an act of urination. A coy, humorous or childish expression, in common use since the 1920s.

I'm just off upstairs for a tinkle.

2. a telephone call. This colloquial usage was inspired by the thin, slow ringing of early telephones.
3. money, cash, wealth. A working-class term heard especially in the late 1950s and early 1960s.

Got any tinkle for me?

tinkle[2] *vb*
to urinate. A childish, coy or humorous euphemism which has been in widespread use since the 1920s, although it probably originated earlier as an echoic nursery term.

tinkler *n British*
the penis. A nursery term from **tinkle**, also applied ironically or derisively in reference to older males.

tinnie, tinny *n Australian*
a can of beer. There has been recent argument in Australia as to whether this term is now archaic or not, but as late as 1988 it was recorded in London among young expatriate Australians.

tin-tacked *n British*
dismissed from one's job. An item of rhyming slang based on the colloquial term *sacked*.

tiny *n British*
a small child, younger fellow-pupil. 'The tinies' is the (usually dismissive or condescending) standard middle-class, prep or public-school designation of children 'lower down' the school.

tip[1] *n British*
a dirty, messy or squalid place. The term has become a popular colloquialism since the 1980s, often describing an untidy bedroom. It is a shortening of 'rubbish tip'.

tip[2] *n, adj*
(a male who is) fashionable, admirable, **cool**. A term used by young street-gang members in London since around 2000.

tiswas, tizwoz *n British*
a state of confusion and/or flustered excitement. Usually found in the expressions 'all of a tiswas' or 'in a (bit of a) tiswas'. This folksy, light-hearted term probably comes from 'it is – it was', that is, expressing a disorientation in time, or else is an elaborated form of the colloquial 'tizz' and 'tizzy'.

tit *n*
1a. a breast. Various Old Germanic languages and late Latin dialects contained related words formed on the root *tet-* or *tit-* (*teta* in Spanish and *téton* in French are modern cognates). 'Teat' was, for many centuries, the standard English form; in the 17th century the alternative spelling and pronunciation tit began to be used. It was only in the 20th century that the variant spellings and pronunciation

clearly differentiated the vulgar and standard usages.

1b. any button, knob, nipple or small protuberance

You have to attach it to the tit on the end.

1c. the sight or touch of a woman's breast(s). An exclusively male vulgarism.

I got some tit.

1d. women in general, seen as sexual partners. An exclusively male vulgarism.

There's loads of tit around.

2. a fool, buffoon. The word has been heard in this sense since the early 20th century in British usage.

'There were two outstanding things about Q.E.D.'s "The Battle Of The Sexes" – Faith Brown. Stuart Hall merely made a right tit of himself.'

(Charles Catchpole, *News of the World*, 5 February 1989)

tit about/around *vb British*
to mess about or behave in a disorganised or ineffectual manner. One of many similar expressions such as **arse about**, **fanny about**, **fart around/about**, etc.

titfer *n British*
a *hat*. One of the best-known examples of rhyming slang (from the cliché 'tit-for-tat'), the term probably dates from the end of the 19th century and is still heard.

titless wonder *n American*
an unfortunate, feeble or clumsy person of either sex. The expression, also recorded in British armed-services slang, formerly referred literally to a 'flat-chested' woman.

tits-up *adj See* **go tits-up**

tittie, titty *n*
1. a breast. An affectionate or diminutive form of **tit**, in use since the 18th century when it was considered less vulgar than it is today.

2. *See* **tough titty**

tit-wrench *n British*
a stupid, inept or ridiculous individual. The word suggests an imaginary and presumably unnecessary tool.

toadsucker *n American*
a teenage term of abuse which, while offensive, has the advantage of not being obscene.

toast *adj American*
confounded, in trouble. The word nearly always occurs in the form 'I'm toast!', an admission that one is about to suffer, e.g., punishment or humiliation.

toasted *adj American*
drunk or tipsy

'It's not much [money], just enough to go out and get toasted some time you need it.'

(*Working Girl*, US film, 1988)

ToBo *adj American*
worthless, inauthentic, pretentious. A shortening of the **Valley Girls**' standard dismissal 'totally **bogus**'. The formation is based on the pattern of similar phrases such as **MoFo**, etc., and was first recorded in 1991.

Tod (Sloan) *n British See* **on one's tod**

todger *n British*
the penis. A version of the more common **tadger**.

'Orange Y-fronts with a slogan like "my todger is in here".'

(Alternative-comedy act, Jo Brand ('the Sea-Monster'), Montreal Comedy Festival, 1988)

todger-dodger *n British*
a lesbian. The term was posted on the b3ta website in 2004.

to die *adj American*
utterly excellent, wonderful. A **preppie** term, used typically by female speakers in thrilled approval or admiration. The expression, shortened from the colloquial 'to die for', refers to the notion of dying for something or of love for someone and is probably influenced by a usage such as **killer**.

Did you see that boy in the cut-off chinos? My God, he was to die!

It was just to die.

toe-jam *n*
an accretion of dirt between the toes

toerag *n British*
a contemptible person, a scrounger, ne'er-do-well, tramp or thief. Toe-rags were the bindings wound around the feet of convicts or tramps in the 19th century. The word had taken on its present meaning by early in the 20th century in both Britain and Australia. During the 1950s and 1960s toerag was an obscure cockney term; it was given wider currency in the 1970s by TV programmes such as *The Sweeney* and the pop songs of Ian Dury. From the mid-1980s it has been revived by working-class Londoners. In Britain toerag is often used facetiously or slightly dismissively, in Australia it can sometimes

indicate approval of one who acts like a (natural, rather than social) gentleman.

toes *n pl See* **have it (away) on one's toes**

toey *adj Australian*
nervous, agitated. By 2004 the term was in use in the UK.

toff *n British*
a socially superior and/or wealthy person. The word dates from the middle of the 19th century and probably derives from 'tuft' (used of a titled undergraduate at Oxford or Cambridge who wore a decoration on his cap) rather than the later 'toffee-nosed'. The word had an archaic ring in the 1960s and early 1970s but, like other working-class terms relating to money and status, has been revived by modern cockneys and their 'upwardly-mobile' emulators.

> 'Max was trying to build a high-tech laboratory complex, but all kinds of posh people were blocking his path. Basically, nobody loves you if you're common and you presume to take liberties with toffs.'
> (Kate Saunders, *Evening Standard*, 17 May 1989)

toffee *n British*
1. nonsense, empty talk or flattery. This is predominantly a working-class usage, particularly popular in the armed forces and in London. The origin of the image is probably in the idea of something sweet, sticky and attractively wrapped.

> 'She gave me a load of old toffee as usual about what a reputable organisation they are and how they enjoy doing business with us.'
> (Recorded, advertising executive, London, 1988)

2. gelignite. A term used by criminals and terrorists since the 1950s, from the explosive's appearance.

together *adj*
in control of oneself, well organised, adjusted, collected. Derived from the phrase **get it together**, this became a catchword of the late 1960s and early 1970s, designating an approved state of self-possession, inner harmony, etc.; the antonym was **untogether**. The usage is now dated.

togg outs *n British See* **give (someone) togg outs**

toilet[1] *n*
a disgusting, squalid or depressing place. A usage which has been in vogue since the 1980s.

toilet[2] *n, adj British*
(something or someone) inferior, of poor quality, disappointing

> That programme is a load of toilet if you ask me.

> 'He played really fucking badly; he was really toilet.'
> (Recorded, London student, April 2001)

toilet-talk *n*
'smutty', coarse or obscene conversation. An American euphemism of the 1950s which has since been adopted for ironic or jocular use in Britain and Australia.

> 'OK, I'll go next door and you two can get on with your toilet-talk.'
> (Recorded, Devon, 1986)

toke *vb, n*
(to take) an inhalation of a **joint** or pipe of cannabis. This has been a standard term in the marihuana and hashish smokers' vocabulary since the late 1960s. Toke probably comes from the Spanish *tocar*, meaning to touch, although, perhaps coincidentally, the word existed for many years in British underworld slang, meaning prison bread or a small piece or slice, becoming archaic by the 1930s.

tokus *n American See* **tush**

tom[1] *n British*
1. jewellery. A piece of underworld rhyming slang, from **tomfoolery**.
2. a prostitute. In police jargon and in the slang of the underworld and prison this has been a standard term since the 1940s. It derives from a 19th-century use of the nickname Tom to denote a masculine, assertive or aggressive streetwalker.

> '...and he says that the tom couldn't have been where the police officer said she was because she was in bed with him. He was transferred the same day.'
> (Police sergeant, *Inside the British Police*, Simon Holdaway, 1989)

3. an act of defecation. Rhyming slang from 'tom-tit' (the bird): **shit**.

tom[2] *vb British*
to work as a prostitute. A fairly rare extension of the noun sense.

tombstones *n pl*
the teeth. A jocular simile often applied to gapped, uneven or partly discoloured teeth.

tomcat, tomcat around *vb American*
to prowl, usually at night, in search of sexual activity. A term used disapprovingly, usually by women of men.

tomfoolery *n British*
jewellery. A piece of rhyming slang more often heard in the short form **tom**.

Tom Mix *n British*
an injection of a narcotic. A piece of drug abusers' terminology from the 1960s, rhyming on **fix**. (Tom Mix was the star of silent western movies.)

toms, the, the tom-tits *n Australian*
an attack of diarrhoea, or feelings of intense discomfort or dislike. A vulgarism based on the rhyme tom-tits: **shits**. The singular form is more prevalent in British rhyming slang.

ton, a ton, the ton *n*
1a. the ton (or, less commonly, **a ton**) 100 miles per hour. A term, used typically by British motorcyclists, which has been in use since the early 1950s. It was popularised by the press describing the activities of **ton-up kids**. The word was adopted by American hotrodders in the 1960s.
1b. a ton £100, in working-class and underworld parlance
1c. £1,000 in the parlance of City of London financial traders and others

tongue-job, tongue-bath *n*
1a. a French kiss
1b. an act of cunnilingus
Both uses of both terms are from the late 1960s lexicon of **hippies** and pornographers. In the sense of kiss the expression has been supplanted in US teenage and **preppie** usage by **tongue sushi**.

tongue sushi *n American*
French kissing. A **preppie** term inspired by the Japanese raw fish delicacy fashionable from the late 1970s and 1980s.

tonguing *n*
French kissing. A term popular among British teenagers in the 1990s. It was included in *Just Seventeen* magazine's article, 'lingo of lurve' (a guide to the slang of dating) in August 1996.

> *'We weren't actually doing it, only tonguing in the back of the car.'*
> (Recorded, London student, 1995)

tonk¹, tonker *n Australian*
1a. a fool
1b. an effeminate or homosexual male
Both usages date from before the 1950s and are of unknown origin. ('Tong' is an archaic term for the penis but may be quite unrelated.)

tonk² *n British*
a fat or heavily-built man or woman. A term from Caribbean speech, also heard in the UK since 2000, especially among younger speakers.

tonk³ *adj British*
muscular, well-built. Defined by one user as 'beefed-up and hardcore, e.g. Arnold Schwarzenegger'.

tonsil hockey *n American*
1a. French kissing. 'Tongue-hockey' is an alternative form of the expression.
1b. oral sex, usually fellatio. The term was popular among American college students in the late 1990s.

ton-up kid/boy *n British*
a teenage or young adult motorcyclist, a precursor of the **rocker**. Ton-up boys were the bugbears of the popular press in the late 1950s. 'A ton' or 'the ton' was 100 mph, the goal of the leather-jacketed groups who gathered near suburban bypasses and main roads to stage informal speed trials and races or to go for a 'burnup' (to drive as quickly as possible, simply for the enjoyment of speed).

> *'The BBC broadcast of "Morning Service" from Keele University, Staffs, yesterday was interrupted when a record about "ton-up" boys was heard above the hymn singing. A loudspeaker was found hidden behind a stage in the chapel.'*
> (*Daily Telegraph*, 25 January 1965)

Tony Benner *n British*
a *tenner*, a £10 note. The rhyming slang uses the name of the Labour politician Tony Benn. Synonyms are **Ayrton (Senna)** and **Pavarotti**.

Tony Blairs, Tonys *n pl British*
flared trousers. A jocular usage by British adolescents in the later 1990s borrowing the name of the Prime Minister to replace the earlier rhymes **Lionel Blairs** and **Grosvenor Squares**.

tool *n*
1. the penis. The notion of the male member as an implement is very ancient. The word tool itself appeared in Middle English and by the 16th century had been recorded as a sexual metaphor. It was at first an acceptable colloquialism, but since the beginning of the 19th century has been considered vulgar.

> *'Play it safe*
> *Play it cool*
> *Wear a Jiffi*
> *On your tool.'*

(Promotional slogan for *Jiffi* condoms, 1988)

2. a fool. Like many other words designating the male member, tool has the secondary meaning of a stupid (male) person. In the US since 2000 the word has also denoted an inept, unpopular or unpleasant male.

3. a weapon. This usage is now rare, but has given rise to the standard underworld and police jargon expression **tooled-up** (armed with firearms) in British English.

tool around/about vb
to idle or loaf, mess around performing trivial tasks. Originally an upper-class Edwardian phrase, probably from the sense of tool meaning to drive (a coach) skilfully and smoothly, hence to perform without effort. In modern speech there may also be a convergence with the sense of **tool** as the male member, paralleled in the synonymous usage **dick around**.

tooled-up adj British
1a. armed, issued with firearms. A term used by the underworld and the police since the early 1950s. The noun **tool**, denoting a firearm, is now archaic. The expression tooled-up became more widely known in the later 1970s and 1980s after references in the media; it is sometimes extended to denote armed with knives, coshes or other weapons.

'Some of the briefing scenes could have come straight from a movie thriller as the elite Squad members get "tooled up" – issued with snub-nosed revolvers and pump-action shotguns.'
(*News of the World*, 5 February 1989)

1b. equipped with housebreaking implements. A piece of police and underworld jargon.

tool up vb British
to arm oneself
We're going to have to tool up if we take that lot on.

too much exclamation
excellent, exceptional, outstanding. A now dated usage which originated in the **jive talk** of pre-World War II jazz musicians in the USA and became a (sometimes derided) cliché expression of **hippy** enthusiasm.

toont n American
the vagina. A variant form of **tuntun**, recorded in the Midwest in 2001.

toot[1] vb
to take any inhaled drug, but especially cocaine or amphetamine crystals (**speed**). This word had existed in the drug users' lexicon since the mid-1960s, but became widespread in the late 1970s with the increased popularity of cocaine among otherwise 'respectable' people. It employs the predictable simile (as in **bugle**, **hooter**) of the nose as a musical instrument.

toot[2] n
1a. an inhalation or sniff of a crystalline drug
D'you want a toot of this?
1b. a drug normally inhaled, particularly cocaine
This is grade A toot.
2. *Australian* a toilet. The word is pronounced to rhyme with 'foot', and is used by middle-class speakers.
3. a **fart**
'...there is no place, save my apartment, that is safe to let off a toot...'
(Internet chat room posting, July 2004)

tootie-fruitie n See **tutti-frutti**

tootin' adv, adj American
absolutely (right). An adjective used to intensify, as in the cliché expression 'damn/darn tootin'' right', whence the shortened version 'darned tootin'' or simply 'tootin'', meaning correct. The word is ultimately derived from 'rootin'-tootin'', originally meaning cheering and whistling.

toot sweet adv
immediately. The phrase is an anglicised version of the French *tout de suite* ('straightaway'), used jocularly, typically by students.

top[1] vb
to kill or execute (someone). The term, which is part of underworld jargon, has existed since the late 18th century when it referred to hanging.

top[2] adj British
excellent, fashionable. A vogue term of approbation among adolescents from the late 1980s. In this sense, the word was probably adopted first in the north of England, later spreading to all other regions. **Mint** and **fit** were other fashionable synonyms from the same period.

'... do you enjoy being a pop star?
I think it's top, me.'
(Liam Gallagher of Oasis interviewed in *NME*, 30 September 1995)

top bollocks *n pl*
female breasts. A vulgarism used by males in Britain and Australia since the early 1960s.

top man *n British*
a vulgarly or unfashionably dressed male. The ironic term, heard among adolescents and young adults, particularly students and **yuppies** since the late 1980s, refers to the Top Man stores which sell low-price fashion clothing.

top shatter *n British*
a leader, commanding male. An item of black street-talk used especially by males, recorded in 2003.

The top shatter is the number one bad boy.

torch[1] *vb*
to set fire to something, usually to get rid of incriminating evidence or as part of an insurance fraud

'But torching the building made little difference to the neighbourhood. There are three other crack houses within easy walking distance.'
(*Sunday Times*, 10 September 1989)

torch[2] *n*
an arsonist, especially one who is paid to burn down buildings in order to collect fire insurance. The word, which is part of police and underworld jargon, is also used as a verb.

torch job *n*
an act or case of arson

torn up, to'up *adj American*
drunk. An expression used on campus in the USA since around 2000.

tosh *n British*
1. a term of address to a stranger, invariably used by a man to another man. This working-class word, now obsolescent, was a favourite with **spivs** and young toughs in the 1950s and early 1960s. It can be used with bravado, in rough comradeship or provokingly. In this sense it possibly derives from Scottish or Cornish dialect, in which it meant smart or well-dressed.
2. nonsense. A 19th-century public-school and university term that was obsolescent, except in affected usage, during the 1960s and 1970s, but was revived in the 1980s. It often forms part of phrases such as 'tosh and tarradiddle' or 'tosh and twaddle', equating with 'stuff and nonsense'. The origin of this sense of the word is obscure; it may be an imitation of

a snort of derision (as in 'tish' or 'bosh') or derive from 'toshy', meaning over-dressed.

'He gave me some sort of explanation, but it was basically a load of old tosh.'
(Recorded, film producer, London, 1986)

toss[1] *n British*
1. something futile, worthless or useless. A word usually found in the phrase 'a load of old toss'. It denotes the semen ejaculated in masturbation, and is influenced also by **tosh** meaning nonsense.
2. an obnoxious and/or foolish person. The term is a shortening of **tosser** or **toss-bag**.

toss[2] *vb*
1. to deliberately lose a match, game or contest (usually as part of a gambling conspiracy). A racier version of 'throw'.
2. to search and/or ransack premises in pursuit of evidence of crime or of booty. An underworld and law enforcers' term.
3. *Australian* to defeat. A term used particularly in sport; it probably derives from the image of a wrestler or bull tossing an opponent, or simply from the standard sense of 'toss aside'.

toss-bag *n*
an idle, worthless, foolish and/or obnoxious person

tosser *n British*
an idle, worthless and/or foolish person. A mainly working-class term of contempt which enjoyed a particular vogue in the later 1970s. It is a synonym of **wanker** and derives from the verb **toss off**.

'Yis wan to be different, isn't tha' it? Yis don't want to end like these tossers here. Amn't I righ'?'
(*The Commitments*, Roddy Doyle, 1988)

tossing *adj British*
an intensifier for use with nouns in the same way as the more vulgar **frigging**, **fucking**, etc. The term is heard in working-class speech, especially in northern England.

toss off *vb*
to masturbate. This verb, used transitively or intransitively, has been in use since before its first recording in 1735 to refer to male masturbation. In modern English slang the word is restricted to British and Australian speech.

toss one's cookies/tacos *vb American*
to vomit. Jocularisms popular among college students in particular.

toss-pot *n*
1. a drunkard or habitual heavy drinker. This term of disapproval or affectionate abuse has been a British colloquialism for hundreds of years. The pot in question is a jar of ale, which is tossed down the throat.
2. a foolish, weak, unpleasant and/or incompetent person. Users of the term in this sense probably confuse it with **tosser**, falsely identifying the verb origin **toss off** with its sense of to masturbate. In Australia the expression toss-pot is sometimes used as a meaningless term of hearty address.

total *vb*
to destroy completely. A widespread term, especially among teenagers, since the 1960s; it derives from the notion of a 'total wreck' or a 'total loss' in official accident reports. Originally an Americanism, it is now heard elsewhere.

> '*I was so out of control I totalled the car, crashed it somehow into the side of the road.*'
> (John Philips, *Papa John*, 1986)

totally *adj*
an all-purpose, deliberately ambivalent usage (in the same way as **very**), often heard as an exclamation by female adolescents in the US. It frequently, but not necessarily, indicates approbation

> *It's, like, totally!*

to the max *adv American*
to the greatest extent, utterly. A **Valley Girl** term typically occurring in exclamations such as '**grody** to the max' (utterly awful), but is sometimes used on its own to mean absolutely or completely.

> *Was it really awful? To the max!*

toto *adj British*
completely, totally. An item of **parlyaree** recorded in the TV documentary *Out* in July 1992. It is Italian for 'all'.

> *Everyone could see she was toto blotto.*

tottie, totty, totsie *n British*
a girl or women in general, seen as potential sexual partners. The word meant a prostitute or woman of easy virtue in the 19th century and is probably an affectionate diminutive of Dorothy. It is still a fairly common term all over Britain, particularly among working-class males and servicemen.

> *a nice little tottie*

touch *adj*
good. The word, sometimes used in the 1990s as an exclamation of solidarity, affection, etc. (originally accompanying the literal touching or slapping of hands), has, since 2000, also been used adjectivally by UK teenagers and gang members.

> *touch blade*
> *That new game is so touch.*

touch down *vb*
to have sex (with). The term, which probably originated in black American usage as a sports metaphor, invariably refers to male success in seducing/penetrating females.

touch (someone) for (something) *vb*
to solicit, cadge. This colloquialism, used almost invariably in connection with a loan, has been recorded since 1760. **Touch up** is a less common alternative form, particularly in the USA.

touch-respect *exclamation British*
an all-purpose greeting or indication of approval in use among teenage gangs. The term, an elaboration of the earlier **respect**, was recorded in use among North London schoolboys in the 1990s.

touch up *vb*
1. *British* to caress sexually, grope. A phrase (often used derogatively) prevalent among adolescents.
2. to **touch** (someone) for (something) (in the sense of solicit a loan from)

tough *adj*
1. excellent. A vogue term from the early 1990s, applied particularly to music.
> *tough sounds*
2. unpleasant, disgusting, ugly, etc. A vogue term of disapproval that originated in the language of black street gangs in the early 1990s and was adopted by other adolescents.

> '*He's well tough.*'
> (Recorded, London schoolboy, 1994)

tough bounce/buns *n*
hard luck. These are rueful or, alternatively, unsympathetic versions of the colloquial 'tough luck'. The expressions originated in American speech.

tough titty *n*
hard luck, a raw deal. The expression is most often heard as an unsympathetic dismissal of another's complaint.

toup, toop *n American*
a toupée or wig

touristas n pl American
an alternative spelling of **turistas**

tout n British
an informer. A Northern Irish expression, used typically by the IRA or its supporters of a turncoat or **grass**.

towel-head n
an Arab. A predictable pejorative term. **Rag-head** is a more widespread synonym.

'Some towel-head from Hizbullah marched up and down the street twice.'
(Republican Party Reptile, P. J. O'Rourke, 1987)

town bike/pump n
a local woman supposedly available for sex with all and sundry. A form of this masculine term of contempt occurs in all English-speaking countries; the first variant employs **ride** as a sexual metaphor; the second is American.

townie, towny n British
a member of an urban underclass, working class or youth subculture characterised e.g. by tattoos, jewellery, sports clothes, etc. Like its near-equivalent, **chav**, the term came to prominence in the UK media in 2004. It had previously been used by teenagers in distinguishing youth 'tribes', also including goths, skaters, etc.

toy n
a novice or unskilled practitioner. The term is part of the jargon of graffiti artists.

toyboy n
a young male lover of an older woman. A vogue word from 1987 which started as a code term among sophisticates and was eventually popularised by the press.

trabs n pl British
trainers, sports shoes. The term was in use among adolescents in Liverpool in 2003.

tracks, trackmarks n pl
needle marks or scars on the limbs of addicts of hard drugs resulting from regular injections into the veins

'You got more tracks on you baby than the tracks of this train.'
(Lyric from 'Been on a Train', Laura Nyro, 1970)

trade n
a sexual partner or partners, particularly a paying customer of a prostitute. A generic term for custom or customers in the jargon of male and female streetwalk-ers, the word has sometimes been extended in the **gay** lexicon since the late 1960s to refer to any sexual partner.

'He'd been having the trade back and finally his landlady said "You've been bringing people back, haven't you?". She looked disapproving.'
(Kenneth Williams, quoted in Joe Orton's Diary, 25 April 1967)

tradesmen's entrance n British
the anus. A vulgar euphemism often used jocularly, dating from the 1940s when even middle-class houses might have a rear or side entrance for hawkers, deliveries, etc.

tragic adj
1. disappointing, unattractive
2. embarrassingly and/or reassuringly unfortunate

Peter Andre's chart career? Tragic.

In its slang sense the word is an intensified successor to **sad**.

trailer-trash n American
(a member of) the white underclass. The phrase became fashionable in the later 1990s, both to denigrate poor whites of the sort who are characteristically forced to live in trailer-parks and to describe a fashion for cheap, garish and kitsch accessories. A synonym for poor **white trash**.

train n
an act of serial sexual intercourse. The word is usually used as part of a phrase such as 'do a train (on someone)'.

trainspotter n British
an unfashionable, excessively earnest, unattractive individual. The phrase, originally referring to hobbyists who collect train numbers, became a vogue term as a synonym for **anorak** and **nerd** in the mid-1990s, before being used as the title of Irving Welsh's cult novel, Trainspotting.

train surfing n
joy-riding on the top or outside of mainline or underground trains. A lethal teenage prank of the 1980s in the USA and, more recently, Britain.

tramp adj British
inferior, inadequate, shabby. An all-purpose pejorative, formed from the noun, in use particularly amongst younger schoolchildren since the later 1990s.

'... this is a tramp school anyway.'
(Truanting schoolboy interviewed in the Sunday Times, 27 October 1996)

trampling n

dancing, especially energetically. The term was used by clubbers and salsa aficionados in the UK in 2004.

tranks, tranqs, trancs, tranx n pl

tranquillisers. The abbreviations are employed by drug abusers rather than the estimated three million people in Britain suffering from dependency on prescribed drugs.

tranny, trannie n British

1. a transistor radio. An abbreviated form which has survived beyond the dated full phrase from the 1960s.

   'Records were less affordable in those days (a "trannie" and Radio Caroline being the nearest thing to free music).'
   (Maureen Nolan and Roma Singleton, Very Heaven, 1988)

2a. a transsexual
2b. a transvestite

Both shortenings were part of the **gay** lexicon of the 1980s.

3. a (photographic) transparency. This is particularly popular in the parlance of designers and publishers.
4. a transport café
5. a Ford Transit van. Formerly the means of transport for many (humbler) pop groups.

trash and ready adj

attractive, exciting. The term is applied typically to someone who has dressed up and embellished themselves in a showy or deliberately vulgar style. The phrase originated in the US but was used by UK females in 2003.

trashed adj American

drunk. A teenage and **preppie** term on the familiar lines of **destroyed, smashed**, etc.

   'I'm getting trashed, man. Isn't that what you're supposed to do at a party?'
   (10 Things I Hate About You, US film, 1999)

trashed out adj American

exhausted. A popular phrase among teenagers and students since the 1970s. The term recalls synonyms such as 'shattered' or **wrecked**.

tray adv See **très**

tray-bits, the n Australian

an attack of diarrhoea. A 'tray-bit' is a British term for a threepenny piece from the turn of the 20th century (from **parlyaree**; '-tray' is from the Italian for three, tre). The phrase was adopted in Australia

as rhyming slang for **the shits**. Widespread in the 1950s, the expression is now obsolescent.

treach adj

a hip hop term of approbation. Its origins are uncertain, but it is probably a shortening of 'treacherous', by analogy with **wicked** and **bad**.

   'This month's music selections are frightfully def, totally treach and all those other hip hop clichés.'
   (I-D magazine, November 1987)

treads n pl British

shoes, trainers. The term was posted on the b3ta website in 2004.

treat vb American

to seduce. An item of black street slang of the 1990s.

tree n American

cannabis, marihuana. A predictable borrowing of the word by college students and others, perhaps influenced by the earlier use of **bush**.

tree-hugger n American

an environmentalist or green activist. A derogatory term which featured in the 1992 Montana State Election debate. Synonyms are **prairie-fairy, eagle freak**, etc.

trembler n British

a burglar alarm. This example of the jargon of cat burglars was recorded in FHM magazine in April 1996.

très adv

very. The French word is used for comic effect, e.g. 'très cool'.

Trev n British

an unfashionable, crass male. Defined by one user as 'a loser boy'. Like **Darren**, a more recent synonym for **Kevin** and **Wayne**.

trews n pl See **troos**

trey-bits, the n Australian

an alternative spelling of **the trays, the tray-bits**

tribal chieftain n British

an unpleasant and/or obnoxious person. An elaboration of the earlier **chief**, in playground usage since 2000.

trick[1] n

1a. a prostitute's client

   'Sandy had invited two girlfriends to live with them who gave Ordell "rent money", twenty per cent of what they made entertaining tricks, so it wasn't like Ordell was pimping.'

(Elmore Leonard, *The Switch*, 1978)

1b. a session or transaction between a prostitute and client

These senses of the word have been current in the USA since the first decade of the 20th century. They derive from the notion of an entertainer's 'turn' or stratagem. Trick has appeared in British English since World War II, often in the phrases 'on a trick' or **turn a trick**.

2. *American* a promiscuous female. An expression used on campus in the USA since around 2000.

> *Mary slept with the whole team; she's such a trick.*

trick² *vb American*

to sell sexual favours for money. This derivation from the noun form has not crossed the Atlantic.

> *Whenever she runs out of dope she goes out tricking.*

trick³ *adj*

1a. fancy, attractive and sophisticated. A 1980s term used by enthusiasts in fields where high technology is admired.

> *'A legendary homemade speed machine dominated the bike park last summer: a Kawasaki-powered, Harris-framed, turbo-charged, nitrous oxide-assisted rocket. To bikers, this bike is "trick", very trick.'*

(*Independent*, 6 April 1988)

1b. attractive, fashionable. From the mid-1990s the term was adopted by adolescents as a synonym for **cool**. The phrase 'totally trick' was used in a TV advertisement for plastic toy effigies of the 'Butt-ugly Martian' cartoon characters in April 2001.

trick (out) *vb American*

to decorate, embellish, customise. The term has been in vogue in hip hop culture and among car and motorcycle enthusiasts since the 1990s.

trick cyclist *n*

a psychiatrist. A humorous alteration of the standard word, evoking, like **shrink**, a suspicious contempt for the profession. The phrase was first heard in the 1930s.

> *'They are suspicious of the "trick cyclist" (nearly every policeman I have met uses the phrase to describe psychiatrists).'*

(*Town* magazine, March 1964)

trickified *adj Caribbean*

cunning, crafty

tricksy, trixie *adj, n*

(behaving like) an ostentatious, pretentious or otherwise obnoxious female, **flossie**. The term is used by females of those they disapprove of.

triff *adj British*

terrific, wonderful, exciting. This shortening, like the more widespread **brill**, became a vogue term among teenagers in the 1980s.

trim¹ *n British*

a female, especially an attractive girl. A briefly fashionable phrase used in **hip** circles and among medical students, etc. in the early 1990s. It was probably adapted from the (somewhat dated) black American use of the word to denote the female genitals or women as sex objects.

trim² *vb American*

to kill. The term was employed in the US film, *Plain Clothes*, in 1988.

trimmed *adj*

cheated, swindled. In the parlance of gamblers the word implies the neat removal of a dupe's (excess) money or winnings.

trip *n*

1a. an experience of a 'psychedelic' drug such as LSD. A typical LSD trip would last around 6–8 hours, during which time the user would undergo profound sensory and psychological changes. The image evoked is that of an 'inward journey'.

> *'Leary himself has been on over 300 trips although he has abstained for nearly a year.'*

(*Sunday Times* colour supplement, 1 January 1967)

1b. a single dose, tablet or capsule of LSD

2. a state of mind, state of affairs or personal experience. The original 1960s counterculture sense of an LSD experience was soon broadened to encompass these meanings. The word was used in a variety of sub-senses, in expressions such as 'a guilt trip' (a bout of remorse), 'lay a trip on someone' (subject someone to one's own preoccupation, obsession or problem), 'a heavy trip' (a devastating or oppressive experience) or 'on one's own trip' (preoccupied with oneself or introverted).

trip (out) *vb*

to experience the effects of LSD or a similar hallucinogenic drug. The term was coined in California in the early 1960s to describe the period (often around 8 hours) under the influence of the drug wherein one is 'transported on an inner voyage'.

tripehound n British
a term of abuse, now often used affectionately but formerly used with real venom, particularly in the north and Midlands of England. The image is that of an offal-eating dog.

tripped-out adj
1a. under the influence of LSD or a similar hallucinogenic drug
1b. exhibiting signs of euphoria or eccentricity caused by, or typical of, the use of LSD

tripping¹ adj British
strange, weird. This adjective, unknown before the 1990s, denotes a generally bizarre situation, thing, person, etc., rather than referring specifically to the simulation of the effects of LSD.

tripping² n American
enjoying oneself, having fun. In the slang of black hip hop aficionados the 1960s term for LSD usage has been generalised.

trippy adj
exhibiting or suggesting the euphoric, surrealistic effects of 'psychedelic' drugs such as LSD. The word, based on **trip**, was heard from about 1967.
    Listen to this – it's got a really trippy guitar solo.

trog¹ vb British
to trek, walk energetically or wearily. An armed-services' term which passed into civilian usage in the 1970s. It is probably a blend of 'trek' and 'slog'.

trog², trogg n British
a simplistic, (literally or figuratively) low-browed person, someone of restricted intelligence or no social graces, a 'Philistine' or 'Neanderthal'. This shortening of 'troglodyte' (a cave-dweller) was used in the armed forces in the early 1950s and particularly by jazz enthusiasts, **beatniks** and students in the late 1950s and early 1960s to describe those who were dull, boorish or out of touch. Since around 2000 in adolescent usage the term has denoted an unpleasant and/or unattractive female. Users have claimed it is a blend of **troll** and **dog**.

Trojan n American
a condom. The word is a trademark name used generically in the USA in the same way as Durex in the UK.

troll¹ vb, n British
(to take) a prowl, wander or **cruise**. This alternative form of 'trawl' has existed since the 15th century. It acquired the sexual sense in the 1930s and was a vogue **gay** term of the 1960s.
    'Orton insisted the trolling fed his work; but it also fed Halliwell's rage.'
    (John Lahr, preface to Joe Orton's Diaries, published 1986)
    'I don't just get married because I enjoy trolling down the aisle.'
    (Joan Collins, TV talk show, 1988)

troll² n
an unpleasant and/or unattractive person. The standard term, denoting a mythical monster or goblin, has been applied especially to females in UK and US usage since the 1990s.

trolleys, trollies n pl British
underpants. A fairly rare public-school expression. It is of uncertain origin but may be related to the archaic 'trolley-bobs', a nursery version of trousers. (In her diary entry for 8 January 1934, Barbara Pym mentions buying trollies at Marks and Spencers.)

trollied, trolleyed adj British
drunk. The term, recorded in 2001, may be derived from the phrase 'off one's trolley' or from **trollies** in the sense of visible, undignified and/or comical underpants.

trombone n British
a telephone. A rhyming alternative to **dog (and bone)**.

tronk n British
a foolish, clumsy or contemptible person. A rare schoolchildren's and student's term, possibly related to the Australian synonym **tonk**.

troos, trews n pl
trousers. The preferred term among many British teenagers and students since 2000.

troppo adj Australian
unhinged, deranged, crazy. The word is an abbreviation of 'tropical' and is usually heard in the phrase to 'go troppo', originally referring to someone overcome by tropical heat but now generalised to mean something like **over the top**. The word originated among armed-service personnel in World War II.

trots, the n British
an attack of diarrhoea. The expression, heard since World War I, evokes swift

but controlled movement to the lavatory.

troub, troubs n British See **trub**

trouble (and strife) n British
a *wife*. A piece of cockney rhyming slang which is still in (mainly jocular, ironic or self-conscious) use; it is now generally shortened simply to 'trouble' by Londoners.

trough vb British
to eat. A humorous middle- and upper-class verb evoking (but not necessarily involving) gluttony.

trounced adj British
drunk. One of many synonyms in use among students since 2000.

trouser[1] vb British
to pocket something. A humorous alternative term from the 1980s.

'Strobes then insisted on accompanying Chancellor to the prize-giving in Milan, and trousered the cheque himself.'
(*Private Eye* magazine, 17 March 1989)

trouser[2] n British
a generic term for males as sex objects. A 1980s women's version of '(a bit of) **skirt**', satirising the 'predatory' male expression.

trouser bandit n British
a male homosexual. A humorous, though pejorative, euphemism, evoking the image of a predatory or promiscuous **gay** male. 'Bum bandit' and **arse bandit** are alternative versions.

trouser chuff n British
a **fart**. A mock-childish term used by adolescents in the 1980s and popularised in the best-selling *Viz* comic.

'Johnny Fartpants' "trouser chuffs" always get him into meddlesome scrapes – losing his pocket money or causing the San Francisco earthquake of 1906...'
(*Time Out* magazine, December 1988)

trouser snake n
1. the penis. A young person's joky euphemism adopted by adults; the full version is **one-eyed trouser snake**.
2. a disreputable or reprehensible person. This sense of the expression was typically used in the 1980s by American girls as a term of disapproval applied to males, emphasising the treachery inspired by 'snake' rather than the sexual aspect of the image.

trout n See **old trout**

trouting n British See **out trouting**

trout-pout n British
the result of lip-enlargement injections. The term was given wide circulation by media comments on the TV actress Lesley Ash's cosmetic enhancement in 2001.

trub n British
trouble. A shortening used typically in middle-class badinage.
We've been in a spot of trub recently.

trucking n See **keep on trucking**

true-say, true-dat exclamation
indications of agreement, acceptance, approval. From black speech used in e.g. street-gang code and its imitations.
'True-say, but what can you do about it? Nothing!'
(Recorded, contributor to www.wass-up.com, November 2003)

trump vb British
to **fart**. The term, popular since the late 1990s, is based on the noun **trumpet**.

trumpet n British
1. a **fart**. A children's word which enjoyed a vogue in the late 1980s.
'Lucy did a trumpet.'
(Recorded, 10-year-old boy, Devon, 1986)
2. a telephone. A rare synonym of **trombone**, **the blower**, etc.

trunk[1] n
1. *American* the backside. By analogy with the trunk (UK: boot) of a car. The term has been popular since 2000, sometimes in the phrase 'junk in the trunk', i.e. a 'packed' or very prominent posterior.
2. *also* **trunker** or **trunky** the penis. By analogy with either the trunk of a tree or an elephant's trunk.
Man, I slammed my trunk into her.
He gave her a trunky.

trunk[2] vb
to have sex (with), penetrate. Derived from the noun form, the usage was recorded in 2004.
He claims he trunked her.

trust[1] n British
money. The slang usage, possibly from trust-fund, has been in vogue since around 2000.

trust[2] vb British
to lend (money)
Trust me a Pavarotti, will you?

tsotsi n South African
1. the South African patois as spoken in Cape Town and Johannesburg, especially by black speakers. The language is a combination of English, Afrikaans, Xhosa and Sotho.
2. a stylish black male, a young gangster

T.T.F.O. phrase British
an item of doctor's slang, as written facetiously on a patient's medical notes. The letters stand for 'told to fuck off'.

tub n
1a. a boat
    'Can't this tub go any faster?'
    (Friday 13th part VI, US film, 1986)
1b. a car, truck, bus, etc.
2. a 'tub of lard'; a fat person. A widespread colloquialism.

tube n
1. the Tube the London Underground railway system, from the tubular construction of the tunnels. This nickname dates from the turn of the 20th century.
2. the hollow formed by a breaking wave. A surfer's term from which the term of approbation, **tubular**, is derived.
3. Australian a can of beer. (**Tinnie** is a slightly later synonym.)
    'Alex Buzo, who is minder of the Australian language among his other activities, records that it is 20 years since he last heard beers referred to as tubes.'
    (Observer magazine, 13 December 1987)
4. the tube television, from the cathode ray tube
5. British a person. A vogue word among teenagers in the late 1980s; it was a synonym for **dude**, although it sometimes had the added sense of someone foolish or gormless.

tube it vb American
to fail an examination, test, task, etc. This common campus expression is based on the colloquialism 'down the tubes' in the sense of lost or ruined.

tube steak n American
the penis. A euphemism heard in **hip** circles in the 1980s, from black street usage of the 1970s. It was originally a jocular term for a frankfurter sausage.

tubular adj
an all-purpose term of teenage approbation, deriving from riding the **tube** as being the highest form of surfing experience. Like many 1960s surfing terms this

expression (often intensified as 'totally tubular') was adopted by **Valley Girls** in the later 1970s and subsequently became a vogue usage in international English in the 1980s.

tuchis n American See **tush**

tuck, tucker n
food. The first version of the word is typical of British public-school vocabulary, the second Australian. Both date from the 19th century and probably derive from the verb to 'tuck in(to)', which originally implied the humorous notion of tucking food surreptitiously into oneself or behind one's clothing.

tucked up adj British
1. imprisoned, incarcerated. A homely euphemism for a grim reality in the tradition of London working-class usages.
    'Adjusting back to normal society is not easy when you've been tucked up for a bit.'
    (Recorded, ex-prisoner, London, 1986)
2. cheated, duped. A London working-class usage paralleling the more widespread **stitch (someone) up**.

tuckered (out) adj
exhausted. This is originally an American term deriving from an archaic sense of the verb 'tuck', signifying rebuke or reproach. (In Old English tuck also had the sense of to ill-treat.) Now, as heard in such phrases as 'plumb tuckered out', the word has folksy overtones.

tuck-tuck n British
a 'break' at school, from the old schoolboy use of **tuck** to mean food

tuck (someone) up vb British
1a. to defeat, capture
1b. to confound, dupe
This all-purpose phrase is in London working-class usage, particularly amongst criminals and the police. The image is that of putting a helpless child to bed.

tud, tut n British
rubbish. The word was used by clubbers and some teenagers in 2000. It may be a dialect term in origin but its etymology is unclear.
    a load of old tud
    It's no tud.

tude n American
(a bad) **attitude**; a surly, defiant or negative disposition. A short form of the type (i.e. **the burbs**, **nabe**, **perp**, **tard**) fashionable in adolescent circles in the late 1970s

and 1980s and, more recently, in (often facetious) journalese usage.

tug n British
1. an arrest or detention of a suspect (in the jargon of the underworld or police officers), a **collar**

'E won't be expecting a tug at that time of night.

2. an act of manual sexual stimulation of a male, usually by a female. A less common synonym of **hand-job** in use particularly in Australian speech in the 1990s.

tukus n American See **tush**

tumble n
1. an act of sexual intercourse. This fairly inoffensive expression is often elaborated to 'tumble in the hay'.
2. British an attempt, try. In working-class usage 'give it a tumble' is the equivalent of 'give it a whirl' (the Australian expression is 'give it a **burl**').
3. arrest, capture or detention. In criminal and police parlance in both Britain and the USA the word is used in these senses by analogy with a fall suffered by a racehorse or sports contender.
4. See **take a dive/tumble/fall**

tummy banana n
the penis. A nursery expression adopted, or perhaps invented for jocular use, by adults. The phrase was first heard in middle-class circles in the early 1970s.

tuna n American
1a. a girl or woman. Users of the term, who include teenagers and **preppies**, are often unaware of its origins in the senses which follow.
1b. sexual activity
1c. the female sex organs
The use of the seafood metaphor (popular in the USA long before it was readily available in Britain) as a euphemism for femininity or femaleness is inspired by the piscine quality of the female sexual odour.
2. marihuana. The reason for this usage is unclear; it may simply be a transference of the idea of tuna as a delicacy or staple food.

tuneage n American
music. A mock-pompous coinage using the **-age** suffix and recorded among college students in the mid-1990s.

tune in vb
to attune to one's environment, achieve harmony with one's peer group, the counterculture and/or the cosmos. This **hipster** and **beatnik** term became part of the catchphrase slogan of the **hippy** movement; 'turn on, tune in, drop out'. Unlike the other two verbs, tune in was not itself adopted into mainstream colloquial speech.

tuntun n American
the vagina. The word is used by hip hop aficionados and students. Its origins are obscure, but it may be a form of **tuna 1**. **Toont** is a variant form.

tup vb British
to have sex (with). The country persons' term for the copulation of a ram with a ewe (from the Middle English word for ram, *tupe*) is, by extension, used vulgarly of humans.

turbo-crush n British
an infatuation. 'Turbo-' here is used as an intensifier in the same way as the contemporary and more common 'mega-'. 'To have a turbo-crush on someone' was a vogue expression among younger British adolescents in the mid-1990s.

turd n
1. a piece of excrement. A descendant of the Anglo-Saxon word *tord*, the term was freely used until about the 17th century, by which time it was being avoided in polite speech and writing. It is still considered vulgar by many speakers, although, when referring e.g. to dog droppings, it is now sometimes used even in broadcasts.
2. an unpleasant and/or despicable person. In this sense the word has the same connotation of obnoxiousness as its literal and figurative synonym, **shit**.

turd burglar n British
a male homosexual. One of several jocular but hostile phrases of the 1980s (such as **fudgepacker** and **brownie-hound**), used by heterosexuals to suggest the faecal aspects of sodomy.

turf[1] n
a street gang or street drug dealer's territory

'In fact he's a lookout, a lookout for cops and strangers, for other dealers stealing "turf".'

(*Guardian*, 5 September 1989)

turf[2] vb British
to throw away, rid oneself of (something or someone). A slang form of the collo-

quial 'turf out', used by e.g. medical personnel.

If you don't want it, just turf it.

He thought he was going to be there for ever but he got turfed after a couple of days.

turistas, the turistas, touristas *n American*
an attack of diarrhoea. *Turista* is Spanish (or Mexican) for tourist.

turkey-neck *n American*
the penis. From the supposed resemblance.

'When your mother's crying at the funeral, I'm gonna goose her with my turkey-neck.'
(*Barfly*, US film, 1987)

turn a trick *vb*
to service a (prostitute's) client. The phrase, evoking a neat execution of a deception, stratagem or performance, has been in use since the early years of the 20th century.
See also **trick¹ 1a**

turned-on *adj*
1. aware, **hip** or liberated. A term of approbation of the 1960s, deriving from the notion of being 'turned-on' by a mood-altering drug. **Switched-on** was a British alternative form.
2a. sexually aroused. A slang phrase of the 1950s which has become a common colloquialism.
2b. stimulated, fascinated. A generalisation of the previous sense of the term.

turn-off *n*
a depressing, deflating, disappointing or unexciting experience. The phrase was coined by analogy with its opposite, **turn-on**.

'It's really nice that you want to be well groomed, but you get hair in the food. Hair in the food is a turn-off, Joan, sweetie.'
(*The Serial*, Cyra McFadden, 1976)

'I find all that sort of thing [male body-building] a complete turn-off.'
(Recorded, female social worker, London, 1987)

turn on *vb*
1a. to take a drug. The term first referred to hard narcotics, but was later applied to cannabis and LSD. It was originally based on the notion of stimulus at the throw of a switch.
1b. to allow oneself to experience a heightened or more liberated reality. One of the three 'commandments' of the alter-

native society of the late 1960s; 'turn on, tune in, drop out'.

'Within a year the league [for Spiritual Discovery] will have a million members who who will turn on with LSD every seven days.'
(Timothy Leary, *Sunday Times* colour supplement, 1 January 1967)

turn-on *n*
1a. a drug, specifically a user's drug of choice
What's your turn-on?
1b. anything arousing or exciting, a sexual stimulus. A back-formation from **turned-on**.
I love shoes – patent leather stilettos are a real turn-on.

turn (someone) over *vb British*
1a. to cheat, rob
I never thought my best mate would turn me over.
1b. to attack, beat up
1c. to raid and/or search premises
All three sub-senses are in working-class use, particularly in London. The first two have been heard since the 1950s, the third from the mid-19th century.

turtle *n*
1a. a passive sexual partner, especially one willing to offer oral or anal sex. The term is in use among prisoners, criminals, etc., and is often applied to male prisoners who offer sexual favours in return for tobacco, etc.
1b. a woman regarded as a sex object
'Lesley Morris, 23, said sailors called the WRENS sluts, slags, splits and turtles.'
(*Daily Mirror*, 4 February 1997)

turtles *n pl*
gloves. An item of rhyming slang (from 'turtle doves'). This example of the jargon of cat burglars was recorded in *FHM* magazine in April 1996.

tush, tushie *n American*
the buttocks, backside. These are inoffensive terms used in the family and elsewhere. They derive from the Yiddish *tochis*, also written *tokus*, *tukus* or *tuchis*, which in turn derives from the Hebrew *tokheth*.

tut *n British*
a version of **tud**

tutti-frutti, tootie-fruitie *n*
an effeminate, frivolous or ridiculous male. This slang use of the name of the Italian ice cream dish (vanilla with pieces of glacé fruit) originated in the USA

where **fruit** denotes a **gay** male. (*Tutti frutti* is Italian for 'all fruits'.)

T.V. *n*
transvestism or a transvestite

twang *vb British*
(of a female) to masturbate. The term was used by UK students in 2000.

twang (the wire) *vb*
to masturbate. This word, used only of men, was originally an Australianism with rural overtones.

twanger *n American*
the penis

twannie *n British*
a stupid, obnoxious person. The term is a combination of **twat** and **pranny**.

twat[1], **twot** *n British*
1. the vagina. A word first recorded in the 17th century. The etymology is obscure but it probably derives from a rural dialect term.
2. a foolish or obnoxious person. The word has had this sense (firstly in London slang) since the late 19th century. Until the early to mid-1960s the word was in widespread use in this context, often amongst schoolchildren and some adults who were unaware of its provenance (and probably thought it an intensive form of twit).

> 'What kind of creature bore you/was it some kind of bat?/they can't find a good word for you/but I can/twat.'
> (*A love story in reverse*, poem by John Cooper Clarke, 1978)

twat[2] *vb British*
to hit, beat up

> 'The drummer went to help and he got twatted as well.'
> (*Fresh Pop*, Channel 4 TV, 17 December 1996)

twatted *adj British*
1a. drunk
1b. tired
1c. destroyed
Originally meaning 'struck' or 'cuffed', the term has been extended to cover other senses of 'damaged'. **Cunted** is a more offensive version.

tweak *vb American*
1. to suffer physical symptoms of drug withdrawal. This 1980s term evokes the irritation and spasmodic nature of drug-induced distress, as well as recalling words such as 'twitch' and 'weak'.
2. to adjust or fine-tune. A piece of jargon applied to motor mechanics and computers, for instance.

tweaked *adj American*
eccentric, deranged. An adolescent vogue term of the 1990s.

twerp, twirp *n*
an insignificant, silly and/or obnoxious person. An invented word which appeared in the 1930s and gained widespread currency in the 1950s.

> 'My stuff is outrageously conceived and devastatingly realised.
> Oh do shut up you boring little twerp!'
> (*Biff* cartoon, 1986)

twig[1] *vb British*
to understand, 'catch on'. A formerly raffish term which, since the late 1960s, has become a fairly common colloquialism. This usage has been recorded since the 18th century and derives either from 'tweak' in the sense of snatch or grasp or from a Gaelic verb meaning to comprehend.

twig[2] *n See* **drop off the twig**

twig and berries *n American*
the male genitals. An expression used on campus in the USA since around 2000.

twillie, twilly *n British*
a foolish, clumsy or stupid person. An adolescent term in use since the early 1970s. It is a blend of 'twit' and 'silly'.
> a complete twillie

twimp *n American*
a foolish and/or insignificant individual. A high-school term of mild abuse from the late 1980s, blending 'twit', **twerp** and **wimp**.

twimpoid, twimpo *n British*
a silly, foolish person. These teenage and pre-teenage vogue terms of disapproval or insult from the 1990s are British versions of the American **twimp**.

twinkie, twinky, twink *n American*
1a. a male homosexual or effete, fey or eccentric man
1b. a cute, attractive person
Both senses of the words derive from the trademark snack food *Twinkies*, a sort of cupcake. The word has echoes of 'twinkle-toes', 'twinkling' and 'Tinkerbelle'. Twink is sometimes used as a (usually male) nickname in Britain for someone with sparkle

or vim.

2. a $20 bill. An item of black street-talk which was included in so-called **Ebonics**, recognised as a legitimate language variety by school officials in Oakland, California, in late 1996.

twirl n British
a prison officer. An item of prisoners' jargon recorded in the 1990s. 'Twirl' in the sense of a (skeleton) key is an archaic piece of underworld argot dating back to the 19th century.

twirp n
an alternative spelling of **twerp**

twist n American
a girl or attractive young woman. This term, used typically by underworld or working-class speakers, is a rare example of American rhyming slang, from 'twist and twirl': girl.

> 'M-m-m – goodlooking twist!'
> (Panic on the 5.22, US film, 1974)

twisted adj American
intoxicated by drink or drugs. An expression used on campus in the USA since around 2000.

twister n American
a person with supposedly perverted sexual taste or preferences

twitch n British See **get a twitch on**

two and eight n British
1a. a fit of agitation

> 'What with coming home to find the place burgled, then all these bills arriving, I was in a right two and eight.'
> (Recorded, middle-aged woman, London, 1988)

1b. a dishevelled, disorganised or grotesque person

> Look at 'er, she's a right two and eight.

Both senses of the term are London working-class rhyming slang for a **state**.

two-bit adj American
cheap, penny-pinching, worthless. This Americanism of the mid-19th century is now occasionally used even in countries where 'two bits' does not signify 25 cents (a 'bit' is one-eighth of a dollar).

twoccer, twocker n British
a joy-rider, car-thief. This term of criminal slang comes from the offence recorded on charge sheets as 'taken without owner's consent', and refers to the culture of **hotting** which grew up in working-class areas in the 1990s.

twonk n British
a foolish and/or unpleasant person. A term of abuse employed by adolescent males around 2000.

two-pot screamer n Australian
a person more than usually unable to cope with the effects of strong drink. A term of disapproval used by hearty males in particular.

> 'Hi! My husband's pissed again – he's always been a two-pot screamer.'
> (The Wonderful World of Barry McKenzie, Barry Humphries and Nicholas Garland, cartoon strip in Private Eye magazine, 1968)

two stops short of Dagenham adj British
deranged, eccentric. A pun recorded in 2002, Dagenham in East London is 'two stops short of **Barking**' on the underground line.

> I tell you, she's two stops short of Dagenham, that one!

Compare **Upton Park**

twot n British
an alternative spelling of **twat**

U

U.B.I. *n British*
'unexplained beer injury'. An item of jocular medical shorthand, as supposedly written on a patient's notes.
See also **N.F.N.**

Uganda *n See* **discuss Uganda**

uggers *adj British*
ugly. A term popular with adolescents since the late 1990s using the long-established familiarizing suffix **-ers**.

ugly pills *n*
an imagined source of repellent physical characteristics, manners or behaviour. The words usually form part of a sardonic speculation that the person in question has been 'taking ugly pills'.

u-ie *n*
a U-turn. The expression is used by skateboarders as well as drivers, usually in the form 'do a u-ie' or 'hang a u-ie'.
See also **hang a louie**; **hang a ralph**

uncle[1] *n*
1. *British* a pawnbroker. A use of the word which arose in the 18th century, referring (probably ironically) to the moneylender's avuncular assistance. The term was still heard in London in the 1950s and may survive. From the 1980s it was heard in the British TV soap opera *EastEnders*.
2. *American* a cry of concession. To 'say uncle' or 'cry uncle' is to surrender or admit defeat, in playground games for instance. The reason for this choice of word is obscure.
3. *American* the law-enforcement establishment when seen as benevolent, protective or rewarding by crooks
All three main senses of the word derive from the notion of an uncle as a potential protector or provider of funds (in the third case perhaps reinforced by 'Uncle Sam'). There are many other examples of this, for instance in theatrical jargon where the word equates with 'angel'.

uncle[2], Uncle Dick *adj British*
sick. One of many rhyming-slang expressions using 'uncle' and a convenient rhyming Christian name.
'You look a bit uncle to me.'
(*Minder*, British TV series, 1984)

Uncle Mac *n British*
heroin. London drug-users' rhyming slang for **smack**. 'Uncle Mac' was a presenter of children's radio programmes from the 1930s to the 1960s. This sinister borrowing dates from the late 1970s.

uncool *adj*
unacceptably or unfashionably intrusive, assertive, dull, reckless, conventional, etc. A generic negative complement to the all-purpose term of approbation, **cool**.
'Weekend hippies and the like who think "what a groovy joy-ride" and are very, very uncool.'
(*International Times*, April 1968)

underarm *adj British*
1a. underhand, **dodgy**
1b. illegal, illicit
The use of underarm in these senses stems from the literal sense of passing or carrying something concealed under the arm, reinforced by the supposed offensive nature of the armpit. ('Under the arm' is an archaic expression, once used by vagrants and marginals and meaning bad or inferior.)

underchunders *n pl Australian*
male or female underpants. A humorous vulgarism which employs **chunder** (vomit) as a rhyme, rather than for sense (unless the original image was of a sickening item of clothing).

undercrackers *n pl British*
male or female underpants
'The problem with Carole Caplin…is not…that she may or may not have an inside track on the PM's undercrackers.'
(*Guardian*, 9 March 2004)

underdaks n pl Australian
male underpants. The Australian equivalent of the north of England expression **underkecks**, from **daks**, the trade name of a popular brand of casual trousers.

underground n, adj, adv
(belonging to) the 'alternative society' or counterculture, as opposed to bourgeois society. A term from the 1960s adopted from the wartime usage when applied to clandestine resistance movements. (The term 'underground railroad' was earlier used for the system of sympathizers/safe houses by which escaped slaves were taken from the southern states to the North before emancipation.)

under heavy manners adj, adv
in a state of oppression. A phrase from the counterculture patois of Jamaica which became known in Britain and elsewhere due to its use by reggae musicians in the early 1970s.

underkecks n pl British
male underpants. An extension of the (mainly northern English) use of **kecks** to mean trousers.

underware n
personal files in a computing system. A piece of jargon in use among computer specialists in the mid-1990s.

undie-grundie n American
the grabbing and twisting of a victim's underwear. A form of jocular attack used by school and college students in the US.

unforch adv British
unfortunately. Described in 2003 by a London student as 'used by muppets who mean unfortunately'.
Compare **obv**

unglued adj
an alternative version of **untied**

unhip adj
unaware, culturally and/or socially out-of-touch, unfashionable. The opposite of **hip**. The word has rarely been heard since the early 1970s, except among the remnants of the 'counterculture'.

unit n
1a. the genitals. An unromantic 1970s and 1980s term used by the self-consciously liberated or promiscuous to refer to the (usually male) sex organs.
1b. a potential or actual sexual partner or conquest. A cold-blooded piece of singles-bar jargon from the mid- to late

1970s, similar in usage and connotation to the more common **item**.
'Would ya look at that li'l unit in hotpants, though!'
(R Crumb cartoon, *Head Comix*, 1970)

units n pl American
an abbreviated form of **parental units**

unload vb
1a. to defecate
1b. to **fart**
A vulgarism which is heard all over the English-speaking world but which is particularly popular in Australia.

unmentionables n pl
1a. underwear
1b. the genitals
A mock-Victorian euphemism for taboo personal items. The expression was used fairly seriously in the early 1900s; since at least World War II the usage has invariably been facetious.

unplugged adj British
behaving naturally and unself-consciously rather than boisterously, particularly towards a partner or friend. This sense of the word, heard among adolescents in the later 1990s and usually referring to male behaviour, is inspired by the use of the term to describe rock and pop musicians performing informal and relaxed acoustic sets as opposed to more contrived electrified stage shows.

unravelled adj
an alternative version of **untied**

unreal adj
1a. unbelievably good, excellent
1b. outrageous, excessive or unreasonable in behaviour
Both usages are from the jargon of teenagers, firstly (since the 1960s) in the USA and later elsewhere in the English-speaking world. The expression in fact originated in the **beatnik** era when unreal was an exclamation of hallucinated delight or admiration.

unt-cay n American
the vagina. An item of **pig Latin** based on **cunt**.

unthinkables n pl British
1a. underwear
1b. the genitals
'She left her door open and I got a glimpse of her unthinkables.'
(Recorded, male university student, London, 1988)
A students' facetious mock-Victorian euphemism coined in imitation of the ear-

lier **unmentionables**.

untidy adj Australian

drunk. A humorous euphemism.

untied adj

in disarray, confused. Often occurring in the phrase **come untied**, the expression has recently been heard less often than its synonyms **unglued** and **unravelled**.

untogether adj

disorganised, confused, diffuse. This popular **hippy**-era term more often than not refers to the personality or mood of someone who is not in equilibrium emotionally, intellectually or psychically. It postdates its opposite, **together**. Untogether is now rarely heard, but survives in the sociolect of those reaching adolescence in the late 1960s.

up adj

1. American 'dried', having forgotten one's lines. A theatrical term of uncertain origin.

2. exhilarated or intoxicated, **high**

up against the wall exclamation

a shout of rage, defiance or menace. This Americanism, chanted on anti-war or Black Power demonstrations in the late 1960s and early 1970s, and invariably followed by the epithet **motherfucker**, was intended to evoke the righteous rage of a revolutionary mob about to summarily execute their oppressors, and to parody the police instruction when 'spreading' a suspect or captive.

upchuck vb

to vomit. A humorous reversal of **chuck up** (itself based on 'throw up'), this expression surfaced in the USA in the 1920s and, having spread to British and Australian speech, has enjoyed a limited currency ever since.

up each other/one another adj, adv Australian

engaged in mutual flattery, 'in cahoots'. The image is that of mutual sodomy, colourfully suggesting an unhealthy or illegally close relationship (often in a political or business context).

Compare **up oneself**

upfront adj

bold, assertive, open, straightforward, trustworthy. The word is usually used approvingly of someone acting honestly or without guile.

uphill gardener n British

a male homosexual. The term is one of many pejorative synonyms (**stabber**, **fudge-nudger**, **rear-gunner**, etc.) denoting 'active' or 'predatory' homosexuality, heard since the 1990s.

(all) up in someone's grill adj American

See **grill²** 1a

up on blocks adj, adv British

menstruating. The expression, used typically by males since 2000, borrows the image of a car which is temporarily out of operation and immobilised in a garage. The reference is to a female who is unavailable for e.g. sex during her period.

up oneself adj Australian

self-satisfied, smug, high-handed. A vulgar version of 'full of oneself', evoking auto-sodomy. Now also heard in the UK.

'They're all up themselves, that lot.'
(Referring to members of a university department, teacher, Melbourne, 1988)
'Anyone who thinks their signature is worth £175 is getting up himself.'
(Guardian, 2 March 2004)

Compare **up each other/one another**

uppers n pl

stimulant drugs such as amphetamines (i.e. **pep pills**, **speed**) and cocaine, as opposed to **downers** (barbiturates and sedatives)

He acts as if he's on uppers.

uppie, uppy adj British

exhilarating, exciting, powerful. A term from the lexicon of **rave** and dancefloor culture in the northwest of England in the late 1990s.

uppy adj

aggressive, assertive. The term, often used in the phrase 'getting uppy', is heard throughout the English-speaking world but particularly in Lowlands Scottish speech.

up shit creek adj

in serious trouble. Shit creek was a 19th-century nickname (probably coined by British or American sailors) for any stagnant or dangerous backwater or river. The expression is often embellished to 'up shit creek without a paddle', sometimes with the addition of 'in a barbed wire canoe'. 'Up the creek' is a less offensive version.

up the duff adj British

pregnant. A working-class synonym of **up the poke/pole/spout/stick**, here employing the long-established British metaphor of pudding. Duff is an old-fashioned boiled or steamed pudding; the word is a dialect version of 'dough'. It has an all-purpose sexual sense (encompassing gratification, the penis, semen or a woman and baby).

up the guts *adj Australian and South African*
pregnant. A vulgar version of **up the duff**.

up the poke/pole/spout/stick *adj British*
pregnant. These expressions are in mainly working-class use. They are all vulgar, simultaneously evoking the male and female sex organs and the idea of a baby being lodged or jammed. They can describe either the act of conception, as in 'he's put her up the stick', or the condition of being pregnant, as in 'she's up the stick again'.

uptight *adj*
1. tense, repressed, humourless, unrelaxed. A black slang term which is probably in origin a short form of 'wound-up tight' or 'screwed-up tight'. The term was adopted into the **hippy** vocabulary to express the unliberated, repressed characteristics of **straight** society, particularly the authority figures thereof. Since the early 1970s uptight has passed into (mainly middle-class) colloquial usage, although by the late 1980s it had begun to sound rather dated.

> *'The cops? Oh, just about as uptight and corrupt as in Britain.'*
> (Terry Reid interviewed in *Oz* magazine, February 1979)

2. *American* satisfactory, in good order. In black American street-talk the expression retains a second, rare and positive connotation, possibly deriving from 'locked-up tight', meaning fixed, settled, under control or, alternatively and more probably, from a sexual sense of being 'coupled' or 'snuggled-up tight'.

> *'It's   uptight,   everything   is   all right/Uptight, it's out of sight.'*
> (Chorus lyric from 'Uptight' by Stevie Wonder, 1963)

Upton Park *adj British*
(slightly) crazy. The jocular expression is based on the fact that Upton Park underground station is 'two stops short of **Barking**'.

Compare **two stops short of Dagenham**

up to one's pots *adj British*
drunk. An expression in use among the **gay** theatrical community since the 1960s.

urban surfing *n*
riding on the outside of a moving car, bus, train, etc. A dangerous fad of the later 1980s among adolescents, first in the USA and later elsewhere.

Uri (Geller) *n British*
(a drink of) Stella Artois lager, playing on the name of the famous illusionist. **David (Mellor)**, **Paul (Weller)** and **Nelson (Mandela)** are synonyms, all popular with students since the late 1990s.

u.s. *adj British*
useless. Mainly used by middle- and upper-class speakers, the term can apply to objects or people.

> *'This female razor thing is absolutely u.s.'*
> (Recorded, female, Bath, 1986)

user *adj*
a habitual drug user, especially referring to a heroin addict

using *adj*
addicted to heroin or habituated to another hard drug. A euphemism employed by law enforcers and drug abusers.

> *Looks like she's using again.*

u.v.s *n pl American*
ultra-violet rays, sunshine. A **preppie** and **Valley Girl** usage found in phrases such as 'catch/cop/grab/soak up some u.v.s'.

V

V *adj British*

very. Often heard in middle-class speech, as in 'v. good', 'v. difficult', etc.

vadge *n*

the vagina. A vulgarism (it also occurs in the form **fadge**) in use among adolescents in the 1990s and listed in *Viz* comic in 1994. **Vige** is an American synonym.

vagitarian *n British*

a lesbian. The term was posted on the b3ta website in 2004.

Vals, Valley Girls *n pl American*

a Californian (and later more widespread) youth culture of the early 1980s, based on the habits, mannerisms and distinctive vocabulary of teenage girls from the San Fernando Valley region of outer Los Angeles. The Vals, daughters of affluent parents working typically in the media, music industry or professions, had developed a sybaritic lifestyle in which consumerism ('recreational shopping') and leisure activities were elevated to a social code. Vals employed a colourful hyperbolic repertoire of slang, typically expressed in a high-pitched, breathless drawl. Their lexicon was partly invented and partly adopted or adapted from the argot of surfers, college and high-school students and other sources. (**Grody, gnarly** and **to the max** are examples). Many of these terms became teenage vogue expressions on a wider scale in the mid-1980s.

'The greatest creative work that any Val does is trying to think of a good slogan for her [car number] plate.'

(*Harpers and Queen* magazine, 1983)

Valspeak *n American*

the jargon of **Valley Girls**, as spoken in California in the early 1980s, and subsequently elsewhere

'Valspeak is an almost impossible farrago of surfer expressions, Midwesternisms and irrational neologisms, delivered in nasal lockjawed whining tones.'

(*Harpers and Queen* magazine, 1983)

vamoose *vb American*

to leave, go away, get moving. The word, familiar since its use in cowboy-era fiction and subsequent film and TV drama, is a corruption of the Spanish *vamos* ('we're going') or ¡*vamonos*! ('let's go!').

OK, I think it's time we vamoosed.

vamp *vb, n*

(to behave as) a seductress. The word is usually employed only semi-seriously to denote an individual (usually, but not invariably, female) affecting a languid, mysterious and predatory air. The term arose in 1918, inspired by the vampire legend as interpreted by such film stars as Theda Bara.

vamping *n*

showing off, behaving ostentatiously. A key term in the lexicon of club culture, hip hop, street gangs, etc. since the 1990s. It derives from the verb to **vamp** (from 'vampire'), denoting the seductive displays of 1920s film stars.

vamp up *vb British*

1a. to intensify, make more effective, improve or renovate

1b. to improvise, ad-lib

These colloquial usages are from the standard informal musical sense of 'vamp' (an improvised accompaniment, ultimately from the archaic French *avantpied*) and not, as is often assumed, from the verb to **vamp** (to pose as a temptress).

V and T *n British*

(a) vodka and tonic

vanilla *adj*

innocuous, orthodox. The adjective was applied, from the early 1980s, to otherwise illicit behaviour such as 'vanilla lesbian(ism)', 'vanilla sex', etc.

varder, va(h)da(h), vardy, vardo *vb British*

to see, look (at). These are forms of the Romany verb to watch (originally rendered as *varter*), used especially in the 1950s and 1960s in the slang of the street market, fairground and theatre. The word was briefly exposed to a wider audience following its use by the **camp** characters Julian and Sandy in the Kenneth Horne radio comedy shows of the 1960s.

va-va-voom *exclamation, n American*
this imitation of a revving engine or explosive take-off is used to suggest overwhelming sexual potential or allure. The word was particularly popular (among males) in the 1960s and often featured in *Mad* magazine, usually as the name of a starlet. The phrase was re-popularised by a TV commercial for Renault cars starring footballer Thierry Henry in 2004.

veeks, vix *n British*
a motor vehicle. An item of black street-talk used especially by males, recorded in 2003. It is probably an alteration of vehicle(s).

veep *n American*
a V.I.P., 'very important person'

veg, vedge-out *vb*
to vegetate, idle or loaf. A predominantly adolescent usage, heard in the 1980s, which was first recorded almost simultaneously in the USA and Australia.
I think we'll spend next week just vegging out in front of the TV.

veggie, vedgie *n, adj*
(a person who is) vegetarian

velcro *n*
1. a lesbian. The use of the trademark term dates from the late 1980s and is derived from the supposed similarity between the lesbian practice of pressing pubic areas together and Velcro fasteners, consisting of two pieces of rough fabric.
2. *also* **velcroid** *American* an intrusive or 'clinging' person, especially a neighbour. A piece of adult or family slang using the trademark name of the fabric-fastening material.

velcro-head *n*
a Negro. A phrase from the 1980s, deriving from the supposed likeness between Velcro (a trademark name for a fabric-fastening material) and a black person's hair. Like **rag-head** and **towel-head** as applied to Arabs, the term is invariably pejorative.

velveeta *n, adj*
(something) **cheesy**. A pun, first recorded on US campuses in the early 1990s, using the brand name of a cheese spread.

ventilate someone's shorts *vb American*
to give someone a severe telling-off or dressing-down. A colourful campus phrase of the 1980s invoking the image of a miscreant with their backside (and underwear) shredded by a blast of buckshot.

Vera (Lynn) *n British*
(a glass of) gin. Rhyming slang based on the name of the patriotic wartime singer, still heard in the 1990s, often in conjunction with **supersonic**.
Compare **Veras**

Veras *n pl British*
cigarette papers. This shortening of the London rhyming-slang expression 'Vera Lynns', meaning **skins**, was popular among younger cannabis smokers in the 1990s.

verbal(s) *n, n pl, vb British*
(to tell) a lie(s). Deputy Assistant Commissioner David Powis, in his *Field Manual for Police* (published in 1977), claimed that 'a verbal is an oral statement of admission or incrimination which is invented by the arresting or interviewing officer and attributed to a suspect'. The word can also be used in the phrases 'work the verbal' (synonymous with **work the oracle**), 'put the verbal in' or 'put the verbals on'. These are all items of police jargon in current use.

verboten *adj*
forbidden, prohibited. The German term has been used, usually facetiously, in English dialect since World War II as an intensive form of its literal translation.
Talking to his girlfriend is absolutely verboten.

very *adj American*
1a. a term of approval, admiration, etc.
Wow, that bag is, like, very!
1b. a non-commital comment or response
What was the hairdo like? Well it was, like, very.
These witticisms, formed by excluding the expected qualifying adjective for effect, occur in the affected or mocking speech of adolescents and teenagers in the US, particularly females. (**Totally** is employed in the same way.)

vet n American
a veteran (soldier). A term best-known in the context of the post-Vietnam War era.

vex vb
1a. to anger, infuriate
Don't vex me!
1b. to become infuriated
She be vexin'?
The standard word has become modified in the slang of younger speakers since 2000, probably influenced by black usage.

vibe n
ambience, atmosphere, mood, the latest news. A shortening of **vibrations** popular in the **hippy** era, vibe was applied catholically to anything that was 'in the air'; from an intuitive empathy ('I like it here. There's a really good vibe about the place'.), to an item of hot gossip ('Hey man, what's the vibe about Mary?'). The plural **vibes** was a more widespread near-synonym.

vibe on vb American
to be sympathetic toward, understand, appreciate someone. A **hippy** term deriving from the notion of having good vibes about someone.
'Some people would say things like, "Oh, that boy's gonna really be great. You don't know how talented that boy is". And the others would say, "Yeah, yeah, yeah, uh-uh, sure". They didn't really vibe on me.'
(Stevie Wonder, *Musician* magazine, 1984)

vibes n pl
feelings, ambience, atmosphere, mood. A key term and concept in the **hippy** psychic repertoire, vibes denotes the unseen and unheard, but nonetheless experienced **vibrations** linking individuals with each other and with the cosmos. The word originated among jazz devotees and **beatniks** and survives in the post-hippy era in limited and usually facetious usage.

vibrations n pl
invisible emanations or forces, experienced as psychological sensations; feelings, ambience. A word (and notion) in evidence since its use by 19th-century spiritualists, but in very limited currency until it became part of the vocabulary of jazz musicians, **beatniks** and, most significantly, **hippies**. The word was generally shortened to **vibes**.

vic n American
a victim, dupe. An underworld term heard in the 1990s.

vicious adj
impressive, powerful, exciting. A teenage term of approval, admiration or satisfaction on the lines of the more widespread **bad** and **wicked**.
That's some vicious venue, know what I mean?

vige n American
the vagina. An alternative form of **vadge** and **fadge**.

village n, adj British
1a. (a person who is) slow-witted, stupid. This middle-class term, often used by middle-aged speakers, is a shortening of 'village idiot'.
I've always considered her rather village.
1b. inferior, of poor quality. A middle-class term, used by schoolchildren and college students but probably borrowed from parents, said to be based on notions such as 'village cricket'.

villager n British
an unsophisticated person, **chav**. The term has been popular since the late 1990s.

villain n British
a criminal. The standard police slang designation of a lawbreaker, villain has been used in this way since the inter-war years.
'He found two villains in possession of stolen goods. They offered him a substantial bribe and he devised a way to get them out of trouble.'
(Former detective, *Inside the Brotherhood*, Martin Short, 1989)

-ville suffix
a termination used in **hip** talk, **beatnik** slang and later teenage usage. It denotes a place, situation or state of affairs. **Endsville** (the ultimate in either boredom or pleasure) and 'Dullsville' (boredom only) are typical examples. The French form *ville* (a town, from the Latin *villa*) was used by early American settlers, like '-city' or '-burg', to create placenames.
Compare **-city**

vinegar strokes n pl British
the pelvic thrusting just before the achieving of male orgasm. An item of sexual slang which has been common in armed-forces' usage since World War II, though it has recently been given more widespread prominence by alternative

comedians such as Frank Skinner, as well as by references in *Viz* comic.

> *'Aye, he'd just got to the vinegar strokes when he were interrupted.'*
> (*The Viz Big Fat Slags Book*, 1994)

vines *n pl American*
clothes. A term which probably arose in the **beatnik** era and was still heard among adolescents in the 1990s. **Rags**, **threads** and, more recently, **garms** are synonyms.

> *Hey, tasty vines.*

vino *n*
wine. This is the Italian and Spanish translation of the English word.

vogu(e)ing *n American*
showing off, behaving ostentatiously. The term, which probably originated in black street slang, denoted a particular style of imitation catwalk posing adopted by hip hop aficionados and later by the singer Madonna in the 1980s.
Compare **profiling**; **styling**

voice *n See* **throw one's voice**

vom *vb, n*
(to) vomit. A shortening typically used by teenagers and students.

vung *n South African*
a car

W

wabblefats *n American*
an alternative spelling of **wobblefats**

wabs *n pl British*
female breasts. A term, like the synonymous **waps**, **baps**, **smams** and **chebs**, popular among younger speakers since 2000.

wack¹ *adj*
inferior, worthless, unpleasant. A vogue term in use in the black hip hop and **rap** subcultures in the early 1980s. The term is probably derived from **whacky**. By the 1990s it was employed as an all-purpose pejorative, also in use among British and Australian adolescents.

wack², wacker *n British*
a term of address between males in the working-class speech of the Liverpool area. The word may be connected with **whack**, meaning a share or portion (as in 'pay one's whack').
See also **whacker**

wacko *n See* **whacko**

wackser, waxa *n, adj British*
(something or someone) excellent, impressive. A vogue term among teenage gang members in provincial England since 2000, sometimes used as an exclamation.

wacky *adj See* **whacky**

wacky baccy *n British See* **whacky baccy**

wad *n*
1a. a bundle of banknotes, a large quantity of money. Wad had been used in this sense all over the English-speaking world since the end of the 19th century. In Britain the word was heard principally in working-class speech before being adopted as a vogue term in 1988 following its use by the alternative comedian Harry Enfield. One of his **Loadsamoney** character's catchphrases was '*wanna see my wad?*', shouted before brandishing a roll of notes.
1b. *British* a bun or (thick) slice of bread

-wad *combining form American*
a termination (denoting a despicable and/or disgusting person) seen in such compounds as **jerkwad**, **dick-wad** and **butt-wad**. The wad in question originally referred to tissues used as a receptacle for bodily excrescences. **-weed** is a disguised version of the same suffix.

wadge *n British*
a variant spelling of **wodge 1**

wag *vb Australian*
to play truant. A variant of the older British form 'hop the wag', in which the wag in question is a shortening of waggon.
> '*And don't you go wagging school this afternoon either – I might be bringing Frank round.*'
> (*Richmond Hill*, Australian TV series, 1988)

wag it *vb British*
to play truant. A modern version of the phrase 'hop the wag', in which the wag in question is a shortening of waggon. The Australian term **wag** and its extension **wag off** are other modern derivations.
> '*"All these kids", says Marjorie disapprovingly. "Wagging it, I suppose".*'
> (David Lodge, *Nice Work*, 1988)

wag off *vb*
to bunk off, play truant. This 1980s variant on the old phrases 'hop the wag' and 'on the wag', used by schoolchildren, is heard in Britain and Australia. (The word was defined for viewers in a report on *Newsround*, a BBC TV children's programme, in June 1988.)
Compare **wag**; **wag it**

wa' gwan? *exclamation See* **whagwan?**

wake *adj*
an alternative spelling of **wayk**

waldo *n American*
a fool. An American personification, similar to the British **wally**, in use among teenagers and college students.

walk *vb*
1. to go free. A term popularised by its use in US TV crime dramas and the like.

Just give us the names we want and we'll let you walk.

2. to escape, leave, disappear

'And the guy walked. (He walked with twenty million dollars but he walked.)'
(*Serious Money*, play by Caryl Churchill, 1987)

walkabout *n, adv See* **go walkabout**

walk of shame *n*
a journey home after a night of supposed debauchery. The phrase, popular on US campuses, has been in UK use since around 2000. It typically describes someone sneaking back to their room after surreptitiously spending the night with a sexual partner.

wall *exclamation*
a statement of incomprehension or bafflement. In use among **cyberpunks** and **net-heads**, it originated in the jargon of professional computer specialists.

wallop *n*
strong alcoholic drink. A light-hearted term inspired by the supposed effect of alcohol (although, until recently, the word more often denoted beer than spirits).

a pint of wallop

wallopers *n pl British*
police officers. A nickname from the 1950s, now obsolete in Britain but occasionally heard in Australia.

'Please, please Sid. You'll have the wallopers in here in a minute.'
(*Hancock's Half Hour*, British comedy series, October 1959)

wally, wallie *n British*
1. a pickled gherkin. This old working-class name for a bottled delicacy is still heard in London. It may be a variation of 'olly', a corruption of 'olives', to which the gherkins were likened by earlier unsophisticated eaters.

'Want a gherkin, Doll?... Charlie calls them Wallys, I call them gherkins.'
(East Ender, *Sunday Times* colour supplement, 2 June 1968)

2. a foolish, ridiculous, clumsy and/or unsophisticated person. This word emerged from obscurity into great popularity between 1976 and 1978 and many theories as to its origin have since been advanced. What seems certain is that the word originated in working-class London

usage. The word began to be used in the school playground and in the media from about 1978 (with a meaning very similar to its almost contemporary American counterpart, **nerd**). The term may derive from the earlier sense of a pickled gherkin (**dill** is a synonym in both senses) or from an obscure dialect origin (the archaic Scottish dialect *waly draigle*, meaning a weakling, has been proposed). **Punks**, who helped to popularise the expression, cited an eponymous Wally, a friend and fan of the Sex Pistols and other coevals; it also seems possible that the usage simply arose because of what was felt to be the inherent comicality of the Christian name.

'The George Formby Appreciation Society in plenary session. Until you have seen this herd of wallies, all long past their sell-by dates and playing their ukeleles in time to a film of their diminutive hero, you haven't lived.'
(John Naughton, *Observer*, 15 January 1989)

3. a cry or chant, heard e.g. at rock concerts (particularly of the **punk**, post-punk, **hardcore** variety). This phenomenon recalls the street and playground cry 'ollie, ollie, ollie!' heard in London in the 1950s and 1960s and recorded in cockney use as long ago as the 1870s as a shout of recognition or derision.

wamba, womba *n British*
money. A vogue word in 1988 and 1989, emerging from London working-class argot into more general usage. Wamba, like many other obscure or dated synonyms (**rhino**, **moolah**, **spondulicks**, etc.), came into use in the financially-oriented atmosphere of the later 1980s. The word is most probably an alteration or mishearing of **wonga**, perhaps in imitation of an exotic 'tribal-sounding' word such as the archaic Amerindian 'wampum'.

wand-waver *n American*
a male sexual exhibitionist, a **flasher**. A term in use among police officers, prostitutes, etc. **Wienie-wagger** is an alternative.

wang, wanger *n*
the penis. These are more recent spellings of **whang** and **whanger**; words which emerged around the turn of the 20th century. They probably derive from an echoic British dialect word meaning beat, hit or slap, with a secondary meaning of strike in the figurative sense of impress or

surprise. Although a vulgarism, wang is often considered less offensive than **prick** (but probably more offensive than synonyms such as **dong**, **willie**, etc.) Unlike many similar terms, wang does not have the additional sense of a fool.

wanger, wanga n British
a schoolchildren's euphemism for **wanker**. This expression from the late 1980s is apparently sufficiently disguised to allow its use in the presence of adults or even on broadcasts such as the British children's TV series Grange Hill.

wank vb British
1. to masturbate. This very widespread vulgarism (with some recent exceptions, still taboo in the printed and broadcast media) is, perhaps surprisingly, of obscure origin. It seems to have entered the spoken language in the late 19th century, significantly at a time when the word **whang** was emerging as a vulgar term for the penis. Wank (earlier spelled 'whank') is probably derived from the same source; 'whang' as a dialect word first meaning hit, beat or slap. Wank may simply be a variant pronunciation or a development of the earlier word, influenced by 'whack' and 'yank'. Since the 1960s the word has been used of and by women as well as men.
2. to behave in an ostentatious, self-indulgent and/or futile manner. A usage deriving from the interpretation of masturbation as purposeless and/or offensive.

wanker n British
1. a masturbator. For the probable etymology of the word see **wank**.
2. an inconsequential, feeble, self-indulgent or otherwise offensive person. The term of abuse or disapproval (most frequently applied to males) has been in use since the early 20th century, but became extremely common in the 1970s. In the USA the word is known, but its force as a taboo term in Britain is often underestimated by American speakers.

wankered adj British
extremely drunk. A popular word with students and other adolescents in the 1990s.

wank off vb British
to masturbate. A longer version of the more widespread term **wank**.

wankshaft n, adj British
(something or someone) unpleasant, obnoxious. In playground usage.

wank stain n British
a tedious, insignificant and/or obnoxious person. This vulgarism seems to have arisen in the 1970s among adolescents; in the 1980s it became a popular term of abuse, particularly among students. The less offensive shortening, **stain**, was a vogue term from the late 1980s.

wanky adj British
meagre, inadequate, disappointing. A popular term amongst schoolchildren, also used in the TV comedy Men Behaving Badly in 1995, formed from **wank(er)** and possibly influenced by **manky**.

wannabe n
an aspirant or imitator. A fashionable Americanism of 1986 and 1987 which was quickly adopted in the UK The wannabe, typically a teenager or young adult, exhibits an envious or ambitious desire, characterised by phrases such as 'I wannabe like Madonna', 'I wannabe thin', 'I wannabe in the Seychelles', etc.

> 'There are two types of Wannabee. The first kind are the clones – the stagedoor Georges, the Cindy Lauperettes, the Apple scruffs, the Madonna Wannabees (aka Wannabes) – the devoted fans who ape their idols as closely as possible. The other kind are the young urban upstarts with a desperate lust for fame.'
> (I-D magazine, November 1987)

waps n pl British
female breasts. A term popular among younger speakers since 2000.

warby n, adj Australian
(something or someone) filthy, inferior or defective, coarse. This Australianism is a survival of a Scottish dialect term for a maggot, archaic in Britain since the 19th century.

warehouse vb British
to hold or attend an **acid house** party

> 'The philologically inclined will note that in Tony's world the word "warehouse" has turned into a verb. "Yea", says Tony, "I warehouse, you warehouse…we was warehoused …" Essentially what it means is this: to overwhelmingly swamp with people.'
> (Evening Standard, 9 October 1989)

See also **warehousing**

warehousing *n British*
the practice of arranging or attending **acid house** parties, also known as **orbital raves**; a youth subculture phenomenon of 1988 and 1989

wark *adj*
an alternative spelling of **wayk**

warm fuzzies *n American*
affection, comfort, friendliness, compliments. A light-hearted phrase from the 1970s, adopted by the business community to denote praise applied deliberately as a motivator. The notion is that of something warm, and perhaps furry, to be nuzzled as a reward or consolation.

warm the bed *vb British*
to mobilise personal contacts to ensure a deal. The phrase occurred in the slang of City of London financial traders in the 1990s.

war-paint *n*
make-up, female (earlier theatrical) cosmetics. A humorous usage heard all over the English-speaking world since the mid-19th century.
  She's next door putting on her war-paint.

wart *n*
an irritating, bumptious or unpleasant person. A term often applied by schoolchildren to younger pupils.

wash *n British*
crack. Washing refers to the chemical purifying of cocaine (with ether for instance) for **freebasing** or in order to produce the more potent **crack**.

WASP *n*
a 'white Anglo-Saxon Protestant', a member of the traditionally dominant ethnic group in the US establishment. This was probably the first of many acronyms, first denoting ethnic subgroups (such as **JAP**), and later social subcultures (**yuppie**, etc.) The term WASP originated in the 1960s.

waste (someone) *vb*
to kill (someone). A euphemism inspired by 'lay waste'. In the 1950s US street gangs used the word to mean defeat, while criminals used it to mean kill. In the Vietnam War era the term first signified to devastate and then to annihilate and kill someone.

wasted *adj*
1a. exhausted, drained of energy
1b. intoxicated by drugs (or, occasionally, alcohol), **stoned**. This is an extension of the sense of to devastate or annihilate

(arising in the late 1960s), on the pattern of synonymous terms such as **wrecked**, **smashed**, **blitzed**, etc.
1c. *American* penniless, broke. A now obsolescent sense of the term, heard in the 1950s.

water sports *n pl*
urination as part of sex play. A euphemism from the repertoire of pornographers and prostitutes.

wax (out/up) *vb Australian*
to share. The verb, heard in the early 1990s, probably derives from the notion of **whack**, meaning a portion or share. A synonym is **whack-up**.

waxa *n, adj See* **wackser**

wax the dolphin *vb American*
(of a male) to masturbate. A humorous euphemism employed by adolescent males since the 1990s.

way! *exclamation*
a contradiction of 'no way!', popularised by the cult US film *Wayne's World* in 1992

way- *combining form*
this intensifier, signifying 'extremely', was fashionable in youth subcultures in the late 1980s and early 1990s, particularly in the catchphrase **way-cool**

way-cool *adj*
admirable, fashionable. A catchphrase whose usage followed the usual course in moving from street subcultures in the early 1980s to pubescent schoolchildren in the mid-1990s.

wayk, wake, wark *adj British*
abbreviated forms of the catchphrase term of approbation **way-cool**, in use among teenagers in the later 1990s, often in the form of an exclamation

Wayne *n British*
an alternative personification to **Kevin**. Wayne and his female counterpart, usually **Sharon**, supposedly embody crassness, bad taste, etc. Generic epithets deriving from the late 1970s and popular in the 1980s, the names were generally thought to epitomise working-class adolescents or young adults and were used derisively by those who considered themselves socially superior or more sophisticated. **Trev** and **Darren** are more recent versions.

way-out *adj*
extreme, excessive, exotic, eccentric. A vogue term first among pre-World War II jazz aficionados, later among **beatniks**.

The phrase was picked up by more conventional speakers to refer to unorthodox behaviour and has become a fairly common, if dated expression.

wazoo *n American*
the anus. This humorous euphemism, usually used figuratively rather than literally, is most often heard in the phrase 'up the wazoo'.

> *I wasn't expecting it but I got it right up the wazoo.*

wazz¹ *n British*
an act of urination. A variant form of the more common **wizz**.

> *'I've got to go for a wazz.'*
> (London cab driver, *Guardian*, February 1994)

wazz² *vb British*
to urinate. The word also occurs in the phrase 'it's wazzing (it) down', i.e. it is raining hard.

wazz³ *adj British*
inferior, worthless, disappointing. Teenagers have used the term since around 2000.

> *The stuff they sell is, like, truly wazz.*

wazzed *adj British*
drunk. A more recent coinage by analogy with **pissed**.

wazzock *n British*
a fool, buffoon. A term widespread outside the London area in the late 1990s.

weasel¹ *n*
1. a sly, devious, unprincipled and/or vicious person
2a. *British* a dodge, stratagem or half-truth
2b. *British* a tip, a reward achieved by trickery

The weasel is used as a by-word for deviousness in all English-speaking areas. Historically, even its name embodies this; the Old English *weosule* is related to the Latin *virus* and originally meant a slimy liquid or poison.

weasel² *vb British*
1a. to behave in a devious, sly or underhand way
1b. to carry luggage in order to earn or extract a tip

The verb sub-senses are specific instances of the more prevalent notion of untrustworthiness and unscrupulousness associated with the animal.

weasel words *n*
insincere, devious or unscrupulous talk. This well-established usage probably derives from the weasel's claimed ability to suck the contents from an egg without shattering the shell, hence the notion of evasion.

wedding tackle *n British*
the male genitals. A humorous phrase which is an elaboration of the earlier 'tackle', heard in this context since the 18th century. Wedding tackle is a euphemism which is considered inoffensive enough to be broadcast and printed, as well as used in conversational contexts. It was popular during the 1980s but probably dates from much earlier. (Partridge dates the synonym 'wedding kit' to 1918.)

wedge *n*
money, wealth. In the 18th century wedge specifically referred to silver, which criminals melted down and reconstituted as 'wedges' (ingots or bars). The term was used throughout the 20th century by working-class speakers, including street traders and criminals. Perhaps unconsciously influenced by **wad** and 'edge', the word has enjoyed a renewed popularity, like most of its synonyms, in the money-conscious environment of the 1980s.

> *'I've come into a bit of wedge.'*
> (*Budgie*, British TV series, 1971)

wedged(-up) *adj British*
financially well-endowed, wealthy or 'flush'. A racy working-class back-formation from **wedge**, meaning money. Wedged(-up) or 'well-wedged' were adopted in the **yuppie** era by middle-class speakers.

> *'... the senior partner who spends his lunch hours not at a sandwich bar but at a casino, and every so often comes back "wedged up with more than just a round of tuna mayonnaise".'*
> (*Sunday Times*, 15 December 1996)

wee¹, wee-wee *n*
urine or an act of urination. A nursery term in use for the last 90 or so years. The word is an invention, probably influenced by **pee**, 'wet', the word 'wee', meaning small (as opposed to **big jobs**), and the sound of urination.

wee², wee-wee *vb*
to urinate. An inoffensive nursery term, often used facetiously by adults.

weed, the weed *n*
1. marihuana. The plant *cannabis sativa*, which yields marihuana leaves, grows

like a weed in warm dry climates and somewhat resembles nettles.

'They get a £10 bag of weed and put it all in the spliff, then they get catatonic.'
(*Panorama*, BBC TV, 19 June 2005)

2a. tobacco. When preceded by 'the', the word is often used when referring to the harmful nature of the plant and its derivatives.

Back on the weed again?

2b. a cigarette. A usage popular among American teenagers.

3. *British* a weak, ineffectual person. This usage, beloved of schoolboys in the 1950s and 1960s, is inspired by the visual comparison with a thin etiolated plant.

4. the weed *British* a system of extra, unofficial work or a scheme yielding unofficial or illicit income. This sense of the word, used by workers and fairground employees among others, is probably obsolete now. It is related to the following verb form.

-weed *combining form American*
a disguised or milder version of **-wad**, attached to the same words, as in **dickweed**, **puss-weed**, etc.

weedy *adj British*
weak and ineffectual

weenie *n American*
an alternative spelling of **wienie**

weenie-wagger *n American See* **wienie-wagger**

weezer *n American*
a weak, eccentric and/or infirm person. The word, perhaps a combination of **wimp** and **geezer**, was adopted as the name of a US rock band in the early 1990s.

weight *n*
1. *British* one pound of hashish or marihuana. The drug dealers' and users' jargon term since the early 1960s; it is a shortening of 'pound weight'.

He sold them a weight of black.

2. *American* narcotics. The word in this context originally had the sense of a necessary or measured amount, but is often generalised to mean heroin or, more recently, marihuana, cocaine, etc.

I need some weight.

weighted off *adj British*
imprisoned. This synonym for **sent down** has been recorded in this form since at least the 1980s. In the form 'weighed off' it is much older, referring to the assessing of the criminal and subsequent passing of the sentence carried out by the judge or prison governor.

weirdie, weirdo *n*
a non-conformist, eccentric, a **beatnik** or **hippy**. The terms have been used, typically by disapproving adults, since the end of the 1950s; weirdie was the standard British version ('bearded weirdie' was an elaboration) until about 1966 when the American equivalent weirdo became more prevalent. The standard English word 'weird' (from the Old English *wyrd*, meaning fate) not only describes the appearance and behaviour of 'deviants' but was a vogue word among beatniks themselves, meaning impressive and acceptable as well as bizarre.

weirding *n British*
a more recent version of the American **weird**(ing) **out**

weird out *vb American*
to behave eccentrically, undergo a disturbing change of mood. An extension of the use of 'weird' in **hipster**, **beatnik**, **hippy** and later teenage parlance, originally frequently used in a drug context, the phrase currently more often refers to unpredictable or temperamental displays by children, parents, etc. To 'weird someone out' is to disorientate or confuse them.

weisenheimer *n American*
a know-all, 'wise-guy', **wiseacre** or **wiseass**. The word, dating from the first decade of the 20th century, is an elaboration of the standard term 'wise' into a quasi-German or Yiddish surname (on the lines of Oppenheimer, etc.)

welch, welsh *vb*
to fail to repay a loan or wager or to evade another obligation. Now virtually standard English, this term originated as 19th-century racecourse slang inspired by the archaic belief concerning the dishonesty or meanness of the inhabitants of Wales.

I knew he'd welch on the deal.

welfare-jockey *n American*
a recipient of state subsidies, unemployment pay, etc. A pejorative term employed by the right-wing comic writer P. J. O'Rourke, among others.

well *adv British*
very. A vogue usage among adolescents and younger schoolchildren since about 1987, from the slang of the streets (used

by black **youth** and some white working-class adults) of the earlier 1980s. Typical instances of the word as an intensifier are 'well good' and 'well hard'.

well-hung adj
having large genitals. A vulgarism applied to males (only very rarely used of large female breasts) for at least two hundred years.

> 'No male streakers are naff, least of all stupendously well-hung men who invade the pitch at a Test Match and upset Richie Benaud.'
> (The Complete Naff Guide, Bryson et al., 1983)

See also **hung**
The pun 'well-hanged' appeared in Shakespeare in 1610.

wellie[1], welly n British
1a. force, impetus, power. The word often occurs in the phrase 'give it some wellie'.
1b. brute strength, brawn as opposed to brain

> 'It was just welly, welly, welly. The ball must have been screaming for mercy.'
> (Ron Yates characterising Wimbledon FC's style, Independent, May 1989)

2. a dismissal, the sack, as in 'get the wellie/the order of the wellie'
3. a condom. A term from the late 1980s using the name of one piece of protective rubberwear for another. Also known as a **willie-wellie**.
4. a **green welly**
Wellie, as a diminutive of 'wellington (boot)', became a household word in the 1970s. It was quickly applied to figurative or metaphorical uses of the word or notion of 'boot', both as a noun and, later, a verb. The first instances of the use of the word have not been definitively identified, although the Scottish comedian Billy Connolly popularised the term, closely followed by several radio disc-jockeys.

wellie[2] vb British
1. to kick out, dismiss, sack
2. to defeat, bully or attack
These are back-formations from the noun form of the word, heard since the end of the 1970s.

well-oiled adj
drunk. A colloquial synonym for **lubricated**.

well on adj
1a. drunk
1b. intoxicated by drugs

In both senses the euphemism was fashionable in the late 1990s.

welsh vb British
an alternative spelling of **welch**

wenching n
(of a male) having sexual relations with females. A term typically employed in the UK by adult males but adopted for ironic or jocular use by adolescents.

wenchy, wench adj American
obnoxious, condescending. Used particularly of and by women, the term is based on a specifically American colloquial sense of 'wench' as a forward, shameless or troublesome female. (In archaic dialect usage in Britain, the word, deriving from an Old English word for a child, had for several centuries signified a promiscuous or immoral woman.) By 2004 the words were being used in the UK as a generalised term of disapproval.

Wendy n British
a feeble, ineffectual or contemptible person; a **weed**, **swot** or misfit among schoolchildren. The word was typically applied to schoolboys by their contemporaries in the 1980s. The name is supposed to epitomise 'girlishness' and, like Tinkerbelle, probably owes its resonance to a character in Peter Pan by J. M. Barrie.

wet[1] adj British
1a. ineffectual, irresolute, feeble or foolish. A characterisation common in service and public-school usage since the early 20th century.
1b. (of a Tory) having liberal views as opposed to being resolutely 'Thatcherite'. The schoolboy term began to be applied in 1980 as a term of disapproval to MPs with reservations about the style and substance of the current cabinet policies.
2. (of a woman) sexually aroused. Also expressed as **damp**.

wet[2] n British
1a. a weak, irresolute or foolish person
> Oh Nigel, you're such a wet!
1b. a Tory who was not a wholehearted supporter of the policies of Margaret Thatcher. The word was used by the Prime Minister herself in 1980.

wetback n American
an illegal immigrant from Latin America. The term refers specifically to those swimming the Rio Grande, the river which forms the Mexican–US border. It dates from the 1940s.

wet scene *n American*
a gory killing. An item of police and secret-service jargon of the 1970s.

> 'hellacious wet scene'
> (Jonathon Kellerman, *Over the Edge*, 1987)

wetter *n British*
a knife when carried or used as a weapon. An item of black street-talk used especially by males, recorded in 2003, so called because the blood wets the blade.

whablow *exclamation British*
a vogue greeting originating among black youth around 2000, but recently more widespread

whack¹ *n*
1. *British* a quantity or portion. The word is imitative of a slapping or smacking (down); here used in the sense of dumping or depositing spoils onto a table or other surface.

> *He insisted on his full whack.*

2. *American* a contract killing. A variant of **hit**.
3. heroin. A later variant form of **smack**.
4. *American* a **whacky** person.
See also **wack¹**

whack² *vb American*
to kill. A racier and more recent coinage based on the well-established use of **hit** in this sense.

whacked *adj*
1a. abnormal, deviant, crazy
1b. unpleasant, unacceptable
A more recent version of **whacky** and **wack**.

whacker *n*
1. a **whacky** person, an irresponsible or eccentric individual
2. an alternative spelling of **wack** or **wacker**

whacko, wacko *n, adj*
(someone who is) crazed, eccentric, insane. This racier version of the colloquial **whacky** has been heard since the mid-1970s. It was popularised by press references to the singer Michael Jackson as 'Wacko Jacko'.

> *We got enough to handle without her going whacko on us.*

whack off *vb*
to masturbate. A vulgarism heard all over the anglophone world. Like many synonymous terms it employs the notion of striking or slapping.

whack-up *vb*
to share, apportion. The phrase is heard particularly in Australian speech.

whacky, wacky *adj*
crazed, eccentric, insane. This now widespread colloquialism seems to have originated in northern English dialect meaning a fool (either by analogy with 'slap-happy' or as an imitation of 'quacking' speech). The word was particularly popular in the 1980s.

> 'The Wacky Patent of the Month is devoted to recognising selected inventors and their remarkable and unconventional inventions.'
> (*www.colitz.com*, June 2005)

whacky baccy *n*
marihuana. A humorous nickname from **whacky** (eccentric or crazy) and **baccy** (tobacco).

whagwan?, whatagwan?, wha's gwanin? *exclamation British*
a vogue greeting (a dialectal version of the bonding catchphrase 'what's going on?') originating among black youth around 2000, but recently more widespread

whale *n See* **play the whale**

wham-bam-thank-you-ma'am *n*
a catchphrase used to characterise a brusque, cursory sexual act. The expression was heard among American servicemen in World War II (probably adopted from cowboy parlance). Currently the phrase is most often employed disapprovingly by feminists and others to describe a selfish or boorish male attitude to sex.

> *I was hoping for something interesting or exciting, but it was just wham-bam-thank-you-ma'am.*

whammers, wammers *n pl British*
female breasts. An adolescent vulgarism heard in the late 1980s.

whammy, the whammie *n American*
a supernatural power, spirit or curse, responsible for punishment or retribution. A fanciful evocation, adapting the colloquial term 'wham', imitative of a heavy blow. The word is sometimes part of the phrase 'to put the whammy on (someone or something)'.

> 'Sarge, you got the whammy on me!'
> (*Bilko*, US TV series, 1957)

whang, whanger *n*
the penis. These are earlier (and still current) spellings of **wang** and **wanger**.

whap vb American See **whop**

whaps adj British
bad. The word, of uncertain origin, although it may be related to **whoop**, was used by London schoolchildren from the late 1990s.

what it is! exclamation
an all-purpose exclamation of greeting, approval or solidarity, which originated in black American speech at the end of the 1980s, and by the late 1990s was being heard in British school playgrounds. 'What it like?' was a similar ritual greeting used by members of rival black street gangs, the Crips and the Bloods, in Los Angeles.

what to go? exclamation British
a phrase used by teenage gangs as a provocation or invitation to fight. A synonym is **do me something!** Both phrases are often followed by 'then?!' The term was recorded in use among North London schoolboys in the 1990s.

what ya saying exclamation British
a vogue greeting originating among black youth around 2000, but recently more widespread

wheelie n
a manoeuvre in which a vehicle is driven at speed on its back wheel(s) only. The term may apply to bicycles, motorcycles or cars (in the case of cars the term may apply only to the spinning of the rear wheels).

> 'Stealing and nicking gives you lots of pleasure and money for everything. And it's easy … you just get an old lady in your sights and do a 360-degree wheelie on her moustache.'
> (Teenage mugger, Observer, 22 May 1988)

wheelman, wheels-man n
a getaway driver. A piece of criminal and police jargon in use in all English-speaking areas.

wheels n
a car or means of transportation

wheeze (off) vb American
to destroy, defeat, frustrate. This adolescent usage often occurs in the phrase 'wheeze off someone's gig', meaning to frustrate their efforts, spoil their enjoyment, etc.

whiff¹ vb
1. to sniff (cocaine)
2. British to smell bad. A synonym of **niff**.

whiff² n
cocaine

whiffy adj British
having an unpleasant smell. **Niffy** is a synonym.

> It's a bit whiffy in here, isn't it?

whinge¹ n
a complaint, a bout of self-pity

> 'His "memoirs" are really an extended whinge at how terribly he's been treated by the corporation – seldom offered any work, never appreciated enough, sneered at by pinkoes, and so on.'
> (Private Eye magazine, 27 October 1989)

whinge², winge vb
to complain or make excuses, especially in a wheedling tone. A blend of 'whine' and 'cringe' which existed for some time in Australian usage before becoming established in Britain in the second half of the 1970s. The word was originally often found in the Australian phrase 'whingeing Pom', describing the perpetually complaining British immigrant.

> 'English people love a good queue, and they love a good disaster; they seem to love a good moan. I think the notion of the "whingeing Pom" is true. But I've become a whinger too, since I've been here.'
> (Australian nurse, NOW magazine, March 1988)

whip n American
a car. An expression used on campus in the USA since around 2000. A luxury car is a '**phat** whip'.

whipped adj American
a shortened, hence disguised and more acceptable version of **pussy-whipped**

whip some skull on (someone) vb American
to perform fellatio. A phrase (using **skull** as a substitute for **head** in a similar context) which was often used as a ribald exclamation by college boys and **hippies**, among others, in the late 1960s and early 1970s.

whirl(e) amount n British
a large quantity. This synonym for 'lots' or 'loads' is usually used in connection with money. The term was recorded in use among North London schoolboys in 1993 and 1994.

whirling pits, the n British
a feeling of giddiness and/or nausea, tinged with hallucination, brought on, for

instance, by the combination of alcohol and a drug such as hashish. The expression describes a condition characterised by lying on one's back, unable to move, while one's stomach heaves and the room whirls about one's head. **The helicopters** is a synonym.

whistle *n British*
(of clothes) a suit. From the rhyming-slang phrase 'whistle and flute'. This term dates back to before World War II and has survived into the early 21st century. It was used by London **mods**, for instance, and is now heard among students as well as working-class Londoners. Since the 1950s the phrase has almost invariably been abbreviated to the one word.

white ant *vb Australian*
to denigrate, undermine. The phrase is based on the action of the Australian termite and was given prominence by its use in TV soap operas such as *Neighbours*.

white bread *n, adj American*
(a person who is) virtuous, well bred, but dull and insipid. A dismissive term, usually applied to straitlaced or ingenuous people, from the **preppie** lexicon. The word is also used in marketing jargon, meaning bland or inoffensive.

white-hat *n American*
the term was defined in 2002 as follows: a genre of high-school and college-aged boys primarily from New England. Identified by their social uniform of khaki trousers, white trainers, a plaid flannel collared button-down shirt with a white cotton T-shirt underneath and a white baseball cap that has either a sports team or fraternity logo on it: white-hats are usually members of a fraternity and are condemned by non-members for their lack of individuality.

white lady, the white lady *n*
1a. cocaine
1b. heroin

"'I've been through pot, white lady and blue lady forms of synthetic heroin and I can't go through this much more", says Jean Hobson.'
(*Sunday Times*, 10 September 1989)

Often used to denote a spectre in folklore, the phrase is employed here to romanticise or dramatise the white powders or crystals in question.

white lightning *n*
1. raw spirit, illicitly distilled grain alcohol. The phrase evokes the sudden, devastating effects (and perhaps the accompanying visual disturbance) of the substance in question.
2. a generic nickname given to white tablets or 'microdots' of LSD in the late 1960s and early 1970s, in the same fashion as 'orange sunshine' or 'blue cheer'

whitener *n*
1. *British* cocaine. A **yuppie** term.
'There are guys who blow out, sure, stick too much whitener up their nose.'
(*Serious Money*, play by Caryl Churchill, 1987)
2. *Irish* a version of **white-out**, recorded in the Irish Republic in 2004

white-out, whitey *n*
a bout of nausea and/or feeling faint as a result of ingesting drugs and/or alcohol. The expression, which is airline pilots' slang for an abrupt loss of vision due to snow, refers to a sudden pallor.
Dave chucked a whitey so he went home.

whites *n British*
a 'class A' illicit drug; heroin, cocaine or **crack**. An item of black street-talk used especially by males, recorded in 2003.
dealin' whites
get me some whites

white space *n*
free time. **Yuppie** jargon of the late 1980s inspired by blank spaces in an appointment book, but ultimately deriving from the jargon of graphic designers, printers, typographers, etc., in which white space refers to areas deliberately left blank in a page layout.
I think I have some white space towards the end of the week.

white telephone, big white telephone *n*
the toilet bowl or pedestal. The term occurs in phrases such as 'making a call on the big white telephone', evoking the image of someone being noisily, and usually drunkenly, sick. The phrases probably originated in US campus slang of the early 1970s, which also gave synonyms such as **pray to the porcelain god**. One phrase combining both notions is 'call God on the big white phone'.

white trash *n*
1a. poor whites living in the southern states of the USA. A term coined by black speakers in the mid-19th century to refer

to their neighbours, either pejoratively or ruefully. The term was also used by whites and survives into the early 21st century; it is often used with connotations of degeneracy and squalor.

See also **trailer-trash**

1b. the decadent rich or sophisticated individuals, the 'jet set' or their hangers-on and imitators. The phrase has been extended to refer contemptuously to cosmopolitan socialites (often in the phrase 'International White Trash'). **Eurotrash** is a derivative.

'She came from South Los Angeles, near Watts, every day and her parents had saved all their lives to buy her in among this rich white trash.'
(Julie Burchill, *The Face* magazine, March 1984)

whitey *n*

1. *American* a white person. A predictable term used by black speakers to or of individuals and of the white community in general. It is usually, but not invariably, pejorative or condescending. **Pinkie** is a less common Caribbean and British form.

2. a **white-out**

whizz *n*

1. *See* **wizz**[1]

2. *See* **Billy**

whoop, woop *adj British*
bad. An all-purpose term of disapproval in use among London schoolchildren at the end of the 1990s. It may be related to **whoopsy**.

whoopsy, whoopsie, whopsy, woopsie *n British*
an act of defecation, excrement. A nursery term sometimes used facetiously among adults, usually in the phrase 'do a whoopsie'.

whop, whap *vb American*
to hit, beat, thrash. The terms (used for over 200 years) are echoic and are sometimes extended to mean defeat or trounce.

They whopped us good.

whore *n*
a prostitute. The word has been used in this sense since about the 12th century; before that time it denoted an adulteress and, earlier still, a sweetheart. The ultimate derivation of whore is the Latin *carus*, meaning dear or beloved. In Germanic languages this

became *horr* or *hora* (Old Norse) and *hore* (Old English).

'Thugs, whores, cabbies, street Arabs, gin jockeys – these are by nature conservative folk.'
(*Republican Party Reptile*, P. J. O'Rourke, 1987)

whorehouse *n*
a brothel

'Pundits summarize [the history of Manila] as "four hundred years in a convent, fifty years in a whorehouse".'
(*Republican Party Reptile*, P. J. O'Rourke, 1987)

who ya bouncing *exclamation*
an exclamation of irritation, defined by one user as 'what the f*** do you think you're doing, bumping into me!' It was recorded in 1999

wibble[1] *vb British*
to behave or speak in an irresolute, confused and/or tedious manner. A middle class adult and Internet usage, popular since 2000.

'...fruitcake Anna Nicole Smith has been rambling away again – sticking up for fellow former fatty Kirstie Alley. "Everyone's so mean to her", wibbled Anna...'
(*Metro*, 30 July 2004)

wibble[2] *n*
meaningless and/or tedious speech. In this sense, probably inspired by the use of the word in the UK TV comedy *Blackadder* and *Viz* comic, wibble is commonly employed on the Internet to describe tedious small-talk or irrelevance.

wick[1] *n*

1. *British* the penis. This sense of the word combines the candle wick as a phallic image and the London rhyming-slang phrase **Hampton Wick** (for **prick**). Hampton Wick is a small community in the Southwest London suburbs, familiar to cockneys of the past hundred years as being on their route to the nearby riverside, Hampton Court or Bushy Park. Wick is rarely found alone, but rather in the phrases **dip the wick** or 'get on one's wick'.

2. *Irish* nonsense. The standard English word (originally meaning a flammable material) is used in colloquial Irish to mean 'rubbish', hence this extended meaning.

wick² *adj*

1. *Irish* uncomfortable, embarrassed, ashamed. This usage may derive from the phrase 'get on one's wick', meaning to annoy or irritate, or from the second noun sense above.

feeling wick

2. *British* an abbreviation of **wicked**, meaning good

wicked *adj*

good, excellent. A US term of approbation adopted by UK teenagers. Originally in black and street-gang usage, the word is now employed by analogy with **bad** but in this sense is probably much older, dating from the turn of the 20th century. By 1989 wicked had become a vogue term, even among primary schoolchildren (sometimes used in the emphatic form 'well wicked', meaning extremely good, and it may alternatively be spelled 'wik-kid').

　'[Oxford University] aristocrats disguise themselves with lingo like: "It's wicked, guy".'
　(*Evening Standard*, 16 June 1988)

widdle¹ *n British*

an act of urination. This middle- and upper-class nursery term is a blend of **wee** and **piddle**.

widdle² *vb British*

to urinate. A combination of **wee** and **piddle**. This nursery term was given prominence when employed by Prince Philip to describe the actions of an ape during a visit to London Zoo.

　'Now sneak pictures of Prince William, apparently widdling into a hedge, are published in colour on the front page of the unsavoury Sunday People.'
　(Victoria Mather, *Evening Standard*, 22 November 1989)

wide-o *n*

a disreputable, dishonest individual. The term is a variant form of the colloquial term 'wide-boy', where 'wide' denotes someone untrustworthy, devious or dishonest.

wide-on *n*

a feminine, feminist or jocular female version of **hard-on**

widget *n*

a device, small contraption or product. This synonym for, and adaptation of the word 'gadget' has been in use since before World War II in the USA. In Brit-

ain it has been widely used since the 1970s to denote a hypothetical, otherwise unnamed product in business simulations, calculations, planning, etc.

widgie *n Australian*

a female equivalent/counterpart of a **bodgie** (**teddy boy**). The widgie was a less respectable Australian version of the **bobby soxer**, characterised by the wearing of hair tied into a ponytail, a long skirt or blue jeans, often accompanied by 'delinquent' behaviour. The name is said to be a diminutive of 'widgeon', as used as a term of endearment.

widow *n, adj British*

(an) American. A piece of now almost obsolete London rhyming slang from around World War II, playing on Widow Twankey (a character in the pantomime *Aladdin*): **Yankee**.

widows' and orphans' fund, the *n American*

money given as bribes. A police euphemism. In Britain the 'policeman's ball' has been employed in a similar euphemistic role.

wienie, weenie, wiener *n American*

1. a frankfurter type sausage. The word is a contracted form of 'wienerwurst' (a Vienna sausage).

2. the penis. A term which is usually derisive, inspired by the small size and flaccidity of the sausage of the same name.

3. an ineffectual, foolish or tedious person. This sense applies particularly to **swots** in the argot of students.

wienie-wagger, **weenie-wagger** *n American*

1a. a male masturbator

1b. a male sexual exhibitionist, a **flasher**. **Wand-waver** is an alternative.

　'He's just a wienie-wagger … that's what the cops call them.'
　(*Lady Beware*, US film, 1987)

wife-beater *n*

1. *American* a white undershirt, typically ribbed and sleeveless, thought to be emblematic of uncouth males. An expression used on campus in the USA since around 2000.

2. *British* a slang term for Stella Artois lager. The origin of the term is unknown but is possibly related to domestic abuse as a result of drinking too much.

　a pint of wifebeater

wifey n American
a female partner. The term is typically used with irony and affection rather than patronisingly or dismissively.

wigga, wigger n
a white person who adopts the mannerisms, appearance and culture of blacks. The word blends 'white' and **nigger** and was first coined by blacks to describe white participants in hip hop and **rap** subcultures. The word is used appreciatively as well as neutrally or pejoratively.

> 'Wiggas wannabe black: the word may be only a letter different from a serious case of racial abuse, but London's super-cool young whites carry it with pride.'
> (Evening Standard, 21 March 1994)

wigged adj American
a 1990s variant form of **wiggy**

wiggle n
a sexual act. An item of student slang in use in London and elsewhere since around 2000. The word has been used in the same sense by US **rappers** and hip hop devotees.

wiggle-room, wriggle-room n American
freedom to manoeuvre, especially in a delicate situation. The term was common in the 1990s in armed-forces' and professional usage.

> You've got to let us have some more wiggle-room.

wiggling n
having sex. An item of student slang in use in London and elsewhere since around 2000.

wiggy adj
crazy, eccentric, irresponsible. The word, from the **beatnik** lexicon, was often used approvingly as a synonym for **wild**. It derives from the use of 'wig' to mean the head or brain and the notion of 'flipping one's lid'. (**Liddy** is a less common synonym.)

wig out vb
to go crazy, 'lose one's **cool**', 'flip one's lid'. A term from the argot of the **beatnik** era, based on wig as used as a jocular term for the head or brain in pre-World War II **jive talk**.

wikkid adj
an alternative spelling of **wicked** (in its vogue youth sense of admirable)

wild adj
exciting, impressive, excellent. This was a vogue term among jazz aficionados, **hipsters** and **beatniks** of the 1950s in the USA. It is inspired by the use of wild to mean enthusiastic in the phrase 'wild about something'. The transferred use of wild as a term of approbation mainly survives in adolescent and pre-teenage speech.

wilding n
running amok. A black youth vogue term, seemingly first published in the New York Times, 22 April 1989.

> 'A beautiful woman jogger viciously gang-raped and left in a coma by a mob of "wilding" youths in New York's Central Park has woken from the dead.'
> (People, 14 May 1989)

Wilf n British
a fool. A mild term of (usually) jocular or affectionate abuse from London working-class speech. The word, typically heard in a school context, is either based on the supposedly inherent comic nature of the name Wilfred, or on the use of that name for a character in the cartoon strip The Bash Street Kids, appearing in the Beano children's comic since the 1950s.

> Come on, don't be such a Wilf!

wiling n See **wylin'**

William n British
the police, a police officer. A personification based on **the Old Bill** and usually used facetiously or ironically.

willie n British
the penis. A schoolchildren's word which is usually used coyly or facetiously by adults. It is a personification, like many similar terms (**peter**, **John Thomas**, etc.), in this case first recorded in 1905.

> '"genital cold injury" … is described as "Arctic Willy" in the current edition of The British Medical Journal.'
> (Independent, 22 December 1989)

willied adj British
drunk. An item of student slang in use in London and elsewhere since around 2000.

willie-wellie n British
a condom. A humorous expression (**wellie** is a wellington boot), playing on the notion of protective rubberwear.

Willy Wonka vb British
to have sex (with). A term used by younger teenagers in 2001. The phrase comes from the name of a character in a Roald Dahl story and 1971 film based on it Willy Wonka and the Chocolate Factory.

wiltshire *n British*

impotence. A middle- or upper-class embellishment of 'wilt', heard since the early 1970s.

It was a case of wiltshire, I'm afraid.

wimp *n*

a feeble, weak or timid person. This now well-established term first appeared as a term of derision employed by US high-school and college students in the mid-1970s. Its exact origins are obscure: suggested derivations are from 'whimper'; from a British undergraduate term for a girl (which was, however, in very limited use and was obsolete by 1930); from the name Wimpy, given to a character in the Popeye cartoons; or from a blend of 'weak', 'simple' or **simp** and 'limp' or **gimp**. By the late 1970s the word had spread to adult speech and beyond the USA.

'Well, goodnight Ralph. It was nice meeting someone so sensitive, aware and vulnerable. Too bad you're such a wimp.'

(*Real Men Don't Eat Quiche*, Bruce Feirstein, 1982)

wimp out *vb*

to act in a feeble or cowardly manner. A later coinage based on **wimp**, by analogy with the many phrasal verbs employing 'out' (**freak out**, **weird out**, etc.)

Listen, just pull yourself together; this is no time to wimp out.

wimpy, wimpish, wimpo, wimpoid *adj*

feeble, weak or cowardly. Formed from the noun **wimp**.

windbag *n*

a person who is garrulous, loquacious or full of empty rhetoric. An old and well-established colloquial expression.

'Mr Kinnock appears to be sinking under a barrage of criticism to the effect that he is an ill-educated Welsh windbag carried high by chippy class hatred.'

(*Evening Standard*, 25 July 1989)

winding *n*

dancing. A term used in club and hip hop culture since the 1990s.

window *n*

1a. an opportunity

1b. a period available for meetings, appointments or other tasks

This fashionable jargon term of the **yuppie** era derives from the use of window in space engineering to denote a set of parameters in time and space. The term was carried over into data processing and other semi-technical usage.

window-licker *n*

a slow-witted, unfortunate and/or irritating person. A popular term among adolescents and in office slang from around 2000. The image is said to be that of a handicapped person peering from inside a bus.

wind someone up *vb British*

to provoke, tease, deceive someone. A London working-class usage which became fashionable at the end of the 1970s in raffish circles. It described the sort of straightfaced manipulation of a victim which discomfits increasingly; the image is probably that of winding up a clockwork toy or tightening a winch. By the early 1980s the phrase was in widespread colloquial use and was generalised to encompass mockery, deliberate irritation, etc.

It took me a few minutes to realise that she was winding me up.

wind-up *n British*

a provocation, teasing or deception. A London working-class back-formation from the verb **wind someone up**, which became a fashionable term in the late 1970s, spreading into general colloquial usage around 1979. (An expert at this kind of deliberate irritation is a 'wind-up artist'.)

wing it *vb*

1. to improvise, ad lib. Rather than being inspired, as is sometimes thought, by the phrase 'on a wing and a prayer', this usage almost certainly comes from a 19th-century theatrical term 'to wing', meaning to learn one's lines at the last moment (while standing in the wings, literally or metaphorically).

2. to leave, go away

wing-nut *n*

a person with protruding ears. The jocular pejorative, heard in all English-speaking areas but particularly the USA, has been applied to Prince Charles, among others.

wing-wong *n British*

an object or contraption, the name of which is unknown or forgotten. The expression is probably a nursery term, also used among some adults.

winkie, winky *n*
1. *British* the penis. A nursery term which is probably a diminutive of **winkle**.
2. *American* the backside, buttocks

winkle *n British*
the penis. This nursery term is based on the supposed resemblance between a (peri)winkle (a seafood delicacy traditionally associated with working-class outings) and a child's member.

winnet *n British*
an alternative term for **dingleberry**

winning action *n British*
a successful sexual encounter. A euphemism employed by university students since 2000. A synonym is **action gagnée**.

wino *n*
an alcoholic or habitual drunk. A term particularly applied to vagrants. (In the USA cheap domestic wine is the standard means of intoxication for tramps and poor alcoholics.)

wipe *vb*
1. to kill or destroy. A racier version of the standard phrase 'wipe out'.
2. *Australian* to snub, ignore or **blank (someone)**. This usage was prevalent in the 1950s.
3. *American* to be repellent, inferior or worthless. A more recent synonym of **suck** and **blow**, in use principally among adolescent speakers.

> *'This planet both wipes and sucks – in that order.'*
> (*Third Rock From the Sun*, US TV comedy, 1995)

wiped out *adj*
1a. exhausted
1b. intoxicated by drink or drugs
2. devastated, ruined, defeated
These senses of the phrase are all based on the standard meaning of annihilate or massacre.

wipe out *vb*
1a. to fall off a board or be capsized by a wave. A surfer's term.
1b. to fail, particularly in a decisive and/or spectacular way
The second sense is a transference of the first, which came to prominence during the surfing craze of the early 1960s.

wipe-out *n*
a failure, particularly a sudden and/or spectacular one

wired *adj*
1. tense, edgy, manic. The word combines the notion of highly strung with that of electrified. It arose among amphetamine (and later cocaine) users in the 1970s, originally in American speech. The word was subsequently adopted in the USA in a non-drug context to denote someone overstimulated or anxious.

> *'Frankie man you're all wired, you're all pumped up – you know you're not thinking straight.'*
> (*Satisfaction*, US film, 1988)

2. *American* well-connected, integrated in a social or information network

wiseacre *n American*
a know-all, insolent or smug person. The word is an anglicisation of the Dutch *wijssegger* (literally 'wise-sayer', originally meaning soothsayer).

wiseass *vb, n American*
(to behave as) a know-all, an irritatingly smug or insolent person. This vulgar version of 'wise-guy' has been heard since the early 20th century. (The word wise has flourished in American speech because of reinforcement from the synonymous Dutch *wijs* and the German *weise*.)

wiseguy *n American*
a member of a mafia family or organised crime syndicate. This item of East Coast US criminal jargon was made famous by Hollywood films of the 1980s and 1990s.

> *'It was a glorious time. There were wiseguys everywhere.'*
> (*GoodFellas*, US film, 1990)

wisenheimer *n American*
an alternative spelling of **weisenheimer**

witchy *adj*
mysterious, uncanny, fey. This term probably originated in black American speech; it became fairly widespread in the **hippy** era, describing a bewitching or other-worldly quality or atmosphere.

with-it *adj*
fashionable. A vogue term of the early to mid-1960s which, in its sense of stylish or up-to-date, is still used by the middle-aged in particular, but now sounds dated. It derived from the phrase 'get with it', an essential item of pre-World War II **jive talk** and post-war **beatnik** parlance. In its sub-sense of 'on the ball' or in touch with events, the phrase may be used by speakers of all ages.

'The "Galerie 55"... has a madly with-it cabaret of saucy "chansons paillardes".'
(*About Town* magazine, September 1961)

witten *n British*
an alternative term for **dingleberry**

wizz¹, whizz *n British*
amphetamine sulphate, **speed**. The term, which dates from the later 1970s, is used by the drug abusers themselves.

wizz² *vb American*
to urinate. An echoic term.
'What can I do?
Wizz in one of the empty beer bottles in the back.'
(*Dumb and Dumber*, US film, 1994)

wob *n British*
a piece, chunk, lump. A term in mainly middle-class usage since the 1980s. It is a coinage presumably inspired by **wodge**, 'gob(bet)', 'knob', etc.

wobblefats, wabblefats *n American*
an obese person. A term of abuse heard mainly among adolescents.

wobble off *vb British*
to leave, depart. The term, which does not necessarily imply moving slowly or unsteadily, was recorded in 1999.
Why don't you wobble off and get the car?

wobbler, wobbly *n British*
a bout of erratic, neurotic or extreme behaviour. The term usually occurs in the phrase **throw a wobbly/wobbler**. The wobbling in question is probably the unsteadiness or trembling of a disturbed or uncontrolled subject and the usage may have arisen among medical or psychiatric personnel. The word has been widespread since about 1980.

wobbly eggs *n pl British*
temazepam tablets, in the parlance of young drug users in the 1990s. The gelatin-covered capsules of a tranquilliser are roughly ovoid, and both they and their users can be said to wobble.

wodge, wadge *n*
1. *British* a lump or slice. The word is a blend of 'wad' and 'wedge' and has been in use since at least the mid-19th century.
2. money. In this sense, recorded in 2002, the word is probably a variant from of **wedge**.

wog *n*
1. *British* a foreigner. The word was first used to refer to dark-skinned inhabitants of other countries and is still usually employed in this sense. First recorded in the late 19th century, some people believe the term is derived from the initials for 'Westernized Wily Oriental Gentleman', a condescending euphemism supposedly applied to Indians or Arabs working for the British colonial authorities. An equally plausible source is the word 'golliwog' (originally 'golliwogg'), denoting a black doll with curly hair; a character invented by the children's writer Bertha Upton in the late Victorian era. The word is common in Australia and not unknown in the USA.
'The only reason I was opposed to them calling me a wog was because I realise that in this country the word is used adversely against dark-skinned people.'
(Marsha Hunt, *Oz* magazine, July 1969)
2. the wog *Australian* an alternative version of **wog gut**

wog gut *n*
an upset stomach, diarrhoea, a **gyppy tummy**. A World War II armed-services term surviving mainly in Australian usage, also in the form 'the wog'.

wok¹ *vb*
to have sex (with), penetrate. A term used by young street-gang members in London since around 2000.

wok² *n British See* **chimney-wok**

wokking *n*
smoking **crack**

wolf *n*
a predatory male. This word has been used since the early 1900s in the USA to denote an aggressive womaniser and, in the **gay** and criminal subculture, an aggressive, promiscuous and/or violent male homosexual. Since the 1960s the heterosexual sense has been adopted in other English-speaking areas.
'A self confessed wolf, with the morals of a tom-cat.'
(The judge in the Argyll divorce case, speaking in March 1963)

womba *n British*
an alternative spelling of **wamba**

wombat *n*
1. *American* an eccentric and/or grotesque person. The name of the bear-like Australian marsupial has been used in this way since the late 1970s, probably because of the animal's exoticism and comic-sounding name.
2. an incompetent, ineffectual and/or irritating person. In Internet and office slang

the term is an acronym, the letters standing for 'waste of money, bandwidth (or brains) and time'.

womble n British
a foolish, clumsy or unfortunate person. Since the appearance of the books and television puppets of the same name in the early 1970s, the word has been appropriated, particularly by schoolchildren, to refer to someone considered feeble, contemptible or a misfit. **Gonk** and **muppet**, both names of grotesque creatures, have been used with the same connotations.

> 'She hangs around with wombles.'
> (Recorded, schoolgirl, London, 1986)

wombled adj British
drunk. An item of student slang in use in London and elsewhere since around 2000.

wonga, wong n British
money. A common expression since the 1990s (in the 1980s **wamba** was probably more widespread), this may derive from the 19th century use of the Romany word *wongar*, which literally denotes 'coal', to signify money in the argot of travellers, peddlers, etc.

wonk n American
a **swot**, in **preppie** and high-school jargon. The word is probably an arbitrary coinage, although it may possibly derive from the British taboo term **wanker**.

woo, wooshious adj
excellent. A vogue term of 2003 and 2004.

wood n
1. *American* a shortened form of **peckerwood**
2. *British* an erection, as in **get wood**

woodentop n British
a uniformed police officer. A term of mild derision used by plain-clothes detectives and disseminated through TV police shows. The Woodentops were a family of puppets featured on British children's television in the 1950s. There is also an obvious parallel with 'woodenhead', meaning a fool.

> 'You'd better get your uniform cleaned – you'll be down among the woodentops next week.'
> (*Rockcliffe's Babies*, British TV police series, 1989)

woodie, woody n American
1a. an American estate car or station wagon. Wooden exterior trim was a feature of the models manufactured in the 1930s, 1940s and 1950s.
1b. any vehicle used by a surfer for transporting people and boards to the beach. Old or customised estate cars were originally favoured for this purpose.

> 'I've got a 34 wagon, and we call it a woodie/ You know, it's not very cherry, it's an oldie but a goodie/ Well it ain't got a back seat or a rear window/ But it still gets me where I want to go.'
> ('Surf City' written by Jan Berry and Brian Wilson, recorded by Jan and Dean, 1963)

2. an erection. The same notion is conveyed by the British expression **get wood**.

woof¹ n British
an attractive woman. The word, posted on the Internet as an item of new slang in March 1997 by *Bodge World*, may be a variant form of **oof**.

woof², woofter n British
variant forms of **poof** and **poofter** heard since the mid-1970s

woof (one's custard) vb
to vomit. The word is echoic (in colloquial usage it may also describe 'wolfing down' food).

woofie, woofy n American
(someone who is) stylish, in the know. The word is probably somehow related to the black slang concept of 'woofing' (itself derived either from the imitation of a dog's bark or from 'wolf'), as used to describe someone who is behaving in a boastful or intimidating manner.

woof ticket n American See **buy a woof ticket**

wool n American
1. the female pubic hair
2. women considered as potential sexual partners. Used in this sense the term is a vulgarism, particularly among middle-aged males.

> She sure is a good-looking wool.

woop adj See **whoop**

woopsie n British
an alternative spelling of **whoopsy**

Woop-woop n Australian
a very remote region. A synonym for 'the back of beyond' or 'the middle of nowhere', also expressed as (beyond the) **black stump**. The term was first recorded in the 1920s and was probably an imitation of a native Australian name.

wop *n*
an Italian. This derogatory term originating in the USA is now common in all English-speaking areas. The word was first applied to young dandified ne'er-do-wells, thugs or pimps in New York's Little Italy in the first decade of the 20th century. It derives from the Sicilian dialect term *guappo*, itself from the Spanish *guapo*, meaning handsome.

'"At our last New Year's Eve party, we had 65 wops, and five Brits", says Maro. "They behaved atrociously, all huddled up in a corner".'
(Maro Gorky, *Harper's and Queen* magazine, November 1989)

word!, word up! *exclamation*
an all-purpose term of agreement, solidarity, greeting, etc. (inspired by 'word of honour' or 'the good word'), which appeared first in black street culture of the late 1980s and subsequently in **rap** lyrics, where it was used as a form of punctuation. Someone asking 'word up?' is making the informal greeting 'How are you today and what's happening, my friend?' In the UK *The Word* was adopted first as the title of a radio programme on the station Kiss FM and then for a controversial TV youth programme of the early 1990s.

'What do you think?'
'Word'.
'Enjoying wide usage this winter is my favourite word "Word" (as in "Word up, man, you be illin'").'
(Charles Maclean, *Evening Standard*, 22 January 1987)

wordhole *n American*
the mouth. **Pie-hole** and **hum-hole** are synonyms.

word up *vb American*
to speak out, tell the truth, say something meaningful. A street slang expression from the early 1980s, originating in black speech.

worked *adj American*
tired. An expression used on campus in the USA since around 2000.

working girl *n*
a prostitute. A euphemism in use among prostitutes themselves as well as police officers, **punters**, etc.

'He said that he'd just met her in a hotel, but I'm pretty sure that she's a working girl.'

(Recorded, financial advisor, London, August 2001)

works *n*
a hypodermic syringe, in the language of **junkies**. The term may also apply to the other paraphernalia of drug-taking, but usually specifies the means of injection.

work the oracle *vb British*
to invent an oral statement of guilt on the part of a suspect. A term from police jargon (synonymous with 'verbal').

'I wondered if his return was a consequence of his reluctance to verbal, to "work the oracle" as it is sometimes called...'
(*Inside the British Police*, Simon Holdaway, 1983)

worst, the *n*
1. something considered contemptible, pitiful, miserable, inferior. A straightforward application of the standard word in use among American teenagers and others.

God, that movie – it's the worst!
2. something excellent, admirable, superlative. This sense of the word is used by analogy with **bad** in its black street and youth culture sense of good. The worst was used in this sense by adolescents in the 1980s.

wowler *n British*
an alternative form of **howler**

wowser, wowzer *n Australian*
a spoilsport, puritan or 'wet blanket'. A word which has been recorded in American usage, but not in Britain; wowser originated in the late 19th century and is of uncertain origin. Most suggested etymologies refer to 'wow' as a roar or bark of disapproval or an exclamation of shocked surprise.

wrap *n*
a portion of a drug such as an amphetamine, **ecstasy** or **crack**. Measured amounts of the drug are wrapped in paper or tinfoil for sale to consumers. This term has been in use in Britain from 1989.

wreckaged *adj British*
drunk. An item of student slang in use in London and elsewhere since around 2000.

wrecked *adj*
intoxicated by drink or drugs. A coinage which parallels such dramatic usages as **smashed, bombed, blitzed, destroyed**, etc.

wrinkly, wrinklie *n, adj*
(a person who is) old. A popular term among adolescents since around 1980, the word is often used of (middle-aged and elderly) parents. Synonyms are **dusty**, **crumbly** and **crinkly**.

wrong *n British*
a foolish, unfortunate or unpleasant person, a misfit. In use among adolescents since 2000.

wrongo *n American*
the equivalent of the British **wrong 'un**. A fairly rare term.

wrong 'un *n British*
1. a criminal, ne'er-do-well or other undesirable character
2. something to be avoided, a nuisance. The term has been a common working-class colloquialism since the later 19th century.

wullong *n British*
a very large penis. An item of black street-talk used especially by males, recorded in 2003.
Compare **bullong**

wuss *n American*
a weak, feeble person and, by extension, a dupe. A word used by college students and young people from the 1960s and probably inspired by 'puss', 'pussy' or 'pussy-wussy', all used as terms of endearment to a kitten.

wussy *n American*
a variation (and probably the origin) of the more common **wuss**

'Come on, toxic waste won't kill you. Don't be such a wussy.'
(*Armed and Dangerous*, US film, 1986)

wu-wu, woo-woo *n American*
the female genitals. An imitation nursery euphemism in adult use.

'You might have to show your wu-wu.'
(Hollywood agent quoted in ITV documentary, *Hollywood Women*, December 1993)

wuzzock *n British*
a version of **wazzock**

wylin' *n*
the term was defined by a UK adolescent in 2002 as follows: '…behaving very badly, drinking too much and shooting people! Hard-livin' R 'n' B types would go out wylin''. It is almost certainly the same word as the **wilding** of the 1980s.

XYZ

X *n*
1. a kiss. A teenagers' term, from the use of the letter x to symbolize a kiss at the end of a letter. The word is used in phrases such as 'give us an x' or, as an affectionate exclamation, 'x, x, x!'.
2. the drug **ecstasy**

X-er *n American*
a member of **Generation X**. The term was briefly popular between 1992 and 1994.

> The narrator of the book is the archetypal X-er. He lives in a rented bungalow (X-ers don't have mortgages) …

X-filed *adj British*
rejected (by a partner), jilted. The expression puns on the cult US TV series on the paranormal (*The X-Files*) and the notion of an 'ex' partner being filed away. The phrase was used by teenage girls in particular in the late 1990s.

x-out *vb*
1a. to cross out, cancel
1b. to kill, eliminate, **rub out**
(The phrase is pronounced 'ecks-out'.)

x-rated *adj*
1a. salacious, taboo, extremely daring or pornographic. Often used nowadays with at least a degree of irony, the expression is an extension of the categorisation applied to films deemed suitable only for those over 18.

> We had this real x-rated date!

1b. terrifying, horrifying, dreadful. A second sense inspired by the term's application to horror films.

> She's got this x-rated boyfriend.

xtc *n*
an alternative spelling of **ecstasy** (the amphetamine-based disinhibiting drug), in vogue in the late 1980s

yaas *exclamation See* **yass**
yack *vb, n See* **yak**
yacka, yacker *n See* **yakka**
yackers *n British*
money. A variation on **ackers**, in mainly working-class usage.

yaffling irons, yaffling spanners *n pl British*
cutlery such as knives, forks and spoons as used at the table. The humorous phrase is widespread in the armed forces and derives from the archaic dialect term *yaffle*, probably imitative in origin, meaning to consume or eat voraciously.

> Grab your yaffling irons and let's get scrumming!

yah, yaah *n, adj British*
(someone who is) ex-public school, a **hooray**. The term, particularly popular in Edinburgh since the early 1990s, derives from the class's characteristic drawling of the word 'yes'. **Rah** is a synonym.

yahoo *n*
a lout, oaf. The word, imitating a wild shout, was used by Jonathan Swift in *Gulliver's Travels* as the name of a race of brutish humans. The modern usage varies slightly in the English-speaking countries. In Britain the word often denotes a boisterous, inconsiderate youth, and is used of **hoorays**, students, etc.; in Australia the word generally equates with **yob**; while in the USA the word may depict a stupid and/or coarse person.

yah-yo *n American*
cocaine, in the street language of the late 1990s. It was included in so-called **Ebonics**, recognised as a legitimate language variety by school officials in Oakland, California, in late 1996.

yak, yack
1. *vb, n* (to indulge in) incessant talk, idle chatter. The word imitates the sound of monotonous, grating and/or inane speech. Nowadays variants of the verb

form such as 'yak away' or 'yak on' are often preferred.

> *'How much longer are you going to be yakking into that damn phone? We're late.'*
>
> (Recorded, middle-class woman, Bristol, 1989)

2. *n* a laugh, joke or instance of humour. **Yok** is an alternative form, favoured in fashionable journalism.

3. *n* **the yak** *American* cognac, brandy. The use of the term reflects a vogue for expensive cognacs among US **rap** and hip hop stars, such as Busta Rhymes and Puff Daddy, from 2002.

Compare **Hennessey**

yakka, yacka, yacker *n Australian*
work. The word is a native Aboriginal proper name.

yakkety-yak *vb, n*
(to indulge in) incessant talk, idle chatter. An elaborated form of **yak** heard especially in the USA and enshrined in the pop song of the same name (written by Jerry Leiber and Mike Stoller and a worldwide hit for the Coasters in the late 1950s). The term often denotes gossip as well as chatter or talk.

ya mamma, ya mam *exclamation*
defined by a UK teenager in 2004 as 'a way to diss someone or to answer an insult'

yammer *vb*
1a. to wail, complain or jabber fearfully
1b. to talk or shout insistently

Yammer is probably a modern descendant of an Anglo-Saxon verb meaning 'to murmur or lament'. Its use is reinforced by the influence of words like yell and stammer and, in the USA, by the similarity to the German and Dutch *jammeren*, which means to whine or lament and derives from the same Old Germanic root as the English cognate.

yang *n American*
the penis. This term may be an alteration of the more established **whang**, influenced by the verb to 'yank', or is perhaps a shortened form of the post-1970s expression **yinyang** (itself possibly containing the Chinese *yang*, meaning masculine principle).

> *'Hanging around toilets waiting for some poor guy to reach for a cop's yang by mistake.'*
>
> (*The Switch*, Elmore Leonard, 1978)

yangyang *n American*
a variant form of **yinyang**

yank (off) *vb*
(of a man) to masturbate. A fairly rare but geographically widespread term.

yank (someone around/someone's chain) *vb American*
to mislead, deceive, harass or irritate someone. The image on which the expression is based is that of a chained or leashed animal or prisoner being thoughtlessly or maliciously jerked about or led in different directions. (Phrases commencing with **jerk** are used in the same way.)

Yank, Yankee *n*
an American, a native or inhabitant of the USA. Yankee is the older form of the word and seems to be connected with the early Dutch settlers in Connecticut and the rest of New England. It may be a familiar form (Jan-Kees) of the common forenames Jan and Cornelius, a diminutive Janke ('Johnny'), or an invented epithet Jan Kaas ('John Cheese'), all applied to Dutchmen in general. Other suggestions are that it is from a nickname given to English-speaking pirates and traders by the Dutch, or a deformation of the word 'English' by Amerindian speakers. It may possibly be connected with *yonker*, which is Dutch for young (noble-)man. In the USA Yankee is used as an epithet by which old-school southerners damn northerners and also as a straightforward designation of an inhabitant of the northeastern states.

yank someone's crank/weenie/zucchini *vb American*
to mock, mislead or irritate someone. These expressions are all vulgarisations of 'pull one's leg'.

yap¹ *vb*
to talk incessantly and/or inanely. An echoic term also used to depict the persistent high-pitched barking of small dogs.

yap² *n*
1a. incessant talk, idle chatter
1b. the mouth

This echoic term is often heard in the form of the British working-class exclamation 'shut your yap!'.

2. *American* a country bumpkin. This sense of the word is from an archaic British rural dialect term for a simpleton.

yard *n*
1. the penis. A usage said to be archaic by most authorities, but still revived from time to time by those in search of a robust or rustic-sounding euphemism.
2. the Yard *British* Scotland Yard, the headquarters of the London Metropolitan Police
3. *American* one thousand. Also one hundred (dollars).
4. Jamaica. A nickname used by the local inhabitants, probably deriving from the notion of 'my own backyard'.
5. a home
'This is going to be someone's yard – it used to be a morgue, unfortunately.'
(*Exodus: The Diary*, Channel 4 TV documentary programme, 12 November 1995)
6. *American* money

yard (on) *vb American*
to cheat, be unfaithful to (one's spouse). A black American slang term, deriving from the notion of adulterous trespassing in someone's back yard.
Compare **backdoor man**

yardbird *n American*
1a. a military recruit or other person assigned to menial outdoor duties
1b. a convict, prisoner
1c. a hobo frequenting railyards

yardie *n Jamaican*
1a. a member of a secret Jamaican crime-syndicate or gang, said to operate in Britain and the USA since the late 1980s
1b. a person from Jamaica or the Caribbean. In Jamaica itself the term has had this more generalised meaning, it comes from the use of **yard** to denote Jamaica or someone's home (probably deriving from 'my own backyard').

yards *n British*
a home, flat or accommodation. From Caribbean usage, since around 2000 this form has been more fashionable than the singular.
I'm heading for my yards man.

yarko *n British*
a synonym for **chav**, in vogue in 2004. The derivation of the term is obscure but it seems to have originated in East Anglia.

yarning *n British*
telling stories, especially tall stories. The word, based on the phrase 'to spin a yarn' (itself from nautical rope-making or spinning cloth), is heard particularly among adolescent girls since the later 1990s and probably originated in black usage.
'Yarning is telling your girlfriends all about this amazing bloke you met on holiday and what a deep experience you had…when nothing actually happened.'
(Recorded, London student, 2003)

yarra[1] *adj Australian*
crazy, mad. There is a psychiatric hospital at Yarra Bend in the state of Victoria.

yarra[2] *n Australian*
a stupid and/or obnoxious individual. This usage derives ultimately from the Yarra river, upon which Melbourne is situated, and refers either to the opacity of its water or, like the adjectival form, to a psychiatric hospital on its banks.

yass, yaas *exclamation*
an exclamation of derision, defiance or provocation in black Caribbean English. It is a conflation of '(up) your **ass**'. The expression was briefly adopted by some black Americans and white British speakers in the early 1970s. (The Rolling Stones' use of the term ya-yas in the title of their 1970 live album, *Get yer Ya-Yas out*, was a misreading of this expression.)

Yasser *n American*
an erection. A shortened form of 'Yasser Crack-a-fat', an expression punning on the phrase **crack a fat** (to have an erection) and on the name of the late Palestinian leader, Yasser Arafat. The word was used by male college and high-school students in the later 1990s.

yatter, yatter on *vb*
to talk incessantly, frivolously or inanely. This colloquialism is a blend of **yap**, **yak**, 'chatter' and 'natter'.

yatties *n pl*
girls. A term from Caribbean speech, also heard in the UK since 2000, especially among younger speakers.
She hangs out with those posh yatties.

yawn[1] *n*
something extremely boring, dull or uninspiring. A colloquial term, particularly prevalent in middle-class usage. It is either a noun, as in 'the film was a total yawn' or an interjection, as in 'they took us round the exhibition – yawn!'. A racier alternative is **yawnsville**.

yawn[2] *vb, n*
(to) vomit. Although particularly popular in Australia, where it is often embellished

to **technicolour yawn**, the usage also exists in Britain and the USA.

yawnsville n
a boring thing, person or situation. An American teenage expression adopted in Britain and Australia. It uses the common slang suffix **-ville** to denote a place, situation or state of affairs.

yecch! exclamation American
an alternative form of **yuck!**

yecchy adj American
an alternative form of **yucky**

Yehudi adj British
authentic, trustworthy. A jocular item of middle-class rhyming slang using the name of the late Israeli musician Yehudi Menuhin to mean genuine.

yell n British
1a. a good joke or source of hilarity
That's a yell!
1b. a riotous party or good time
We had a real yell last night.
Both usages were heard among young people from the late 1970s. The first is also in use in upper-class and theatrical milieus.
2. an instance of vomiting
He's up in the bathroom having a yell.

yellow adj
cowardly, afraid. This now common term is of obscure origin. It is an Americanism of the late 19th century which was quickly adopted into British and Australian English. (In English slang of the 18th and early 19th centuries, yellow meant jealous and/or deceitful.) Some authorities derive the modern sense from the activities of the sensationalist 'yellow press'; other suggestions include a racial slur on the supposedly docile Chinese population of the western US or a reference to a yellow-bellied submissive reptile or animal, but it seems more likely that it is an extension of the earlier pejorative British senses.

yellow-belly n
a coward. This phrase, adopted by modern schoolchildren from the language of western movies, was probably coined after the turn of the 20th century. The use of the word **yellow** to denote cowardice is a 19th-century development.

yen sleep n
a waking trance state brought about by the smoking of opium or, by extension, a drowsy, restless sleep resulting from opium or heroin withdrawal. An expression from the 1950s jargon of drug abusers. The Chinese word yen, meaning smoke or opium, is also the source of the English word for a yearning.

yenta, yentl n
a shrewish woman, a gossip or crone. The word is a middle-European Jewish woman's name or title (probably related to forms of the word 'gentile'). The yenta became a comic figure in Jewish folklore, particularly in the American Yiddish theatre before World War II.

yeti n British
a primitive, repellent or stupid person. A term from the repertoire of schoolboys, army recruits, etc. since the 1970s. The word can be used both with facetious affection (e.g. as a nickname) or to express strong contempt.

yey, yay, yeyo n American
cocaine

yid n
a Jew. The word is the Yiddish term for a Yiddish-speaking Jew (Yiddish being a Germanic dialect influenced by Hebrew). When used in English the word is invariably racist and derogatory.

yike n Australian
a brawl or violent quarrel

yinyang, ying-yang n American
1a. the anus
1b. the sex organs
Yang and **w(h)ang** are both common expressions for the penis. Yinyang may be either an embellished version of these, a genuine nonsense nursery word for any unnameable thing or part (it was used in a pseudo-Chinese music-hall chorus in the earlier years of the 20th century) or, alternatively, an adult imitation thereof influenced by 'yang' and 'yin' as describing the Chinese masculine and feminine principles respectively (given currency in the early 1970s via the *I Ching* and subsequently in therapy and sex manuals).
2. a fool, dupe, an inept person, a **yoyo**. This use of the term probably postdates its other sense of the anus or genitals, by analogy with most other words of similar meaning.
'Well, if it's a yinyang you want, you've got three much better guys for this job.'
(*Vice Versa*, US film, 1988)

yip n American
cocaine

yippy, yippie *n*
a **hippy** activist, a member of the so-called 'Youth International Party' founded by Abbie Hoffman and Jerry Rubin in 1968, the date of the Chicago Democratic Convention where they put forward a pig as a presidential candidate. This short-lived movement was a loose coalition of radicals, anarchists, libertarians and left-wingers concerned with 'situationist' and confrontational political methods. The term was sometimes applied to other politically involved hippies and was one of the sources (albeit a heavily ironic one) of the later word **yuppie**.

> *'Yippy politics, being made up as it goes along, are incomprehensible.'*
> (*Oz* magazine, 1970)

yo *exclamation*
an all-purpose greeting, also indicating solidarity, enthusiasm, etc.

yob, yobbo *n British*
a thug, lout, brutish youth. This is one of the only pieces of **backslang** to enter the popular lexicon; it was heard occasionally in working-class and underworld milieus from the 19th century until the early 1960s, when it became a vogue word and was extensively used in the newly-liberalised entertainment media. 'Yobbishness', 'yobbery' and even 'yobboccracy' are more recent derivations, often used to refer to brutal behaviour in a social and political context as well as in connection with juvenile delinquency and hooliganism.

> *'The London International Financial Futures Exchange, terrible place, full of the most frightful yobs.'*
> (*Serious Money*, play by Caryl Churchill, 1987)

yo-boy *n British*
a hooligan, adolescent male. The term was recorded in the south of England, particularly in the Slough area, from the mid-1980s and is probably a variation of the older term **yob**.

yock *n*
an alternative spelling of **yok**

yodel *vb, n*
(to) vomit. An expression used particularly by teenagers and college students.

yodel in the canyon/valley *vb*
to perform cunnilingus. The first version is a jocular expression originating with American college students in the 1960s and now heard elsewhere. The second version is Australian and British.
Compare **yodel**

yoff *vb British*
to vomit. An item of student slang in use in London and elsewhere since around 2000.

yogurt-weaver *n British*
a derisive term for individuals involved in or keen on handicrafts, 'ethnic' pastimes, New Age remedies, etc. The term was posted on the b3ta website in 2004.

yoink *vb American*
to steal. It is probably an alteration of 'yank'.
> *Who yoinked my beer?*

yok, yock *n*
a laugh, chortle or instance of humour. A racier version of **yak** or 'yuk', popular for instance with rock-music journalists.
> *There's lots of yoks in this new movie.*

yomp *vb British*
to tramp across rough country wearing or carrying heavy equipment. This item of arcane military slang became known to the general public at the time of the war between Britain and Argentina over the Falkland Islands in 1981. The word is now used, by non-military hikers and others, more or less as a synonym for 'trek'. It is either an invented blend, influenced by words like 'tramp', 'hump', 'stomp' and 'jump', or an imitation of the sound of boots slamming into muddy ground.

yoni *n*
the vagina. This Sanskrit word (originally meaning 'abode' or 'womb' and later the female equivalent of a religious phallic symbol) is sometimes used jocularly or by writers on sexual matters in place of a taboo or clinical-sounding alternative. It has been familiar to Western readers since the publication of the *Kama Sutra* and other Hindu texts in the early 1960s.

yonks *n British*
a very long time, ages. This now popular word began to be heard in the early 1960s, mainly in middle-class usage. Its exact etymology is obscure; it may be a children's deformation of 'years' or an alteration of 'donkey's years'.
> *God, I haven't seen her for yonks.*

yop vb British
to tell tales, inform on someone. The origin of this 1990s playground usage is obscure.

york vb
to vomit. The term is both echoic and jocular like its synonyms, including **erp**, **ralph**, **buick**, etc.

you-dat exclamation British
an all-purpose greeting or indication of mutual respect or approbation. **Respect** itself and **touch-respect** are synonyms. The term was recorded in use among North London schoolboys in 1993 and 1994.

youngblood n American
a black youth. The term, inspired by its literary use referring to Amerindian braves, is used particularly of a junior member of a street gang. In the late 1980s the word was often shortened to **blood** (which also derives from 'blood brother').

young fogey/fogy n British
a youngish person of self-consciously traditional attitudes, manners and aesthetic ideals. Young fogey, by humorous analogy with the colloquial 'old fogey', characterised another social subgroup of the 1980s. Personified by the fastidious and conservative novelist and critic A. N. Wilson, these mainly male members of, or aspirers to the upper-middle-class re-create in their lifestyle and outlook the more refined pre-1960 establishment values (i.e. [high] Anglicanism, literary dabbling, a liking for traditional cooking/clothing, etc.)

'These days a "party" is often a sedate à deux affair at the latest Young Fogy nightspot.'
(*Sunday Times*, Men's Fashion Extra, October 1989)

youth n Jamaican
a young hero, young gangster or, still in the singular form, young people in general. A specialised usage of the standard English term, it is often pronounced 'yoot'.

'There's nothin' round here for the youth. No wonder they out on the street looking for trouble.'
(Recorded, Jamaican woman, London, 1988)

you wish! exclamation British
an all-purpose cry of derision or provocation, particularly in response to an expression of an unrealistic hope or desire. The term was recorded in use among North London schoolboys in 1993 and 1994.

yoyo n
a silly, eccentric or frivolous person. This use of the word, which may be said affectionately of a dizzy nonconformist or contemptuously with the straightforward meaning of a fool, originally referred to someone who vacillated or behaved in an irresolute manner.

yo-yo mode adj, n
(in) a state of chaos or confusion. The term occurs in the language of computer users. It is often in the form of an exclamation, 'full yo-yo mode alert!', cried when a system is going 'haywire'.

yuck[1] n
1. something or someone disgusting
2. an alternative spelling of **yuk**

yuck[2] adj
an alternative spelling of **yucky**
In American English this echoic approximation of retching is often transcribed as 'yecch'.

yuck! exclamation
an exclamation of repelled distaste or disapproval

yucky, yukky, yecchy adj
unpleasant, disgusting, sickly, cloying. A very popular word, particularly among children and teenagers since the mid-1970s, it derives from **yuck** as an exclamation of distaste.

yuk n
an alternative form of **yok**

yukker n British
a small child or baby. The term was recorded in 2002.

yumyum(s) n
anything considered irresistible, such as a potential sexual partner, an illicit drug or a sum of money. A less-respectable usage of the colloquial and childish lipsmacking exclamation meaning 'delicious'.

yuppie n
an acronym for 'young urban professional' (later also interpreted as 'young upwardly-mobile professional') with an added -ie ending in imitation of **hippie**, **yippie**, **surfie**, etc. The word was coined sometime between 1978 and 1980 to denote a new social phenomenon which needed to be distinguished from the existing **preppies**. The yuppie, originally

identifiable in New York City by a uniform of a business suit worn with running shoes, is an ambitious work-oriented materialist, usually highly paid and extremely receptive to consumer fashions. The term quickly became established all over the English-speaking world, epitomising the 'aspirational' mood of the 1980s.

> 'Yuppie scum fuck off/Kill a yuppie today.'
>
> (Graffiti protesting the gentrification of the East End, London, 1988)

za *n American*
a pizza, in the jargon of **preppies**

zaftig *adj American*
an alternative spelling of **zoftig**

zak, zac *n South African*
money. The same word, possibly from the Dutch/Afrikaans term for a bag (of coins), has been recorded in Australia, where it refers to a small amount of money.

zap *vb*
1a. to overwhelm, destroy, obliterate (literally or figuratively). The term derives from a comic-book sound effect applied to the action of ray-guns in the 1950s and 1960s.
1b. to target an individual or organisation for protests, picketing, situationist political action, etc. A word from the lexicon of radical **gays** in the 1970s.

> 'The Sisters of Perpetual Indulgence… used to go out and zap various things dressed as nuns.'
>
> (Gay activist, Out on Tuesday, British TV documentary series, 1989)

zapper *n*
a TV remote control. This term established itself in some households in the 1980s. It was coined perhaps to convey the power and relish experienced by viewers now able to switch channels or turn off at a touch.
See also **Frank**

zappy *adj*
energetic, speedy, dynamic, decisive. A back-formation from **zap**.

zazz *n American*
glamour, showiness

> *plenty of zazz*
> *Give it more zazz.*

zebbled *adj British*
circumcised. An item of playground slang of obscure origin.

zeds *n British*
sleep. This use of the term is probably a back-formation from the phrases **stack some zees/zeds**, **cop some zeds/zees** or **bag some zeds/zees**, all meaning to sleep.

zee *n American*
a Japanese sports car, in the argot of black street gangs of the late 1980s

> 'I saw a guy I knew, my age, had a Blazer [a Chevrolet Blazer – 4-wheel drive jeep]. Another guy got a "zee".'
>
> (**Crack** dealer, Independent, 24 July 1989)

Zelda *n American*
an unattractive female. An expression used on campus in the USA since around 2000. The original reference may have been to Zelda Fitzgerald, writer F. Scott Fitzgerald's deranged wife, or simply the borrowing of a supposedly odd or outdated first name.

zen *n*
LSD. The term dates from the 1960s but has been revived, particularly in differentiating the drug in question from **ecstasy**.

zen out *vb*
to enter a blissful, contemplative or inert state. The phrase, based on the notion of mindlessness in Zen meditation, was ascribed to the singer Lisa Stansfield in the *Daily Telegraph* magazine in October 1993.

zeppelin *n*
1a. a large cannabis cigarette; a **joint**
1b. a large penis
Both senses are inspired by the size and shape of the original Graf Zeppelin airship. The second sub-sense may be influenced by the similar use of the slang term **joint** for both a **reefer** and the penis.

zero-cool *adj American*
extremely impressive, admirable, nonchalant, etc. An intensive form of **cool** probably coined by **hipsters** or **beatniks**, now in use among adolescents.

zero out *vb American*
1a. to run out of money, to go broke or bankrupt

> 'But, dad, I'm totally zeroed out.'
> (Maid to Order, US film, 1987)

1b. to 'hit rock bottom', reach one's lowest point
1c. to fail utterly

zes n American See **z's**

zhlub n American
an alternative form of **slob**

zhooshed, zhush'd adj British
elaborately dressed and/or made up. The term has been used in **parlyaree** since the 1960s, e.g. to describe the teasing and primping of hair and eyelashes before emerging for a social occasion. The word's origin is unclear; it may simply be an imitation of the sound of appreciative smacking of the lips or an intake of breath.

zilch¹ n
1a. nothing. The word became common in US speech in the later 1960s, spreading to Britain in the 1980s. It is either an invented alteration of 'zero' or from subsense **b**.
1b. a nonentity. Zilsch or Zilch is a Yiddish/German family name borrowed for a comic character featuring in *Ballyhoo* magazine in the USA in the 1930s.
2. the name of a dice game

zilch² vb American
1a. to defeat utterly
1b. to fail utterly
Both usages, found in adolescent speech, are based on the earlier noun form.

zillion n
a very large number; a humorous coinage by analogy with 'million', 'billion' and 'trillion'. (**Squillion** is a similar mythical number.)

zine n
a magazine, particularly a post punk-era 'fanzine'. The clipped form of the word is typical of the tendency for shortening words among American adolescents from the 1980s (as in **za**, **rents**, **the burbs**, etc.)

zing vb American
to deliver a sudden attack, retort, etc. This use of the word is derived from the colloquial sense of to fly, spin, hum or perform zestfully.

> '"Did you hear him zing my lawyer?" Mr. Gotti asked reporters. "Bruce should hit him on the chin".'
> (Mafia trial report, the *Times*, 7 February 1990)

zinger n
something or someone extremely impressive, spectacular, energising, exciting, etc. The word comes from the use of 'zing' to mean a shrill, high-pitched sound and a lively, zestful quality.

zip n
1. nothing. Originally often used for a score of zero, the sound of zip evokes brusque dismissal. It has become a fashionable term in racy speech, as have its synonyms, such as **zilch** and **zippo**. Originating in the USA, zip is now heard in the UK.
2. *also* **zippy** an insignificant or worthless individual. An expression used on campus in the USA since around 2000. From the previous sense.

zip it vb
to shut up, keep quiet. A shortening of **zip one's lip**.
> 'Zip it, Fred!'
> (*All of Me*, US film, 1984)

zip one's lip vb
to shut up, keep quiet. A racier update of **button one's lip**, typically used as a brusque instruction.

zippo n
nothing. An embellished form of **zip** in the sense of zero. Zippo, originally an Americanism, is now heard elsewhere (albeit less often than **zip**).
> 'I checked and re-checked and got zippo.'
> (*Hooperman*, US TV series, 1986)

zit n
a spot or skin blemish. This Americanism has become well established in British usage since the later 1980s, featuring for instance in a TV commercial for anti-acne cream using the slogan 'blitz those zits!'. The etymology of the word is obscure.

zizz vb, n
(to) sleep or rest, nap. A British coinage dating from the 1920s. The word echoes the sound of light snoring or susurration associated with sleep.

zlub n American
an alternative form of **slob**

zod n American
a dullard, fool, nonentity. A 1980s teenage term of unknown provenance.

zoftig, zophtic, zaftig adj American
pleasing, luxurious, voluptuous, succulent. The words are Yiddish forms of zaftig, originally meaning 'juicy', from the German *saft*, meaning juice. The expression was extended to refer admiringly or lasciviously to women, before

acquiring the general sense of pleasurable or satisfactory.

zoid *n*
a foolish, clumsy or despised person. This teenage expression is an invention, probably influenced by such terms as **zomboid** and 'bozoid'. It originated in the USA, but by the late 1980s was heard in British schools, usually denoting a misfit.

zombie *n*
1. a dull, vacuous or inert person
2. a UFO or a rogue or unidentified object or signal
Both senses derive from the voodoo walking-dead of Haitian folklore.

zombified *adj*
1a. tired
1b. uncoordinated, incoherent
In both senses the word is common among adolescents in all English-speaking areas.

zomboid *adj*
dull, stupid, inert or intoxicated. A coinage from **zombie** using the 'pathological' suffix **-oid**.

> 'I mean any man who more-or-less turns the American genocide squad into a bunch of nodding, scratching hepatitic zomboids can't be all bad.'
> (Hashish dealer quoted in *IT* magazine, July 1972)

zoned, zoned out *adj*
stoned, **spaced out**, semi-conscious. Originally a piece of US drug-users' jargon, the word may now be employed in a non-narcotic context to mean worn out.

zone out *vb*
to lose consciousness or concentration, to become intoxicated. A drug users' expression related to the notion of **spaced out** and perhaps influenced by the mythical 'twilight zone'. The term has become generalised for use in more innocuous contexts.

> 'I didn't really notice – I guess I must have been zoning out.'
> (Recorded, American sub-editor, London, 1989)

zonked, zonko *adj*
intoxicated, overwhelmed, stunned. Zonked began as a term evoking the result of a blow to the head (a 'zonk', similar to a **bonk**), referring to the effects of drink or drugs. The word is now in widespread use and may refer to more innocent sensations such as surprise or exhaustion.

> 'I was zonked on enormous quantities of drug cocktails. Once you're on those things it's almost impossible to get off them.'
> (Former patient in a psychiatric hospital referring to his treatment, *Time Out*, February 1988)

zoob, zoobrick, zubrick *n*
the penis. The several forms of the word are all derived from the Arabic slang (in which there are variant forms, usually rendered as *zob* or *zip*).

zoo daddy *n American*
a divorced father who rarely sees his child or children. An item of family slang which refers to the supposed practice of accompanying offspring to the zoo when visiting rights are being exercised.

zoom *n*
an amphetamine (**speed**) or cocaine. A drug abuser's nickname. The term refers to the exhilarating **rush** experienced by those using these stimulants.

zoot *n*
1a. marihuana
1b. a marihuana cigarette, **spliff**
It is not clear whether the word as used since 2000 is a back-formation from **zooted** or an archaic usage revived for a new generation. The term was posted on the b3ta website in 2004.

zooted *adj American*
intoxicated by drugs or alcohol. The coinage, probably influenced by **toot** and perhaps **zonked** or **zoned (out)**, appeared in the 1980s, originally seemingly referring specifically to the effects of cocaine.

zophtic *adj American*
an alternative spelling of **zoftig**

> 'A pill and a cup of coffee and Im [sic] being already zophtic so who's complaining.'
> (*Requiem for a Dream*, Hubert Selby Jr, 1979)

zos *n South African*
food. Recorded as an item of Sowetan slang in the *Cape Sunday Times*, 29 January 1995.

zotz[1] *n American*
nothing. A synonym for **zip** and **zilch**, used in the *Prizzi* novels by Richard Condon.

zotz[2] *vb American*
to destroy, kill. 'Zot' was an earlier word for a short, sharp blow.

'Are we just going to wait until one more hooker gets zotzed?'
(*I Love A Man In Uniform*, Canadian film, 1994)

zow *n South African*
a yokel or an oaf. Recorded as an item of Sowetan slang in the *Cape Sunday Times*, 29 January 1995.

z's *n American*
sleep. From the use of 'z' to indicate the rasping sound of snores, hence sleep, in cartoons. The word, when pronounced in the American way, is usually part of phrases such as 'grab/cop some z's'.

zucchini *n American*
the penis. This Italian term for courgettes is also used throughout North America to refer to the vegetable in its singular form. In addition to its culinary usage, it is also a fairly widespread jocularism for the male member.

zulu *n, adj British*
(a person who is) black. A term of abuse current, for instance, in the army in the 1980s.

'zup? *question form, exclamation American*
an abbreviated form of 'what's up?'. This greeting was fashionable in teenage speech of the 1990s.